BELLE STARR

ALSO BY MICHAEL WALLIS

The Best Land under Heaven: The Donner Party in the Age of Manifest Destiny

Los Luceros: New Mexico's Morning Star

David Crockett: The Lion of the West

The Wild West 365 Days

Billy the Kid: The Endless Ride

Oil Man: The Story of Frank Phillips and the Birth of Phillips Petroleum

Route 66: The Mother Road

Pretty Boy: The Life and Times of Charles Arthur Floyd

Way Down Yonder in the Indian Nation: Writings from America's Heartland

Mankiller: A Chief and Her People
(with Wilma Mankiller)

En Divina Luz: The Penitente Moradas of New Mexico

Beyond the Hills: The Journey of Waite Phillips

Songdog Diary: 66 Stories from the Road
(with Suzanne Fitzgerald Wallis)

Oklahoma Crossroads

The Real Wild West: The 101 Ranch and the Creation of the American West

Heaven's Window: A Journey through Northern New Mexico

Hogs on Route 66: Best Feed and Hangouts for Roadtrips on Route 66 (with Marian Clark)

The Art of Cars (with Suzanne Fitzgerald Wallis)

The Lincoln Highway: Coast to Coast from Times Square to the Golden Gate

Belle Starr, Fort Smith, Arkansas, 1886.

BELLE STARR

The Truth Behind the Wild West Legend

MICHAEL WALLIS

Liveright Publishing Corporation

*A Division of W. W. Norton & Company
Independent Publishers Since 1923*

Copyright © 2025 by Michael Wallis

All rights reserved
Printed in the United States of America
First Edition

For information about permission to reproduce selections from this book, write to Permissions, Liveright Publishing Corporation, a division of W. W. Norton & Company, Inc., 500 Fifth Avenue, New York, NY 10110

For information about special discounts for bulk purchases, please contact W. W. Norton Special Sales at specialsales@wwnorton.com or 800-233-4830

Manufacturing by Sheridan
Book design by Lovedog Studio
Production manager: Anna Oler

ISBN 978-1-63149-477-2

Liveright Publishing Corporation
500 Fifth Avenue, New York, NY 10110
www.wwnorton.com

W. W. Norton & Company Ltd.
15 Carlisle Street, London W1D 3BS

1 2 3 4 5 6 7 8 9 0

TO HAZEL ROWENA MILLS
HER DILIGENCE MAKES ME A BETTER WRITER

CONTENTS

MAP: BELLE STARR COUNTRY   xi

INTRODUCTION   xiii

Part I

1. IN THE COUNTRY OF THE SIX BULLS   3
2. YOUNG MYRA IN CARTHAGE   14
3. "THE WAR THAT NEVER GOES AWAY"   29
4. ALL TORN ASUNDER   40
5. MYRA ON THE SCOUT   49
6. TURNING POINT   58

Part II

7. GONE TO TEXAS   75
8. ARMED AND DANGEROUS   82
9. JIMMY AND MAY   91
10. ON THE SCOUT   103
11. SOUTHERN CALIFORNIA: AN "ISLAND" IN THE SUN   113
12. LIVING THE OUTLAW LIFE IN TEXAS   123
13. SHEER GREED   138
14. JIM REED'S LAST HURRAH   147

| 15. | REPERCUSSIONS | 164 |
| 16. | OUT OF THE SHADOWS | 175 |

Part III

17.	THE GLARE OF THE LIMELIGHT	185
18.	THE LEGEND TAKES ROOT	194
19.	THE BIRTH OF BELLE STARR	208
20.	HELL ON THE BORDER	218
21.	MYTH VERSUS REALITY	238
22.	THE LEGEND GROWS	253
23.	THE CURTAIN FALLS	277
24.	WHO KILLED BELLE STARR?	293

EPILOGUE: PRINT THE LEGEND	307
ACKNOWLEDGMENTS	337
NOTES	341
BIBLIOGRAPHY	403
ILLUSTRATION CREDITS	425
INDEX	427

BELLE STARR COUNTRY

Map showing important locations in the life of Myra Maibelle Shirley (Belle Starr).

Introduction

Of all the noted women ever mentioned by word or pen, none in history have been more brilliantly daring nor more effective in their chosen roles than the dashing Belle Starr, champion and leader of robbers, herself a sure shot and a murderess, who never forgot an injury nor forgave a foe.[1]

—S. W. Harman, Hell on the Border, 1898

WHO WAS BELLE STARR? MANY PEOPLE HAVE ASKED that question, and many have attempted to answer it through books, articles, dime novels, films, songs, and stories. Those tales, spun from a mixture of fact and fiction, are still passed down among the keepers of legend and myth. Arguably the most famous female outlaw of the nineteenth century, Starr was celebrated and cursed far and wide across the American West.

Shortly after her mysterious death in 1889, Starr became well known throughout the nation and beyond because of a highly imaginative book published by Richard K. Fox, editor of the *National Police Gazette*.[2] The book described Belle as "a combination of the very worst, as well as some of the very best traits of her sex. . . . Of her it may well be said that Mother Nature was indulging in one of her rarest freaks, when she produced such a novel specimen of womankind."[3] The public devoured this greatly romanticized story and happily forked over two bits for a "handsomely and profusely illustrated" copy of *Bella Starr . . . The Bandit Queen, or the Female Jesse James*.[4] And so the legend of Belle Starr was born—to this day, many people think of her as the "Bandit Queen."

Often cited as a historical reference despite its flagrant inaccuracies, *Bella Starr* was the first of scores of books that soon followed, each presenting its own unique—and mostly imaginative—interpretation of Belle. All sorts of crimes and mayhem were laid at her feet, as were wild tales, such as the rumor that her daughter, Pearl, was the spawn of outlaw Cole Younger—a complete fabrication.

In truth, Belle never killed a single person and never robbed a stagecoach, train, or bank. She used the surname Starr for less than nine years of her life after marrying Sam Starr, son of legendary Cherokee outlaw Tom Starr.

Despite the many misconceptions about Belle Starr's life, she did have an unquestionable lust for adventure and was known to associate with outlaws. As Belle once said, "I am a friend to any brave and gallant outlaw."[5] Although she certainly had run-ins with the law, the only crime she was ever convicted of was horse theft. For punishment, Judge Isaac Parker, the "Hanging Judge" of Fort Smith, Arkansas, sent her to the House of Correction in Detroit, Michigan, for one year. She was released early because of good behavior. Belle immediately returned to the Cherokee Nation in eastern Indian Territory and once again crossed that very thin line separating miscreants from the virtuous. Belle's passion for horses sometimes extended to horses belonging to other people.

At a time when women had few opportunities in what was most definitely a man's world, Belle stands out as a shining example of resilient females who were not afraid to speak up and take their place as equals to their macho male counterparts. Belle reigned as a queen to many, but not the kind associated with genteel Victorian society. She rode another path, and she often rode it hard.

This is the story of how a young woman, shell-shocked by a cruel war and the death of her beloved brother, became the most infamous female outlaw of the American West, whether or not she deserved such a title. She was branded as a she-devil and an avenging angel, and the elusive truth about Belle Starr remains tangled in myth and folklore.

Many journalists, authors, and filmmakers have attempted to represent the life of Belle Starr over the years since her legend was first heard. Only a few got it half right, and most fell miserably short. Even respected historians have consistently perpetuated many sensational myths about every aspect of her public and private life.

The truth is that for many years, historians—mostly men—refused to tell it like it was for women of the American West. Women such as Belle Starr, who often lived their lives outside the law, rejected the conventional images of womanhood in the West—a dutiful prairie Madonna wearing a gingham bonnet in a covered wagon or a soiled dove plying her trade in a saloon or brothel.

Historian Susan Armitage describes the West as a mythical place.[6] In this romanticized world, Armitage wrote, "a cast of heroic characters engage in dramatic combat.... Occupationally, these heroes are diverse... but they share one distinguishing characteristic—they are all men." Overwhelmingly, they were White men who stereotyped women and failed to comprehend unconventional females such as Starr.

Belle Starr chose not to live her life by the Victorian ideal that women were limited in their abilities to survive in a man's world and expected to focus only on their domestic duties. She allowed her rebellious spirit to guide all her movements.

There are many facets to this woman. She is a reminder that in truth, there were some white hats, some black hats, and always plenty of gray hats. Belle Starr wore all three colors.

PART I

CHAPTER 1

In the Country of the Six Bulls

To unravel the life and legend of Belle Starr, the journey must begin in southwestern Missouri. She was born there in 1848 in the bottomlands of black loam and prairie soil watered by springs that started rivers. This vast region became known as the "Country of the Six Bulls."[1]

The origin of the name "Six Bulls" was debated for years around hunters' campfires. Some early visitors believed it honored a mighty Indian warrior who had killed six monstrous bison bulls. Others attributed the name to frontier trailblazer Edmund Jennings, who had left Tennessee and set out alone on foot into the wilderness in the late 1700s.[2] For fifteen years, he lived on peaceable terms with the Indians he encountered. He hunted, fished, and trapped while his loved ones in Tennessee had given him up for dead.

When Jennings finally returned to visit Tennessee after many years of living among Indians, he was clad in buckskin and moccasins and had difficulty speaking his native language. In strained English, he regaled friends and family with tales of his adventures in what he called the Country of the Six Bulls.

Jennings said "bulls," but this was a mispronunciation of the word *boils* and referred to six bubbling spring-fed streams and tributaries—Cow Skin Creek, Shoal Creek, Indian Creek, Center Creek, Spring River, and the North Fork. Nonetheless, stories of the plentiful water and fertile soil were compelling to land-hungry emigrants.[3] "There is no part of the western country that holds out greater advantages to the new settler than the

Missouri Territory," Scottish botanist John Bradbury wrote in his journal, published four years before Missouri was admitted to the Union in 1821 as a slave state.[4]

The accounts of Bradbury, Jennings, and other adventurers helped to spark a migration of settlers to the Six Bulls. The first significant wave of immigrants began to arrive in the 1820s, and settlement soon spread up the river valleys into central Missouri. By the 1830s, White settlers had ventured into western Missouri from Kentucky, Tennessee, Virginia, North Carolina, Ohio, Indiana, and Illinois.

Among those lured to Missouri was the family of John and Elizabeth Pennington Shirley, who later became the parents of Belle Starr. Although the Shirleys came to Missouri from Indiana, they both had ancestral ties to the South. John Shirley traced his immediate lineage to Washington County, Maryland, directly south of the Pennsylvania border and on the Mason-Dixon Line—a symbolic cultural boundary between the northern free states and southern slaveholding states.[5] Formed in 1776, Washington County was the first county in the new nation to be named for Revolutionary War general George Washington.

John's father, Christian Shirley, was born in 1773 in Washington County. However, John's grandparents Johann Peter Shirley (Shalle) and Anna Elizabeth Kelker (Kolliker) were born just north of the Mason-Dixon Line, in Lancaster County, Pennsylvania Colony, in 1741 and 1736, respectively.[6] Shortly after their marriage in 1765, they moved south to the colony of Maryland, where Peter Shirley (who used his middle name) found work as a miller. Eventually, he and Anna raised three sons and a daughter: Christian, Jonathon, Balser, and Mary, nicknamed Polly.[7]

Christian, the Shirleys' firstborn, was twenty years old when he wed Roseanna (Rosannah) Canote, born in Maryland in 1776, a daughter of John and Rosanna Hunse Canote.[8] In the early 1790s, Christian, Roseanna, and many of the Shirley and Canote kinfolk, including their parents, left Maryland for neighboring Virginia. Not everyone in the Shirley family made the move, however. Christian's mother, Anna Kelker, moved instead to her ancestral homeland in Switzerland, where she died in Zurich in 1800.[9] The other Shirleys and John Canote's family moved to

Virginia's Shenandoah Valley, tucked between the Blue Ridge Mountains on the east and the Allegheny Mountains on the west. They soon acquired property and established farms in sprawling Augusta County.[10]

For many years, hemp and tobacco had been the leading cash crops in the Shenandoah Valley. The demand for hemp as a source for sailcloth and textiles had swelled during the American Revolution. By the time the Shirleys arrived, production of both crops was on a downward slide. But wheat, easier to manage than hemp, was on the rise. By 1800, the valley had doubled its export of wheat, shipping out four million pounds.[11]

Whether the Shirleys planted wheat or hemp or other crops such as flax, indigo, rye, or oats, they relied on enslaved laborers. Unlike the Tidewater aristocrats in eastern Virginia with their stately tobacco plantation manors, the farmers in western Virginia with smaller operations did not require large numbers of field hands. Although the crops they grew were labor intensive, the valley farmers and their families worked in the fields alongside their enslaved laborers. Often, a farmer would make an agreement with a plantation owner to "rent" a few laborers to ensure that crops were harvested in time to turn a profit.[12] The lack of profits, however, took a toll on the Canotes and Shirleys.

Despite the close family ties, an issue about money caused a rift between the families. In 1797, John Canote Jr., brother of Christian Shirley's wife, Roseanna, filed a lawsuit against Peter Shirley, Roseanna's father-in-law. The dispute was over ownership of a bay mare. Several members of the Shirley family, including Christian, were deposed during the legal proceedings. In the end, the final judgment in the suit was in favor of Peter Shirley.[13]

Tension between the families eased, but their financial problems continued. The Shirleys had no choice but to sell the land in Virginia and move farther west, just as several other Shirley family relations had done years before. And so the Shirleys struck out for Kentucky—Peter and his sons Christian and Jonathon. They bought farmland in Madison County, where "the Bluegrass meets the foothills of the Appalachians."[14] They acquired the land from the widow and children of Michael Shirley, Peter's older brother.

Born in Germany in 1732, before the family moved to America and settled in Pennsylvania, Michael had served as a colonial soldier in a Virginia regiment during the Revolutionary War. He had moved to the Kentucky wilderness in 1780, five years after Daniel Boone had blazed the Wilderness Trail through the Cumberland Gap. A surveyor by trade, Michael acquired tracts of land along the Kentucky River but was killed by Indians in 1784 while surveying what became Madison County.[15]

In Kentucky, Christian's son John Shirley came of age. While riding over endless meadows and pastures of bluegrass and white clover, Shirley developed his lifelong love of well-bred horses, a passion that would be passed on to his children, including the future Belle Starr. John had barely reached his adolescence in Kentucky when, true to form, the restless Shirley family once again uprooted their households and crossed the Ohio River in time to be included in the 1810 Indiana Territory census.[16] They bought farmland in what originally was the Shawnee tribe's hunting grounds, later named Floyd County.

In 1816, Indiana became the nineteenth state. Two years later, on April 6, 1818, John Shirley married Nancy Fowler in Clark County. The groom was twenty-two, and the bride was twenty-one.[17] In the next eight years, Nancy bore four children—Mary Ann, in 1819; Elizabeth, 1820; John Finley, circa 1821; and Preston, 1826.

By the time Preston had learned to walk, John was entangled in an extramarital relationship with a young woman named Frances (Fanny) Minnick. In 1828, Fanny bore him a daughter, whom they named Clarissa.[18] Although divorce was not socially acceptable at that time, John's flagrant marital misbehavior was beyond the pale. The marriage of John and Nancy Shirley officially ended in divorce on April 27, 1829, three weeks after Nancy's thirty-second birthday and what would have been the couple's eleventh wedding anniversary.[19]

Most people in antebellum America considered divorce an abomination and a threat to the well-being of society. There was, however, a widely accepted view that at least some redemption could be achieved by returning to the marital altar.

"[W]hen they made new 'marriages' that demonstrated their commitment to the conventional order of marriage, courts saw little reason to challenge the order they had reestablished in their lives," wrote Hendrik Hartog, professor of law at Georgetown University.[20]

If the hope of redemption held much sway with John Shirley, then he got his chance only eleven days after his divorce from Nancy was final. On May 8, 1829, John married twenty-four-year-old Fanny in a simple civil ceremony in Floyd County, Indiana.[21] For several years, John, Fanny, and their daughter, Clarissa, resided on what was called the Knob, a bluff rising over the Ohio River. Sadly, Clarissa took ill and died on March 30, 1836. "The Daughter of J. and F. Shirley d. Mar 30, 1836, in her 8th year" was chiseled on her tombstone in a cemetery at the Knob.[22]

At the time of Clarissa's passing, John and Fanny's relationship was rapidly deteriorating. Within the year that followed, it completely collapsed. Much like what happened while he was wed to Nancy, this second marriage ended mainly because of John's philandering. A young Kentucky belle had caught his eye and captured his heart.

Fanny filed for divorce on the grounds of adultery. For her counsel, she hired Henry P. Thornton, a respected attorney and a signer of the Indiana state constitution. John chose Hugh L. Livingston as his legal representative.[23] At the time, Indiana was known to have the most liberal divorce laws in the nation. Judges were prone to grant a divorce decree "as a matter of course in every case where the defendant did not appear to oppose it."[24] All an applicant was required to do was offer proof of residency. Indiana became a "divorce mill" for unhappy couples who flocked to the state to secure quick divorces.

Dissolving a marriage might have been fairly easy in Indiana, but the result was usually devastating for women. Indiana adhered to the English common-law tradition that "considered women as perpetual juveniles,"[25] meaning that once a woman married, she surrendered many civil and property rights. "A woman's gender and marital status were the primary determinants of her legal standing in Indiana and much of America from 1800 to 1850," wrote Indiana state historian Timothy Crumrin.[26]

On April 27, 1837, a Floyd County jury heard Fanny's petition for divorce. After "mature deliberation," they found John Shirley guilty of adultery and decreed that "the bands of matrimony therefore existing between John Shirley and Frances Shirley be dissolved."[27]

Less than two weeks later at a civil ceremony in Greene County, Indiana, presided over by justice of the peace Moses Ritter, John Shirley took Elizabeth (Eliza) Pennington as his third bride. Eliza had been born in Louisville, Kentucky, in 1816, two years before John's first marriage.[28] Younger than some of John's children, Eliza was twenty-one, and John was forty-two.

The old saying "the third time's a charm" worked for John Shirley. He and Eliza were married for about forty years and had six children of their own, all born in Missouri. One of them would become Belle Starr.

THE YEAR 1837 PROVED to be momentous for John Shirley. He was pleased when his young son, Preston, unlike his three siblings, chose not to remain with his mother but joined his father. John Shirley's bride, Eliza Pennington, gave birth to their first child, Charlotte Amanda, that year.[29] However, it was also the year that a crippling financial crisis staggered the Shirley family and virtually the whole nation. The Panic of 1837 touched off a prolonged economic depression that lasted for several years. In some large cities, desperate mobs raided warehouses to get food. Many people, including some prominent businessmen, lost everything as hundreds of banks closed.[30]

Indiana was in financial ruin. Several important public-works projects, including the creation of a major canal, had to be abandoned. A London newspaper declared that Indiana was "the land of promise for all the knavery and thievery in the known world." The citizens were branded as "plundering vagabonds."[31] In 1841, Indiana declared bankruptcy.

By then, John Shirley was long gone. He had recognized that the best plan of action was to do what generations of his forebears had done—move on. In 1839, John procured a yoke of oxen and loaded his family and their belongings into wagons. He took with him the few enslaved workers he had acquired in Kentucky. Besides daily household tasks, the enslaved workers tended to the Shirleys' prized Kentucky-bred horses.[32]

John had heard the stories and listened to the accounts of a land of promise on the other side of the great Mississippi River, deep in southwestern Missouri. That became the Shirleys' destination. They left Greene County, Indiana, and headed due west for the Country of the Six Bulls.

A contributing factor in choosing Missouri might have been Eliza Pennington Shirley's family. Her origins and much of her family history have always been a mystery. It was often said but never proved that she was related to the Hatfields, a family that many years later gained notoriety during the famous feud with the McCoys. Eliza's father and mother remain unknown, but there is cause to believe that the Shirleys moved to Missouri because her parents were already there. According to historical records from Jasper County, Missouri, a John Pennington and his unnamed wife resided in an area where the John and Eliza Shirley first settled.[33]

"He (John Pennington) appears, from mention in old histories, to have been a man of at least middle age," wrote revered Missouri historian Ward Loren Schrantz. "This constitutes no proof that he was the father of Eliza Pennington Shirley, yet settlers were still but few and it perhaps was no mere coincidence that the Shirleys came to a neighborhood where there already were Penningtons."[34]

For whatever reasons the Shirleys came to the Country of the Six Bulls, they likely paused to rest at the newly named village of Sarcoxie, formerly Centerville. The name had been changed in 1839 to honor a chief of the Delaware Indians who had lived near a spring in the area before the coming of White settlers. The hamlet—once described as "a collection of log huts where vice and profanity rules [sic]"—had become a regular jumping-off point for emigrants headed west.[35]

The Shirleys would have camped east of Sarcoxie at Cave Springs, an early settlement where a large spring flowed from a cavern with two large underground chambers. As many as twenty families could stay there for a few days, while the heads of families scouted for homesites.[36]

John Shirley left his family and rode northwest into what soon became known as Jasper County. He did not go far before he located a promising site on the south side of Spring River, one of the Six Bulls streams. John walked the land, came upon a fine spring in a grove, and spied a shallow in the river that would be known as Shirley's Ford. The land was only a few miles east of the western border of Missouri, "beyond which was nothing but emptiness and Indians."[37]

Missouri had been the home of many Indian tribes, including the Osages, whose lands at one time included Jasper County. For thirty years after the Louisiana Purchase in 1804, the tribes living in Missouri signed treaties with the federal government relinquishing all claims to their Missouri lands. By the late 1830s, the tribes had all been relocated to Kansas Territory and Indian Territory, the future state of Oklahoma.

During the winter of 1836–1837, hunting parties of Osages, Shawnees, and Delawares persisted in returning to their former homeland in the Six Bulls area. Missouri Governor Lilburn Boggs, a Kentucky native, ordered them removed because their presence was "distasteful to the settlers."[38] This resulted in the so-called Osage War, a bloodless confrontation between the Osages and a company of state militia. It ended unceremoniously when the Indians agreed to depart without a shot having been fired.[39]

Shirley and other settlers drifting into the lower Spring River country had little to fear from Osage warriors who periodically came back to hunt game and trade with White settlers. Convinced that he had found the ideal location for his homestead, Shirley dashed back to Cave Springs to retrieve his family.

Once they arrived, they set up a temporary camp near the spring. Shirley, with help from young Preston and the enslaved laborers, began to clear land and cut timber for a home. Using round logs, they quickly constructed a family cabin and, for the enslaved people, a freestanding cabin with dirt floors. Within a few years, as the family grew, a more substantial two-story squared-log home was erected. It had wooden plank floors and a proper stone chimney and fireplace with a mantel.[40]

Missouri was a public-domain state where unclaimed land was surveyed and then granted or sold by the government through federal and state land offices. The Shirley land had not yet been surveyed by the government. That meant it could not be offered for public sale, and the

Shirleys could not gain legal title. To circumvent the problem, John Shirley relied on what was known as "squatter sovereignty."[41]

By staking a claim, building a home, and planting crops, Shirley and other squatters could retroactively obtain title to the government land they occupied once it was properly surveyed. A partial survey of the eastern part of future Jasper County was launched in 1836, three years before the Shirley family's arrival. It would be another ten years before the survey of the western part of the county, including the Shirley property, was completed. That allowed great numbers of settlers to make filings with the land office in Springfield and secure title to their lands.[42]

Confident that he would eventually have clear title to the land, Shirley put his enslaved laborers to work transforming prairie into cultivated fields that yielded an abundance of corn and grain crops. They planted a fruit orchard and built a sizable barn, corncrib, hog pens, and stables. Shirley also bred and sold horses and was known to trade with Indians passing through.[43]

As more settlers, mostly from the South, poured into the area, the Missouri legislature passed a bill in 1841 authorizing the creation of Jasper County, named in honor of Sergeant William Jasper, a hero in the Revolutionary War.[44] The first session of the Jasper County Court was held in the hewed-log home of George Hornback on the Spring River, twelve miles southeast of the Shirleys' homestead. At the meeting, John Shirley was appointed overseer of some of the county's first roads, marking the debut of his name in the county records.[45] In 1841, the county road commissioners, at their inaugural meeting, ordered a road built "commencing at the township line south of John Pennington's and ending due South of William Babb's mill."[46]

In early 1842, the county court began to meet at the Pennington home, on a hill south of Spring River. The land south of and adjoining Pennington's residence was chosen for the permanent seat of justice for Jasper County. The new county seat was named Carthage, after the ancient Phoenician city-state on the North African coast.[47]

When the land for the town square was being surveyed, a large crowd of newly minted Carthaginians gathered to watch crews stake off the

Map of Jasper County, Missouri, circa 1870s, birthplace of Myra Maibelle Shirley (Belle Starr).

dimensions. John Shirley and his family were likely present when John Pennington, pleased that the new town would be adjacent to his home, made an appearance. Many years later, the story was still told of how Pennington greeted the throng of onlookers and visited with the surveyors. He pulled up a survey stake and poured whiskey from his flask into the hole. "Now she'll make a town," he proudly told the crowd.[48]

The Shirley family had more to be proud of in 1842 than the birth of Carthage. That year, John and Eliza welcomed their second child—a son named John Allison M. Shirley. The family called the baby by his middle name, Allison, but as he grew older, he became known as Bud, a nickname that stuck for the rest of his life.[49]

Life for the Shirleys went reasonably well until the spring of 1844. That March, a series of steady, long-continued rainstorms turned Spring River into a roaring surge of floodwater that swept away sprouting crops, livestock, and rail fences. Less than a month later, the family suffered yet another blow.

John Shirley ran afoul of the law, and a grand jury indicted him on two counts. One charge was for doing business on Sunday, and the second and more serious accusation was for selling corn whiskey to an Indian. When the cases came up in circuit court, he pleaded guilty to Sabbath-breaking and paid a dollar fine and court cost. Shirley requested a continuance on the liquor charge. It was granted after he posted a $500 bond. The case finally came up again in 1846. Fortunately for Shirley, a motion to quash the indictment was sustained.[50]

The criminal charges and court appearances apparently did not have a negative impact on Shirley's standing in the community. On the heels of the dismissal of the second charge, the county court saw fit to appoint Shirley as road commissioner, a public office he held intermittently for the next twenty years. Although he was both plaintiff and defendant in numerous legal actions on business and financial disputes in civil courts, Shirley never again faced a criminal charge.[51]

By the mid-1840s, many Americans, especially those with painful memories of the Panic of 1837, believed the time had come for the nation to spread across the continent. They convinced themselves that God had bestowed on them the right to grow and prosper by advancing the frontier westward. The phrase "Manifest Destiny" became the nation's watchword. In 1846, the movement gained momentum, and the United States—led by land-hungry President James K. Polk—went to war with Mexico.[52]

In Missouri, a call went out for volunteers to join the corps of mounted dragoons that was being speedily organized. Preston Shirley was not one of them. He remained on his father's farm and made plans for starting his own family. On May 26, 1847, twenty-one-year-old Preston married sixteen-year-old Mary Arella Chelson. Mark Robertson, a circuit-riding minister of the gospel in the Methodist Episcopal Church, solemnized the rites of matrimony.[53] Preston built a home on land generously provided by his father.

The Shirleys' log house seemed empty with Preston gone. His departure left John and Eliza with only nine-year-old Charlotte Amanda and five-year-old Bud. But there were more children to follow.

CHAPTER 2

Young Myra in Carthage

THE NEW YEAR OF 1848 HAD JUST BEGUN WHEN TEMPERAtures plummeted, and a bone-chilling rain fell across the Country of the Six Bulls in southwestern Missouri. By late January, the persistent rain had turned to sleet and snow, which froze as it fell. By February, everything was coated with ice. "It did not thaw until the latter part of March and during all this time the trees and shrubs sparkled and glistened all through the day and by moonlight, making a scene like a fairy garden," waxed an early chronicler of Jasper County history.[1]

Romanticized prose did not tell the whole story, however. Such a bad winter storm seriously disrupted daily life for Jasper County residents. No one ventured outside except farmers and enslaved laborers to tend to livestock and collect ice for cooking and drinking water.

On the bitterly cold Saturday of February 5, 1848, all members of the Shirley family were huddled in their log house northwest of Carthage near the frozen Spring River. That day, Eliza Shirley gave birth to her third child—another daughter.[2] There is no record of who tended to Eliza, but it can be assumed that a female enslaved worker called Annie who had been brought to Missouri with the Shirleys helped with the baby's delivery.

Eliza and John named their healthy baby girl Myra. The name is based on the Latin *myrra*, meaning myrrh, a fragrant tree resin used throughout history as a perfume, incense, or medicine.[3] Over time, various middle names were attributed to Myra, including Belle, May Belle, Maebelle, Maibelle, Mae, and Mary. However, Myra was the name she was known by as a child and young woman, and she was identified solely as Myra Shirley on the 1850 and 1860 census schedules of Jasper County.[4]

As the Shirleys celebrated the arrival of the new family member, good news from Mexico was beginning to spread across the land. On February 2, the United States and Mexico signed the Treaty of Guadalupe Hidalgo, ending the Mexican-American War.[5] President James Polk's dream of westward expansion had been realized; through the treaty, the nation would acquire more than five hundred thousand square miles of valuable territory.[6]

By the time Congress ratified the peace treaty with Mexico in March 1848, news had broken in Jasper County that considerable quantities of gold had been discovered at Sutter's Creek, a branch of the American River in the lower Sacramento Valley of California. In Jasper County, 1848 and the storied gold rush of 1849 became known as "the time of the gold excitement." It was estimated that family members of at least half the households in the county headed west to the goldfields.[7] Some were never heard from again. Others returned empty-handed. A few struck it rich.

In Carthage, John Shirley heard the stories of instant wealth and riches that awaited all those who went to California. Unlike his neighbors and friends, Shirley was not inclined to go after gold. He and Eliza had three children to care for, one of whom was infant Myra. At about the time Myra was born, John also become a grandfather. Mary Shirley, wife of his eldest son, Preston, gave birth to Christian T. Shirley, named for the baby's great-grandfather.[8]

John Shirley stayed put. He finally got around to filing a claim on his eight hundred acres southeast of the future townsite of Medoc. On June 30, 1848, he was granted a patent and assumed ownership of the property.[9]

If Shirley had had any interest in mining, he could have pursued it without leaving the county. Significant deposits of lead—in great demand since the War of 1812—were discovered in Jasper County. In the late 1840s and for many years afterward, "gray gold," as miners called it, was a major source of income for the region. Mining camps—such as Lone Elm, just north of the future city of Joplin—sprang up during the early days of the lead bonanza.[10]

"Little did the emigrant think, as he made his way over the hills of southwestern Missouri, in the hope of finding home and wealth in the gold fields of the Pacific slope, that he need but stop, tickle the earth with pick and shovel, and reap a most bountiful reward," F. A. North wrote in 1883.[11]

Lead was found only eight miles from the Shirley home, but mining lead appealed to Shirley about as much as seeking gold did. He would continue to make his living by working the rich topsoil and selling horses. Shirley did, however, profit from the gold excitement and lead mining in other ways—the demand for horses increased, and cattle prices rose.

In September 1849, the Shirleys welcomed their fourth child, Edwin Benton. Myra was nineteen months old by then. She became an aunt once again when her half brother, Preston, and his wife, Mary, had another son, John—named for the baby's grandfather.[12]

In 1850, one of John's daughters from his first marriage, Elizabeth, responded to her father's invitation and moved to Jasper County with her husband, Williamson Dunn Alexander, and their four small children. Only four years younger than her stepmother Eliza, Elizabeth had married in Indiana in 1836.[13] The Alexanders soon settled and farmed land southwest of the Shirley homestead, by then known as Shirley's Ford.[14]

Shirley continued to horse-trade, both literally with well-bred steeds and figuratively with real estate. In the next decade, he bought and sold small tracts of land for a good profit. His holdings were appraised by the 1850 census at $600. By 1860, that had increased to $4,000 in real estate and $6,000 in personal property.[15] By the standards of the day, the Shirleys were considered prosperous.

On June 1, 1850, Shirley's name appeared on a deed in a land transaction with Henry (Harry) Washington Younger, a successful businessman and one of the largest landowners in western Missouri, with holdings in Jackson, Cass, and Clay Counties.[16] The Youngers and Shirleys were acquainted when Shirley sold Younger 160 acres of his Jasper County land. Younger was the patriarch of a large family that included sons Thomas Coleman (Cole), James Hardin (Jim), John, and Robert (Bob). In due course, they formed an infamous outlaw band known as the Younger brothers.

By 1851, Shirley decided the time was right to invest in property in the emerging town of Carthage. His first purchase was a $500 lot on the town square. Title to the property was in the name of young John Allison M. ("Bud") Shirley, for whom it was an investment. John Shirley then bought three adjoining lots and built a rental house for extra income. He now owned almost all of the north side of the Carthage town square.[17] His son Preston was busily making his own property acquisitions. Besides procuring more farmland, he paid only thirty-five dollars for a vacant block of land on the northeastern edge of Carthage.[18]

"The Shirleys apparently always paid off their mortgages in this antebellum period," wrote historian Ward Schrantz. "Their land ownership and retention record, if taken by itself, would seem to indicate that they were reasonably substantial people in a financial way for the time. Yet there seems no question that they frequently were hard-pressed for cash."[19]

The Shirley family, whether "land rich and cash poor" or not, continued to grow. In 1852, another son was born. Eliza and John named him Mansfield, supposedly after Thomas Mansfield, a newly elected Missouri legislator from Jasper County.[20] Later that year, John Shirley's oldest child from his first marriage—Mary, born in 1819—moved from Indiana to Jasper County with her husband, Richard Hunter, whom she had married in 1836. The Hunter children were close in age to their half aunts and uncles, the offspring of Eliza and John.[21]

Although he had become a significant property owner in Carthage, John Shirley remained on his land for a few more years. He had plenty of help. At one point, Shirley owned as many as eight enslaved laborers. They handled domestic chores, groomed horses, cared for the livestock, and worked in the crop fields.

Many settlers in the region were of limited means and could not afford to keep enslaved people. An able-bodied enslaved man could fetch $1,000 or more at auctions outside the county courthouse on the town square. At the auctions, appraisers examined men, women, and children much as they would livestock.

Like other farmers with enslaved workers in Jasper County, Shirley needed only a few field hands. Outdoor labor in the humid Missouri summers could be brutal. In the early 1850s, area farmers and their enslaved laborers were plagued by swarms of bloodsucking horseflies as large as honeybees. Often called blue-tail flies from the old minstrel tune of the 1840s, they attacked any warm-blooded mammal, inflicting painful bites on horses, cattle, and humans. All plowing was done by moonlight when the flies were dormant. During the day, horses and oxen were kept covered in barns.[22]

Adjusting the work schedule for beleaguered field hands might have been regarded as a considerate act of kindness, but it also was an advisable investment strategy. Because of western Missouri's proximity to antislavery Kansas, mistreatment of enslaved workers could result in their escaping to find sanctuary across the border. Proslavery meetings were held in Jasper County, and vigilante committees were organized in response to the perceived abolitionist threat in Kansas. Sanctimonious settlers, with sizable hemp and tobacco plantations in the region of Missouri known as "Little Dixie" and the counties along the western border, created a rationale for owning human beings.

"We have considered slaves as mere property, to show how absurd are the ravings of fanatics, the idle dreams of poets and novelists, which represent slaveholders as not only monsters, but idiots, reveling in the destruction of their property," stated a report published in 1854 by the Platte County (Missouri) Self-Defense Association. "But when it is remembered that the affection which naturally springs up between the master and slave, is little less than that of parent and child, it is easy to explain the seemingly strange results shown by the census. Kindly treated, carefully tended, they grow healthy and happy: unlike the miserable free negro, they are neither insane nor idiots."[23]

The pejorative and paternalistic arrogance of slavery advocates only encouraged enslaved people's desire to escape bondage. Professional hunters and buyers of enslaved people made the rounds through all the counties each year searching for recalcitrant individuals. Local owners anxious to rid themselves of unruly laborers or habitual runaways were always ready to bargain. Most of those enslaved laborers were taken south in heavily guarded gangs and sold at a profit to large plantations prepared to maintain control and mete out strict discipline.

Like other slave states, Missouri laws governing slavery were severe, and punishment was swift and drastic because of the continual fear of insurrection. Depending on the gravity of an alleged offense, punishment ranged from lashing and beating to castration and hanging. In one instance, a habitually disobedient enslaved person was thrown overboard from a riverboat and drowned. As Schrantz pointed out, "Punishment for individual crimes of a major nature often were outside the law."[24]

In August 1854, the Shirley family, including six-year-old Myra, probably bore witness along with thousands of their fellow citizens to such punishment "outside the law."[25] Remembered as the most barbaric act of retribution in Jasper County history, it became deep-rooted in the memories of every person present.

That summer, Dr. John Fisk, a highly respected physician with a farm near Carthage, received a substantial amount of cash in a business transaction with John B. Dale. One of Dale's enslaved hands, known only as Colley, witnessed the exchange and hatched a plan to get the money. He recruited an accomplice, Bart, an enslaved man owned by John J. Scott. That evening, Colley went to the Fisk home. He told the doctor that Dale's child was very ill, and he had been sent to ask that Fisk come to the boy's bedside. Believing the ploy, Fisk saddled his horse and took his medicine case. He and Colley had not ridden very far when Bart sprang out of the brush and pulled Fisk from his horse. Colley struck Fisk twice in the head with an ax, killing him. Not finding any money on the doctor's body, Colley and Bart went back to the Fisk house. They raped Fisk's wife, killed her with the ax, and strangled her two-year-old child. A search of the premises yielded a bit of cash and a watch. Before fleeing the scene, the two men set fire to the house.[26]

It did not take long to learn the identities of the killers. Colley's nervous behavior aroused suspicion, and a search of his cabin turned up bloody clothing. Colley denied any role in the crimes, but after an intense interrogation and the threat of hanging, he confessed. He revealed the hiding place in a corncrib where he had stashed about thirty dollars in cash and the doctor's watch. Sheriff T. F. Thompson took the prisoner into custody. Because there was no county jail, Colley was chained to a stake in Thompson's yard, and guards were posted.[27]

Meanwhile, Bart had taken to the brush and was on the run. When he turned up missing from the Scott farm, Sheriff Thompson put together a posse that included John Shirley. They scoured the countryside in pursuit of Bart, who was not familiar with the area and was easy to track. A group of children, likely Myra and her siblings, came upon the fugitive hiding in a sumac thicket on Shirley's farm, not far from the family home. The children ran to tell Shirley, and the posse quickly captured Bart.[28] A committee of citizens—described as "infuriated people not being willing to wait for the law to take its course"—determined there was no need to wait for a court to convene. Punishment had to be prompt. They took control of Colley and Bart, immediately declared them guilty, and sentenced them to die.

The only decision remaining was the form of execution. Some folks were in favor of lynching the convicts, but the majority thought hanging was too good for them. A vote was taken on Carthage's public square. The tally was two to one in favor of burning Colley and Bart at the stake, as a warning to other enslaved workers.[29]

On the chosen day, an enormous crowd gathered to witness the dual execution in a hollow less than a mile from the town square. The surrounding hillsides formed a natural amphitheater for comfortable seating. The crowd of three thousand to four thousand people came from many surrounding counties and even from Indian Territory. Many of them brought food and drink. Farmers forced their enslaved workers to see firsthand the delivery of Old Testament justice. The scene seemed more like a revival or camp meeting than a public execution.

The massive assembly jeered when the condemned men were marched in shackles into the middle of the hollow and chained to two large iron posts. Colley and Bart's eyes scanned the faces around them as if looking for someone familiar.

"Dry sycamore wood was piled up around them in a circle but not touching them and about waist high," one of the witnesses, Timothy Meador, remembered in a newspaper interview published in 1897. "Then light shavings were added to the heap and the whole was fired by four or five persons simultaneously. The flames leaped up around the doomed men like a blast from a furnace, sucking their breath away and they were dead in a quarter of a minute."[30]

When the fire burned down, little remained of the men's bodies. As the spectators left in a celebratory mood to return to their homes, ominous dark clouds rolled in the heavens, heralding a severe thunderstorm accompanied by heavy rain and deadly lightning. Everyone fleeing the storm in wagons and on horseback was quickly drenched and in desperate need of shelter from lightning. The storm "added to the terrors of the day and many of the visiting men and women died soon afterwards from the effects of the journey and the sight," according to a writer from nearby Lawrence County, referring to fatalities from lightning.[31]

Many years later, in recalling the events of that time, Schrantz wrote, "It is quite possible that little Myra Shirley saw that day the first of the many scenes of violent death she was to witness during her life."[32]

THE BRUTAL AND MERCILESS execution of Colley and Bart convinced John Shirley that the time had come to leave his farm for the safety of Carthage. He had contemplated the move for some time and had been buying up property on the square and elsewhere in town. The Fisk murders and the events that followed—especially the capture of one of the fugitives on his property—concerned Shirley. He feared that the very real possibility of increasing numbers of enslaved runaways posed a threat to his family's safety. The easiest local path to antislavery Kansas crossed the Shirley land. Less than a month after the public burning of Colley and Bart, Shirley carried out his plan. By mid-September 1854, he had vacated the Spring River farm and moved his family to Carthage.[33]

In 1856, Shirley sold the farm to George W. Broome for $3,000.[34] Broome, a young, unmarried, wealthy Georgia native, already owned substantial property holdings and a large enslaved workforce to handle livestock and farming. He continued to grow his fortune as a speculator, buying and selling farmland.[35]

Besides the perceived threat of enslaved runaways, another reason the Shirleys moved to Carthage was to broaden educational opportunities for their children. Myra had reached school age, and her younger brothers would soon follow. Starting in the 1840s, a few school districts were established and a scattering of one-room log schoolhouses appeared in Jasper County.

In the antebellum years, it was difficult to attract qualified teachers to backwoods communities on the Missouri frontier. Consequently, "teachers were paid poorly and very inadequately prepared for their work," asserted Missouri governor John Cummins Edwards, who left office in 1848, just in time to join the California gold rush.[36] Many years later, Missouri historian Floyd C. Shoemaker noted, "Virtually all it took to be a teacher in early Missouri was the ability to make a good goose-quill pen and to be a good judge of the toughness and durability of a bunch of hickory switches."[37]

Myra likely attended a log-cabin public school not far from the Carthage town square but soon was enrolled at a private school on the second floor of the Masonic Hall. William Cravens, the main teacher, was considered more competent than public schoolteachers. The tuition for each student ranged from a dollar to a dollar and a half per month.

"She [Myra] was a bright intelligent girl but of a fierce nature, and would fight anyone, boy or girl, that she quarreled with," one of Myra's classmates remembered. "Except for this trait she seemed a nice little girl however."[38] Indeed, Myra had no problem making friends at school. The other children appreciated her intelligence, musical talent, and spunk.

Myra cherished her family. She looked up to her older sister, Charlotte Amanda, who at nineteen left the Shirley household in 1857 to marry Jesse B. Thompson.[39] Myra also doted on her younger brothers, Eddie (Edwin) and Mansfield, and helped care for baby Cravens, born in 1858 and lovingly nicknamed "Shug."[40] Her big brother Bud (John Allison), however, was her favorite sibling. He became her champion and best riding companion.

In Carthage, Myra's love of horses and her equestrian ability were obvious to everyone who knew her. She had learned to properly ride sidesaddle on her father's fine Kentucky steeds and often rode that way throughout her life. Bud and Myra spent countless hours roaming the countryside and racing through the dirt streets of town. Known for his marksmanship as a hunter, Bud taught Myra how to handle firearms. By the time she reached adolescence, she had become a fearless rider and a crack shot. Old-timers who swapped tales on the Carthage square bragged that Myra could shoot a bumblebee off a thistle at thirty yards with her pistol.[41]

As his family adjusted to town life, John Shirley continued to buy property throughout the 1850s, including a vacant one-story building on the north side of the town square that had served as Jasper County's first courthouse since 1842. In 1854, a more substantial two-story brick courthouse was built in the center of the square. When Shirley completed his purchase of the six lots making up the entire north side of the square and the complete block of lots north of the square, he was said to have been the largest property owner in Carthage.[42]

Most Carthaginians held Shirley in high regard. In 1855, he was again appointed a county road commissioner, a clear indication of the public's confidence in him.[43] That trust was important to Shirley when he revealed his bold plan to build and operate a first-rate hotel on the town square.

Aware that establishing a hostelry on the frontier required a considerable investment, Shirley kept as much of his capital in liquid form as possible. He mortgaged four enslaved workers to generate extra cash, including Ike and Lavina, a married couple who had accompanied the Shirley family from Indiana to Missouri. They were pledged as collateral for a $500 loan, and two additional enslaved workers were also mortgaged for another $500. Shirley paid off both mortgages within three years.[44]

Shirley transformed existing structures and started new construction on his property in the town square, much of it with the labor of enslaved workers. But as he and other proslavery citizens upheld human bondage and promoted educational opportunities for White children only, signs of change were occurring elsewhere. In the eastern United States, the voices of abolition and educational reform grew louder.

At Shirley House, also called the Carthage Hotel, John Shirley built a livery stable and corrals and operated a blacksmith shop to accommodate guests who arrived on horseback or by stagecoach. An advertisement heralding the new hotel regularly appeared in the local newspaper:

> **CARTHAGE HOTEL**
> North Side Public Square
> John Shirley, Proprietor.
> Horses and Hacks for Hire.
> A good stable attached.[45]

Shirley quickly became the consummate innkeeper host. Although he was never issued a dram-shop license, the hotel had no shortage of strong drink. Liquor was dispensed freely to guests thanks to three saloons on the courthouse square and a grocer who sold whiskey by the barrel. Travelers feasted on hearty tavern fare prepared by Eliza Shirley's hardworking enslaved women, who lived with their husbands and children in lean-to quarters built onto the west side of the hotel.[46]

The Shirley House's location on the square in the county seat made it a convenient haven for the many lawyers and litigants who came to Carthage for legal proceedings in the courthouse. The hotel also attracted cross-country pilgrims, drummers, circuit riders, drifters, cattle drovers, and politicians. For the curious and spirited Myra, life as a hotel child amid such a diverse assortment of humanity was exhilarating.

Myra became more excited when the much-anticipated Carthage Female Academy, which had been in planning for several years, prepared to open. Intended as an institution to be "patronized by the best families of the county," the school was to be constructed three blocks south of the public square.[47] It would have been an easy walk for Myra.

The struggle to make the academy a reality required plenty of patience and persistence. It began in earnest in 1851, when the more prosperous citizens of Carthage launched the funding campaign for the establishment of an all-female institution. It was intended to be an alternative to the private coeducational school above the Masonic Hall that Myra attended. Advocates of the proposed academy petitioned former Vermont governor William Slade for guidance. He was known as a strong proponent of public education, and during his term as governor, he advanced a program of education reform.[48]

A born and bred New England Yankee, Slade was a curious choice as an adviser for the citizens of Carthage. The majority of Vermonters considered slavery barbaric and opposed the "peculiar institution," a euphemistic term used by White owners of enslaved people.[49] In 1777, the Vermont constitution had been the first in the United States to ban adult slavery. Slade was an ardent abolitionist and outspoken critic of slavery.[50]

By 1847, Slade had cofounded the Board of Popular Education with Catharine Beecher, one of the most vocal advocates for improved education in the nation. She was the sister of Harriet Beecher Stowe, the abolitionist famous for her groundbreaking 1852 novel *Uncle Tom's Cabin*, often recognized as the spark that ignited the Civil War.[51] That book was very likely absent from John Shirley's library.

The publication of *Uncle Tom's Cabin* provoked heated debate across the nation. Slavery supporters argued that Stowe was a radical reformer who "belongs to the school of Women's Rights . . . one which would place women on a foot of political equality with men and cause her to look beyond the office for which she was created—the high and holy office of matrimony."[52]

Women with progressive viewpoints, such as Stowe, galled self-styled chivalrous men just as much as the zealous abolitionists upset them. Both threatened two time-honored and revered institutions of the South that were considered divine—human servitude and venerated ladies.

At first glance, any productive dialogue between eastern "radicals" and proslavery Missourians seemed highly unlikely. However, the memorable phrase coined in 1850, "politics makes strange bedfellows," proved to be true.[53]

Slade and Beecher reviewed the Carthaginians' request for procurement of a teacher and decided to help. Their goal was to recruit, train, and dispatch women teachers into the West to civilize the young in frontier schools and "advance the cause of Christian Education . . . to the occupancy of destitute places."[54] Carthage, perched close to Indian Territory, met the criterion of being a destitute place.

After completing the National Board's six-week tuition-free training course at Hartford, Connecticut, Miss Mary E. Field was sent west to open a school in Carthage.[55] She pledged to teach there for at least two years, and the board paid for her transportation to Missouri.

The new schoolmarm with an odd accent was provided with classroom space in a building on the south side of the town square. She found enough students to keep her in Carthage for two years. No records of her tenure were left behind, but her departure might have resulted from culture shock caused by an inability to adjust to daily life in such a foreign environment.[56]

"For whatever reason she ceased [teaching]—probably marriage or return to Vermont—it was not for lack of patronage for a move for a bigger and better school of the same sort was immediately launched," according to Schrantz.[57]

The departure of Miss Field prompted the frustrated proponents of a bona fide private school for young women in Carthage to renew their efforts. That time, however, they did so without seeking further assistance from what they then considered Yankee do-gooders. Instead, the academy supporters made frequent trips to the state capital, Jefferson City, to lobby legislators and other government officials.

Those efforts paid off. In 1855, the Missouri legislature passed an act incorporating the Carthage Female Academy and placing it under the management of a board of trustees, all of them prominent Carthage citizens. The Jasper County Court sold the trustees a prime building site for one dollar and donated a forty-seven-acre tract that was sold, with the proceeds going to a school construction fund.[58]

A newspaper advertisement of the time succinctly described the school. "The academy is a two-story brick building, large and commodious and equal in all respects to the best in this part of the country. It is located in a retired part of town, surrounded by ample grounds, pleasantly shaded. The rooms [four on each floor] are furnished in the most approved style for school purposes."[59]

Myra Shirley was one of the first students enrolled. Samuel D. Knealand was appointed as the principal. Alice Walker and D. P. Hurley were entrusted with teaching Myra and the other young ladies of Carthage whose families could afford the tuition. Yearly payments varied from eighteen to thirty-five dollars, according to the number of academic classes the student took. Extra charges of as much as fifty dollars per class covered individual instruction in oil painting, ornamental needlework, piano, melodeon, and organ.[60]

The academic curriculum was rigorous. Courses included music, reading, spelling, grammar, arithmetic, algebra, deportment, and classical languages—Greek, Latin, and Hebrew. In antebellum southern society, knowledge of the classics was considered important for an elite man or woman. An extra charge included French—the language of great social importance—"considered essential for young ladies of quality."[61]

Private academies and seminaries for females had become a cultural phenomenon across the nation by the mid-nineteenth century. Until then, educational opportunities for young women had been scarce. For many years, the literacy rate for American women was half that of men, but the federal census of 1850 revealed that women had drawn even with men in literary skills.[62]

In spite of progress in the education of females, significant regional differences separated the schools in New England and the cities of the Midwest from academies in southern states, including rural Missouri. As one southern father explained in 1858, the goal was "the development of the girls into a *lady*, healthy in person, refined in feeling, pure in morals & humble in religion."[63]

John Shirley undoubtedly expected the Carthage Academy to prepare Myra for becoming a wife and mother, and not for entry into a profession. That would have been unladylike. Southern ladies of a certain social class and standing were thought to be more feminine than other women. They had to be protected and idolized and put on a pedestal. Eliza Shirley—Myra's mother—was such a woman, a true Kentucky belle.

A bright and clever girl, Miss Myra was said to have done well in her studies at the academy. Although she might not have fully mastered a foreign language, she developed a lifelong appreciation for art and poetry. She also excelled as a singer and pianist and frequently entertained guests at her father's hotel.

"In these few ante-bellum student years she acquired that faint cultural veneer which seemed later to help her make an outstanding person in a crude society where culture of any kind whatsoever was deemed noteworthy," wrote Schrantz, based on interviews with Myra's friends. "Myra Belle doubtless was a familiar figure in the local life of the small community. A pretty little girl that, keen as a scalping knife, well educated, able to play the piano or melodeon and sing, a good rider and able to shoot too—yep, quite a girl, that kid of old John Shirley."[64]

CHAPTER 3

"The War That Never Goes Away"

THE 1860S DAWNED WITH MYRA SHIRLEY ON THE BRINK of adolescence. She would have to grapple with her identity and independence as a young woman, matters that could be perplexing and exhilarating. She was a confident child capable of riding a thoroughbred at breakneck speed and playing the piano for an audience of hotel guests. With every advantage and a spirit of adventure, the world appeared to be hers for the taking. Instead, her life was suddenly interrupted by all-out war between the northern states and southern slave states.

Fueled by years of pent-up malice and intransigence, the cataclysm swept across the land with the vengeance of a "terrible swift sword."[1] The hopes and dreams of the entire nation morphed into a four-year apocalypse of biblical proportions. In the words of Union general Phil Sheridan, it was the kind of warfare in which "[n]othing should be left to the people but eyes to lament the war."[2] In later years, it was described as "the war that never goes away."[3]

Long before the Confederate States of America was formed as an unrecognized "country" in 1861, the threat of open warfare had grown until it metastasized. The root cause of the war remains one of the most controversial topics in American history. Even before the war ended, scholars and members of the public argued over whether slavery was the primary cause of the Civil War.

On March 21, 1861, the vice president of the newly created Confederacy, Alexander H. Stephens, delivered an extemporaneous address in defense of slavery to a large audience at the Athenaeum in Savannah, Georgia. It became known as the "Cornerstone Speech," in which Stephens declared that the Confederacy's "foundations are laid, its cornerstone rests upon the great truth that the negro is not equal to the white man; that slavery subordination to the superior race is his natural and normal condition."[4]

The same ominous war clouds hovering over the Deep South had gathered on the Mason-Dixon Line and the western borderlands. The clouds were especially threatening over Missouri, a slave state since it had entered the Union in 1821. Even though Missouri settlers required fewer enslaved laborers for their farms than plantations farther south, they vehemently defended their right to own enslaved people and supported the extension of slavery to new states and territories. Like some other Jasper County farmers, John Shirley, a native of the South who had grown up in a family that depended on forced labor, believed he was entitled to own enslaved workers.

Shirley and other slavery advocates in Missouri were particularly interested in their western neighbor entering the Union as a slave state. As early as the 1840s in Kansas Territory, abolitionists established a branch of the Underground Railroad that became an enticing destination for enslaved runaways from Missouri. Abolitionists also threatened Missourians who pursued fleeing enslaved people across the border. However, because of the huge amounts of money invested, the tracking down of human chattel continued.

Tension between the two sides intensified as nerves and tempers frayed. The breaking point came in 1854 when a reluctant United States Congress passed the Kansas-Nebraska Act, opening the territories to broader settlement. More important, the measure adhered to the principle of "popular sovereignty," allowing residents rather than the federal government to decide for themselves whether to allow slavery within their borders.[5]

Before the ink had dried on the bill signed by President Franklin Pierce—a supporter of proslavery settlers—it became painfully clear that although the act had passed Congress, it had failed in its purposes.

According to noted Missouri historian Floyd Shoemaker, Missourians were fearful that "if Kansas should become a 'hotbed of Abolitionism,' then Missouri would be surrounded on three sides by free-soil country; in this case, it required no prophet to see what would become of the Missourians' manpower."[6]

When the law went into effect, an election was called to choose a delegate to Congress and representatives for the Kansas territorial legislature. Both sides of the slavery issue immediately reacted by mustering their forces and descending on Kansas.[7]

The Shirleys likely knew and supported many of the armed Missourians. Often referred to as Border Ruffians, some came from Little Dixie, a region in central and western Missouri settled mostly by families from southern states who owned enslaved workers. Others were from the Six Bulls country and surged into the new territory to cast fraudulent votes under the guise of calling themselves Kansas "residents." To give the appearance of bona fide settlers, some of the intruders built crude huts on the land they claimed.

Antislavery Free-Staters followed suit. They came from northern states as far away as Massachusetts to sway the Kansas elections by making speculative land claims and posing as residents.[8]

Failure to draft a constitution amenable to all citizens in Kansas Territory resulted in sham elections, rival territorial governments, and two opposing legislatures. It also led to disputes that quickly degenerated into brutal violence and guerrilla warfare. The territory became known as "Bleeding Kansas," a fitting moniker that also could have been given to neighboring Missouri.[9]

Many writers and historians have used the propaganda sobriquet "Bleeding Kansas" to lament the loss of life of the antislavery populations of Missouri and Kansas. It has been established, however, that more proslavery men and women died during the long border war than did those on the antislavery side. Both sides found ways to justify violence.[10]

By the summer of 1855, more than twelve hundred antislavery New Englanders had emigrated to Kansas Territory. Many of them were armed with brand new breech-loading Sharps rifles supplied by abolitionist preacher Henry Ward Beecher, a sibling of Harriet Beecher Stowe. The rifles were called "Beecher's Bibles" after Beecher asserted "the true moral agency" of the Sharps rifle and claimed "there was more moral power in one of those instruments, so far as the slaveholders of Kansas were concerned than in a hundred Bibles."[11]

Undaunted by the abolitionists' superior firepower, proslavery proponents wanted to protect their livelihood and way of life, including the use of enslaved laborers. Northern abolitionists and antislavery Missourians rationalized that the termination of slavery and the vanquishing of slaveholders could cleanse the southern populace, and blood sacrifice could purge the evil of human slavery. Extremists and terrorists existed among the Free-Staters as well as the abolitionists. Few heroes could be found.

At first, the Missouri-Kansas border troubles did not directly impact the citizens of Jasper County, Missouri. Most of the activity took place farther north. Eventually, gossip and rumors about border raids and the divisive slavery question turned bitter and rancorous. Folks started to choose sides, and political discourse turned into heated arguments. The carrying of firearms became more common.

Acts of violence increased, such as in 1858 when a Kansas man was hired to teach school in Sarcoxie, the strongest proslavery town in Jasper County. Only a few families in the community were not southern sympathizers. The teacher's strong abolitionist views were revealed when he began to lecture about the evils of slavery and read *Uncle Tom's Cabin* with his pupils. He was promptly told to resign. He refused. A citizens' delegation confronted him and again ordered him to leave town. After refusing a second time, the teacher was escorted to a patch of woods, given a thick coat of hot tar and chicken feathers, and sent on his way.[12]

Such incidents contributed to the rancor in Missouri and other border states. Over time, the animosity caused irreparable damage. People turned against their neighbors, and lifelong friendships were splintered. Divided allegiances destroyed families, pitting siblings against one another in what came to be called the "Brothers' War."[13] The Shirley family became one of the casualties.

IN THE CHAOTIC YEARS before the Civil War, John Shirley found himself in a precarious situation that became increasingly difficult to navigate. The Virginia-born Shirley owned enslaved workers, but he also was a public figure in his community and a busy innkeeper. Partisan politics, the Kansas troubles, and the question of slavery were frequent topics of conversation and heated debate at his hotel and on the streets of Carthage. The vast differences of opinion among Shirley's customers and friends forced him to maintain a delicate balance between his livelihood and his personal and political beliefs. As a host bent on retention of trade, Shirley took a neutral tone in public. In private, he likely tried to sympathize with the views of the person with whom he was talking.[14]

However, the most challenging of the balancing acts Shirley had to manage was within his family. Not all the Shirleys had the same political allegiances, especially when it came to the struggle between North and South. The discord resulted in pitting siblings against one another and children against their father.

Preston, or Pres, and his older sister Mary Ann—children from John Shirley's first marriage—had moved to Missouri to be near their father. As much as they loved him, neither they nor their spouses saw eye to eye with Shirley about politics and slavery. Pres and his sister Mary Ann made no secret of their opposition to human servitude and their strong belief that it should be abolished.[15]

"Preston was developing some dangerous anti-slavery ideas, possibly partly as a result of the influence of his wife's family, but more pronounced since Dick Hunter and his wife, Mary, one of John's daughters by his first marriage, had come west in 1852," wrote historian Ward L. Schrantz. "Dick and Mary were both anti-slavery, yet not as much as Pres was becoming."[16]

As early as the presidential election of 1856, the Shirley family's ideological divide became public when Pres chose not to vote for his father's favorite candidate and the eventual winner, Democrat James Buchanan.

Instead, Pres openly supported John C. Frémont, the famed explorer of California and the West and the first presidential candidate of the newly formed Republican Party.[17]

Frémont's abolitionist views appealed to Preston. However, Frémont's father-in-law, Thomas Hart Benton—a powerhouse who had represented Missouri in the United States Senate for thirty years—remained a loyal Democrat and endorsed Buchanan. Ultimately, Frémont was excluded from the ballot in Missouri and a dozen other southern and border states.[18] The only presidential choices for Missourians were Buchanan and Millard Fillmore, the former United States president and a candidate of the American, or Know Nothing, Party.

Although Preston Shirley had been denied the opportunity to vote for his preferred candidate, the gossip about his support of a political party that opposed the extension of slavery likely caused his father some embarrassment. John Shirley and his children Pres Shirley and Mary Shirley Hunter avoided talking about their political differences at family gatherings, but the tension must have been palpable for Myra and her younger brothers.

By the time another presidential election cycle rolled around in 1860, four presidential candidates were in the race: Democrat Stephen A. Douglas of Illinois, Constitutional Union candidate John Bell of Tennessee, Southern Democrat John C. Breckinridge of Kentucky, and Republican Abraham Lincoln of Illinois. That time, all the candidates were on the Missouri ballot.[19]

In Jasper County, there was little doubt that most voters would support anyone but Lincoln. The more vehement slavery supporters wanted Breckinridge of the Southern Democrats, an extreme proslavery group that threatened secession of southern states from the Union if Lincoln won. When the votes were tallied nationwide, Lincoln was elected as the sixteenth president of the United States. In Jasper County, the most votes went to Bell with 424, followed by Douglas with 407 and Breckenridge with 192. Lincoln finished in last place with only 38 votes.[20]

Preston Shirley likely voted for Lincoln, but if he did so it was not in Jasper County or anywhere else in Missouri. Months before the November 4, 1860, election, Preston was long gone to Texas.[21] He had grown weary of the way people treated his wife and children once the word got around about his Republican affiliation. A woman who lived near the Preston home had offered to pay $500 toward the expenses of anyone who would go to Springfield, Illinois, and kill Lincoln; some of Preston's acquaintances offered to match the amount.[22] It was all "whiskey talk," but Preston worried that such bravado, as well as the sneers and ridicule aimed at him and his family, would lead to violence.

Still a dutiful son, Preston went to Carthage to seek John Shirley's counsel and discuss the pros and cons of relocation. The pros won. Then Preston, his wife, Mary Arella, and their three sons—Christian, Oliver, and one-year-old George—left Missouri. They moved to Burleson County, Texas, and established a farm near the town of Lexington. Although Texas seemed an unlikely refuge for Preston because of his political beliefs, the generally accepted story at the time was that he thought he could avoid the impending war by going south.[23]

Myra Shirley, about to enter her teens, must have been bewildered by the sudden departure of her half brother and cousins. Everywhere she turned, the political bombast that dominated conversations added to the confusion and uncertainty about the future. "Myra at school, at home, at the hotel and on the streets heard talk of secession, and of the chivalry of the south and of glorious southern womanhood, and of 'Old Ape' Lincoln and what he might do after he was inaugurated president," wrote Schrantz. "She heard talk about whether or not Missouri would secede. But her father, John Shirley, was guarded in his talk about secession. He had his business to think about. It was principally in this that his life's savings were tied up."[24]

On January 28, 1861, prior to Lincoln taking office in March, outgoing president James Buchanan signed the bill admitting Kansas Territory to the Union as a free state. The abolitionists had prevailed, but John Shirley and the proslavery faction in Missouri realized there would be a resulting escalation of violence along the state border.

With the election of Lincoln, it had become painfully clear that a war between the northern and southern states was inevitable. Southern states were already passing ordinances of secession from the Union and lobbying border states to join a new confederacy in which slavery would be unchallenged. Missouri—the gateway to the West—was a ripe plum for the picking because of its strategic location, large population, and abundance of natural and human resources.

Missouri was the only proslavery state north of the Mason-Dixon Line. The newly elected governor, Claiborne Fox Jackson, was pro-Confederate and an ardent secessionist. In his inaugural address, he boldly proclaimed, "The destiny of the slave-holding states of this union is one and the same. So long as a state maintains slavery within her limits, it is impossible to separate her fate from that of her sister states. Missouri will not be found to shrink from the duty which her interests, and her sympathies point alike in one direction, and determine her to stand by the South."[25]

Governor Jackson did not speak for all the state's citizens, however. Most Missourians wished to remain neutral. At a secession convention that met in Saint Louis in March 1861, the delegates overwhelmingly decided to remain with the Union.[26] Missouri would not secede or go to war against her sister states of the South, the convention decided.

Although many people believed the war was wrong, they opposed the federal government's forcing states to remain in the Union. This resulted in a split within the Missouri state government. It became apparent that the two opposing forces would collide, leaving Missouri in turmoil for four years and well beyond.

"The struggle for Missouri was one of the most prolonged and violent conflicts of nineteenth-century America, extending beyond the boundaries of the Civil War," wrote Civil War historian Elle E. Harvell. "In fact, Missouri was the very seedbed of the Civil War."[27]

There was nothing remotely *civil* about the war in Missouri. From 1861 to 1865, more than twelve hundred battles and engagements would be fought within the state.[28] Only Virginia and Tennessee exceeded that total. From the start, the fighting in Missouri was especially vicious and personal. That was partly because the drums of war were beaten by newspapers from both sides, echoing across the state.

Those drums beat loud and clear in Jasper County. On March 29,

1861, Christopher Columbus Dawson, an advocate of the slaveholding interest and the bellicose editor of the *Southwest News* in Carthage, published an editorial that stated, "Abraham Lincoln is six feet four in physical stature and four feet six in mental stature."[29] That same day, newly inaugurated President Lincoln sent more troops to reinforce Fort Sumter, South Carolina, where two weeks later, a Confederate artillery barrage marked the official start of the war. Missouri secessionists itching for battle promised that any invading federal troops would be welcomed "with bloody hands to hospitable graves."[30]

Missouri governor Claiborne Fox and other Confederate sympathizers maintained a secessionist state government even after a provisional Unionist government was established. The Confederate States of America officially totaled eleven states, but two of the thirteen stars on the Confederate flag reflected the Confederacy's claim on Missouri and Kentucky.[31] The popular marching song "The Bonnie Blue Flag," written in 1861 in tribute to the Confederacy's unofficial banner, devoted a lyric to Missouri.

And to Missouri we
Extend both heart and hand
And welcome her a sister
Of our Confederate band.[32]

Patriotic tunes were harbingers of an ominous future. Missourians, hardened by fear, anger, revenge, and hatred, took on a long and bloody ordeal inside the boundaries of their state that raged within the larger national war.

Throughout the winter and spring of 1861, volunteer militias representing both sides of the conflict formed across Missouri. A considerable number of Union men from Jasper County took off for Kansas to enlist in the Sixth Kansas Regiment Volunteer Cavalry being mustered into service at Fort Scott. Southern sympathizers organized their own "companies of minute men" and began drilling and training for combat at several towns in Jasper County, including Sarcoxie, Minersville, Sherwood, Medoc, and Carthage.[33]

The Carthage company was sworn into service by Captain Emmett MacDonald, an Ohio native and Saint Louis attorney. MacDonald's volunteer militia battalion was based in Vernon County, fifty miles to the north, with orders to patrol the region and protect the border.[34]

Named the Border Rangers, the Carthage volunteers elected Jesse L. Cravens, a prominent merchant, as captain. One of the first men to enlist was John and Eliza Shirley's son, John Allison "Bud" Shirley, a strapping nineteen-year-old. His skills with horses and with firearms would be put to good use in the cavalry command. The men supplied their own horses and small arms but trained with wooden swords until they could obtain sabers. Every Saturday, the Border Rangers met to drill and receive military instruction. A notice in the *Southwest News* of March 29, 1861, plainly stated, "The Border Rangers drill every Saturday from this on. Let everyone be at his post tomorrow as there is important business to transact."[35] Bud Shirley and many of his cohorts reported as ordered.

Myra and her schoolmates at the Carthage Academy became a regular audience at the drills, beaming with pride as the men and boys went through their paces. Myra had nothing but scorn for any young men from Carthage who failed to join the Border Rangers. She also turned up her nose at her former friends who dared to ridicule the rangers.[36] Any such disrespect was an affront to her dear brother Bud.

Myra was somewhat puzzled when she learned that James Hunter had joined the Border Guards, the company formed in Medoc near the old Shirley home. Hunter was the son of Mary Hunter, Myra's half sister. Despite being ten years older than Myra, Hunter always teasingly called her "Aunt Myra."[37] Myra was surprised when Hunter was appointed first lieutenant of the company because she knew he was a Yankee at heart. Jim Hunter had cast one of the thirty-eight votes Lincoln received in Jasper County, but Hunter's sole mission was to protect Missouri from Kansas raiders.

"Myra Shirley probably snorted when she heard that Jim Hunter was in the Medoc 'Border Guards,'" wrote Schrantz. "He was an unconditional Union man. How silly could people be? He actually thought those companies were being formed to protect the border. Everybody in Carthage knew better than that. These were going to be southern soldiers if there were a war."[38]

That was precisely what happened. A pro-Confederate delegation of prominent Carthaginians went to Medoc and urged the Border Guards to join Governor Jackson's insurgent army to defend Missouri from Union troops. Captain A. J. Talbot, in command of the Border Guards and a strong southern sympathizer, was in full agreement, as were most of the other men.[39]

The Shirleys were forced to deal with the internal strife that impacted so many Missouri families. They would soon have even more concerns as war came to Jasper County and Carthage. Their lives were about to change drastically, and the events set to occur would eventually make young Myra Shirley a legend of the American West.

CHAPTER 4

All Torn Asunder

On the night of July 1, 1861, as the suffocating humidity began to calm down, an enormous comet broke through the cloud cover and appeared in the northern sky over Missouri. It had been visible to naked eyes for months, with sightings reported from Africa to Montana. President Lincoln had followed the course of the ball of fire from a window in the White House. For a brief time, the entire planet was within the comet's long tail.[1]

"We have a flaming comet in the sky," wrote southern diarist John Beauchamp Jones. "It comes unannounced and takes a northwestern course. I dreamed last night that I saw a great black ball moving through the heavens, and it obscured the moon . . . men ran in different directions, uttering cries of agony."[2]

Union troops making their way from Saint Louis to the Six Bulls country watched in awe as the comet plowed across the heavens. Dogs and coyotes howled throughout the night. Many people believed that the end of the world had come. A dire omen of death and destruction, the comet was viewed as a portent of the pending bloody combat. Classified by astronomers as the Great Comet of 1861, it became known as the War Comet, the most spectacular celestial body of the nineteenth century.[3]

Carthaginians were aware of the much-ballyhooed comet and mindful that intruders of another stripe—Union soldiers—had made their way to Jasper County. Federal troops marched into Sarcoxie on June 28, 1861. They promptly chopped down the tall wooden pole flying a large Confederate flag and set it ablaze.[4] But a flag also flew in Carthage.

"People knew that a war was in progress but without realizing very clearly just what war was—as was natural for persons who had yet to view it at close range," wrote historian Ward Schrantz. "It all seemed unrealistic somehow, though the Confederate flag which fluttered lazily on its pole south of the courthouse showed where the major sympathies of Carthage lay."[5]

As was true throughout Missouri, the Fourth of July turned into a day of ambivalence in Carthage. Myra and her siblings did not attend a picnic or parade. Like everyone else in town, they did not venture outside. The feelings of many pro-Confederates, such as the Shirleys, were summed up by a soldier who wrote in his diary that day, "Once the Sons of the South hailed its [July 4] coming with joy, but now we heed it not, as the United States are no more."[6]

Ironically, the anniversary of the birth of the nation came to Jasper County just one day before the war that would decide the future of that Union. On the evening of July 4, eleven hundred Union soldiers appeared and camped at James Spring on the southeastern edge of Carthage.[7] Before the columns of soldiers reached the town square, someone lowered the Confederate flag and tucked it away. That night, approximately six thousand pro-Confederate Missouri state militiamen camped eighteen miles north.[8] The Battle of Carthage was about to commence.

On July 5, the state guard troops broke camp two hours before sunrise and marched south toward Carthage. They were under the command of Missouri governor Claiborne Fox Jackson, the only time a sitting United States governor has led troops into battle.[9] In Jackson's mind and heart, Missouri was no longer part of the Union.

Jackson's forces consisted of several thousand infantry, cavalry, and artillery troops. Some companies had only shotguns and squirrel rifles they had brought from home. At least two thousand recruits were unarmed.[10] All of them were primed and eager to take on the smaller Union force of mostly German immigrants from Saint Louis, commanded by Colonel Franz Sigel.[11]

Prior to the war, Sigel—a "small, red-bearded, nervous man"—had been a professor of mathematics and history at the German-American

Institute in Saint Louis.[12] He also was an accomplished military tactician and a decorated commander of as many as thirty thousand troops during the German Revolution of 1848. Revered by the large German community in Saint Louis, Sigel assembled a formidable regiment that included many German army combat veterans.[13] Although he was outnumbered, Sigel was confident that his "Yankee Dutch," as the Confederates called them, would make short work of the despised "Missouri rabble."[14] His infantrymen were equipped with powerful .69-caliber military muskets rifled for minié balls, conical projectiles that were far more accurate than round-ball ammunition and greatly increased the range of the weapons.[15]

In the early hours of July 5, the well-armed Union troops quickstepped north through the town square en route to battle. Although many residents stayed in their homes or shops with the curtains drawn, some pro-Union citizens showed up to cheer the troops passing in review. Myra Shirley and her family watched from the hotel windows until the rear guard was out of sight.[16] Their main concern was for the safety of Bud, the brother whom Myra idolized. He was somewhere out there riding for the southern cause against the Yankee interlopers.

Before long, the rival armies formed battle lines on a plain about ten miles north of Carthage. An artillery duel was soon under way. Both sides employed artillery, infantry, and cavalry, making it one of the earliest full-scale land engagements of the war, preceding the first major land battle—the Battle of Bull Run (or Manassas)—by sixteen days. The *New York Times* would later describe the battle at Carthage as "the first serious conflict between the United States troops and the rebels."[17]

The rumble of cannon fire could be heard in town just as the few guests at the Shirley Hotel were served breakfast. The loudest of the big guns was "Old Sacramento," a cannon the Missourians had seized in 1847 at the battle of Sacramento Creek during the Mexican War. Reportedly cast from melted-down silver church bells, "Ol' Sac" produced a distinctive ring that could be heard for miles.[18] The roar of the cannons grew louder. A veil of black smoke drifted southward and hovered over the square. Before long, Myra likely breathed the smell of battle as the pungent stench of exploding gunpowder seeped into the hotel lobby.

Archy Thomas, a soldier in the Missouri State Guard from Carroll County, described the start of the battle in his unpublished memoir, signed "An Eyewitness":[19]

> State troops filed to the left of the road formed in order of battle, planting the cannon on the side of the hill with their infantry to support them. When ready the order was given and off went the misiles [sic] of death and destruction from the cannon mouth. With the loud roar of distant thunder, in quick succession roar followed roar from each battery and we could see at every fire the state battery made a swarth [sic] open through the columns of the federal troops and again and again discover the officer rally the men, but again and again would the state cannon belch fourth [sic] death among them until they fled.

This battle, pitting Missourians against one another, turned into a nearly fourteen-hour series of running engagements and skirmishes in the unforgiving July heat. Most of the combatants had little water and no breakfast. A contingency of state guard cavalry happened upon a thicket of blackberry bushes and took time to satisfy their appetites before resuming the chase of the "Dutch."[20] Then they doggedly attacked Sigel's outnumbered Yankee forces and ultimately pushed them toward Carthage.

James Hickey, a young farmer who lived south of town, rode into the square late that afternoon and came upon a group of about twenty-five women just east of the Shirley Hotel. "They were gathered around, talking excitedly and wondering what was going to happen to the town. The noise of the battle had got close by this time,"[21] Hickey recalled many years later. Although he did not give any specific names, it was likely that Eliza Shirley and her teenage daughter, Myra, were in that crowd.[22]

The women scattered in different directions just as some state guard cavalrymen entered the town from the north. Gunfire erupted.[23] Windows shattered in the courthouse, and bullets thudded into the Shirley Hotel.

"Federal skirmishers now came falling back through the square, firing from behind buildings," wrote Schrantz based on eyewitness accounts.

"In pursuit, slipping from house to house, came state guard skirmishers, shooting from the concealment of fences or around the corners of buildings, then reloading and firing again. More powder smoke drifted into the Shirley Hotel. There was gunfire all around. . . . Men darted across the rear yard. Muskets were crackling around the stables and other outhouses. Stray bullets entered through windows, smacked violently against the hostelry's inside walls."[24]

By then, John Shirley had ushered Eliza, Myra, his three young sons (Edwin, Mansfield, and Cravens), enslaved workers, and guests to the safety of the hotel cellar, where they remained until the shooting eventually stopped. When they emerged and peeked outside, they saw the square full of mounted cavalry and a throng of thirsty men bunched around the public well southeast of the Shirley Hotel.[25] The fighting had moved on. Sigel and his troops were in retreat.

Eliza and Myra rushed outside to tend to the battle-weary men and boys. They brought buckets of water and food that the enslaved women had busily prepared in the hotel kitchen. "As our troops came into town," recalled George Venable almost a half-century later, "the ladies, God bless them, brought large waiters [trays] filled with good things to eat and our boys did full justice to the feast."[26]

Myra spent much of the day toting water and vittles to the southern militiamen trudging into the square.[27] Maimed soldiers hobbled to the courthouse, which had been converted into a hospital. Archy Thomas, the militiaman who later wrote of the battle in his memoir, was one of them. He had received a flesh wound in his arm during one of the skirmishes.

"The citizens and especially the ladies of Carthage were very much rejoiced that the state troops had driven out the federals," wrote Thomas. "One lady running out when the balls were flying thick and heavy, shouting hurra[h] for Jef [sic] Davis, liberty and independence forever, down with the dutch [sic] and cheering on the boys to brave and noble deeds."[28]

Wagons brought litter cases to transport the wounded from the southeast of town as the action was concluding. Interior doors were taken down to use as operating tables for two local doctors who worked alongside regimental surgeons. The county clerk's office in the southwest corner of the first floor became a surgery. By flickering light, the surgeons amputated mutilated arms and legs and tossed the severed limbs into a pile just outside the window. Soldiers buried them in a shallow trench hastily dug in the courthouse lawn.[29]

"Dead from the fighting in and about the town were being collected by male civilians and brought in," veterans of the battle later told Schrantz. "They couldn't be left out with the town's hogs running at large as they did. But the town's roving hogs were perhaps dying themselves about that time. The minds of the disorganized soldiers were on food."[30]

The Shirley Hotel took in large numbers of hungry soldiers. Eliza and the enslaved women—Annie, Lavina, and Lena—toiled well into the night to feed as many as possible.[31] Myra helped serve the food but also volunteered at the courthouse hospital, comforting the wounded. Her mind was on her brother, and she asked every man she encountered if he knew Bud Shirley or had any notion of his whereabouts. None of the Shirley family members got much sleep when they finally fell into their beds in the wee hours.

Dawn broke on July 6 to answered prayers. A gaggle of Carthage Border Rangers rode into town on lathered horses after a long night ride. Among them was an unscathed and smiling Bud Shirley. He rushed to the hotel, where he was greeted by his father and young brothers and hugged and kissed by his tearful mother and sister. Bud sat down to breakfast and related how the rangers had been on patrol well to the south and did not get back in time for the battle.[32]

Despite countless artillery salvos and musket volleys, the number of casualties in Carthage was surprisingly low. The commonly accepted tally of federal losses came to thirteen killed and thirty-one wounded, and the state guard had thirty-five killed and 125 wounded.[33] Both sides declared victory. Union forces claimed they had won because of Sigel's ability to escape a much larger force with minimal casualties. Governor Jackson's volunteers, however, considered Sigel's hasty departure a full-blown retreat. They claimed victory because of having forced the Dutch to flee the county. The battle lifted the spirits of southern sympathizers and state guard forces.[34]

Whether they had volunteered or not, private citizens from each side had been drawn into the war. Noncombatants had to make choices and declare allegiances. Before the dead were buried, armed state guardsmen went to the homes of known northern sympathizers and placed adult males under arrest. They were taken to a secret location to be held for questioning and released in the morning. The more loquacious pro-Union residents were warned that the time had come for them to leave Jasper County at once—or face the consequences.

The threats were taken seriously, and a steady stream of "Yankee lovers" departed to Saint Louis or returned to their home states in the Northeast. Most of the refugees went west to Kansas, the closest and most convenient pro-Union haven. Several of those who left were friends of the Shirleys, and some were kin.

Just a few weeks after the battle, Myra's half sister, Mary Shirley Hunter, told the rest of the family that she and her sons had been given notice that it was time to depart. The Hunters were recognized as abolitionists and supporters of the hated Abraham Lincoln. Since the death of Mary's husband, Richard Hunter, in February 1861, her son Jim had run the farm with help from three younger brothers. Jim had been a lieutenant in the Border Guards but resigned because of his political views. Since then, horses had been stolen from the Hunter place, and Jim's life had been threatened repeatedly.[35]

Just as Preston Shirley had done before he left with his family for Texas, Jim Hunter rode into Carthage to confer with his grandfather John Shirley. Once again, Shirley discussed various options and the pros and cons of such a move. In the end, he agreed with Jim that Indiana, their family home before moving west, would be the best choice.[36]

On July 21, 1861, Jim Hunter, his mother, and his younger brothers—Cornelius, Thomas, and Richard—abandoned their farm. They spent that night with their family at the Shirley Hotel. Myra had mixed feelings. She liked Mary and her four sons, especially Jim. But Myra understood that they were Unionists and needed to move elsewhere for their own safety.

The Hunters left the next morning in their wagon pulled by sturdy oxen. Several days later, while camped on a riverbank near Saint Louis, the younger boys went swimming. They "contracted an illness," and Cornelius and Thomas soon died. Devastated by the loss, the grieving family buried the boys and continued their journey. Once in Indiana, Jim provided a comfortable home.[37] However, just a year-and-a-half later, he left his mother in his brother Richard's care and enlisted as a Union private in Company I, Second Indiana Volunteer Cavalry. Jim fought in several battles and in 1864 was with the troops led by General William T. Sherman on his "March to the Sea."[38]

"It was well for the Hunters that they left [Missouri] when they did," wrote Schrantz. "Within a few days the state guard foraging parties were in their old neighborhood, loading their wagons and forming their herds from the farms of those reputed to be federal adherents."[39]

Not all the violence and terrorism in Jasper County was aimed at pro-Union folks. Federal soldiers and citizen marauders swore revenge for their losses as well. As a result, many farmers driven out of Missouri headed to Fort Scott, Kansas, and enlisted in Union cavalry regiments.

One of the first acts of blatant violence occurred in Jasper County in August, when armed abolitionist horsemen from Kansas raided the farm of George Broome, who had purchased the Shirleys' farm when they moved to Carthage. Broome was known to own many enslaved workers and many thoroughbred horses. The raiders rode up to Broome's home, and when he came to the door, shot and killed him. They stole a large amount of money, gathered every horse they could find, and burned the former Shirley home to the ground.[40]

Broome had been a popular figure in Carthage, and news of his murder stunned his friends and associates, including John Shirley. "Despite all early bloody threats, Broome had been the first civilian slain in Jasper County since the outbreak of the war," wrote Schrantz. "His death made a tremendous impression, and the anger and terror engendered by it sent additional recruits to the southern armies."[41]

Death and destruction would become common in Missouri. Myra and her family witnessed the inglorious reality of a nation waging war against itself. Irrevocable choices were made. The results of those decisions showed the Shirley family that unlike the promise of the old hymn, there was no "balm in Gilead to make the wounded whole," only wounds that would never heal.[42] The next few years would have a devastating impact on young Myra Shirley and—for better and for worse—would shape the rest of her life.[43]

CHAPTER 5

Myra on the Scout

DURING THE TUMULTUOUS SUMMER AND AUTUMN OF 1861, Myra Shirley's childhood slipped away. Her exposure to horrible acts of violence and the ever present sight and smell of death created invisible wounds. War had become a normal part of her life. The bullet-pocked walls of the Shirley Hotel and battered buildings on the square were constant reminders of what had happened and what was to come.

John and Eliza Shirley must have been anxious about their son Bud answering the call to arms and concerned for the safety of their other children. The Shirleys had likely given up hope that Myra would become a model of culture and refinement in the mold of the stereotypical "southern belle."

This uniquely southern archetype that flourished in the antebellum years called for the idealized female to transition from being a daughter to a devoted and graceful wife. Historian Anne Goodwyn Jones provides a succinct description: "She is the fragile, dewy, just-opened bloom of the southern female. . . . Then she becomes a lady, and a lady she will remain until she dies—unless, of course, she does something beyond the pale."[1]

Myra was bright and engaging but regularly strayed beyond the pale of acceptable female behavior. Although the natural order of society called for females to be submissive and obedient to men, women saw their roles changing, particularly with the nation at war. Women on both sides were not merely spectators but contributed to the war effort. They endured economic hardship, took over the management of farms and plantations, nursed wounded soldiers, and accomplished other unaccustomed tasks.

Many women took exception with zealots such as Orestes A. Brownson, often called "America's first great Catholic intellectual," who considered Black people and women inferior to White males.[2]

"Woman was created to be a wife and mother; that is her destiny," Brownson wrote. "She was born to be a queen in her own household, and to make home cheerful, bright, and happy."[3]

It is highly doubtful that young Myra Shirley would have put any stock in Brownson's opinions. She probably would have been much more inclined to agree with Frederick Douglass, the former enslaved worker, avid abolitionist, and champion of women's rights, who wrote in 1866, "To me, the sun in the heavens at noonday is not more visible than is the right of women, equally with man, to participate in all that concerns human welfare."[4]

In August 1861, the Confederate victory at the Battle of Wilson's Creek southwest of Springfield, Missouri, encouraged many pro-Confederate women to respond to a call for assistance in the war effort.[5] For a time, the battles at Carthage and Wilson's Creek had secured southwestern Missouri for secessionists and bolstered the recruitment of civilian females to volunteer in support of the southern cause.

"It was for this cause that the rich blood of your sons, brothers, kindred and friends was poured out like water on the bloody fields of Carthage and Springfield," Colonel John T. Hughes of the Missouri State Guard wrote in a communiqué to the citizens of the Fourth Military District of Missouri. "We want to ask our noble, generous-hearted and patriotic women (and thank God the country is full of them) to have a thousand suits of fall and winter clothing made up for our soldiers, as we advance into the Missouri Valley."[6]

By all appearances, Myra wanted to pitch in, especially if those efforts could help her cherished big brother Bud; she missed her regular jaunts through the countryside with him. However, sitting in a sewing circle of women and girls stitching uniforms, darning socks, or picking lint to make bandages would likely not have appealed to Myra. She wanted a much more active role. If she had been a few years older and could have pulled it off, she probably would have taken up arms and ridden with

Bud. Instead, she decided to put her equestrian skills to good use by carrying any useful information she picked up around town to her brother and his comrades hiding in the countryside. Her anxiety grew whenever Bud rode off with his cohorts to engage their sworn enemies. She lived in constant fear that he would never return.

By 1861, the earlier years of Bleeding Kansas paled in comparison to the vicious guerrilla war on the Kansas-Missouri border. It has been referred to as "a war of stealth and raid, without a front, without formal organization, with almost no division between the civilian and the warrior."[7] In many cases, guerrilla fighters turned out to be thieves and adventurers who murdered, pillaged, and raped civilians. Numerous bloodthirsty protagonists were on both sides, all seeking retaliation and revenge.

Pro-Confederate Missourians despised James Henry Lane, the first United States senator from the free state of Kansas. He commanded what he dubbed the "Kansas Brigade," fifteen hundred volunteers who took part in a rampage of terror and mayhem in the slave state of Missouri.[8] Two bands of citizen scouts made up much of Lane's force: the Jayhawkers, named for a mythical bird that stole from other bird's nests, and the Red Legs, ruffians who wore maroon leggings fashioned from pilfered sheepskin leather tied just below the knee.[9] Charles R. "Doc" Jennison—considered the most brutal and unscrupulous of the Jayhawkers—was the founding commander of the Red Legs.[10] This secretive group of the most ardent abolitionists often accompanied Jayhawkers on raids into Missouri.

On the Confederate side of the guerrilla war, irregular insurgents operating outside the military chain of command were known as bushwhackers. They operated independently of the regular Confederate troops but assisted them at various skirmishes. They also made retaliatory raids on the farms and homes of any suspected pro-Union residents. The Union command considered them "no better than thieves and robbers."[11] Bud Shirley was a confirmed bushwhacker.

A generally accurate description of the various paramilitary factions operating in the borderlands came from C. M. Chase, reporter for the *True Republic Sentinel* of Sycamore, Illinois, traveling through Missouri and Kansas in the early 1860s:

General James Henry Lane was the leader of the Kansas Jayhawkers.

Jayhawkers, Red Legs, and Bushwhackers are everyday terms in Kansas and Western Missouri. A Jayhawker is a Unionist who professes to rob, burn out and murder only rebels in arms against the government. A Red Leg is a Jayhawker originally distinguished by the uniform of red leggings. A Red Leg, however, is regarded as more purely an indiscriminate thief and murderer than the Jayhawker or Bushwhacker. A Bushwhacker is a rebel Jayhawker, or a rebel who bands with others for the purpose of preying upon the lives and property of Union citizens. They are all lawless and indiscriminate in their iniquities. Their occupation, unless crushed out speedily, will end in a system of highway robbery exceeding anything which has existed in any country.[12]

On September 23, 1861, Lane—known as the "Grim Chieftain"—and his Kansas Brigade proved themselves indiscriminate killers when they descended on Osceola, Missouri.[13] The Jayhawkers looted and burned houses and businesses, bombarded the courthouse, and robbed the bank.

During the sacking of the town, nine citizens were given a quick drumhead trial and summarily executed in the town square.[14]

"Missourians," Lane had said, "are wolves, snakes, devils, and damn their souls, I want to cast them into a burning hell! We believe in a war of extermination."[15] As the sun went down, Osceola was a smoldering ruin.[16]

The Jayhawkers and Red Legs were not the only purveyors of violence and terror along the Kansas-Missouri borderlands. Depredations on the civilian population by irregular pro-Confederate guerrillas came with the same cruelty and fierceness that had been dealt by their Union counterparts.

Many bushwhackers were men of southern heritage committed to oppose Union occupation and defend home and hearth. Others, however, were opportunists and brigands with no noble purpose who reveled in robbery and sadistic violence.

"Missouri was neither north or south," wrote Samuel Byers, a Union officer who served with the Fifth Iowa Volunteers. "She was simply hell, for her people were cutting one another's throats and neighboring farmers killed each other and burned each other's homes. One half of the male population of Missouri was trying to kill the other half. They were not opponents from different sections fighting, but near neighbors, and nothing seemed too awful or too cruel for them to do. How I pitied the women and children in the State in those awful days."[17]

One of the primary contributors to the depredations in Missouri and Kansas was William Clarke Quantrill. A former Ohio schoolteacher, Quantrill led a band of mostly teenage farm boys on a tear through Union border strongholds in both states. They rode under Quantrill's standard—the ominous black flag intended to show that no quarter would be given.[18]

To pro-Confederate Missourians, Quantrill and his fellow partisan rangers were heroes who stood up to Jayhawker harassment and Union occupation. Quantrill always had his share of defenders, including some Civil War historians who have claimed that he has always been terribly maligned. They argued that Quantrill and his guerrillas "became the victims of a thorough character assassination," as historian Donald Gilmore wrote.[19]

Jayhawkers and bushwhackers were equally ruthless in a war fought without quarter.[20] Citizens lived in constant terror that they would be caught in the fierce and deadly cross fire. However, to Kansans of that time, Quantrill was the devil incarnate, and his band of boys and men epitomized cruelty.

One of the most feared and hated of all those who rode with Quantrill was William T. Anderson, a ruthless guerrilla leader who "took to the brush" out of pure hatred of Union sympathizers. Known as "Bloody Bill," Anderson had no regard for human life. It was said that he broke into tears and frothed at the mouth during battle.[21] Anderson explained his behavior in a rambling letter to pro-Confederate newspapers, writing:

"I have chosen guerrilla warfare to revenge myself for wrongs that I could not honorably revenge otherwise. I lived in Kansas when this war commenced. Because I would not fight the people of Missouri, my native state, the Yankees sought my life, but failed to get me. Revenged themselves by murdering my father, destroying all my property, and since that time murdered one of my sisters and kept the other two in jail for twelve months."[22]

Bloody Bill Anderson killed, tortured, and mutilated scores of civilians and Union soldiers. In several instances, Anderson scalped his victims and cut off their noses and ears for trophies. Some people later claimed that he suffered from delusional paranoia that exacerbated his sadistic personality.[23]

Numerous books and stories have asserted that John Shirley's hotel was a popular resting and meeting place for Anderson, Quantrill, and other mythologized bushwhackers. Quantrill and his raiders made appearances in Jasper County and passed through Carthage. Historian Ward Schrantz reported that on at least two occasions—including one in 1862 when Union troops occupied Carthage—Quantrill and his men paused at the Shirley Hotel but did not sleep there.

"Dashing into town hoping for a surprise, the guerrillas had found the Missouri militia who held the place ensconced in the courthouse and all ready for them," wrote Schrantz. "These visitors were great heroes to Myra.... And they talked about killing people just as casually as other folks might about killing chickens. And they were so polite—real southern gentlemen they seemed to her. She played the piano and sang for them."[24]

John Shirley was likely relieved when Quantrill and his men rode out of town. Shirley's allegiance was to the South, but he also had a business to run. He knew it was important to keep a neutral public face.[25] Depending on which side occupied Carthage at any given time, more Union troops than southern soldiers either dined or were billeted at the Shirley Hotel.

Some people have claimed erroneously that Bud Shirley rode with Quantrill and Anderson. Sources have even stated that Bud was a captain in Quantrill's command. Other published accounts maintain that Myra Shirley acted as a spy and courier for Quantrill, bringing him critical military intelligence gleaned from talkative Union soldiers and other sources in Carthage. None of the reports directly connecting Bud and Myra to Quantrill has ever been substantiated or proved credible, however.[26]

It is true that hundreds of women on both sides served as spies during the Civil War. If caught, those spying for either side could be tried and punished by a military tribunal. In many instances by both armies, however, captured spies were subject to execution without trial and were summarily killed.[27]

Myra was not a spy for Quantrill, but she dutifully carried out her share of "scouting" for her brother and his partisan comrades. She engaged soldiers and even officers in seemingly innocent conversations and collected information about the enemy's plans, troop sizes, and supply operations.[28] When riding into the countryside to forage for food for her brother or deliver the sad news to a farm wife that she had become a widow, Myra usually proceeded to Bud's camp with fresh intelligence gleaned from unsuspecting Yankees.

"No one would shoot a girl, and Myra's horse could run as well as any in the country, nor was there anyone who was a better rider than Myra Shirley," wrote Schrantz. "So, Myra rode freely on this errand or that for her parents, or to keep in touch with brother Bud the Bushwhacker and to tell him the latest news. There was no longer any civil government or law in Jasper County, or any pretense of either."[29]

Long after the grim years of 1862–1863, Schrantz noted that "old John Shirley, treading a tortuous path of apparent neutrality kept his Carthage hotel in operation and his family fed" while Myra rode her own path as a busy scout for the local guerrillas.[30]

ON FEBRUARY 5, 1863—Myra Shirley's fifteenth birthday—an event took place that would become the most publicized incident in her wartime life. On that day, Myra is said to have ridden lickety-split from Newtonia, in Newton County, Missouri, back to Carthage because her brother was in danger. Bud was visiting home, and she had to warn him that the Newtonia federals had learned of his location and were on their way to capture him.[31] Whether the story of Myra's adventure is true does not change the fact that what purportedly transpired that day became part of her ultimate legend. Myra Shirley's Newtonia ride has been recounted in varying detail in several published books and articles.

"Some writers have deemed this tale . . . to be sheer fiction," wrote Schrantz. "Actually, once numerous obvious inaccuracies are corrected, it fits in well with time and circumstances and sounds both logical and likely. The present writer has no doubt that it possesses a solid background of truth."[32]

In the most popular version, Myra was visiting friends in Newtonia when the local Union commander caught wind of her presence and heard she had helped her brother Bud sneak home to visit his family in Carthage. The officer ordered Myra placed under arrest and prepared to send troops to Carthage to seize her brother. Myra was taken to the residence of H. M. Ritchey,[33] an imposing brick house which had survived the recently fought battle of Newtonia and served as the Union headquarters. Local citizens said Quantrill had spent a night in the residence with some of his men. Despite the Union sympathies of the owner, Quantrill reportedly spared the building from the torch because of the Ritchey family's cordial treatment.[34]

Myra was brought to the mansion under duress, but despite rough treatment, the clever teen quickly took stock of the situation. Relying on her wits and the talent she had learned as a little girl, she impressed the officers and guards by playing the piano for them late into the night. The following morning, the Union major in charge released her, apparently believing she was harmless. His troops had left earlier that morning to arrest her brother, so he was sure Myra did not have enough time to return home and warn Bud.[35]

But the bluecoats had underestimated Miss Shirley's riding prowess and her knowledge of the territory. Vowing that she would beat the soldiers to Carthage, Myra shunned the regular route from Newtonia to Carthage, taking every shortcut she knew, riding at breakneck speed through backcountry woods and fields. Myra arrived at the Shirley Hotel well before the detachment of soldiers and alerted Bud, who escaped.[36]

The Shirley family breathed a collective sigh of relief. Bud had had many close calls, but once again, he had avoided capture. For now, his luck held.

CHAPTER 6

Turning Point

BY APRIL 1863, MANY RESIDENTS OF CARTHAGE HAD loaded everything they could into wagons and taken their leave. Pro-northern folks headed to nearby Fort Scott, Kansas, or some other Union refuge. Pro-southerners followed suit, but they chose more hospitable locales of their liking, such as the slave state of Texas. It might have crossed John Shirley's mind that his best course of action would have been to abandon his hotel and move the family. But in a display of the frontier stoicism and resolve of their forebears, Shirley decided his family would stick it out as long as they could.

The Shirleys' friend James Petty, whose home was nine miles northeast of Carthage, was commissioned a captain in the Confederate army that spring. To assemble a company, Petty recruited from the ranks of local partisans and bushwhackers. One of the first young men Petty approached was Bud Shirley, a seasoned guerrilla and an ideal candidate for cavalry combat.[1]

"Bud Shirley thought it over," wrote Ward Schrantz, who interviewed veterans of Petty's company years later. "Just being 'on the scout' with the local boys wasn't so good any more. The recent federal expedition along the stream valleys showed that this could become a very tough life. Perhaps it was time to become a Confederate. The name of John Allison M. Shirley was accordingly entered on the roll of Captain Petty's company. Most of Bud's companions in the brush joined him."[2]

Each of the recruits was responsible for furnishing a horse and acquiring his own weapons and ammunition. Many of them rode with a Sharps carbine slung on their backs and a brace of Colt Navy revolvers in their belts. The company of about thirty or forty men was sworn to the service of the Confederate States in a ceremony on the Carthage town square.[3]

In late spring 1863, Captain Petty and his men rode out of town and prepared for further skirmishes with the "damned Yankees," but they would not be gone for long. On June 26, Petty and some of his company, including Bud Shirley and George B. Walker, returned to Carthage. In 1922, Ward Schrantz interviewed Walker, then seventy-nine years old, about the events of that day.[4]

"Bud Shirley, one of our men who lived in Carthage, had ridden toward town to see his family who lived on the north side of the square at the hotel which his father kept," related Walker. "Bud . . . was medium size, dark complexioned and . . . weighed probably about 160 pounds. Bud was as good a companion and as brave a man as you could find anywhere. His age was about 22 [twenty-one]. He had a younger sister, Myra, who was about 16 [fifteen] and although she was small for her age, she was rather a pretty girl and everybody liked her."[5]

According to Walker, Myra had told Bud that six federal soldiers were staying at a residence in Carthage. Commander Petty was eager to confront them. He and a party of ten soldiers rode into town and headed to the house, not far from the courthouse square.

"We dashed up to the house with drawn pistols, Petty in the lead with Shirley on one side of him and me on the other," recalled Walker. "A militiaman stepped out of the door as we galloped up, snatched a rifle from beside the door, and fired. The bullet struck Captain Petty squarely in the head and he slid from his horse, instantly killed. Both Shirley and I snapped our pistols at his slayer and either of us could have gotten him except that the caps failed to explode. We always had difficulty getting good pistol caps and the ones we now had were wretched ones . . . thus they sometimes became worthless and failed us when we needed them most."[6]

More militiamen, roused by the gunfire, emerged from the house. Shirley and Walker realized that instead of six enemy soldiers, at least thirty-five had been crowded into the house eating dinner.

"There was a lively fusillade for a moment," continued Walker, "they firing and we firing and snapping. The shooting was pretty wild, however, except for the militiaman's first shot, the militia being surprised by our sudden attack and we being surprised by their unexpected number."[7]

In the commotion, Walker was the only one of Petty's command to be wounded; a ball passed through his right arm. He stayed in the saddle and raced out of town with Shirley and the others, leaving their dead commander behind.[8] Myra almost certainly breathed a deep sigh of relief when she learned that Bud and his mates had departed town. She also realized she had underestimated the number of militiamen in the house, and it had resulted in Petty's death.

"Jim Petty was dead," wrote Schrantz. "He was lying there by the house where he had been shot, but he was going to be carried up town. Someone would need to ride and tell Mrs. Petty. That someone was Myra."[9]

The Shirleys had no notion of Bud's whereabouts after he fled Carthage. They were somewhat relieved when a night rider brought word that with Petty's company in disarray, Bud Shirley had resumed the perilous life of a bushwhacker.

Only days later, in late June or early July, Bud ventured into Sarcoxie with fellow guerrilla Milt Norris.[10] Although Norris was from Sarcoxie, the two young men wisely chose not to go to his family home in case Yankees were lurking nearby. They were likely aware that because Sarcoxie had always been a pro-Confederate stronghold, Union troops constantly patrolled the area. Company C, Seventh Missouri Provisional Enrolled Militia, under the command of Captain Green C. Stotts, was stationed a few miles northeast of town at Cave Springs.[11]

"They [the Union militia] had been hearing of these two men [Bud Shirley and Milt Norris] coming to Sarcoxie and were watching for them," recalled eyewitness Sarah Scott Musgrave.[12] She had lived in Sarcoxie and witnessed the many comings and goings of the young guerrillas from the house of a woman identified only as Mrs. Stewart.

Just before dusk, Shirley and Norris tethered their horses in a clump of brush behind a fence. As quiet as thieves, they slipped into the Stewart home for a hot supper.

"I had lived in Sarcoxie and knew all about the town and guided the group of our men who went into town that night to catch some guerrilla said to be sleeping in a house there," Thomas Callaway Wooten, one of the Union militiamen, related many years later. "We went up by the old mill and tied our horses there, then went on foot around to the other side, opposite from Cave Springs, then into the town and surrounded the house."[13]

The Company C detachment led by a junior officer had not been as stealthy as hoped—the young men inside the house had discovered their presence. Suddenly, before the militiamen could make a move, a door to the Stewart home burst open, and Shirley and Norris ran out and dashed for their horses with pistols blazing.

The startled soldiers fired wildly, but one man, Gilbert Schooling, took careful aim. He held his fire until the bushwhackers started to vault the plank fence. Then he softly squeezed the trigger, and John Allison Shirley, Myra's beloved Bud, fell dead on the other side.[14]

"Norris got a rifle ball scratch on his side as he went over the fence, but he was not much hurt and escaped in the brush, where he could not be seen," recalled Musgrave. "I went over and helped take care of the body [of Bud Shirley]. Next morning the militia returned and burned Mrs. Stewart's home for harboring bushwhackers, and also burned Mrs. Walton's home nearby, as she had also assisted in entertaining the bushwhackers."[15]

In all the confusion after the shooting, Norris retrieved his mount and rode directly to the Shirley Hotel in Carthage.

"Norris could hardly have been sure that [Bud] Shirley was dead," wrote Schrantz. "All he could have known was that he had been hit and did not get away. The word that reached the family that night must, therefore, have been that Bud had been shot and if not killed had been captured. That was a sad night in the Shirley home—particularly so for Myra. She had ridden to tell other families of casualties, and now someone had come to them with news of Bud's death or capture."[16]

The next morning, more news arrived from Sarcoxie. After a sleepless night, Myra realized her worst fear had come true—her brother was confirmed dead, shot in the back by federal militia. There would be no more long rides on the prairies and meadows with Bud. He would be twenty-one years old forever.

Later that day, John Shirley and his younger sons hitched up a wagon. Eliza, Myra, and likely their enslaved worker Annie followed the well-worn road to Sarcoxie. On arrival, they were directed to the house where Bud's body had been taken. Sarah Scott Musgrave and several other women sympathetic to the Confederacy met them and told them what they knew about Bud's death.

"Shirley's mother and Myra Shirley, the sixteen-year-old [fifteen-year-old] sister of Shirley, appeared at Sarcoxie, the latter with a belt around her waist from which swung two big revolvers, one on each side," Musgrave stated. "She was not timid in making it known among those whom she saw that she meant to get revenge for her brother's death."[17]

Schrantz, who interviewed Musgrave when she was ninety-three years old, later suggested that she possibly had some memory lapses in telling the story of Bud Shirley's death and Myra's reaction. But Schrantz contended that Musgrave's recollection of Myra being armed and making threats to seek retribution for her brother's death appeared credible.[18]

"That Myra talked just as Mrs. Musgrave said seems entirely possible," Schrantz wrote. "In view of her reputed temper and the poignancy of her grief, she likely would. But it does not necessarily follow that such threats were uttered in public on the open street. It is far more likely that they were made only in the presence of Mrs. Musgrave and other women of the town, southern sympathizers all—who were with the body of the slain man."[19]

It also is likely that Myra had come to Sarcoxie armed. Because of the long clandestine rides she often took in service of the bushwhackers, it was quite probable that her brother had given her revolvers for protection.[20]

Once Bud's body was placed in the wagon, Eliza and Myra returned to Carthage and prepared for the funeral. Bud was dressed in his best suit and placed in a coffin in the hotel lobby. Several mourners paid their respects, mostly the families of other young men who had died in the war. Some of Bud's pals and his younger brothers carried the coffin to the City

Cemetery, near the academy building where Myra had attended classes. As his mother and sister sobbed, John Allison Shirley was buried under the oaks.[21]

Myra Shirley never completely recovered from Bud's death. In the coming weeks, she learned that the loss did not lessen with time. Not only had Bud disappeared from her life, but a part of Myra had also gone with him. The death of her brother would mold her as she became an adult, shaping her opinions, prejudices, and attitudes about government and the law.

To survive, the Shirley family had to cope with their loss and grief while going through the motions of daily routines. Adding to their troubles came news from the main battlefronts that did not bode well for the Confederacy.

July 1863 marked a significant turning point for the Union war effort. During the first few days of that month, as the Shirleys tried to come to grips with their personal tragedy, northern forces won the Battle of Gettysburg in Pennsylvania. Arguably the most important battle of the war, this defeat of the Confederate army forced General Robert E. Lee to abandon his plan to bring the war into northern soil. This victory was followed immediately by the Union army's successful forty-seven-day siege of Vicksburg, Mississippi, which enabled federal forces to establish total control of the entire length of the Mississippi River.[22]

"John Shirley perhaps felt that the war would soon be over," wrote Schrantz. "If he did, he was not alone in that thought. Deserters from the Confederate armies in Arkansas, dispirited by the turn of events, began drifting into the region, joining some guerrilla bands or becoming independent bushwhackers seeking only to exist and with no particular desire to fight."[23]

Sirius, the Dog Star, ruled the night sky, marking the dog days of August 1863. Some observers had come to believe that it was the last summer for the Confederacy west of the Mississippi. Even the staunchest southern sympathizers in Jasper County had become uncertain about the future. Their pessimism grew when Union Captain Milton J. Burch and two companies of the Eighth Missouri State Militia Cavalry trotted into Carthage. The troops dismounted on the town square, unsaddled their mounts, and picketed them on the courthouse lawn. They then proceeded to unload supply wagons into the courthouse. It became clear to the townsfolk that the Yankees were back in Carthage to stay.[24]

The brick courthouse became a barracks and headquarters for Burch. Militiamen turned the old academy building on the south side of town into a second barracks for one of the companies. The appearance of the Union garrison lured new civilian residents to Carthage, most of whom had been farmers loyal to the Union who had initially left for safety.[25] Now they felt reasonably comfortable that the presence of so many northern soldiers offered protection for their families. Ironically, the Shirleys also benefited from the surge of soldiers and refugees.

"John Shirley's hotel very likely had paying tenants," wrote Schrantz. "It is probable, also, that Captain Burch and his officers ate at the Shirley house while their men—there being no unit cooks—arranged with families of the town to prepare their issue rations in palatable form for hire."[26]

By mid-August, the Union soldiers comfortably hunkered down at Carthage had fallen into a routine. By day, cavalry patrols regularly hunted bushwhackers and intimidated pro-Confederate civilians. In the evening, soldiers took their ease in the streets of Carthage, flirting with local girls. Some of the militiamen shared rations with children who had little food.[27]

At the Shirley Hotel, Myra resumed her mission of intelligence gathering by chatting with officers and enlisted men while she played the piano. "And, by one means or another, word was transmitted to the sullen guerrillas outside of all that concerned the Union soldiers and their intentions," wrote Schrantz.[28]

Neither Myra, her father, nor the federal forces occupying Carthage had the slightest inkling that far to the north, a turning point in the border war was about to take place.

∽

MOTIVATED BY THE 1861 Osceola Massacre, rebel guerrilla leader William Quantrill decided it was time for retribution. On the morning of

William Clarke Quantrill was a guerrilla chieftain and the catalyst for a criminal dynasty that lasted more than seventy years.

August 21, 1863, Quantrill led about 450 of his well-armed raiders in a brazen assault on Lawrence, Kansas, to avenge the outrages that Kansans had committed against pro-Confederate Missourians. Lawrence was the logical target because it was an abolitionist stronghold and the hometown of despised Senator James Henry Lane, the Jayhawk leader and architect of the Osceola bloodbath.[29]

In Lawrence that August morning, most of the homes and stores were ransacked, many buildings were burned, and 160 to 200 men and boys older than fifteen were shot and killed. Lane, one of Quantrill's primary targets, escaped in his nightshirt and found cover in a cornfield as gunfire and shouts of "Remember Osceola!" rang in his ears.[30]

"At Lawrence it was butchery from the first charge to the last shot," recalled Richard Cordley in 1895. "The killing was indiscriminate and mostly in cold blood."[31]

The day after the Lawrence raid, survivors surveyed the smoldering ruins and began to bury the dead. Some of them took time to lynch a lone guerrilla captive.

The equilibrium of Missouri had become completely unbalanced. Mayhem and unbridled cruelty would continue for years. The dark angel, as frontier families referred to death, had found a comfortable home in the bloody borderlands.

"No fiends in human shape could have acted with more savage barbarity than did Quantrill and his band in their last successful raid," Kansas governor Thomas Carney wrote in an August 24 letter to Major General John M. Schofield, commander of the Department of the Missouri, headquartered in Saint Louis. "I must hold Missouri responsible for this dreadful fiendish raid. No body of men large as that could have been gathered together without the people residing in Western Missouri knowing everything about it. Such people cannot be considered loyal, and should not be treated as loyal citizens."[32]

Moved by the governor's plea for help, Schofield immediately sent a dispatch to Brigadier General Thomas Ewing Jr., commander of the District of the Border, which included Kansas and western Missouri. Schofield ordered six companies of the Eleventh Missouri Cavalry to join Ewing in pursuing Quantrill and his raiders, stating, "Spare no means by which he may be destroyed."[33]

Ewing unveiled his infamous directive on August 25, 1863, four days after the Lawrence raid. General Order No. 11 mandated that all inhabitants of the western Missouri counties of Jackson, Cass, Bates, and the northern half of Vernon—regardless of allegiance—would be evicted from their homes and farms. They were ordered to move to communities near Union military posts or anywhere in Kansas except the counties on its eastern border. The Missourians affected by the order were required to give oaths of loyalty to the Union and move within fifteen days—or face the consequences.[34]

Ultimately, the order impacted at least twenty thousand rural residents. The drastic reprisal strategy became known as one of the harshest and most repressive punitive measures ever imposed on American citizens.

"It is well-known that men were shot down in the very act of obeying the order, and their wagons and effects seized by their murderers," wrote George Caleb Bingham, the famed Missouri artist and a vehement critic of Order No. 11. "Dense clouds of smoke arising in every direction marked the conflagrations of dwellings."[35]

The area subject to the stipulations of the Union order became known as the Burnt District. In many places, all that remained of homes were burned fields and charred chimneys, called Jennison's Tombstones after "Doc" Jennison, infamous Jayhawk commander. The ruins stretched for miles, relics of unbridled violence.[36]

The southern edge of the Burnt District was sixty miles north of Carthage, but not all Union troops and renegade Kansas guerrillas observed the boundary.[37] Both sides of the conflict burned farmhouses, barns, and hay crops in Jasper County.

The Shirleys had more cause to worry. Because Carthage was still garrisoned with Union soldiers, more pro-northern people continued to return to town in late summer 1863. They strutted on the courthouse square and jeered at refugees streaming through the county headed due south.

The approaching autumn offered only slight hope. In Jasper County, fields that had gone fallow or had been burned yielded no harvests. People no longer trusted their neighbors and sometimes not even their own kin.

But then good news for Missouri's southern sympathizers came almost out of nowhere. On October 2, 1863, Confederate Colonel Joseph O. "Jo" Shelby and his seasoned cavalry raiders charged north from Arkansas into Missouri and picked up reinforcements near Pineville. Eventually the Iron Brigade, as the outfit came to be called, swelled to more than fifteen hundred men.[38]

Besides wreaking havoc behind enemy lines, the daring raid was meant to raise the fighting spirit of Confederate forces west of the Mississippi, bolster recruitment, and boost the morale of pro-Confederates. A slim chance also existed that such a bold incursion might provoke an insurrection in the slave state.

Shelby's first target was Neosho, Missouri, only eighteen miles from Pineville and garrisoned by a small Union force of the Missouri State Militia Cavalry and the Enrolled Missouri Militia. Quickly realizing that they were outmatched by the overwhelmingly large Confederate brigade, the Union troops barricaded themselves in the courthouse. After two cannonballs crashed into the building, the federal commander surrendered unconditionally. Shelby's men collected fresh horses, food stores, and weapons.[39]

"Halting in Neosho only long enough to distribute the arms and ammunition, I pushed on rapidly for Sarcoxie, resting on Jones Creek some five hours, and fed my command," Shelby later wrote in the official report of his monthlong raid. "October 4, passed through the blackened and desolate town of Sarcoxie, whose bare and fire-scarred chimneys point with skeleton fingers to heaven for vengeance."[40]

As Shelby made his circuitous ride through Missouri, skirmishing with federal troops and burning homes and barns, he bore witness to the toll the war and his actions had taken on the citizenry.

Shelby wrote, "All along the road the inhabitants had their household furniture taken from their houses, and waiting in silence and sorrow for us to apply the torch, it having been represented to them that my command was laying the country to waste. . . . On the road we met delicate females fleeing southward, driving ox teams, barefooted, ragged, and suffering for even bread."[41]

Apparently the two companies of the Eighth Missouri Militia Cavalry led by Captain Milton Burch, based in Carthage, had not yet learned of Shelby's movements. On October 3, Burch and forty troopers left Carthage to escort a party of northern refugees and, if possible, take on a group of guerrillas thought to be operating in the area. After ordering some of his men to accompany the refugee wagons to Carthage, Burch and his force rode off in pursuit of bushwhackers. They located a camp and pursued the fleeing rebels, managing to kill ten of them and capture two, along with twenty-five horses.[42]

"The militia captain [Burch] then started to return to Carthage meaning to go by way of Neosho," wrote Schrantz. "Upon nearing the town he sent two men ahead . . . they learned that the place was full of Confederate troops said to be bound for Carthage. Hoping to arrive at Carthage first, Burch abandoned his captured horses and pushed north at top speed, avoiding the roads." According to Schrantz, Burch "immediately commenced preparing to give them [the Confederates] a warm reception."[43]

Unknown to Burch, there was much more to fear than Shelby's Iron Brigade. On October 5, William Quantrill and at least five hundred of his heavily armed guerrillas broke camp after bivouacking less than twelve miles west of Carthage.[44] Many of them still carried money and plunder taken in the Lawrence raid.

Fortunately for them, Quantrill and his raiders had no interest in paying a call on Carthage. They were heading south to spend a quiet winter nursing wounds in rebel-friendly Texas and stayed overnight on Shoal Creek near the Missouri-Kansas line. At dawn on October 6, they gobbled down what one raider called "a fine breakfast—bread made of flour and water and twisted around a stick and cooked, broiled bacon and coffee."[45] They soon were in their saddles, making an encore call on Kansas before turning south to Texas.

By early afternoon, Quantrill's advance guard neared Baxter Springs, Kansas, and encountered some Union teamsters from nearby Fort Blair, often referred to as Fort Baxter. After killing the teamsters, the guerrillas made an assault on the small earth-and-log Union outpost. The outnumbered garrison fought valiantly and sustained many casualties but managed to keep their attackers at bay through the gallantry of Lieutenant James Burton Pond.[46] For his extraordinary heroism in action, he was promoted to major and in 1898 was awarded the Medal of Honor.[47]

While Pond was repelling the raiders, Quantrill and his men had moved out onto the prairie, where a wagon train guarded by Union soldiers was approaching from the north. In the distance, the rebels spied General James G. Blunt, en route from Fort Scott, Kansas, to Fort Smith, Arkansas. The general's escort consisted of one hundred men of the Third Wisconsin and Fourteenth Kansas Cavalry, including military bandsmen.[48]

Many of the guerrilla raiders were dressed in federal uniforms, causing Blunt to believe they were friendly troops out on a drill. When he realized his mistake, it was too late. Quantrill and his group quickly formed a battle line and charged ahead. The federal troops broke and ran and were slaughtered like sheep. Blunt narrowly escaped, and ninety-three of his men were shot and killed, including the wounded. The dead included a twelve-year-old boy, a journalist, and fourteen musicians who frantically waved white handkerchiefs in surrender but were gunned down nonetheless.[49]

Late in the afternoon, Quantrill and his men left Baxter Springs. They continued about fifteen miles due south on the Texas Road. They then passed through Indian Territory, killing more than 150 Indian and Black Unionists that they encountered.[50] On October 12, the rebels reached the Confederate lines in Texas.[51] By then, large numbers of pro-Confederate refugees also were Texas bound, including many citizens of Carthage.

On the evening of October 5, Captain Burch and the two cavalry companies at Carthage had received new marching orders from Major A. A. King, commanding the Sixth Missouri State Militia Cavalry. In reaction to dispatches from the field concerning Shelby and his whereabouts, King and his men were riding south "in the direction of Newtonia to find out what was going on there, not realizing that the Confederate raiding column had already passed."[52]

Although King was unsure of Shelby's exact location, he thought it wise to have Burch leave Carthage and join in the pursuit of the Confederate raiders. Burch was obliged to obey the order and was no doubt eager to be in the field pursuing Shelby.

King and Burch would have been surprised to know that on October 5, Shelby and his raiders were only eighteen miles east of Carthage. They were burning down Bowers Mill, a gristmill on the Spring River just west of Mount Vernon, where Burch had been ordered to send his wagons and baggage.[53]

On the morning of October 6, Captain Burch and his two companies of mounted militia rode eastward out of Carthage on the Bowers Mill Road, with a long string of wagons trailing behind.[54] They would not return.

On October 7, sixty Union soldiers from Baxter Springs wandered into the Carthage town square. They had left the day before with eight wagons foraging for food.[55]

"They were close at hand when the roar of the battle [at Baxter Springs] broke out," wrote Schrantz.[56] The Union soldiers—fearful that they would be discovered—quickly unharnessed the mules and left the wagons. They rode for their lives to the east, under the assumption that Carthage was still garrisoned by Union troops. In the early morning hours, when they arrived on exhausted horses and mules, they were doubtless disturbed to find the federals gone. They knew if guerrilla scouts came upon the abandoned wagons, an enemy force would pursue them. The men quickly fed and watered the animals and ate a hasty breakfast provided by sympathetic townsfolk. Soon the sixty Union soldiers resumed their flight westward in the direction of Fort Scott.

The forage party was barely out of sight when bushwhackers galloped into Carthage with guns drawn. They might have been in pursuit of the Yankee forage party, but if so, they did not continue the chase. The bushwhackers dismounted and proceeded to put Carthage to the torch. They likely began by setting fire to the courthouse.[57]

"On the morning of October 7, 1863, almost before the party, which had left the forage train near Baxter Springs, had got out of town, the rebels rode into the place; and set fire to the court house and all the other brick as well as log houses," wrote Leon Boyd, a Missourian who had served alongside elements of the Third Wisconsin Calvary.[58]

Contrary to Boyd's report, not all the buildings were burned that day. For the time being, the Shirley Hotel was spared, as were other homes of recognized southern sympathizers. Likely one of the first residences burned was the log home of strong Unionist Norris C. Hood on the west side of the square.[59]

While several men set fires throughout the courthouse, other bushwhackers torched stores and homes. John Shirley and his family witnessed the devastation from the safety of the hotel lobby. They were especially distressed when they saw smoke pouring from the direction of the academy building, where Myra had gone to school.

"The courthouse and the academy belonged to the people of the county, mostly southern like themselves," wrote Schrantz. "It was southern people who would be hurt the most. John Shirley's hopes probably collapsed with the courthouse—its ruin typified the impending ruin of the town. So long as it stood, it had seemed to him a symbol of stability. Now Bud was dead and buried. Myra was half a guerrilla and not improving in the environment of war or through the associations forced on her by the circumstances. As for the boys, they were becoming little savages. They were good boys, of course, but they had seen people killed and had laughed."[60]

John and Eliza Shirley doubtless had talked through their options soon after the burning of Carthage, perhaps even as the buildings around them smoldered. They must have known that eventually the federal army would return, and as southerners, the Shirley family would pay a steep price. They had only one sensible option—going south.

PART
II

CHAPTER 7

Gone to Texas

DURING MUCH OF THE NINETEENTH CENTURY, IT WAS NOT uncommon to see the letters "G.T.T." painted or carved on the doorways of houses in some parts of the country, especially in the South and the border states. It was a sign that the occupants had packed up and "Gone to Texas."[1] When bill collectors looked for defaulters but found only an empty house with that carving, they knew the occupants had taken "French leave"—evading creditors—and gone to Texas. And when a pro-Confederate Missouri family found themselves in the cross fire of war and needed a fresh start, they too were gone to Texas.[2]

That was precisely what the Shirleys did. In early October 1863, they headed to Texas.

Once they decided to join the refugees, the Shirleys and their slaves quickly prepared for an arduous journey of several weeks. Eliza Shirley and Myra probably hid money and valuables in their clothing because women would likely not be searched if anyone stopped them on the road.[3]

Two or three ox-drawn wagons would have been needed to accommodate the party and their possessions. John Shirley likely drove one wagon, and perhaps an enslaved man or Eliza drove another. Myra likely would have ridden horseback so she could help control the horses tethered to the wagons and scout ahead to select campgrounds.[4]

When the wagons rolled away from the shuttered Shirley Hotel, the route on the east side of the square provided one last look at the ruins of the courthouse. The Shirleys would have passed the burned Cravens store and then bumped southward by the remains of the Carthage Female Academy, where Myra had gone to school.

Burned rubble was everywhere. The regrets, visions of death, and bittersweet memories must have been overwhelming. The family, especially Myra, had not stopped mourning Bud's death three months earlier. Out of respect for the slain John Allison Shirley, John and Eliza had changed the name of their youngest child, five-year-old Cravens, to John Alva Shirley. Most of the time, he went by the affectionate nickname Shug, or sometimes Doc.[5]

If they had not done so earlier, the family surely paused at Bud Shirley's grave beneath the oaks before they left Carthage. Tragically, the Shirleys had lost their beloved Bud but—according to records uncovered 160 years later—by the end of 1863, they would have an addition to the family. Riding in one of the wagons headed for Texas was the enslaved eighteen-year-old Annie, six months pregnant with a baby likely fathered by John Shirley or one of his sons.[6]

This discovery, which has never been publicly revealed, brings to light an entirely new dimension to the John Shirley family story.

The family's African American lineage first surfaced in late 2022. The Shirley Family Association, an international organization designed to preserve the worldwide Shirley family heritage, shared the results of DNA testing they had conducted for a genealogical project researching the potential for African American ancestry.[7]

The six-page report about the John Shirley family's enslaved lineage was based in part on official records. However, it should be noted that some of the findings are "quite likely" but "not proven."[8] For instance, in the case of Annie's baby conceived in Missouri, the true identity of the father is questionable. Some Texas birth and death certificates as well as census records list Mansfield Shirley as the father. However, at the time of Annie's pregnancy in 1863, Mansfield was only eleven years old. Although there have been rare instances of boys as young as ten fathering children, the chances are far greater that either John Shirley or one of his older sons—perhaps even Bud before his death—was responsible for Annie's pregnancy.[9]

In October 2022, the name Annie Shirley (sometimes called Leanne or Dinah) first appeared in the updated Shirley Family African American lineage research site. Texas death records list her date of birth as August 17, 1845, in Georgia, the daughter of Henry Miles and Mary Lu Jones. However, federal census records "conclusively identified" Missouri as her birthplace. Further information about her parents—presumably enslaved—has not been found, and records of when Annie became one of John Shirley's enslaved workers remain unknown.[10]

It is unknown whether the relationship that resulted in Annie's pregnancy was mutually consensual. Like other enslaved women, Annie would have had little power to reject the sexual advances of her master or his sons. Despite the circumstances of her child's conception, however, it is likely that she was afforded comfort during the long journey to Texas.

The timing of the Shirleys' departure proved fortuitous. On October 17, ten days after the guerrillas had set the town ablaze, Colonel Jo Shelby and his column of cavalry raiders rode into Carthage. They established a camp just north of town at the stately two-story brick home of W. B. Kendrick. Shelby's men found "wood, water and forage in abundance," and they wisely "slept booted and spurred."[11]

At daybreak, the Confederates needed only to saddle their horses and brandish their weapons when General Thomas Ewing appeared with a sizable Union force to halt Shelby from continuing his retreat. After a running skirmish that lasted more than an hour and has sometimes been called the second Battle of Carthage, Shelby and his men broke free and continued their escape in the same direction the Shirleys had taken only a few days earlier.[12]

No record has been found of the Shirley family's journey to Texas and the route they followed. The most likely path would have been the road south to Neosho and then across into Arkansas at a point north of Elkhorn Tavern. They would then have picked up the Butterfield Overland Mail Company route, a stagecoach service authorized by Congress. This popular operation ran from 1858 until 1861, carrying US mail and passengers from Saint Louis to San Francisco, covering three thousand miles in twenty-five days, the longest mail route in the world.[13] With the onslaught of the Civil War, all services had ceased on the southern route. The trail, however, remained a wagon path for soldiers, refugees, and travelers until its demise with the completion of the transcontinental railroad by the end of the 1860s.[14]

When the Shirleys entered Arkansas and passed near Elkhorn Tavern in October 1863, they would have seen scarred trees and the bullet-pocked walls of the tavern that had once been a trading post and popular rest stop for travelers. All had changed on March 7–8, 1862, when the tavern became a makeshift hospital during a major clash between Union and Confederate forces. As sometimes happened, the two sides could not even agree on what to call their skirmish. Southerners named the action the Battle of Elkhorn Tavern, and northerners called it the Battle of Pea Ridge, after the small nearby community.[15]

After leaving Elkhorn Tavern, the Shirley party would have found comfort just ten miles south on the Wire Road at Callahan's Tavern, the first official stop in Arkansas for the old Butterfield line. Callahan's offered hot meals, cold mountain spring water for humans and beasts, and grease for wagon axles.[16]

The road continued south through the communities of Cross Hollows and Bloomington, called Mudtown by travelers whose wagons regularly became stuck in deep ruts made by heavy lumber wagons hauling rough pine timber to nearby sawmills.[17] Throughout northwestern Arkansas, public houses, hotels, campgrounds, and private residences catered to travelers such as the Shirleys.

When they reached Fayetteville, the Shirleys would have stayed only long enough to procure water and supplies and see to their horses and oxen. The town was crawling with Union soldiers who had fought southern forces in an indecisive battle at Fayetteville in April 1863.[18]

Ahead, travelers faced the sixty-five miles of road crossing the rugged Boston Mountains to Fort Smith, one of the most difficult legs of the trek to Texas. The trail narrowed and the grade became steeper as the wagons slowly ascended the highest ridge crests. This stretch usually took at least a full day, but the rest of the path to Van Buren on the Arkansas River was downhill. The river crossing would have been made on a crude ferry.[19]

On the other side was Fort Smith, at the confluence of the Arkansas and Poteau rivers. Established as a western frontier military post in 1817, Fort Smith had developed into a base for migrants headed west. In October 1863, Fort Smith, like Fayetteville, teemed with Union soldiers. They had taken control a month earlier after a skirmish with Confederate troops.[20]

Refugees crossing the Missouri border into Arkansas had entered a Confederate state that would not be readmitted to the Union until 1868, three years after the end of the war. Their destination—the Confederate state of Texas—would not be readmitted to the United States until 1870. Between Arkansas and Texas, the Butterfield route ran almost two hundred miles southwesterly through Indian Territory, the future Oklahoma, which would not become a state until 1907. In 1863, most of the twelve Butterfield Stage stations in Indian Territory remained viable and able to accommodate refugees.

On that leg of the journey, "the good roadbeds in the valleys, shallow crossings on the larger streams, and easy passes through the outlying ridges of the San[s] Bois and the Winding Stair Mountains . . . made it the best and the most direct route for travel from Fort Smith across the Choctaw and Chickasaw country to the Red river and points southwest," wrote Oklahoma historian Muriel H. Wright.[21]

After crossing a toll bridge over the North Boggy River and reaching the old Boggy Depot, the Butterfield road drew close to the Texas line and soon converged with the Texas Road, another important route that entered Indian Territory far to the north just below Baxter Springs, Kansas. Some authors have suggested that the Shirleys took the Texas Road the entire way to reach Texas, but because of the location of Carthage, the Butterfield Stage path would have been the more convenient route for the family to use, especially with a pregnant woman in their party.

No matter which route the Shirleys followed, they would have used Colbert's Ferry—known as the nation's northern gateway to Texas—to cross the Red River. Located seven miles downstream from Preston, Texas, the ferry was owned and operated by Benjamin Franklin Colbert, a Chickasaw citizen and the owner of twenty-six enslaved laborers.[22]

The Shirley wagons had to traverse a short stretch of log corduroy road on the muddy riverbank that led to the waiting ferry. One at a time, the wagons were ferried across the Red River by Colbert's enslaved workers wielding long poles in the shallow water.

When the wagons rolled onto Texas soil, the Shirleys likely breathed long sighs of relief before making a beeline to the home of Preston and Mary Arella Shirley and their three sons. Preston, John Shirley's eldest son, had left Jasper County in 1860 because of death threats over his abolitionist beliefs. He and his family first settled in Burleson County in east-central Texas, about fifty miles east of the state capital at Austin.[23]

Cotton and corn crops flourished in Burleson County. When the Civil War broke out, the growing enslaved population boomed. The war generated an influx of planter refugees with their enslaved laborers. At the same time, many of the county's Unionists concluded that their best course of action would be to support the Confederacy.[24]

Unhappy that Burleson County had become overrun by Confederates, Preston Shirley packed up his family and moved north to Dallas County, known for its rich soil and food production. That county, however, also attracted droves of slaveholders looking to avoid the invasion of Union troops because Texas was distant from the battles raging in the Deep South. Preston stuck it out for a few years. His name appears on the Dallas County tax assessment rolls for 1861 and 1862.[25]

Despite their political differences, John Shirley and his family must have been delighted to reunite with Preston and Mary Arella and see how much their boys had grown. John's family likely stayed with Preston while looking for a homesite of their own. John and his enslaved workers built temporary quarters, perhaps dugouts or sod houses, while they got the lay of the land. Their temporary homestead was near Grape Vine (called Grapevine after 1914), a community named for the profusion of wild mustang grapes that flourished in the area.[26]

Although the Shirleys were a long way from Missouri, it must have been comforting to know that by late 1863, Missouri's Confederate capital in exile was in the east Texas town of Marshall, just north of Carthage, Texas.[27] Missouri governor Thomas C. Reynolds and the fugitive

Confederate government had little claim to legality in Missouri. However, thousands of Missourians such as the Shirleys who "went South" during the war were proud that Marshall had become known as the "last capital city of 'rebel' Missouri."[28]

Some sources claim that the Shirleys left Grape Vine and moved to land near Mesquite in northeastern Dallas County. John Shirley's name appeared on the Dallas County tax rolls starting in 1864, where it was recorded that by that time, he owned seven enslaved workers, valued at $4,000; $325 in Confederate treasury notes; and livestock valued at $735.[29]

In due course, the Shirleys settled about a mile east of a town that appeared suitable for their needs. They quickly came to find out that it also was a refuge for hell-bent ruffians proud to make their home with the rogue rebels of Texas. The hamlet was called Scyene [sye EEN].

On December 30, 1863—the brink of a new year—the Shirleys had barely unpacked when Annie Shirley gave birth to a healthy baby boy, born into slavery like his mother. She named him George Washington Shirley.[30]

In the past, John Shirley had been known to sell the children of his enslaved workers. An 1855 deed book from Missouri holds an account that Shirley "sold to Archibald McCoy for one dollar Negro boy, Jordan, and Negro girl, Leanner, slaves for life."[31] But Shirley had no intention of parting with a child that was part of his family bloodline. George Washington Shirley would live for more than eighty-seven years, and he would never know for sure which of the Shirley men was his father.

CHAPTER 8

Armed and Dangerous

SCYENE, THE TEXAS TOWN THAT THE SHIRLEYS NOW CALLED home, was tough as a hickory nut and bore a bastardized name. Located ten miles southeast of Dallas, the hamlet had been known as both Prairie Creek and Thorpville until 1854 when residents chose a new name—Seine, after the famous river that cuts through the heart of Paris, France.[1] But when paperwork establishing the new post office was drawn up on June 1, 1854, the name was recorded as Scyene.[2] The name had likely been mispronounced and hence misspelled by someone speaking with one of the drawling dialects that had developed in the Lone Star State. Phonetics issue or not, no one bothered to correct it—Scyene it would stay.

When the Shirleys relocated to Scyene, they found a town with a post office, a half dozen saloons, a few churches, some mercantile stores, a wagon maker, and a two-story frame building used as a school and Masonic lodge and for social events.[3] Scyene also was one of two stops in eastern Dallas County for stagecoaches traveling the Scyene Road—once a buffalo trail—that linked Dallas to the west with Jefferson, Texas, and Shreveport, Louisiana, to the east.[4] Travel of any sort on the road was nearly impossible when a heavy rain fell. The creeks were swollen, and a low-water log crossing over White Rock Creek and the chalky dirt roadbed became slippery.[5]

∽

THE SHIRLEYS' DECISION TO move proved to be a blessing. On September 22, 1864—less than a year after the family had left for Texas—a band of guerrillas once again attacked Carthage. That time, the Shirley Hotel was not spared.[6] An unnamed witness painted a stark portrait of what Carthage looked like after the second assault:

"Only five dwellings had escaped destruction.... The old chimneys became the nests of owls, which hooted gloomily and forebodingly over the silent and desolate scene. The deserted public square and streets, overgrown with weeds were given up to wolves and deer."[7]

On his new property, likely leased east of Scyene, John Shirley and his enslaved laborers built a clapboard house, barn, stable, and livestock pens with milled timber harvested from cedar groves and a hardwood forest near the Trinity River bottomlands.[8] The woodlands and thickets yielded deer and feral hogs.[9]

Cotton had long been the most popular crop with area farmers, but during the war, the Confederate government had encouraged more corn production to feed troops.[10] Likely that was why John Shirley chose to raise corn; with corn, he could simultaneously turn a profit and feed his own family. In early 1865, Shirley, with help from his sons and enslaved laborers, plowed the rich soil with oxen. After the last frost, Shirley's first Texas corn crop was planted.[11]

About the time corn began to poke up from the black Texas soil, an event took place far to the east in Appomattox, a small town in central Virginia, that marked the beginning of the end of the bloodiest war in American history. On April 9, 1865, General Robert E. Lee surrendered his Army of Northern Virginia to General Ulysses S. Grant, creating a blueprint for other Confederate generals to follow.[12]

When President Abraham Lincoln's assassination stunned the nation only six days after Lee's capitulation, some diehard southerners celebrated, but the surrender process continued. Over the next few weeks, other Confederate generals followed Lee's example and surrendered tens of thousands of fatigued and disheartened troops.

Some rebels in Texas, however, were not ready to stop fighting the bluecoats. On May 12–13, 1865, more than a month after Lee's surrender at Appomattox, Texas Confederates led by the daring Colonel John Salmon "Rip" Ford defeated a larger force of Union troops on the Rio

Grande in south Texas. The Battle of Palmito Ranch became the final land battle of the war.[13]

The war had come to an end after four horrendous years. There was much jubilation in the North, but large numbers of southern soldiers and civilians were not ready to acknowledge defeat to the "damn Yankee" conquerors. For them, the Civil War never ended. Many in those ranks were Texans.

Distant from the main theatres of war, Texas had been spared major Union invasions and the resulting devastation in much of the South. Nevertheless, Texas paid a dear price for joining the Confederacy. Of the more than seventy thousand Texas men and boys who took up arms for the South, an untold number perished on battlefields and in prison camps from wounds or disease. Amputations became the most common surgical procedure in battlefield hospitals and resurrected the old nickname "sawbones" for military surgeons.[14]

"More terrible than the number of casualties was how they were inflicted—not by foreign enemies, but by fellow citizens," wrote historian Geoffrey C. Ward.[15]

A Confederate military surgery manual issued in 1863 said, "Opium is the one indispensible [sic] drug on the battlefield—important to the surgeon, as gunpowder to ordinance [sic]."[16] Hypodermic syringes, introduced in the 1850s, became the best method for dispensing liquid morphine.[17]

Many surviving soldiers struggled with addiction, especially in the South. They turned to opiates for comfort. In 1868, in a book written "chiefly for the benefit of opium-eaters," Horace B. Day wrote, "Maimed and shattered survivors from a hundred battle-fields, diseased and disabled soldiers released from hostile prisons, anguished and hopeless wives and mothers, made so by the slaughter of those dearest to them, have found, many of them, temporary relief from their sufferings in opium."[18]

In both the North and South, soldiers that had become used to the presence of death found it difficult to return to civilian life. Some of them had lost touch with reality. Many suffered from constant insomnia or delusion and no longer had any concept of time. Some veterans were so disturbed by nightmares of the war that they left their homes and took to the open road, going "tramping," as it was called.[19]

Suicide rates dramatically increased after the war, mostly among young male veterans.[20] The number of patients committed to psychiatric hospitals—then known as lunatic asylums—increased.[21] Former soldiers who displayed a tendency for violence were placed in prisons with the general population. The prevailing belief was that mental illness was only temporary. It was something to get over, like a cold.[22]

Significant numbers of Yankee and rebel survivors returned home with their nightmares—and their guns. Union soldiers had the option of buying their "arms and accouterments," and Confederate troops had either brought their personal weapons when they enlisted or picked up discarded guns from battlefields. The articles of surrender stipulated that Confederates give up all weapons, but that policy was rarely enforced.[23]

Many veterans from both sides—trained to kill and hardened by the violence they had witnessed or committed—were armed and often dangerous when they mustered out. In the postwar years, homicide rates among veterans soared across the nation. There were reports of veterans, forever terrified of being killed, constantly carrying handguns and even keeping weapons nearby when they slept.[24]

The situation became especially chaotic in Texas. Confederate veterans who had not received pay for months made the long trek home to find the huge enslaved workforce now freed. The former Confederates also encountered occupying federal troops implementing the policies of Reconstruction. During the arduous years of 1865 to 1877, the federal government focused on rehabilitating Texas and other Confederate states politically, economically, and socially.[25] The effort to reintegrate the former slave states often led to violence. Bitter and embarrassed by their defeat, many southern soldiers adopted the rule of every man for himself.

"We of Texas know to what an alarming extent crime has reached," the *Galveston Daily News* lamented in an August 1865 editorial. "Men of all grades seem to have entered on the career of crime."[26]

The Shirley family learned that even before the Civil War, Scyene was said to be a "sporty town" and "the rendezvous of the reckless riders of the Southwest."[27]

Early settler W. S. Burris recalled in 1924, "I have stood in our door and seen a bunch of rowdies come into town, tank up, shoot and yell a few times, kill a few dogs, rope some of the dudes and have what they called a good time for a few hours. . . . A few days later, after getting sobered up, each of them would come into town and pay for the stuff used and the damage done. . . . Usually, no one was hurt in these frivolities, no fights occurred, just a good time enjoyed."[28]

After the war, thousands of rough riders came to Scyene from Missouri, Arkansas, Kentucky, and Alabama. The town had become "the headquarters of free livers, free riders, and free raiders" living high while lying low "within the noisy precincts of the 'hot town on the hill.'"[29]

Scyene kept its image as a tough town but also became a sanctuary for desperate men who committed crimes elsewhere, especially in Dallas. "Merely to show their contempt of Dallas and its police force and police restraint, the wild and woolly sons of the prairie would visit Dallas at intervals, load up on the fighting whisky and then attempt to 'shoot up' the town," according to a *Dallas Daily Times Herald* report.[30]

In time, a different breed of unreconstructed Confederates found the way to Scyene—and made a lasting impression on the Shirley family.

BY THE CLOSE OF 1865, the South was grappling with the reality of a nation without an economy built on enslaved workers. As a result, many people hungry for a panacea to their problems remained firm believers in southern exceptionalism and White supremacy. They found comfort in what became known as the "Lost Cause," an ideology that venerated the southern way of life in what they rationalized as the just and noble tenets of the Confederacy. Followers of the romanticized philosophy maintained that the war had not been about ending slavery but about a struggle for states' rights in the face of overwhelming Yankee aggression.

"And by the sheer virtue of losing heroically the Confederate soldier provided a model of masculine devotion and courage in an age of gender anxieties and ruthless material striving," explains historian David W. Blight.[31]

Robert Penn Warren observed, "We may say that only at the moment when Lee handed Grant his sword was the Confederacy born; or to state matters another way, in the moment of death the Confederacy entered its own immortality."[32]

Texas was especially resistant to the emancipation of its enormous enslaved population and the advent of Reconstruction. The state had become the last stronghold of chattel slavery in the United States. President Abraham Lincoln had signed the Emancipation Proclamation on January 1, 1863, but news of the edict that freed all enslaved people did not officially reach Texas until June 19, 1865. On that auspicious day, Union Major General Gordon Granger arrived in Galveston and issued a proclamation declaring that the institution of slavery was dead. By 1866, the date had become known as Juneteenth (short for "June Nineteenth"), an annual celebration commemorating the end of slavery.

Owners of enslaved workers in Texas had no reason to celebrate emancipation. The federal edict did not immediately change the lives of enslaved people. It did, however, lead to staggering levels of violence, and the homicide rate in Texas soared.[33]

During the Texas Constitutional Convention of 1868, an official report about violence expressed doubt that "such a record of blood can be exhibited in any Christian or civilized State in the world in a time of peace." Many victims were freedmen—as those who had formerly been enslaved became known—who were lynched or shot down in cold blood by mobs and vigilantes with no provocation.[34]

The Shirley family's newly liberated members remained out of harm's way. In 1866, twenty-one-year-old Annie Shirley and her young son, George Washington Shirley, continued to live with the Shirleys and retained the family surname.[35] Like other freedmen who stayed with their former owners, Annie and her son were provided with food, shelter, and protection. Apparently Eliza Shirley and her children accepted Annie and began to refer to her as Aunt Annie. She remained in the Shirley household until the mid-1870s, during which time John Shirley and/or one of his sons fathered five more children with her.[36]

The Shirleys' formerly enslaved members had little fear of violence because many of the men "on the dodge" who came to Texas from Missouri were acquaintances of the family. The Shirleys became accustomed to seeing men and boys with pistols in their belts and knives in their boots. They probably reminded Myra of her deceased brother Bud or other young bucks she had known in Missouri. The family remained sympathetic and welcomed them to their home.

Texas had always attracted opportunists looking for a second chance. As bad as conditions were in postwar Texas, much of war-ravaged Missouri had degenerated into a campaign of personal vengeance to settle crimes committed during the war. Not all Missouri bushwhackers and guerrillas made the transition to become law-biding citizens. Some of them turned outlaw. They claimed that the Yankees who controlled the banks, railroads, and real estate had forced them to take drastic measures. As outlaws, they rationalized that they were victims driven to remain gallant resistance fighters. Missouri became known as the "Outlaw State," a breeding ground for a mélange of renegades and the most audacious and legendary brigands in postwar America.

It was no coincidence that the best-known Missouri outlaws had served under William Clarke Quantrill or William "Bloody Bill" Anderson. Half of the 296 men and boys who at one time or another rode under Quantrill's black flag later "pursued criminal careers, served prison sentences, were shot by peace officers or other outlaws, or were executed by state authorities or lynched by mobs."[37]

Contrary to hard-core apologists, survivors of Anderson's viciousness considered Anderson a homicidal maniac, even more ruthless than Quantrill. On September 27, 1864, Anderson and his guerrillas attacked Centralia, Missouri. They shot twenty-three unarmed Union soldiers, mutilated their bodies, and scalped them.[38]

Weeks later, Anderson met his end during a skirmish when a .36-caliber ball tore through his head. Federal troops took Bloody Bill's body to Richmond, Missouri, where photographs were taken of his corpse

This tintype of Confederate guerrilla leader William "Bloody Bill" Anderson was taken in October 1864 at Richmond, Missouri, shortly after Union soldiers had killed him.

holding a pistol. That evening, after decapitating Anderson, soldiers buried his remains and urinated on the unmarked grave.[39]

Quantrill ultimately fell out of favor with the Confederate hierarchy because of his contrary behavior and unorthodox tactics, but he survived until the end of the war. On May 10, 1865, Quantrill was mortally wounded by Union troops on a Kentucky farm. At a military prison infirmary in Louisville, he converted to Catholicism and died at age twenty-seven.[40]

The guerrilla chieftains were gone, but the young men and boys under their tutelage proved to be able students. They had learned the tactics of advance scouting and surprise attack and had honed survival skills that would serve them well in their outlaw days. Their wartime experiences acted as the catalyst for the creation of a criminal dynasty that would last for decades and serve as the basis for many popular outlaw legends of the so-called Wild West.

"Wars breed crime and criminals; and the American Civil War did not differ from others in that respect," wrote Western historian Paul I. Wellman.[41]

Out of this brotherhood of Missouri outlaws emerged a cunning young man who became a folk hero in his own lifetime. No single crim-

Cole Younger is shown near the close of the Civil War.

inal captured the public's imagination and left so deep an impression on American culture as Jesse Woodson James. Born in Missouri in 1847, Jesse and his older brother Alexander Franklin James, or Frank (born in 1843), grew up in a Missouri family of staunch southern sympathizers.[42]

Frank James fought for the Missouri State Guard in the defeat of Union forces at the Battle of Wilson's Creek in 1861. By 1863, he had joined Quantrill's raiders and had taken part in the slaughter at Lawrence, Kansas. Sixteen-year-old Jesse joined guerrillas who fought under "Bloody Bill" Anderson the next year. Both James brothers participated in the Centralia massacre, when scalps were taken as trophies to hang on saddles.[43]

In early 1866, as the James brothers contemplated a future that did not include farming, Frank ran into a former pal from the guerrilla days with Quantrill.[44] His name was Cole Younger, and he and his brothers had also reached a turning point in their lives. Frank introduced Jesse to Cole.

It was the beginning of a fateful relationship that was doomed from the start. Soon enough, young Myra Maibelle Shirley also became shrouded in a cloud of myth through this outlaw liaison.

CHAPTER 9

Jimmy and May

BY 1866, EIGHTEEN-YEAR-OLD MYRA SHIRLEY'S FORMAL education was complete. She had attended the Scyene community school for several months after her arrival, where she quickly learned that education in Texas was not a high priority, especially for girls.[1]

As early as 1850, Melinda Rankin, a Presbyterian missionary and teacher, noted that Texas lacked a "female seminary of high order, to elevate the standard of female education, which has not been made in Texas as prominent an object as its importance demands."[2] A state public school system would not be initiated until 1871, and even then, the Texas Board of Education specified that girls who attended public schools had to devote two days a week to needlework.[3]

Myra was older than most of the students and far ahead of them academically. After having mastered classical education at the Carthage Academy, Myra was not intellectually challenged by the rudimentary reading, writing, and arithmetic curriculum taught in a one-room school in rural Texas. Art, music, literature, and Greek were not offered. Her classmates likely found that just speaking and writing proper English was like learning a foreign language. Myra soon grew bored and eventually dropped out.[4]

She did not have to worry about turning to needlework full time after leaving school—her father had plenty of tasks for her. John Shirley bought farm acreage and town lots and even briefly considered opening a hotel such as the one he had left behind in Carthage, but that plan never materialized.[5] Shirley's stud horses and crop fields kept him busy enough and provided plenty of work for the few former enslaved laborers that remained, as well as Myra and his three sons—Edwin, sixteen years old; Mansfield, thirteen; and Cravens, now called John Alva, or Shug, seven.[6]

John and Eliza Shirley—fretful that the rowdiness of Scyene might be a negative influence—did all they could to keep their boys out of trouble, especially the two oldest. Local citizens noticed their mischief and misbehavior and their big sister's deportment. By Texas standards for female conduct, Myra, with her "scathing tongue and quick temper, was considered wild," according to Oklahoma writer Glenn Shirley.[7] Her bluntness and snappy retorts would have caused folks to say that Myra was "a caution," in the vernacular of the time.

At eighteen, Myra was fully capable of making her own decisions despite the machismo attitude of many Texan men, who expected women to be docile. In her free time, she frequently raced her fine steed on the Scyene Road and cantered along Mesquite Creek. She also enjoyed visiting her half nephews at Preston Shirley's place and was friendly with her fellow Missourians in the area.[8]

"Old-timers would tell that the Shirleys and the other Missourians were not well-liked at Scyene," wrote local historian Gwen Pettit. "They were clannish, had learned to keep their mouths shut during the old conflicts in Missouri and were thought to be unsociable."[9]

Those "other Missourians" had been acquainted with or were at least aware of the Shirley family from years past before they relocated to Texas. Others frequently came to Texas to visit kinfolk or escape arrest warrants. Those included Jesse and Frank James, the Younger brothers, and others who had ridden as rebel guerrillas during the war. None of them, however, could have known how their lives would intertwine and become an essential component of post–Civil War history—let alone subjects of folklore and myth.

From after the Civil War until the turn of the century, storytellers and hack writers began to turn the American West into the so-called Wild West in the minds and imaginations of the public. That process never truly ended—there has always been debate about how wild and violent life really was on the American frontier. Some historians still maintain that much of the violence associated with the Wild West was exaggerated. Other historians contend that the violent nature of the frontier was encouraged and widespread.

Most credible sources on the nineteenth-century American West agree that it was an era when history became legend, and legend became myth. That was particularly the case when it came to the public's perception of outlaws. Oscar Wilde, Irish poet and playwright, summed it up perfectly in a letter written in 1882 during a one-year lecture tour of America. After making many stops throughout the West, Wilde wrote, "Americans are certainly hero-worshipers and always take [their] heroes from the criminal classes."[10]

The folk-hero outlaw archetype was not unique to the United States: It was a widespread phenomenon that existed in many societies throughout the world for centuries. In post–Civil War America, however, a multitude of problems created a bumper crop of criminals who became heroic champions of the socially and economically oppressed classes. Those problems included failed Reconstruction programs, economic disparity, disrupted social conditions, widespread political corruption, and disenchantment with authority.

"Banditry simultaneously challenges the economic, social and political order by challenging those who hold or lay claim to power, law and the control of resources," wrote historian and scholar Eric Hobsbawm.[11]

In 1959, Hobsbawm created and popularized a term for outlaws who were touted as champions of the oppressed and downtrodden: He called them *social bandits*. They were regarded as defenders of the people and often were compared with the legendary Robin Hood. Like the heroic outlaw of English folklore, the social bandit had been forced to become a criminal, but he robbed only the rich and gave to the poor.[12] Historical evidence, however, offers only a few examples of social outlaws performing charitable acts.

Some acquaintances the Shirleys had known in Missouri, including the James and Younger brothers, had evolved into textbook examples of social outlaws, capable of committing high crimes while casting them-

In 1864, seventeen-year-old Jesse James rode with William Quantrill's guerrillas.

selves as heroic criminals with only good intentions. Their metamorphosis from guerrilla fighters to folklore outlaws was seamless.

By late 1865, Jesse and Frank James had returned home to Clay County, Missouri. Jesse was still recovering from a gunshot wound he had received near the end of the war, and Frank had returned from Kentucky. He had been with Quantrill in May 1865 when the guerrilla chieftain was shot and killed. Frank finally surrendered to Union authorities, took the oath of allegiance, and was paroled.[13]

By the winter of 1866, several of Jesse and Frank's former comrades at arms also had returned to Missouri and congregated with the James brothers to renew friendships. That was when Frank James reconnected with twenty-one-year-old Cole Younger, who had returned to Missouri after spending the last part of the war in California and Texas.

"It was while at this time I saw Jesse James for the first time in my life, so that sets at rest all the wild stories that have been told about our meeting as boys and joining Quantrell [Quantrill]," Younger wrote in his 1903 memoir. "Frank James and I had seen service together, and Frank was a good soldier, too. Jesse, however, did not enter the service until after I had gone South in the fall of 1863, and when I saw him early in the summer of 1866 he was still suffering from the shot through the lung he had received in the last battle in Johnson County in May, 1865. . . . We were thrown together more or less through my friendship with Frank James."[14]

The foundation had been formed for what would become known as the James-Younger gang. It would not be long before members of the gang and other ex-rebels would find their way to Scyene, Texas, and to the Shirley home. A few had already done so before the war ended. All of them were welcomed.

JAMES REED WAS AMONG the many guerrilla veterans who visited Scyene in 1866. He made a beeline for the Shirley family's residence to reunite with fellow Missourians he had not seen since 1861 in Carthage when the Reed family left Missouri, bound for Texas.

The Reeds had lived in Missouri since 1818. They had moved there from Knox County, Kentucky, when Jim Reed's father, Solomon Reed, son of Samuel and Ann Jones Reed, was one year old.[15] Eventually, Samuel's brothers Solomon and Matthias Reed followed with their families and settled in nearby counties.[16] They developed friendly trading relationships with numerous Indian tribes in the area, including Osage, Sac and Fox, Miami, and Potawatomi. Eventually, many of the White settlers learned to speak the Osage language fluently.[17]

Jim Reed's mother, Susan Demanda Brock, born in Missouri in 1821, had married Solomon Reed in 1838. The newlyweds settled in Vernon County, Missouri, and soon were joined by other family members. They acquired promising farmland near the mouth of a tributary of the Little Osage River called Hoyle's Branch, which soon became known as Reed's Creek.[18]

As was the practice of farming families, Solomon and Susan Reed had a large family—eight sons and six daughters. Their sixth child, born in Vernon County on February 6, 1845, was James Commodore Reed. His middle name came from one of Susan's brothers, William Commodore Perry Brock.[19]

Much like her husband's parents, Susan Brock Reed's parents also had been southern born and bred. Her father, Perry Green Brock, a native South Carolinian, and her mother, Margaret Ann "Peggy" Scott, born in Tennessee, had married in Kentucky and started a large family.[20] About the same time as the Reeds had left the Bluegrass State, the Brocks had moved to western Missouri.

By the mid-1850s, tensions over slavery had increased along the Missouri-Kansas border. Beginning in 1858, when Kansas Jayhawkers and Red Legs stepped up their incursions into Missouri, members of the Brock family, including Susan Reed's parents and several of her siblings, left Missouri and moved to Texas.[21] When his in-laws departed, Solomon Reed did not immediately follow suit. He remained on the farm with his older sons but sent his wife and their younger children south to Carthage, supposedly out of harm's way. Susan rented one of John Shirley's houses north of the town square, and the two families became well acquainted during the brief time the Reeds lived there.[22]

By 1861, with the nation about to be torn asunder by war, Solomon and Susan Reed gathered their brood and set out for Wise County, in northeastern Texas, forty miles south of the Indian Territory border.[23] The Reeds acquired land and built a home near Susan's parents and other family members at Prairie Point. Missourians had established the town in the late 1850s at the crossroads of two stagecoach lines.[24]

The Reeds soon realized that life in Texas would be just as dangerous as in Missouri. Once the war commenced, all federal troops were removed from the Texas frontier, and local men and boys left the area to fight for the Confederacy. This resulted in outlying settlements in Wise County being at the mercy of Indians determined to get their land back.

Wise County "was on the edge of civilization, with the Kiowa and Comanche Indians dominating almost everything," wrote a Reed descendant many years later. For defense purposes, the Reeds and Brocks built their cabins in a circle, a tactic known as "forting up."[25]

Early in the war, old men and boys did their best to protect the civilian population from attacks by Indians and occasional bandits. The Indian raids became more numerous, prompting many people to declare Wise County the scene of some of the bloodiest battles between Indians and settlers recorded in Texas history. Conditions improved only somewhat for the settlers when home militia companies, or minutemen, were authorized and placed under Confederate regulations. The small detachments were responsible for pursuing Indian raiders and recovering stolen livestock.[26]

"On moonlight nights, . . . the minute companies would patrol the county . . . ," wrote Clifford D. Gates in his history of Wise County.[27]

Most Brock and Reed males old enough to ride and shoot joined the Frontier Guards, protecting settlers from Indian raids, or Company B, 15th Texas Cavalry, organized in summer 1862 under the command of George Bible Pickett. Some served in both.[28]

Solomon Reed's oldest sons—Francis Marion (Marion), Samuel Benton (Benty), and William Scott (Scott)—enrolled as privates, as did several of their cousins and friends. Scott served with the 15th Texas Cavalry and in 1864 joined Captain Ben B. Haney's Company A, Wise County, First Frontier District, from Cooke County. That same year, Marion Reed enlisted in Captain Thomas Whaley's Company, First Frontier District.[29] As Marion later put it, "We cast our fate with the southern cause."[30]

In his memoir of the war, Colonel Robert Marvin Collins described the formation of Pickett's B Company as "a very nice lot of young men, boys, and middle aged men."[31] "Some had single barreled shotguns, some had squirrel-rifles and some had buck and ball muskets. In one thing only were all armed alike, and that was with big knives. The blade was from two to three feet in length and ground as sharp as could be. The scabbards for the great knives were, as a rule, made of rawhide with the hairy side out, and worn on the belt like a sword."[32]

Jim Reed did not ride with his brothers in the war. He joined William Quantrill's Partisan Rangers. Reed's name appeared on several Quantrill rosters that also listed Jesse and Frank James and Cole and Jim Younger.[33] In his memoir, Cole Younger acknowledged that Reed served with him during the war but provided no further details. Reed joined the raiders when he was about seventeen or eighteen during one of Quantrill's winter layovers in north Texas. Reed took part in some of the guerrilla activities in Missouri and elsewhere.

The Reeds would endure many losses in the early 1860s.[34] Like the Shirley family, the Reeds also dealt with the death of a son in 1863. On February 2, Jim Reed's older brother Samuel Benton Reed was killed while serving the Confederacy in Wise County. Then on May 22 of that year, Jim Reed's father, Solomon Reed, died in Wise County at age forty-six. Family chronicles stated that Solomon Reed "was killed in 1863," which would indicate a violent death.[35] He was buried near his son Benton and other kinfolk in the Teague Cemetery in Texas. Many years later, a granite gravestone was erected in Solomon Reed's honor at the Rider-Fairview Cemetery near Rich Hill in Bates County, Missouri.[36]

On October 7, 1863, Susan Brock Reed—who had been pregnant at the time of her husband's untimely death five months earlier—gave birth to a daughter. Susan named the girl Fatima Jane, after her favorite sister, Fatima Jane Brock, who had wed David Reed, a cousin of Solomon Reed. The family referred to the baby as Tima, or Timey, and some of them called her "Poor little Timey no father."[37]

Life in Wise County was never the same for the Reeds and Brocks as they banded together and struggled through the last years of the war. Decatur, the Wise County seat, had become a refuge for settlers fearful of Indian raids. The population of Prairie Point and other small communities sharply declined as people left.[38] Some members of the Reed and Brock families returned to Missouri, and others moved to Benton County, Arkansas. Susan Reed and her sister and brother-in-law, Fatima and David Reed, stayed in Texas. They moved east to nearby Collin County, thirty miles south of the Red River, and settled south of McKinney, the county seat.[39]

By the time Jim Reed had concluded his guerrilla service, his mother and other family members were in Collin County. Reed would have been familiar with the area from having spent time there and in other north Texas locales while serving with Quantrill.[40]

Once Jim had had time to catch up on family news, his thoughts turned to the old friends from Missouri who had also relocated to Texas.

The stage was set for a visit to the Shirley family, a short ride away in Scyene. He would once again see Myra Shirley, the little girl who had caught his eye in Carthage.

But Jim Reed did not find that little girl in Scyene, for Myra had grown into a comely young woman. Myra had not forgotten Mister Reed, who had become a strapping young man. The time and turmoil that had passed since they had last been together had not changed their attraction to each other. Myra was still his May, as he called her, and James was still her Jimmie—the first man she ever loved.

Theirs was a whirlwind courtship. After only a few months, the couple made a commitment to wed. Despite tales that John Shirley opposed the marriage, their families were supportive and gave their blessings. "Fate threw them together again," according to Jim's brother Marion Reed.[41]

"There is nothing in the facts to indicate that the marriage of Myra Maebelle Shirley and James C. Reed was anything other than a marriage of children of two families that were friends," wrote Texas historian Gwen Pettit.[42]

Many writers have repeated a wild tale that Myra eloped and was married to James Reed on horseback, with a member of his "outlaw gang" performing the ceremony. This rumor came from the fictionalized book published in 1889 by Richard K. Fox. Entitled *Bella Starr, the Bandit Queen, or the Female Jesse James*, the book has been the main source of misinformation about Myra, and many of its fabricated legends still dominate the public's perception of her.[43]

In fact, "Mira" M. Shirley—although the writing on the marriage license could be misread as "Mina"—and James C. Reed were legally married in 1866 in Collin County, Texas, where Reed's mother lived at that time.[44] The young couple applied for a marriage license on October 31, as attested by J. M. Benge, county clerk, and they were married on November 1 by the Reverend S. M. Wilkins, pastor of Corinth Presbyterian Church in Collin County.[45]

It is not known whether the ceremony was held in the courthouse, the church, the pastor's home, the home of the bridegroom's mother, or elsewhere, but it presumably was not conducted on horseback amid

James Reed and Myra Shirley's marriage record, Collin County, Texas, October 31, 1866.

an "outlaw gang."[46] Jim Reed's older brother Marion recalled in an 1889 newspaper interview that he had attended the wedding.[47] Wilkins certified on the marriage license that he had performed the ceremony, but when the document was filed in the courthouse afterward, the date of filing was left blank.[48] Myra Shirley was eighteen years at the time of the marriage, and Jim Reed was twenty-one.

The newlyweds lived in Scyene with Myra's parents at first, and Jim Reed helped with the Shirley hog and stud farm. In 1867, he worked for a while as a salesman for a Dallas saddle and bridle maker and said he wanted to buy land near Scyene and raise horses and cattle.[49] That plan did not work out.

By early 1868, Jim Reed's widowed mother and her younger children had moved back to Missouri. They settled at Rich Hill. Before long, Jim and Myra Reed also joined his family in Missouri. Myra helped her mother-in-law with household chores and tended to the children.[50]

Soon the Reed family grew even larger. In early September 1868, Jim and Myra welcomed their first child—a daughter born at the Reed home in Missouri.[51] They named her Rosa (Rosie) Lee Reed. When Myra declared that the baby was her special pearl, the name stuck—at various times in her life, almost everyone called her by the nickname of Pearl.[52]

One of the most persistent myths still perpetuated about Myra is that she had an affair, if not a marriage, with Cole Younger and that he was the father of her daughter.[53] The heads of the two families were certainly acquainted; the Youngers had had some business transactions with Myra's father, John Shirley, in Missouri before the Civil War.

However, in a newspaper interview conducted in 1889 while he was in prison, Cole Younger was quoted as saying that the story of his relationship with Myra Reed was "an entire fabrication from beginning to end.... In the first place, I have never been blessed with a wife, and was never so depraved as to keep a mistress. I never had more than five minutes' conversation with her in my life and never saw her after we left Scyene in 1872 with our herds."[54]

Younger continued to deny the rumors that he had been involved with Myra Shirley in his memoirs, writing, "In the spring of 1864, while I was in Texas, I visited her father, who had a farm near Syene [Scyene], in Dallas county. Belle Shirley was then 14 [sixteen], and there were two or three brothers smaller. The next time I saw Belle Shirley was in 1868, in Bates County, Mo. She was then the wife of Jim Reed, who had been in my company during the war, and was at the home of his mother. This was about three months before the birth of her eldest child, Pearl Reed, afterward known as Pearl Starr, after Belle's second [sic] husband."[55]

Younger's knowledge of Myra Maibelle's later life was sketchy, partly because he was in prison at that time. Although he told reporters in 1889 that Belle had started the rumors that she had been his wife and "the girl Pearl was our child," no proof has been found that Belle ever made such statements.[56]

Part of the confusion might have resulted from Belle's later relationship with Bruce Younger, half uncle of the Younger brothers of the outlaw gang. Cole Younger seems to have been unaware of her connection with his half uncle.

Myra was in love with her husband, Jim, and enjoying her time as a new mother. A neighbor, Gertrude Higgins, later recalled having watched

Myra Reed on her way to Bethel Baptist Church, riding sidesaddle with baby Rosie in her arms. Higgins had been impressed by "Myra's devotion to her daughter and the fine clothes she provided for her," wrote historian Glenn Shirley. "Even during the sermon Myra would look at her little girl instead of the preacher."[57] Perhaps this brief interlude in Missouri left Myra with sweet memories that she could turn to in the dark and dangerous years ahead.

CHAPTER 10

On the Scout

THE AFTERGLOW OF FIRST-TIME MOTHERHOOD PROVED fleeting for Myra Reed. While she savored her time in Missouri with her newborn daughter, life for the Shirley family in Texas had gone sour. Shortly after Rosa's birth in Missouri, Myra's younger brother Edwin Benton Shirley was shot and killed as a common horse thief. He was eighteen years old.[1]

Edwin Shirley had always loved horses, and like his big sister, he had become an accomplished horseman at an early age. Much of his time had been spent caring for the fine horses that his father, John Shirley, sold and bred. The problem was that young Ed also took a keen interest in other people's horses.

On May 3, 1866, Ed had been charged with two counts of horse theft in Dallas County, Texas. Apparently he failed to learn his lesson. On October 24, 1866, he was again charged with horse theft in Dallas County, but this time along with an accomplice—Mansfield Shirley, Ed's fourteen-year-old brother.[2] It remains unknown whether the Shirley brothers were ever apprehended or adjudicated. Many criminal cases fell through the cracks during Reconstruction.[3]

Nonetheless, taking someone's horse was an especially serious offense that deprived the victim of transportation. Horse thieves were thought of as vile scoundrels lacking any sense of decency; to be called a horse thief was the worst insult.

Yet contrary to Old West legend, horse stealing in most states and territories, including Texas, was not a capital offense. Culprits found guilty in a court of law were seldom—if ever—legally hanged.[4] Many horse thieves, however, never made it to a jail cell or courtroom—vigilantes or antihorse-thief associations often took matters into their own hands.

"The thief was most often found hanging from a tall tree with a note pinned to his shirt identifying him as a horse thief," wrote historian Robert Turpin. "It was a warning to other would-be horse thieves to think twice before taking another man's horse."[5]

Ed Shirley managed to avoid being strung up like a field-dressed deer. He could not, however, outrun a bullet. As the *Dallas News* bluntly stated, "Ed Shirley, a noted horsethief, was shot off his horse near Dallas in 1868."[6]

When word of Ed's death reached Myra Reed in Missouri, she likely returned to Texas out of respect for her slain brother, who was laid to rest in the Pleasant Mound Public Cemetery.[7] Myra's visit would have provided an opportunity for John and Eliza Shirley to meet Rosie ("Pearl") Reed, their new granddaughter. Time spent with the baby might have helped to ease some of the pain the Shirleys felt over the violent death of another son.

Back in Bates County, Missouri, Myra's husband, Jim Reed, concluded that there must be a better way to make a living than growing corn and raising hogs. A farmer's life held little appeal for Reed after his experiences as a guerrilla raider. His restlessness must have been apparent to Myra.

Reed was seldom at home. He spent a great deal of time racing horses and gambling in Arkansas and Indian Territory. Wagering on fast horses had become a popular pastime of the frontier.[8] Reed looked for ways to fund his sporting passions.

Before his daughter had reached her first birthday, Jim Reed had turned outlaw. He joined a group of bootleggers and horse thieves who operated in Arkansas, Indian Territory, and Texas. Like his wife's younger brothers in Texas, Reed had gone "on the scout." In the vernacular of the time, that meant he was doing his best to keep a low profile

James Reed, a Missouri-bred outlaw, was the first husband of Myra Shirley.

and avoid law officers or anyone else who could have interfered with his nefarious deeds.[9] In eastern Indian Territory and along the western Arkansas border, such outlaws often were called "owlhoots," traveling at night under cover of darkness on the owlhoot trail.[10]

REED WAS NOT THE only former guerrilla who had gone on the scout. Many other Missourians had taken to the owlhoot trail, such as Jesse and Frank James and the Younger brothers—Cole, Jim, Bob, and John. The members of the James-Younger gang were in a league of their own. Unlike Reed and his cohorts, the Jameses and Youngers did not settle for running illegal whiskey or stealing horses. Starting in the late 1860s, they quickly became the most notorious bank and train robbers in the nation.[11]

The James and Younger names had been linked to bank robberies as early as February 13, 1866. At about 2:00 p.m. on that snowy afternoon, thirteen mounted men rode into Liberty, Missouri, the seat of Clay County, a few miles north of the Missouri River. The riders reined in their horses when they reached the Clay County Savings Association, a two-story brick building on the northeast corner of the town square.[12]

Two riders clad in blue soldier overcoats dismounted and walked to the bank. The others remained astride their mounts. Because of the weather, only two employees were in the bank when the men entered and warmed their hands at the wood-burning stove. When the robbers stepped to the counter and asked to change a bill, they suddenly brandished revolvers and demanded the contents of the vault. Within minutes, the brigands exited the bank lugging a grain sack that held nearly $60,000 in greenbacks, bonds, and gold and silver coin.[13]

The robbers mounted up while their fellow gang members screamed rebel yells and fired their guns into the air to create a diversion. In the commotion, George Wymore, a nineteen-year-old student at William Jewell College, was killed by an errant shot in the chest as the gang thundered down Franklin Street firing guns. They headed to the ferry waiting at the Missouri River to make their escape before the posse—slowed by the blinding snow—could track them.[14]

The Clay County authorities and Robert Love, president of the Clay County Savings Association, declared that the bank robbery was the work of former rebel bushwhackers.[15] The offer of substantial reward money produced suspected culprits. All of them had ridden with William Quantrill or Bill Anderson. Among the names bantered about were Archie Clement, often called "Anderson's scalper," and Jim Anderson, Bloody Bill's older brother.[16]

Clement was named as leader of the pack, a position he still held on October 30, 1866, when $2,000 was stolen from Alexander Mitchell and Company, a private bank in Lexington, Missouri.[17] Clement, with a price on his head for the Lexington bank robbery, was finally killed on December 13, 1866. "Little Arch" met his demise on an icy street in Lexington when he engaged in a running gun battle with a militia detachment.[18]

The James and Younger brothers were named as suspects in several Missouri bank robberies over the years, but no official records have ever been located that tied either family to those crimes.[19]

The first verifiable bank robbery credited to the James-Younger gang occurred on March 20, 1868, an unseasonably warm day in Russellville, Kentucky.

"They rode splendid horses, and were as completely armed and equipped as the most daring and accomplished highwaymen could desire," reported the *Nashville* (Tennessee) *Banner* on March 22, 1868.[20] Detectives were called in to investigate. Three of the robbery suspects named were Jesse and Frank James and Cole Younger.

"It is fairly certain that Frank, Jesse, and Cole were present that day," Marley Brant, biographer of the Younger brothers, wrote of the Russellville robbery.[21]

As had been true of other crimes connected to Cole Younger, he vehemently protested accusations that he had helped rob the Russellville bank. He claimed he was not even in Kentucky at the time.

"When the bank at Russellville, Ky., was robbed, which had been laid to us, I was with my uncle, Jeff Younger, in St. Clair County [Missouri], and Jim and Bob [Younger] were at home here in Lee [Lee's] Summit [Missouri]," Younger wrote in his fanciful autobiography that often was referred to as his "alibi book."[22]

After the Russellville robbery, the Jameses and Youngers laid low. During the hiatus, Cole Younger tended to family business and, with help from his three brothers, cared for his ailing widowed mother as she prepared to relocate to a warmer climate in Texas.[23] The James brothers headed to California for rest and recuperation with a beloved uncle.[24]

―

ALTHOUGH SOME WRITERS LATER tried to connect Jim Reed with the robberies associated with his old Missouri guerrilla pals, no official records or credible evidence substantiates such claims. Without providing any proof, some writers suggested that Reed used the alias "James White" when he rode with the James-Younger outlaws during the 1860s. They contended that Reed had been complicit in the bank robberies at Lexington, Savannah, and Richmond, Missouri, and the holdup at Russellville, Kentucky.[25]

"James-Younger biographers consistently have James White participating in these robberies and include White's brother John in the Richmond affair," wrote historian Glenn Shirley. "Warrants were issued for both, but a Missouri justice of the peace acquitted them for lack of evidence. James White was a different man entirely. On October 30, 1866, the date of the Lexington robbery, Jim Reed was obtaining his marriage license in Collin County, Texas."[26]

As the James and Younger brothers were gaining notoriety, Reed was brushing shoulders with another outcast while actively pursuing his own life of crime, mostly in Arkansas and Indian Territory. By 1868, Reed had been introduced to the infamous Tom Starr, who for many years had been a pariah to the Cherokee Nation.[27]

Starr's father, James Starr, and his extended family had supported the controversial and fraudulent 1835 Treaty of New Echota between the Cherokee Nation and the federal government. The treaty cleared the way for the Cherokees' removal from their ancestral home in the Southeast to Indian Territory.[28] As staunch supporters of the Treaty Party who favored removal, the Starrs moved westward before federal soldiers—in 1838 and 1839—forcibly removed those opposed to the treaty, called the Ross Party.

The Ross Party was named after Cherokee Principal Chief John Ross, whose authority was undermined when a small group of Cherokee elites made a deal with the federal government to cede their territory through the Treaty of New Echota. Once the two contentious groups settled in Indian Territory, tempers on both sides flared. The Ross Party maintained that the people who had signed the treaty had no authority to do so, and the document was fraudulent. Treaty signers were considered guilty of a capital offense, and many were killed, including James Starr.[29]

During the bitter intratribal war, Tom Starr carried out a string of bloody reprisal killings. In 1843, Starr and two of his brothers attacked Benjamin Vore, member of the rival Ross faction, at his home and trading post near Fort Gibson, Indian Territory. They killed Vore, his entire family, and a hapless traveler who was present. After looting the home, the Starrs burned the residence and the victims.[30]

R. P. Vann, descendant of a politically prominent Cherokee family, later recalled, "Tom Starr. . . . told me about burning the Vores and their house and told me while it was burning a little boy about five years old came running out and begged him not to kill him and Tom said he just picked him up and threw him in the fire."[31]

In 1845, Tom Starr stepped up the revenge slayings. He often bragged that he had tracked down and killed thirty of the thirty-two men who rode in the party that had attacked his father. The other two died before Starr could find them. For many years, Starr wore a rawhide necklace studded with the dried earlobes of the men he had killed.[32]

Principal Chief John Ross signed an official decree that offered $1,000 "for the apprehension and delivery" of Tom Starr—dead or alive—for the Vore murders and other "depredations committed upon the property of certain citizens of this Nation." Starr remained safe and on the scout, however, because of the support of his Treaty Party allies.[33]

Yet even some of those on the same side as the Starrs in the vicious Cherokee civil war recognized Tom Starr's violent and cruel nature. John Rollin Ridge, who had witnessed his own father's murder by the same faction that had killed Tom Starr's father, closely followed Starr's exploits.

"Robberies, house trimmings [burnings], and all sorts of romantic deeds are attributed to this fellow, and the white people in town and around say they had rather meet the devil himself than Tom Starr," Ridge wrote in an 1846 letter to his cousin Stand Waite. Later, during the American Civil War, Waite became a Confederate brigadier general with whom Starr served as a scout for the First Indian Brigade.[34]

In 1846, the United States government forced the factions in the Cherokee Nation to sign a truce. President James Polk had grown weary of "the horrid and inhuman massacres which have marked the history of the Cherokees for the last few years." Polk decreed that the tribe's "internal feuds still exist which call for the prompt intervention of the Government of the United States."[35]

Subsequently, the two warring factions and the Cherokee Old Settlers, who had moved to Indian Territory much earlier, drafted a peace treaty that was ratified by Congress and ultimately approved. The treaty included a special clause that offered a complete pardon to all Cherokee citizens who had committed crimes, including murder and arson. Most tribal members understood that the clause was intended to stop the further escapades and rampages of Tom Starr.[36]

"Rarely has a government or a nation been forced to the extremity of entering into a treaty of peace with one of its own subjects," wrote historian brothers Harry F. and E. S. O'Beirne in 1892.[37]

Starr was fifty-five years old when he met Jim Reed. Starr had moved from his home in Going Snake District of the Cherokee Nation shortly after the truce was called in 1846. He had relocated on land along the Canadian River in the southern part of Canadian District.[38] By that time, much of Starr's blood lust had been satisfied, but his propensity for illegal acts had not been fully sated.

"Tom conducted a lively business in whiskey, cattle, and horse thievery," wrote Glenn Shirley. "He became firmly entrenched in a wild, remote domain on the South Canadian. Jim Reed undoubtedly participated in some of the Starr gang's looting excursions during 1868 and 1869, in which stolen cattle and horses were driven south through the rugged San[s] Bois country of the Choctaw Nation to Texas markets below the Red River or sold to white fences around Tom's former stomping grounds at Evansville, Arkansas."[39]

"Cherokee lawmen attempting to make arrests in Indian Territory had no jurisdiction if the outlaw stood on the Arkansas side of the Line," wrote Arkansas journalist Denele Pitts Campbell. "Similarly, federal marshals authorized out of Fort Smith were the only whites who had any jurisdiction in Indian Territory. Local lawmen like the Washington County sheriff couldn't arrest anyone on Indian land. This made Evansville, Cane Hill, and other Washington County border towns hot spots for outlaw activity."[40]

Thanks to Tom Starr's tutelage, Jim Reed became well acquainted with Evansville and the other locales in the region where men on the scout were welcomed. While Myra and her infant daughter remained comfortable in Missouri, her husband apparently found pleasure just over the line from Indian Territory. He risked his illicit earnings playing keno and high-stakes poker in the saloons of Evansville, where it was said that "gamblers and thugs congregate," and "nearly every morning the dead body of some Indian or transient white man would be found."[41]

Reed also found his way to Fort Smith where, since 1850, settlers, frontiersmen, soldiers, and Indians had pitched tents on "Race Track Prairie" and wagered on swift horses.[42] When Reed went home to check on Myra and Rosie, he likely attributed the money he shared to his good fortune at the racetrack and not to horse theft and whiskey running. Whether Myra took her husband at his word remains unknown. By late 1868, however, there could have been no doubt that Myra—and many lawmen—had become aware of Reed's felonious lifestyle.

Reed had been joined on the owlhoot trail by one of his older brothers, William Scott Reed, known as Scott, a Confederate veteran. The Reed brothers associated with John King Fisher and his gang of horse thieves and bootleggers who operated in Arkansas, Indian Territory, and northern Texas.[43] The Fisher who welcomed the Reeds to his band was not the notorious Texas gunslinger who had the same name and a colorful reputation for working both sides of the law.[44] The J. K. Fisher who befriended the Reed brothers hailed from the Fisher family of Washington County, Arkansas, where the Fishers competed in the whiskey-running trade with another local clan, the Shannons. Bad blood had existed between the families for some time, but it erupted into full-blown warfare that led to grudge killings and vendettas.[45]

"In 1868 a deadly feud arose between the Shannons and Fishers and their friends," according to a history of Washington County, Arkansas, published in 1889. "All the parties at the time lived at or near Evansville and were considered desperate characters."[46]

On December 2, some of the Fisher gang, including Scott Reed, rode into Evansville, where the Shannons ambushed them. During the mêlée, Scott Reed was shot and killed.[47] When Jim Reed learned of his brother's death, he made plans to avenge the slaying.

In 1889, Francis Marion Reed, the eldest Reed sibling, spoke publicly about his brother Scott's death and how Jim Reed reacted.[48]

"In 1868 brother Scott was assassinated in Arkansas by some Shannon boys, between whom and a family of Fishers there had previously been some killing done," Marion Reed told a reporter. "Brother Jim went immediately to the scene of Scott's murder and allied himself with the Fishers and participated in the killing of two of the Shannons in retaliation."[49]

In truth, Jim Reed's retaliation took place on June 2, 1869, six months to the day after Scott Reed had been gunned down. The two men killed were not Shannon brothers but two members of their gang, Noah Fitzwater and Newton C. Stout. After Jim Reed, John Fisher, Cal Carter, Charles Bush, and John Coleman waylaid Fitzwater and Stout, some of the Fisher gang raced back to Indian Territory.[50] One of the Shannon brothers reported that after ambushing his two men, "the murderers then hastened across the Cherokee line, whooping and swearing after crossing the line that they were home."[51]

The Fisher gang did not have much time to gloat. Posses were formed, warrants issued, and rewards offered. Jim Reed had become a wanted man on the run.

CHAPTER 11

Southern California: An "Island" in the Sun

A FTER THE DUSTUP WITH THE SHANNON BUNCH IN EVANS- ville, Arkansas, Jim Reed had wisely slipped into the shadows of Indian Territory. It was never proved that any of Reed's bullets had been among the twenty-one that had cut down Noah Fitzwater or the six rounds that had struck Newton Stout.[1] Posses were on the prowl for the Fisher gang, however. Reed's presence at the scene of the killings was more than enough for the Shannons to make him a target.[2]

At the time, some people speculated that Reed had holed up with Tom Starr on the Canadian River. Others contended that Reed had ridden to his mother's home in Rich Hill, Missouri, where he gathered Myra and Rosie and returned to Texas. A third theory seemed the most logical. It suggested that Reed had indeed gone to Missouri but stayed only long enough to make a plan with Myra. They concluded that their best choice was to head to California, "the land of milk and honey."

Perhaps the Reeds knew that other Missourians who had ended up on the wrong side of the law had relocated temporarily to California. Cole Younger stated years later that he was "on the Pacific slope" visiting his uncle Coleman Younger when the Civil War ended in April 1865.[3] But Cole Younger's trip to the West Coast might have been more than just a "visit" to relatives. Younger knew Confederate Captain Henry Kennedy, who had traveled to California, Nevada Territory, and Arizona Territory in 1864 and found "many southern men ready to enlist."[4] In addition, various plots existed "to take or buy ships in California and Canada to use against U. S. shipping and to serve as pirate operations and take gold that was shipped from California."[5]

Younger returned to Jackson County, Missouri, in the fall of 1865 "to pick up the scattered ends of a ruined family fortune."[6]

Jesse and Frank James spent the winter of 1868–1869 hiding out near El Paso Robles ("the pass of the oaks") at La Panza Ranch, which their uncle, Drury Woodson James, had owned since 1860.[7] The bank robbery in Russellville, Kentucky, in March 1868 "made a brief sabbatical from the outlaw business seem advisable," and the two brothers supposedly traveled to San Francisco.[8] From there, they reached Paso Robles by stagecoach and worked as cowhands on their uncle's ranch in the fall and winter before heading east "to resume their banking careers." Jesse James went by the name "Scotty" on the ranch.[9]

Drury Woodson James later denied knowing that Jesse was a wanted man. In 1869, D. W. James and his business partner sold La Panza Ranch,[10] and James bought a half interest in the Paso Robles hotel, bathhouse, and the surrounding 4,300 acres.[11]

In late 1869 or early 1870, Jim, Myra, and little Rosa moved to California, probably by stagecoach. Although stagecoach travel was slow and fraught with difficulties and the danger of attack by Indians or bandits, it was much faster than traveling by boat. Rail travel in the West was not yet extensively available.

On February 5, 1870, Reed, who had little formal education, wrote a letter filled with misspellings to his brother Marion in Missouri:

Well Marion again I drop you a few lines this leaves all well and hope it may find you all the same. I have no nuse to rite. I have ritten severl letters and got no answer yet. Marion I rote to you to pay that money to Billy Reed and Jasper [probably Jim Reed's younger brother Jasper Columbus Reed]. But if you haven't pleas send it to me. Uncle [Henry Reed] is broke and I am needing money very bad. Now if you have payed it out let it go and I will wate on uncle. You can deposit it and send a check by male. I will close by sending my love to all. I remain your afectionate brother until death.

James C. Reed.

A postscript says, "I have givin you mi address severl times but for fear you haven't got it I will give it again." And at bottom, in Myra's handwriting, is "Cucamongo, Sanbernadino Cty., Lower Cal."[12]

Cucamonga ("sandy place"), in San Bernardino County near the base of the San Gabriel Mountains, was the site of the Rancho Cucamonga land grant in 1839 to Tubercio Tapía, who established California's first winery on his land (the second winery in the United States). Several roads met at Cucamonga, including a Butterfield Stage route. A community called Grapeland was settled there in 1869 but began to decline in the early twentieth century.[13]

On March 25, 1870, in a longer letter to his brother Marion, again riddled with misspellings, Jim Reed writes:

Well, Marion, I will write you a few lines. I believe I have ansered all of your letters. I have never give you any satisfaction [illegible words] in regard to things in general. I have never ben satisfied hear It have been very dry and [illegible words] come hear until lately we have had fine ranes and the grass is growing fine. The berries is green with all kinds of grass this is the partyist [prettiest] country I eaver seen and If we could have rain, it would be the best in the world. It is like Texas in regard to raining. I have not ben hear long enough to no wheather this state will hold me or not though if it proves satisfactory after 3 or 4 years I will stay hear for life. The weather is pleasant and the climat is good the water is good timber is very scarce in placis [places] though I have pleanty of timber sutch as it is. All Hell cant split it we have plenty of Pine lumber ship [shipped] hear from Oregon it is worth $30 a thousand I am fensing some the land I Bought was unimproved land. Uncle Henry is liveing with me. Him and

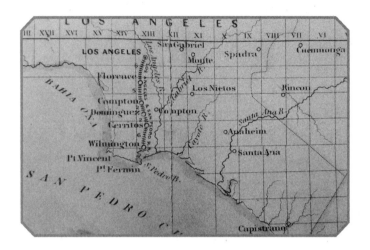

Jim and Myra Reed's home was in southern California in the early 1870s.

I have not got any money. I have spent about all I had when I Come hear. I am afraid to rite for any of mi friends to come hear I am afraid they would not like [it] though I think this would be a as good a place to ware out a life time as anywhere land is selling from 7 to 20 Dollars per acor [acre].[14]

Reed also tried to interest Marion in joining him in California:

I think you could do well hear as you as have there and maby better. I have got as good a piece of land as is in this country and I [illegible words] and if you Can git hear and borrow five hundred Dollars and go in with me we will go in the stock business all kind stock payes well hear. I would be glad if you could come right off a man can make money hear if he has money to comens [commence] with. Uncle Henry wants Billy to come.[15]

Reed continues, "I will close for the present give mi love to mother and the children. This leaves us as well as [illegible]. May [Myra] has been sick for some time though she is able to be up some of the time. I hope this may find you all well. You must excuse bad riting and spelling.

I remain your brother until Death. James C. Reed."[16] Below his signature, Jim Reed adds, "I have got the fatist [fattest] little Bay you eaver seen," referring to a bay horse.[17]

The illness that Reed mentioned in his letter might have been a complication of pregnancy; in April 1870, Myra had her second child, a daughter.

By the time the 1870 federal census was taken, the Reeds had left Cucamonga and were living in Los Nietos Township. The census gave this information for their household of five people: James, head of household, age twenty-four [twenty-five], farm laborer, born in Missouri; Mary M., age twenty [Myra Maibelle, twenty-two], "keeping house," born in Missouri; Rosa, age two [she would turn two in September 1870], "at home," born in Maryland [almost certainly a misinterpretation of the census taker's notes, which should have read MO for Missouri rather than MD for Maryland]; Eliza W., age two months, "at home," born in April in California; and Henry Reed, age thirty-five, "at home," born in Kentucky. Thus we can deduce from baby Eliza's age that the census taker visited the Reed household in June 1870. The census notes were compiled on ledger page 23 on August 11, 1870.[18]

Federal censuses list Myra Shirley as two years old in 1850 and twelve in 1860, so her reduced age on the 1870 census is either the census taker's error or an early example of Myra's tendency to shave years off her age.

No further mention has been found of little Eliza, who apparently was named for Myra's mother. She supposedly died as an infant in California. On February 22, 1871, the Reeds' son, Edwin Benton[19] (named for his uncle Edwin Benton Shirley), was born in California, only ten months after Eliza. It is not known whether Eddie was a full-term baby or premature.

Myra and Jim Reed jointly wrote a letter to Marion Reed from Los Nietos in about December 1871.[20] Most of the letter is in Myra's delicate script, with a shorter note from Reed toward the end. The letter begins:[21]

> *I take my pen in hand to write you a few lines this morning. We are all enjoying the best of health. Indeed it is a rare thing for anyone to be sick in this country. Marion, we have received but two letters from home in a long time; and they were old. Oh so*

old I guess they had been written some two or three months. I presume you would like to know how we have been getting along lately. When we left Sanbernadino, we rented a place in Los Nietos. Los Nietos is an Island, and as such is said [to be] the last bastion of California.[22] *We then rented the place to a gentleman by the name of Wolf. He gave us one hundred and thirty dollars for possession. Jimmie [Jim Reed] has bought land here on the Island, and I guess we will make a permanent home. Here I am perfectly satisfied. I think in a few years we can have as lovely little home as the state can boast of. We don't care a cent if it never rains. We have the lead on raising everything we wish too, as we have plenty of irrigating water. Jimmie is going to put out an orchard the first thing and then a vine yard. You never seen such corn as grows here. It beats any land to produce I ever seen.*[23]

The letter continues:

Marion[,] Jimmie is very anxious for you to come out here. He paid thirty dollars an acre for our land, and he is compelled to raise $400 next month. It would confer a great favor on us if you could collect what is coming to us back their [there] and come out here. Hays wrote us that you had an idea of going to Texas; do no such thing, come here[,] Marion, and if you don't like, you shall loose [lose] nothing by it. Jimmie is gathering corn and wanted me to write a letter and have it ready for him to take to the P. O. when he comes in. Jimmie says to tell you to make it in by Christmas anyhow. I want you to be shure and take dinner with us on Christmas day. I would not knowingly misrepresent things to you. Jimmie thinks you could do well here, and we would both be pleased to have you come. Press [probably her brother, Preston Shirley] wrote that he was coming out here, but I guess it was more talk than any thing else.[24]

The letter continues, "I have wrote to Manda[,] Sally[,] [probably James Reed's sisters Susan Demanda Reed and Sarah Francis (Sallie)

Reed] your ma and Aunt Letty since I got a letter. I intend to quit writing. Do you blame me? Old Phillips (the old cuss) never condescends to write a line. Jimmie wrote him a scorcher last night. I guess he thinks Jimmie won't come back their [there] soon. He might be disagreeably surprised some day. When we get our land all paid for we will ask the world nothing else. Oh Marion an Orange Orchard is *so* pretty."[25]

Myra then mentions Rosa and the baby boy but not Eliza, who presumably had already died. "Rosie sends her love to all. I have not [page torn]. She often talks of her days with Uncle Marion; she knows her letters and can say over the whole Alphabet. She has got a little set of dishes and three dolls[,] a ball[,] and two hoops and a steel whistle. I will send Tima [James Reed's youngest sibling, Fatima Jane Reed, born in 1863 after her father's death] one of her little saucers. The baby is not very well. He is teething and looks very pale this morning."[26]

Finishing her part of the letter, Myra says, "Write soon[,] Marion[,] and give us all the news. Give my love to all and I want them all to write soon and often. In Haste, May."[27]

Jim Reed added his comments on the remainder of the page, reiterating the upcoming need for money.

Marion I ritten to you some time ago and have not received any answer yet. I want you to rite as soon as you git this and talk Business. I have bought 47 acres of land and I have one payment to make the first of January which is $400. I have got $200 on hand and stock that will bring it if I can git that that is back there. Marion this is a good country and I am shure you can do well hear the Climate is good I no you can't help likeing this is a good[28]

The letter abruptly ends there.

The Reeds' new home, Los Nietos in Los Angeles County, is one of the oldest communities in southern California. *Los Nietos* translates from Spanish as "the grandsons." The town was established on La Zanja, later referred to as Rancho Los Nietos, one of the earliest Spanish land grants and the largest (three hundred thousand acres) in Alta California. A solider, Manuel Nieto, had received the grant in 1784.[29]

The ranch remained intact for fifty years. In 1833, the Nieto heirs petitioned Mexican governor Jose Figueroa for a partition. In 1834, Figueroa declared the Rancho Los Nietos grant to be under Mexican rule and ordered it to be partitioned into six smaller ranchos—Los Alamitos, Las Bolsas, Los Cerritos, Los Coyotes, Santa Gertrudes, and Palo Alto.[30]

In 1836, Los Nietos had two hundred inhabitants. The area had good soil and water and could support livestock and crops such as corn, barley, and beans.[31] Much of the population lived in adobe houses. The area slowly began to develop. By 1860, a Butterfield stagecoach line was operating between Los Angeles and Saint Louis via Arizona, New Mexico, northern Texas, Arkansas, and Missouri. The trip took nineteen days,[32] about eight of which were consumed in traversing Texas.[33]

Los Nietos School District was established in 1862, and a Methodist circuit centered on Los Nietos was founded in 1867. The community grew up around Rancho Los Nietos and its constituent Rancho Santa Gertrudes. Los Nietos had a post office and was listed as a township in the 1860 and 1870 federal censuses, with its area comprising most of the old Rancho Los Nietos, stretching from the Puente Hills south to Long Beach. Census records report Los Nietos's population as 605 in 1860 and 1,544 in 1870.[34]

After the "turmoil and transformation of the Gold Rush era of the 1850s" and the flooding, drought, disease, and "general degradation" of the first half of the 1860s—not to mention the Civil War—the Los Angeles area changed dramatically.[35] The real growth of the area was said to date from 1869; there was a great demand for housing. That same year, the region's first railroad was completed from Los Angeles to the "rudimentary harbor at San Pedro/Wilmington," which soon was boosted by federal funding for dredging and breakwater projects.[36]

It was a crucial and tumultuous time. A smallpox epidemic raged in Sonora, and drunkenness and shootings were rampant.[37] The first reported riot in the Chinese community occurred in Los Angeles, sparked by a fight between two rival gangs and resulting in the hanging and shooting of nineteen men.[38] The stealing of horses and mules in southern California was common. Many of the thieves were thought to be former Confederate soldiers.[39]

The 1870 population of Los Angeles was about 5,700, and southern California was becoming more welcoming to newcomers. Santa Monica was just beginning to attract attention as a seaside resort "for the tired city man," and residences and tents were popping up at the mouth of Santa Monica Canyon. By 1871, summer boat excursions were available to Santa Catalina Island, and a carrier-pigeon service from the island was inaugurated. Pigeon racing was a popular sport among rival owners. One bird made the trip of about twenty-nine miles from Catalina to the mainland in only fifty minutes.[40]

It is doubtful that Jim Reed and his family went to Santa Catalina Island or raced pigeons during their short time in southern California. As things turned out, they did not stay in that area "for life." Evidently Reed's view that a man can make money if he has money to start with took a sudden twist that sent the Reeds back east, shattering their hopes for a permanent, "lovely little home" in California.

According to some sources, Jim Reed was accused of committing various crimes in California, including robbery, counterfeiting, and murder.[41] An article published later in the *Dallas* (Texas) *Daily Commercial* said that Reed had robbed a man of a large sum of money.[42] Other sources say Reed held up a stagecoach near San Diego while he was involved in counterfeiting. California law officers learned of the warrant issued for his arrest before he had moved to California. Rewards offered for his capture "made him a valuable target for bounty hunters. He was again forced to flee."[43] It is also possible that the Reeds, who were struggling to come up with a $400 payment, defaulted on their loan and lost their California property.

Cole Younger, long acquainted with the Reed and Shirley families, later commented on their return to Texas—although perhaps exaggerating his own role. He said, "In 1871 [or very early 1872], while I was herding cattle in Texas, Jim Reed and his wife, with their two children, came back to her people. Reed had run afoul of the Federal authorities for passing counterfeit money at Los Angeles and had skipped between two days. Belle [Myra] told her people she was tired roaming the country over and wanted to settle down at Syene [Scyene]. Mrs. Shirley wanted to give them part of the farm, and knowing my influence with the father, asked me to intercede in behalf of the young folks. I did, and he set them up on the farm, and I cut out a lot of the calves from one of my two herds and left with them."[44]

Jim Reed wrote to his brother Marion from Denton County, Texas, on January 19, 1872:

With pleasure I write you a few lines to let you no I have not forgot you. This leaves all well. I am living on Perry Burnett's old place on Denton Creeke. I was at Decater [Decatur] yesturday. Times is dull hear but better than have ben for some time. I was at Prairrie Point that Country is improveing some land is lo [low] worth from 2 to 5 Dollars that is unimproved land. I will stay hear or in this part.[45]

The letter continues,

Write soon and let me no if Sollie [probably Reed's brother Solomon Lafayette (Lafe) Reed] is there or not. I am uneasy about him and whether Hall payed you any money or not. I seen old Hunter as I come south at Neosho [Missouri] he sayed he would give Collonel Hunter what he was owing me. I don't have any confidents in any one hardly. . . . I will close for the present write as soon as you get this. Give my best respects to all. I remain your Brother as Ever. James C. Reed.

Reed then wrote a name and address: "Direct, Mrs. M. M. Shirley, Denton P. O., Denton Co., Texas." M. M. Shirley were Myra's initials and maiden name. And finally, Myra wrote a note in elegant backhand, sideways on the margin of the second page of the letter: "Marion[,] I have not forgotten you, and I want you to write to me. Give my love to your wife and the children. I would love to see all of you. M. M. Reed."[46]

And so the Reeds resumed their tumultuous life in Texas.

CHAPTER 12

Living the Outlaw Life in Texas

IN THE WINTER OF 1871-1872, THE REEDS—FRESHLY SETtled on Denton Creek in Denton County, Texas—frequently visited family and friends at Scyene, in neighboring Dallas County. John and Eliza Shirley finally met Myra and Jim Reed's baby son, Eddie, and were reacquainted with his big sister, Rosie. Myra also met her half brother, James K. Shirley, a toddler born in 1869 to Aunt Annie and probably fathered by John Shirley.[1] The reunions at the Shirley residence gave everyone a chance to catch up with one another. They had an abundance of news to exchange, and not all of it was good.

During the Reed family's interlude in California, Myra not only had to bury her infant daughter, Eliza, but also had lost another brother, Mansfield Shirley. In early December 1869, Mansfield had been indicted for horse theft in Dallas County for a third time.[2] On the scout, he stayed clear of Texas and managed to avoid arrest—until his time ran out. In early 1870, Mansfield was killed in Indian Territory during a gun battle with law officers. He died just short of his eighteenth birthday and was laid to rest far from home and family in an unmarked grave in Indian Territory.[3] John and Eliza Shirley were left with only one surviving son, Cravens (renamed John Alva), or Shug, as he was called. Barely in his teens, Shug appeared to be hell-bent on following the example of his brothers who had taken to the outlaw life.

By 1870, other Shirley family members had left Texas. Preston Shirley returned to Jasper County, Missouri.[4] He and his wife, Mary, moved back to family land they still owned and commenced farming. It is unknown how long Preston and his family stayed in Missouri, but according to census records, they had returned to Texas and settled in Cooke County by 1880.[5] By then, only one of their three sons, Oliver, remained at home.[6] Pres apparently had the same itch to keep moving as his father. It is likely that Pres took part in the first Oklahoma land rush of 1889, the only land run into the Unassigned Lands of Oklahoma Territory. His name appears in the 1890 Oklahoma territorial census.[7]

Although Myra's family had been further depleted in her absence, several familiar Missourians who had settled in the Scyene area remained, including members of the Younger family. In 1868, Cole and his brothers had moved their ailing mother, Bursheba Younger, from Missouri to the warmer clime of Texas.[8]

"The town of Scyene was selected, as there were other Missouri families nearby and so that Bursheba would not have to adjust to a totally foreign environment," wrote Younger family biographer Marley Brant. "The Younger boys had many friends in Texas, and the Shirley family of Carthage, Missouri, were some of them."[9]

Bursheba Younger was pleased to have much of her family close by. However, after the winter of 1869–1870, she became despondent and wanted to return to her beloved Missouri to spend her final days.[10] Her sons obliged, but Cole remained in Texas while his three brothers accompanied their mother to Jackson County. They stayed until Bursheba died in Lee's Summit, Missouri, on June 6, 1870—her fifty-fourth birthday. After her death, her sons returned to Texas, where Cole remained in the cattle business.[11]

The Youngers had become familiar figures in Scyene and other Dallas County towns. They frequently were seen in the company of "G. W. Howard," likely an alias for Jesse James, and "C. P. Alexander," better known as Frank James.[12] The James brothers also had family and old friends in Texas, including their sister, Susan Levina James.

Four years earlier, on December 7, 1869, about the time the Reeds had moved to California, the James brothers had been publicly identified as the outlaws who had robbed the Daviess County Savings Association in Gallatin, Missouri. In the process, Jesse reportedly shot and killed bank owner John W. Sheets, whom he mistakenly believed was Samuel P. Cox, the killer of Bloody Bill Anderson.[13]

The James brothers were no longer just suspects—they had been branded as wanted outlaws. In response to the charges, Jesse and Frank launched a public-relations campaign to clear their names. Taking a cue from Cole Younger's standard practice of denial, Jesse vehemently disavowed any wrongdoing. He even penned a letter of protest to Missouri governor Joseph W. McClurg, who on Christmas Eve 1869 had ordered a militia organized to capture or kill the James brothers.[14] The *Liberty Tribune* saw fit to publish the epistle, in which Jesse claimed to have several character witnesses—"the best men in Missouri"—who would provide a rock-solid alibi for the James brothers.[15]

"I well know if I want to submit to an arrest I would be mobbed and hanged without trial," James wrote. "Governor, when I can get a fair trial, I will surrender myself to the civil authorities of Missouri. But I will never surrender to be mobbed by a set of bloodthirsty poltroons."[16]

Some people still loyal to the Old South worshiped the James brothers as caring bandits motivated solely by political and social injustice, despite any evidence to the contrary. At the same time, the Jameses' criminal association with the Younger brothers had grown stronger as they carried out bank, stage, and train robberies in several states. By the mid-1870s, however, public opinion had turned against the James-Younger gang. Nevertheless, they knew safe harbors awaited them with family and old comrades in Texas or Indian Territory, such as Tom Starr's place on the Canadian River.

BECAUSE OF A STEADY flow of refugees hiding out from justice, Scyene's reputation as a rowdy town remained intact. At the same time, nearby Dallas was already well on its way to becoming a full-fledged city. Its proximity to the frontier made it an important market for the skins and tongues of the immense bison herds roaming the plains.[17]

"During the years that preceded the coming of the railroad, and until the systematical extermination of the great herds had ended, it was the center of the buffalo trade," wrote John William Rogers in his history of Dallas. "In the sixties [1860s] and seventies [1870s], hundreds of men on the prairie did nothing but hunt buffalo. A good hide brought $2 while dried buffalo tongues were popular food locally and considered a delicacy in the East. The rest of the carcass had so little commercial value that it was left to rot or be devoured by wolves.[18] By 1875, when the buffalo trade reached its peak, Dallas had become the largest market in the world for buffalo skins."[19]

By then, Dallas was "beginning to put on the airs of a city," according to the *Texas Almanac* of 1872.[20] That same year, the Texas & Pacific Railroad reached Dallas. A year later, that line was intersected, making Dallas one of the state's major cities.[21]

The railroads, however, bypassed Scyene. What had been a thriving town with a post office, mercantile stores, school, and churches soon went into decline. Citizens left in search of better opportunities, but some families, including the Shirleys, remained.

Jim and Myra Reed were ready to move on from Denton County but had no intention of returning to Scyene. Neither was Reed interested in hunting buffalo or working for the railroad, and he had given up on farming.

Authors and historians have completely overlooked a significant familial connection from the early 1870s, before the Reeds departed Denton County. It has been confirmed in Shirley and Canote family genealogical records, but this discovery has not appeared in any published work until now.

Myra Reed was related by blood to Sam Bass, another infamous outlaw cloaked in legend. She and Bass were second cousins through their paternal Shirley-Canote grandmothers.[22]

Born in Indiana in 1851, Bass was orphaned at an early age and raised by an uncaring uncle, David L. Sheets. In 1869, Bass struck out on his own to work in a Mississippi sawmill. A year later, he moved to Texas and found employment as a ranch hand southwest of Denton. Bass had always had a way with horses, but the cowboy life was not up to his boyhood dreams. He moved to Denton, where he briefly groomed stable horses at a fancy hotel.[23] Then Sheriff William F. "Dad" Egan hired him to care for

Living the Outlaw Life in Texas ✣ 127

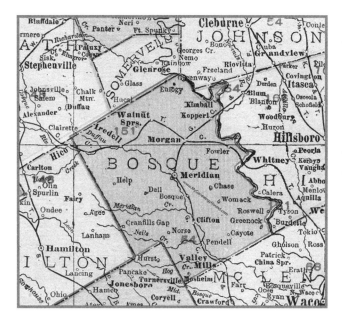

After they left California in the early 1870s, Jim and Myra Reed settled in Bosque County, Texas.

his livestock and property. Bass also worked as a freighter hauling supplies between Denton and the railroad towns of Sherman and Dallas.[24]

When Bass was not working for the sheriff of Denton County, he spent most of his time and much of his money on fast horses that raced at the dirt track on the outskirts of town. "Gradually Sam became more and more absorbed with horse racing and finally he obtained a racing pony for himself," wrote John William Rogers.[25] Sam's fleet horse was a two-year-old gray named Jenny that became known as the "Denton Mare" after she won races at San Antonio and throughout northern Texas.[26]

Whether Myra Reed and Sam Bass were aware of each other or ever met might never be known. They both had a passion for fast horses and resided at the same time in Denton County for at least a year. The overlap occurred only a few years before Bass turned outlaw and carried out train and bank robberies. Bass died in a shoot-out with Texas Rangers on July 21, 1878, his twenty-seventh birthday.[27]

By the summer of 1872, the James Reed family had bid farewell to Denton County and headed to Bosque County in central Texas. Named for the Bosque River—*bosque* is the Spanish word for "woodlands"—the county was about sixty miles south of Dallas.[28]

The storied Chisholm Trail entered the county east of the Bosque River. It had become the most famous cattle trail beaten out by millions of Texas longhorns driven to Kansas railroad towns and northern markets in the first twenty-five years after the Civil War.[29] The trail traversed the county's open cattle ranges and grassy prairies studded with mesquite and cedar that flourished along the Bosque River and its tributaries. Many settlers also had success capturing wild horses from the great herds that roamed the prairie.

When the Reeds arrived, they found that Bosque County offered opportunity but also had hardships and perils. For many years, settlers had understood that constant vigilance was a top priority for their safety. Comanches and Kiowas made forays through the county and occasionally attacked settlements and stole cattle.

"I never did see an Indian although they made raids all over the county in those days," recalled Susan Frances Lomax of her family's time in Bosque County in the 1870s. "We rented land across the Bosque River the first year. . . . We had to take our mules up a ravine moonlight nights as the Indians made their raids on those bright nights. One time in my life I was sorry to see the moon shine."[30]

Random grudge killings, vicious feuds, and vigilante lynchings also occurred regularly in Bosque County. Much of the violence was perpetuated against African Americans. In 1870, an Austin newspaper reported that "there appears to be about two killings a week in Bosque. Two men were lynched for cattle stealing, and two other men killed. There are no laws and no civilization in Bosque."[31] The Texas governor ordered the state militia to the county to keep the peace, but most of the soldiers were African Americans, which enraged racists.

Despite what some folks might have called a cauldron of trouble, Jim and Myra Reed were fully prepared to make Bosque County their home. In August 1872, they bought 160 acres of land fifteen miles east of the county seat of Meridian, on South Coon Creek, a tributary of the Bosque River.[32]

The Reeds handed $750 cash to William and Mary Cox, longtime settlers on Coon Creek, and moved into their sturdy log house. Their closest neighbors, the Conine family, lived on the adjoining 160 acres, purchased from the Coxes' son, Tom Cox.[33] Known throughout the area for making fine saddles, the younger Cox had moved to Iredell, a settlement in northwestern Bosque County, where he became a Baptist preacher.[34]

Will Conine and his family welcomed the Reeds and quickly became fond of the new neighbors. In later years, Conine wrote about the Reed family in his journals. His memories provided an opportunity to learn about a side of Myra and Jim that had never been revealed:[35]

We liked the Reeds all right. Reed was very good looking, tall, wiry, jolly and intelligent, vim and full of life. His wife was good looking, very intelligent, dressed well, and passed well. They had two pretty children, Rosie and Eddie. They afterwards called her Pearl. She sure was a pretty little girl. Eddie was a pretty little curly headed boy.

Reed and his wife visited us often and we visited them. He soon had a pretty good bunch of horses and cattle. Mrs. Reed was a splendid rider and could handle a six-shooter all right. Reed and her used to get on their horses and ride up to our house and sit until late bed time once or twice every week. They were real interesting too. If she liked any one she would die for them. She never visited among the rough set much while she lived there.

She owned a very fine race horse. She liked to ride. I used to lope across the prairie with her every now and then. She always seemed to enjoy the ride. It was common for her to get on her horse and lope up to our house. She often spent Sundays with us.

[My] brother Emmett, 6 or 7 years younger than me, was badly crippled and had to walk on crutches for several years. She made a great pet of him. After she left there she would send or bring him some nice present every now and then. Once she brought him a real nice album with her and her children's pictures in it.[36]

Weary of roaming the country with her husband and children, Myra must have been optimistic about the move to Coon Creek. It likely seemed that her dream of enjoying a stable family life had at last come true. Sadly, it would not last long.

MYRA AND JIM REED settled into a Bosque County community composed of law-abiding settlers and residents of dubious repute. Jim Reed tended to fall into the latter category.

"There was not another place in the U.S. that had a harder name than Coon Creek did," wrote Will Conine. "At that time a very pretty open prairie country with clean running creeks, good black land, fine grass, green grass in abundance. It used to be a common thing if a man was going across that country for some one to tell him not to drink the water out of Coon Creek if he did he would be sure to steal a horse or cow before he got back. That had been the stamping ground for all kinds of outlaws for years. It was a rendezvous for train and bank robbers, horse and cattle thieves, or any other kind of outlaws from Missouri to Mexico."[37]

Many of the log houses scattered along Coon Creek attracted "very tough people" who tended to stay in one place for a while and then move on. Outlaw refuges were scattered all around the county, including along Childress Creek, Cedron Creek, and Lunsford Branch and at the edge of thick cedar breaks.[38]

"It was not hard for bad men to get protection or good hiding places," Conine wrote. "The outlaws and cattle thieves from all parts of the country seemed to feel at home."[39]

Soon after the Reeds got their bearings, it was time to sow winter wheat. Instead of borrowing oxen to break the prairie soil, Reed used his horses for plowing. It turned out that his plow horses were also very fast; he could put them to good use at the racetrack on North Coon Creek.[40]

"Reed was anything but lazy and liked the farm and stock and so did his wife," recalled Conine. "They seemed to take an interest in all kinds of stock and had good judgment. He bought considerable bunch of cattle." Reed's cattle brand was the design of a curry comb, the grooming brush used to remove shedding hair, scurf, and sweat from a horse's body.[41]

Reed might have found aspects of his domestic life satisfying for a while, but before his first crop of wheat was harvested, he had slipped back to his former ways. His behavioral changes were described in an 1874 story in the *Dallas Daily Commercial*: "For a while his [Reed's] generous manners won the esteem of his neighbors. Soon, however, ugly rumors floated throughout the neighborhood, the stock disappeared in that section, and he drew around him the worst class of men, and his place became a rendezvous for the horse thieves and desperadoes from all sections."[42]

Among the arrivals at the Reed place in the winter of 1873 was Reed's brother, Solomon Lafayette Reed, known as Sol, Solly, Lafe, or Ed.[43] He was twenty-two years old, six years younger than Jim Reed. Sol showed up with Thomas John McKeehan Jr. from Bates County, Missouri, who had served in a Confederate cavalry unit and—like many other diehard rebels—had remained "unreconstructed."[44] In 1868, McKeehan, best known as Jack, had joined the Reed family circle when he married Sarah Reed, one of the Reeds' sisters, in Vernon County, Missouri.[45]

Some of the Fisher gang cronies that Jim had ridden with in Indian Territory and Arkansas also came to Bosque County. One of the most notorious was Missouri native Calvin H. Carter (Cal), whose usual alias was Charles Farmer.[46]

The Reed brothers and their cronies often gathered at Smiths Bend, a small community near where North Coon Creek emptied into the Brazos River.[47] After a day of racing their plow horses at the nearby track, the Reed brothers regularly stopped at a store tucked away in the timber. The owners sold groceries and supplies, but the main draw was the quart house, a distillery retail store where jugs and glasses could be filled directly from whiskey barrels.[48] After a few quaffs of ripe spirits to test the proof, the patrons traded gossip and brags.

Likely it was at the quart house where the Reeds caught wind of an opportunity to acquire a bundle of greenbacks. Their target was Dick Cravey, a forty-three-year-old farmer who maintained a home for his wife and six children at the small community of Cove Spring. Cravey looked to be an easy mark.[49]

On a cold February evening in 1873, Jim and Sol Reed, Jim Porter, and possibly one more rode to Cove Spring. They dismounted, drew their weapons, and approached the Cravey cabin.

"Dick Cravey had carried $4,000 from Meridian to his home in the western part of the county," wrote Will Conine. "It was said that only two men knew that he had that money at his house. One of them was a relative of Jim Porter's."[50]

"They were one day too late to get the money," continued Conine. "Cravey's brother left for eastern Texas that morning with $3,000 of the money. He [Cravey] had $800 in a trunk. Cravey ran out of the house. They followed him and shot him. While they were killing him an old negro woman that was on the place run to the trunk got the money and went to a neighbor house. They must have thought that he [Cravey] carried the money with him when he ran from the house. It was believed that was why they killed him. Some thought that Porter was afraid he had recognized him and that was the reason they killed him. They ransacked the house. I reckon there is no doubt but they were the ones that killed him."[51]

According to Conine, his father and a family friend named Jeff Smith served on the grand jury that considered the case against the Reeds and Porter. "I never heard Father say whether there was an indictment or not," Conine wrote. "All though Father and Jeff Smith both were satisfied that they were the men that killed him [Cravey]. Neither of them seemed to doubt it."[52] Apparently, there was no resolution to the case.

Shortly after the Cravey killing, fifteen or twenty men rode up to the Conine family home. They dismounted, took the saddles off their mounts, and staked and hobbled their horses. The men had been riding hard, and they and their horses were covered in sweat.[53]

"Father said lets go see who they are," Conine recalled. "One or two of them had gone to the house. When we got over there we found a fine solid looking bunch of men. Father was acquainted with nearly all of them. They were Dick Cravey's old friends. They were on the lookout for Jim Porter and the Reeds. They were uncertain about the Reeds, as they did not much believe that they were in the county at that time. But they had been pretty sure of getting Jim Porter. I heard some of them say to Father that if they had got him that they would have swung him up."[54]

Neither the vigilantes nor the sheriff's posses were able to track down the suspected killers of Dick Cravey. Eventually the trail grew cold, and the murder remained unsolved. Crimes ranging from cold-blooded murder to chicken theft often slipped through the multitude of cracks in the state's judicial system.

It was not unusual for justice to be meted out at the end of a mob's rope rather than on a sheriff's gallows. Many criminals were never punished in a court of law. Corruption and incompetence in law enforcement and the judicial system often resulted in acquittals because of some technicality or lack of evidence.

"Murderers were hauled into court but escaped punishment despite the overwhelming weight of evidence against them," wrote history professor John Ross.[55]

Jim and Sol Reed had managed to escape vigilante and civil justice after the Cravey killing. But less than six months later, the brothers killed in cold blood yet again. The victim was Ambrose Wheeler, whose family cut a wide swath in Bosque County. Wheeler ran a cattle ranch and was known for turning out superb racehorse stock. Will Conine had fond memories of Wheeler, despite his reputation for procuring other people's cattle on the range.[56]

"He [Wheeler] always had plenty of free grub for every body that came along hungry," Conine recalled. "When any one overtook him with a lot of their cattle in his herd that he had stole from them he was the most accommodating man you ever saw. He fed you good, cut your cattle out and helped you drive them back and was so nice with you, you couldent [sic] help believing him to be a bully good fellow. You never knew but you were eating your own beef when you were eating with him. But he was so friendly. It tasted good any way."[57]

The Reeds' troubles with Wheeler stemmed from a disagreement over a close finish of a horse race that had pitted Jim Reed against Joe Butler and Jeff Smith, two prominent racehorse owners. By race time, a good deal of money had been put up and many bets made for Tom, one of Myra Reed's horses, and for Fannie Bales, the horse sponsored by Butler and Smith.[58]

The race ended in what was known as a blanket finish, so close that a single blanket could have covered both horses when they crossed the line. Both sides claimed victory and the prize money. Wheeler was one of the judges, and when he decided in favor of Fannie Bales, Reed was furious. His rage was aimed at Wheeler as well as Butler and Smith.[59]

Rumors surfaced that Butler and Smith had intercepted correspondence intended for Reed that contained compromising information about some of Reed's criminal activities. They shared what they learned about Reed with others, including Wheeler. Reed became suspicious and anticipated trouble.

One evening, Jim and Sol Reed were drinking at the quart house when they were told that a party of armed men intended to surround the building and shoot them when they emerged. Before the armed men could get into position, however, the Reed brothers had slipped away. They quickly moved through a thicket into a corn patch close to Wheeler's house and made their escape.[60]

"Reed was finally convinced that Wheeler was working to get him killed," wrote Conine.[61]

Jim and Sol Reed began to trail Wheeler, waiting for an opportunity to strike. They found their best chance on August 17, 1873—a Sabbath afternoon—when Wheeler was returning home from Meridian.[62] He was astride his racehorse named Brown Dick when he spied the Reeds riding toward him. Wheeler broke into a run, and Jim Reed, riding Myra's good four-mile horse, Tom, gave chase.[63]

"Wheeler had been in several bad shooting scrapes and had showed bravery in every one of them, but it seemed that he would rather risk a good run that day, but old Tom was too long winded for him," wrote Conine.[64]

After Reed shot Wheeler out of the saddle, it was reported that for good measure, he cut out the dead man's tongue. The Reeds took Wheeler's saddled horse and rode off to one of many hideouts in north Texas and Indian Territory.[65]

That time, however, murder warrants were issued for the Reed brothers. On September 16, 1873—a month after Wheeler's death—Texas governor Edmund J. Davis declared that the brothers had become "fugitives from justice" and announced a $500 reward for their capture, delivery to Bosque County, and conviction.[66]

The Reed brothers were never apprehended for the Wheeler murder. Sol Reed, however, had had his fill of the outlaw life and soon headed back to Missouri. He continued to be accused of criminal acts. In a letter dated May 24, 1875, Jesse James attempted to implicate Sol Reed and four other men in the December 8, 1874, robbery of a Kansas Pacific Railway train near Muncie, Missouri, a crime that matched elements typical of the James-Younger gang. No evidence was found to support James's alibi claim that Sol Reed had been a participant.[67]

Sol Reed married Jude Dean Davis on April 7, 1874, in Vernon County, Missouri, and was never again charged with or arrested for a crime. He spent the balance of his life as a law-abiding Missourian. On August 26, 1922, he died peacefully in his bed at age seventy.[68]

Unlike his younger brother, however, Jim Reed had no intention of changing his ways. At age twenty-eight, he made no further pretense of trying to live a lawful life. Myra likely had reached the same conclusion about her husband and how his actions had so greatly altered their lives and the lives of her children. However, she appeared to have not yet given up on her marriage. Myra likely still loved her Jimmie and wanted to believe that he still loved his May.

After a hectic fourteen months in Bosque County, the Reeds loaded a wagon with their belongings and went to Scyene. Myra left her children with her mother for safekeeping and accompanied Reed to Tom Starr's home in Indian Territory.[69]

By that time, Starr was in his mid-fifties and well established in the Canadian District of the Cherokee Nation. Many years before, when he had resided in Going Snake District, he had married Katy (Caty) Mouse, and they had two children. Their son, Squirrel Starr, was born in 1836 and daughter, Nancy Starr, in 1838.[70]

Despite Tom Starr's staunch support of the Confederacy when the Civil War erupted, Squirrel Starr—like others in the politically divided

Cherokee Nation—had fought for the Union. He enlisted as a private in the Second Indian Home Guard, a volunteer infantry regiment organized in Kansas in 1862 and commanded by Colonel John Ritchie.[71] Before the war, Ritchie had been involved with the Underground Railroad and had aided abolitionist John Brown and a group of escaped enslaved workers in avoiding capture.[72] Squirrel Starr was assigned to Captain James H. Bruce's Company C, one of two predominantly Cherokee companies. Squirrel was almost thirty years old when he "died in service" in 1863.[73]

Tom and Katy Starr's daughter, Nancy, wed Eli Baldridge in 1858 and later that year gave birth to a daughter named Sallie. Only a few years later, the child was orphaned after the deaths of her parents. Eli passed away in 1861 and Nancy in 1862, from unknown causes. Members of the Baldridge family raised the little girl.[74]

Tom Starr had divorced Katy long before the deaths of his two adult children. In 1840, he married Catherine Reese, born in 1816 to Charles Tasker Reese and Eleanor (Nellie) McCoy Reese in the old Cherokee Nation in Tennessee.[75] Catherine accompanied Starr to the Canadian District where, over the next twenty-three years, they raised eight sons and two daughters and regularly gave shelter to outlaws and misfits such as James Reed.[76]

Reed had frequently found sanctuary at Tom Starr's stout log house in the remote southwestern corner of the Cherokee Nation. The strip of tribal communal land that Starr occupied, about two miles wide and twelve miles long, was on the north bank of the Canadian River where it made a hairpin southerly turn. The area was called Younger's Bend.[77]

It remains unknown who came up with the name Younger's Bend. Some sources claimed that the name likely predated Starr's arrival in the area and referred to someone named Younger but not related to the Missouri outlaws. Most people cling to the erroneous belief that Myra Reed was the source of the name because of the tall tales that she had had a romantic relationship with Cole Younger and that he had even fathered her daughter.[78] Another popular theory maintains that Tom Starr called the area Younger's Bend in tribute to Cole Younger, who reportedly counted on Starr's hospitality when he rode as a Confederate raider and later in the company of the James brothers during their outlaw years.[79] What was never in dispute was that Younger's Bend was tailor-made for anyone who sought rest and recuperation and did not want a public presence.

When the Reeds stayed with the Starr family in 1873, most of Tom and Catherine's ten children had left home. One of the girls, Jane, had died, and five of the older sons and daughters—Lucinda, James Nutch, Ellis Bean, William Truxie, and Charles Reese—had married, built homes in the area, and started families of their own. Only the four youngest children remained in the household—Cherokee, nineteen; Tom Jr., sixteen; Samuel (Sam), thirteen; and Wenona, nine.[80]

The Starr children became self-reliant at an early age. The sons were good riders and hunters, and although lacking much formal education, they developed skills not taught in schools. They could track game, make a fire without matches, and move through brush as silently as a fox. The stars, sun, and moon were their compasses. Tom Starr was a good teacher who drew from his own experiences. It was often said that anyone who spent even a few minutes in his presence never forgot him.

In the early 1870s, Louise Norwood Rider—a young Cherokee girl—met Tom Starr. He had been on the scout and stopped at her aunt's house for something to eat.

"She gave him what she had, including corn bread and meat and he sat down on the porch to eat it and when she asked if he was afraid, he said he would watch out," Rider recalled more than forty years later. "While he was sitting there eating a deer came up the lane from the woods and passed the house and he [Starr] got up and said he must be going and soon some men came from the same way looking for him. When he came to the woods, he would enter if the birds were singing but if they were not he would not enter as they would stop their singing just as frogs stopped croaking at the approach of strangers."[81]

While staying at Younger's Bend, Jim Reed met other outlaws when they paused to rest their horses, have a hot meal, and listen to Tom Starr's endless stream of stories.

Myra also listened and was mesmerized.

CHAPTER 13

Sheer Greed

BY THE TIME TOM STARR HAD REACHED HIS SIXTIES, HE had become a living legend in Indian Territory, especially in the minds of his fellow citizens of the Cherokee Nation.

"He seemed another world apart," a Philadelphia newspaper reporter wrote of Starr when he encountered him in Tahlequah, Indian Territory. "He was a very conspicuous figure as he passed along the street . . . no one giving him a nod of recognition, but everyone turning to look back at him after he had passed, and to whisper to his neighbor, 'That's old Tom Starr.'"[1]

Some Cherokees had become convinced that Starr possessed mystic powers. Many of them had heard tales of the ferocious and cunning Starr and feared him. His friends and neighbors, however, found Starr a misunderstood victim unfairly branded as an outlaw by tribal enemies and imaginative journalists. That was why he slept with a brace of firearms at his side and his dependable hounds always on alert.[2]

"It has been written by misinformed writers that Tom Starr . . . was a common outlaw and guilty of many crimes, which is untrue," John Henry West, one of Starr's neighbors on the Canadian River, said during a 1937 interview that obviously overlooked Starr's violent past. "Tom Starr was not guilty of anything except what he was driven to in defense of his people or himself. I never knew a better man nor had a better neighbor."[3]

Two years after Starr's death at seventy-seven in 1890, brothers H. F. and E. S. O'Beirne described the duality of Starr's public percep-

Tom Starr was a legendary Cherokee outlaw and the father of Sam Starr.

tion in a book chronicling the history of Indian Territory tribes.[4] The O'Beirnes wrote another overtly favorable description of Starr, ignoring his violent past:

> Starr . . . had too many friends willing to sacrifice much for his sake. . . . It is true that he was often associated with lawless men, who, like himself, were fugitives from justice. . . . He used them when it suited his purpose, and they never failed to assemble at his call. His favorite signal was the scream of the night owl, which he imitated to perfection.[5]

On an autumn night in 1873, three visitors to Younger's Bend—Jim Reed, William D. Wilder, and Marion Dickens (also known by various aliases, including Myron Dixon and Burns)—likely heard that banshee cry of an owl and immediately went to Tom Starr's cabin. There, they hatched an ambitious criminal scheme. It promised great reward but also plenty of risk. Starr verified a persistent rumor that had been circulating throughout Indian Territory. According to him, Walter "Watt"

Grayson, a wealthy Creek rancher, had hidden more than $30,000 in cash and gold in the nearby Choctaw Nation. For enterprising thieves such as Reed and his friends, Grayson's fortune promised to be theirs for the taking.[6]

Although Starr was the architect of the crime devised that night, Reed, Wilder, and Dickens were recruited to carry it out. In return for his tip about Grayson, the three likely promised Starr a taste of the proceeds from the robbery.[7] "Tom Starr planned it [the Grayson robbery] but the others got the money," William H. Balentine, Starr's neighbor, told historian Carolyn Thomas Foreman in a 1933 interview.[8]

Grayson's home was only a few miles south of North Fork Town, a Creek Nation settlement founded in the mid-1830s at the junction of the North and South Canadian rivers, just west of the merge with the Arkansas River.[9] North Fork Town prospered as a trade center for travelers, seekers of California gold, and citizens from the nearby Cherokee and Choctaw nations.[10] However, in 1872, the Kansas and Texas Railway bypassed North Fork Town, sending the community into a rapid decline. Within only a year, most of the population and merchants had left in favor of the nearby emerging railhead town of Eufaula, named after an earlier Creek settlement in Alabama.[11]

Watt Grayson had lived in Indian Territory since the 1830s, when the Creeks were forcibly moved there after having ceded their ancestral lands in Alabama and Georgia to the United States government. The Graysons were a prominent mixed-blood family in the Creek Nation long before they moved west.[12] They traced their ancestry through male Scottish ancestors rather than along matrilineal Creek clan lines.

Watt Grayson's Scottish father, Robert Grierson, was born in 1748 into a family of considerable wealth and influence closely associated with the nobles of Scotland. Grierson and several of his siblings moved to the American colonies in the 1760s.[13] After he was licensed as a trader in Georgia, Grierson set off for what became Alabama, where he formed successful relationships with Muscogee Creeks and Cherokees, trading guns, blankets, and pots for deerskins.[14]

By 1775, Grierson had acquired an established trading post in east-central Alabama, a Creek settlement called Hillabee.[15] That year, Grierson made a strategic business move when he married a seventeen-year-old Creek girl named Sinnugee. The couple raised eight children. The youngest was Walter B. Grierson, best known as Watt, born in 1791.[16]

Although Grierson was his surname at birth, the word was difficult for Creeks and their enslaved workers to pronounce. By the time of the family's removal to Indian Territory, the name had morphed into Grayson.[17] However, another view is that the name change "had been an intentional move to distance themselves from the multi-racial problems that were beginning to emerge," according to Creek historian Don C. East. Some people believed Robert Grierson had many children with women other than his wife.[18] Slave ownership and intermarriage were not uncommon among the Creeks and the other southeastern tribes in Indian Territory. As a result, intimate relations often occurred between the Grayson family and their enslaved workers. Some of Watt Grayson's siblings wed Black, Indian, and mixed-race spouses, "ultimately producing tri-racial offspring by the next generation."[19]

Several Grayson family members owned enslaved people related to them by blood, including first cousins. Watt Grayson's nephew, George Washington "Wash" Grayson—a future Creek Nation chief who was characterized as being "the most prominent and intelligent of all Creek Indians of his time"—advocated the denial of equal citizenship to Creeks with African ancestry.[20]

"In the case of the Graysons, over the course of the nineteenth century, race drove a wedge between family members, separating those with African ancestry from those without, and driving the two sides apart until they denied their common origins," wrote historian Claudio Saunt.[21]

Watt Grayson had been buying and selling enslaved workers as early as 1827, when he sold an entire family of nine people to one of his brothers for $1,500.[22] In 1854, one of Grayson's enslaved workers, known only as Jim, was accused of murdering two Creek men. He was deemed guilty and sentenced to death. He was seated unbound on a log, and his head was covered with a blanket. Two members of Jim's family fired rifle balls into his body and helped carry him to his grave.[23]

By the outbreak of the Civil War in 1861, Watt Grayson was one of the largest owners of enslaved people in the Creek Nation.[24] At war's end, the federal government negotiated treaties with all the southern tribes that had been moved to Indian Territory. In 1866, the Creeks, some of whom had allied with the Confederacy, were required to emancipate their enslaved workers and offer them tribal citizenship.[25] Despite having lost his enslaved workforce, Grayson convinced many of the freedmen, including some with familial ties to the Graysons, to remain in his employ at his ranch.

Jim Reed and his accomplices might not have been aware of the presence of able-bodied men at the Grayson place. Apart from Grayson's great wealth and the close proximity of his ranch to Younger's Bend, they likely knew little about the man they intended to rob. Reed had been on the scout since earlier in the year, after the murders of Dick Carvey and Ambrose Wheeler in Bosque County, Texas. Reed's impulsive decision to commit a crime against a high-profile Creek Nation citizen only a few months later fit his chronic pattern of risky behavior.

On November 16, 1873, Reed revealed the Watt Grayson robbery plan to Myra. There is no record of her reaction to the news at the time. However, she eventually provided significant details of the crime in sworn testimony during a deposition before Ben Long, United States commissioner for the Northern District of Texas, on December 16, 1875.[26]

In what was later described as a well-coached statement, Myra testified that " . . . while we were stopping on the Canadian River in the Indian Territory he [Reed] told me that Watt Grayson a Creek Indian living on or near the Canadian River had over thirty thousand ($30,000.00) in gold, and that he meant to have it." She further testified that Reed had been "in company with W.D. Wilder and Marion Dickens, alias Burns."[27]

According to Myra, William Wilder saddled his horse the morning of the crime and left Tom Starr's home near Younger's Bend.[28] Wilder rode directly to Grayson's ranch south of the Canadian River. He told Grayson that he had been looking for cow ponies to buy and asked if he could board with the family for a few days while he inspected their string of ponies. Grayson agreed to that.[29]

About an hour after sunset on November 19, 1873, Jim Reed and Marion Dickens rode up to the Grayson house, where they were welcomed and were invited to enter.[30] They told Grayson they were looking for a friend [Wilder] and thought he might be staying at the ranch. When they were told that he was in an adjacent room, Reed fetched Wilder, and they returned with guns drawn.[31]

"The three men then assembled Grayson's family and a few hired hands into the one room," wrote historian Kenneth Hobbs. "At this point Reed announced that he was not after men but money. He forced Grayson's wife, Susan, to give up her keys. Wilder seized Grayson's shotgun and held it on the victims while Reed opened a trunk." Inside, Reed found more than $2,000 in gold and silver coin and currency.[32]

While Dixon guarded the captives, Reed and Wilder took Grayson outside. They ordered him to surrender the rest of his stash, but he told them that what they had found in the trunk was all of his money, and there was no more. Not convinced, Reed and Wilder marched Grayson to the nearby stable and bound his hands behind his back. Wilder retrieved a lariat from his horse and threw it over a tree limb. Then tied a loop and put it around Grayson's neck.[33]

"Reed said, 'Now old man, I hate to hang you, but if you don't tell me where the money is I am going to kill you,'" according to Hobbs. "Again, Grayson replied that he had no money. The outlaws then pulled on the rope and hung him from the tree. Grayson lost consciousness and when he regained his senses he was lying down. The two men shook him and he got to his feet. Again they asked for money and again he replied there was none. The outlaws then drew Grayson up again by his neck."[34]

Grayson later recalled that after the second hanging, he heard Reed and Wilder talking about him. They thought he was dying and would never tell them where the money was cached.[35]

"They attempted to raise him up, but he could not sit up so they laid him down again," wrote Hobbs. "Then, Grayson heard them say they would hang his wife. At that point he said, 'Wait till I come to myself, and I will tell you where it is.'" Reed and Wilder helped the old man stand

and untied him. Grayson then directed them to where his gold was buried under the house. Reed removed two kettles containing $30,000.[36]

The outlaws divided the gold from one of the kettles into two canvas bags. The rest of the loot was stuffed into saddlebags, pockets, and even inside their boots. They considered using one of Grayson's mules to haul the gold, but the critter proved too wild and unbroken.[37] The three men mounted their heavily laden horses and left.

Grayson, still groggy from the torture he had endured, was unable to pursue the thieves. Some of his hired men and neighbors tracked the outlaws for about twenty miles after crossing the Canadian River into the Creek Nation near North Fork Town but lost them on the road to Fort Gibson.[38]

The morning after the robbery, Grayson posted two letters at North Fork Town. One letter went to his son, Edmond Grayson. Watt Grayson wrote, "On last night I was robbed of every dollar I had in the world by three white men. You will please get a Marshal and come forthwith to my aid in searching for them. I will give an ample reward for them of twenty-five hundred dollars."[39]

Grayson had overstated his financial losses. He claimed that the theft of $32,000 had left him penniless, yet he offered no explanation about the source of the reward money.[40]

Grayson's second letter was sent to longtime friend William H. Rogers, owner of a general store in North Fork Town who had borrowed money from Grayson. Once again, Grayson mentioned the "loss of every dollar I had in the world"[41] and asked Rogers to "notify all U.S. Marshals to be on the lookout for three men." As he had done in his letter to his son, Grayson gave a description of the outlaws: "One riding a bay mare with white spots on her sides and perhaps a star in the forehead. The man light complexion with sandy hair and whiskers. Another with brown eyes, brown hair and whiskers, with a Roman nose. Wearing gray clothes rather worn. Age about 30 or 33. The third light hair and little whiskers same color. Low and tolerably heavy set."[42]

Within a few days, accounts of the Grayson raid appeared in several

Arkansas and Indian Territory newspapers. Most of the reports exaggerated Grayson's torture and editorialized for an increase of law enforcement in the territory. Several stories also erroneously reported that the robbers had made off with less than $4,000 instead of $32,000.[43]

By far the most outrageous of all the falsehoods and legends that emerged from the Grayson robbery were the many claims that Myra Reed not only took an active role in the crime but also did so disguised as a man.[44] This flagrant fabrication later appeared in other articles and books, including some biographies. Watt Grayson and his family members and hired hands present during the robbery never mentioned a fourth outlaw in the gang or a woman dressed as a man. Likewise, the men who had ridden in pursuit of Reed, Wilder, and Dickens never spoke of a fourth outlaw during subsequent legal proceedings.

While the Grayson robbery was taking place, Myra Reed was at the Starr home, worried about the fate of her husband. That was revealed in her 1875 deposition before US Commissioner Ben Long in Dallas.[45] She testified:

"On or about the 20th day of November A.D. 1873 in the morning they returned all together, the above mentioned Reed, Wilder, and Dickons [sic] alias Burns and came near where I was stopping and stopped in the woods and sent for me. I went to them and they told me that they had accomplished their object and had the money to show for it, and they sat down upon the ground and began counting it. I saw they had a large amount of gold, they counted it and divided it in my presence, and to my best recollection they had about ten thousand ($10,000.00) in gold apiece, making $30,000 in gold. They also had some currency—all of which they said they took from Watt Grayson the night before."[46]

Myra's testimony made no mention of why the money was not divided at Tom Starr's house and why she had been summoned to join the men in the woods. It remains unclear whether Reed, Wilder, and Dickens returned to Starr's house after they divided the money or left Indian Territory without giving Starr a share of the loot. Whether or not they adhered to the old adage about no honor among thieves, they followed their best course of action and rode due south through Indian Territory to Texas, taking Myra with them.

It turned out to be the last long ride May and Jimmy would take together.

CHAPTER 14

* * * * * * * * * * * *

Jim Reed's Last Hurrah

DURING SEVEN CHAOTIC YEARS OF MARRIAGE, THE BOND between Myra and Jim Reed had steadily deteriorated. Myra had known of her husband's outlaw deeds from the start, yet she held out hope that he would eventually come to his senses. That never happened. By late 1873, her last bit of hope had died.[1]

After the Watt Grayson robbery in Indian Territory, the Reeds crossed the Red River into Texas together but then went their separate ways. Myra, anxious to be with her children, rode directly to her parents' home in Scyene.

Earlier in 1873, the Shirleys' former enslaved worker Annie Shirley had given birth to two more babies—Sterling Price Shirley and Robert E. Lee Shirley—twin boys named for Confederate heroes and probably fathered by John Shirley.[2] Although their date of birth is unknown, Dallas County, Texas, death records show that Sterling Price Shirley died in Dallas on January 28, 1927, and Robert E. Lee Shirley on June 8, 1935.[3]

It remains unclear how Eliza Shirley and her children reacted to John Shirley's long and open relationship with a former enslaved woman. However, Aunt Annie and her seven children lived and worked in the Shirley household until 1880, when she moved her family to establish residency in Dallas.[4] It is not known whether Myra tolerated her father's adultery, but she brooded about Jim Reed's chosen way of life.

Reed stayed clear of Myra and remained on the scout. He and his outlaw accomplices headed to familiar haunts and hideaways in Bosque County. On December 18, 1873, Reed sold his 160 acres on Coon Creek to his accomplice, William Wilder, for $750, the same price that he and Myra had paid for it in 1872. Wilder moved in with the family who had rented the place from Reed, but Wilder lived there off and on for only two months before he sold the property.[5]

Sometime in early 1874, Reed returned to the Scyene area to be closer to his estranged wife and children. The couple remained married while living apart. Despite outstanding warrants for his arrest for murder and robbery in Texas and Indian Territory, Reed had no intention of changing. He was caught in a downward spiral. "[N]o influence seemed sufficient to check his viciousness," claimed a Dallas newspaper in 1874—not even his "highly educated and accomplished" wife.[6]

One transgression, however, Myra apparently could not abide—the betrayal of marriage vows. During the winter of 1873–1874, her disappointment in Reed turned to rage when she found out about his brazen liaison with nineteen-year-old Rosanna (Rosa) McCommas. Reed had met and subsequently seduced the girl, who was from a prominent Dallas County family in Scyene, where she had been living with relatives.[7] Once rumors of the affair made the rounds, Scyene and nearby Dallas were filled with gossip.

Named for a deceased aunt (Rosanna McCommas Cox), the younger Rosanna was the granddaughter of Amon McCommas.[8] The family patriarch, McCommas was an ordained minister, prosperous farmer, and civic leader who had settled on the northern frontier of the Republic of Texas in 1844. The next year, he founded the first Christian Church in Dallas County, where he delivered fiery sermons and baptized multitudes of the faithful in the nearby Trinity River.[9] His family and associates referred to McCommas as "Elder" Amon, to distinguish him from his son Amon Jr., Scyene postmaster and owner of a mercantile business, who was Rosanna's uncle.[10]

Although separated from Myra but still wed to her, Reed had proposed marriage to the love-struck Rosanna before absconding with her to San Antonio in early February 1874. Myra never saw Reed after that.[11]

Rosanna's sudden disappearance became a topic of discussion in Scyene. Citizens gathered at the local schoolhouse on February 7 "for the purpose of devising ways and means for the better security of life and property."[12] They drafted resolutions aimed at curbing the lawlessness that had become "so prevalent in our midst.... [O]ur present laws seem to have no terror to evildoers, rendering our lives and property insecure."[13]

In a petition to the legislature, the Scyene citizens—although "not wishing to resort to lynch law and vigilante committees"—called for changes in the Texas criminal code. One proposal included making horse theft a capital offense punishable by death. Another requested implementation of "the whipping post, the branding iron or some other such punishment as the Legislature in their wisdom may devise, thereby making the law a terror to wrong-doers."[14]

After the citizens' meeting in Scyene, the *Dallas Daily Commercial* urged the police force to hire more officers. The editorial criticized the practice of paying officers a bounty for each arrest in addition to their salaries, which encouraged trivial arrests instead of focusing on more serious crimes.[15]

February 1874 proved to be a significant month for Reed. On February 12, he and his brother Sol—long gone to Missouri—were finally indicted for the 1873 murder of Ambrose Wheeler in Bosque County, Texas.[16] Only two days later, Jim Reed was named as one of the three outlaws responsible for the November 19, 1873, robbery of Watt Grayson in Indian Territory.

Based on an eyewitness's physical description of the robbers, Deputy Marshal L. E. Bracken swore in a writ issued in Fort Smith, Arkansas, that Reed had been one of the perpetrators of the crime.[17] Bracken erroneously identified Reed as Robert Reed. He also claimed that Reed's partners had been John Boswell, also known as William Boswell or Charles Bush. Instead of William Wilder, the lawman mistakenly swore that Cal Carter, Reed's old pal from the J. K. Fisher gang, had been the third accomplice.

Meanwhile, Reed and his young lover had safely established themselves in San Antonio. They rendezvoused with William Boswell, Cal Carter, Marion Dickens, and Dickens's wife.[18] The six of them "rented a house, and all lived together, having and paying for everything in common, and living happy as one household."[19]

By 1874, San Antonio was no longer a sleepy army garrison but had evolved into a bustling trade center and the largest city in Texas, with a population of more than fifteen thousand.[20] Jim Reed, Rosanna McCommas, and the rest of the entourage had found "the Paris of the wilderness.... Its bright lights were a beacon that shone across the chaparral. It was brightest after dark."[21]

Gas lamps glowed in the crowded plazas, and streets were filled with drovers gathering herds of longhorns before long treks up the trails through Indian Territory to northern railroad towns. There were cockfights to wager on and icy kegs of Saint Louis–brewed beer to swig. Spanish and German conversations echoed along with cowboy yells in the scores of beer gardens, gambling lairs, saloons, bordellos, and billiard parlors. Town boys trapped wild pigeons and hunted rats bold enough to fight dogs and kill cats. The night air was scented by a mix of horse manure, roasted kid goat, and the pungent aroma of chili con carne, ladled into bowls by the city's famous "chili queens" who tended concoctions of fiery peppers and chunks of meat that cooked for hours in iron kettles over mesquite fires.[22]

For safety's sake, the Reed party maintained a low profile. The two women mostly stayed at the house unless foraging for food and supplies. "The men frequented a 'loafing place' known as Price's Saloon while they spent their time watching the banks and waiting for an opening from February until the first of April, passing under the assumed names, respectively, of William James (Jim Reed), Charles Farmer (Cal Carter) and J. C. Nelson (William Boswell), Dickens alone passing under his own name," according to an August 10, 1874, newspaper account.[23] After a few months, however, any plan for a bank robbery had been shelved in favor of a different opportunity.

On April 1, 1874, Dickens and his wife slipped out of the rental house. They rode to San Marcos, about halfway between San Antonio and Austin, and camped on the banks of the San Marcos River. The next day, Reed, Carter, and Boswell joined them.[24]

"Here, Reed, who seems to be an enterprising cuss, traded horses with a citizen by the name of Woolfork, he agreeing to pay Reed twenty-five dollars to boot in cash for [to give] his wife [Rosanna McCommas]. On Monday [April 6], the women and Dickens moved to the Woolfork's [sic], and in the evening the other men left town," according to the *Austin American-Statesman* of April 17, 1874.[25]

Because of the newspaper's assumption that the woman accompanying Reed was his wife, rumors spread that Myra had been with Reed on his latest escapade and had used the innocent Rosanna McCommas's name as an alias. Some journalists and authors bought into the tale. "Undoubtedly it was spite, or envy, coupled with the diabolic sense of humor she [Myra] often displayed," wrote Harry Sinclair Drago, a pulp writer who perpetuated the myth.[26]

Myra Reed was nowhere near San Marcos in April 1874. She was at home with her children in Scyene, unaware of Jim Reed's whereabouts. Only a few days later, however, Myra would learn what her wayward husband had been up to since leaving Dallas County.[27]

At dusk on April 7, Reed, Carter, and Boswell robbed an S. T. Scott Company stagecoach loaded with passengers and carrying several bags of United States mail. The stage had departed from San Antonio early that morning for Austin, about an eighteen-hour journey.[28]

After leaving San Marcos, the stage had crossed the Blanco River when the three mounted bandits appeared, brandishing six-shooters. They told the driver, Bill Anderson, that they were looking for a man who had killed their brother and wanted to see if he was aboard the stage. Anderson obeyed the outlaws' orders and drove the stage to a secluded area.[29] The details of what occurred next were chronicled in the *Austin Democratic Statesman*.[30]

> The stage had on board nine passengers, viz: Mssrs. McLemore, O'Neal, Waters, Brackenridge, Frazier, McDonald, Wells, Munroe and one lady Mrs. Lloyd. . . . Two of the robbers stood before them, each waving a six-shooter in each hand cocked, and ordered them to give up their money, watches, and other valuables.
>
> After having collected all they could from the persons of the passengers, they proceeded to cut open and rifle through trunks,

taking such articles of value as they could get away with speedily; and lastly came the United States mails; after cutting open the sacks and rifling them of their contents, they left them lying scattered around, with the exception of one, which they took away with them. After this they proceeded to cut the horses loose from the stage, and rode off.[31]

The outlaws took about $2,500 in currency and an assortment of personal items, including four gold watches.[32] Newspapers praised Mrs. Lloyd, the sole female passenger, for her grit and how she had outsmarted the outlaws.

"The lady acted with great courage, though several times asked by the robbers which man she was traveling with, or by herself," reported the Waco *Daily Examiner*. "When told she was travelling alone, they demanded her money. At the same time, one of them was rifling her trunk. Mrs. Lloyd very firmly told them if they would not molest her trunk further she would give them her money. They agreeing, she handed one of them her purse, which contained fifty-five dollars. She had in her trunk eighty dollars."[33]

A pursuing posse found letters from the only canvas mailbag the outlaws had taken with them. One letter contained a check for $121.46 drawn on a Galveston bank. It was payable to A. S. Mair, a commission and exchange merchant and real estate developer in Austin.[34] A taunting message from the robbers had been scrawled on the envelope, likely by ringleader Jim Reed.

"'A. S. Mair—We are too long on the rode [sic] to be caught with chaff as this. This orders doo us no good.'" It was signed CUIDADO, a Spanish word from the old outlaw expression "on the cuidado," meaning "running from the law" or "watch your step." A postscript read, "As we don't want to be mean about it. I leave 'em where some dam fool can find 'em."[35]

News of the stage robbery spread across the nation. Even the staid *New York Times* found the crime newsworthy, publishing an all-editions front-page story on April 9 beneath the headline, "A Highway Robbery in Texas—Passengers of a Stage-Coach Robbed."[36]

After the robbery, Richard Coke—the recently elected Democratic Texas governor—sprang into action. On April 8, the legislature was called into session and quickly passed a bill that gave Coke the authority to offer rewards of $1,000 for each of the three robbers. In addition, the United States Post Office Department pledged $3,000, and the stage line offered $1,000.[37]

The promise of $7,000 in rewards for the capture and conviction of the three outlaws inspired the recruitment of large posses and bounty hunters, whose work was dangerous and usually not financially rewarding.[38] Professional law officers usually collected rewards as a way to supplement their incomes. Thomas Purnell—the first United States marshal of the Western District of Texas since the close of the Civil War—headed the investigation and took charge of the manhunt.[39]

The sprawling Western District, formed in 1857, stretched westward across the state to Mexico.[40] Frontier marshals served as the primary source of law enforcement, especially in areas that had no local government. Purnell served the federal court by rounding up wanted killers, escaped convicts, and mail thieves.[41]

After the stagecoach robbery, Purnell and his deputies scoured the countryside in pursuit of the outlaws. On April 17, Purnell identified the robbers in a statement released to local newspapers: "It is now definitely settled that the robbery was perpetuated [perpetrated] by three men from Missouri."[42]

Purnell was only partly correct. He named James Reed and a man called Nelson, who later turned out to be William Boswell. But just as law officers had done in the Watt Grayson robbery in late 1873, the third outlaw was initially misidentified as Cal Carter instead of William Wilder. Purnell had unknowingly given Wilder a pass by naming Carter. The statement went on to discuss J. M. Dickens and his wife and details of Reed's seduction of Rosanna McCommas.[43]

"Dickens, his wife, and the girl McComus [sic], are still in San Marcos," Purnell explained. "Dickens having rented a farm and gone to work; but a strict surveillance is kept over them, and they will be brought to this city [Austin] to-day.... Reed has a friend in the Territory [Tom Starr], to whose house he goes whenever he gets into trouble, and it may be that he is making for that place now, but he is said to be very fond of the girl [Rosanna] whom he seduced, and it may be the loadstone [sic] that will draw him back to Texas."[44]

After Marion Dickens and Rosanna McCommas had been taken into custody and interrogated at San Marcos, Marshal Purnell and his deputies took them to Austin. No further records have been found concerning the whereabouts of Dickens's wife. Reed remained out of sight. On April 20, Dickens and McCommas appeared before the United States commissioner in Austin. They were bound over to appear at a later date in the United States District Court. Bond was set at $2,000 for Dickens and $1,000 for McCommas. Bonds were posted, and both were released from jail while they awaited trial as accomplices in the stagecoach robbery.[45]

Some people refused to believe that Rosanna McCommas—not Myra—had been Reed's companion during that time. In later years, various authors propagated the fiction that Purnell had been hoodwinked and had displayed "remarkable ignorance."[46] They maintained that she and Rosanna had been schoolmates and that Myra had used the girl's name as an alias.[47]

Some contemporary newspapers, however, reported that Rosanna McCommas had been Reed's companion. "The assumption that Belle [Myra] Reed was able to successfully convince law enforcement officers and court officials that she was another person is not very plausible in view of later events which reflect the competency and completeness of the robbery investigation," wrote historian Kenneth Hobbs. "Belle [Myra] Reed was also twenty-six years old and the mother of two children when the robbery was committed, yet the newspapers emphasize the youthfulness of Rosa McCommas by describing her as a young girl."[48]

No official court records survived concerning the criminal cases against the McCommas girl and Dickens. Some historians concluded that the charges were eventually dropped when no evidence was found that they had been involved in the stage robbery.[49]

Rosanna McCommas had managed to escape prosecution, but she had no intention of leaving the man who was responsible for her predicament.

Likely she found it difficult to be separated from Jim Reed and shake memories of their high times together and his promise to make her his wife.

Despite having been hunted by Purnell and his deputies, the impulsive Reed purportedly had every intention of reuniting with his lover. Driven by reckless passion, Reed had never been capable of ignoring risks even if the odds were against him.

⁓

BY LATE APRIL 1874, Thomas Purnell—leader of what one Texas newspaper called a "strong posse"—had stepped up his dogged pursuit of Reed and the stagecoach robbers.[50] However, in the lawmen's haste to solve the crime, they made mistakes in the investigation.

On April 24, Dallas City Marshal Junius "June" Peak spied a man imbibing spirits in a hotel saloon who resembled a photograph of one of the alleged stagecoach robbers. Peak approached the man, who gave his name as Wilder. Despite the man's cooperation, Peak took him into custody and marched him to the city jail, where he was searched and questioned further.[51] When law officers searched Wilder, they discovered papers that identified him as Jim Reed.

Later that evening, Peak apprehended another suspect who also resembled one of the photos of the stage bandits. That man identified himself as Bidwell, but after an hour of interrogation, Peak released him because of insufficient evidence.[52] Bidwell promptly reclaimed his horse and headed for Scyene. A short time later, Peak apparently changed his mind and dispatched two officers to go after Bidwell. The officers found him sleeping in a grove just outside Scyene and hauled him back to Dallas.[53]

After further interrogation of the second suspect, the Dallas law officers were convinced that they had the right men in custody. They wired Purnell in Austin.[54]

"The United States Marshal will be down shortly, and will be pretty apt to be heard from," the *Dallas Daily Commercial* noted on April 27 in a story headlined "Got One of Them!"[55]

On April 28, after Purnell had thoroughly interrogated the two suspects, his opinion was "that the fabric of the evidence was not strong enough to justify the further retention and incarceration of the prisoners."⁵⁶ A newspaper reported that Bidwell's "general appearance and voice [indicated] that he felt freedom to the bone."⁵⁷ His freedom was short-lived, however. Bidwell was arrested for horse theft on May 2 but escaped jail with five other inmates on July 18, 1874. He subsequently disappeared, and his true identity was never established.⁵⁸

When William Wilder was released, neither Purnell nor Sheriff James Barkley realized that once again, one of the robbers of Watt Grayson had been turned loose after having been in custody. Wilder likely breathed a sigh of relief that his complicity had not been discovered. He was also agreeable when Purnell requested to accompany him to Scyene to gather information about Reed's whereabouts.⁵⁹

In Scyene, Purnell sought out one of Reed's sisters-in-law in hopes that "some light may be obtained as to the whereabouts of the bandit chief."⁶⁰ It is unknown whether Purnell visited the Shirley family residence or attempted to confer with Myra Reed.

Still, the Scyene visit proved helpful. While Purnell sniffed around town for any promising leads, he spent time with the McCommas family. Purnell discovered that Rosanna McCommas had not yet returned to Scyene but was staying at the home of John T. Morris in Collin County, Texas.⁶¹

Morris, born in 1824 in New York, eventually migrated to Texas. He settled in Collin County and married Eliza Jane Fisher.⁶² Like other pro-slavery families, the Fishers had moved to Texas from Missouri.⁶³

In the early 1870s, Morris, his wife, and their daughter, Nora, had taken up residence on farm acreage about five miles south of McKinney, the county seat.⁶⁴ Purnell's interest in the Morris family likely increased when he learned that not only was Rosanna McCommas a guest of the Morris family, but Eliza Morris was also reportedly Jim Reed's cousin.⁶⁵

Purnell returned to Austin and dispatched three of his best deputies to Collin County to be on the lookout for Reed and to keep tabs on the Morris farmhouse.⁶⁶ Reed was familiar with Collin County. His mother and other family members had lived there during the Civil War before they returned to Missouri. Reed had married Myra Shirley in that county in 1866.

Since Reed had kinfolk in Collin County and Rosanna was with them, her presence might entice him to drop his guard and come calling. Purnell's hunch almost paid off after his deputies received a credible tip that "Reed and a companion"—likely Cal Carter—planned to spend Saturday night, May 23, at the Morris residence.[67]

On that date, after dark, a well-armed party of about twenty-five men—including the three deputy marshals and Collin County law officers led by Sheriff William W. Merritt—quietly surrounded the Morris house. The plan had been to spend the night in their positions and, by show of force, confront and capture the two outlaws when they emerged in the morning.[68]

That plan was scuttled. The deputy marshals became impatient and decided to use the cover of darkness to storm the house and arrest the outlaws. A Collin County sheriff's deputy urged the federal officers to at least alert Sheriff Merritt and the others of the change in plans, but they determined that such a warning was not necessary.[69] The three deputy marshals and a few others moved out of the brush and crept toward the Morris house. The *Dallas Weekly Herald* reported what transpired:

> They were halted by some of the other parties and gave the countersign, but unfortunately it was not understood by the parties hailing, and they fired a volley into the party, severely wounding one and slightly wounding another of the detectives [federal deputies]. Subsequently, it was ascertained that the robbers [Reed and his unnamed comrade] that the party was in search of were not in the house, but were camped a short distance off, and, on hearing the firing, took to their heels.[70]

In the mêlée, US Deputy Marshal Sam Martin had received a wound in his leg but was up on crutches after a few days.[71] US Deputy Marshal William Heresberg, however, had been struck by a shotgun blast. He was taken to the Saint Charles Hotel in Sherman, Texas, where he died.[72]

Less than two weeks after the botched ambush, the true identities of the stagecoach bandits were revealed publicly. On June 5, 1874, the federal grand jury in Austin returned true bills of indictments for mail robbery against "Jim Reid [sic] otherwise called William Jones and Robert Miller, one Cal Carter, and one William Boswell, otherwise called William Rogers and William Nelson."[73]

After escaping into the night when the posse's gunfire broke out at the John Morris place, Reed and likely Cal Carter had fled north to Indian Territory.[74] Reed pulled together a half dozen willing recruits familiar with committing acts of larceny and violence.

By mid-July, Reed and his band appeared in Going Snake District of the Cherokee Nation. Reed soon found a likely mark—William Harnage, a wealthy Cherokee citizen rumored to have substantial money and valuables secreted in his residence. Reed decided on the same tactics that had been used in the robbery of Watt Grayson.[75] On July 13, 1874, Harnage was away from his home when the crime commenced. A few days later, the *Cherokee Advocate* told the story.

> Harnage of Going Snake District was robbed of about $1,600. . . . It appears that two men came to the house about night fall and asked to stay all night. They were permitted to stop, and a while after supper the tramp of horses feet was heard. . . . Several strange men made their appearance, seized a hired man, conducted him into the house with a pistol [and] bade [him] not to open his mouth under penalty of death. They then proceeded, eight in number, to burst open the trunks and chests, to drag the bedding upon the floor and to search the premises generally. They succeeded in getting all the money about the place. . . . Every effort will, and should be made to discover and bring the scoundrels to justice.[76]

More details of the crime appeared in a July 16 letter that John B. Jones, the United States Indian agent at Tahlequah, sent to the United States deputy marshal at Fort Gibson, Cherokee Nation.[77] Jones wrote that the robbers had taken "about $1,600 or 1,700 dollars in gold and $25 or 30 in Greenbacks, an Enfield Rifle gun, a fine double shawl for ladies, a hat & a ladies Shatchel [sic] & a very peculiar powder horn." According to Jones, the thieves also took saddlebags, a revolver, and clothing from Harnage's hired man, Thomas Madras.[78]

Based on eyewitness descriptions, Jones identified the ringleaders of the Harnage robbery as "Cal Carter, Bill Fisher, Reed & one other of that gang. . . . It is thought that they take refuge at Tom Starr's [home]."[79]

A posse of United States deputy sheriffs and Cherokee Nation police descended on Starr's sanctuary on the Canadian River, but Reed had slipped away.[80] He beat a path back to Texas, where he remained near the top of the most-wanted list in the state.

Reed rode to Lamar County on the Red River in northeastern Texas instead of returning to Collin County to see Rosanna McCommas at the Morris residence. He bunked at the home of Henry Russell, an old acquaintance who lived about twenty miles northwest of Paris, the county seat.[81] Reed had spent little time in the area and had few worries of being recognized, although a photograph of him and Rosanna McCommas made during their time in San Antonio had been circulated in newspapers across the state.[82]

Authors and historians have continued to misidentify the young woman in the photograph as Myra. In truth, in early 1874, Reed and Rosanna McCommas posed for the portrait at the downtown San Antonio studio of Henry A. Doerr, the most prolific photographer of nineteenth-century San Antonio.[83]

"Reed frequently walked in open day through the streets of Paris and rode about the neighborhood without disguise," according to the *Denison Daily News*.[84]

It seemed he had found a safe haven with his friend Russell in Lamar County. His continued success at dodging the law in Indian Territory and Texas likely had boosted his confidence. Still, he longed to be with Rosanna and wrote letters to her in care of William and Eliza Morris in Collin County. Reed's letter writing did not stop there.

On August 2, 1874, the *Dallas Daily Herald* published a letter it had received the day before, purportedly written by James Reed. It appeared below the headline, "A Warning to Our Police."[85]

The San Antonio (Texas) Express of July 22, 1874, correctly identified the daguerreotype of James Reed and Rosanna McCommas, the "girl he seduced about Dallas." They posed for the portrait at the San Antonio studio of Henry A. Doerr. McCommas has often been misidentified in this photograph as Reed's estranged wife, Myra Shirley Reed.

To the Detectives and Police that is trying to ketch the men that Robbed the Stage near Sanmarcas, when you come for me come to fite and be cearful the Path is clear in whitch you travel you Have proved you are a set of Cowrdly murders at Hart and fur the way you have treated mi Lady [Rosanna McCommas] I will knock the skeets from under some of you. I have got you marked and as fur that little Reward if U am not worth more than that I am not worth a Nickel and lookout fur Breakers.

James C. Reed[86]

Immediately after Reed's letter was published, he convinced Henry Russell to go to Collin County and deliver letters to Rosanna and Morris. Reed hoped Rosanna would return with Russell to Lamar County. Russell obliged and rode to the Morris family home. On August 5, much to Reed's surprise, Russell returned without Rosanna but with John Morris.[87]

"The way that I found out his whereabouts was through a letter he wrote to his wife [Rosanna], and myself, and sent by Russell, which delivered to her and then came to my home with the letter to me," Morris later testified. "I came back with Russell to his home where we found Reed. His wife did not accompany us—she played sick—she is not his real wife, however."[88]

No adequate explanation has been found as to why Rosanna did not go to Reed. Perhaps Morris prevented her or, as historian Rick Miller suggested, maybe she was "choosing to play sick and apparently no longer keen on being with Reed."[89]

About the time Reed's letter was published, his pal John Morris showed up at the Russell place for a visit. Reed and Morris had time to catch up on news from Collin County. They had not seen each other since the April 23 debacle at the Morris home when a federal deputy was fatally wounded. Reed confided that he had planned yet another home robbery of an elderly man in Arkansas, similar to the other raids he had committed. Before the night ended, Reed had enlisted Morris as a partner in crime.[90]

The following morning, August 6, 1874, Reed gave Russell about $600 in twenty-dollar gold pieces to hold for him until he returned.[91] After breakfast, Reed saddled his favorite horse, Rondo, and rode northeast with Morris.

However, Morris had no intention of helping Reed carry out another robbery, and Reed had no idea he was about to be betrayed. The promise of a reward for the apprehension of Reed had proved too tempting for Morris to ignore. Morris later related that he had planned Reed's capture soon after he came to the Morris home in April to see Rosanna. Angry and embarrassed over the accidental killing of a law officer that night, Morris quickly offered his services to the Texas authorities.[92]

Purnell and Sheriff Merritt commissioned Morris as a special deputy and authorized him to "work up the case" against Reed and gain his confidence.[93] That was precisely what Morris had done by hosting Rosanna and corresponding with Reed. On that August day as he and Reed rode to Arkansas to carry out the planned robbery, Morris realized that he had to take Reed into custody before they crossed the Red River. Morris' status as a special deputy would not be recognized in Indian Territory.[94]

In late afternoon, Reed and Morris encountered a farmer who told them they were still more than twenty miles southwest of the Red River crossing, a popular route for horse thieves and desperadoes headed to Indian Territory.[95]

Reed and Morris had ridden only a few miles more when Morris suggested that they pause for supper at the home of S. M. Harvey.[96] After they dismounted, Morris recommended that they not take their pistols inside the house out of courtesy to their host. Reed agreed and hung his gun belt on Rondo's saddle horn.

The pair approached the house, and Harvey greeted them. As was the custom of the time, he invited the strangers to spend the night. When supper had been prepared, Reed and Morris were asked to take seats at the dining table.

"I got done eating before Reed and went back into the main room, and explained to Harvey, Reed's character, and asked him to assist me in his arrest, which he agreed to do," Morris later explained in a written statement. "Mr. Harvey and I then went out to the horses where we took the pistols off of Reed's and my own horse."[97] He continued:

> We went to the dining room where Reed was still eating. I said to Reed, "Jim, throw up your hands." He said he would do so, but ran under the table, and raised up with the table and ran towards the door with the table in advance. I shot two holes through the table. After he dropped the table I shot him in the right side. He ran his hand in his pocket to draw a cylinder as I thought. I shot four times and hit him twice, once a scalping shot in the head and once in the right side. He had an extra cylinder which he carried in his pocket. After he got out of the house, he ran up to me and grabbed me—my pistol refusing to fire—and as he rushed against me, I fell and he fell too. I then called Mr. Harvey to assist me in his arrest, which he did and we thus secured him.[98]

They carried Reed back inside the house, where Morris later testified that Reed told him, "You have killed as brave a man as ever lived."[99]

Morris added that Reed then turned to Harvey and said, "Tell my comrades I died like a man." Harvey asked if he had really committed all the crimes that Morris had attributed to him. Reed replied, "I never killed any man except in self-defense, and in defense of my property."[100]

Reed lingered about twenty minutes. Near the end, he asked Morris for water. He gave him a drink, unbuttoned Reed's bloody shirt, and washed his head and chest.[101] Soon, Myra Shirley Reed's estranged husband, James Commodore Reed, died on the floor of a stranger's kitchen. His reckless life had lasted twenty-nine years.

CHAPTER 15

Repercussions

JIM REED'S SLAYING IMMEDIATELY BECAME FRONT-PAGE news across Texas and beyond. "The career of crime through which this man [Reed] has passed is but imperfectly known, and many dark and bloody deeds will only at the judgment be found charged to his account," opined the *Dallas Daily Commercial*.[1]

The circumstances of his death had come as no surprise to anyone who knew him, including his family. It is unknown, however, how Myra Reed reacted when she learned that she had become a widow. Despite the breakdown of their marriage, the loss of Jimmie likely saddened Myra. She apparently had been a faithful wife since 1866, and he was the father of her children—Rosie, Eddie, and Eliza, who had died in infancy in California.

In later years, author S. W. Harman concocted a scenario that claimed the authorities had summoned Myra to identify Reed's body.[2] Supposedly, when Myra "received word to come and take charge of her husband's dead body her eyes took on a hard look and she said, 'They've killed him for the reward but they will never get it,' and rode to the house where the body lay."[3]

According to Harman's tale, she approached the body and "gave a glance at the face of her loved one and without the least sign of emotion, but with a scornful curve of her lips quietly remarked: 'I am very sorry gentlemen, that you have made such a mistake and killed the wrong man; very sorry indeed. John Morris, you will have to kill Jim Reed, if you desire to secure the reward offered for Jim Reed's body.'"[4]

Harman's book *Hell on the Border: He Hanged Eighty-Eight Men*, published in 1898, has been called one of the better books on outlaws and lawmen. But some historians and writers have reservations about Harman's accuracy. "When he wrote about Belle's early days, he knew nothing about them and never bothered to look them up," wrote Homer Croy, ironically an author who also was prone to bias and factual error.[5]

Myra had been separated from Reed for more than six months, and she did not see him in death or claim his body.[6] Contrary to Harman's assertion, there was no difficulty identifying Jim Reed. Shortly after his death, Morris—assisted by a badly shaken S. M. Harvey—lashed the corpse belly down over the saddle of Reed's horse, Rondo, and rode directly to the county courthouse in Paris. At the coroner jury's inquest the next day, Lamar County Sheriff John A. Gose, who had known Reed from Civil War days in north Texas, examined the body and made a positive identification.[7]

Morris testified about his involvement as a special deputy in Reed's pursuit and the details of what had transpired at the Harvey farm. The coroner's jury report stated, "We are of the opinion from the evidence, that the killing was justified by the said Morris, and it further appears from the evidence that said Morris was fully authorized to make said arrest; and in view of the above facts we recommend that the said Morris go hence without delay."[8]

Reed's remains were placed in a metallic coffin, loaded onto a flatbed wagon, and taken to Collin County for burial.[9] Unfortunately, the drayman transporting the coffin mistakenly went to the wrong burial ground and had to retrace the route. The body had not been embalmed and had started to bloat because of the August heat. The strong odor caused the drayman to stop, pull the coffin off the wagon, and leave it on the side of the road.[10]

When Collin County Sheriff William Merritt learned that Reed's body had been abandoned on the roadside, he and a party of men retrieved the coffin. It was taken to Potter's Field Cemetery, also known as Settler's Field, in McKinney for interment in an unmarked grave.[11]

Jim Reed had been killed and left to rot in a forgotten grave, but reports about him remained front and center in countless newspapers. On August 19, 1874, one of the more dubious accounts of Reed's death appeared in the *Kansas City Times*.¹² It was a letter dated August 16 from Sherman, Texas, allegedly written by John Morris. The letter read in part:

> As I am the man who killed James H. [sic] Reed, the Austin and San Antonio stage robber . . . , I feel it is my duty, as Reed's dying confession was made to me, to send a few lines to Missouri for publication, to let the public know that the James and Younger brothers have been persecuted in Missouri. Reed made a confession, and I believe he spoke the truth, for I cannot believe that one so brave as Reed was would speak anything but the truth, when he was positive that he had only a few moments to live.
>
> He would not implicate any one but himself. He said he had robbed stages in Nevada, California, Oregon and Arizona, and that he was the leader of the Iowa train robbery, the leader at Ste. Genevieve and at Gad's Hill; but he declared to the last that [Arthur] McCoy, the James and Younger brothers had no hand in these robberies.
>
> I had been pursuing Reed for several weeks on the charge of robbing the Austin stage, and I came upon him at noon when he stopped for dinner, in Lamar County, Texas, fifteen miles northwest of Paris. Reed resisted and I was forced to shoot him. He lived for two hours after being shot. He was very brave and deserved a better cause than the life he had led since the war. During the war he served in [General Joseph O.] Jo Shelby's "Iron Brigade," and no better soldier ever lived.
>
> Reed said that he had never robbed a poor man, and that he was not afraid to die. He had $1,000 in gold on his person when he was killed. He said that he had $20,000 in gold buried, but refused to tell where it was.
>
> Respectfully,
> John T. Morris, Deputy Sheriff of Collin County, Texas[13]

The letter sounded "suspiciously like a fabrication that a person sympathetic to the James and Younger brothers might write, perhaps even an editor," reported historian Hobbs.[14]

One editor who might have been the letter writer was John Newman Edwards. A hero of the Confederacy who had served as adjutant of General Joseph Shelby's Iron Brigade in the Civil War, Edwards founded the *Kansas City Star* in 1867.[15] He wrote impassioned editorial tributes to Jesse James and his band of robbers and had been known to pen letters that promoted James as a chivalric folk hero.[16]

"The *Times* and other papers with which he [Edwards] was associated through the years were the mediums for publication of most of the letters alleged to have come from Jesse James," wrote James biographer William A. Settle. "Whether Jesse really wrote any of the letters is not known, but Edwards' connection with them is established."[17]

Author T. J. Stiles also made a compelling case that Edwards likely wrote the "Morris" letter to shine a better light on James. "Undoubtedly Jesse appreciated the efforts of secessionist newspapers to defend him, but he must have been amused to read a story in the *Kansas City Times* on August 19, 1874, that claimed to prove his innocence," Stiles wrote. "The story would have been doubly amusing because Jesse was already planning his next strike, in the very heart of his old hunting grounds."[18]

John Morris was not amused by the letter and dashed off a rebuttal to the editor of the *Kansas City Times* to set the record straight.[19]

> Denison, Texas. Aug. 21, 1874
> To the editor of the Kansas City Times:
>
> I saw in a copy of your paper a few days ago what purports to be a confession of James C. Reed to Morris, the Deputy Sheriff of Collin County, Texas. I am the deputy sheriff who arrested Reed, and who shot him in his attempt to escape. Reed lived about twenty minutes after he was shot. He had on his person $60 in gold. He made no confession.
>
> Reed said nothing about the Younger brothers, the James brothers, or [Arthur] McCoy; nor did he say anything about the Iowa train robbery, the Gad's Hill robbery, or anything about the money he had.

I make this statement to correct the errors in the communication alluded to.

I am, truly yours,
John T. Morris
Dep. Sheriff, Collin County, Texas[20]

Morris wrote the repudiation letter in Denison, Texas, where he had been summoned to offer his knowledge of Henry Russell at a hearing before United States Commissioner Charles E. Maurice.[21] After Reed's death, Russell, who had given Reed shelter, was arrested and charged as an accessory in the San Antonio stage robbery. The hearing in Denison had been called "to determine whether jurisdiction should rest with the State or Federal government since the case involved looting the United States mail."[22] Curiously, none of the law-enforcement agencies had filed charges against Russell for aiding and abetting Reed.

Russell's legal counsel was Henry W. Lightfoot, who had settled in Paris, Texas, in 1872 and had become a prominent figure in Texas politics.[23] Lightfoot's law partner, Samuel Bell Maxey, had served as a Confederate brigadier general and in 1874 was chosen for the first of two terms in the United States Senate.[24]

Lightfoot and the opposing prosecutors examined several witnesses at the preliminary hearing, including Morris, whose testimony took almost an entire day.[25] Myra Reed surprised courtroom spectators when she arrived from Dallas County to appear at the hearing. Described by a reporter as "the bona fide Mrs. Reed"—likely a snide reference to Reed's lover, Rosanna McCommas—Myra had been called to verify that Reed and Russell had been close friends for at least five years. After she had performed her civic duty, Myra promptly returned to her children without visiting Reed's unmarked grave.[26]

On August 19, the same day the bogus Morris letter appeared in the *Kansas City Times*, the Russell hearing concluded. The commissioner ruled that Russell must post bail of $1,000 and promise to appear at a later date in Tyler, Texas, headquarters for the United States District

Court for the Eastern District of Texas at the time.[27] Russell returned to his home in Lamar County and disappeared from public view.[28]

"No further information could be found to learn the disposition of the case against Henry Russell," wrote historian Hobbs. "In view of the earlier facts concerning the robbery, the evidence against Russell was not very substantial."[29] Other sources contended that Russell likely would have been acquitted if he had gone to trial.[30] It remains unknown whether a trial was ever held. On November 17, 1878, a fire swept through Tyler's business district and destroyed the records for the United States District Court.[31]

State and federal law officers, including Collin County Special Deputy John Morris, continued to hunt Reed's partners in crime.

Morris was anxious to collect some of the promised reward money for having ended Reed's criminal career. After a month had passed without news about the payment of the reward, Morris asked Collin County Sheriff William Merritt to intercede on his behalf. On September 7, 1874, Merritt sent a letter to Texas governor Richard Coke.[32]

Dear Sir: I write to you in the interest of John T. Morris, the man who killed Reed, the stage robber. Morris is absent at your city to procure the reward as offered for the capture of Reed. Having heard that it was circulated by some that Morris was a man of bad character, I thought I would write you what I knew of him. I have lived three years in two miles of Morris and known that he made his living by the use of his own hands. His wife was a cousin of Reed's and Reed imposed himself upon Morris by stopping with him when he passed through the country before Morris knew anything of his depredations. At my solicitation and others, Morris feeling the sting of disgrace by reason of Reed's having made his house a stopping place, followed him with the intention of capturing him, but was forced by circumstances to kill him, a thing that Morris very much regretted having to do. I write this to you as much for the vindication of Morris's name for honesty as his pecuniary interest. Morris made a good and honest soldier during the war, as many of our citizens here will attest. And of a man whom I believe to be honest and whose action I have fully endorsed on this Reed matter, and as such I beg leave to subscribe myself.[33]

While waiting to collect the full reward of $3,000, Morris pursued Cal Carter and William Boswell, the other stagecoach robbers still at large.[34] The confusion had been sorted out about which of Reed's accomplices took part in the Watt Grayson robbery and the San Antonio–Austin stage robbery. Although originally both Carter and Boswell had been indicted along with Reed for the stage robbery, lawmen had concluded that neither of them had had a hand in the earlier robbery of Watt Grayson in Indian Territory.[35]

That discovery had been made prior to Reed's death, when United States Deputy Marshal William H. Anderson had become intrigued by the similar witness descriptions of William Boswell and Marion Dickens and by William Wilder's resemblance to a daguerreotype of Cal Carter.[36] Further investigation satisfied Anderson that his hunch had been right. He quickly convinced United States Marshal Thomas Purnell that Wilder and Dickens had assisted Reed in the theft of more than $30,000 from Watt Grayson in 1873.[37]

Satisfied that he had correctly identified Reed's true accomplices, Anderson wrote Grayson and obtained descriptions of the robbers and the personal items they had taken, including weapons and purses used to hold some of the stolen money. Anderson later recovered one of the purses that Grayson identified as his wife's and two shotguns that the outlaws had sold after returning to Texas. It was believed that Anderson recovered the purse from Rosanna McCommas, to whom Reed had given it.[38]

"I then went to Eufala [Eufaula] Indian Territory where I met Watt Grayson," Anderson later explained in a sworn deposition before United States Commissioner Ben Long at Dallas. "I told the facts to him. He then employed me to arrest the robbers if possible and bring them to justice, and to recover any of the money that I might find in their possession."[39]

Anderson was not the only one whom Grayson had recruited to track down the thieves. A. J. King, who worked on Grayson's ranch, was also in hot pursuit.[40] Grayson had ordered him to scour the countryside for the outlaws. King secured an appointment as a special deputy United States marshal and procured arrest warrants from the United States Court for the Western District of Arkansas at Fort Smith.[41]

Informants told King that Dickens had planned to make a run to Eagle Pass, Texas, on the Mexican border, a popular river crossing for fugitives fleeing the United States.[42] King later testified that he stopped his pursuit at the Mexican border when Dickens went beyond his jurisdiction.[43] It seems that no one heard of Dickens again. Some sources believe that he died in Mexico, but no records have been found concerning his death. The only mention of Dickens appears in a notation penciled in a William Wilder criminal-case file. It simply states, "Burns dead,"[44] referring to Dickens' alias. With Reed dead and Dickens unaccounted for in Mexico, King's attention turned to William Wilder.

Federal deputies William Anderson and George Holland already had a bead on Wilder, who had returned to Bosque County. He laid low with the family living at the Reeds' old house, which he had also once owned.[45]

Will Conine, a longtime friend of the Reeds, wrote about Wilder's time on Coon Creek.

> Mrs. Reed [Myra] was down there several times during the summer 1874. She found out that Wilder and his bunch had it in for us. She told us that she told him [Wilder] that we were the best friends that she ever had in that country and if any body wanted her friendship that they must not bother us and I think she meant it too.
>
> Not long after that she was back. She went to her old home where Wilder lived and staid [sic] with them several days. She was in a good two-horse buggy, had good team. On Sunday she wanted to drive out some distance to see some one. Wilder was in the buggy with her. They passed our house and stoped [sic] in front. She got out and come in to tell us howdy. Wilder stayed in the buggy. She seemed glad to see us.
>
> She talked to father to one side a short time. She told him that the US Marshal would be after Wilder, that he [the marshal] would

come to our house and depend on us to help him out. She stopped in the evening to say good-bye and talked a short time. She went back to Dallas the next day.[46]

About two weeks later, just as Myra had predicted, deputy marshals Anderson and Holland showed up at the Conine home. Because Will's father, R. E. Conine, was away on business, Anderson asked to speak privately to young Will.[47]

"When we went out he took a letter out of his pocket to Father from Mrs. Reed telling him who they [the deputies] were and that they were all right," wrote Conine. "And that she would appreciate any help we would give them. She signed her name May Bell Shirley."[48]

Anderson further explained that Wilder had tried to make a deal with the authorities by promising that he would provide the names of "a bunch of outlaws if they would make it easy for him" and share part of the rewards, according to Conine. "When Mrs. Reed found out that he [Wilder] intended to give some of them away she decided to do some giving away herself."[49]

Conine recalled that Wilder "had a smooth way and a good turn for fooling people."[50] Apparently he had not fooled Myra and had misjudged her allegiance to him as an associate of Reed. Her cooperation with law officers was never officially acknowledged and went totally unreported by the press. That was likely no concern to Myra—anonymity suited her well.

Both Conine and his younger brother, Emmett, assisted the law officers by scouting the house where Wilder had been staying and confirmed that he was still there.[51] Conine rode with the posse when the deputies surrounded the house. Anderson approached with the intention of holding face-to-face negotiations, but Wilder attempted to escape on a saddled horse.

"The posse killed the horse and Wilder ran off on foot, jumping into a gully, but not before a bullet hit him in the thigh," wrote historian Rick Miller. "Anderson crawled nearby and discussed Wilder's surrender with him. When Wilder wouldn't agree, Anderson gave him four minutes, after which the posse would open fire again. Wilder was convinced and surrendered to the lawmen."[52]

Conine failed to mention that in addition to Anderson and Holland, other lawmen also helped to capture Wilder, including United States Deputy Marshal John Henry Minehart. Special Deputy A. J. King, who worked for Watt Grayson, also had arrived in Bosque County at the time of Wilder's capture.[53]

In sworn statements at Wilder's trial, both King and Anderson took credit for Wilder's capture, but each gave a different arrest date in court documents. Anderson claimed Wilder had been arrested on September 29, 1874, but King maintained that the correct date was September 26.[54] The *Fort Smith Weekly New Era* neglected to mention A. J. King and barely mentioned Anderson. Instead, the paper heaped praise on hometown lawman John Minehart.[55]

"Every effort to get any trace of [the robbers] was unraveling until Minehart got on a trail that he has followed with persistency, shrewdness, and caution," overstated the *Fort Smith Weekly New Era* when Wilder was brought to Fort Smith in shackles in early October for trial.[56]

"Wilder, who was captured about a week since, in his confession of the robbery of old man Grayson, states that he and his two companions divided the $32,000 equally between them, but as they were unable to carry it all (it being specie) they buried $8000," reported the *Galveston Daily News*.[57] "He subsequently returned to the place where the money was secreted, but it had been taken away. He supposes his companion Reed, the stage robber, got it."

Several witnesses from Indian Territory went to Fort Smith to identify Wilder, including Watt Grayson, who recognized him as one of the robbers. By late November, the grand jury had returned three indictments against Wilder.[58]

With his confession and the overwhelming evidence, Wilder's trial was brief. Judge Henry C. Caldwell of the Eastern District of Arkansas presided.[59] William Story, judge of the United States District Court for the Western District of Arkansas, had resigned to avoid impeachment after he had been accused of accepting bribes and overcharging the government for court expenses.[60]

On December 8, 1874, Wilder was found guilty. Four days later, Judge Caldwell—known as a merciful jurist—imposed his punishment.[61] Wilder was sentenced to one year of hard labor at the Arkansas State Penitentiary in Little Rock and a fine of $1,000 and court costs.[62]

Many people in the Fort Smith courtroom, especially the federal prosecutor and deputy sheriffs, were stunned by what they considered a lenient sentence. The *Fort Smith Weekly New Era* called out Judge Caldwell in a scathing editorial. "Had he [Wilder] stolen a pony worth fifteen dollars, he would probably have been hung by Judge Lynch," the editor wrote. "Such are the inequalities of the law."[63]

On December 14, 1874, deputy marshals delivered Wilder to the warden of the Arkansas State Penitentiary.[64] Built in 1849, the prison was infamous for "cruel, barbarous, and inhumane" conditions.[65] No records exist regarding Wilder's incarceration or his life after release.

Law officers pressed on with the search for Cal Carter and William Boswell. Lawmen carried arrest warrants for Carter and Boswell for more than a year. "Carter was reported dead, although no details were given," Miller wrote in his summary of Jim Reed and his outlaw band. "Boswell was reported as drowned while crossing a river in Kansas and the body fully identified. The Reed gang was no more."[66]

CHAPTER 16

Out of the Shadows

B Y 1875, MYRA REED HAD LIVED IN THE SHADOW OF DEATH ever since her beloved brother, Bud, had been struck down in a godless war. Many friends and two of her younger brothers had also died violently. Twenty-seven-year-old Myra now faced a future without a husband, albeit a status she had grown accustomed to in the six months of separation that had preceded Jim Reed's death.

Nineteenth-century widows were expected to follow a strict etiquette of mourning that governed their behavior and appearance. "Women and men had different spheres: women in the home and men in the world. Men could not be burdened by complicated mourning rituals because that would limit their ability to take part in society," wrote historian Katherine McDaniel.[1]

However, not all widows followed such customs—especially those who lived on the frontier. "Women traversed the vastness of Western spaces with desires distinctly at odds with those of Victorian gentility," wrote historian Virginia Scharff.[2] Myra Reed was one of the rebels. Estranged from Reed at the time of his death, she did not become one of the "angels in black" who donned widow's weeds and observed a mourning period of at least a year or more.[3]

Myra had no time for an extended period of bereavement, anyway. The prospects for a widow in rural Texas in the 1870s were few and far between, especially for one with two young children. Myra had no choice but to move forward. Jim Reed had left her nothing but bittersweet memories and his favorite horse, Rondo.

"Home is preeminently woman's kingdom, and every 'house-mother,' using the tender German name, should reign uncrowned queen," advised *The Home Manual: Everybody's Guide in Social, Domestic, and Business Life*.[4] For unfortunate females forced to go outside their "kingdom" to join the workforce, job opportunities were mostly for menial labor.[5] Restaurant work also came highly recommended. According to *The Home Manual*, "The requirements are neatness and good appearance generally, with the ability to receive and execute orders with dexterity and dispatch."[6]

Although large numbers of women and children entered the American workforce in the Victorian era, they toiled at lowly and tedious jobs for a pittance.[7] Women in the trans-Mississippi West were excluded from most frontier industries.[8] For many years, the keepers and chroniclers of western history were mostly White males who were inclined to dismiss women as "bit players" with little or no influence.[9]

"Unfortunately, our perception of Westering women have [has] been shaped by male writers who did not read what women themselves wrote about the West,"[10] wrote Sandra Myres, a western American scholar. "Westering women became protagonists of a stereotyped version of the West as false as that of Hollywood Indians."[11]

Emerson Hough, a prolific western writer, perpetuated the stereotype of the idealized frontier woman in *The Passing of the West*, published in 1921:

> The chief figure of the American West, the figure of the ages, is not the long-haired, fringed-legging man riding a rawboned pony, but the gaunt and sad-faced woman sitting on the front seat of the wagon, following her lord where he might lead. . . . Who has written her story? Who has painted her picture?[12]

Myra Reed did not fit the stereotyped images of females of her time. She had a passion for literature and music, combined with an attraction to fast horses and lawless men, that largely shaped her life.

Nancy "Nannie" Fite, a prominent Cherokee Nation citizen and wife of pioneer physician R. L. Fite, saw Myra take part in a horse race at the first Indian International Fair at Muskogee in 1875. Fite later recalled that

Myra "rode her pony bareback with only a surcingle strapped around it." Although Myra did not win the race, Fite never forgot her performance.[13]

Myra's friend Will Conine also admired her horsemanship. "While she lived near us she had a very fine beaded blanket she would fasten that on her horse with a ciringle [surcingle] and ride as well as any circus girl," recalled Conine.[14] "Of course, some people thought them days that it was improper to ride that way. If a woman rode astride she was sure disgraced all the time. She was past redemption."[15]

Glenn Shirley referred to the time after Reed's death as Myra's "mystery years."[16] Shirley was unable to find many credible records of Myra's whereabouts and actions from 1875 to 1880. Other writers had no problem with this lack of dependable evidence. "Undaunted biographers have found a wealth of 'facts,'" wrote Shirley of the inventors of mythical figures of the nineteenth-century American West.[17]

Many of them created outrageous stories that portrayed Myra as the leading hellcat of Dallas in the mid- to late 1870s. Wild fabrications turned Myra into a scheming seductress who used a Dallas livery stable as a front for dealing in stolen horses, a dance-hall hostess, a dealer of high-stakes faro, and someone who bellied up to the bar with the corrupt and the vile.[18] The tall tales were often spawned and kept alive by people who claimed they had known Myra and had witnessed her wild and scandalous behavior.

"Many people in Dallas remember the beautiful, determined woman as she galloped through the streets, her black hair streaming in the wind, her horse caparisoned like an Indian's, with only a surcingle and a blanket,"[19] according to a story in the *Dallas Morning News* about Myra's "masculine career."

Hyperbolic descriptions of Myra Reed became commonplace starting in 1875 and remained so for decades. Even authors who sought the truth eventually perpetuated some of the most grievous myths.

In 1941, journalist and literary critic Burton Rascoe, despite his reputation of being "angrily allergic to legend," claimed that in 1875, Myra left her children in Scyene and took up residence in a Dallas hotel.[20] There, she "dressed and behaved in a spectacular manner," Rascoe wrote:

She purchased a horse and buggy, a riding horse and a stud which she kept in the stables back of the hotel, hiring a Negro as her special hostler and groom. . . . She dressed in black velvet, with long flowing skirts when she rode sidesaddle, and wore white chiffon waists, a tight black jacket, high-topped boots and a man's Stetson hat turned up in front and decorated with an ostrich plume. The only peculiarity about this costume was that around her waist she wore a cartridge belt from which two revolvers were suspended in holsters. She attended the races, the circus, and the county fair. She would enter bars and drink like a man or taken [take] her place at gaming tables for a try of her luck at cards or roulette.[21]

Rascoe, like others before and after him, offered no attributions or credible sources to support his claims. He also suggested that Myra sometimes exhibited a completely different fashion sense. "When the mood struck her, she shocked the women and more respectable citizens of Dallas by changing into beaded and fringed buckskin costume like those worn by Buffalo Bill, and riding at breakneck speed through the streets of the town, scattering everyone to the sidewalk," wrote Rascoe. "The constabulary and the whole town was afraid of her."[22]

Rascoe propagated several outrageous legends about Myra, and even created imaginary scenes and dialogue to back up his claims.[23] In a review published in 1941 in the *Journal of American History*, Willard H. Smith wrote of Rascoe's book, "No footnotes are used, but several quotations, some of them unnecessarily long, are embodied in the text."[24]

Rascoe's errors and exaggerations aside, however, Myra's deportment was far from spotless. During her so-called mystery years, she regularly crossed the line between the lawful and the lawless.

Myra had grown up in a pro-Confederate family on the fringes of the frontier. Experiencing the trauma of war and the death of her brother contributed to her distrust of the federal establishment and authoritarian figures. Her early years had been spent in the company of unreconstructed Confederates and outlaws. Consequently, her male companions came from those dubious ranks.

Nonetheless, her family and friends must have been surprised when Myra took up with Mike McCommas in 1875.[25] He was a nephew of the highly esteemed Dallas County pioneer Amon McCommas and the cousin of Rosanna McCommas, Jim Reed's paramour.[26] Despite being a member of a prominent family, McCommas had a streak of larceny in his heart and—much like Myra—was willing to buck authority figures, especially former Yankees.

Born in Missouri in 1844, Michael J. "Mike" McCommas was the son of Sarah Ann Mitchell and Isaac McCommas, a younger brother of Elder Amon McCommas.[27] Most people called him Mike, but he also went by Mitchell, his mother's maiden name, and some census reports and other records listed him as Mikel, Mitchel, and Mack.[28]

Soon after his birth, the McCommas family left southwestern Missouri for Crawford County in the rugged Ozark region of northwestern Arkansas, on the eastern border of Indian Territory. Mike McCommas and his eleven brothers and sisters came of age on the family farm in Sugar Loaf Township.[29] By 1860, Mike's father and oldest brother, Alexander, worked as teamsters, hauling freight and goods in wagons pulled by oxen or draft horses.[30]

When the Civil War erupted, Mike McCommas fought for the Confederacy. No official records have been found concerning his military service, but when he died in 1913, it was reported that McCommas "was a former Confederate soldier and his remains were buried according to the ritual of the order of United Confederate Veterans."[31] He was laid to rest in the Confederate section of Rose Hill Cemetery in Ardmore, Oklahoma.

Shortly after the Civil War, Isaac McCommas and his family, like other disenfranchised supporters of the Lost Cause, departed Arkansas and moved to Dallas County, Texas, where many of their kinfolk had settled in the 1840s.[32] On September 22, 1866, in Lamar County, Texas, twenty-two-year-old Mike McCommas married Lucy Josephine Anderson, a slightly younger native Texan.[33] Three years later, Josephine gave birth to a son, William McCommas, but the toddler did not make it to his second birthday. He died of an unknown cause.[34]

Josephine gave birth to a second son on January 21, 1872, named Isaac

Mason McCommas after Mike's father.[35] No records can be found that Isaac or his mother had any further relationship with Mike McCommas. Josephine completely vanished from the records, an indication that she might have remarried and used her new husband's name.

Young Isaac McCommas grew into manhood, was thrice married, fathered at least a dozen children, and worked primarily as a carpenter.[36] When he died on June 24, 1940, in Big Spring, Texas, his tombstone was inscribed with the surname he had used throughout his life, despite having been estranged from his father.[37]

In early 1875, when Mike McCommas and Myra Reed connected, chatter about their morals and behavior spread throughout Dallas County. The extent of their relationship was never fully proved, but some writers contended that she became his common-law wife.[38]

"It is one thing for a woman to be faithful to her lawless husband [Jim Reed], but quite another to go about consorting with outlaws to whom she is not bound in wedlock," wrote William Yancey Shackleford (pseudonymous name of folklorist Vance Randolph). "Many friends dropped her [Myra] at this time, and she was no longer invited to respectable homes in Dallas."[39]

Among Myra's chief critics, the upper echelon citizens of Scyene were the most vocal in their condemnation of her and her associates. In early 1875, Amon McCommas Jr. organized and chaired a committee of almost fifty of Scyene's civic and business leaders, including his father, Amon McCommas, to discuss solutions for battling the rampant lawlessness in their community.[40] A similar parley had been held in 1874 "for the purpose of devising ways and means for the better security of life and property."[41] Some recommendations at that time had never been implemented.[42]

The new committee drafted a petition that sought authorization of a legal vigilante effort of "law-abiding men and good citizens, and to go only where the laws of the land will protect us, and in no wise to take the law into our own hands."[43] On March 29, 1875, the petition, filled with misrepresentations about Myra Reed, was delivered to Texas governor Richard Coke.[44] The authors of the petition took point-blank shots at those who were considered the worst offenders.

For several years past the town of Scyene, Dallas County, Texas, and vicinity, has been noted as a place of lawlessness, crime and disorder, as well as a place of resort for horse thieves, desperadoes, and other bad characters—certain parties having located themselves here as a place of rendezvous for such characters, thus giving aid and comfort to thieving and marauding bands infesting all parts of the state. Here is the home of the widow and family of James Reed, the San Antonio bank robber, his widow being no less celebrated in such exploits than her notorious paramour. Here the robber and outlaw himself made his home and sought refuge while resting from his daring and infamous robberies and murders. Here Porter and the Younger brothers, whose names have since become synonymous of infamy throughout the length and breadth of the land, for a time rested secure. Here was murdered Colonel Nichols, a deputy sheriff of this county, and Mr. McMahon, one of his posse, while attempting to arrest Porter and John Younger. Here, for a time, was the headquarters of the notorious desperado Hays, alias Parker, who shot off Judge Hart's arm, and murdered in cold blood James Loving, a peaceable citizen of Dallas County. Here the robber and desperado Wilder, who now lies in prison at Fort Smith, rested while he concocted his infamous plans.

For such characters the latch springs [strings] of the home of this family has even hung out; and as courier, and if need be coworker of the band, she (Mrs. Reed) has done them good service. Donning often male attire, she has ridden hundreds of miles to apprise them of pending danger.

Quite recently she had threatened to burn out any one who proposed to interfere with her nefarious plans, and states, in a threatening letter to one of our citizens, that she has twenty-five men who will do her bidding and annihilate Scyene, if necessary.[45]

On April 1, Governor Coke sent a sympathetic but brief and "eminently noncommittal" reply to the community leaders. "I think your object most praiseworthy—a similar spirit throughout the state would do more than all else to put down lawlessness and crime," Coke wrote. "In pursuing your plans it will be important that your action be in strict accordance with the law. You cannot be too careful about this."[46]

In the petition, Mike McCommas' name was suspiciously absent among those cited as lawbreakers. But even his powerful family could not keep the relationship between McCommas and Myra under wraps for long. Soon, the pair's liaison was fully revealed, and Myra was trapped by newfound notoriety.

PART III

CHAPTER 17

The Glare of the Limelight

IN THE SPRING OF 1875, MYRA REED HAD NOT BEEN CHARGED with any crime, but her marriage to Jim Reed had been enough to put her name at the top of Scyene's most-wanted list. Mike McCommas's close association with Myra had earned him a place on a list of suspected lawbreakers.

"Society in that section of our county has not reached the degree of advanced civilization so desirable in Christian communities," opined the April 15 *Dallas Daily Herald* about the state of affairs in Scyene.[1]

Once they had been cast as incorrigible troublemakers, Myra and Mike McCommas went on the scout. They had not been gone long before they were back in the news. Only a week after the *Dallas Daily Herald* story about troublemakers in Scyene, Myra and McCommas surfaced near Waco, almost ninety miles south of Dallas on the Brazos River in McLennan County.[2] Waco, on a spur of the Chisholm Trail, had developed into a flourishing cattle and cotton marketplace. Besides cotton farmers and cowboys, many saloons, gambling houses, and a red-light district that came to be called the Reservation, the town also attracted its share of outlaws.[3] Horse thieves passing through on their way from southern Texas to Indian Territory had plenty of hiding places in thick brush along creek bottoms.

McCommas and Myra opted for comfort and found shelter at the Kirkpatrick House, a respectable establishment that Naomi Kirkpatrick owned and operated on Austin Avenue.[4] A widow with four children,

Kirkpatrick advertised that her hotel boasted "fresh groceries" and a "good wagon yard."[5]

As in Scyene, Waco's civic and business leaders had tired of widespread lawlessness. In 1873, McLennan County voters had enthusiastically chosen a local Confederate hero, Lawrence Sullivan Ross, to take over law enforcement.[6] "Sul" Ross had risen to the rank of brigadier general while commanding Texas cavalry brigades. He had garnered praise and glory before the Civil War, however, as the leader of a brutal assault against a group of Comanches, an offensive known as the Battle of Pease River.[7]

In 1860, Ross and a company of mounted Texas Rangers had swept down on a small Comanche hunting camp on Pease River in northwestern Texas, taking prisoners and slaughtering at least a dozen people. Among those taken was Cynthia Ann Parker, a young White woman who became one of the most renowned captives in the history of the West.[8] She had been kidnapped by a Comanche raiding party in 1836 and raised as a Comanche, eventually marrying Chief Peta Nocona. They had a daughter and two sons, one of them Quanah Parker, a noted warrior and the last Comanche chief.

Ross and his rangers returned Cynthia to her birth family, but after having lived as a Comanche for almost twenty-five years and then being separated from her two sons, she never readjusted to White society. She tried but failed to escape with her daughter many times to return to the Comanches. When her infant daughter died, the distraught woman lost all hope. In her grief, Cynthia stopped eating and eventually starved to death.[9]

In later years, the so-called Battle of Pease River became known for what it truly was—a massacre. Ross offered five divergent versions about his role in the raid. Claims were made that he had manipulated the facts of his glorious victory to further his image and promote his political career, which by 1884 had culminated in two terms as governor.[10] But in the 1870s, many folks in McLennan County did not care whether the allegations against Ross held any merit. All that mattered was that he had the leadership skills necessary to guide the effort to murder Native populations and curb crime.

During Ross's two years as sheriff, 675 men and women were held in the McLennan County jail, and seventy-six were convicted and sent to the penitentiary. Most of them were apprehended for crimes committed in other counties.[11] Myra Reed and Mike McCommas were two of those on the run from another county. They had scarcely settled into their room or sampled one of Naomi Kirkpatrick's fine dinners when they were discovered.

On April 23, 1875, McCommas was spotted on a city street and was taken into custody without incident. Confusion existed about McCommas's identity.

"A detective named Glenn arrested a man by the name of McCormick [McCormack] for murder[;] to collect a reward he brought him to the sheriff's office," Deputy Sheriff Samuel Newton Clabaugh recalled in 1944, when he was ninety years old. "I was told to take him to jail."[12]

"After locking him up he asked me if I would do him a favor," continued Clabaugh. "I told him yes, if possible. He told me he was traveling with Mrs. Belle Reed and wanted me to tell her if I saw her where he was as she would be in town looking for him if he didn't return to their hideout [the hotel]. I asked him if she was Jim Reed's wife and he said she was. I told him that I had known her in Bosque County. We were notified [by Dallas County authorities] to hold the man and arrest the woman. I notified all livery stables and hotels if a woman of that description came in to notify me at the jail."

Clabaugh continued, "About 8 o'clock that night a party came to tell me she was at Mrs. Kirkpatrick's hotel on Austin Street. I went by and got the sheriff and we went up then walked into the lobby and there she sat with several more people. I pointed her out to the sheriff. She said she wasn't Mrs. Reed but we told her that she was under arrest and then she made an effort to get to her room for her pistol, which we prevented."[13]

The initial news reports about McCommas clearly misidentified him and accused him and Myra of murders they had not committed and were never charged with.

"On last Friday a man by the name of McCormack was arrested by Sheriff Ross, supposed to be an Arkansas murderer," reported the *Waco Reporter* after the arrests of McCommas and Myra.[14] "A telegram was soon after received from the authorities at Dallas, stating that 'Bell Ross,' alias Mrs. Reed, the wife of the notorious stage robber, Reed, killed a short time since in Colin County by a deputy sheriff in attempting to arrest him, was traveling with McCormack, and that she was implicated in one to two murders, and to arrest her. . . . She had a dirk knife and six-shooter but had laid them aside a few minutes before her arrest. Report says she has killed two men. She had letters on her person of a startling character, but the nature of which, for prudential reasons, we shall not make known."[15]

No further records have been found of the alleged murder charges. After Myra and McCommas were identified by their correct names, they were held for horse theft, not murder.[16] McCommas remained in the McLennan County jail, but four days after her arrest, Myra was returned to Dallas, where her troubles with the law continued.[17]

On April 28, 1875, Myra Reed was indicted for arson by a Dallas County grand jury for allegedly having burned down a store four years earlier in Scyene.[18] The store purportedly belonged to Nancy Clorinda Fisher Alexander, known as Nannie.

Born in Illinois in 1844, Nannie was four years old when she moved to Texas with her parents and eight siblings.[19] She wed John Hunter Martin in 1861, but that union ended in divorce. In 1869, she married Charles P. Alexander, who reportedly had some "fleeting run-ins with the law."[20] Stories circulated that Nannie Alexander had spoken out against Myra in public and supposedly organized a march of local women to protest Myra's presence in Scyene.[21]

No records or contemporary newspaper reports have been found of Nannie Alexander's ownership of a store in Scyene or the alleged fire. But the most compelling evidence that the arson accusation was bogus was the timeline. If the crime had taken place as charged in 1871, Myra Reed would not have been in Texas—she was residing in southern California with Jim Reed and their children.[22]

"The charge [of arson] was likely trumped up by her enemies in Scyene," wrote Texas historian Rick Miller.[23] Yet the wheels of frontier justice kept turning until the arson trial.

On May 1, 1875, Dallas County Sheriff James E. Barkley ushered Myra from her jail cell to the courthouse for a bond hearing before Fourteenth District Judge Hickerson Barksdale.[24] A native of Tennessee and former officer in the Confederate army, Barksdale had moved to Dallas in 1870 and became a judge three years later.[25] In Myra Reed's arson case, Barksdale quickly reviewed the arrest report and set her bail at $2,500. As was later noted, that substantial amount was "no doubt reflecting the close attention being paid to her case by prominent voters in Scyene."[26]

Barksdale's hefty bail prompted a local newspaper reporter to write, "There are at present 48 prisoners in the county jail, one of whom is a woman, charged with setting a house on fire some four years ago. In answer to an inquirer, the reporter will say that he certainly thinks the amount of bail—$2,500—in connection of the circumstances, excessive. Her attorneys will move for a reduction this morning."[27]

In seeking a lower bail, Myra's lawyers wisely turned to Judge Silas Hare to hear their case. In 1873, Hare, a veteran of the Mexican War and Civil War, had been appointed a district judge of Dallas, Collin, and Grayson counties.[28] At the hearing, Hare was sympathetic to the request from Myra's lawyers and lowered her bail. In reporting the court's action, an Austin journalist wrote that Myra stood accused "of attempting to burn the whole town... but it was determined by one Hare that she wasn't such a 'singed cat' after all, and her bail was reduced from $2,500 to $1,000."[29] Likely John and Eliza Shirley posted the bond that allowed their daughter to go free.[30]

Clearly, however, freedom did not guarantee any improvement in Myra's deportment. Just two months after her release, Myra was back in trouble. On July 2, 1875, she was charged with disorderly conduct and hauled into Mayor's Court, presided over by William Lewis Cabell, the city's mayor, acting as an ex officio magistrate.[31] A decorated Confederate brigadier general, Cabell had moved to Texas from Fort Smith, Arkansas, in 1872 and was elected to the first of three terms as Dallas mayor two years later.[32]

Myra's hearing was brief. Cabell found her guilty as charged and assessed a fine of fifty dollars plus court costs. A motion for a new trial was overruled, and she immediately gave her notice of appeal to the Criminal District Court.[33] The lower court's misdemeanor case had no impact on the bail of the more serious arson charge. Myra remained free, but her problems continued.

On July 22, Dallas County Deputy Sheriff Harry Farmer arrived in Dallas from Waco with a shackled Mike McCommas, who had been at the McLennan County jail since his arrest on April 23.[34] McCommas faced pending charges in Dallas County in the court of Judge Nathaniel Macon Burford. A hard-core opponent of Reconstruction who had risen from private to colonel as a Confederate soldier, Burford was elected presiding justice of Dallas County at about the same time McCommas and Myra Reed had been apprehended in Waco.[35]

While Mike McCommas pondered his fate in a jail cell, Myra laid low with her family. Her respite was short-lived. During the sweltering dog days of August, the dozen men impaneled to serve on a new Dallas grand jury busily considered other criminal cases that Dallas District Attorney Edwin Gustavus Bower presented. It later became known that Bower—a Missouri native—had been "a comrade of the James and Younger boys" and "remained a steadfast friend to both to the day of his death."[36]

Apparently, Bower's allegiance to fellow Missourians did not extend to other people. On August 12, 1875, Bower got just what he had sought. Most of the grand jurors returned bills of indictment against Myra Reed and Mike McCommas for the theft of a gelding, a castrated horse.[37]

Horse theft—a more serious crime than disorderly conduct—meant that Myra's bail on the arson charge was immediately revoked, and she was taken to a cell in the county jailhouse. Almost three months passed before any news of Myra became public. On November 10, 1875, an anonymous letter of warning sent to Sheriff Barkley was published in the *Dallas Daily Herald*:

> Dear Sir—You ought to treat that lady you have in jail right. I tell you this for your own good. It will be hard for you; you will come up missing one of these fine days if you mistreat her. Remember there is lots of Jim Reed's friends left yet—Don't you never forget

it. But as long as you treat her right you will be treated right, and if you please, see that she is treated as a lady as long as she stays in there. I will see you on the road probably one day, and we will have a good talk over it.

I remain still a friend[38]

The letter was followed by editorial commentary:

The above letter addressed to Major Barkley is a fair sample of the epistles which our officers receive daily. . . . The above letter is simply published to show, like a straw, how the winds blow. In this instance, there is something redeeming, since the party who writes is willing to spare a Sheriff's life for the sake of kind treatment to a woman. Fortunately, for us, if we do have women who unsex themselves, we also have officers who do not fear to perform their whole duty.[39]

The term *unsex*—originated by William Shakespeare in his tragedy *Macbeth*—remained in use in the late nineteenth century to describe free-spirited and independent women who opposed conventional beliefs about ideal Victorian womanhood.[40] Any woman who had become an "unsexed, terrifying violent Amazon" threatened the accepted view of masculinity.[41] Ironically, the newspaper story about Myra Reed described a woman accused of stealing a horse that had been deprived of its gonads.

Barkley must have taken the intimidating letter from one of Myra Reed's friends seriously. At that time, however, there was no shortage of worries on his mind.

"Both the police force and Sheriff Barkley's deputies were experiencing a significant increase in demand for their services," wrote Rick Miller. "Trail herds driven through city streets, shooting, burglaries, complaints of prostitution and gambling, and dealing everyday with drunken disturbances kept both forces busy around the clock."[42]

Security had become an issue at the Dallas city and county jails, and rumors of planned inmate escapes increased in late 1875. On November

18, deputies stopped the third escape attempt at the county jail that month when they found several prisoners with small saws cutting through the iron bars of their cells.[43] The next day, it was announced that forty-five prisoners were tucked away in the county jail, including Myra Reed, charged with arson, Amelia Brown, accused of theft, and a third female, retained as a state's witness in a murder case.[44]

Less than a month after the Dallas newspaper published the warning letter sent to Sheriff Barkley, Myra left her jail cell for several hours. On December 16, 1875, she was brought before Benjamin Long, a former Dallas mayor and the United States commissioner for the Northern District of Texas.[45] Myra had been summoned to give her deposition in support of Watt Grayson's attempt to recover the money that Jim Reed and his pals had stolen in 1873.

In her sworn testimony before Long, Myra confirmed that Reed, W. D. Wilder, and Marion Dickens had terrorized Grayson and his wife before absconding with more than $30,000 in cash and gold. She also testified that she had no part in the robbery but had seen the large amount of gold that the outlaws had counted and divided among themselves in her presence.[46] "That of the amount taken from Grayson, I know of no part that could be recovered, my said husband having spent or disposed of all that he had and having left me in a destitute condition," Myra stated.[47]

United States Deputy Marshal W. H. Anderson corroborated Myra's statement and helped to substantiate Grayson's claim.[48] Myra's testimony was invaluable in the lengthy congressional hearings and court hearings that followed for many more years. It also showed that she had been only a bystander in the crime.

In the end, Watt Grayson's claim was proved and paid, but he never saw a dime. He died on August 1, 1878.[49] Ten years later, after lengthy debate in Congress, the reimbursement of the stolen money was approved. Finally, in 1888—almost fifteen years after Watt Grayson had been tortured and robbed—his money was returned to his estate.[50]

If Myra had even a shred of hope that her participation in Watt Grayson's ongoing effort to recover his stolen wealth would serve her well, she must have been disappointed. She remained jailed without bail on the arson charge. On December 22, the arson case against her was continued at Myra's request, probably to gain more time to prepare her defense.[51]

Tall tales later emerged that to escape her confines, Myra had tried to seduce her jailers, including one who "became so infatuated with her, that he suicided because his attention was not reciprocated."[52] Even unsubstantiated, such lurid fabrications added to Myra's colorful outlaw image.

Myra remained in jail well into the spring of 1876, when she was released on her own recognizance pending the outcome of her arson and horse-theft charges.[53] Both pending cases were continued until June 14, 1876, when the charges against Myra and Mike McCommas for horse theft were placed on the trial docket.[54] After important state witnesses failed to show up in court, the trial had to be continued. The next day, once again, the witnesses "could not [be] located or brought to Dallas in time, one of them being Sul Ross, a noted Texas Ranger."[55]

On June 17, the county attorney announced that he had no choice but to halt the trial and any further prosecution. Both defendants were released fully acquitted.[56] McCommas took his leave, and Myra celebrated her acquittal while preparing for the arson trial to start that week.

Myra's joy, however, soon turned to sorrow. On June 19, 1876, her father suddenly passed away from an undisclosed illness.[57] John Shirley was eighty-two years old and had remained vigorous to the end. Less than four months earlier, on March 28, Laura A. Shirley, thought to be his daughter, was born to former enslaved woman Annie Shirley. The Shirley family patriarch died at his home in Scyene with Eliza, his wife of thirty-nine years, Annie, and some of his children at his bedside.[58]

Myra was in Dallas on the eve of her arson trial when she learned of her father's death. On June 20, she entered a plea of not guilty to the arson charge, a jury was seated, and the trial commenced. It did not last long. After hearing the evidence, the jurors briefly deliberated, and on June 21, foreman Joseph A. Harris announced the decision—not guilty.[59] Myra was a free woman, able to properly mourn the loss of her father, comfort her mother, and return to her children.

CHAPTER 18

The Legend Takes Root

IN A LETTER POSTMARKED AUGUST 10, 1876, ADDRESSED TO the Reed family in Metz, Vernon County, Missouri, Myra Reed summed up the past year of her life. The letter was written on stationary likely purloined from Dallas County Sheriff James E. Barkley. It bore no signature and was undated.[1]

Dear Mother and Brothers and Sisters—I write you after so long a time to let you know that I am still living. Time had made many changes, and some very sad ones indeed. My poor old father has left this world of care and trouble. He died two months ago today. It seems as if I have more trouble than any person. "Shug" [Cravens, or John Alva Shirley] got into trouble here and had to leave; poor Ma is left alone with the exception of little Eddie [Reed]. She is going to move away from here in a few days and then I'll be left alone. Eddie will go with her, and I don't know that I shall ever see him again. He is a fine, manly looking boy as you have seen and is said to resemble Jimmie very much; he is very quick motioned, and I don't think there is a more intelligent boy living. I am going to have his picture taken before he leaves and I will send you one; would like for you to see and know him. I know you would love him for the sake of the dear one that's gone. Eddie has been very sick and looks pale and wan, but I think my boy will soon mend up. Rosie is here in Dallas going to school; she has the reputation of being the prettiest little girl in Dallas. She is learning very fast. She had been playing on the stage here in Dallas theatre and gained a world-wide reputation for her prize performance. My people [the Shirley family] were very much opposed to it but I wanted her to be able to make a living of her own without depending on anyone. She is constantly talking of you all, and wanting to visit you, which I intend she shall sometime.

Jno. L. [sic] Morris is still in McKinney, at large. It seems as if justice will never be meted out to him. Pete Fisher is in Colin City [Collin County], where he has always lived. Solly [Jim Reed's brother] hasn't the pluck and love for Jim I thought he had. I have Jimmie's horse Rondo yet; I was offered $200 for him the other day. If Sol had come to Texas, freely would I have given the horse to him if he had sought revenge [for Jim Reed's killing].

I think Brocks are in Montague County. I will realize nothing from my farm this year. Brock rented it out in little pieces to first one another [to first one and then another], and none of them tended it well, so I made nothing. I am going to sell it this fall if I can.

I am far from well. I am so nervous this evening from the headache that I can scarcely write.

Myra's heartfelt letter to the Reed family revealed many of her fears and concerns. She held very little back, with the obvious exception of her legal difficulties, none of which had ended in convictions.

By late 1876, in the wake of her father's death, Myra had helped her widowed mother, Eliza Shirley, dispose of property, livestock, and other assets so she could move to smaller quarters in Dallas. In her letter, Myra had suggested that her five-year-old son, Eddie, would join his Grandmother Shirley. Instead, he was sent to his paternal grandmother, Susan Brock Reed, in Missouri, perhaps to improve his physical condition and stamina or, as Myra put it, to "mend up."[2]

Myra also explained in the letter that although she resided in Dallas with eight-year-old daughter Rosie, she still owned farmland in Scyene and had leased it to the Brock family, who had not been able to make a go of it. Myra bragged about her daughter's beauty and skill as a performer, including a stage mother's grandiose boast that Rosie had "gained a world-wide reputation for her prized performance."[3] In the late 1890s, a story came to light about a performance in autumn 1876 and Rosie having been "overcome by a sudden rush of blood to the brain and for a time death was feared."[4] This incident supposedly ended Rosie's theatrical dreams, but no records or evidence validating the claim have ever been found.

At one point in her letter to the Reeds, Myra showed a flash of temper when she chastised Sol Reed, her slain husband's brother. She was disappointed that Sol had not returned to Texas to confront John Morris, the man who had shot and killed Jim Reed on August 6, 1874, in Lamar County, Texas.[5] Myra's desire for Morris to suffer punishment wasn't fulfilled until years later. In 1880, Morris and his family moved to Erath County, Texas, where he accepted a job as deputy sheriff.[6] Known to drink too much whiskey and turn into a mean drunk, Morris quickly "established a reputation by killing two men."[7] He was not charged and soon moved farther west, and in 1883, he was elected the first sheriff in newly created Reeves County, Texas.[8]

"Sheriff John T. Morris was wrapped tight," was how historian Bob Alexander described the volatile lawman who had served as sheriff for only seven months "before stupidity had overhauled good sense."[9] On August 18, 1885, Morris took a train from Pecos, the county seat, to the town of Toyah, a gathering place with a trading post and saloons frequented by cattlemen and cowboys from area ranches.[10] Morris was already drunk when he got off the train, and he made his way to the Favorite Saloon. He continued to imbibe and became increasingly belligerent.

When Morris brandished his six-gun and threatened other patrons, word was sent to Texas Ranger Captain James T. Gillespie at the nearby tent camp. Gillespie dispatched a sergeant and three rangers to disarm Morris and detain him until he sobered up.[11] When the sergeant asked Morris for his gun, Morris started to shoot. His first shot missed the sergeant, but Morris fired a second shot that struck and killed Ranger Private Thomas P. Nigh.[12] The other rangers returned fire, striking Morris in the chest five times. He was carried to the Field Hotel and died within twenty minutes. It had taken eleven years, but Myra Reed's hunger for revenge against Morris was finally sated.

In 1876, however, Myra Reed had very little to look forward to and no good prospects in sight. "Faced only with continued harassment, there was no future for her in Dallas County, and it was time to go elsewhere," wrote Texas historian Rick Miller. "She soon left Dallas, only to return for occasional visits, but never in a manner that caused the community to rise up against her."[13]

By late 1876 or early 1877, Myra Reed finally "shook Dallas dust from her boots" and took leave of Texas.[14] With young Rosie in tow, she traveled north into Indian Territory, perhaps pausing to visit Tom Starr and his family at Younger's Bend on the Canadian River before continuing into Arkansas. By horseback or train, they went to Conway, the seat of Faulkner County.[15] They found suitable quarters near the railroad depot in a "large airy room" at the Conway Hotel, sometimes called the Horton Hotel, built in 1875 by Andrew J. Horton. Guests flocked to the rocking chairs on the wide veranda across the east façade.[16]

Myra and Rosie apparently found the rambling two-story hotel to their liking and stayed there for several months. Most of their time was spent visiting one of Myra's former schoolmates from Carthage who resided near Holland, a hamlet eighteen miles northeast of Conway.[17]

After their stay in Conway, Myra and Rosie headed north into the familiar land of Missouri. They visited the Reed family in Bates County, where Myra's son, Eddie, lived with his grandmother. Rosie likely remained with her brother at the Reed home but occasionally joined her mother to visit some of the places Myra had known as a girl.

They trekked through Jasper County, pausing briefly in Carthage, greatly changed since the Shirley family had fled the horribly ravaged town during the Civil War. The town square, once the site of the Shirley Hotel, had been rebuilt, and an opera house with a capacity of nine hundred graced the south side of the square.[18]

A great wave of temperance had swept over Carthage in the winter of

1877, but that was not the case in nearby Joplin, where more than one thousand lead and zinc mines fueled a boomtown culture.[19] The city had become known as "the liveliest place between the Mississippi River and the Rocky Mountains."[20] Joplin's many saloons—open day and night—quenched the thirst of thousands of miners. Many of them cashed their paychecks with barkeeps before heading to bawdyhouses or gambling dens.[21]

One of those miners with a taste for dice, cards, and fast horses crossed paths with Myra in the late 1870s. His name was Bruce Wilson Younger.[22] They likely met in Joplin or in Galena, Kansas, a rip-roaring mining town just west of the Missouri line.[23] Thus, despite the inaccurate rumors in later years that Myra had a child with Cole Younger or was married to him, she did have an intimate connection to Cole's half uncle. Their relationship and subsequent short-lived marriage ended abruptly and ushered in the period of Myra Reed's life that solidified her mythical image.

"Apparently, Myra was not one of those women who could live alone. Or perhaps eroded self-esteem convinced her that she had no place in the world, except as the companion of an unsuitable man," wrote historian Glenda Riley.[24]

Whether or not Bruce Younger was "suitable" for Myra, his infamous surname proved unsuitable to a great number of people he encountered. Most contemporary newspaper articles and many later writers misidentify Bruce Younger as a cousin or brother of outlaws Cole, Jim, John, and Bob Younger. However, Bruce was the much younger half brother of their father, Henry Washington Younger, son of Charles Lee Younger and Sarah Sullivan Purcell.[25]

Charles Lee Younger (1770–1854) had two children, Milton Toney Younger and Elizabeth Darlisco Younger, by his first wife, Nancy Toney, who was twenty-nine when she died in Kentucky in 1807. Only a month later, Younger married Sarah Sullivan Purcell, and they had five children: Lucy Sullivan Younger, Coleman Purcell Younger, Henry Washington Younger (father of the outlaw Younger brothers), Littleton Purcell Younger, and Sydney Ann Sullivan Younger.[26]

Charles Lee Younger and his "beloved wife"[27] Sarah remained married, but he also had an ongoing relationship with Parmelia Dorcas Wilson, by whom he had nine children: Richard, Adeline (mother of the outlaw Dalton brothers), Charles Franklin, Sophie Lee, Mary Agatha Lee, Martha Jane, Thomas Jefferson, Sophronia Lee, and Bruce. Some of his children with Parmelia used the surname Wilson, and others used Younger.[28]

Younger also fathered two children, Catherine Younger and Simpson Charles Younger, with his enslaved worker Elizabeth Simpson, and had two sons, Nathan and Washington, with an enslaved woman known only by the name of Fanny (Fany).[29]

It is not clear how much contact Bruce Younger had with his half nephews, the outlaw Youngers, most of whom were older than he was. However, the shared surname caused confusion in the public mind and trouble for him on more than one occasion when he was mistakenly identified with the gang. But unlike his outlaw relatives, Bruce Younger did not pursue a career of killing people and robbing banks. His tastes were milder—mostly horse racing and gambling.

Bruce Wilson Younger was born in Osceola, Saint Clair County, Missouri, in 1853, the youngest child of Parmelia Wilson and Charles Lee Younger, who died the next year.[30] By the time he turned nineteen, Bruce was being targeted for his half nephews' illegal activities. In 1872, a newspaper item, probably from Paola, Kansas, states, "Bruce Younger, a cousin [half uncle] of the Younger brothers, was arrested at Joplin [Missouri] last Monday on the charge of being concerned with the Missouri Pacific train robbery. Younger has frequented the saloons in Paola the last six months."[31]

Hobbs Kerry was arrested and later confessed to the robbery of more than $15,000 from a Missouri Pacific train at Otterville, Missouri, on July 7, 1876. He named the other robbers but was still sentenced to four years. Kerry named Bruce Younger as an accomplice, which led to Younger's arrest in Sedalia, Missouri. A newspaper report dated August 6, 1876, and republished two days later mentioned the confusion in identity and concluded, "Bruce Younger was not present when the robbery was committed."[32]

The same day, August 8, the *Chicago Tribune* reported that Bruce Younger had been released in Sedalia on August 7 on a writ of habeas corpus "and started home last night. . . . He will stop in St. Clair County [Missouri] to visit his brother at Appleton and his mother near Chalk Level."[33] The *Tribune* continued, "Bruce Younger received his education at Georgetown, in this county [Pettis County, Missouri, of which Sedalia is the county seat], and has three times been arrested on false charges."[34]

The *Chicago Tribune* included details of Younger's father's estate and then said, "The Hon. Waldo P. Johnson was the executor of the estate, and Judge McLean [W. A. McClain] was Bruce's guardian. Mr. Johnson sent Bruce to Notre Dame College, in Indiana," but Younger dropped out after about two weeks.[35] In the relaxed journalistic practices of the era, which liberally mixed hearsay and opinion with fact, the *Chicago Tribune* again cited Johnson, who said Younger "went well-dressed . . . if he had $100 in his pocket, the first thing he would do would be to dress in good style and buy a watch."[36]

In August 1876, several other newspapers also mentioned Bruce Younger's arrest as one of the supposed Otterville train robbers.[37] The *State Journal* in Jefferson City, Missouri, said, "Bruce Younger is a young man, about twenty-four [twenty-three] years of age. . . . In his manner and speech he is very determined and prompt."[38]

Although the James-Younger gang's careers as robbers had ended with the disastrous Northfield, Minnesota, raid on September 7, 1876, "bad press" continued to hound Bruce Younger in his relatively harmless pursuits, as exemplified in Kansas's *Empire City Echo* on June 20, 1878.[39] The *Fort Scott* (Kansas) *Daily Monitor* reported on June 21, 1878, "Mr. Younger says he is sorely aggrieved at the manner in which he is being treated by newspapers, all because he happens to be a cousin [half uncle] of the notorious Younger brothers. . . . Mr. Younger was employed in Deland & Bacon's mill in this city several years ago, and has been employed at other places in this country, and nothing wrong has been shown up against him. All he asks, like a common citizen, is for the press to let him alone."[40]

Like Bruce Wilson Younger, Myra Reed also fell victim to scurrilous press reports. She and Younger both liked horses and racing, so that would have been another tie between them.[41] They were both raised by privileged parents, had multiple sets of half siblings (including some of color), a good education, and a love of fine clothes. Myra also knew Younger's half nephews, the outlaw Younger brothers.

By the late 1870s, Bruce Younger and Myra Reed were living together in Missouri and Kansas hotels, according to some sources. Vance Randolph,[42] writing under the pseudonym William Yancey Shackleford, stated in his book *Belle Starr, the Bandit Queen*, "In 1879 Belle [Myra Maibelle Shirley Reed] appeared at Galena, Kan.—a tough mining-camp a few miles west of Joplin, Mo. Mr. Riley Robinson, retired mining man of Joplin, told me in 1938 that he had often seen Belle in Galena."[43]

Shackleford goes on to quote Robinson's description of Myra: "She was a brunette, medium height, about 130 pounds, well built and shapely. She was not so chunky as the pictures of her that I have seen. She dressed just like the other young women—nothing loud or flashy. She was a good rider, but so were all the women in the country at that time. I never saw her carrying a rifle or wearing a pistol. Belle had a bad reputation all right, even in that tough camp, but I don't know exactly how she got it. Mostly because she run around with Bruce Younger, I reckon. Bruce and Belle lived together in several places here in Joplin, but mostly they stayed at the Evans Hotel in North Galena."[44]

In the interview by Shackleford, Robinson categorized Bruce Younger as a "tinhorn gambler" and said he had never heard whether Younger and Myra Reed were legally married at that time. In Shackleford's book, Robinson described Galena's colorful early years: "'Galena was full of money in the boom times. . . . There was a lot of robbing and fighting and killing and hell-raising all the time. The biggest honkey-tonk in town was called the Round Top, and most of the saloons, dancehalls, whorehouses and gambling joints were on Redhot Street. Belle Starr and Bruce Younger were well known on Redhot Street.'"[45]

Shackleford continued: "Also in 1938 I interviewed Sam Evans, former sheriff at Galena, Kan., whose father was the owner of the Evans Hotel mentioned by Riley Robinson. Mr. Evans . . . admitted that Belle had lived for some time in the Evans Hotel, in 1878 or 1879, and that he remembered her very well indeed. 'Her mother was with her part of the time,' said Mr. Evans. 'Also her brother Doc, that some people called Shug [Cravens, or John Alva Shirley]. And her daughter Pearl was there for a while, too, when she was about eight or nine years old.'"[46]

When Shackleford asked Evans about Bruce Younger, Evans "made a wry face but admitted that Bruce had lived in the hotel while Belle was there. He said that he had never heard of Bruce Younger and Belle being married. As to whether they lived together as man and wife, he said that he didn't know, adding that people minded their own damn' business in those days. 'Bruce Younger was just a cheap gambler who played the joints on Redhot Street,' said Mr. Evans, 'and I never paid him any mind.'"[47] Evans described Myra: "She was a mighty good-lookin' woman, well educated, quietly dressed. She was not tough like the newspapers made out . . . and she wasn't loud and vulgar like the girls are nowadays."[48]

Shackleford continued his interviews with those who allegedly had brushed shoulders with the couple in Galena. "After seeing Evans I called on Mr. W. L. Lumbley, police judge at Galena. He was about 70 years old and said that he had often seen Bruce Younger and Belle Starr in Galena when he was a young man. He had heard a lot of talk about them and figured that they were mighty good people to let alone. Belle was always quietly dressed and well behaved so far as he could see, but she had a bad reputation. 'There was lots of tough people here in them days,' said Mr. Lumbley, 'and probably Bruce and Belle were no worse than the rest of them.'"[49]

One wonders whether the later lurid publicity about Myra and about Bruce Younger colored the reminiscences of those three Galena men quoted by Shackleford almost sixty years after they had known the couple. For example, they referred to her as "Belle Starr," which was not her name when they had observed her in Kansas.

Several years later, the *Galena* (Kansas) *Weekly Republican* mentioned Myra: "In the early day of Short Creek made her headquarters at the Evans house, then situated immediatly [sic] west of where the smelter now stands. She is or then claimed to be, a sister to 'Doc Shirley' who was connected with a gang of counterfeiters and who was implicated in the burning of the Empire house, in Empire City. A full account of the affair appeared in the *Republican* at the time. Belle was rather an attractive woman."[50] Other parts of the article are a prime example of a blend of fact and sensational fiction.

～

SHUG (DOC) SHIRLEY WENT on the scout with some other Texas misfits such as Columbus (Lum) and Dave McCommas, younger brothers of Myra Reed's former running mate Mike McCommas. Shug was often in trouble with the law in Texas, including arrest on an unknown charge in 1876, two arrests for "assault to murder" in 1877, and theft of a mule in 1882 (charge dismissed).[51] It is interesting that Doc Shirley's name was "connected with a gang of counterfeiters" in Kansas, just as Myra's husband Jim Reed's had been in California a decade earlier.

In September 1878, a John Shirley—Shug's name—was linked with Lizzie Hall, a young Dallas girl who had given birth to a baby supposedly fathered by Shirley. "Anxious to get rid of it she called in the services of a negro woman, who attempted to dispose of it, saying its mother had fled the city," according to news reports.[52] "Reporters traced the matter up, and the girl's mother was prevailed upon to take the child and care for it. It is the result of an amour with John Shirley, a dashing beau, who promises to do the fair thing. The affair is town talk."[53]

～

NO DOCUMENTATION FOR A marriage between Bruce Wilson Younger and Myra Maibelle Reed has been found before 1880, but an item from the *Pleasanton* (Kansas) *Observer-Enterprise* on July 19, 1879, states, "Bruce Younger stopped in Pleasanton Saturday long enough to engage a team and start for Pleasant Gap, Mo., where his wife had been visiting. He returned shortly and with his wife is still in Pleasanton. He is made somewhat notorious by reason of his bearing the same name and being a half-brother or cousin [half uncle] of the outlawed 'Younger brothers' of Missouri."[54]

Pleasant Gap was a small town in Bates County, Missouri, the county where Myra Reed's former mother-in-law, Susan Brock Reed, resided.

Myra's son, Eddie, had been living with his Grandmother Reed for several years. It is conceivable that Myra could have been visiting the area, if indeed she was the "wife" referred to in the newspaper article.

In the new decade of the 1880s, the press continued to find Bruce Younger newsworthy, even in small matters. A short item in the *Burlington (Kansas) Democrat* on April 2, 1880, rather gloated on his gambling loss during a visit to that town.[55] Younger's mere presence in a town sparked interest. The "Little Locals" column in the *Parsons (Kansas) Daily Eclipse* on April 7, 1880, was filled with items such as "New potatoes are scarce," "The usual runaway is missing to-day," and "The school bonds carried by a large majority," and one item announced succinctly: "Bruce Younger has returned to the city."[56]

Younger moved on quickly. Only two days later, on April 9, 1880, the *Neodesha (Kansas) Free Press*, said, "Bruce Younger, a sport [gambler] and a cousin [half uncle] of the Younger boys, spent a few days among the sports."[57] The *Junction City (Kansas) Weekly Union* reported on May 8, 1880, a Saturday, that "Bruce Younger, a cousin [half uncle] of the notorious Younger boys of Missouri, has been in Junction City since last Monday."[58]

Five days later, the same newspaper published a longer article with the headline "Bruce Younger." The *Weekly Union* article started out, "This gentleman has been in town about a week, stopping with J. L. Parker of this city. The first news of his presence caused a little amusing trepidation in business circles."[59]

Right after that article was published in Junction City, in northeastern Kansas, Bruce Younger returned to southeastern Kansas. On May 15, 1880, S. L. Coulter, probate judge of Labette County, Kansas, issued a marriage license for Bruce Younger, aged twenty-seven, of Saint Clair County, Missouri, and Maibelle Reed, aged twenty-three [thirty-two], of Vernon County, Missouri. John P. Shields, justice of the peace, certified that he married the two that same day in Chetopa, Labette County, Kansas. The date when the completed marriage certificate was returned to the probate judge was written faintly, but it appears to be May 15 or possibly May 18.[60]

If we can assume that "Maibelle Reed" was indeed Myra Reed, she was not twenty-three years old but thirty-two. It was typical of her to reduce her age by several years. No record has been found of another person named "Maibelle Reed" who might have married Bruce Younger. However, one twentieth-century Younger family member speculated casually on the possibility that the bride "just might have been a Reed in her own right," meaning Reed could have been her maiden name rather than a previous married name.[61] The choice of Vernon County, Missouri, listed on the marriage license as the place of residence of the bride, was not too far-fetched. Some of Myra's Reed in-laws lived there, and she seems to have been on good terms with them and might have spent time there.

The marriage eventually made the newspapers in a rather businesslike legal context. The *Labette County Democrat* in Oswego, Kansas, reported on June 4, 1880, "Judge Drake has turned over the docket, books and papers to Judge Shields. The first official act of Judge Shields was to unite in marriage Mr. Bruce Younger and Maibelle Reed, both of Missouri."[62]

The same issue of the *Labette County Democrat* carried a list of marriage licenses issued in probate court from May 1 to June 1, 1880. The names of fifteen couples were listed, including Bruce Younger and Maibelle Younger. The other fourteen brides, however, were listed under the names they had used before they married. Perhaps because the couple had lived together before marriage, Maibelle might have already been using Younger's name.[63]

An identical list of marriage licenses issued by "Probate Judge Coulter" was published elsewhere in Labette County, in the *Parsons Weekly Sun*, on June 10, 1880. Again, it showed the couple's names as Bruce Younger and Maibelle Younger.[64]

Despite an often-repeated lurid tale that Myra followed Bruce Younger to Kansas, forced him to marry her at gunpoint, and then he immediately vanished, the two obviously had lived together in Kansas for a few years before they married. Perhaps Myra was pregnant, suspected she was, or wanted Younger to think she was. She might have persuaded him to marry her, but he then had second thoughts. Or he might have viewed it as a ruse to force him into matrimony, and he escaped in anger. If that is true, what happened with the pregnancy? Myra had no known children

Office of Probate Judge S. L. Coulter, "true copy" of marriage license for Bruce Younger and Maibelle Reed, May 15, 1880.

after the death of her first husband, but she could have had a miscarriage or abortion that was not mentioned in any records.

Sadly and perplexingly, by the time the list of marriage licenses was published in Parsons on June 10, the union of Bruce Younger and Myra Shirley Reed had already ended, and both had left the area. On June 24, Younger's name was included in a list of people who had unclaimed mail at the post office in Girard, Crawford County, Kansas, "for the week ending June 3, 1880. . . . If not called for in 30 days, they will be sent to the Dead Letter Office Washington, D. C."[65]

The two probably did not obtain a divorce, although Kansas was known for relatively liberal divorce laws at the time. Compared with some other states, Kansas had shorter waiting periods to establish residency and for a divorce to become final, and women petitioners were "not necessarily looked at unfavorably."[66] Divorce laws remained the same in the state from 1868 until 1909.[67] The statutes listed ten grounds for divorce.[68] The right to remarry was "acquired at the end of six months."[69]

Labette County does not have any divorce or annulment record for Myra and Bruce Younger,[70] and on a statewide basis, Kansas did not record divorces before 1951.[71] Likewise, Missouri did not record divorces statewide before 1948.[72] A search of marriage and divorce records in several counties in western Missouri and southeastern Kansas does not show any marriages or divorces for Bruce Younger and any woman,[73] nor do Cherokee Nation records.[74]

Could Younger have been a bigamist, and Myra was outraged when she found out about it and kicked him out? If she and Younger had contracted a bigamous marriage, perhaps they would not have found it necessary to file for a divorce or annulment from each other. One can only guess at the emotional and legal issues that might have been involved.

CHAPTER 19

The Birth of Belle Starr

MYRA REED'S SHORT-LIVED MARRIAGE TO BRUCE Younger was one of the more puzzling and inexplicable episodes in her turbulent life. Even more baffling was that only three weeks after her civil wedding to Younger, Myra married once again.

On June 5, 1880, Myra Reed wed Samuel (Sam) Starr in the Canadian District of the Cherokee Nation in Indian Territory.[1] Starr was a son of Tom Starr, whom Jim Reed had associated with in various illegal dealings in Indian Territory. That was when Myra became acquainted with Sam Starr and his family. Her choice of a third husband surprised many of her family and friends, especially those who had not yet heard of the whirlwind marriage to Bruce Younger.

The June 5 ceremony, performed by Canadian District Judge Abe Woodall, joined in marriage "Samuel Starr a citizen of Cherokee Nation age 23 [twenty] years and Mrs. Bell Reed a citizen of the United States age 27 [thirty-two] years."[2] Court clerk H. J. Vann dropped the "e" from Belle's name, and the ages the bride and groom gave were incorrect. Starr was still five months short of his twenty-first birthday, and Belle was more than eleven years older.

The occasion marked the first known use of the name Belle rather than Myra, Maibelle, May Belle, or May. Perhaps she used a different form of her name on the record of marriage with Sam Starr to make it less obvious that she had married another man only three weeks earlier.

Even though official Kansas and Cherokee Nation records exist for the Younger and Starr marriages, several writers remained skeptical for many

The marriage report of Samuel Starr and Mrs. Bell [sic] Reed, June 5, 1880.

years and either denied the Bruce Younger marriage, ignored the documentation of both marriages, or failed to look for more evidence.

There was no question, however, that the day she wed Sam Starr, Myra Shirley Reed Younger became Belle Starr. It would be the name she carried for the rest of her life. *Belle Starr*—it had a ring to it that she liked, and the makers of myth could not ignore it.[3]

Throughout the nineteenth century, White men who had married Indian women and adopted the traditions of their wives were called, in the parlance of the time, "squaw men"—another way of saying they had "turned Injun" or "gone native."[4] It was rare for White women to wed Indian men. Many White people considered such unions scandalous and a threat to their race.

There had been accusations that Belle Starr "had already broken many of the rules of refined feminine behavior, not to mention actual laws," but any disapproval of her marriage was likely less harsh.[5] Some Cherokees had reportedly warned Tom Starr that his son's bride could be troublesome—the stories and rumors that sprang from Belle's past association with Jim Reed were well known in that region—Cherokees intermarried with Whites more than most other tribes did.[6] In addition, Sam Starr, like the rest of his immediate family and many other tribal members, was not a "full-blooded" Cherokee.

"The Starrs of Oklahoma are descendants from those of Chester County, Pennsylvania, formerly of Oldcastle, Ireland, and a little earlier from England," wrote Emmet Starr in his history of the Cherokee Nation. "The name is derived from the Norman word *Starri*, which means hawk."[7]

Belle had married a mixed-race Cherokee man, but that did not mean she had become a tribal member. Five years prior to her marriage to Starr, a Cherokee law declared that all White persons who married Cherokees after November 1, 1875, "acquired no rights of soil or interest in the vested funds of the Nation as citizens."[8]

At the time of the Starrs' marriage, Cherokees still held their land in common. Tribal law provided that title to the land remained with the Cherokee Nation, but individual Cherokee citizens could "stake a farm or ranch on unoccupied communal land anywhere in the Nation."[9] They could lay claim to the land by making "improvements," such as building homes and barns, erecting fences, and clearing fields. If the tract went unused for two years, ownership would revert to the tribe.[10]

The newlyweds briefly "lived in a little box house"[11] just a few miles south of Porum Gap, a community that later merged with another settlement called Starvilla (or Starville) to become the town of Porum.[12] But the Starrs were not there long enough to even plant a garden—most of their time was devoted to searching for available land for a more permanent homesite.

They quickly found just the right spot—a sixty-two-acre tract of wooded hills and open bottomland on the north side of the elbow bend of the Canadian. North of the allotment rose Hi-Early Mountain, named for an early rancher, and at 1,030 feet, the highest point in the area.[13] Six miles west of their land was Briartown and the nearby John Kettle Settlement, named for a respected Cherokee prophet. Sam's parents, Tom and Catherine Reese Starr, and other family members had long resided there.[14]

Sam and Belle dubbed their new home Younger's Bend, the name Tom Starr had coined for the area. Soon the newlyweds began the resurrection of a cedar-log dwelling with a pitched clapboard shingle roof that had been built years before by Dempsey Hannell, an early Cherokee settler.[15]

*Sam and Belle Starr's house at Younger's Bend,
Cherokee Nation, Indian Territory.*

Then a Cherokee named Big Head lived in the abode for an unknown period. According to tellers of tall tales, the old man supposedly buried $10,000 in gold coin on the property. Outlandish stories were perpetuated that Sam and Belle Starr, among others, diligently dug countless holes in search of Big Head's cache of gold, but to no avail.[16]

The Starrs likely had no time to look for hidden treasure when they moved in. One of Sam Starr's numerous cousins, who had been the last occupant of the one-room cabin, had left the place in disarray.[17] It remained structurally sound and had good bones but required plenty of work to make it habitable.

Although referred to as a log cabin, the structure was a log house. Cabins typically were built of round logs with most of the bark left on, but most log houses had a more finished look, with logs that had been hewed square by an adze and axe. The puncheon floor—heavy slabs of split timber dressed smooth on one side—was solid as bedrock.[18]

"The house was not far from the old Briartown-Eufaula Trail, and stood on a little knoll, facing south," wrote Frederick Samuel Barde, "the dean of Oklahoma journalism," after one of his visits to the Younger's Bend area. His detailed descriptions of the Starr residence and property appeared in various newspapers in the late 1890s.[19] His dispatches and a feature article with accompanying photographs published in the September 1910 issue of *Sturm's Oklahoma Magazine* are considered the most accurate on-site descriptions of the Starr home and area.[20] Barde wrote:

> The single log room was about fourteen feet square, with an old-fashioned fireplace on the west side. The rafters were scarcely seven feet from the floor. To the north was a lean-to kitchen of boards, divided into two small rooms, under which was a cellar. Two small windows, mere lookouts, let in the light; one on the right of the door, and the other beside the fireplace. The veranda that stretched across the entire front of the house was within fifty feet of the timber. . . . Westward several hundred yards lay the yellow river, implacable, dangerous, its waters running among its quicksands. On the opposite side of the Canadian, precipices towered abruptly toward the sky, and there in perfect concealment the gentry that frequented the Starr home lodged by day and kept watch over all the surrounding country.[21]

Barde was fortunate to have seen the Starr home when it was still habitable. He also found various people living in the area who had known Belle and Sam Starr and were willing to share their memories. During visits with Barde, they recalled the white calico cloth with small floral designs that Belle had used to paper the interior walls of the main room. They told him of the portraits of Belle's family and friends, a rack of buck antlers hanging above the fireplace, bear rugs on the puncheon floor, and a shelf of books, including some belonging to Belle's father, John Shirley, that she had saved.[22]

Belle planted a maple sapling on each side of the gate. Over time, they grew to be large trees that offered relief from the scorching summer sun. Less than two hundred yards from the house, a hand-dug well supplied cold, clear water from a "never failing spring."[23] A picket fence enclosed the well, and a watering trough quenched the thirsts of the Starrs' horses. Sam Starr placed a wooden platform over the well to keep out drifting sand

and debris.[24] With help from nearby Starr relatives, Sam built a corncrib and smokehouse and erected corrals for horses and milch cows. He and Belle planted a vegetable garden and cleared three acres for a cornfield.[25]

The Starrs had created a snug haven. It would be their family home for the rest of their lives.[26]

Soon after Belle's daughter Rosa Lee Reed turned twelve in September 1880, she left her Reed relatives in Missouri, where she had been living, and joined Belle and Sam in Indian Territory.[27] Belle's nine-year-old son, James Edwin Reed, best known as Eddie, did not accompany his sister to Younger's Bend but remained with his Grandmother Reed in Missouri, where he would spend much of his boyhood.[28]

Because of her mother's fleeting marriage to Bruce Younger earlier in the year, Rose had sometimes used the Younger surname and continued to do so. For many years, she went by Pearl Younger or Pearl Starr before returning to her original surname of Reed later in life. Belle also sometimes referred to her daughter as her "Canadian Lily," evidently because of her residence on the Canadian River.[29]

Happily reunited with her mother, Pearl helped with chores and rode her well-groomed horse to the log schoolhouse with a clapboard roof just east of Briartown.[30] It was a subscription school, meaning each pupil's family paid a modest tuition of one dollar per month. Mostly Indian or mixed-race children attended, but only for a few months each year because they were needed at home to help with harvests and roundups.[31] Students sat on split-log benches in one small room heated by a large "stick-and-mud" chimney.[32] The school bore no resemblance to the Carthage Female Academy where Pearl's mother had studied foreign languages, music, and art. Pearl's curriculum was basic reading, writing, and arithmetic.

When Pearl wasn't in school, she stayed close to home with Sam and Belle. The Starrs kept mostly to themselves except for visits with kinfolk at Briartown and other small communities in the southern Canadian District and nearby Choctaw Nation.

"Belle did not associate much with her neighbors, nor did she care to," wrote historian Glenn Shirley. "It was her intention then, she wrote years later in a short biographical sketch to John F. Weaver of the *Fort Smith Elevator*, to live a quiet life, a credit to her sex and her family."[33]

In the biographical sketch, Belle wrote:

> After a more adventurous life than generally falls to the lot of woman, I settled permanently in the Indian Territory, selecting a place of picturesque beauty on the Canadian River. There, far from society, I hope to pass the remainder of my life in peace and quietude. So long had I been estranged from the society of women (whom I thoroughly detest) that I thought I would find it irksome to live in their midst. So I selected a place that but few have ever had the gratification of gossiping around. For a short time I lived very happily in the society of my little girl and husband a Cherokee Indian, a son of the noted Tom Starr. But it soon became noised around that I was a woman of some notoriety from Texas, and from that time on my home and actions have been severely criticized. My home became famous as an outlaw ranch long before I was visited by any of the boys who were friends of mine. Indeed, I never corresponded with any of my old associates and was desirous my whereabouts should be unknown to them. Through rumor they learned of it. Jesse James first came in and remained several weeks. He was unknown to my husband, and he never knew until long afterwards that our home had been honored by Jessie's [sic] presence. I introduced Jessie [sic] as one Mr. Williams, from Texas. But few outlaws have visited my home, notwithstanding so much has been said. The best people in the country are friends of mine. I have considerable ignorance to cope with, consequently my troubles originate mostly in that quarter. Surrounded by low down class shoddy whites who have made the Indian country their home to evade paying tax on their land, and who I will not permit to come on my premises. I am the constant theme of their abusive tongues. In all the world there is no woman more persecuted than I am.[34]

The sketch appeared in a lengthy article about Belle published in 1889 that contained little fact but was filled with hearsay, conjecture, and fiction, including the spurious claims that Cole Younger had been Belle's first husband, that she and Jim Reed had not been legally married, and that she had dressed as a man and participated in the San Antonio–Austin stage robbery.[35]

"These would probably have been the kind of unfounded assertions Belle complains about in her text, which makes the juxtapositioning of the two voices—the reporter's and Belle's—so peculiar," wrote folklore scholar Victoria Lee Stefani. "This sketch may have been subjected to some editorial tampering, but for the most part it appears authentic."[36] The belief that Belle had written at least most of the sketch was based in part on comparisons with other writing credited to her.[37]

In the published sketch, Belle clearly hoped to make a case that she had been treated unfairly and victimized by malicious gossipmongers. In response to tales that her home had become an outlaw resort, Belle maintained that she no longer had any contact with "old associates" and did her best to keep her whereabouts unknown.[38] Some people considered that claim disingenuous.

"Outlaws from the states, including the Youngers . . . , had long found the Indian Territory a haven where they were safe from pursuit and could expect to be treated hospitably by Belle's father-in-law, Tom Starr," wrote Stefani. "For Belle to imagine 'the boys' would not learn of her presence there [Younger's Bend] would have been naïve. Still, she might have sincerely hoped to be left alone with her family in 'peace and quietude.'"[39]

SCHOLARS LATER EXPRESSED NO doubts about the validity of Jesse James's stay at the Starr home, but they questioned when. "The time of Jesse's visit to Youngers' Bend is conjecture," wrote historian Glenn Shirley.[40] The most likely time for James to have holed up at Younger's Bend would have been sometime after September 7, 1881. That was after the James gang's last train robbery at Blue Cut, east of Independence, Missouri.[41]

The Blue Cut robbery took place on the fifth anniversary of the disas-

The Younger brothers (from left to right), Bob, Jim, and Cole pose with their sister Henrietta. She was visiting them in the Minnesota State Prison, where they had been incarcerated for thirteen years since the bungled bank robbery in Northfield, Minnesota, on November 26, 1876.

trous raid at Northfield, Minnesota, where the James-Younger gang was shot to pieces in an attempted bank robbery.[42] Two gang members were killed at Northfield, and the James and Younger brothers beat a hasty retreat. Three of the Youngers—Cole, Bob, and Jim—were captured and ended up in the Minnesota State Prison at Stillwater. Bob died of consumption in 1887, and Cole and Jim were paroled in 1901 after having served twenty-five years of their life sentences.[43]

After the botched Northfield robbery, the James brothers kept a low profile until Jesse formed a new gang and resumed train robberies. By October 1881, Jesse James had returned to Missouri from Indian Territory, where he had been planning his next bank robbery. He soon recruited two new gang members, brothers Bob and Charley Ford.[44] It proved to be the worst decision James ever made because the Fords were eager to claim the staggering $10,000 reward offered for James dead or alive—they were just waiting for the right opportunity to make their move.

The opportunity came on April 3, 1882. After breakfast with the Fords, who were guests at James's family residence in Saint Joseph, Missouri, James walked into the parlor and pulled off his coat and two pistols.⁴⁵ When he climbed onto a chair to brush some dust off a picture, Charley winked at Bob, who drew his gun and fired a shot directly into James's head. He tumbled headlong to the floor. Jesse James was thirty-four years old and stone dead.⁴⁶

Except for the mention of his visit to Younger's Bend, there is no record of Belle Starr ever having discussed Jesse James. "In any event, Jesse's visit to Younger's Bend provided the springboard for much novelistic nonsense,"⁴⁷ according to historian Shirley.

In the early 1880s in Indian Territory, however, not all the stories of lawlessness were tall tales—not by a long shot. For many years after the Civil War, outlaws and outcasts found refuge in the territory, where they could nurse wounds, divide loot, and plan future wrongdoing. It was a criminal's paradise and a legal and jurisdictional nightmare. It was said that Indian Territory was "the rendezvous of the vile and wicked from everywhere."⁴⁸

Law-abiding citizens were not immune to the outrages. Neither the companies of Indian lighthorsemen guarding the borders nor Chickasaw and Choctaw vigilantes could quell the rising tide of lawbreakers who flocked to hideouts in the Indian nations. Tribal courts had no jurisdiction over White horse thieves, sex workers, whiskey peddlers, and bushwhackers who poured in.⁴⁹

For many years, the common saying about Indian Territory was, "There is no God west of St. Louis and no law west of Fort Smith." No God, perhaps, but finally a judge did arrive. His name was Isaac C. Parker.⁵⁰

CHAPTER 20

Hell on the Border

ISAAC CHARLES PARKER WAS THIRTY-SIX YEARS OLD WHEN President Ulysses S. Grant appointed him United States District Judge for the Western District of Arkansas, with headquarters at Fort Smith.[1] For years, this Ohio native and Democrat-turned-Republican had resided in Saint Joseph, Missouri. He practiced law, briefly served as a circuit court judge, and represented Missouri in Congress for two terms.[2]

The Western District Court that Parker inherited in March 1875 was in disrepute because of the actions of his predecessor, Judge William Story.[3] Story had accepted bribes and had embezzled and extorted thousands of dollars in undocumented court expenditures. Under threat of impeachment, he quickly moved to Colorado, where he built a large law practice and served one term as lieutenant governor.[4] Judge Henry Clay Caldwell acted as interim judge of the Western District Court until Grant appointed Parker, asking him to "stay a year or two in Fort Smith and get things straightened out."[5]

Parker remained the presiding judge for the next twenty-one years.[6] Parker represented the law west of Fort Smith. At the start of his time on the bench, he held exclusive jurisdiction over much of western Arkansas and all of Indian Territory.

Parker's jurisdiction was approximately 78,500 square miles, including the nineteen western Arkansas counties and Indian Territory. In the 1880s, the Indian Territory jurisdiction was reduced to 22,000 square miles.[7]

To bring order, Parker counted on two hundred United States deputy marshals. It was difficult and dangerous duty. Armed with badges, arrest

Isaac C. Parker served as the federal judge of the Western District of Arkansas from 1875 to 1896.

warrants, Colts, and courage, they patrolled an area about the size of New England.[8] Most of their attention was focused on Indian Territory. Besides tracking down felons, deputies pursued White squatters who violated Indian sovereignty by grazing cattle on tribal lands.

"The introduction of 'spirituous liquors' into Indian Territory was a federal crime, as was timber poaching," wrote historian Stephanie Stegman. "However, the enforcement of such laws proved difficult. The Fort Smith court frequently saw defendants, many of them repeat offenders, charged with whiskey peddling, illicit distillery, and other alcohol-related violations."[9]

Whether a deputy marshal was stalking a hardened criminal or a first-time offender, Parker's standing order remained: "Bring them in alive—or dead."[10] Officers tried to return with live prisoners, for which they could collect expenses and fees.

"If a deputy failed to make an arrest, no matter how long or how much he was out in time and money, he received no payment," wrote National Park Service historian Juliet Galonska. "The paid rate of an arrest was $2.00 regardless of how serious the crime was. Officers were paid the same if they arrested a whiskey peddler or a murderer."[11]

The men who rode for Parker came from various backgrounds. Some were veterans of the Civil War, and others were experienced lawmen. Several deputies had been outlaws or later resorted to crime.[12] According to an 1877 Office of Indian Affairs report, "Some of the present officers of justice clothed with the full authority and majesty of the law, are well-known as formerly horse thieves."[13]

The Dalton brothers, from the outlaw state of Missouri, exemplified lawmen gone rogue. In 1882, the oldest brother, Frank Dalton, was commissioned a United States deputy marshal at Fort Smith. A highly respected law officer, he was killed in the Cherokee Nation while tracking a horse thief and whiskey peddler. Then his brothers Grattan, or Grat, and Bob became deputy marshals, and the youngest, Emmett, rode with several of their posses of law officers.[14]

But by 1890, the Daltons were fed up with the low wages they received for risking their lives in law enforcement—they went on the scout.[15] They knew how to think like criminals. The Daltons eventually formed their own gang and committed successful train robberies. Their luck ran out in 1892 when they attempted to rob two banks at the same time in broad daylight in Coffeyville, Kansas. The townspeople, who had anticipated their arrival, armed themselves, and in the ensuing gun battle, Bob and Grat Dalton were killed.[16] Emmett was wounded, stood trial, and received a life sentence. Pardoned in 1907, he eventually moved to California, where he died quietly in 1937.[17]

Despite knowing that some deputies had been law enforcers and lawbreakers at different times, Parker permitted them and other "officers of variable character and quality" to represent him.[18] Glenn Shirley wrote, "The personal characters of some of his most famous officers would scarcely bear careful scrutiny. But the judge winked at that sort of thing as long as they served the cause of justice in this haven of the worst hellions on earth." What mattered most to Parker was that his men were tough and stood their ground. He could not abide a coward, even if the deputy was "highly moral."[19]

The public had begun to form an impression of the judge before he set foot in Arkansas. Many White citizens suspected that Parker was just another Republican "carpetbagger."[20] It was incumbent on Parker to prove his critics wrong and clean up a crowded criminal docket.

That was precisely what he did. On May 10, 1875, Parker opened the first term of the Fort Smith court and a week later commenced his first federal murder trial.[21] The accused, Daniel Evans, had been charged with the 1874 murder of his companion, nineteen-year-old William Riley Seaboalt Jr., while traveling through the Creek Nation. According to court documents, Evans shot Seaboalt in the head and took his fancy boots and bay horse. United States Marshal John F. Simpson tracked down Evans and brought him to Fort Smith.[22]

On December 10, 1874, Evans's two-day trial resulted in a hung jury because of an eleven-to-one vote for conviction.[23] He was taken back to the communal cells in the dark, dank jail, which had been converted from an old army mess hall and later was referred to as Hell on the Border. The cramped and unsanitary dungeon was in the basement of the courthouse.[24]

Evans did not fare as well at his retrial before Judge Parker. That time, the jury had more than circumstantial evidence to consider. William Riley Seaboalt, the victim's father, had come from Texas as the prosecution's key witness.[25] Seaboalt testified that the boots Evans was wearing were the same boots Seaboalt had given to his son, and he had had a matching pair made for himself. Seaboalt raised his pant legs, exposing boots identical to those the defendant was wearing. Seaboalt explained that a heel had come off his son's left boot. Three horseshoe nails had been used to tack the heel back on, and three more were tacked onto his other boot. When the court bailiff instructed Evans to pull off his boots, those distinctive nails were revealed.[26]

The next morning, after the defense offered rather unconvincing rebuttal testimony and final arguments, Parker gave a lengthy charge of instructions to the jurors and sent them off to decide Evans's fate. They deliberated for less than a half hour before returning with a unanimous verdict: Evans was guilty.[27]

On June 26, Judge Parker pronounced Evans's sentence—death by hanging.[28] Evans was just the first of many defendants who received the ultimate punishment. By the time Parker's first term at the Fort Smith court had concluded, he had sentenced seven more convicted murderers to join Evans on the gallows. Prior to the first mass execution, scheduled for September 3, 1875, one of the eight convicts was shot and killed during an escape attempt, and another was spared because of his youth. His sentence was commuted to life imprisonment.[29]

The week before the execution of the remaining six men, newspaper reporters from surrounding states and Indian Territory flocked to Fort Smith. All the hotels were booked. On September 3, it was estimated that more than five thousand spectators had gathered at the old garrison grounds to witness the hangings.

During a rambling statement to reporters prior to his execution, Evans boasted that he had met Jim and Myra Reed in Texas and had become a member of Jim Reed's gang. Evans maintained that he had taken part in the 1873 torture and robbery of the wealthy Creek rancher Watt Grayson in Indian Territory. He also bragged that he had been present when John Morris shot and killed Reed in Texas in 1874.[30]

"When Jim was killed, I was with him but not in the house," Evans told reporters. "I heard the firing, knew what was up, got on Reed's horse and sloped. Jim was an awful man; large rewards were offered for him in Texas; he had killed over 40 men in his time; he would kill a man for ten dollars."[31]

There was not a shred of truth in any of Evans's claims. Reed had not killed forty men, and Evans had not taken Reed's horse, Rondo, who was returned to Reed's widow, Myra. It is doubtful that Evans ever met Reed. However, once Evans's misinformation was published in the *New York Times* and other newspapers, many people accepted his fantasies as facts.[32] Several authors also promoted the barefaced lie that Belle Starr (Myra Reed at the time of the Grayson robbery) had been at the crime scene dressed as a man.[33]

On the day of his execution, no one present refuted Evans's wild tale. The crowd watched while he and the other five men, wearing black suits, leg irons, and handcuffs, shuffled two abreast to the gallows, which were built of heavy timbers and later dubbed the Gates of Hell.[34] It was the domain of Parker's dour executioner, George Maledon. Eventually

George Maledon, Judge Isaac Parker's dour executioner, was known as the Prince of Hangmen.

known as the Prince of Hangmen, Maledon took great pride in his work, although he was prone to stretching the truth about his record.[35]

"I never hanged a man who came back to have the job done again," he often quipped. "The ghosts of men hanged at Fort Smith never hang around the gibbet."[36]

Maledon carried out the September 3, 1875, mass hanging without a hitch. After the death warrants had been read, the condemned had spoken their last words, and the clergy's prayers were over, the six prisoners—with their arms bound and black hoods over their heads—were lined up on the scaffold death trap. Maledon adjusted the hemp nooses. To ensure quick death, the nooses had been soaked in oil to prevent the hangman's knot with its thirteen wraps from slipping.[37] There was a loud boom as Maledon pulled the lever that sprang the trap door. All six men plunged to their deaths at the end of the ropes.

"Not one struggled," historian Edwin Bearss later wrote. "Maledon had done his work well, every neck was broken by the fall."[38]

The next day, news of the executions quickly spread across the country. A headline in the *New York Times* read:

THE GALLOWS.
SIX MURDERERS EXECUTED.
SKETCHES OF THE CULPRITS AND THEIR CRIMES—ALL REPENT AND JOIN SOME CHURCH AT THEIR LAST.[39]

Parker generally ignored news coverage and focused on his demanding judicial duties. He faced a burgeoning caseload that had grown so large that he held court every day except Sunday, often working more than ten hours a day to clear the docket.[40]

During the November 1875 term of court, six more men were convicted of murder; again, only one was commuted. They faced Maledon on the gallows on April 21, 1876, and were followed by four more convicts five months later. On three occasions during his first year at Fort Smith, Parker sent fifteen men to their deaths "upon the forbidding gallows at Fort Smith, a formidable device that could accommodate twelve victims simultaneously," according to historian Larry Ball.[41]

During Parker's twenty-one years as federal judge at Fort Smith, he presided over 13,490 cases. In more than 8,500 cases, the defendant either pleaded guilty or was convicted. In the 344 capital-crime cases Parker heard, however, of the 160 defendants who received a death sentence, only 79 were ultimately sent to the gallows.[42] Those well-publicized hangings perpetuated Parker's "posthumous yet fiercely unshakable moniker of 'Hanging Judge.'"[43]

Notorious for making arbitrary rulings to clear the crowded dockets, Parker also was accused of intimidating witnesses and leading juries with questionable evidence in his often lengthy court instructions, especially in cases of self-defense. Parker believed that most wrongdoers who claimed self-defense were attempting to evoke sympathy from the jury.[44]

Parker refused to back down from the challenges of his job or acknowledge his inability to adapt to changing legal standards. He believed that his court was "the humble instrument to aid in the execution of that divine justice which has ever decided that he who takes what he cannot return—human life—shall lose his own."[45]

ALTHOUGH MOST OF THE defendants who appeared before Parker were men, it likely surprised no one that Belle Starr eventually ended up in his courtroom. The two figures, forever linked in frontier folklore, seemed destined to meet.

That first face-to-face encounter occurred in 1883 when Belle and her codefendant, husband Sam Starr, stood before Parker accused of horse theft. Although it had been said that those who stole horses were "lower than snakes, vermin, as good and dirty rotten as one can get in life," their crime was not a capital offense—at least not in federal court.[46]

Nonetheless, the Starrs had to prove their innocence. But if they were found guilty, there was hope that the "Hanging Judge" would muster a modicum of compassion.

Judge Isaac Parker had heard about Belle Starr soon after his arrival in Fort Smith when she was still Myra Reed, living in Texas as the wife of outlaw Jim Reed. Many of the stories Parker heard were tall tales.

By spring 1882, there were whispers that Belle Starr's lifelong attraction to horses—a passion shared with Sam Starr—extended beyond their own horses to those owned by others. The Starrs' suspected covetous behavior led to a disagreement between kinfolk and neighbors that probably could have been settled outside court. Instead, it escalated into a federal case, with the Starrs facing larceny charges for horse theft. They were accused of stealing a gray mare from Sam Campbell and a bay horse from Andrew Crane on April 20, 1882, during the spring roundup near Younger's Bend.[47]

For many years, because of the Cherokees' system of communal land ownership, all their livestock grazed on the open range, with cattle and horses roaming and mingling freely. Each fall and spring, area ranch hands joined in a community roundup and sorted the livestock by brand or mark.[48] The various horse owners then took their herds to market. In 1882, the Starrs planned to sell many of their horses in McAlester, more than seventy miles away in the Choctaw Nation.[49]

While gathering horses during the April roundup, Belle asked John

Calhoun West, her husband's second cousin, if she could temporarily pen some horses in his corral.[50] West was half Irish and half Cherokee and for a time had operated a ferry across the Canadian River with his younger brother, Franklin Pierce West. Sarah Harlan, the Wests' grandmother, was the sister of Sam Starr's great-grandmother Nancy Harlan.[51]

"West agreed to help Belle, since he apparently expected to share in the proceeds," wrote historian Edwin C. Bearss. "Then he spotted a large bay horse with a star on its forehead and a rope mark on its left foreleg. This animal, as John and Belle knew, belonged to Andrew Crane, a cripple who lived nearby."[52]

West later stated that he had told Belle to get the horse back to Crane, and likewise, when he spied the Campbell horse in the corral, he urged the Starrs to return it too. They did not heed his words. Crane met with the Starrs and West and demanded the return of his gaited horse or payment of eighty-five dollars. The result was an argument between the Starrs and West. They talked about splitting the cost, but ultimately West refused to contribute. After the horses were sold and weeks of stalemate had passed with no compensation in sight, Crane and Campbell sought relief and brought charges against Belle and Sam Starr in Fort Smith, Arkansas.[53]

On July 31, 1882, Cassius M. Barnes, chief deputy United States marshal at Fort Smith and a future governor of Oklahoma Territory,[54] signed a writ for United States Commissioner Stephen Wheeler. The writ swore to the Starrs' "felonious theft of a horse belonging to one Andrew Crane, a non-citizen resident of the Cherokee Nation" on April 20, 1882.[55]

Based on a report that the Starrs were not at Younger's Bend but were traveling in the Cherokee Nation's Cooweescoowee District, the arrest warrants were dispatched to Lemuel Walker Marks, a deputy marshal based in the town of Vinita.[56] Marks and another deputy set out to arrest the Starrs and bring them to Fort Smith.

Finding the Starrs was no easy task. Because of "the conflicting reports of people along the way," the lawmen did not locate and arrest the Starrs until September 21—almost two months after the warrants had been issued.[57] The pursuit ended without incident near Bird Creek on the brink of the rolling tallgrass prairies and dense thickets of blackjack oaks of the Osage Hills. Commonly called "the Osage," it was an ideal sanctuary for outlaws on the scout.[58]

"The dependable Deputy Marshal L. W. Marks made the arrest at a Negro's cabin near the Osage line," wrote Bearss. "Sam and Belle came in without a struggle, hoping they would be released after a preliminary hearing before the United States Commissioner."[59]

In Fort Smith, the Starrs made bail and immediately attained the services of Cravens & Marcum, a prominent law firm led by two seasoned defense attorneys—Thomas Marcum and William Murphy Cravens.[60] A Kentucky native whose paternal grandfather had been a close companion of Daniel Boone, Marcum had served as a federal colonel in the Civil War.[61] In 1871, Marcum moved to Fort Smith to practice criminal law in the federal court.[62]

The other half of the Starrs' defense team was perhaps even more important to the couple's fate because of William Cravens's ties to Belle Starr that dated to her childhood in Missouri. That relationship remained undiscovered until now and consequently has never been included in the books and articles about Belle Starr.

Cravens was born in 1833 in Fredericktown, Missouri, but grew up southwest of Carthage in Sarcoxie, in Jasper County.[63] When the county was founded in 1841, his father, Jeremiah Cravens, was appointed one of the first three county judges.[64] While Judge Cravens was serving as the presiding judge of the county court, it is probable that he had occasion to frequent the dining room of John Shirley's hotel on the public square and become acquainted with the Shirley family.

William Cravens attended Spring River School in the oldest school district in Jasper County and later enrolled at Arkansas College (now the University of Arkansas) in Fayetteville.[65] After graduation, Cravens returned to Jasper County and briefly taught at the tuition school in the Masonic Hall above a store on the northwestern corner of the Carthage public square.[66] One of his students was the bright young daughter of the proprietor of the nearby hotel, Myra Shirley.[67] It is possible, although unproved, that Myra's youngest brother, Cravens, born in 1858, was named for Carthage schoolteacher William Cravens.[68]

Cravens was accepted at the Cumberland University Law School in Lebanon, Tennessee.[69] By 1860, he had earned his degree and was back in Missouri, practicing law in Neosho.[70] In 1861, Cravens became the prosecuting attorney for an eight-county region, but his legal work was postponed when war broke out. Espousing the southern cause, Cravens volunteered as a private when the state militia was called out. He fought for the Confederacy at Carthage and Wilson's Creek.[71] By 1867, Cravens's law practice was established. It flourished for more than fifty years.[72]

On October 9, 1882, Cravens and Marcum accompanied the Starrs to the preliminary hearing before Commissioner Stephen Wheeler, who also served as clerk of the court and had issued the Starrs' arrest warrants in July.[73] As district court commissioner, Wheeler was empowered to subpoena witnesses to judicial proceedings, to administer oaths, and to take depositions. After reviewing all the sworn testimony, Wheeler determined whether there was enough evidence to warrant sending the case to the grand jury for further consideration. If he found that the evidence was insufficient, he was obliged to dismiss the charges and allow the accused to walk free.[74]

During the Starrs' two-day hearing, Wheeler heard from defense and prosecution witnesses, including the two plaintiffs and some of the Starr family, among them Sam's father, Tom Starr.[75] But the Starrs were disappointed. On October 10, Wheeler ruled that more than enough evidence existed to refer the Starrs to the grand jury for further action. Wheeler also ordered the Starrs to be taken into custody. He set their bail at $1,000 each, which Tom Starr and his brother, James Starr Jr., promptly posted. Sam and Belle Starr immediately returned to Younger's Bend and waited for the grand jury to convene.[76]

On November 6 and 7, the Fort Smith grand jury listened to additional witness testimony and returned a true bill of indictment "for larceny in the Indian Country."[77] The Starrs' bail was continued, allowing them to remain free until their case went to trial in February 1883.

Another skilled attorney, Benjamin T. Duvall—a former Confederate officer and Arkansas legislator—joined Cravens and Marcum in preparation for what promised to be a high-profile proceeding.[78] On November

9, the Starrs' attorneys filed an application for witnesses in the US Court for the Western District of Arkansas, which included Indian Territory. Several people on the defense list had appeared at previous hearings. Although their testimony had not won over the commissioner or grand jury, the Starrs' lawyers had faith in them as credible alibi witnesses.[79]

The Starrs' trial on two felony charges of larceny commenced on February 15, 1883—ten days after Belle's thirty-fifth birthday—in the United States Court for the Western District of Arkansas. Not a seat in the courtroom was vacant. Prosecuting attorney William H. H. Clayton presented the case for the United States. When Judge Parker asked for the defendants' plea, the Starrs, flanked by their attorneys, pleaded not guilty. "Twelve good and lawful men of the District," selected as jurors, had already been sworn in and waited for the proceedings to begin.[80] All were White male citizens of Arkansas.

Curious onlookers strained to catch a glimpse of Belle Starr. Newspapers were ready for the trial, considered by many observers and reporters as "the most interesting that has engaged the attention of this court for a long time."[81] Based solely on hearsay, the *Fort Smith New Era* presented an exaggerated description of Belle that became fodder for the gossip mill. According to the newspaper, "The very idea of a woman being charged with an offense of this kind and that she was the leader of a band of horse thieves and wielding power over them as their queen and guiding spirit, was sufficient to fill the courtroom with spectators."[82]

During the four-day trial, multiple witnesses offered testimonies for the prosecution and the defense. After two days of listening to prosecutor Clayton interrogate witnesses and present his case against the Starrs, the defense lawyers enjoyed some success by arguing their clients' citizenship. They contended that the Western District Court could not legally hear criminal cases between members of Indian nations. The defense also conceded that Belle was under Parker's authority, despite her marriage to Sam, because she was a White woman. But they pointed out that Sam Starr was in another category, as a Cherokee charged with the theft of a horse owned by Campbell, also a citizen of the Cherokee Nation. Consequently, Parker dismissed the theft charge against Sam on a technicality.

Crane, however, proved to the court that despite some Indian blood, he lived as a White man in Indian Territory, so the horse-theft charge against Sam and Belle Starr remained intact.[83]

The defense then tried a ploy that had proved unsuccessful in the previous hearings. They explained that the Starrs could not have stolen Crane's horse in late April 1882 because Starr was "down sick" with measles from March until late May, and his wife had remained at his bedside most of that time.[84]

The defense questioned several witnesses who swore that Starr had been laid up at his father's home in Briartown when the horses went missing. Tom and Sam Starr testified, but that was disastrous.[85] They seemed confused and struggled to recall dates and details, even during direct testimony. The measles alibi quickly fell apart in cross-examination when Clayton pressed Sam and Tom Starr about their lapses of memory and contradictory statements.[86]

Belle chose not to testify in her own defense, but throughout the trial, she remained attentive and frequently dashed off notes for her lawyers. She occasionally glared at the prosecutor, especially when Clayton pressed her husband on the witness stand.[87]

"Once when allusion was made to Jim Reed, her former husband and the father of her child [children], tears welled up in her eyes and trickled down her cheeks, but they were quickly wiped away and the countenance resumed its wonted appearance,"[88] reported one newspaper.

In a last-ditch effort to cause reasonable doubt that the Starrs bore any guilt, Cravens and Marcum launched an attack on the credibility of John West, the prosecution's key witness. "But West held firm and held to his story, Judge Parker and District Attorney Clayton helping him a little," wrote Bearss. "The fate of the defendants was sealed in the minds of the jury."[89]

On February 19, the prosecution and defense presented final arguments and rested. The jurors received the charge of the court and retired to consider the Starrs' fate. After less than an hour, the jurors shuffled back to the courtroom with their verdict. It was unanimous and came as no surprise. The Starrs were found guilty of horse theft—Belle on both counts and Sam on one. Judge Parker immediately revoked the Starrs' bail and committed them to jail to await the final sentence.[90]

On March 8, in separate sentencings, Sam Starr and Belle Starr were given the chance to state why the sentence should not be imposed, but neither had anything further to add. Parker ordered the Starrs to pay all court costs and to be "imprisoned in the House of Correction situated at Detroit in the Eastern District of Michigan." Sam Starr received a one-year term and Belle two six-month terms, and both were given the opportunity to obtain early release in nine months for good behavior.[91]

During the trial, Belle had sent her daughter to stay in Oswego, Kansas, with "Mamma Mc" McLaughlin. McLaughlin was an old friend from Belle's time with Bruce Younger, and her family operated hotels in Oswego and Parsons.[92] From her jail cell on March 18, 1883, the eve of the Starrs' departure for prison, Belle wrote a letter to her daughter.[93] The letter was addressed to "Miss Pearl Younger, Oswego, Kansas (My baby)":

My dear little one:—It is useless to attempt to conceal my trouble from you and though you are nothing but a child [Pearl was fourteen years six months old] I have confidence that my darling will bear with fortitude what I will now write.

I shall be away from you a few months baby, and have only this consolation to offer you, that never again will I be placed in such humiliating circumstances and that in the future your little tender heart shall never more ache, or a blush called to your cheek on your mother's account. Sam and I were tried here, John West the main witness against us. We were found guilty and sentenced to nine months at the house of correction, Detroit, Michigan, for which place we start in the morning [March 19]. Now Pearl there is a vast difference in that place and a penitentiary; you must bear that in mind, and not think of mamma being shut up in a gloomy prison. It is said to be one of the finest institutions in the United States, surrounded by beautiful grounds with fountains and everything nice. There I can have my education renewed, and I stand sadly in need of it. Sam will have to attend school and I think it is the best thing ever happened to him, and now you must not be unhappy and brood over our absence. It won't take the time long to glide by and as we come home we will get you and we will have such a nice time.

We will get your horse up and I will break him and you can ride John while I am gentling Loco. We will have Eddie [Reed] with us and will be as gay and happy as the birds we claim at home. Now baby you can either stay with grandma or your Mamma Mc, just as you like and do the best you can until I come back, which won't be long. Tell Eddie that he can go down home with us and have a good time hunting and though I wish not to deprive Marion [Belle's brother-in-law, F. Marion Reed, brother of Jim Reed] and ma of him for any length of time yet I must keep him a while. Love to ma and Marion.

Uncle Tom [probably Sam Starr's father, Tom Starr] has stood by me nobly in our trouble, done everything that one could do. Now baby I will write to you often. You must write to your grandmother but don't tell her of this; and to your Aunt Ellen, Mamma Mc., but to no one else. Remember, I don't care who writes to you, you must not answer. I say this because I do not want you to correspond with anyone in the Indian Territory, my baby, my sweet little one, and you must mind me. Except auntie; if you wish to hear from me auntie will let you know. If you should write me, ma would find out where I am and Pearl, you must never let her know. Her head is overburdened with care now and therefore you must keep this carefully guarded from her.

Destroy this letter as soon as read. As I told you before, if you wish to stay a while with your Mamma Mc., I am willing. But you must devote your time to your studies. Bye bye sweet baby mine.

Belle Starr.[94]

Belle's letter to Pearl first appeared in print in S. W. Harman's book *Hell on the Border*, originally published in 1898, with a note that it was

"Copied from the original." Harman has been accused of often mixing myth and fact, but credible historians and Belle's descendants agree that the letter appears to be authentic.[95]

"The date at the top of the letter [February 1883] is almost certainly wrong and was probably added by Harman, who was the first to reproduce the letter; Belle left for Detroit on March 19," according to folklore scholar Victoria Stefani.[96] Next to the date appeared the word *Pandemonium*, meaning "all demons," the name given by John Milton to the capital of Hell in his poem *Paradise Lost*.[97] If written by Belle or added by Harman, it might have been a reference to the name Fort Smith newspaper editor Valentine Dell had coined for Indian Territory in 1877. "It was a perfect pandemonium . . . swarming with outlaws and malefactors of every description," Dell wrote.[98]

In the letter to Pearl, "Belle sounds much less like a bold desperado than a mother with rather conventional values, who is concerned about her child and worried about what relatives and neighbors might think," wrote Stefani.[99]

In the early morning of March 19, 1883, Belle and Sam Starr started a journey that would take them more than one thousand miles northwest to Detroit, Michigan, on the Canadian border. The simple headline "Gone to Detroit," above the brief article in the *Fort Smith Elevator*, announced the departure of twenty-two federal prisoners, including the Starrs, all bound for the Detroit House of Correction.[100]

"Belle Starr had a repugnance to the *expose* in marching off with the squad of prisoners, she was courteously furnished with a well-dressed guard and escorted to the depot in bon ton style," reported the *Vinita (Indian Territory) Indian Chieftain*.[101]

The shackled prisoners were loaded onto the "regular railroad prison car" known as "Old Ten Spot."[102] US Marshal Barnes and four of his deputies accompanied the prisoners and kept constant vigil all the way to Detroit.[103] On March 20, the prison train passed through Saint Louis, Missouri, as reported in the *St. Louis Post-Dispatch*, and Belle Starr evidently was not given any special courtesy. According to the newspaper:

A BATCH FOR THE PEN.

Col. Cassius Brooks, Chief U. S. Deputy Marshal, and four deputies, passed through the city this morning from Ft. Smith, Ark., to Detroit, in charge of twenty-two United States prisoners, who are remanded to serve out sentences given them at Ft. Smith. The squad was made up of 6 whites, 7 negroes, 8 Indians and 1 woman, whose name is Belle Starr. The sight of a woman chained to a man and driven along to the 'pen' attracted much attention and it was learned from Col. Brooks that she is one of the most notorious characters of the Indian Territory. She has the reputation of being one of the best bareback riders in that country, a fine shot and expert at any manner of devilment. Col. Brooks says that at one time she was the wife of one of the Younger brothers [wife of their half uncle, Bruce Younger]. She and her husband [Sam Starr] are going up for two years [one year] apiece for horse-stealing. The sentences of the others range from one to four years for manslaughter, larceny and selling whisky.[104]

That same day, March 20, 1883, a long letter to the editor about the Detroit House of Correction, signed by M. J. Murphy (whose company had a contract at the prison) and dated March 15, 1883, appeared in the *Detroit Free Press*. The letter was part of an ongoing dispute between Murphy and Superintendent Joseph Nicholson of the House of Correction about whether the prison was paid for the care of prisoners from other states and territories.[105]

The Detroit House of Correction was considered advanced for its time. It was a model for other penal institutions, including the House of Correction in Chicago, which copied its administration and structure, even building its cells the same size as Detroit's. "The Detroit institution was roughly structured in a cross shape. Males occupied the two hundred cells on the left arm of the cross; women were detained in eighty cells on the right side. Each cell was seven feet long and four feet wide. Prisoners labored in large workshops separate from the cell houses,"[106] according to the institution's first annual report.

In the United States in 1880, 9 percent of prisoners were female, but in the West, it was only about 2 percent.[107] Women in the United States were arrested mostly for petty crimes and were housed in local jails rather than prisons. Most crimes committed by women involved drunkenness, prostitution, and petty larceny, but women were also arrested on charges of abortion, infanticide, murder, and other crimes.[108]

During the 1880s, when Sam and Belle Starr were incarcerated in the House of Correction, male prisoners worked ten-hour shifts manufacturing chairs. Female prisoners did laundry, mended clothing, made shirts, and wove cane seats for the chairs the male prisoners made.[109] Night classes were held, and Saturday afternoon lectures and musical performances were provided.[110] Attending night classes was evidently not optional. In Belle's purported letter to her daughter, quoted above, she mentions, "Sam will have to attend school." It is interesting to speculate on whether the prisoners were performers or audience members at the musical performances—or both. Perhaps Belle put her keyboard skills to use.

Invented accounts of Belle's time in Detroit that later appeared in print described her life behind bars as one of ease because of her prowess at charming the warden and prison matrons. "After her first month of servitude Belle was given the freedom of the place, scarcely any tasks being assigned to her, but poor Sam, who knew not how to charm by his individuality, was compelled to put in the regulation hours at labor," wrote Harman in *Hell on the Border*.[111]

Harman also promoted the notion that the warden was so impressed with Belle's intellect that he "offered to suspend the rules in her case and permit her the untrammeled use of pen, ink and paper in return for her promise to write a book during her term of imprisonment."[112] There is no evidence that Belle ever wrote an account of prison life.

Belle might not have had the run of the prison, but she "made a point of being a likeable, cooperative inmate."[113] Prisoner records at the Detroit House of Correction gave the following information on Belle and Sam Starr:

Belle Starr: *date of admission*: March 21, 1883; *age*: 29 [thirty-five]; *offence*: larceny; *by whom/where convicted*: U. S. Arkansas; *nativity*:

California [Missouri]; *occupation:* domestic; *color:* white; *habits of life:* temperate; *intellectual education:* read and write; *religious education:* Protestant; *health on admission:* good; *sentence:* 1 year; *expiration of sentence:* March 28 [March 8], 1884; *good time expiration of sentence:* good time; *date of discharge:* January 28, 1884; *prior commitment:* [blank]; *weight when received:* 140; *weight when discharged:* 140; *remarks:* sentenced March 8, 1883.[114]

Samuel Starr: *date of admission:* March 21, 1883; *age:* 23; *offence:* larceny; *by whom/where convicted:* U. S. Arkansas; *nativity:* Indian Territory; *occupation:* farmer; *color:* white; *habits of life:* intemperate; *intellectual education:* read and write; *religious education:* Catholic; *health on admission:* good; *sentence:* 1 year; *expiration of sentence:* March 8, 1884; *good time expiration of sentence:* good time; *date of discharge:* January 28, 1884; *prior commitment:* [blank]; *weight when received:* 138; *weight when discharged:* 147; *remarks:* sentenced March 8, 1883.[115]

Several things are of interest in the prison register. Belle, as usual, erased years off her age. Sam Starr was classified as White rather than Indian (he had Cherokee and White ancestry). Belle did not describe herself as a drinker, but her husband evidently admitted that he was. Although some writers have said Belle gained weight during her prison stay, her weight is shown to have stayed the same. Sam Starr, on the other hand, gained nine pounds, but he was a lightly built man, unlike his large and burly father, Tom Starr.

As predicted by Judge Parker at the Starrs' sentencing hearing in Fort Smith, a spotless prison record earned them both early releases. Some sources reported that the couple left Detroit as early as December 1883, in time to celebrate Christmas with the Reed family in Missouri. Official records from the House of Correction, however, show their discharge date as January 28, 1884.[116]

It was a significant date, not only for the Starrs but also for family and friends in the Cherokee Nation. On that particular January 28, a new moon hung in the winter heavens.[117] In that phase, the moon is visible in the night sky only briefly. Low on the western horizon just after the sun goes down, the thinnest sliver of what becomes the waxing crescent moon can be seen. In astronomy, a new moon marks the first lunar phase. It represents the start of a new lunar cycle and symbolizes new beginnings.[118]

The Cherokee people called the January moon the Cold Moon.[119] It marked the season of finding comfort from the chilly air and biting wind. It was a time for hearth fires, self-reflection, remembering ancestors, and preparing for the start of new cycles. There was the promise of fresh beginnings and change.[120]

CHAPTER 21

Myth Versus Reality

IN LATE JANUARY 1884, AFTER THEIR DISCHARGE FROM THE Detroit House of Correction, Belle and Sam Starr made their way south to Indian Territory. They collected fifteen-year-old Pearl in Kansas, where she had stayed with a family friend during Belle's incarceration, and visited the Reed family at Rich Hill, Missouri. Belle's son, Eddie, no longer resided there. After a lengthy stay with his father's mother, Susan Reed, thirteen-year-old Eddie had grown "tired of his humdrum school days" and moved to Texas to spend time with his other grandmother, Eliza Shirley, at her home in Dallas.[1]

During the Starrs' imprisonment in Detroit, the makers of myth had continued to shape a romanticized image of the Wild West as an alternate reality for a frontier that some historians sensed was rapidly vanishing. Many people believed that the United States had a divine mandate to possess all the land from "sea to shining sea."[2] That widely held cultural belief, based on imperialist and racist views, galvanized the eager proponents of expansionism and spawned a systematic acquisition of western lands all the way to the Pacific.[3]

The "perceived demise of the frontier brought about a longing for wilderness and the pioneer spirit."[4] This pervasive malaise later came to be called "frontier anxiety."[5] Writers and artists were among those who were most anxious. They reflected on the disappearance of the old frontier that had been mythologized for so long.

Artist Frederic Remington had joined the chorus of voices eager to keep the mythic West alive. Remington wrote, "I knew the wild riders and the vacant land were about to vanish forever."[6]

Some American authors also sensed the dramatic changes. The Starrs were adjusting to being back at Younger's Bend in 1884 when Mark Twain completed his novel *Adventures of Huckleberry Finn*, "acknowledging the end of the frontier as Huck naively pondered the possibility of lighting out for the [Indian] Territory ahead of the rest."[7]

Author Edgar Wilson Nye also foresaw the demise of a way of life that he preferred. "The march of civilization had taken the joy out of pioneer life," he wrote.[8] In one his pithy essays published in 1887, Nye pointed out that "the Old West was so far gone that a single day's ride could get a man to where he could see daily papers and read them by electric light."[9]

Although electric service arrived in parts of Indian Territory as early as 1889 and electrified streetcars appeared in Fort Smith by 1893, it would be many more years before most rural areas would be fully electrified.[10] Belle Starr would have had to read about Huck Finn's adventures by a kerosene lamp.

When Belle and Sam returned to Younger's Bend, they found their home and property in good shape. Every book was in place, and the floors and windows were scrubbed clean. Sam's father, Tom Starr, had seen to that. In their absence, he had kept a man on the place to look after the house and land.[11]

"The corn and garden patches had been plowed and the livestock well cared for," wrote Glenn Shirley, based on recollections of Starr kinfolk. "Belle repapered the cabin and helped Sam get ready for spring planting. She had little interest in housework but could prepare an excellent meal when in the mood and took pride in making candy and passing along her favorite recipes to her friends."[12]

Despite having served time in prison, Belle maintained amenable relationships with some of her neighbors and her loyal family and friends in Briartown and other communities near Younger's Bend. But because of the chinwags' tales of her lawless ways, some people believed Belle was wily, untrustworthy, and someone to avoid. Instead of trying to improve her image, however, Belle ignored her detractors and continued to live her tumultuous life on her own terms.

"Perhaps she felt that if she was to be labeled an outlaw, she might as well make the best of it," according to researchers Ron and Sue Wall.[13] Historian Glenda Riley came to the same conclusion: "Gradually, Belle seemed to accept her image and even play to it. She wore gold earrings, affected a man's sombrero decorated with feathers, donned a black velvet riding habit for special occasions, and referred to her Colt .45 pistol as 'my baby.' Belle also preferred to ride a black mare named Venus, on whom she used a tooled sidesaddle."[14]

Belle's independent spirit and swagger, coupled with her status as a convicted felon, resulted in far-fetched stories about her being attired in men's clothing and leading a large outlaw gang based at Younger's Bend. Published accounts of questionable origin created by journalists and early biographers were even resurrected many years later by some of Belle's own descendants, including a granddaughter.[15]

In one fanciful tale, Belle supposedly took pity on Mabel Harrison, an orphaned girl from Missouri purportedly related to the Reed family. The Reeds were said to have given the girl shelter after her parents "had been shot down before her eyes."[16] According to those who gave credence to the story, Belle brought Mabel to Younger's Bend, supposedly as a companion for Pearl. Freelance writer Edwin "Eddie" P. Hicks alleged that in the 1890s, Pearl married Mabel's brother, William "Will" Harrison, but soon left him, and they divorced.[17] There are no records of such a marriage and no records of Mabel or her brother ever having lived at Younger's Bend. However, records show that in 1891, Pearl was briefly wed to a Will Harris, an acquaintance from Holden, Missouri, a railroad town east of Kansas City.[18]

Another questionable story contended that Belle enjoyed playing a cabinet grand piano at her home at Younger's Bend.[19] For many years, purveyors of the piano story emerged with their own accounts of having witnessed one of Belle's performances at her home or in a public setting such as the Elk House, a popular hotel in McAlester, the largest town in the Choctaw Nation. Glenn Shirley wrote about the possibility of a piano in Belle's home but noted that it was "a point of controversy" that other biographers gave no credence to.[20] Writer Burton Rascoe found the notion of a piano at Younger's Bend "a fantastic supposition" and said it was a "most improbable story" that Belle played the piano while a guest in Judge Isaac Parker's home.[21]

"Belle's deep love of books and music is a persistent motif in her legend," wrote folklore scholar Victoria Stefani. "Most of her biographers, for example, take firm stands on whether she did or did not have a piano in her cabin at Younger's Bend."[22]

As 1884 came to a close, Belle's mother, sixty-eight-year old Eliza Shirley, and son Eddie Reed, then a handsome young teen, boarded the Missouri, Kansas and Texas Railway Company train ("the Katy") in Dallas and traveled two hundred miles north to Eufaula in the Choctaw Nation, west of Younger's Bend.[23] Eliza stayed with her daughter for several days, enough time to dote on Pearl and get acquainted with son-in-law Sam Starr. At last, Belle not only had her mother but also both of her children with her again.

Unfortunately, the tranquility was fleeting. Just after Belle's mother returned to Texas, trouble came calling at Younger's Bend. In late December, John Middleton—a wanted killer "widely known as one of the most daring outlaws in the land"—unexpectedly appeared at the Starr home.[24]

Although Belle must have been surprised to see him, they likely had met years before at a Reed family gathering in Arkansas.[25] Middleton, a striking man of twenty-five with sandy hair and a thick mustache, was a cousin of Belle's first husband, Jim Reed.[26] Born in Tishomingo, Mississippi, in 1859, Middleton was the son of Richard Robert Middleton and his second wife, Nancy Adline Reed Middleton, a Missouri native and Jim Reed's aunt.[27]

The Middleton family left Mississippi and lived for a time in Alabama before settling in Logan County and later Scott County, Arkansas, north of Fort Smith, on the border of Indian Territory.[28] By the time Middleton reached his teens, it was apparent that he had inherited felonious genes from the Reed side of the family.

At age eighteen, he was convicted of stealing a pair of boots and several pocketknives, and he spent a year in the Arkansas State Penitentiary. After his release, Middleton promptly became a fugitive when he was suspected of burning down the Scott County courthouse at Waldron.[29] On the scout, he headed to Texas and became a proficient horse thief along the Red River in the northeastern corner of Lamar County, not far from where Jim Reed had been shot and killed.[30]

Middleton's frequent trips to Indian Territory and Arkansas attracted the attention of local authorities. In February 1884, he was charged with three counts of transporting stolen horses into Texas and was incarcerated at Paris, the Lamar County seat.[31] His stay in the county jail was brief.

Middleton fell ill with a severe case of diarrhea brought on by unsanitary conditions at the jail. A doctor convinced the county magistrate that Middleton would die if left in his cell.[32] Consequently, he was moved to the private-residence part of the jail, where head jailer Newt Harris and his wife, Rebecca, could care for Middleton. After dinner one evening, the "gravely ill" Middleton allegedly made a miraculous recovery. He quietly left and disappeared into the night.[33]

It later became apparent that Lamar County Sheriff George Mack Crook and some of his deputies had orchestrated Middleton's escape. Crook had lost his reelection bid in the August 1884 Democratic primary to James H. Black. Refusing to accept the results, Crook ran on the general ballot on November 4, and once again, Black soundly defeated him.[34] Despite the two defeats, Crook vowed that "the damned son of a bitch [Black] will never be sheriff of Lamar County."[35] Middleton, who had been seen coming and going from the county jail after his escape, was recruited to make sure Crook's promise was carried out.

On November 16, the day before Black was to assume office, Middleton, armed with a pistol and shotgun, rode to Blossom Prairie, a railroad community nine miles east of Paris. He pulled up in the yard of a two-room house where Black resided with his wife and children. Middleton called out to Black, and when he appeared at the door, eighteen pellets from a shotgun blast struck him in the chest, and he fell dead.[36]

Black's brazen assassination stunned Lamar County. A large posse was formed, and an angry crowd of five hundred people attended a public meeting in Paris and pledged a special fund of $1,500. Other county residents pledged an additional $2,500.[37] A committee of prominent citizens appointed to oversee the fund sought detectives and "man trackers" to bring the killer—or killers—to justice.

The hefty reward money caught the attention of one of the most renowned bounty hunters in Texas—John Riley "Jack" Duncan. The Kentucky native and former butcher started his law-enforcement career in 1876 with the Dallas police force. His prowess as an exceptional manhunter grew the next year when he worked undercover for the Texas Rangers and gathered information that eventually led to the arrest of John Wesley Hardin, a notorious outlaw and gunslinger.[38]

Duncan served with the Texas Rangers for only four months. After he received his share of the $4,000 reward for Hardin's capture, he concluded that instead of wearing a badge, he could earn more money as a bounty hunter. He opened a detective agency in Dallas.[39]

A woman in a Dallas bordello shot Duncan in the lung with his own gun in 1878, but he survived. However, two years later, while walking on Main Street in Dallas, he suddenly began to hemorrhage and was rushed by hack to his father's residence. Physicians concluded that the bullet that remained in Duncan had caused the hemorrhage. He was not expected to live, but an emergency tracheotomy saved his life, and a silver tube was inserted into his throat to enable him to breathe and speak.[40]

Duncan could still function effectively as a sleuth and once again proved himself by determining who had had the most to gain by killing James Black. Duncan concluded that the most obvious culprits were former sheriff Mack Crook and his deputy allies.

"It was quickly determined that a desperado named John Middleton, an escapee from the Lamar County jail, had been the triggerman, but Duncan unearthed sufficient evidence to suspect former sheriff [Mack] Crook, his jailer Newt Harris, and two of his deputies, Jim Yates and Lewis Holman, as being complicit in the murder,"[41] wrote Robert K. DeArment.

After accumulating more incriminating evidence, Duncan and new Lamar County Sheriff Bill Gunn locked up Crook and his accomplices. Yates and Holman were granted immunity for their testimonies, and

Crook and Harris were indicted for complicity in Black's murder.[42] Harris died in jail in 1888 after his first trial resulted in a hung jury. On November 28, 1888, a jury in Sherman, Texas, found Crook guilty of having been an accomplice in the murder of James Black and set his punishment to confinement in the state penitentiary for life.[43]

In 1885, the Lamar County citizens' committee had presented Duncan with $2,800 for his services in the Black murder case. But reward money for the apprehension of the actual killer was still offered, and Duncan pressed on with his search.[44]

Duncan and newly appointed Lamar County Deputy Sheriff James A. "Polk" Burris rode to Indian Territory, the logical place for Texas fugitives to find refuge.[45] As they went farther north, they picked up Middleton's trail and were convinced they had made the right decision. In late December 1884, however, about the time Middleton found his way to Sam and Belle Starr's home, his trail went cold, and Duncan and Burris returned to Texas.[46]

Many biographers subsequently came up with wild stories about the escapades of the Starrs and Middleton during the winter of 1885. Some of them even suggested that Belle had grown tired of Sam and started a romantic relationship with Middleton.[47] There also were tales of the Starrs and Middleton going on a crime spree that included robberies of the Seminole Nation and Creek Nation treasuries. More credible sources countered that "no substantive contemporary accounts or official records" support such claims.[48]

In April 1885, Duncan, accompanied by Lamar County Deputy Sheriff J. H. Milsap, returned to Indian Territory and resumed the search for Middleton.[49] When they reached the South Canadian River near Younger's Bend, they wisely enlisted the services of John C. West, a member of the Cherokee Lighthorsemen who had recently been commissioned as a United States Indian policeman.

Although the Wests were related to the Starrs and for many years lived near them in the Briartown area, there was bad blood between some members of the families. Most of it stemmed from John West's criminal complaint and subsequent testimony in the horse-theft trial of Sam and

Belle Starr that resulted in their going to federal prison in Detroit.[50] West was the Starrs' chief nemesis, as was his younger brother Frank West, who had also joined the Cherokee tribal police.[51]

West explained to Duncan and Milsap that Middleton's younger brother, James F. Middleton, and their father, Richard R. Middleton, had recently moved to Briartown. However, West had already met with them and was convinced they were not aiding and abetting John Middleton.[52]

Born in in 1857 in Tishomingo, Mississippi, James Middleton came to Indian Territory in 1885 and settled about four miles west of Briartown, not far from the Tom Starr residence.[53] Richard R. Middleton—long estranged from his wife in Arkansas—also moved to Briartown, where he lived until his death in 1887.[54]

"I became acquainted with Sam Starr and his wife, Belle Starr, when I first came to Indian Territory as I rented a place from them the first year I was here," James Middleton related in a 1937 interview, a year before his death at his Briartown home.[55] "All our business transactions were always satisfactory, and during my four year acquaintance with them . . . I never saw anything in her life that caused me to think she was a bad woman."

West, Duncan, and Milsap did not share James Middleton's assessment of Belle Starr's deportment. They also were confident they would find their quarry at the Starrs' home at Younger's Bend. One chilly morning in April 1885, Duncan determined it was time to make their move. Heavily armed and prepared for a siege, they made their way to Younger's Bend. At the cabin, there was no sign of Middleton or Sam, only Belle—with a pistol on her hip—and her two sleepy teenage children.[56]

"She supposedly cursed her sworn enemy, John West, for leading lawmen to her place," according to historian Rick Miller. "There is no information indicating that Belle and Duncan knew each other from her former days in Dallas. Exercising what was probably good discretion, given Belle's legend, the lawmen took her pistol away from her before she might get the idea of trying to use it, although they returned it to her when they left. She heaped considerable abuse on the three for trying to nab Middleton; however, after they were gone, she likely wasted little time in getting word to the fugitive that this wouldn't be the last time the lawmen visited."[57]

Wary of other troublesome visitors showing up at their door, Belle and Sam knew it was time for Middleton to find refuge elsewhere. He readily agreed. Arkansas appeared the best choice. Middleton had kinfolk from the Middleton and Reed families living just outside Paris in Logan County, Arkansas. In neighboring Yell County, Belle's old friend Pete Marshall and his family lived at Chickalah, a community south of Dardanelle, on the Arkansas River.[58] Belle was familiar with the area from previous visits with Pearl that occasionally included taking the vapors and soaking in a popular hot spring.[59]

In early May, Belle and Pearl tethered their mounts to the rear gate of a wagon pulled by a team of horses. They took their seats on the wagon bench beside the driver, Frank Cook, a young petty thief who did odd jobs for the Starrs.[60] They set out from Younger's Bend for Chickalah. Besides saddles and tack and trunks filled with personal belongings, the wagon cargo included John Middleton, concealed beneath a sheet of canvas. Sam Starr and Eddie Reed rode alongside the wagon to the crossing of the South Canadian River and stayed with them for the remainder of the day.[61]

The plan was for Middleton to stay hidden until they approached Fort Smith. At that point, Middleton would leave on Pearl's horse and "take a circuitous route beyond the settlements where he might be seen, cross the Poteau River, then go directly east through Booneville to his old home in Logan County."[62] The others would follow the usual trail to Fort Smith and then take the Arkansas River route to Logan County. Pearl would retrieve her horse from Middleton, and the wagon party would proceed to Chickalah.

The seemingly well-laid plan went awry the first night. When the party made camp for the night, "some trivial act" attributed to Middleton so angered Pearl that she refused to loan him her horse for his solo journey.[63] The exact nature of Middleton's supposed indiscretion has never been revealed or fully explained. At the breakfast campfire, attempts to change Pearl's mind failed. In addition, it was highly unlikely that Belle would have allowed Middleton to gallop off on her beloved steed, Venus.

Fortunately, a solution was at hand. Fayette Barnett—a White rancher married to a Choctaw woman—was out tending his cattle, saw smoke, and rode into camp to see who was there. Belle explained that they needed another horse, and the neighborly Barnett said he could provide one. He rode off and soon returned leading a sorrel mare he had caught on the range.[64]

Eddie Reed led the horse into the woods where Middleton had been hiding. Middleton was not pleased when he saw that the mare was blind in the right eye and had not been shod. Middleton had no other choice, however, so he begrudgingly handed Eddie fifty dollars for Barnett, who pocketed the money and rode away. Barnett failed to tell anyone that the mare was not his to sell. She belonged to another area rancher, Albert G. McCarty, and bore his brand.[65]

Belle provided Middleton with a saddle that she had purchased for Pearl at Eufaula. Although he had a pair of six-shooters on his hips, he borrowed another pistol from Belle and left his shotgun in the wagon before riding off toward the Poteau River.[66]

After the campfire was extinguished, Sam and Eddie rode back to Younger's Bend. Belle and Pearl continued east to Arkansas with Frank Cook. Along the way, the party encountered two of Belle's friends from Eufaula—James Johnson and William Hicks—who later testified in court that they "met her [Belle] on the road and nooned with her."[67]

When the journey resumed, Belle paused to visit with other acquaintances they came upon. By the following evening, the wagon party had reached Fort Smith and spent the night at a hotel. In the morning, they pushed on to Logan County and the anticipated rendezvous with Middleton.[68] When they reached the designated meeting place, however, they saw no sign of Middleton. Belle likely decided that his longer evasive route had slowed him down, and it was in her and Pearl's best interest to keep moving. After a short wait, the party moved on toward Yell County.

On May 7, Henry Tallay, a resident of Pocola, in the Choctaw Nation on the eastern border of Indian Territory, found a riderless horse wandering through the brush on the bank of the rain-swollen Poteau River. The sorrel mare was saddled, and a cartridge belt and .45-caliber Colt revolver hung on the saddle horn.[69] Tallay noticed that the horse was blind in one eye.

The dried muck and silt that covered the mare's hide and tack indicated that she had attempted to cross the river and that her rider had been swept off. Tallay knew that crossing the Poteau River could be treacherous. It was prone to flooding in the spring and fall when it became "wild and flowing rapidly enough to 'dislodge' a man from his horse."[70]

Tallay returned to Pocola with the sorrel and recruited some local men, and they launched a search for the missing rider. On May 11, Tallay found the body of a man washed up on the muddy bank about two hundred yards downstream from tracks that showed where the horse had entered the river.[71] No identification was found on the man, who was thought to have been in his late twenties. His body was badly decomposed, and buzzards had eaten away part of the face and heavy mustache, making facial recognition difficult. He was dressed in a vest, dress shirt, woolen trousers, and boots. Two holstered Colt pistols hung on a gun belt around his waist. In his pockets, Tallay found a ten-dollar bank note, eleven dollars in silver coin, a silver watch, two jackknives, and a comb.[72]

Tallay placed the corpse in a crude coffin and buried it in a shallow grave near the river. He returned to Pocola with the dead man's possessions and notified authorities in Fort Smith. A description of the mare and of the man's clothing and belongings was sent to O. D. Weldon, editor and business manager of the *Fort Smith Elevator*.[73] A story about the grisly find on the Poteau River appeared in the newspaper on May 15, 1885. Weldon, a regular correspondent with several major newspapers, dispatched the story to the *St. Louis Globe-Democrat* and the *Arkansas Gazette* in Little Rock.[74]

"It is now thought, beyond a doubt, that the drowned man found in the Poteau River . . . is none other than John Middleton, the outlaw, for whom there is a $500 reward in Lamar County, Texas, where he murdered the sheriff some time since," announced the front-page story in the *Gazette*.[75]

After reading this story at his home in Indian Territory, Al McCarty went to Fort Smith to alert law officers that the horse was his. He then went to Pocola and retrieved his one-eyed sorrel.[76]

Meanwhile, Duncan, Milsap, and West set out from Fort Smith to the gravesite on the Poteau River to positively identify of the body. *Elevator* reporter Weldon tagged along.[77] They located the shallow grave and used field hoes to rake away the loose dirt. When the lid of the makeshift coffin was lifted, they knew it was Middleton, despite the decomposition. The body's size, hair color, and scar on one knee matched his description. Before reburying the corpse, the lawmen cut off a lock of hair and took the string of beads and rattle hung around his neck. Once they met with Tallay and examined the saddle and other personal effects found with the body, they were even more convinced that the dead man was Middleton.[78]

"His identity was further established by the pistols found on him. One of them being a weapon which these same officers had taken from Belle Starr, the mistress of Middleton, in April last, but had returned it to her," Weldon wrote in a dispatch to his newspaper. "Middleton was known to have had this pistol in his possession. The other two pistols were Middleton's."[79] In the same story, Weldon stated that Middleton "won the heart of Belle Starr, wife of Sam Starr, and she became his mistress." By referring to Belle as Middleton's mistress based on conjecture, he gave credence to existing gossip and hearsay.[80]

Like many journalists of that time, Weldon was not known for impartial and accurate reporting. Although some newspapers and periodicals tried to meet professional standards of accuracy and impartiality, much of the journalistic content in the late nineteenth century consisted of sensationalized reporting and manufactured facts.[81] As historian James Baughman wrote, "Editors unabashedly shaped the news and their editorial comment to partisan purposes."[82] Weldon knew scandal and violence sold newspapers, and Belle Starr made good copy.

Weldon returned to Fort Smith with the lawmen as soon as they completed the investigation in the Choctaw Nation. According to Weldon, they were "satisfied that the country would never more be afflicted by the presence of John Middleton."[83]

Back in Fort Smith, Duncan, Milsap, and West rested their horses and then headed east to Yell County. Based on good intelligence, they found Belle Starr's camp in the mountains south of Dardanelle after a hard day's ride. Belle and Frank Cook, in the midst of cooking supper, were the only ones there. Pearl was visiting Reed cousins in nearby Logan County.[84]

Belle told Duncan that she already had learned of Middleton's death. One of his brothers had ridden over from the family home in Logan County to bring her the news.[85] "Belle says she left Middleton on Wednesday, May 6th, five miles from where he was drowned, and that he must have met his death about 12 o'clock that day," Weldon wrote, based on what Duncan had told him. "She also says that Middleton had $400 in the belt that was on the horn of the saddle; that the belt and pistol belonged to her. Says she don't believe Middleton was drowned but was killed and thrown in the river. The beads and rattle that were attached to his neck she put there herself."[86]

While Duncan and Milsap questioned Belle, West turned his attention to Cook. In West's saddlebag was a warrant for Cook's arrest on a charge of larceny for the robbery of a mercantile store at Wealaka, a busy Creek Nation trading center. Samuel W. Brown, a prominent chief and leader of the Yuchi (Euchee) tribe, owned and operated the store.[87] The heist had taken place in late April, shortly before Cook left Indian Territory in May with Belle and Pearl.

Cook was said to be one of three men who made off with several hundred dollars, watches, pistols, and other goods. "They were not masked but rode up boldly to the store in broad daylight, robbing not only the store, but the clerks and bystanders," eyewitnesses told reporters.[88]

Authorities believed that John Middleton was with Cook, but much speculation occurred about the identity of the third robber. Some reports also maintained that there were more than three outlaws, and other people were certain that there had been only two. As in the past, suspicion was attached to Sam and Belle, but no proof existed. Even so, more than fifty years later, they were included in a list of perpetrators based on hearsay.

"Belle was considered the brains of the plot and Sam was her tool," Tulsa attorney S. R. Lewis, who as a boy had heard the tales of early lawmen, related in a 1937 interview. "It was known that Sam became 'flush' with money about this time."[89]

The most scandalous version of the robbery was fueled by relentless rumors that Belle had kindled a romantic liaison with Middleton that led to her eloping with him. It became public in late May when Fayette Barnett, the rancher who had sold Middleton the one-eyed stolen horse, was arrested at Eufaula for "introducing spirituous liquors" in Indian Territory.[90] During questioning, Barnett admitted that John Middleton and Frank Cook were two of the men wanted for robbing the Wealaka store.

"Middleton wished to live with Belle Starr and Barnett was to have her daughter," according to the *Muskogee Indian Journal*. "He [Barnett] was to take his cattle west and sell them, and then meet the party at a rendezvous in Arkansas, where they hoped to live unmolested. But Barnett's capture spoiled the plan."[91]

No evidence supports the story. It also seems highly unlikely that the often overprotective Belle would have allowed her teenage daughter to take up with Barnett, an older man with a Choctaw wife.[92] What seemed more likely was the prospect that Barnett's theft of Albert McCarty's horse and its sale to Middleton would eventually be connected to Belle. At her camp close to Dardanelle, however, the law officers took only Cook into custody. He readily confessed to his part in the robbery after a search of his belongings turned up boots, firearms, and other items taken from Sam Brown's store at Wealaka.[93]

On May 19, at nearby Russellville, Arkansas, Duncan wired confirmation of Middleton's death to authorities in Dallas.[94] Duncan, Milsap, and West rode to Wealaka in Indian Territory with Cook in shackles, where store clerks identified him as one of the robbers.[95]

Cook was returned to Fort Smith and on June 2, 1885, appeared in court to answer for his part in the robbery at Wealaka. He had already confessed, so there was no need for a trial. Cook pleaded guilty to the larceny charge and received a one-year sentence to the House of Correction in Detroit, where Sam and Belle Starr had been incarcerated.[96] Cook's father-in-law, Albert Carr, a highly respected farmer and rancher in Indian Territory, brought a charge of horse theft against Cook, but it was dismissed.[97]

In June 1885, after the brush with law officers at her camp, Belle made her way to the site on the Poteau River where Middleton had drowned. Middleton's brother, James, and his father, Richard, accompanied her. They secured some of Middleton's personal items, exhumed the badly decomposed body, and reinterred it in a properly dug grave near the river.[98]

Once Cook was in the hands of "Uncle Sam," as the *Fort Smith Elevator* reported, Duncan and Milsap collected the reward money offered by the Creek Nation and their share of the reward from the citizens of Muskogee. Their job was done, and they returned to Texas.[99]

Although the tenacious Duncan and Milsap had left Indian Territory, the Starrs' enemy—John West—remained. His deep-seated hatred of Sam and Belle was matched only by their fierce loathing of him. There was never a doubt that West would persist in his quest to put the Starrs once again behind bars. Even if they could somehow stay clear of West, Belle and Sam knew they still had to fret about the United States deputy marshals who rode for Judge Isaac Parker.

CHAPTER 22

The Legend Grows

IN LATE MAY 1885, BELLE AND PEARL RETURNED TO Younger's Bend and were greeted by Sam and Eddie. It is likely that Belle found little comfort being back home, for good reason.

Belle's concern was soon validated. Based almost solely on hearsay, Sam remained a suspect in the April 1885 robbery of Samuel Brown's mercantile at Wealaka in the Creek Nation. But the warrant issued on June 15, 1885, for his arrest was never served.[1] Sam Starr had slipped away from Younger's Bend and was officially declared a "fugitive from justice," back on the scout.[2]

There were many hiding places in the Canadian River communities and surrounding hills. Sam stayed "a jump ahead of John West and his Indian deputies, and evidence that he participated in the [Wealaka] robbery was lacking."[3] Always cautious, Sam occasionally sneaked into Younger's Bend to visit Belle and retrieve fresh clothing and supplies. He even eluded capture when he was named, along with Felix Griffin and Richard Hays, as a suspect in another crime—the October 30, 1885, burglary of the Andrew J. Moore store and post office at the settlement of Blaine in the Choctaw Nation.[4]

A few weeks later, Sam was elsewhere when Indian police arrested Richard Hays, Felix Griffin, and his cousin Luna Griffin for horse theft. All three were tried and convicted in Cherokee circuit court in late December. They were sentenced to four years in the Cherokee National Prison at Tahlequah, the only penitentiary in Indian Territory from 1875 to 1901.[5]

The time behind bars for the three outlaws was brief. On January 14, 1886, they escaped in what was "thought to have been a put up job."[6] Felix Griffin supposedly sought safe haven at Younger's Bend, but for unknown reasons, he and Sam Starr "fell out and had a shooting scrape, Felix getting shot in the right hand."[7]

Yarn spinners and journalists came up with a variety of causes for the duel between Sam Starr and Felix Griffin, but none was ever proved. When the Cherokee police recaptured Griffin a few months later, it was reported that his "left arm [had been] rendered useless by a gunshot [and] his 'set to' with Sam about retired him from active pursuits of any character."[8] For much of the winter of 1886, Sam kept in touch with his family but mostly stayed out of sight.

At Younger's Bend, Belle grappled with the consequences of having aided and abetted John Middleton. She knew John West continued to pursue the Middleton investigation and had narrowed his focus to anyone suspected of having helped the slain outlaw. In mid-January 1886, Belle learned that a court order issued four months earlier alleged that on May 3, 1885, she and Fayette Barnett did "feloniously steal, take and carry away from the lawful possession [of] Albert McCarty one horse of the value of one hundred dollars."[9] McCarty signed a complaint, and warrants were issued on September 11, given to formidable United States Deputy Marshal Bass Reeves—possibly the first Black federal lawman commissioned west of the Mississippi.[10] Formerly enslaved in Texas, Reeves could not read or write. He signed warrants, writs, and subpoenas with only the mark X during his thirty-two years as a law officer in Indian Territory.[11]

SOME SOURCES SPECULATED THAT Reeves and Belle were on friendly terms and that Reeves got word to Belle that it would be best to turn herself in. According to lore, when Belle found out that Reeves had her arrest warrant, she dashed to Fort Smith and surrendered to authorities rather than face Reeves. When she appeared in Fort Smith, Belle supposedly announced that she "did not propose to be dragged around again by some federal deputy."[12]

At the time, Reeves had problems of his own. On January 19, 1886, Reeves was arrested for the first-degree murder of his camp cook, William Leech, in October 1884. At an inquest held just after the incident, it had been ruled an accidental shooting, and no charges had been filed.[13]

Then on May 21, 1885, John Carroll, newly appointed US marshal for the Western District of Arkansas, opened an investigation into Leech's death and ordered Reeves to be arrested for murder.[14] Many of Reeves' fellow officers knew that the charge was politically and racially motivated.[15]

Reeves' bond was set at $3,000, but he was unable to come up with it until after he had served six months in prison.[16] His trial before Judge Isaac Parker began in October 1887. In earlier cases, Reeves had arrested nine of the prosecution's dubious witnesses. On the witness stand, Reeves explained that the shooting had been accidental, and the jurors agreed. They returned a unanimous verdict of "not guilty," and Reeves was reinstated as a deputy marshal.[17]

Unlike Reeves, Belle Starr had no problem making bail when she was indicted for larceny by the same grand jury that had come after Sam Starr. Her alleged accomplice, Fayette Barnette, was "ignored by the grand jury," and the larceny charge against him was dropped.[18]

Belle appeared before Judge Parker on February 8, 1886, three days after her thirty-eighth birthday. "She attracted general attention, as she sat in court with a white, broad-brimmed man's hat, fastened on the side with red feather, jauntily sitting on the side of her head," wrote a Little Rock reporter. "She was accompanied by her daughter Pearl Younger [Reed], who is the constant companion of her mother." Belle entered a plea of not guilty, and Parker set her trial for the September court term. She filed an application for witnesses, posted bond, and was released.[19]

In the courthouse, Belle and Pearl were meeting with a bail bondsman (identified only as "Mr. B") when a reporter for the *Fort Smith Times* approached and asked for an interview. A reporter for a rival newspaper observed what transpired next and scribbled down Belle's reply:[20] "Belle's bright eyes flashed fire and seemed to send a little fire clear into the reporter's marrow bones. 'Well sir, you're the fellow I've been wanting to meet for sometime—I saw the article you published about me when I was here before and it seems you know a [damned] sight more about my business than I do.'"21

Belle raised her riding crop "as if to strike the unfortunate and alarmed knight of the quill," but the bail bondsman intervened. "The amazon's wrath subsided, the angry flash left her cheek and ... that interview was spoiled."22

Immediately after leaving Fort Smith, Belle made a beeline to Barnett's place, where she made it clear that she was innocent and expected him to help prove it at her trial. Barnett, thankful that he had escaped the horse-theft charge and no doubt fearful that Belle might turn on him, wholeheartedly agreed. He promised not only to appear as a defense witness but also to pay her legal fees.23

The same federal grand jury that had no-billed Barnett and indicted Belle also indicted Sam Starr and Felix Griffin for the October 1885 robbery of the store and post office in Blaine.24 Sam remained at large.

ON FEBRUARY 27, 1886, near Cache, a Choctaw community on the Canadian River, three well-armed men entered the home of Wilse W. Farrill, a prosperous farmer, by claiming to be deputy marshals. They brandished pistols and rifles as they rummaged through a trunk and took forty dollars in cash. The robbers then barged into a neighboring house and made off with a pistol and then stole a horse grazing at a third residence before riding away.25

Several persons witnessed the whirlwind raid, but only eighteen-year-old Lila McGilberry provided any useful information for law officers. She was "scared pretty good" but described one invader "with a rifle, wearing a kind of grey overcoat" and another with "a six-shooter in each hand, wearing pants and overcoat and a kind [of] white hat." She also recalled that the robber with the two pistols did not have a male voice but appeared to be "a woman dressed like a man."26

Predictably, all fingers pointed to Belle Starr. Once again, newspaper reports exaggerated her actions and the supposed threat she posed to the public.

In early March, a posse composed of Indian police officers led by John West and Canadian District Sheriff William Vann raided the Starrs' home at Younger's Bend. Besides the Starr family, they reportedly found nine other men on the premises, but most of them fled when the posse arrived.[27]

"They captured one, a white man named Jackson, and after disarming him released him," according to the *Muskogee Indian Journal* of March 11. "The others, the ones wanted, escaped, Sam Starr jumping his horse off a bluff twenty feet high, and swimming the river. . . . These men [the posse] are determined, however, to break up this band of cut-throats, robbers and horse thieves, and say they will never let them rest in peace."[28]

West and his men searched the Starr home and property for the missing pistol and horse but found nothing. No arrests were made. West took a revolver from Belle before departing, perhaps soothing the frustration of leaving without Sam Starr in shackles.[29]

Several days later, a criminal complaint filed before United States Commissioner James Brizzolara at Fort Smith accused Belle Starr of being the "gang leader" in the February 27 raid of the three homes near Cache in the Choctaw Nation.[30]

Born to Italian parents in Virginia in 1848, Brizzolara was the same age as Belle and, much like her, had led a colorful life and was known for his "indefatigable energy."[31] He became city attorney for Fort Smith in 1875.[32]

On March 10, after reviewing the complaint against Belle, Brizzolara issued a warrant for her arrest and subpoenas for several witnesses, including Lila McGilberry.[33] Deputy United States Marshal Benjamin Tyner Hughes served subpoenas to the witnesses, all of whom gave sworn statements in court on March 24. Hughes, however, was unable to find Belle. He scribbled on her arrest warrant "returned with no service, Tyner Hughes, Apr. 1886." Commissioner Brizzolara issued a new warrant for Belle's arrest on April 27.[34]

Two weeks earlier, Deputy Marshal William H. Irwin had been shot and killed in the Choctaw Nation while escorting Felix Griffin to the federal prison at Fort Smith.[35] Griffin, a former pal of Sam Starr's, was arrested for escaping from the Cherokee National Prison after an armed-robbery conviction. Witnesses later named Frank Palmer and

Jack Spaniard as the two gunmen who killed Irwin and freed Griffin.[36] Both Palmer and Spaniard were linked to the Starrs.

In mid-May, Irwin's killing might have been on the minds of Tyner Hughes and Deputy Marshal Charles Fletcher Barnhill as they made their way to Younger's Bend to arrest Belle.[37] When they neared the house, Pearl—sitting on the porch—spotted them and went inside to warn Sam, who was home for a visit. Belle turned down the lamps, and Sam quietly slipped out and vanished into the brush.[38]

Belle greeted the lawmen and informed them that they were out of luck—her husband was not there. Hughes replied that this time, they had come to arrest her for robbery in the Farrill case. Belle looked over the warrant and "consented to accompany the officers to Fort Smith."[39] She packed some necessities and saddled Venus. Pearl rode with Belle and the deputies for about ten miles before returning home.

In Fort Smith, Belle immediately contacted William M. Cravens and Thomas Marcum, the lawyers who had served her well in previous legal matters. Appearing before Commissioner Brizzolara, Belle firmly denied the larceny charge. She applied for several defense witnesses whom she predicted would testify under oath that at the time of the robbery, she was attending a community dance in Briartown.[40]

After posting bail, Belle chose not to return immediately to Younger's Bend. Her decision to spend a few days shopping and socializing in Fort Smith catapulted her name well beyond her stomping grounds. Belle had underestimated the power of the press.

By the mid-1880s, newspapers across the country carried items that mentioned Belle Starr. Most of the stories originated in local and area papers and were picked up by other newspapers, sometimes crediting the source and sometimes not. Reports of the same incident—or alleged incident—would appear in papers in several states within a few days. But Belle's reading audience soared on May 22, 1886, when the new edition of the *National Police Gazette* hit the streets of New York and was sent to thousands of mostly male subscribers across the country, including the clientele of almost every newsstand, hotel, barbershop, saloon, and brothel.[41] On page 16 appeared a dramatic freestanding

"A Wild Western Amazon" is the wood engraving that helped fuel the Belle Starr legend.

wood engraving of a woman with long, dark hair streaming in the wind, brandishing her hat in her left hand as she speeds past cheering onlookers on her wild-eyed steed. Below the illustration, titled "A Wild Western Amazon," the caption read: "The noted Belle Starr is arrested on the border of the Indian Territory and being released on bail vanishes on horseback."[42]

The legends that were building around Belle in the 1880s were ideal fodder for the *National Police Gazette*, founded in New York City in 1845. Early issues published detailed crime narratives, including names, aliases, physical descriptions, and even home addresses of alleged offenders.[43] In 1856, the founders sold the *Gazette* to a former New York City police chief, and he made changes that propelled the magazine to national popularity. Story coverage expanded to lurid sex crimes and

On May 23, 1886, Belle Starr, seated sidesaddle with an unloaded revolver strapped around her waist, awaits trial for horse theft in Fort Smith, Arkansas. Also pictured is Deputy US Marshal Tyner Hughes, often misidentified in this photograph as Belle's husband Sam Starr.

gossip about illicit affairs of political and business figures. The editorial staff grew, and eventually the *Gazette* had correspondents in every major US city.[44]

After more ownership changes, a brash Irish immigrant named Richard Kyle Fox became proprietor and editor in 1876. Fox soon became known as the "Father of the Tabloid." Under his leadership, the *Police Gazette* became one of the most widely read papers of the day, famous for sensationalistic journalism and provocative illustrations.[45] A good example was the woodcut depicting the romanticized image of Belle Starr.

Copies of the May 22 issue of the *Police Gazette* had not yet reached frontier readers when a cabinet-card photograph was taken of Belle the very next day by a large-format camera in front of Roeder Brothers Photography, 115 Walnut Street in Fort Smith. To this day the most famous of the few authentic images of Belle Starr known to exist,[46] it shows Belle sitting sidesaddle on her horse Venus. She is wearing a "snugly fitting brocaded riding jacket" and "long flowing skirts reaching down the left side of her horse almost to the ground."[47] A silk scarf is tied around her neck, and her hat brim is pinned up and festooned with feathers. She wears leather gloves and holds a riding crop in her right hand. An unloaded pearl-handled pistol in a single loop scabbard, or holster, is displayed prominently on Belle's right hip.

Deputy Marshal Tyner Hughes, one of the two law officers who had arrested Belle and brought her to Fort Smith, is in the photograph on horseback next to her.[48] Numerous writers and researchers have claimed that the mounted male rider was Sam Starr, but Starr was on the scout in the Cherokee Nation at the time the picture was taken. Other sources were emphatic that Belle's sidearm was a prop provided by the photographer and was not loaded, ignoring the fact that she was out on bond and permitted to be armed—she had just bought two revolvers while shopping in town.

Hughes is poker-faced and looking off to his left, perhaps uncomfortable at being photographed. Belle is holding Venus' reins and staring intently at the photographer, either J. H. Roeder or his brother, F. T. Roeder. O. D. Weldon, the local newspaper editor who also worked as a correspondent for the *Saint Louis Globe-Democrat*, had contracted the Roeders to take Belle's photograph.[49]

The Roeder brothers' work was not over. The next morning, May 24, they were hired to photograph Belle again, with an outlaw—Bluford Duck, whose Cherokee name was Sha-con-gah Kaw-wan-nu. Throughout Indian Territory, he was better known as Blue Duck.[50]

At that time, Duck resided in jail at the federal courthouse in Fort Smith, charged with the senseless murder of Samuel Wyrick on June 23, 1884.[51] During a drunken ride in Flint District of the Cherokee Nation, Duck and a rogue companion, William Christie, came upon Wyrick plowing a field, and for no apparent reason, shot him several times. It was further alleged that after emptying his revolver, Duck reloaded and continued on his way, taking pot shots at other people he happened upon.[52]

United States Deputy Marshal Frank Cochran arrested Duck and Christie, and they were brought to trial before Judge Isaac Parker in

January 1886.[53] The jury heard the arguments and determined there was not enough proof to convict Christie, who was acquitted. For Duck, there was enough evidence to show that he had been "on a drunken rampage, determined on having blood." He was found guilty, and a motion for a new trial was denied. On February 27, Judge Parker sentenced Duck to hang from the gallows. He set Duck's execution date as July 23, 1886.[54]

Duck's legal counsel was Thomas Marcum, one of Belle's lawyers. In a move to spare his convicted client's life, Marcum—who often served as a public defender in federal court—filed an appeal with President Grover Cleveland for Duck's commutation from a death sentence to life in prison. Anxiously awaiting a response, Marcum gathered testimonials of support from Duck's family and friends.[55]

It is not clear why Marcum thought associating Duck with Belle Starr might help his cause. Nonetheless, Marcum took advantage of Belle's presence in Fort Smith and requested that she appear in a photograph with Duck. Belle agreed and showed up at Roeder's studio in a more subdued wardrobe than she had worn the day before.

Deputies escorted Duck to the studio in manacles, and the photographer arranged the portrait with Duck seated and Belle standing next to him. In the finished cabinet card, Belle, wearing her fancy hat, stands expressionless, with arms folded at her waist. Duck, also wearing a hat, sits with his left hand resting on the chair arm. The manacle around his wrist is plainly visible. There is no record that Belle and Duck even spoke to each other.[56]

It was Duck's good fortune that his attorney's appeal to President Cleveland postponed the execution for a few months. In the end, Cherokee Nation leaders who lobbied for Duck "saved his neck." In September 1886, the appeal was successful. President Cleveland—"because of some doubt of his [Duck's] guilt"—commuted the sentence from death to imprisonment for life.[57] In early October, Judge Parker committed Blue Duck to the Menard Branch of the Southern Illinois Penitentiary at Chester, Illinois, "for the term and period of his natural life." Blue Duck served less than nine years, however. He was suffering from consump-

Shackled outlaw Bluford "Blue" Duck and Belle Starr pose for a staged studio portrait at Fort Smith, Arkansas, on May 24, 1886. Despite later rumors, Belle had no relationship with Duck. This occasion was the only time she was in his presence.

tion with only weeks to live when President Cleveland pardoned him on March 20, 1895, to die among family and friends.[58]

It is debatable whether Belle's posing with Duck helped or hindered his case for commutation. The resulting photograph of the pair certainly did not improve Belle's reputation. It supported bogus rumors that she and Blue Duck were lawless lovers, when in truth, it was the only time they ever met. Still, many writers at that time and for years to come promoted as truth the torrid and fictionalized love story of Blue Duck and Belle Starr.

"Blue Duck must have possessed the manly vigor with which he has been credited, for Belle went all out for him," wrote author Harry Drago in 1964. "She has been described as a nymphomaniac. Perhaps she was. At least sexually she appears to have found no inconvenience in endless variety."[59]

Drago had been inspired by Paul Wellman, whom he praised as "a writer for whom I have an enduring respect."[60] The author of many novels and a variety of nonfiction books, Wellman often received mixed reviews, however. One critic wrote that "Wellman had great trouble portraying women, revealing himself as an anti-feminist."[61] In writing about

Belle Starr in *A Dynasty of Western Outlaws*, Wellman described her as "the 'bandit queen,' who seemed to have an appetite for new bedmates exceeded only by that other celebrated 'royal' nymphomaniac, Catherine the Great of Russia."[62]

The misogynistic Wellman's unproved claim not only insulted Belle but also Russia's longest-reigning female ruler. "Indeed, stories of sexual promiscuity denigrate the legacies of many powerful women," wrote Alicja Zelazko, associate editor at *Encyclopedia Britannica*. "I would argue that these narratives were all probably fabricated by a patriarchy determined to diminish a powerful woman's accomplishments."[63]

Drago and Wellman were but two of the many people who made unfounded claims about Belle's lust for sexual partners. In 1996, a former superintendent of the Fort Smith Historic Site, without any corroboration, wrote that Belle had a "short romance with Blue Duck" and was the lover of outlaws Jack Spaniard and James Kell French.[64]

On the morning of May 25, 1886, Belle checked out of her Fort Smith hotel and had Venus saddled and brought from the livery stable. The *Fort Smith Elevator* described her departure: "Belle Starr left for her home on the Canadian River on Tuesday morning. . . . Just before starting home she showed us a fine pair of black-handled Colt's revolvers, 45 calibre [sic], short barrel, which she had purchased at Wersing's the evening previous for $29 cash."[65]

Another Fort Smith newshawk—hungry for a full-blown feature story for the *Dallas Morning News*—had convinced Belle to sit for an interview on the night of May 24, 1886. He was described as "a correspondent for several southwestern dailies."[66] The newsman was John F. Weaver, a well-known Fort Smith journalist who also worked as a correspondent for other newspapers.[67]

The 1886 story contained the same first-person account, allegedly written by Belle, that appeared at the end of a *Fort Smith Elevator* story by Weaver on February 15, 1889. According to Weaver, Belle's account in the 1886 article remained in his desk drawer until he wrote about her in 1889. However, substantial blocks of identical text directly attributed to Belle were included in both stories. As Weaver explained in 1889, "The following sketch of her life was written by Belle herself, and handed to a reporter of this paper over two years ago but we never had occasion to use it. We published it now *ver batim* [sic], as evidence of her intelligence and education."[68]

The story, with no byline, had been published originally in the *Dallas Morning News* on June 7, 1886. It appeared beneath the headline:

THRILLING LIFE OF A GIRL
BELLE STARR, WHO SHELTERS OUTLAWS

For the past week, the noted Belle Starr has been quite an attraction on the streets of this city. . . . Belle attracts considerable attention where she goes, being a dashing horsewoman, and exceedingly graceful in the saddle. She dresses plainly, and wears a broad-brimmed white man's hat, surrounded by a wide black plush band, with feathers and ornaments, which is very becoming to her. She is of medium size, well formed, a dark brunette, with bright and intelligent black eyes. . . . While here, she kindly granted your correspondent a long interview concerning her past life, but made it plainly understood that she had but little use for newspaper reporters, who, she claims, at various time, have done her great injustices.[69]

Belle proudly showed the interviewer her newly purchased .45-caliber revolvers, which she called her "babies." She added, "Next to a fine horse, I admire a fine pistol. Don't you think these are beauties?" The reporter wrote, "Belle is a crack shot, and handles her pistol with as much dexterity as any frontiersman."[70]

When the reporter asked Belle for a "brief sketch of her career," what followed was a recitation in the reporter's own words highlighting Belle's life from her birth in Missouri to the present. She denied the various crimes she had been accused of but admitted that "her husband [Sam Starr] is, at all times, on the scout to avoid arrest, and there are several charges of larceny, robbery, etc., against him, which have been trumped up by his enemies." Belle spoke of her daughter, Pearl, "whom she calls the 'Canadian Lily,'" and of Venus, the horse she had owned for five years and refused to sell "time and time again" even to the highest bidders.[71]

Near the end of the newspaper account, the reporter made a claim that was never proved to be true but that nourished the originators of the Belle Starr myth:

"Belle related many incidents of her life that would be of interest and says she has been offered big money by publishers for a complete history of it but does not yet desire to have it published. . . . She has a complete manuscript record, and when she dies, she will give it to the public. She spends most of her time writing when at home."[72]

That claim spawned a flood of rumors of a secret book by Belle that has never been uncovered and likely never existed. As Glenn Shirley wrote, the correspondent's dispatch was "full of half-truths and errors but the source of much Belle Starr nonsense."[73]

However, the final paragraph of the *Dallas Morning News* story rings true and best sums up Belle's attitude at that time. It also indicates that the memory of her beloved rebel brother, Bud, shot dead by Yankees, had not diminished:

"You can just say I am a friend to any brave and gallant outlaw, but have no use for that sneaking, coward class of thieves who can be found on every locality, and who would betray a friend or comrade for the sake of their own gain. There are three or four jolly, good fellows on the dodge right now in my section, and when they come to my home, they are welcome, for they are my friends, and would lay down their lives in my defense at any time the occasion demanded it, and go their full length to serve me in any way."[74]

After Belle departed Fort Smith in late May and crossed back into Indian Territory, she found that Pearl and Eddie were at Younger's Bend, and Sam was still on the scout. When Belle finally got her hands on a copy of the *Dallas Morning News* that included her interview, she was "irritated to no end."[75]

For many years, some local raconteurs insisted that when Belle returned to Fort Smith in late June to answer for her alleged role in the Farrill robbery, she came upon the reporter and viciously lashed him with her riding quirt.[76] Unlike Belle's previous clash with a reporter, no such incident appeared in any records or newspaper reports, likely because it never happened.

The June hearing in Fort Smith to take witness testimony in the Farrill robbery case was brief. Plaintiff Wilse Farrill could not identify Belle as one of the robbers of his store. Neither could his sons and employees. Lila McGilberry, the young woman responsible for having involved Belle in the crime in the first place, testified that she had never seen the defendant before that night of the robbery. But she maintained that the robber in men's clothing who "did not talk like a man" was Belle Starr. "I seen the defendant here yesterday and knew it was her," she testified.[77]

During cross-examination, Belle's skilled lawyers shredded the testimony. Other witnesses described the three robbers as "good sized men" who were not as small as Belle. Their testimony was so convincing that none of the defense witnesses was called to back up Belle's alibi that she was at a community dance at the time of the crime. She was cleared, and the charge was dismissed.[78]

Once again, Belle made the trip home and found her husband still absent. Like Jack Spaniard, Frank Palmer, Felix Griffin, and other wanted fugitives, Sam Starr found it in his best interest to stay scarce. He dodged a band of lawmen led by Sheriff William Vann and Deputy Marshal Frank Smith and a posse of Indian police under the command of Captain Sam Sixkiller. During Belle's stay in Fort Smith, dealing with her own legal matters and posing for photographs, the two posses had combined and swooped down on Younger's Bend "to clean out the gang of thieves there."[79]

To the lawmen's chagrin, only Belle's son and daughter were at the Starr home when they arrived. But a few days later, Felix Griffin met his match. Bullet Foreman, a well-known Cherokee citizen and longtime operator of a ferry on the Arkansas River at the mouth of the Illinois River, recognized Griffin at the ferry crossing and got the drop on him. On July 2, Foreman delivered Griffin to the United States marshal at Fort Smith and received a $500 reward.[80]

Less than a week later, Belle Starr was back in the public eye. On July

8, the *Arkansas Democrat* cast her as a "Notorious Female Outlaw of the Indian Territory" in an editorial with no byline:[81]

"Belle Starr has gained for herself a wide and extended reputation; if not a favorable one, it certainly makes her a heroine. Her home is an obscure nook in the Indian Territory, surrounded by a wild, romantic country where the panorama of nature at once inspires admiration and awe. Under different training and surrounded by different circumstances, she might have been a Maid of Orleans . . . , to be loved and praised by the generations of the future; but fate has not be willed it, and the plucky little woman must content herself as the acknowledged queen of outlaws and ruffians. . . . Time and time again she has been arrested, but her ingenuity has as often secured her release. . . . She will not give the reporters scraps of her life because she considers that a history of her career is worth a fortune, and she will one day publish it in book form."[82]

Throughout the summer, Belle did not stray far from home. It was time to ready herself to stand trial in September for the theft of Albert McCarty's one-eyed mare.

Meanwhile, the grand jury in Fort Smith dealt with some of Sam Starr's associates. Jurors passed on the murder charge against Felix Griffin, but on August 24, they indicted him for the robbery of the Blaine store and post office. Griffin posted bond and returned to Indian Territory. The grand jury also indicted Jack Spaniard and Frank Palmer for murder. Both remained at large. Spaniard laid low at a hideout in the Creek Nation, and Palmer fled the area and was never captured.[83]

Belle's trial for larceny was set to begin in September. Because Pearl and Eddie were scheduled to appear as defense witnesses, Belle left Venus at Younger's Bend, and they traveled to Fort Smith in a wagon. After securing hotel rooms, Belle visited with friends and conferred with her lawyers.

The trial had hardly begun when Judge Parker suddenly halted the proceedings. Word had reached Fort Smith that law officers had shot Sam Starr on September 16. Belle's attorneys petitioned the court for a recess so she could return at once to Indian Territory.[84]

"Belle Starr, who is here on bond awaiting trial, has received a letter from her home on the Canadian River stating that her husband, Sam Starr, who has been dodging the officers for years, had been badly wounded in a conflict with the Indian police," reported an *Arkansas Gazette* dispatch from Little Rock. "Belle said that her information was that the police fired on and wounded Sam, killing his horse, without demanding his surrender and that about 50 shots had been exchanged in the fight. Belle has the court's permission to be absent until next Wednesday [September 22] and will leave in the morning for her husband's bedside."[85]

When Belle and her children reached Younger's Bend, they were told that while hunting for Sam in the Canadian River bottoms, a party of law officers, including Sheriff Vann and Frank West, observed a lone rider loping through a cornfield. West knew it was Sam Starr and told the others he was confident that his cousin would never lay down his weapons. Without calling for Sam to surrender, West fired a volley of shots.[86]

Sam was struck and cried out. His horse was also shot and screamed with pain. Sam grasped the saddle horn as he and the horse fell hard to the ground. The officers swept down on the field. Sam was unconscious, with blood oozing from his head and another wound in his side. The horse was dead, shot through the neck.[87] West recognized the mare. Sam had been riding Belle's beloved Venus, likely to rest his own horse.

The lawmen secured a wagon at a nearby farmhouse and stanched Sam's wounds to keep him alive. West and Vann raced off to find medical aid and left two deputies as guards. Apparently Sam's wounds were not as serious as they looked. When Sam regained consciousness, he disarmed both deputies and escaped on one of their horses. It was said that as he rode away, Sam shouted, "Tell Frank West he'll pay for killing Belle's mare."[88]

Forty-six years later, R. P. Vann, younger brother of Sheriff Vann, falsely claimed, "Tom Starr and his gang overpowered the officers and took Sam away with them."[89] However, R. P. Vann was not a member of the posse, and there is no evidence to support his version of the escape.

Sam made his way through the cover of the river bottoms and went into hiding at the home of one of his brothers near Briartown, where Belle found him. She helped care for Sam's wounds and cursed Frank West for having killed her cherished Venus. But her time to mourn was brief—Belle had to hurry back to Fort Smith to resume her trial for horse theft.

True to his pledge, Fayette Barnett—the actual thief—paid Belle's legal fees and appeared as a key defense witness. Under oath, Barnett covered both his and Belle's tracks when he testified that he had been present when John Middleton paid "a stranger" fifty dollars in gold for Albert McCarty's mare.[90]

As in Belle's larceny trial in June, the jury spent little time in deliberation. They found her "not guilty as charged in the within indictment."[91] Soon after the trial, it was reported that Barnett deserted his Choctaw wife and "made a fortune in the liquor trade" in New Mexico Territory.[92]

At last, Belle was legally absolved. She rushed back to Sam. Inspired by her own vindication, Belle implored her husband to stop running from the law and turn himself in to federal authorities before he was killed. But Sam "'vowed to go to hell first' before surrendering."[93] Belle persisted. She explained that if the Indian police captured him and he was tried in tribal court, the risk of severe corporal punishment or execution was almost certain. She also pointed out that if he surrendered to a United States deputy marshal, he would be under the protection of the United States and could be freed on bond. Even if he went to trial before Judge Parker and was convicted, a prison sentence was far better than death.[94]

After further consideration, Sam agreed that his best course was to turn himself in to a federal officer. Belle sent word to Deputy Marshal Tyner Hughes. On October 4, 1886, Hughes, bearing the felony bench warrant issued nine months earlier, took Sam into custody at Briartown.[95]

Citizens of Fort Smith must have been surprised on October 7 when they spotted the notorious Sam Starr, unarmed and unshackled, riding up the avenue to the federal courthouse. He was riding next to Deputy Hughes and in front of Belle, who was said to have had "her revolvers belted at her waist and hat feathers waving in the breeze."[96]

Later that day, Sam appeared before United States Commissioner Stephen Wheeler for arraignment based on the issuance of the grand-jury indictment for "breaking into Postoffice [sic] and larceny of postoffice money."[97] Sam entered a plea of not guilty and was ordered to put up bail of $1,000 to stay free for his next court appearance, set for 10 a.m. November 1.[98] Belle covered the bail-bond requirement.

Prior to Sam's surrender to Hughes, Belle had sought commitments from Alex Burns, a nearby friend, and Frank J. Arnold, who was described as one of the Reeds from Logan County, Arkansas. Both men appeared in Fort Smith and were present at the arraignment. They signed a recognizance bond pledging the surrender of assets, including property and livestock, if Sam failed to reappear in court.[99]

Sam was granted his freedom until the November court proceedings. After being on the scout for most of the year, he was more than ready to spend time in Fort Smith with his wife.

The citizens of Fort Smith were excitedly gearing up for the Seventh Annual Fair of Western Arkansas and the Indian Territory. The fair opened on October 12 with a stirring address from Arkansas governor Simon P. Hughes.[100] During the five-day run, thousands of spectators from throughout the region flocked to Fort Smith to take in exhibits, marching bands, balloon ascensions, and grand illuminations that filled the night skies.

One of the most popular attractions was W. W. Cole's New Colossal Show, a circus featuring trapeze artists, acrobats, clowns, performing lions, elephants, and a white hippopotamus. It was said to be "the most stupendous menagerie ever gathered and exhibited under tents."[101]

Born the son of a contortionist father and a high-wire artist mother, William Washington Cole believed a sideshow exhibition was "the sizzle that sells the steak."[102] Curiosity seekers crowded displays that exploited the abnormalities of people with birth defects, disfigurements, and mental challenges. There was a buzz around Fort Smith when newspapers callously described a "veritable living skeleton . . . being wheeled around the city in his perambulator."[103]

Paying to gawk at "human oddities" held no appeal for some fairgoers, including the Starrs. When Belle learned that the Cole circus was combined with William Frank "Doc" Carver's Famous Original Wild West Show, she and Sam found the ideal place to spend the next five days.[104]

Carver had begun his career as an entertainer and exhibition marksman in 1878. By 1883, after touring Europe with his sharpshooter act, Carver briefly partnered with William F. "Buffalo Bill" Cody in an early Wild West show that failed.[105] Cody often inflated his own importance and helped to form the Wild West myth. Carver went further when creating his own public image.

"In later years he [Carver] invented an early life for himself that was not only remarkable, but so falsified as to cast doubt upon his known abilities," according to western history coauthors Joseph G. Rosa and Robin May. "The truth, of course, is less dramatic."[106]

Belle probably could not have cared less about the veracity of Doc Carver—"Undaunted Scout, Traveler and Wizard Rifleman"—or his troupe of "Renowned Scouts, Cowboys, Indians, Texas Rangers and Mexican Vaqueros."[107] What caught her attention was the opportunity to enter some of the riding contests and participate in reenactments.

To enter any events, the Starrs needed approval from the Fair Association of Western Arkansas. The association's president just happened to be Judge Isaac Parker.[108] After having recently released Sam Starr on bail and proclaimed Belle innocent of robbery charges, Parker gave the couple permission to perform.

When news broke about Belle and Sam Starr's participation at the fair, arrangements were quickly made to include them "in a sort of wild west show."[109] It proved to be a crowd pleaser.

"The weather is beautiful and a successful fair is assured," wrote a Little Rock reporter. "Belle and Sam Starr will attend and give an exhibition of their daring horsemanship. They took a turn around the speed ring this afternoon."[110]

By chance, the Carthage Light Guard Band, from Belle's hometown in Missouri, attended the fair and provided the stirring music at the Starrs' performances.[111] The band not only won the $400 grand prize in a competitive grandstand performance, but Belle visited some members who recalled her as a schoolgirl racing across the countryside with her big brother Bud. W. J. Sewall, a member of the cornet section, later described Belle as "a dark, leathery-faced woman of remarkable agility and horsemanship."[112]

When the band returned to Missouri, the *Carthage News* reported the musicians' impressions of Belle's performances. "Riding a horse bareback at full gallop, she broke clay pigeons and glass balls with rifle fire while in motion, varying the performance by leaping from the animal while moving at full speed, breaking more glass balls and clay pigeons from the ground with her rifle, then leaping back on her animal as it galloped past her again, still at full speed and continued her firing."[113]

The high point for Belle came on October 15, Merchants' Day at the fair. Reportedly at the request of Judge Parker, Belle was chosen to lead the band of robbers for the reenactment of a stagecoach holdup. To add to the excitement, Parker consented to be one of the passengers riding in the stage.[114] One newspaper described the faked robbery as "similar to that in the 'Wild West' shows" and praised how "Belle Starr led the robbers, and exhibited her great skill in handling a charger under excitement and her aptness with a six-shooter. She went at it in a natural way. Sam Starr also appeared in the play."[115]

Some writers greatly embellished the account of Belle's equestrian skills when they injected a tale that Belle intended to use the reenacted stagecoach robbery as cover to assassinate William H. H. Clayton. He had been the federal prosecutor at the 1882 trial that resulted in the Starrs' imprisonment.[116] Belle supposedly slipped a live cartridge into her pistol loaded with blanks so she could shoot Clayton during the pretend attack on the stagecoach. When word came that Clayton was unable to join Parker in the stagecoach, Belle allegedly removed the live round and replaced it with a blank. One imaginative author even claimed that she later told Clayton of the assassination plot.[117]

That incident did not appear in any contemporary newspaper coverage, and no record or evidence of its having occurred has ever been produced. In fact, it is ludicrous to give the murder scheme any credence. Clayton was Sam Starr's lawyer. In 1886, Clayton was not in office but in private practice. M. H. Sandels had become the prosecuting attorney.[118] It is highly unlikely that Belle would have wanted to harm one of her husband's lawyers.

After the fair closed, the Starrs, no doubt exhilarated by the roles they had played and with the cheers of the crowds ringing in their ears, rode back to Younger's Bend to share their own accounts with Pearl and Eddie.

In Fort Smith, Sam's lawyers, Clayton and Thomas Marcum, prepared for his trial. On their client's behalf, they made application for defense witnesses "without whose testimony deft. [defendant] cannot safely proceed to trial. . . . The deft. says he has not the means & actually unable to pay the fees of said witnesses."[119] Judge Parker approved the application, and Sam and Belle returned to Fort Smith in November for the trial. However, because of the difficulty that deputy marshals had in locating prosecution and defense witnesses, Parker delayed the trial and continued the case until February 1887.[120]

Instead of returning home straightaway, the Starrs stayed in Fort Smith to support Sam's father, Tom, who was quartered in the federal jail. Over the years, the notorious patriarch of the Starr family had stayed clear of legal troubles. The one vice he was not willing to curtail, however, was running whiskey. In time, his luck turned, and authorities came calling at Briartown.

Tom Starr had dodged serious jail time in 1884 on a charge of introducing five gallons of whiskey into Indian Territory; a US deputy marshal simply failed to find him to serve a warrant. In late 1885, he was arrested for introducing and peddling four gallons of illicit liquor. He pleaded not guilty and was released on $300 bond.[121] Trial on that charge was still pending when on November 2, 1885, Starr was caught in the act of selling one gallon of whiskey. That same day, he ended up in the federal prison at Fort Smith.

The grand jury passed on Starr's 1884 charge but returned indictments on the two other cases.[122] Sam and Belle were present for Tom's arraignment before Judge Parker on November 23. Sam's lawyers could not help Tom out of his predicament. To the surprise of many courtroom spectators, Tom entered a guilty plea. Parker gave him a one-year sentence on the first count and a six-month sentence and fifty-dollar fine on the 1886 charge.[123] On November 27, Tom Starr was transported to the Southern Illinois Penitentiary at Menard.[124]

By the time Sam and Belle returned home, the anguish Sam felt over his father's imprisonment had turned into full-blown rage. Much of his anger came from his own legal problems, most of which he credited to Frank and John West. By mid-December, Belle feared that Sam might forfeit his bail and go back on the scout to seek revenge.

In hope of finding some relief for her troubled husband, Belle talked him into attending the annual Christmas dance hosted by Lucy Surratt and her husband, Henry Surratt, at their home near Whitefield (formerly called Oklahoma) in the Choctaw Nation. Pearl and Eddie were eager to see friends at the dance. On December 17, the family foursome left Younger's Bend on horseback and crossed the Canadian River. They arrived at the Surratt place, on a rise above Emachaya Creek, by early evening.[125]

There was a good turnout of folks from miles around, including many of the Starrs' friends. "Aunt Lucy" Surratt, as she was called, laid out plenty of food and drink, and lively fiddle and guitar music ensured a crowded dance floor. Some people in attendance that evening recalled that Belle took a turn on an old pedal organ while her children danced, and onlookers stomped and shouted.[126]

Sam, not one to do much dancing, was drinking hard. He took it all in from a chair near the organ and the front door. Outside, the Surratts stoked a big log fire for guests to keep warm while taking a break in the chilly night air. At some point, Frank West arrived. Before going inside, he went to the fire and was told that his cousin and enemy, Sam Starr, was at the dance. West ignored the advice that it would be wise to get back on his horse and leave.[127]

Moments later, Sam stepped outside and spotted West hunkered by the fire. Sam approached him, and they exchanged words. Sam cursed West for wounding him and killing Belle's horse, Venus, but what exactly happened next is not clear. Some onlookers claimed that Sam drew his gun and shot first. Others said both men fired at almost the same time.

On December 22, a Muskogee newspaper reporter shared an eyewitness account: "Sam pulled his revolver, and West drew his as soon after as he could, but not until he received a mortal wound [in his neck], from which he staggered; but, recovering, he sent a ball through Starr, and then fell dead. Sam staggered for about ten feet and then he, too, fell a corpse."[128]

According to another newspaper report, after having been shot, "Sam turned and throwing his arms around a small tree held himself on his feet until life was extinct, when he fell over stone dead."[129]

Belle rushed to Sam's lifeless body. It was said that she knelt and held his head in her arms, telling Sam that "she would willingly die in his stead if it were possible. . . . There were no tears in her eyes, but her face was white and she cursed Frank West. However, that may be, both men died game within minutes after sighting each other,"[130] recalled a guest at the dance.

Later that night, the body of thirty-four-year-old West was placed in a wagon and taken home to his wife and two children. He was buried just east of Briartown in McClure Cemetery. The following morning, a wagon took Sam's body to his father's home. Tom was in prison in Illinois. Sam Starr, only twenty-seven years old, was laid to rest in the Starr Cemetery. Most of his family was buried there, southwest of Briartown overlooking the Canadian River, just miles from Younger's Bend.

CHAPTER 23

The Curtain Falls

JANUARY 1887 ARRIVED IN INDIAN TERRITORY, AND ONCE again, Belle Starr was a widow. Now two of her three marriages had ended abruptly in deadly gunplay. Secluded at her home, she grieved for Sam and contemplated the future. As usual, the prospects were not promising.

Cedar boughs still decorated Sam's grave in the Starr Cemetery when Belle received more devastating news—the Cherokee Nation tribal council had questioned her continued residency at Younger's Bend. The council ruled that because of Sam Starr's death, Belle had no claim to the dwelling and the surrounding property. She and her children had no Cherokee blood. They were considered White intruders in the Cherokee Nation and had to move.[1]

Belle had no intention of ever leaving her sanctuary on the South Canadian, but she took the tribal ultimatum seriously. Her solution was to find a tribal citizen to join her family at Younger's Bend.

Belle recruited a young man she had known since he was a teenager who frequently showed up at Tom Starr's home near Briartown. He was a nephew of July Perryman of the Creek Nation but was mostly of Cherokee blood, and he used several names. He was born Bill July and often went by Jim July. Tom Starr considered him an adopted son and called him July Starr. On occasion, he called himself Jim July Starr.[2] Contrary to some reports, Belle did not bestow the Starr surname on him.

"Jim July, or Starr, is a splendid specimen of the half-breed, tall, powerfully built and courteous in manner," was one reporter's description of him. "He possesses some excellent natural traits."[3] Educated in Indian schools, July was literate in English and spoke several other Indian languages besides Cherokee and Creek. He wore his hair long and often braided, and much like Sam Starr, he "had the same air of reckless indifference, which excited Belle."[4]

July accepted Belle's invitation to cohabit as her de facto husband. It was reported that he had been "acquainted with Belle Starr about six years, and was married to her about ten months after his cousin, Sam Starr, was killed, an old Cherokee Judge performing the ceremony."[5] Even though no official records for their marriage have been found in Canadian District of the Cherokee Nation or in the surrounding area, July moved into Younger's Bend in 1887. Their union was considered "legal in every respect under an old Cherokee custom and good in federal courts as common law."[6] Belle proudly announced the addition to her household to family and friends. The news did not go over well with Pearl and Eddie.

When July moved to Younger's Bend, he was twenty-four years old, fifteen years younger than Belle, who had turned thirty-nine on February 5. Pearl was going on nineteen, and Eddie had turned sixteen on February 22. Only a few years younger than July, Belle's children resented the new living arrangement.[7] Pearl and Eddie would never accept July as their "stepfather," and he wisely did not try to take on that role.

July's presence at Younger's Bend exacerbated a growing rift between Belle and her children. Eddie Reed was restless and rebelled against Belle's strictness and her demands for him to toe the line and avoid trouble. She often disapproved of Eddie's choice of chums and his deportment.[8] In spite of his mother's rigid rules, young Eddie, who sported a dashing mustache, was said to have "exhibited all the wild characteristics of his father, and under the tutelage of Sam Starr he had gained a liberal education in scouting."[9]

While Belle struggled to keep her son on the straight and narrow, she also tried to regain control of her daughter. During Belle's frequent absences from home, her "Canadian Lily" had blossomed into a young woman who attracted many potential suitors. One caught her fancy—Robert McClure, a Cherokee man less than two years older than Pearl.

Born in 1867 in Monroe County, Georgia, he was one of James and Rebecca McClure's nine children.[10] In 1880, the family had left their ancestral home in Georgia and relocated near Briartown. They joined family members who had settled there after their removal to Indian Territory in the 1830s. Robert's parents were well acquainted with the Starrs, and some McClure descendants believe the McClures might have been related "in some way" to the Starr and West families.[11]

Robert McClure met Pearl when they both attended the log schoolhouse at Briartown. By 1885, they were spending more time together, and before long, they became steadfast lovers. McClure gathered his courage and showed up at the Starrs' home seeking permission to make Pearl his wife. A stunned Belle told him that would never happen. Belle wanted her daughter to wed a man of wealth and not a farm boy without any income.[12] Pearl and McClure were devastated by Belle's reaction. Pearl pleaded with her mother to allow them to marry. Instead, Belle took steps to break up the young couple. Various accounts of how she carried out her plan have been put forward.

One version claimed that Belle sent Pearl to stay with the Marshalls, her family friends in Chickalah, Arkansas.[13] Belle then sent a letter to McClure, supposedly written by Pearl, explaining that she had taken her mother's advice and married a rich man. "Heavy of heart that Pearl could forget him so soon," McClure turned his attention to seventeen-year-old Elizabeth "Lizzy" Weaver, whose family had moved to Briartown from Ohio. When Pearl returned from Chickalah, she learned, "much to her chagrin," of McClure's recent marriage to Lizzy.[14]

In spring 1886, McClure discovered that Pearl had returned and was not married after all—it was all a ruse that Belle had orchestrated. McClure offered to "seek a legal separation" from his wife to end their marriage, but by all accounts, Pearl "refused to listen."[15] McClure's marital status, however, did not fully quench the fiery passion he shared with Pearl. In the summer of 1886, while Belle was busy with legal matters in Fort Smith, Pearl became pregnant.[16] She kept her condition secret throughout the rest of the year while Belle dealt with the courts and the death of Sam Starr.

By February 1887, Pearl could no longer hide her pregnancy. Belle exploded in anger, which turned to burning rage when Pearl refused to name the father. Belle's options were limited. The mother-to-be was too far along to use one of many strong purgatives available to induce spontaneous termination. It was also too late to find a physician willing to perform a clandestine surgical abortion.[17]

A pregnant unwed woman was considered "damaged goods." In her condition, Pearl held little appeal for any eligible man, especially one of means. Belle did not give up, however. She and Pearl went to see a prosperous older gentleman who operated a livery stable in Fort Smith.[18] In the past, he had shown some interest in marrying Pearl and still did so even after he was told of the pregnancy. Likely feeling trapped, Pearl was troubled by their age difference and spurned his proposal of marriage.

Back at Younger's Bend, Belle decided the best remaining solution was to send Pearl to live with the Reed family. Before her daughter's departure, Belle made it clear that after the birth, Pearl was welcome to come home, but under no circumstances could she return with the infant.[19]

Pearl packed her belongings. At Fort Smith, she boarded a northbound train to Missouri, where Marion Reed, her father's oldest brother, greeted Pearl and placed her belongings in a buggy. They went to the Rich Hill home of her grandmother, Susan Reed, where Pearl had been born in September 1868.[20]

As winter gave way to spring, Susan, almost sixty-seven years old, felt poorly.[21] She was advised to find relief for her crippling arthritis by "taking the waters" at Siloam Springs, a health resort in northwestern Arkansas on the eastern border of Indian Territory.[22] The healing power of the water "as clear as crystal" in Sager Creek attracted throngs of health seekers who suffered from afflictions including rheumatism, asthma, malaria, jaundice, and even constipation.[23]

Uncle Marion escorted Pearl and her grandmother to Siloam Springs.[24] They took rooms at the Lakeside Hotel, a two-story brick building built in 1881, a year after the town had been established.[25] The hotel boasted comfortable accommodations, good food, and attentive staff members who catered to every need. Guests sitting on the wraparound porch were provided with lap blankets. Nearby, a pipeline housed in a stone wall channeled curative water to spouts that filled the cups and jugs of all imbibers who sought comfort.[26]

By April in northwestern Arkansas, chilly days lingered, but winter had lost its grip. Throughout the countryside, redbud trees blossomed, soon followed by dogwoods. It was the season of renewal and new beginnings. In Siloam Springs, Pearl was ready to give birth. The time came on Friday, April 22, 1887.[27] At 6:30 that morning near the town of Clarksville, sixty miles east of Fort Smith, a renegade tornado slashed across Johnson County. In minutes, twenty people died and one hundred were injured.[28] To the northwest, Siloam Springs had rain and thunder but avoided lethal weather.

That blustery spring day, likely in a hotel room with her grandmother and a midwife in attendance, Pearl gave birth to a healthy baby girl. Her name had been chosen long before she arrived. Pearl named her daughter Mamie McClure, after Pearl's favorite aunt, Mamie Reed Young of Wichita, Kansas.[29] A popular name in the 1880s, Mamie was of Greek and Latin origin and meant "pearl" or "star of the sea."

Shortly after the birth, Uncle Marion Reed escorted Pearl, Mamie, and Susan Reed to the family home at Rich Hill. Pearl begged Susan and other Reed kin to tell Belle that "she had left for some place unknown." But Pearl did not leave. Instead, she and "little Mamie"—as the Reeds called the baby—remained at Rich Hill.[30]

Although Belle had made it clear that she never wanted to see her daughter's love child, perhaps that was a front to conceal her concern for Pearl. At Younger's Bend, Belle must have been thinking about her daughter, especially when the expected date of the birth came and went. But Belle also had to deal with problems at home. She was occupied with her son's antics and with concerns about Jim July. Once again, she had become involved with a man prone to breaking the law.

In July 1887, Indian police tracked down Jim July and took him into custody for horse theft.[31] The arresting officer was John West, brother of Frank West, who had died in the gunfight with Sam Starr. A warrant for July's arrest was issued by Commissioner John Quincy Tufts, who conducted preliminary hearings at Muskogee, Indian Territory, on cases bound for the federal court at Fort Smith. The warrant charged that "Bill July alias Jim Starr did in the Indian Country . . . on or about the 27 day of June, take carry with the intent to steal one horse valued at $125, the property of J. H. McCormick, a white man and not an Indian."[32]

At the August 30 hearing before Commissioner Tufts, prosecutors alleged that July had slipped into a campsite twenty-five miles west of Okmulgee in the Creek Nation and had stolen a large nine-year-old black mare belonging to McCormick, a resident of Coffeyville, Kansas. According to witnesses, July had been seen in "the vicinity [of the camp] posing as a trader or gambler."[33]

July was not riding the stolen horse when West apprehended him but was mounted on a smaller mare that he had bought from Fox Taylor near Fort Gibson. To verify July's story, West went to Taylor's home, where he found McCormick's black mare and learned that July had swapped the stolen horse for Taylor's mare and fifteen dollars.[34] July was jailed at Fort Smith, where he would remain until he found "sufficient bail in the sum of $500."[35]

Belle—conspicuously absent at July's hearing—did not rush to Fort Smith to post bond. She let July stew in his cell for a while to ponder the consequences of his actions. Since Sam's death, Belle had tried to quell the gossip and slander about her lifestyle and conduct, including the never-ending rumor that she had led an outlaw gang operating out of her home at Younger's Bend. July's arrest was a bit of a setback, but nonetheless, her campaign began to pay off.

Robert Latham Owen, a distinguished attorney in Indian Territory, publicly supported Belle and acknowledged her effort to redeem her reputation. In 1885, Owen had been appointed to head the Union Indian Agency, with headquarters in Muskogee, after John Tufts resigned the post to become a United States commissioner. On July 6, 1887, Owen wrote a letter to Belle that was published in several Indian Territory newspapers.[36] The letter was brief but left no doubt about Owen's opinion of Belle:

Mrs. Belle Starr
Oklahoma, I. T.

   Madam: The complaint against you for harboring bad characters has not, in my opinion, been established and is now dismissed. I hope sincerely that you will faithfully carry out your promise to this office not to let such parties make your place a rendezvous.

Yours respectfully,
Robert L. Owen
United States Indian Agent[37]

Owen, a progressive Democrat, became a prominent national figure, and in 1907, he was elected one of the first senators representing the new state of Oklahoma.[38] Given Owen's standing and reputation, his letter likely lifted Belle's spirits and gave her morale a much-needed boost.

Still, Belle would not help her new husband, whom she treated like a delinquent son. On September 5, thanks to some friends, July posted his $500 bond. He was released from jail and dashed back to Younger's Bend, seeking Belle's forgiveness. After a stern reprimand from Belle, July promised to stay out of trouble. Later, at his arraignment in November, July entered a plea of not guilty. The court allowed his bond to stand and continued his case to the following August.[39]

Through the rest of the winter of 1887–1888, none of the usual drama occurred at Younger's Bend. July and Eddie quietly went about their lives. Several of Belle's longtime detractors from the settlements in the South Canadian River valley began to see her in a different light.

Frederick S. Barde, described as "one of Oklahoma's most ablest [sic] newspapermen,"[40] interviewed people who had known Belle when he wrote his profile of her in 1910.[41] According to Barde, even people who knew her to be "merely a harborer of thieves . . . had a bit of sympathy for her. She was human at heart, and in the thinly settled region where she lived, no woman was more generous to the sick and unfortunate. There are still persons living in old Indian Territory who feel that she was more sinned against than sinning." Some folks told Barde that Belle became "a victim of surroundings from which she could not escape."[42]

In early 1888, Belle could no longer ignore Pearl's prolonged absence. July offered Belle no comfort, and Eddie constantly reminded his mother that she was the real cause of his sister leaving home. Finally, Belle wrote to her former mother-in-law in Missouri, seeking information about Pearl. In a brief letter of response, Susan Reed replied that Pearl and Mamie had moved to an unknown location.[43]

Susan Reed lied to Belle to protect Pearl and her child. Although she did not reveal Pearl's whereabouts, Susan knew exactly where Pearl had found a haven for herself and her daughter, by then one year old. They were in Wichita, quietly living with Pearl's aunt and Mamie's namesake, Mamie Reed Young.

While Belle continued to search for her daughter, Eddie decided to go on the scout with Mose Perryman, a young man from a prominent Creek family and purportedly kin to Jim July. The pair of novice outlaws rode into the Creek Nation on July 11, 1888, where they did "feloniously steal, take and carry away from the lawful possession of Jim Lewis, a negro and not an Indian, one horse of the value of thirty dollars."[44]

Ten days later, United States Marshal John Carroll swore out a court order for the arrests of Reed and Perryman to appear before Commissioner James Brizzolara at Fort Smith. Carroll assigned United States Deputy Marshal G. G. Tyson to help track down the alleged horse thieves. Tyson was unable to find Perryman but came upon Ed Reed at a farmhouse, lying wounded by a gunshot wound in his head. After interrogating Reed, Tyson gave "reliable information," attached to the writ that summarized what had transpired after the horse theft:

Reed and Perryman left the neighborhood the same day [July 11] and got as far as Patrick Ferry on the Ark. [Arkansas] River. Being near night, they couldn't cross . . . and went back to the point of Brushy Mountain to camp. . . . After Ed Reed has gone to sleep Mose Perryman shot him in the head, the ball entering near the nose and coming out the ear. Perryman then went to Philo Harris to stay all night, and Mrs. Harris discovered the print of bloody fingers on his coat sleeve. She called his attention to it, and he, Mose said that while they were asleep some unknown party crept up and shot at them hitting Ed Reed. But Reed swears Perryman shot him and wants a writ for him.[45]

Tyson added a note to the complaint confirming that Reed's "statement is supported by Mr. Harris & wife, put them down as witnesses. The negro Lewis came up day before yesterday and got his pony back that was in Ed Reed's possession. Ed is now at Mr. Wallaces [sic] house, badly wounded."[46]

For the time being, Tyson decided to not serve the warrant because of Reed's condition. Instead of taking him into custody, Tyson summoned Belle. She and July were allowed to take her son to Younger's Bend to recuperate.[47] The hunt for Perryman, now accused of attempted murder, continued.

Despite the anger and disappointment she felt, Belle doggedly nursed her son. She also came up with a ploy to lure Pearl back to Younger's Bend without bringing Mamie. In a letter to Susan Reed at Rich Hill, Belle exaggerated Eddie's condition. She explained that he had been shot, and if Pearl wanted to see her brother before he died, she had to come home as soon as possible. Belle also urged Pearl to leave her child behind during her visit. Along with the message, Belle included twenty dollars to cover travel expenses.[48]

Belle's scheme worked. Susan Reed forwarded the letter and the money to Pearl. When she learned of her brother's serious condition, Pearl was distressed and in a quandary. Although she and her baby had never been apart, Pearl decided it would be in everyone's best interest to leave little Mamie in the care of her aunt,[49] who wholeheartedly agreed.

Pearl reached Younger's Bend and after Belle welcomed her warmly, Pearl rushed to her brother. It was obvious that Belle had exaggerated the seriousness of his wound, and he was not close to death. Despite her mother's deception, Pearl stayed so she could help Ed make a full recovery and persuade him to not end up like their father.

Meanwhile, law officers continued their pursuit of Mose Perryman, wanted for horse theft as well as for shooting Ed Reed. On August 4, Deputy Marshal Tyson located and arrested his quarry on both charges and took him to Fort Smith.[50] Once Perryman was apprehended and jailed, his family, with the assistance of Jim July, pressured Ed to drop the charge of attempted murder. In return, the Perrymans promised to assist Ed in any way they could and provide defense counsel.[51]

Ed had no money of his own, and Belle refused to pay for lawyers, just as she had done when Jim July was in trouble. Ed could not pursue the charge against his accused accomplice. On August 7, after spending three days in jail, Mose Perryman made his bond on the larceny charge and was released. His case was continued for six months, to February 1889.[52]

It took two months for Ed to fully recuperate. Pearl remained his primary caregiver, but she missed little Mamie and longed to be with her again. During that late summer and early autumn, Belle tried to rehabilitate her relationship with her daughter. She proudly showed Pearl the letter from Robert Owen that proved "she was now in good standing with federal authorities and the Indian police."[53]

In late September, Belle convinced Pearl to take a short break from nursing Ed, who was almost fully recovered, to attend the Indian International Fair at Muskogee.[54] Held annually in September or October at the fairgrounds east of town, the highly anticipated event attracted huge crowds from Indian Territory and neighboring states.[55]

The Indian dances, horse races, and livestock and agricultural displays must have been a welcome diversion for Pearl and Belle. On September 27—"the chief day of the fair"—the pair decided to become part of the entertainment. After the afternoon shooting contests, Belle and Pearl made their appearance in the program finale.[56]

"Two lady equestrian contests concluded the day's programme," noted the *Vinita Indian Chieftain*. "The daughter of the notorious Belle Starr was one of the riders and she used no saddle. As the 'wild Indians,' so extensively advertised, did not show up, Belle was substituted as the leading attraction."[57]

The performance was a showstopper, and the crowd roared approval.

Belle and Pearl likely talked about their riding exhibition all the way home. That autumn, Belle and Pearl ventured out to community dances at Eufaula, Whitefield, and Briartown. Ed was back on his feet but refused to go, so July spruced up and escorted the women. "It was like old times," observed Glenn Shirley, "the past mistakes forgotten, and mother and daughter seemed happy."[58]

The family might have appeared happy, but tensions continued to brew beneath the surface. The question of Pearl's child still loomed, and Ed was obliged to answer to the horse-theft charge in Fort Smith now that he was back in good health.

On October 13, Ed appeared for arraignment before Commissioner Brizzolara. Testimony showed that when Ed had been shot, he was found in possession of "a sorrel pony branded G. L. on hip & shoulder."[59] The owner, "General Jim" Lewis, identified the horse as the one stolen from his home in the Creek Nation.

Brizzolara bound Ed over to a special grand jury that considered the evidence and indicted him on November 13. Instead of obtaining legal counsel for him as they had promised, the Perrymans and July did nothing to help. Outraged by the betrayal, Ed decided to prove that Mose Perryman was the lone thief and sought defense witnesses to back up his claim.[60] In his petition to the court, Ed explained that he could not proceed to trial without testimony from Will Meek, Vicey Grayson, and Nancy Grayson. The petition read in part:

> By Vicey Grayson & Nan Grayson he [Ed] can prove that from Eleven until the middle of the afternoon on the day said pony was taken from General Lewis, which was taken about eleven o'clock in the day, the defendant was at their house and was riding a bay horse, the one alleged to have been stolen being a sorrel.... By Will Meek he can prove that he [Meek] was present when this defendant made a trade with Mose Perryman and that Mose owed the defendant $25 and sold him the sorrel pony in payment of the Debt. That Perryman told this defendant that the title to said pony was good.[61]

Ed sought the court's understanding. He could not pay the fees to cover the travel of the three witnesses, and instead asked for them to be subpoenaed at the expense of the United States. Judge Isaac Parker and District Attorney Monti Hines Sandels, a future associate justice of the Supreme Court of Arkansas, sympathized with young Reed. His application for witnesses was approved, and the trial was set for the March 1889 term of court. Instead of waiting for trial in jail or putting up a cash bond, Ed was released on his own recognizance.[62]

When Ed arrived home, he did not hide his anger for the refusal of Jim July and Belle to help him. His resentment grew with each passing day, as did Pearl's desire to return to her child. Aware of this, Belle diligently worked to make sure Pearl would never leave Younger's Bend. For several months, Belle had monitored her family's incoming and outgoing mail with the postmaster at Whitefield. Her instructions were clear. She would collect all mail, and "under no circumstances" would any of it be given to either of her children.[63] In that way, Belle controlled all communications between Pearl and the Reed family.

After reading letters sent from Mamie Reed Young, Belle learned that Pearl's child was in her care in Wichita. She then stepped up her campaign to persuade Pearl to put up her daughter for adoption. Ultimately, Belle was successful. Pearl gave up her child.

In later years, as Pearl neared the end of her life, she vehemently denied that she had any role in giving up Mamie for adoption. She put the blame entirely on Belle. She insisted that the turning point came when Belle sent Pearl's Aunt Mamie and the Reeds in Missouri a barrage of letters threatening to have the child stolen and given to a caravan of roving gypsies.[64] According to Pearl, her aunt was so upset and frightened that she took the girl to an orphanage. Pearl also maintained that she refused to sign a document surrendering custody of Mamie and authorizing her adoption, implying that Belle forged her signature.[65] "I would never sign a paper to give one of my children away," Pearl wrote in 1924. "I ran screaming from the house without looking at the paper."[66]

Whoever signed Pearl's name, on November 18, 1888, nineteen-month-old Mamie McClure was placed in the Wichita Children's Home.[67]

The two-story facility had opened that year as the city's first orphanage to "support and care for destitute and homeless children" twelve years old and younger.[68] Overwhelmed with grief, Pearl might have hoped that Mamie would go to a loving family who would cherish the little girl and make her feel wanted and special. Maybe Pearl found a way to get beyond denial and anger to justify her own guilt and rationalize Belle's behavior.

Pearl remained with her mother for the sake of her brother, still facing trial for horse theft. As the year ended, Eddie's difficulties with Belle increased. She took him to task for trying to intercept mail at the post office behind her back and supposedly resorted to corporal punishment. S. W. Harman contended in his book, primarily founded on fictitious tales, that when Belle suspected Ed of mistreating her horse, she grabbed her quirt and "stalked to the house and into the room where Ed lay in bed asleep and gave him an unmerciful whipping."[69]

It is doubtful that Belle took a riding crop to her son, but the chasm between them deepened that fall and came to a head in late November. Possibly to cool tempers, mother and son sought a change of scenery. Both departed Younger's Bend bound for destinations in different directions. Ed packed his belongings, bid his sister good-bye, and moved in with the Jackson Rowe family across the South Canadian River in the Choctaw Nation.[70] Belle booked passage on a train and headed south to familiar territory in Texas. She visited her mother, Eliza Shirley, in Dallas and friends living near Cisco in Eastland County.[71]

Belle returned home for the holidays in December, and along the way, drew the attention of the *Dallas Morning News* and other newspapers in Texas and Indian Territory. Her brief absence had been noticed. The rumor mill churned out a story that Belle had been murdered.[72] The supposed victim quickly squelched the report of her demise.

"There is no truth in the reported assassination of Belle Starr," reported Little Rock's *Arkansas Journal* of December 13. "She is living quietly with her daughter in Younger's Bend, in the Territory, and says she has only one desire, and that is to be left alone for the remainder of her life."[73]

In a cruel twist of fate, Belle's wish for a peaceful life was not to be. That would become apparent soon enough, although 1889 got off to a

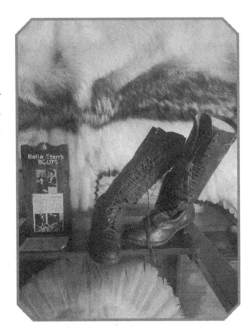

On January 24, 1889, Belle Starr took her lace-up work boots to Levie Keller, a cobbler and owner of a dry-goods store near Younger's Bend in Indian Territory.

quiet start at Younger's Bend. Eddie remained with the Rowe family in the Choctaw Nation. He missed being with Pearl but sometimes saw her when she went riding or ran errands for her mother. As for Jim July, his main concern was the February court date in Fort Smith and keeping Belle happy. She dealt with daily chores but managed to find time for trusted neighbors.

On January 24, Belle rode to Whitefield. She took her lace-up work boots to Levie Keller, a cobbler and owner of a dry-goods store. There was no question that the boots belonged to Belle. At the top of each boot, a leather bell was stitched inside a large inlaid leather star. Belle asked Keller to put on new half soles and to repair a heel, and he said the boots would be ready by the end of February.[74]

February promised to be busy, starting with Jim July's larceny trial in Fort Smith. Eddie Reed's eighteenth birthday was coming up later in the month, and Pearl hoped he would show up for a visit. But before that, Pearl would have to help celebrate her mother's forty-first birthday on February 5.

Early Saturday, February 2, July set out for Fort Smith for his trial. Although Belle had no intention of attending the proceeding, she rode

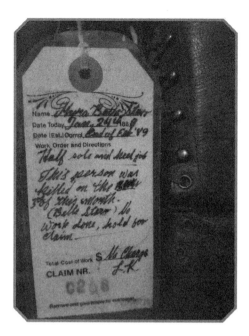

Belle Starr was murdered on February 3, 1889. The boots she had left for repair were never claimed.

partway with July so she could pay a bill at a store on King Creek across the Canadian in the Choctaw Nation. Belle paid off the entire account balance of seventy-five dollars and decided to ride a bit farther with July. They stopped at the home of the Nail family, friends on Sans Bois Creek twenty miles east of Whitefield, to spend the night. After breakfast the next morning, July continued to Fort Smith, and Belle turned back to return home.[75]

Before noon, she stopped again at the store on King Creek to feed and water her horse. The couple running the store asked Belle to join them for lunch. To the proprietor and his wife, Belle seemed downcast. When they asked what was bothering her, she said she was fearful of being killed by one of her enemies. They tried to cheer her, but Belle only grimaced. She asked for a pair of scissors and cut her silk neck scarf in two diagonally, giving half to the merchant's wife as a keepsake. Without another word, she mounted her horse and rode away.[76]

Belle left the store in the early afternoon of February 3 and arrived at Jackson Rowe's house at about four o'clock. The Rowe family's Sunday gatherings attracted many neighbors. Eddie, who was staying with the Rowes, had just left to join a friend across the river and was unaware of his mother's arrival. Robert and Jerusha Barnes and their brood of children were camped in the yard. They were well known to Belle, and Barnes had been at Lucy Surratt's home the night Sam Starr and Frank West killed each other. Jerusha Barnes was preparing supper and knew how much Belle liked her sour cornbread.[77]

Belle enjoyed the warm cornbread while visiting with other local folks as they came and went that afternoon. Most of them she knew well and liked. But sitting on the porch was Edgar Watson, a feisty redheaded tenant farmer with cruel eyes. Watson was no friend to Belle Starr. Shortly after she appeared, he took his leave and headed to his nearby cabin.[78]

The sun was close to setting when Belle grabbed another piece of cornbread, mounted her horse, and rode away. No one knows, but perhaps her mind was on Pearl at home fixing an early supper, or maybe Belle thought about her own forty-first birthday two days away.

Belle's horse splashed down the road home, which was wet and muddy from days of heavy rain. She did not see the weeds part along the split-rail fence flanking the river lane. She did not hear the hammer click back and lock. Then a loud boom—as sudden as a thunderclap—broke the silence, echoing through the thickets and across the meadows. Another boom followed. Belle fell onto the muddy road. She never knew what hit her.

CHAPTER 24

Who Killed Belle Starr?

NO ONE WITNESSED BELLE STARR'S MURDER OTHER THAN her assassin. Residents of the South Canadian River bottoms who heard the thunderclaps of a shotgun were stunned when they learned the victim's identity. Belle had been depicted as a "wild Amazon" who veered from her gender role and was ever fond of her troublesome visitors, but those who knew Belle saw her in a different light.

The first person who came upon Belle lying on the road was twenty-two-year-old Milo Ard Hoyt, son of Babe Hoyt, a Choctaw who operated a ferry at the nearby South Canadian crossing. Nicknamed "Frog" because of his long legs, young Hoyt had been at a community dance in the Cherokee Nation and was headed home.[1]

When he reached the landing on the north side of the river, he found the ferryboat tied to the bank and unattended. Hoyt had no choice but to spur his horse forward into the water and swim across. He had just sat down on the south bank to empty his boots when a saddled horse without a rider dashed by and leaped into the river. The horse bounded up the north bank and raced toward Younger's Bend. Concerned about the rider, Hoyt mounted his horse and rode south to investigate.

"The sun was about half an hour high," Hoyt later recalled. "Passed Alf White's place. I was alone. About a half mile from the ferry I seen her [Belle] lying on her face stretched out across the road. I heard no shots . . . thought the horse had thrown her. I never went up to her, but turned around and went back to the boat. Miss Pearl was at [the] boat when I went back."[2]

Pearl Reed had been preparing supper when she heard hoofbeats. She saw her mother's horse in the yard and noticed fresh blood on the saddle. There was no other sign of Belle. In a panic, Pearl mounted the lathered horse and raced for the Canadian bottoms.

"I went to the river, crossed over & met Milo Hoyt," Pearl later testified at a hearing in Fort Smith. "He told me about Belle lying [in] the road. I got behind him on his horse & he took me to Alf Whites & from there I went to the body alone. It was almost dark when I got to her. She was not quite dead. She never spoke. She was lying on her side & face, kind of across the road. Her whip was in her hand. She was shot in the back with buckshot & left side of her face & arm with fine shot. . . . There were three buckshots in her back close together."[3] Those wounds proved fatal, and Belle soon died.

It was fully dark when locals Alf White, Benjamin Statham, and Charles Acton—a tenant farmer who had leased land from Belle—joined Pearl at the death site. They lifted Belle's body from the mud, laid her in a wagon, and returned to the White residence. White's wife, Martha, had them place Belle on a bed as neighbors arrived to view the corpse and comfort Pearl.[4] Ray England, who had known Belle, showed up with Jackson Rowe and volunteered to sit with the body all night and keep vigil. In the morning, England and others began to search for tracks at the death site, hoping to identify Belle's killer.

One of the trackers was Eddie Reed, who had spent Sunday night at the home of his friend Andy McAntz. Eddie learned of his mother's death the next morning when he returned to the Jackson Rowe place, where he had been staying.[5] He immediately rode to Alf White's home to see his mother's body. Then, after seeing for himself where she had been killed, he joined the others in searching for tracks or signs that could lead them to her murderer.

Before the sun had risen Monday, Charles Acton rode to the closest telegraph station, at Eufaula, and wired the news of Belle's violent death to Jim July, who was standing trial in Fort Smith. "No particulars were given and nothing to show who did the deed," according to a newspaper report. "There was bad blood in Jim Starr's [Jim July's] eye when he heard the news."[6]

Defense attorneys petitioned the court to put the legal proceedings on hold so July could return to Younger's Bend, and "without delay he saddled his horse, provided himself with a quart of whiskey, struck out on a run for home, saying somebody was going to suffer."[7]

Later that morning at Alf White's home, neighbors wrapped Belle's body in quilts and placed her in Jim Cates's wagon. Cates and his brother Wiley Cates headed north. They crossed the Canadian and did not stop until they reached Belle's home.

As was the frontier custom, several women from the area came to prepare Belle for burial. They washed her body and scented it with a balm oil of cinnamon and turpentine.[8] She was dressed in "her best riding outfit" and laid in a pine coffin built by John L. Cates, another of the Cates brothers from Whitefield. The coffin was "padded with cotton, covered by black shrouding, trimmed with white lace."[9] They crossed her arms on her chest, and placed in her right hand one of her "babies"—a pearl-handled pistol.

Jim July made it back to Younger's Bend on Tuesday and sat by Belle's coffin until the next morning, February 6, the day of the funeral.[10] It was bright and clear. Ed Reed helped to dig his mother's grave in the clay close to the log house overlooking the river valley. By noon, mourners had gathered in the yard to pay their last respects.

There was no service and—despite later reports—not a preacher in sight. No eulogies were spoken, no hymns sung, and no Cherokee dirges chanted. The pallbearers, described as "grim visage Indians heavily armed," emerged through the door with the coffin.[11] They carried it to the grave, set it on the ground, and removed the lid.

The mourners formed a single file and quietly passed by the coffin. According to some accounts, many of those present followed the Cherokee burial practice of dropping a few grains of cornmeal into the coffin.[12] Perhaps that simple gesture reminded Belle's family and closest friends of her fondness for sour cornbread, her final meal.

Pearl and Ed were the last ones to approach the coffin. They lingered a few minutes, saying their final good-byes. Then the lid was nailed down and the coffin was lowered into the ground. "The gravediggers began shoveling clay and stone over what was mortal of this sometimes cruel, vengeful, and yet in many respects, kindly woman," reported *The Tahlequah Telephone*.[13]

Once the grave was covered, some mourners headed for their horses and buggies. Others stayed to visit and offer condolences to Pearl and Ed. That was when Jim July made his move. Out of respect for Belle, he had waited until after her burial, but the time had come to confront the audacious killer who probably had showed up for the burial to avoid being the target of suspicion. July suddenly produced his Winchester rifle and in one swift move pointed the cocked weapon at tenant farmer Edgar Watson. Trembling with rage, July snarled, "You murdered my wife!"[14]

Watson and his wife, Jane, were shocked, and like the other startled spectators, were no doubt certain that July was going to pull the trigger. Watson cowered behind Jim Cates, putting him in the line of fire. Cates shouted, "Throw up your hands and don't get us both killed."[15] Watson wisely complied. Cates and Eddie Reed grasped Watson's arms to prevent him from running, but he offered no resistance.

July had no warrant, but he believed he had reasonable cause to arrest Watson in the absence of a law officer. Supposedly, Watson's only comment was that "if he [July] killed him [Watson] he would kill the wrong man."[16] Most of the people present that day disagreed. The consensus of the local men who had investigated Belle's murder and tracked her killer was that Watson was the culprit.

Watson had few, if any, friends and had kept a low profile since showing up in the South Canadian River valley in early January 1888.[17] Claiming that they hailed from Arkansas, Watson, his wife, and three young children arrived in a wagon and rented some farmland from Milo Hoyt in the river bottoms downstream from Younger's Bend.

Although the Watsons might have sharecropped briefly in Franklin County, Arkansas, their trek began in Florida after Watson reportedly cut a man to pieces with a knife during a drunken altercation in Columbia County.[18] Fearing arrest, Watson and his family fled northwest and ended up in Indian Territory.

Edgar Artemus Watson (he also used the initial "J" for Jack) had been on the run all his life. Born in South Carolina in 1855, he took flight to Florida at an early age with his mother and sister because of his abusive father, Elijah Watson, a violent alcoholic and "celebrated brawler" who brutalized his wife and children.[19] Edgar came of age in Columbia County, where his first wife, Ann Mary Collins, died at age seventeen in 1879.[20] Three years later, he married twenty-eight-year-old Jane Dyall.[21] By then, Watson had begun "to mirror his father's abusive and violent actions by getting into numerous fights."[22]

Watson denied having had any role in Belle's murder. He willingly agreed to be taken to Fort Smith the next day but asked that he not be left alone with July. That evening, the Watson family camped near the Starr home. Ed Reed, Jack Rowe, and Ben Statham took turns keeping watch to be sure Watson did not leave. The next morning, July, Ed, and Rowe took Watson to Fort Smith.[23]

They arrived on February 8 for a hearing before United States Commissioner Stephen Wheeler. July presented his prisoner and signed an affidavit that stated, "Edgar A. Watson, a white man, did in the Indian Country, within the Choctaw Nation . . . on or about the 3 day of February 1889 feloniously, willfully, premeditatedly and of malice aforethought kill and murder Belle Starr, against the peace and dignity of the United States."[24]

Wheeler endorsed the writ and authorized July to serve subpoenas for several federal witnesses, including Eddie and Pearl, and at least ten more people who had personal knowledge of the murder and the subsequent search for the killer. In retrospect, it was curious that Commissioner Wheeler did not order a United States deputy marshal to serve the subpoenas. Instead, he entrusted their delivery to Jim July, a defendant in a larceny trial that had been put on hold.

Watson failed to post bail and was conveyed to the federal jail, where he remained until the next hearing, on February 22.[25] Before then, Watson and July had spoken to reporters from various newspapers. In one jailhouse interview, Watson continued his denial of guilt: "I knew very little of Belle Starr, though for some reason, I had known not what, [she] had been prejudiced against me."[26]

Belle's family knew precisely why she was at odds with Watson. Problems between them had begun several months before the murder. It started when Watson came to Belle to see about moving his family from the Hoyt property across the Canadian to sharecrop a piece of Belle's land. At first Belle hesitated. As Glenn Shirley later wrote, "There was an aura of cruelty about him that Belle did not like."[27]

Watson's wife, Jane, however, was gracious and friendly. Belle viewed her as a potential good neighbor and reluctantly accepted Watson's rent payment so they could make the move in December 1888.[28] Soon Belle and Jane began to spend more time together. Belle would visit the Watsons' tenant farm, and Jane often came calling at the Starr home.

During one of their afternoon chats, Jane confided that her husband had been accused of murder in Florida, forcing the family's flight to Arkansas and then to Indian Territory. Belle was concerned by this revelation. If the authorities found a wanted killer living on her land, it would appear that she was harboring a fugitive.

Belle tried to return the rental money, but Watson refused to take it back. She mailed the money to Watson with a note informing him she had already leased the tenant acreage to a newcomer. Watson sought out the man and intimidated him with wild stories about Belle and her outlaw lair. The man became fearful and called off the deal. Belle was so infuriated that when she encountered Watson again, she cautioned him to be careful or the Florida authorities might come sniffing around. It was then that Watson realized his wife had revealed "his dark and terrible secret."[29]

He left Belle without another word, and by January 1889, the Watsons had moved to one of Jackson Rowe's tenant cabins in the Choctaw Nation. It was at the Rowe place on February 3, 1889, where Watson saw Belle and made a quick exit before she left.

On February 8, Jim July told reporters his version of Belle's murder. "When she rode up to the [Rowe] house several men were sitting around in the yard, among them E. A. Watson, whose home was about 150 yards away."[30]

July continued, "A few minutes later after Belle arrived[,] Watson left the crowd and went home. About half an hour after he left[,] Belle mounted her horse and started, the road leading around the field of Watson. As she turned the corner at the back of the field her assassin was inside the fence. . . . After she had passed by, he shot her in the back with a load of buckshot, knocking her from her horse. He then jumped over the fence, and as she lay prostrate in the mud, he fired a load of turkey shot into her side, neck and face and the frightened animal she was riding dashed off home."[31]

When pressed for a motive for Watson having "[committed] the dastardly act," July offered his theory. "I don't know further than the fact that they had a falling out sometime previous . . . and I believe Belle knew [more] about him than he cared to be divulged. I think he was a fugitive from justice, and knowing her reputation for friendship with outlaws he had divulged to her his character, and having incurred her dislike he murdered her. . . . She has had no trouble lately and was on good terms with all her neighbors. I think Watson murdered her, and I will use every effort to prove it on him."[32]

All the subpoenaed witnesses showed up in Fort Smith for the February 22 evidentiary hearing before Commissioner James Brizzolara. It was his task to hear the testimony to determine whether just cause existed to indict Watson and try him for murder. Assistant District Attorney C. L. Jackson sought the grand-jury murder indictment. He was opposed by prominent and well-connected Fort Smith attorney William Moore Mellette, representing Watson.[33]

The hearing stretched into two days. Several witnesses said they believed Watson was the killer, and others denied any knowledge of bad blood between the defendant and the deceased. Much of the testimony was hearsay, based on rumors or secondhand reports.[34] Although no one had witnessed the murder, the prosecutor established the chronology of events leading up to Belle's death. Testimony also confirmed that mutual animosity and Watson's fear of Belle revealing his past might have motivated him to take her life. The most convincing evidence connecting Watson to the crime, however, came from witnesses who had followed the killer's tracks soon after the discovery of Belle's body.[35]

In his early years in Florida, Watson had become notorious for his quick temper and his reputation for getting even.[36] He also was known for his distinctive physical appearance—a burly six-footer with red curly hair and a beard, deep blue eyes, ruddy complexion, and, oddly enough, very small hands and feet in proportion to his stature. Watson wore a size seven boot.[37]

According to witness testimony, Ed Reed, Jim Cates, and Ray England found a set of footprints at the murder site that had been made by one person and led to "within 100 yards of Watson's house."[38] The men measured the tracks, which appeared to have been made by a size seven boot.[39]

Watson swore that after he had left Jack Rowe's on February 3, he went home and stayed there. "My shotgun was home that evening in the rack," Watson told Commissioner Brizzolara. "My gun was loaded with buck shot in both barrels." He further testified that he had had no problems with Belle. "We had never had any difficulty. She never said a cross word to me. . . . I never thought about my gun that day. I had nothing to do with killing. Knew nothing about it."[40]

Ansel D. Terry, who worked for Watson as a hired hand in exchange for room and board, appeared as a defense witness with good reason to provide his employer with an alibi. Terry claimed that when the two shots were fired, he saw Watson at the fence calling the hogs and not wielding a shotgun.[41]

Jim July and Belle's children were apparently confident that the prosecutor had proved that enough credible evidence existed to bring Watson before the grand jury and then to trial before Judge Isaac Parker. But they were wrong.

Mellette's contention that his client was innocent rang true to Brizzolara. He found Watson to be a "quiet, hard-working man whose local reputation was good."[42] Despite the strong testimony about the boot tracks, the commissioner noted that witnesses could not say beyond a reasonable doubt that they knew for certain who had made the tracks.

Brizzolara declared the evidence "all circumstantial" but held off on a final ruling when Assistant District Attorney Jackson pleaded for more time to find additional witnesses.[43] "The evidence was all circumstantial and rather disconnected," reported a Fort Smith newspaper. "The commissioner is withholding his decision in the case until more witnesses are produced and Jim Starr [Jim July] is now out summoning them. It looks at present as if they had the wrong shoat by the ear."[44]

Instead of dispatching deputy United States marshals, the commissioner left the task to Jim July. Belle's family and friends must have been disappointed that no law officers ever actively investigated her murder.

July was unable to come up with any more damaging testimony. On March 4, Brizzolara ordered Watson to be discharged.[45] Fearing retribution, Watson returned to his home only long enough to pack up his wife and children and depart Indian Territory, never to return.

The Watsons went back to Arkansas. Their visit was brief. Watson was arrested for horse theft but escaped from prison and fled the state with his family.[46] By 1890—despite Watson's prior problems—they had returned to Florida. In no time, Watson was back in trouble. In the town of Arcadia, while Watson was embroiled in a dispute over land, he killed a man with a knife, claiming it was self-defense.[47] No witnesses came forward to contradict the alibi, and once again, Watson got away with murder.

In 1892, with his wife and children in tow, Watson became a sugarcane farmer in the Ten Thousand Islands region, a labyrinth of mangrove and saw-grass marsh in the vast Everglades.[48] It was the ideal refuge for army deserters, refugees from the law, and poachers of alligators and plumed birds. It was where Watson would spend the rest of his life. While his sugarcane plantation turned out kettles of tasty syrup called Island Pride, Watson earned the moniker of "Bloody Ed."[49] He was suspected in the murders of numerous men and women.

"Watson never paid any of his workers, and instead when they asked for their money, he would kill them and toss their bodies into the river where the locals of Chokoloskee and Everglades City began to find them," wrote newspaper columnist Savannah Oglesby. "No one knew

Notorious serial killer Edgar A. Watson, who was acquitted in the ambush slaying of Belle Starr, is shown as he appeared before vigilantes shot him to pieces in Florida in 1910.

where the bodies originated from since all of Watson's workers were from out of town."[50]

Watson's wife, Jane, who had befriended Belle Starr, died at age thirty-eight in 1901. Three years later, Watson wed his third wife, seventeen-year-old Edna Catherine Bethea.[51] By then, Watson was entangled in all sorts of unproved rumors and tales. Ironically, the man whom many people believe had killed Belle Starr became a mythical figure in the folklore of the Everglades.

"Edgar Watson is believed to have killed, or to have caused to be killed, at least eight men and two women," wrote Thomas Neil Knowles in "The Everglades' Bandit Killer."[52] "By word of mouth, he was firmly established as the Everglades' most infamous killer. He was never tried and found guilty of any of the murders attributed to him. As was the case with the 'Bandit Queen,' he may have been maligned by rumor and hyperbole. Yet, as Belle Starr's fate attests, associating with Edgar Watson all too often proved to be a fatal experience."

The term *serial killer* did not exist in the early 1900s, but today, some residents of southern Florida consider Watson to have been "a classic serial killer . . . suggesting he suffered from multiple personality disorder."[53] Others think he was a victim, but even Watson's advocates—who swear that he did not kill the more than fifty people attributed to him—do not question that he was Belle Starr's killer.

Watson would eventually be held accountable for his crimes. The time came on October 24, 1910, at the Smallwood Store, a combination post office and market on the southern tip of Chokoloskee Island.[54] A posse of local citizens confronted Watson—who was armed with a pistol and carrying a shotgun—and accused him of a multitude of murders and misdeeds. Watson advanced toward the crowd and fired, but his shotgun misfired. The posse blazed away and riddled Watson with thirty-three bullets. "Bloody Ed" was fifty-four, seventeen days short of his next birthday.

~

AS IN EVERY ASPECT of Belle Starr's forty-one years of life, there have always been skeptics who have questions about her death, including whether Edgar Watson was the assassin. The federal government's failure to prove Watson's culpability was interpreted as proof that someone else had killed Belle.[55]

Over the years, several other candidates have been proposed. Most were quickly discounted. Some claims were preposterous, such as one that surfaced in 1970 from A. J. Robinson, a seventy-two-year-old from Topeka, Kansas.[56] He told reporters that when he was twelve, his grandmother, Nannie (or Nana) Devena, admitted to her family that she had been in a nasty feud with Belle and had killed her "villainous neighbor" with an "old muzzle-loader." Robinson had no further details and no evidence to back up the story. "All I have to go on is her word," he admitted.[57] Proved or not, the tale appeared in Sunday newspapers for the reading pleasure of a public that had been raised on frontier myth.

The failure to convict Watson led to suspicion of Belle's family and friends, including her own children and Jim July. Pearl was quickly eliminated based on Frog Hoyt's alibi testimony. Some folks believed Ed Reed killed Belle out of rage over her harsh treatment of him that led to their estrangement. However, at Watson's hearing, Ed "furnished a provable account of his whereabouts at the time Belle was slain." The authorities in Fort Smith "gave no credence to the rumor that he had killed his mother."[58]

Surprisingly, Belle's fourth husband, Jim July, made the suspect list despite having been on trial in a Fort Smith courtroom at the time of Belle's death. The tale was spread by the notorious Edgar Watson. He contended that July had slipped back to the Canadian River valley, where he "borrowed Watson's double-barreled weapon to kill a wolf."[59] After Belle's body was found, Watson said he went to the site where Belle was killed and saw the tracks of Jim July's distinctive "sharp-heeled boots."[60] Apparently Watson did not realize that July's feet were larger than size seven.

Another story—perhaps originated by the West family, longtime foes of the Starrs—was that old Tom Starr had killed Belle. It was implied that he did so to punish Belle for leading his son, Sam, astray, ending in his violent death in a gunfight.[61] The local populace gave no credence to the tale. Starr was physically incapable of killing his former daughter-in-law. In early 1888, he was in ill health when released from prison in Illinois. Back in Briartown, Starr rested and rarely left his home. He quietly died on October 7, 1890, surrounded by his family. He was laid to rest near his son Sam in the Starr Cemetery.[62]

In the early 1950s, James Middleton's name surfaced as Belle's executioner. Supposedly he blamed Belle for the 1885 death of his older brother, John Middleton, and sought revenge.[63] Based on questionable secondhand and thirdhand accounts, the accusation never gained traction—and for good reason. Middleton family members "categorically denied that Jim had killed Belle." If the tellers of the ill-conceived tale had conducted actual research, they would have found James Middleton's praise of Belle. "I never saw anything in her life that caused me to think she was a bad woman," Middleton said in a 1937 interview.[64]

The identity of Belle Starr's killer has never been "incontrovertibly determined," but the "prevailing theory is that she was murdered by Edgar A. Watson."[65] He remains the only viable suspect to this day.

In 1990, author Ron Hansen wrote a fitting benediction for Watson that appeared in the *New York Times*: "Aggressive and gregarious, without ethics or introspection, . . . dangerously addicted to untamed power, Edgar Watson finally seems to represent . . . America at its worst."[66]

No one was ever convicted of the murder of Belle Starr.

EPILOGUE

• • • • • • • • • • • •

Print the Legend

THE AMBUSH MURDER OF BELLE STARR GUARANTEED HER place in Wild West myth. The woman born Myra Maibelle Shirley had been shot dead, but Belle Starr rode on. Her death ensured her immortality.

As with a variety of other frontier figures such as Jesse James, Wyatt Earp, and Billy the Kid, the story of Belle Starr was reformulated into tales largely based on fabrications and factual inaccuracies. The combination created a substitute for historic reality.

As one pundit noted, "She [Belle] was killed because in myth her persona is too far removed from the boundaries of normal domesticity, so far afield from the matrix of heterosexual normality that was being reinforced at this very moment in U.S. history."[1]

On February 6, 1889, the day Belle was laid to rest, her death was front-page news across the nation. Not one newspaper got the story right, including the revered *New York Times*, regarded as "the national newspaper of record." Under the headline "A Desperate Woman Killed," the page-one story bore a Fort Smith, Arkansas, dateline:[2]

> Word has been received from Eufala [*sic*], Indian Territory, that Belle Starr was killed there Sunday night. Belle was the wife of Cole Younger. . . . Jim Starr, her second husband, was shot down by the side of Belle less than two years ago.
>
> Belle Starr was the most desperate woman that ever figured on the borders. She married Cole Younger directly after the war, but

left him and joined a band of outlaws that operated in Indian Territory. She had been arrested for murder and robbery a score of times, but always managed to escape.[3]

The only morsel of truth in the obituary was the correct date of Belle's death. That same day, the *New York Sun* published a similar story. It also was filled with errors and mistruths, such as the "marriage" to Cole Younger and the suggestion that Belle had resisted arrest and was shot by deputy marshals.[4]

The stories about Belle in the *Times* and *Sun* caught the eye of Richard Kyle Fox, the flamboyant editor and publisher of the *National Police Gazette*, headquartered on Franklin Square in New York. Fox had been aware of Belle Starr for several years and had included a dramatic illustration of her astride a galloping horse in the *Gazette* of May 22, 1886.[5]

Eager to increase circulation, Fox scrambled to get the news of Belle's murder to his growing audience of readers. He used another "titillating woodcut illustration" of Belle in the February 23, 1889, issue.[6] The dramatic illustration—captioned "A Coward Got the Drop on Her"—depicted Belle on horseback pitching forward after having been shot from behind. It read in part: "Belle Starr, a noted female desperado, queen of the border outlaws."[7]

Fox was far from finished capitalizing on Belle Starr's death. By recreating the life story of his self-proclaimed "Bandit Queen," Fox could further "enflame the imagination of his readers" and boost circulation.[8] He promptly dispatched Alton B. Meyers, an itinerant journalist and *Gazette* correspondent, to Fort Smith.[9]

As soon as Meyers arrived in Fort Smith, he set out to get the story. After a bit of snooping, he learned that Jim July was nowhere to be found. To avoid the resumption of his trial in Fort Smith, July had gone back on the scout. Meyers next turned to Belle's children, Ed and Pearl, but they refused his interview requests, as did Belle's mother, Eliza Shirley, who was staying with her grandchildren at Younger's Bend.[10]

Undaunted but also aware of his mission to deliver a riveting story as soon as possible, Meyers sought out anyone with a Belle Starr yarn to share, the more outrageous the better. In addition to using unreliable sources, Meyers resorted to unashamedly fictionalizing Belle's life.

Without revealing any details, he claimed that he had uncovered a secret journal that Belle had supposedly kept for almost twenty years. There was no explanation about where it was found and no proof of its authenticity. To this day, the alleged journal has never been seen. Long passages from the mysterious journal presented as first-person verbatim quotations, allegedly written by Belle, appear throughout Meyers's text. In actual fact, what he wrote was almost entirely fiction. Meyers's mind and imagination had created all of it in his hotel room.[11]

The story of Belle's supposed journal had first surfaced in 1886. In a questionable *Dallas Morning News* story, Belle supposedly told a reporter that she "spends most of time writing when at home" and had "a complete manuscript record."[12] Although publishers had offered her "big money" for her life story, she did not want it published until after her death. The existence of the journal was subsequently discredited by several sources, including biographer Glenn Shirley, who wrote that the tale had created much of the "Belle Starr nonsense."[13]

Meyers was not the only one who claimed to have discovered Belle Starr's journal. News of another claimant broke on February 18, 1889.[14] On that date, Harry F. O'Beirne, a newspaper editor from Atoka, in the Choctaw Nation, announced that he had found Belle's journal at the Starr ranch near Younger's Bend. By the following day, the story had appeared in several newspapers.[15]

"Advices from Indian Territory say that the journal of Belle Starr, the noted female bandit, has been obtained from the Starr ranch, which Belle intended to publish as an autobiography," according to the *St. Joseph* (Missouri) *Weekly Herald*.[16]

The Daily Arkansas Gazette, a newspaper more familiar with Belle Starr, questioned the veracity of O'Beirne's claim of discovery.[17]

By early summer 1889, Meyers had completed his story about Belle and sent it to the *Gazette* editorial offices in lower Manhattan. Fox quickly read it and loved every word. Whether he contributed to the text is unknown. There was no author attribution for Meyers, which led many people to believe that Fox, the publisher, was also the writer. The decision was made to not serialize the biography in the weekly *Gazette* but to bring it out as a bound booklet.[18]

Within months of Belle's death, the sixty-four-page wire-stitched booklet, printed on the same pink paper used for the weekly *Gazette*, was rushed to press and published.[19] *Bella Starr, the Bandit Queen, or the Female Jesse James, A Full and Authentic History of the Dashing Female Highwayman, with Copious Extracts from Her Journal, Handsomely, Profusely Illustrated* was released as a special mail-order publication costing twenty-five cents a copy.[20]

It read like a bad novella riddled with contrived dialogue and factual errors. Besides giving Belle the name Bella, the book gave the surnames of Shirley and Reed as Sherley and Read. The opening paragraph—loaded with purple prose, hackneyed phrases, and elaborate fabrications—set the stage for a wildly imaginative account which has skewed public perception of Belle Starr ever since. It reads:

> Of all women of the Cleopatra type since the days of the Egyptian queen herself, the universe has produced none more remarkable than Bella Starr, the Bandit Queen. Her character was a combination of the very worst as well as some of the very best traits of her sex. She was more amorous than Anthony's mistress; more relentless than Pharaoh's daughter, and braver than Joan of Arc. Of her it may well be said that Mother Nature was indulging in one of her rarest freaks, when she produced such a novel specimen of womankind. Bella was not only well educated, but gifted with uncommon musical and literary talents, which were almost thrown away through the bias of her nomadic and lawless disposition, when in a strange country, and under an assumed name, she brightened the social circle for a week or a month, and then was, perhaps, lost forever.[21]

In the book, Meyers wrote, "Myra describes a terrible contest between the good and bad elements of her nature."[22] In a fabricated "journal" entry from the early years of her life, Meyers quotes her as saying, "My life is a wreck. A great necessity is within me. I must either drift high upon the waves of notoriety, or sink to the level of common life. The latter I can never do. Should I fail to gain a positive reputation for virtue and talent, I shall seek a superlatively bad one, through the channels of vice—dreadful and reckless darting. I must rise above the reach of my sex that men may tremble at the mere mention of my name. Oh! God! That I could content myself with being simply good and leave greatness for others to achieve."[23]

In 1892, while the Fox book continued to sell and seed a crop of myth-makers, Harry O'Beirne resurfaced. He boasted that he not only had found Belle's journal but had written a book about her life.[24]

Unlike the Fox book, no copy of O'Beirne's alleged book, *Bell Starr's Life*, has ever been found, nor was it mentioned in books and articles about Belle that use the Fox book as a source.

The Fox book, *Bella Starr*, often cited as a historical reference despite its lurid approach, became the template for writers, journalists, and filmmakers who chose to not thoroughly research, fact-check, or present the truth.

A line from John Ford's classic Western film *The Man Who Shot Liberty Valance* summed it up: "This is the West, sir. When the legend becomes fact, print the legend."[25]

That quote fit Belle Starr to a T.

Jim July

On February 25, 1889—three weeks after Belle's death—H. J. Vann, clerk of the Canadian District of the Cherokee Nation, presided at a hearing to consider "The Verbal Will of Belle Starr" and determine the ownership of the Younger's Bend property.[26] Morris Kraft and Charles Acton appeared as witnesses. The elderly Kraft operated a general store in Whitefield and ran some cattle in the river bottom. He had been a frequent guest at the Starr home and had "endeared himself" to Belle and Pearl.[27] Acton was a tenant of the Starrs and had been on good terms with Belle and Jim July. Acton also had helped track Belle's killer and had appeared as a federal witness at Edgar Watson's hearing in Fort Smith.

Kraft and Acton testified at the Vann hearing in support of Belle's wishes. Both men swore "that they heard Belle Starr say on several occasions a short time before her death and while in her sound mind, state if anything should happen or befall her, or that she should die and leave the improvements on which she was then living not disposed of the said improvement would be James Starr's [Jim July's]."[28]

Jim July never established a claim to the land improvements on the Canadian. In fact, after the failure to obtain a murder indictment against Edgar Watson, July never went back to Younger's Bend. He also neglected to return to Fort Smith for his horse-theft trial that had been continued after Belle was killed.

"Jim July Starr, as he pleases to call himself when at home, is on bond for horse-stealing, and he is endeavoring to wear his case out by absenting himself just at times when he is wanted," according to a front-page story in the *Dallas Morning News* of August 22, 1889.[29]

July stayed on the scout and briefly took up with an outlaw band operating out of Talala, a small Cherokee Nation community northwest of Claremore in what later became Rogers County, Oklahoma.[30] By late summer 1889, after reportedly having visited New Mexico Territory and made stops in Texas, July showed up at Ardmore, a frontier town and trading post in the Chickasaw Nation.[31] There, he was implicated in a tall tale conceived by Edgar Watson, who claimed that the true killer of Belle Starr was Jim July.

Before the vengeful Watson fled Indian Territory, he approached United States Deputy Marshal James Robert "Bob" Hutchins, who had been on the job less than a year. Watson managed to convince Hutchins that July had borrowed Watson's shotgun to shoot wolves but instead used the weapon to murder Belle.[32] Of course, this could not have occurred because when Belle was murdered, July was standing trial in Fort Smith and did not to return to Younger's Bend until after Belle's demise.

Hutchins' claim that July had murdered Belle was completely fictitious, yet he managed to wrangle yet another arrest warrant and went on the hunt. Accompanying Hutchins was Bud (Bub) Trainor, a shifty character who had ridden with an outlaw gang in the Cherokee Nation and had been accused of many crimes, including the murder of Deputy United States Marshal Dan Maples in 1887.[33] Trainor eluded prosecution when the crime was pinned on Ned Christie, a respected Cherokee blacksmith and tribal leader.[34]

Jim July, much like Ned Christie, also had been blamed for a homicide he did not commit. On January 22, 1890, Trainor and Hutchins, eager to collect a reward, caught up with their prey not far from Ardmore.[35]

"For eight months officers have watched for him [Jim July], and last week they located him in a cabin, which they covered with Winchester rifles, leaving their horses back in the brush," according to a newspaper report. "Starr [July] discovered them in time to mount his horse and get a start, leaning forward in the saddle and shooting back with his pistol. The officers returned fire with their Winchesters, one of them passing through the saddle tree and lodging in Starr's [July's] back, bringing him to the ground."[36]

Badly wounded and with his horse killed, July was turned over to United States Marshal Heck Thomas, who was taking a load of prisoners to Fort Smith by rail. When the party briefly stopped at the Paris, Texas, depot to change trains, July caught the eye of a reporter, who wrote, "Lying in agony caused by the effects of a wound he received," July explained that he had "skipped my bond last spring and have just had it renewed."[37]

Back in a prison hospital bed at Fort Smith, July had more to tell reporters. According to the *Fort Smith Elevator*, July's primary bondsman, J. H. Mershon, had withdrawn the reward for July's arrest after July sent a wire from Ardmore explaining that he "had agreed to come in and make a new bond. . . . I filed the bond and sent it to you and was fixing to come. Can prove name. If I die have Trainor and Hutchins tried for murder. They shot me foul."[38]

By Sunday, January 26, 1890, a doctor pronounced July's case hopeless. Conscious to the end, he died that evening without a murmur. He was twenty-seven. His body was not claimed, and he was buried in the potter's field at Fort Smith.

Bub Trainor and Bob Hutchins were subsequently arrested and jailed at Purcell in the Chickasaw Nation.[39] On February 26, 1890, United States Marshal J. J. Dickerson took the shackled prisoners to Paris, Texas, where they were held without bail, charged with the murder of Jim July. Unfortunately, a case against the accused killers could not be proved. Trainor and Hutchins were freed.[40]

Bruce Younger

Belle Starr's husbands Jim Reed, Sam Starr, and Jim July all died from gunshot wounds, but that was not the case for her third husband, Bruce Younger. Unlike the others, Younger died with his boots off in a sickbed in Colorado about six months after Belle was murdered.

In the wake of a whirlwind three-week marriage to Belle in 1880, Bruce pursued his chosen profession for pleasure and profit and gambled his way across Kansas. Younger drifted from town to town, never remaining in one place very long. Often, he did not stay long enough to collect his mail. His name appeared in newspaper lists of unclaimed mail at the post offices of cow towns and cities, starting only weeks after Younger and Belle had parted ways.[41]

Even after Younger made appeals to newspapers about his peaceful intentions, reporters continued to keep an eye on him for any possible connections he might have with criminal gangs.

Younger had to keep on the move because his surname was linked to the still unsavory reputation of his half nephews, the outlaw Younger brothers. Although the Younger gang no longer existed and the brothers had been killed or incarcerated, the public reaction must have been a painful reminder to Bruce Younger. A mere mention of Bruce Younger in a newspaper often set off a firestorm with readers, demonstrating that the Younger name still packed a punch years after the outlaw gang had been put out of business in 1876 at Northfield, Minnesota.[42]

Any scrap of information or misinformation was enough to generate a story about Younger, and other people even dropped his name for their own advantage. On several occasions, he was blamed for crimes he did not commit and was eventually proved innocent. Some newspapers even printed retractions, clearing Younger of any wrongdoing. Younger continued to be newsworthy throughout the 1880s.[43]

Younger's movements and activities were so well covered by the press that it is interesting to wonder whether any news of him reached Belle in Indian Territory. Likewise, at the same time, the press was reporting on and sensationalizing her life. Did Younger hear anything about the legal troubles Belle and Sam Starr encountered in the 1880s or Sam's death in 1886?

In 1889, surely Younger could not have missed the widespread news of the killing of Belle Starr. Within days of her death, newspapers in several states had picked up on the Younger family's connection with her and carried detailed articles containing some germs of truth and much lurid misinformation. However, as popular with the press as both Belle Starr and Bruce Younger were, it seems odd that reporters did not track down Younger to get his comments on Belle and her violent death. Perhaps they could not find him or he was too ill to be interviewed.

Bruce Younger reportedly died in Colorado City, Colorado, in late August or September 1889,[44] although an unverified record gives the year as 1890. He would have turned thirty-six years old in 1889. No official cause of death has been found. Family members believed that Younger had gone to Colorado for his health. He was known to be an imbiber of alcohol, so perhaps his death had been caused by drinking. Did he contract tuberculosis (known as "consumption" at the time), the cause of many people moving to the mountains of Colorado and New Mexico Territory to seek a cure?

Some unsubstantiated reports claimed that at the time of his death, Younger left behind an unnamed woman he had lived with who was presumed to be his wife, as well as an unnamed child purportedly attending Notre Dame University, in South Bend, Indiana. Obviously, if there was such a woman, it was not Belle Starr, who had been separated from Younger for years. No records have been found of a Younger offspring, presumably a son, since Notre Dame did not allow female undergraduates until 1972.[45]

However, it has been learned that at only fourteen years of age, Bruce Younger himself was admitted to Notre Dame University for the academic year 1867–1868.[46]

Bruce Younger's time as a college student was brief. Records show that "after two weeks stay there, he escaped from college restraint."[47] Perhaps the university's strict regulations prompted the brevity of his tenure at Notre Dame. Besides the prohibition of tobacco and intoxicating beverages, the long list of rules urged students "to endeavor to improve the purity of their language" and "behave with the dignity and propriety of gentlemen."[48] None of the restrictions appealed to a young man with a passion for racing horses and games of chance.

Even Bruce Younger's death did not cease the colorful publicity about him. In 1893, newspapers nationwide published wildly inaccurate articles that men seeking ore had found a "petrified corpse" in a New Mexico Territory cave. They claimed they had come upon the remains of Bruce Younger.[49]

Citing a source in Kansas City, Missouri, one of the many stories about the grisly discovery appeared in the *Chicago Tribune*: "About fifteen years ago, when the officers were hot after the James and Younger boys, Bruce Younger left his home in Missouri and took refuge in a cave in the Guadalupe Mountains in Southern New Mexico [Territory]. A negro whom the Younger family had raised went with him and regularly carried food and ammunition to the fugitive in the cave. . . . It was in this cave that the body was found."[50]

Petrified bodies had become all the rage around the country in the 1890s. Newspaper stories reported discoveries and exhumation of the petrified remains of men, women, and children in several states. Subsequent examinations indicated that some corpses were quite old, but others were decried as hoaxes.[51]

Published stories perpetuated the tale that the fossilized body a group of citizens from Gainesville, Texas, had purchased for $6,000 was the remains of Bruce Younger. They planned to display the grisly souvenir at the 1893 World's Columbian Exposition in Chicago.[52] Several ancient mummies were exhibited there as well as the petrified body of a primeval human found in a Kentucky cave. None of them was Bruce Younger.[53]

Anyone who knew Bruce Younger, including his family, knew that he did not end up as a mummified corpse. The petrified body that had been discovered in New Mexico in 1878 (although not reported until 1893) could not have been that of Bruce Younger, who was obviously still living in 1878.

"There are a few, however, who know that one of the Younger boys is buried in Evergreen Cemetery in this city," according to the *Colorado Springs Gazette* of April 23, 1893. "Bruce Younger ... died at Colorado City [later part of Colorado Springs] and [was] buried in September, 1890. He had been living in Colorado City for a year or two and was a prominent character among the sporting fraternity. He used his proper name and it is said, he was never mixed up in the wrong doing of his brothers [half nephews]. He was a powerful man physically and was notorious among his acquaintances for the amount of whisky he could drink. At the time of his death, he was without money, and the sporting people of Colorado City supplied funds for his burial, a notorious woman of the town supplying the most."[54]

Younger's sister Sophronia Lee Younger Kirkpatrick also rejected the claim that the mummified mystery man was her younger brother. She told reporters that during the winter of 1885, Younger lived at her home in Kansas City, Missouri. "Then he went west," she said. "I know what I am saying." Kirkpatrick had a postal card that Younger had written when he first took sick in Colorado and never recovered.[55]

Although Evergreen Cemetery in Colorado Springs has no record of Bruce Younger's burial and a death certificate has not been found, it is possible that he was buried there, perhaps in an unmarked grave.[56] It is ironic that after years of minute attention in newspapers to Bruce Younger's activities and whereabouts, his specific death date and burial were apparently not reported definitively. After all, he had been well known in his own right, not just for his puzzling role in the life of Myra Reed before she launched a new identity as Belle Starr.

Elizabeth (Eliza) Pennington Shirley

By Eliza Pennington Shirley's later years, her life had changed drastically from the days when she and John Shirley were prosperous farmers and business owners raising a family near Carthage, Missouri. Her elder daughter, Charlotte Amanda Shirley Thompson, had been living in Mexico for thirty years and died in 1894, the same year as her mother. Eliza's younger daughter, Myra Maibelle Shirley (Belle Starr), had been killed in Indian Territory in 1889. Three of Eliza's four sons had been killed by gunfire at various times, and the youngest, known as Shug or Doc, also was dead, according to his mother.[57]

With her family diminished in size and her husband deceased in 1876, Eliza Shirley moved from Scyene, Texas, to Dallas and disposed of property in Scyene.[58]

After Eliza's death, a Dallas newspaper reporter supposedly interviewed "Aunt" Annie Shirley, a formerly enslaved worker of John and Eliza Shirley, who had come with the family when they moved from Missouri to Texas. Annie was quoted as saying "that her master [John Shirley] was rich at one time, and left a great deal of property at his death, but that his widow had no money sense, and she soon ran through with what he left. She and her youngest son spent six years in traveling, spending money in regal prodigality. For several years before her death, she was in very straightened [straitened] circumstances."[59]

Whether or not Eliza Shirley "had no money sense" and spent money "in regal prodigality," she certainly had no financial resources left in her last few years. "As early as January 1893, the Ladies Aid Society at the Methodist Episcopal Church South" (later known as First Methodist Church), in Dallas, Texas, "was paying $2 rent for Mrs. Shirley every couple of months. The society decided in April 1893 to give Mrs. Shirley $3; her rent had gone up." By "November 1893, Mrs. Shirley's rent was again $2."[60]

The Ladies Aid Society continued to help Eliza Shirley to the very end of her life. On January 2, 1894, "Mrs. Swink" of the Ladies Aid Society "was paid $2 from the poor fund for Mrs. Shirley's room rent. She reported Mrs. Shirley badly injured from effects of a fall and that she is being attended by the ladies of the Floyd Street Methodist Episcopal Church."[61]

Eliza Shirley did not survive her injuries. On January 4, 1894, she died "at the residence of Mrs. Charlotte T. Poyner, 636 Pacific Avenue,"[62] apparently a boardinghouse. The Ladies Aid Society learned of it on January 8 when "Mrs. Swink reported Mrs. Shirley's death which it occurred since last meeting, and she had paid only $1 due on her room rent and gave the other dollar to those having the burial in charge. The expense of which had been paid in full as she had learned."[63]

Eliza Shirley was still well known enough in Missouri for an obituary (although highly inaccurate) to be published in a Carthage newspaper, and her notoriety as the mother of Belle Starr garnered notices in newspapers in Kansas and elsewhere.

Eliza was buried in Trinity Cemetery (later renamed Greenwood Cemetery), "a green oasis in the shadow of downtown Dallas, where many prominent Dallasites were buried in the nineteenth century."[64] It was the solitary end of a life of prosperity, accomplishment, loss, and grief.

James Edwin (Eddie) Reed

Ed Reed, son of Belle Starr from her first marriage to Jim Reed, turned eighteen years old on February 22, 1889, less than three weeks after his mother had been killed. Only four months later, on June 26, he and Ed Lear were arrested and jailed in Fort Smith, Arkansas, and were charged with horse theft. Because of his mother's widespread fame, stories of Reed's own misdeeds instantly spread throughout the region.[65]

According to newspaper articles, Reed had already been under indictment for several months but was on bond when he and Lear were charged with stealing two horses in the Choctaw Nation. They traded off the horses in Logan County, Arkansas, resulting in their arrest. "Lear acknowledged" the trade of the stolen horses, but "young Reed, like his late mother, is shrewd and stoical, says he don't know what he has been arrested for."[66]

One article painted a worse picture: "Reed is wanted on a dozen charges, and with the conspicous [sic] bravery that has made him famous in the criminal history of the west he openly marched into the city [Fort Smith] with a number of stolen horses and proceeded to sell them. The surrender was made by a deputy marshall [sic] and a detective who caught Reed in a stall of a livery barn and compelled him to surrender."[67]

Reed "was found guilty in the Federal Court this morning [July 11, 1889] on a charge of horse stealing. . . . He is being tried this afternoon on another similar charge. Young Reed has figured in the Federal Court here since he was 10 years of age, and is as chronic a horse thief as his father and mother before him. There is also a charge of larceny pending against his sister, Pearl Younger."[68]

In relaying the news of Reed's conviction, several newspapers—obviously all based on the same source—commented that "his conviction so early in his criminal career indicates that he is not as good a general as his mother in coping with the law."[69]

On July 31, 1889, twenty-five federal prisoners, including "Edward [sic] Reed (Belle Starr's son)," left Fort Smith for the penitentiary in Columbus, Ohio.[70] His sentence was for seven years, but he apparently was released in about 1893.[71]

Reed made some attempt to live a more orderly life in 1894, when the Katy Railroad hired him as a guard to protect trains between Wagoner and McAlester, Indian Territory.[72] However, Reed's incarceration evidently had not deterred him from returning to his old ways, if contemporary newspapers reports of his drunk and disorderly escapades in the winter and spring of 1895 were true.[73]

Then on June 7, 1895, Cherokee lawmen arrested Reed "while [he was] plowing in a field in the Cherokee nation, and his hands showed blisters from the work. He was unarmed and made no resistance. He is charged with stealing a car load of cattle from Dan Hare, near Waggoner [Wagoner, Cherokee Nation]."[74]

Hare had "perjured himself in attempting to make bond for Fayette

Hudson, and last week swore in open court that he did not own a single head of cattle. Reed has been scouting for two months and blames the newspapers" for his arrest, based on notoriety in his own right and as the son of lawbreaking parents.[75] In the opinion of the *Vinita* (Indian Territory) *Indian Chieftain*, "there seems to be a very poor case against Ed" in the alleged cattle theft.[76]

Events soon seemed to take a twist. On July 18, 1895, the *Vinita Indian Chieftain* published a long column about proceedings at the US District Court in Fort Smith, including a short item about Reed: "Ed Reed recognized to Sept. 7 in sum of $500 as attached witness."[77] Texas attorney and historical writer Rick Miller explains that Reed's being "'recognized . . . in sum of $500 as attached witness'" probably means "that he was a 'material witness' who could give testimony in some pending case. As such, he could be held in custody until that hearing, but a bond of $500 could then be posted, allowing his release subject to that appearance in court. Failure to appear in court at the proper time would mean a forfeiture of that bond, an order for his arrest, and some sort of court sanction (fine or jail)."[78]

It is unclear which legal case Reed was designated as an "attached witness" for, but he soon found himself on the right side of the law, as did several other reformed lawbreakers during the territorial era. George Crump, US marshal for the Western District of Arkansas, gave Reed "a sixty day marshal commission . . . on the assurance that he could and would do some good work."[79] Reed stated that he desired "to settle down and become a good citizen."[80]

One of the reasons Reed might have decided to settle down and become a good citizen was his marriage to Jennie Cochran, "a pretty Cherokee schoolteacher from Claremore," daughter of Alec Cochran.[81] Jennie had been born on November 8, 1875, near Stonewall in the Chickasaw Nation of Indian Territory and later moved with her family to Oologah and then Claremore, both in Cooweescoowee District of the Cherokee Nation.[82] Jennie and Ed Reed "bought a small house on the east side of" Wagoner, where Reed was stationed as a deputy marshal.[83]

Reed's sixty-day appointment as a deputy evidently was extended. In

Ed Reed (right), Belle Starr's son, and Edgar Clark of Denton, Texas, are shown with an unidentified man (left). The portrait was taken circa 1890 at the W. H. Catterlin Studio in Claremore, Cherokee Nation, Indian Territory.

addition to other cases, in March 1896, he arrested "Watt Wafford, (col) [colored]" for cattle theft,[84] ironically, the crime for which Reed had been arrested only nine months earlier.

Reed's short career as a deputy marshal ended violently. According to some accounts, his father-in-law, Alec Cochran, "had been poisoned some time earlier by bad liquor obtained from the 'Gibbs brothers' saloon and gambling room, operated in the rear of their cigar store" in Claremore.[85] However, Cochran lived long enough to tell Reed what had happened. Reed was determined to end the "illegal activity" in the store. Selling liquor to Indians in Indian Territory was against federal law, and Claremore was in his jurisdiction as a deputy. Reed entered the store at about 7:00 p.m. "filled up with hop ale" and "in a dangerous mood" but then left and came back at about 8:30 p.m. on Monday, December 14, 1896.[86] He was then killed by "two shotgun blasts at close range."[87] (If that is true, a shotgun now in the possession of a descendant of Gibbs is allegedly the one that was used to kill Reed.)[88]

However, other newspapers say Reed himself had been "creating a disturbance." Reed, "well loaded with whisky," entered the saloon and started to shoot.[89] Before leaving, he said if John Clark, a bartender, was still there when Reed came back, he would kill him. When Reed came back a few minutes later, "Clark shot two bullets from a 45-caliber Colt's revolver crashing into him. One shot took effect in the neck and the other in the left breast, just below the heart. Reed died about 11 o'clock."[90]

Whatever the circumstances, Reed's life ended in a shooting, like the lives of so many in his family—his father, mother, stepfather, and four uncles. His death brought negative reactions from people who were skeptical of his recent attempts to live a good life.[91]

But again, opinion was divided. The *Claremore Progress* said Reed's "varied career is at an end" and praised him as a "courageous and fearless officer" of the law.[92]

"Reed's wife arrived in Claremore Tuesday about 11 o'clock, coming overland, but nothing was done until the arrival of his sister on Wednesday. He was interred in the Hendrick's Cemetery that evening," December 16, 1894, the *Progress* article concluded. Edwin Reed, twenty-five years old, was buried in Cochran Cemetery (evidently another name for Hendricks Cemetery) south of Claremore,[93] with a gravestone that showed his name as "J. E. Reed" and an inaccurate birthdate of February 22, 1877, instead of the correct date of February 22, 1871.[94] His short life had taken many turns since his birth in sunny southern California, where his parents had hoped to establish a "lovely little home" for their young family.

Reed's wife, Jennie Cochran Reed, later married Alexander Lewis McDaniel of Claremore, and they later lived in Blanchard in south-central Oklahoma.[95] She died in the Indian Health Service hospital in Lawton, Oklahoma, on December 11, 1959, almost sixty-three years to the day since the turbulent life of her young husband Ed Reed had ended in bloodshed.[96]

Rosa Lee (Pearl) Reed

When Belle Starr was killed on February 3, 1889, the storymongers did not stop spinning lurid tales about her, but she was no longer a living target for their sensationalism. Some of them transferred their energies to a ready-made substitute—Belle's twenty-year-old daughter Rosa Lee Reed, known as Pearl. She was young, attractive, and already somewhat scandalous as the mother of an out-of-wedlock daughter almost two years old and adopted out.

Some of the publicity about Pearl resulted from the jailing and court case of Edgar A. Watson, suspected of Belle's murder. Belle's husband, Jim July, and Pearl, called Pearl Younger in some documents, were in Fort Smith, Arkansas, for the hearing on February 20, 1889, with ten witnesses against Watson.[97]

After the end of the hearing, at which Watson was not bound over for trial, the focus of public interest shifted to the alleged activities of Pearl (erroneously identified in some articles as the daughter of Cole Younger). This included the unlikely tale that she had organized a party of "125 whites" to enter the first Oklahoma land run, in the so-called Unassigned Lands, on April 22, 1889.[98] Some newspapers, however, did not fall for the implausible story, stating flatly, "There is no truth in it."[99]

Two years later, Pearl's reputed activities were similar to those that her mother had been accused of years earlier—law officers were reported to have chased through the streets of Gainesville, Texas, after a young man and Pearl, who was carrying a Winchester and two six-shooters and dressed in male attire.[100] The two were accused of having stolen "two fine horses from a farmer near St. Joe" before escaping into "Chickasaw country" in Indian Territory. "She handles a Winchester and six-shooter with perfection, is a fine equestrian and bold[,] daring[,] and fearless," the stories gushed.[101]

As with her mother, inaccurate reports of Pearl's activities were picked up by newspapers throughout the region, evidenced by reports in Kansas and in Oklahoma Territory that she had been arrested in Paris, Texas, for horse stealing[102] and a story that she had been captured near Quanah, Texas.[103]

Just as her one-time stepfather Bruce Younger had done in Kansas, Pearl turned to the press to correct the misinformation. An article in the *Daily Arkansas Gazette* on April 2, 1891, stated:

Belle Starr's daughter, Pearl (right), poses with two unidentified bordello companions.

The sensational dispatches recently sent out from Gainesville, Tex., and published all over the country, to the effect that Pearl Younger, daughter of the late Belle Starr, was in the horse-stealing business, dressed in male attire, is all bosh. Pearl Younger lives at Tamaha, in the Choctaw Nation, about forty miles from this city [Fort Smith, Arkansas]. Seeing the reports published about her, she requests that they be contradicted. She says she has no desire to follow in the footsteps of her late mother. She is leading a quiet life among her friends in the Territory.[104]

A much longer article in the *Arkansas Democrat*, supposedly an interview with Pearl, also quotes her as saying the story about horse stealing was untrue.[105]

Later that summer, about a month before Pearl's twenty-third birthday, her life took a different turn with the first of her several brief marriages or alliances. The *Muskogee* (Indian Territory) *Phoenix* reported succinctly on August 6, 1891, "Despite denials it is a fact that Miss Pearl

Reed, daughter of Belle Starr, was recently married to Mr. Will Harris of Holden, Mo. The license was issued by T. N. Foster of South McAlester [Indian Territory], and Parson Barnhill, who lives five miles south of Whitefield, I. T., performed the ceremony."[106]

But Pearl seemed to be living a double life. Only one week later, on August 13, the *Phoenix* dropped a bombshell in another one-paragraph article: "Mrs. Harris, alias Pearl Reed, the daughter of the notorious Belle Star [sic], was before Commissioner Foster at South McAlester last Thursday, charged with illegal cohabitation with Joe Colburn at Tamahaw, Choctaw Nation. Her attorneys, Wilson and Moore, succeeded in getting her discharged from the accusation of cohabitation, but she was held for fornication."[107] One wonders if this was the same Foster who had issued Pearl's marriage license the previous week.

Pearl worked as a prostitute in Van Buren, Arkansas, allegedly to earn money to get her brother, Ed, out of legal trouble. Later, despite having claimed that she did not want to attract notoriety like her mother, Pearl could not resist capitalizing on the Starr name. She was a prostitute in Fort Smith and then established her own bordello on the Row, Fort Smith's waterfront street, that left no doubt as to who ran the business—the building was identified by a bright red star surrounded by lighted pearls. It was a successful business, and she purchased additional houses of ill repute and invested in saloons and other property.[108]

Pearl's name (with different surnames at different times) appeared for years in numerous newspaper stories and court documents for having been "too noisy and conspicuous at an early hour," disorderly conduct, and other allegations.[109] Some charges against Pearl were more serious, involving physical violence such as beating up female "inmates" who worked at her bordello.[110] In 1911, she was convicted of robbery and sentenced to one year in the penitentiary, but the conviction was appealed.[111]

Simultaneously with her career as a businesswoman and madam, Pearl was a wife (or mistress) and mother. She and Fort Smith businessman Charles Kaigler were the parents of a daughter, Ruth D. Kaigler, born on June 30, 1894.[112]

Then on October 10, 1897, in Fayetteville, Arkansas, Pearl married a German who worked as a pianist at her bordello, Count Arthur E. Erbach.[113] Pearl bought a large home in a fashionable neighborhood of Fort Smith and hoped to establish herself as a respectable married woman with a family.

But her hopes for her home life were tragically short-lived. Erbach became ill with typhoid malaria. He was hospitalized at St. John's Hospital in Fort Smith before a son was born to him and Pearl, on August 24, 1898.[114] Erbach died on September 13, 1898, at "the river front resort at No. 223 Water street"[115] at age twenty-nine and was buried the next day at City Cemetery (Oak Cemetery) in Fort Smith. Pearl's baby, Arthur E. Erbach, whose address was given as 800 Second Street, died on July 28, 1899, at age eleven months. He was buried next to his father on July 29. The cause of the baby's death was not given.[116]

Pearl married gambler Dell Andrews on May 5, 1902, in Fayetteville,[117] and they had a daughter named Jennette Steele Andrews on November 8, 1902. Andrews had a raucous career in his own right, as evidenced by colorful newspaper coverage. Pearl tried to divorce him as early as 1904 and 1905 (once giving her name as Belle Andrews), but the court figured out that she was the notorious Pearl Starr and threw the case out because of her lifestyle.[118] In 1908, Pearl filed a divorce petition and appeal for custody of Jennette, stating that Andrews had never contributed to her support, had run through most of her assets, and had abandoned his family in August 1904 without provocation and left for Texas. He was last heard of living in Flagstaff, Arizona, Pearl stated.[119] She and Andrews were finally divorced on April 2, 1908.[120]

Although Pearl continued to operate bordellos and other businesses in Fort Smith, she wanted to protect her daughters from scandal. She acquired a home in Winslow, Arkansas, a resort town in the Boston Mountains, and hired a couple as housekeepers. Pearl made sure Ruth and Jennette were the best-dressed girls in the Winslow school and had music lessons and other cultural advantages. She took the train from Fort Smith to visit them as often as possible.[121]

Photographs from the era show Pearl, growing stouter with the years, her lovely young daughters, and her substantial homes and businesses.

Fort Smith eventually became less tolerant of the lifestyle of madams such as Pearl, and she moved to Bisbee, Arizona, a copper boomtown, where she acquired a chattel mortgage in October 1916 when she bought furniture.[122] She picked up with her old career by establishing a house of ill repute in Upper Brewery Gulch in Bisbee but was convicted in 1918 of the misdemeanor of operating a "disorderly and ill-governed house."[123]

In Bisbee, Pearl reverted to her maiden name, Rosa Reed, gradually dropping the Pearl Starr name and its connection with her own colorful past and with her mother. The 1924 *Bisbee District Directory* lists her as Rosa Reed (widow of James), living at 14 Tate Hill, P. O. Box 2523, Bisbee. As far as is known, she was not the widow of anyone except Arthur E. Erbach, who had died a quarter of a century earlier.[124]

Late in her life, Pearl wrote to the orphanage in Wichita, Kansas, where her first daughter, Mamie, had been taken many years before. The child had been adopted by David Epple and his wife, Nannie Garten, of Newton, Kansas, and renamed Florence Pearl Epple, known as Flossie. She had been raised in Newton. Pearl's letter eventually reached Flossie Epple Hutton, who was married to Charles Hutton and had been living in Topeka, Kansas, for several years. She had been unaware of her biological parentage. She replied to the letter and established a correspondence with Pearl. Hutton and her only child, a teenaged son named Robert Hutton, went to Arizona to meet Pearl in 1924.[125]

At about that time, Pearl moved from Bisbee to Douglas, Arizona, where she was manager of the Savoy Hotel at 511 Ninth Street for the last nine months of her life. She took out a chattel mortgage on April 10, 1925.[126] In June 1925, she suffered "a paralytic stroke."[127]

About three weeks later, on July 6, 1925, Pearl (under the name Rosa Reed) died in the county hospital in Douglas, Cochise County, at age fifty-six years ten months (her death certificate inaccurately shows her age as fifty-eight). Her birthplace was given as Missouri, her father's name as merely Reed with no first name, and his birthplace, mistakenly, as Oklahoma. Her mother's maiden name, erroneously and anachronistically, was given as Belle Starr, born in Missouri. Pearl was described as a resident of the Savoy Hotel and a widow. The cause of death was given as hemiplegia and arteriosclerosis. E. W. Adamson was the attending physician. The informant was listed as Mrs. Ed Drewitt (Pearl's daughter Ruth Kaigler) of the Savoy Hotel.[128]

Pearl Reed's funeral was held on July 8, 1925, in the chapel of the Porter and Ames Mortuary in Douglas with the Reverend J. E. Howard officiating.[129] Funeral costs were $16 for the burial dress, $20 for the lot, $5 for the minister, and $275 for the service, totaling $316.[130]

After an unusual upbringing and a tumultuous life, the daughter of James Reed and Myra Maibelle Shirley Reed was buried under the name Rosa Pearl Reed in a marked grave in Plot K-195-4 of Calvary Cemetery in Douglas on July 9, 1925.[131] The moniker was a combination of her birth first name, nickname, and maiden name.

After Flossie Epple Hutton met Pearl in 1924, she began to research her connection to Belle Starr. Her lengthy two-part article in the *Dallas (Texas) Morning News* of April 30 and May 7, 1933, written under the byline of "Flossie" without a last name, mixes factual tidbits with unsubstantiated material, much of which seems to stem from the infamous Fox *Bella Starr* book of 1889 or other sources based on that book.

Hutton's 1933 articles evidently attracted the attention of writer and Ozark folklorist Randolph Vance, who was researching Belle Starr with the intention of writing a book about her. He found out Hutton's identity and corresponded with her briefly. She seemed ambivalent about wanting her connection to Belle Starr to be known but nevertheless said she too was writing a book about her. Randolph replied that in that case, of course he would not expect Hutton to provide him with any information for his own research, and the correspondence ended.[132]

Randolph published his book *Belle Starr, the Bandit Queen: The Career of the Most Colorful Outlaw the Indian Territory Ever Knew* in 1946 under one of his pseudonyms, William Yancey Shackleford.[133] Randolph is now widely recognized as the author of the book.

Flossie Epple Hutton, however, never published a book about her famous grandmother Belle Starr. Hutton died on August 7, 1943, in Topeka at fifty-six years old, the same age her mother, Pearl, had been when she died.[134]

Pearl Starr's two younger daughters, Ruth Kaigler and Jennette Steele Andrews, were each married several times. Ruth had one daughter, Veleska Myra Walt, who had no children.[135] Jennette had one known child, a daughter, Delores Vignolo, who was born when her mother was an unmarried teenager. Ironically, just as Belle Starr had not wanted Pearl to rear an illegitimate child, Pearl did not want Jennette to do so either and sent the baby to an orphanage. Later, Jennette arranged for Delores to join her. Delores had no known descendants. (According to an unproved rumor, Jennette might have had one more child later.)[136]

Thus the descendants of Robert Hutton's only child, Flossie Mae Hutton,[137] represent the only known surviving line of descent from the 1866 marriage of James C. Reed and Myra Maibelle Shirley and from their daughter Rosa Lee Reed, Belle's beloved Pearl.

Pearl's encounters with the law were more extensive and more serious than those of her infamous mother, perhaps indicating a darker and more violent side to Pearl's personality. She also showed an increasing tendency to attract publicity at whatever cost to the truth, stating unequivocally in an early interview that she was the daughter of Jim Reed but years later touting the erroneous old tale that Cole Younger was her biological father. Pearl apparently did not curtail her flamboyant lifestyle until her final legal troubles and poverty left her no choice but to live and die in "genteel poverty."

Younger's Bend

Almost a year after Belle Starr was laid to rest near the cabin at Younger's Bend, her grave was looted. The perpetrators—who were never identified or apprehended—took "her jewelry . . . and a very fine pistol buried with her."[138]

As a result, Belle's daughter, Pearl, flush with money earned as a prostitute, took steps to protect her mother's resting place. In 1893, Pearl had already tried to finance her brother's legal defense, but when Eddie

Print the Legend ✥ 331

Belle Starr's original grave marker at Younger's Bend, Cherokee Nation, Indian Territory.

learned that she had earned the money working as a harlot, their relationship was irreparably damaged, and they went their separate ways.[139]

Prior to Eddie's death in 1894, Pearl hired a mason who "walled up [Belle Starr's grave] with two feet of stone, the wall filled with broken rock, and two large, well-fitted slabs of limestone tilted over the vault in a V, like the roof of a house."[140]

Once the wall and tomb were erected, Pearl paid skilled stonecutter John Dailey [Daly] twenty-five dollars to procure and engrave a large white marble slab that would be cemented into the stone wall at the head of the grave.[141] At the top of the slab, he carved the figure of a horse to represent Belle's beloved mare, Venus, with a BS brand on the shoulder. Above the horse's rump, he cut a large star, and below the horse's head, he chiseled a handbell, the kind schoolmarms used to summon students. At the bottom of the tombstone, a carved hand clasped a bunch of flowers.[142] An inscribed epitaph and poem read:

BELLE STARR
BORN CARTHAGE, MO.
FEB. 5, 1848
DIED
FEB. 3, 1889

Shed not for her the bitter tear,
Nor give to the heart vain regret.
Tis but the casket that lies here.
The gem that filled it sparkles yet.[143]

Most people attributed the poem to Pearl, but she did not write it. Many marble carvers in the nineteenth century frequently used variants of that poetic inscription. The verse appeared on tombstones from the gold rush days in California and on markers at graveyards along emigrant trails. Stonecutters commonly used the same poem—sometimes word for word—on monuments at several cemeteries near Younger's Bend, such as Briartown, Porum, and Whitefield.[144]

Younger's Bend became a popular destination for visitors once Belle's gravesite was rehabilitated. Although various Cherokee individuals and families dwelled there at times, a steady stream of curiosity seekers, fascinated by books and articles about the infamous "Bandit Queen," made pilgrimages to her final resting place.

On June 12, 1895, a party of visitors enlisted John Cates, the man who had built Belle's coffin, to guide them to the grave, according to newspaper reports.[145] "The grave has been well taken care of, and is in the front yard of residence, not more than 25 feet from the door, which is now occupied by W. H. Porter and father. Some say it was once the resort of the James [brothers] and Youngers [brothers], but this is exceedingly doubtful. It was then an ideal place to hide, but now is a peaceful hamlet, occupied by enterprising farmers."[146]

Oklahoma journalist Frederick Barde paid his respects at Younger's Bend in 1899, the tenth anniversary of Belle's death. In 1910, Barde returned. Based on his observations and interviews with area residents, he wrote a seven-page article for *Sturm's Oklahoma Magazine*.[147]

> The road wound up and around a rocky hillside, and the house of cedar logs came into full view. The gate hung between two beautiful maple trees planted by Belle Starr when she went there with her Cherokee husband, Sam Starr. A step more and some came to a lowly house of stone—the grave of Belle Starr. It was built of rock from the nearby hills; slabs tipped towards each other formed the roof. At one corner grew a hollyhock—with blood-red flowers. The grave looks toward the west. The headstone, firmly fixed in stone and mortar, has been chipped by relic hunters until the edges are rounded.[148]

Over the years, the property and the grave had negligible maintenance. The log house remained largely intact, but by the late 1920s, it was no longer fit to live in and on the verge of collapse. So was the barn. In 1933, both structures were torn down, and the house was replaced by a small frame dwelling.[149]

Despite the structural losses at Younger's Bend, people continued to visit Belle's grave. In winter 1936, reporters Joe Synar and Richard Venator made an appearance to stand at "the tombstone which marks the grave of the most daring female desperado in history."[150] In their sensationalized feature story in the *Muskogee Daily Phoenix*, they shared stories gleaned from "the oldtimers who knew her personally" but also knew how to spin yarns for a couple of city fellows.[151]

In 1938, Claude Hamilton, a barber in Sterling, Colorado, made a discovery in his tonsorial parlor that changed his life and had a profound impact on the future of Younger's Bend. Hamilton claimed that while sweeping up hair clippings beneath a couch, he spied a map that likely had been dropped by a customer. To his great surprise, it was a map that led him to a cache of buried treasure. Hamilton was hooked. He was determined to continue treasure hunting.[152]

Hamilton had heard tales about the outlaw riches supposedly waiting to be unearthed at the Younger's Bend area in Oklahoma. He bought some land near Younger's Bend and established a barbershop in Porum.[153]

In 1939, Hamilton bought the Starr property at a sheriff's delinquent tax sale.[154] Hamilton was obsessed with finding the alleged hidden treasure in the area. He continually searched the property and the nearby canyons and hills, sometimes even using dynamite in hopes of uncovering hidden riches that were never found.[155]

Hamilton came to respect Belle Starr's resting place. He never probed the gravesite but tried to preserve and protect it from vandals and souvenir hunters eager to break off a piece of marble. Hamilton became so frustrated by the numerous intruders that he planted wild brambles around the grave and posted "No Trespassing" signs.[156]

In the 1960s, Hamilton and his wife, Ada, noticed a substantial rise in visitation. Much of the increase resulted from the United States Army Corps of Engineers dam on the South Canadian River and the creation of Lake Eufaula—an instant tourism attraction.[157] After the dam—which permanently changed the course of the South Canadian—was completed in 1964, the lake became the largest reservoir in the state and one of the largest human-made lakes in the world.

Although the creation of the lake covered several historic sites in the area, the Belle Starr grave and surrounding property remained high and dry. By the late 1960s, however, Hamilton faced more desecration of the gravesite.

After the marble tombstone that Pearl had erected to honor her mother was broken into pieces, Hamilton hauled "two sizable chunks" that remained to his barbershop in Porum.[158] He paid $325 to have a duplicate marker made and surrounded the entire plot with a six-foot-tall chain-link fence. Strands of barbed wire adorned the top of the fence to discourage any climbers.

After Hamilton died in 1970, his widow, Ada, remained in the small frame home close to Younger's Bend. For a time, a sign in the front yard advertised her guided tours of Belle's resting place, but one day, it vanished.[159]

Ron and Donna Hood's passion for history fueled their dream to purchase and preserve the Starr property at Younger's Bend and reconstruct Belle Starr's burial site.

In 1986, Associated Press reporter Gil Broyles of Tulsa showed up at Ada's home while researching a story about the legendary bandit queen. "I charge a dollar," Ada told him, with the caveat, "I don't know anything about Belle Starr."[160]

In a story that appeared nationwide, Broyles wrote, "Belle Starr remains an enigma. Her sonorous name is more widely known now than when she was made out to be the female epitome of lawlessness west of Fort Smith. Television movie reruns show Hollywood's glamorous vision of a six-gun-toting Belle, enlarging upon a legend begun by the sensation-seeking press of the late 19th century."[161]

After Ada Hamilton's death in the early 2000s, her children continued to oversee the Starr property. But when vandals cut the fence surrounding the grave, the site was exposed to trespassers who left graffiti, beer cans, and trash. Eventually, the slabs of the grave roof collapsed, and the concrete replica marker fell flat on the ground.[162]

When it appeared that the Starr land and grave were on the verge of being thrown on the trash heap of history, someone with a passion for healing and history emerged just in time. In 2010, Ron Hood, an orthopedic surgeon, and his wife, Donna, purchased the Starr property from the Hamilton family.[163] The Hoods immediately began to plan the restoration of the property and gravesite.

"My family has been here [Oklahoma] for five generations and been intertwined with the state's history," Hood later explained. "The property was in great disrepair and I thought that was a shame. What's the value of history if no one can see it? History doesn't come alive unless you can touch it."[164]

The Hoods put up with copperheads and ticks while they cleared brush and debris and removed fences. Using historic photographs and the help of an expert stonemason, Hood repaired and restored Belle Starr's grave to "its original state."[165]

Hood later moved his family and his orthopedic practice from Tulsa to Muskogee. He bought an 1850s log cabin in California, Missouri, and had it disassembled and moved to Younger's Bend, where it was redesigned by Tulsa architect Gene Starr (a Starr family descendant) and erected to resemble the original log house.[166] It serves as a second home for the Hoods.

The Oklahoma Historical Society has placed a historical marker at the foot of the property. It includes Belle Starr's quote:

"On the Canadian River . . . far from society, I hoped to pass the remainder of my life in peace."[167]

Acknowledgments

THE ADAGE OFTEN ATTRIBUTED TO SPORTS COLUMNIST RED Barber says it best: "Writing is easy. Just sit down, open a vein, and bleed." I know that to be true. While writing twenty books, I have opened countless veins. This book was no exception.

Telling the story of a legendary frontier figure is especially challenging. The many myths and lies that surround them need to be carefully unwrapped and taken apart so that the true—and invariably better—story can be told.

That was my mission in writing about the life and times of the woman best known as Belle Starr. Fortunately, I had my own posse with me as I tracked down the elusive Belle.

At my side during the wild ride was my dear wife and forever partner, Suzanne Fitzgerald Wallis. She has always provided encouragement and refuge as well as honest and helpful criticism. Our two felines—Juniper and Martini—are constant literary muses.

A lion's share of gratitude goes to Hazel Rowena Mills. This book is dedicated to her because of all her contributions as a researcher and editor, not only for this book but for most of my other published works. Rowena has never let me down, and I know she never will. Thank you, dear friend.

Another good friend, Allen "Storm" Strider, was by my side from day one. We journeyed through Belle Starr country, visiting old haunts, ghost places, historic sites, and research depositories. If I am riding shotgun in Storm's vehicle, I am confident we will uncover unadulterated literary treasure. We always do.

I salute my late agent and brother-in-law, James Fitzgerald, who did not live to see this book's birth. He now lies in the adobe earth of our beloved New Mexico.

Massive thanks to the editorial team at Liveright Publishing, a division of W. W. Norton, executive editor Bob Weil, my longtime editor and friend, and editors Gina Iaquinta and Maria Connors. Gina and Maria deserve special thanks for their guidance and patience. I truly appreciate their counsel and assistance.

Rebecca Karamehmedovic, a founding partner of Sway, will always be remembered as the woman who tracked down and secured permissions for all photographs and images, including some that are rare and difficult to locate. Rebecca puts the best bloodhounds to shame.

Ron and Donna Hood, who own and protect Belle Starr's grave and homesite at Younger's Bend on the South Canadian River in Oklahoma, deserve a standing ovation for all the assistance they gave me. The memory of Ron guiding me through time and space at Younger's Bend is eternal.

My colleagues in the Wild West History Association came through for me throughout the entire process of researching and writing this book. Kudos to Roy Young and Charlotte Steele for providing many images from the Robert G. McCubbin Collection and the Phillip W. Steele Collection. In addition to photographs, the Steele Collection also provided me with an unpublished manuscript about Belle Starr's early years by Ward L. Schrantz, a newspaper editorial writer for the *Carthage* (Missouri) *Evening Press* from the late 1940s until his death in 1958.

I appreciate the encouragement of other WWHA members, including Elizabeth Weathers, Kurt Haus (like Roy Young, one of my fellow Pizzlers), Matthew Bernstein, editor of the WWHA Journal, Donna Harrell, and Nancy B. Samuelson. *Muchas gracias* to Mike Koch, a talented Oklahoma writer who introduced me to the invaluable research files of Texan Rick Miller, a superb author and Old West authority. Miller also supplied an abundance of original research and a plethora of sage advice.

A host of institutions and research sites deserves praise, including the National Archives, the Shirley Family Foundation, the Kansas Historical Society, the Missouri Historical Society, the Oklahoma Historical

Society, the Tulsa Historical Society, the Fort Smith Historical Society, the Powers Museum, the Western History Collection at the University of Oklahoma, and the Tulsa (Oklahoma) City-County Library System.

Steve Rice, of Map Ink, Norman, Oklahoma, created the helpful Belle Starr Country map to guide readers.

Last, I offer everlasting thanks to my close friends on the home front who kept me going as I opened veins—Nita Dragoo, Mollie Williford, Steve and Sue Gerkin, and my irreplaceable wingmen, Ken Busby and Rhys Martin. I owe all of you an enormous thanks.

Notes

Introduction

1. S. W. Harman, *Hell on the Border* (Fort Smith, AR: Phoenix Publishing, 1898), 557–58.
2. Richard K. Fox, publisher, *Bella Starr, The Bandit Queen, or the Female Jesse James*, facsimile of the 1889 edition (Austin, TX: Steck, 1960).
3. Fox, *Bella Starr*, 5.
4. Fox, *Bella Starr*, book cover.
5. *Dallas* (Texas) *Morning News*, June 7, 1886, 4.
6. Susan Armitage, "Through Women's Eyes: A New View of the West," in *The Women's West*, eds. Susan Armitage and Elizabeth Jameson (Norman: University of Oklahoma Press, 1987), 17.

Chapter 1: **In the Country of the Six Bulls**

1. Joel Thomas Livingston, *A History of Jasper County, Missouri, and Its People*, vol. 1 (Chicago: Lewis, 1912), 4.
2. Livingston, *History of Jasper County*.
3. Livingston, *History of Jasper County*.
4. John Bradbury, *Travels in the Interior of America, in the Years 1809, 1810, and 1811* (London: Sherwood, Neely, and Jones, 1817), 266.
5. John Mackenzie, "A Brief History of the Mason-Dixon Line," APEC/CANR, University of Delaware. The name "Mason-Dixon Line" came into popular usage when it was first used in the Missouri Compromise of 1820 to designate the entire boundary between free states and slave states.
6. Betty M. Shirley, ed., *Belle Starr and Her Roots* (Cupertino, CA: Shirley Family Association, 1989), 3, 6. Betty Shirley founded the Shirley Family Association in 1978. She published the book in 1989 in commemoration of the 100th anniversary of Belle Starr's death.
7. Shirley, *Belle Starr and Her Roots*, 6.
8. Shirley, *Belle Starr and Her Roots*.
9. "Anna Elizabeth (Kelker) Shelley (1736–1800)," WikiTree.
10. Shirley, *Belle Starr and Her Roots*. Shortly after the family's move to Virginia, a Maryland court ordered Peter Shirley to repay 28 pounds he had borrowed from an unnamed party in Washington County, plus 5 pounds in damages.
11. David Brown and Mike Gregory, "Agriculture in the Upper Shenandoah: An Outline from the 18th Century to the Present," unpublished paper, Washington and Lee University, 2015, 8, 9, 12, 13.

12. Laura Peters, "Historian: Valley Slavery Story 'Not Pretty,'" *Staunton* (Virginia) *News Leader*, November 15, 2015.
13. Shirley, *Belle Starr and Her Roots*, 6.
14. John E. Kiebar, ed., *The Kentucky Encyclopedia* (Lexington: University Press of Kentucky, 1992), 602.
15. Shirley Family Association, "30. Michael Shirley."
16. Shirley Family Association, "30. Michael Shirley."
17. John Shirley–Nancy Fowler Marriage Record, Book A, page 21, April 6, 1818, Clark County, Indiana, Marriages, 1808–1897.
18. Shirley Family Association, "31. Peter Shirley (cont.), 1(iii). Christian Shirley."
19. Shirley Family Association, "31. Peter Shirley (cont.), 1(iii). Christian Shirley."
20. Hendrik A. Hartog, "Marital Exits and Marital Expectations in Nineteenth Century America," *Georgetown Law Review* 80, January 1991, 126.
21. "Floyd County, Indiana, Marriages, 1802–1892," FHL Film #1411883, Genealogy Trails. According to some sources, John and Fanny were married on May 22, 1829. The official county records, however, list the date as May 8.
22. Shirley Family Association, "31. Peter Shirley (cont.), 1(iii). Christian Shirley." Other than the tombstone in an abandoned cemetery at the Knob, there are no other records or family accounts of Clarissa Shirley.
23. Shirley Family Association, "31. Peter Shirley (cont.), 1(iii). Christian Shirley."
24. "Divorce Mill," Indiana Public Media.
25. Timothy Crumrin, "Women and the Law in Early 19th Century," Conner Prairie.
26. Crumrin, "Women and the Law in Early 19th Century."
27. Shirley Family Association, "31. Peter Shirley (cont.), 1(iii). Christian Shirley."
28. Marriage Records of Greene County, Indiana, Book C, 32, certified copy by Frankie Justus Jr., Clerk of Greene County Circuit Court.
29. Phillip W. Steele, *Starr Tracks: Belle and Pearl Starr* (Greta, LA: Pelican, 1998), 21. Several other sources erroneously claim 1828 as Charlotte Shirley's year of birth, ten years before her correct birthdate.
30. "Panic 1837," Armstrong Economics.
31. James H. Madison and Lee Ann Sandweiss, *Hoosiers and the American Story* (Indianapolis: Indiana Historical Society Press, 2014), 70.
32. Madison and Sandweiss, *Hoosiers and the American Story*.
33. Ward L. Schrantz, *The Background of Belle Starr*, unpublished manuscript, n.d., 6, 7. From the Phillip W. Steele Collection, courtesy of Charlotte Steele and Roy Young.
34. Schrantz, *Background of Belle Starr*.
35. *Goodspeed's History of Newton, Lawrence, Barry and McDonald Counties, Missouri* (Chicago: Goodspeed Publishing, 1888), 278.
36. Joel Thomas Livingston, *A History of Jasper County Missouri, and Its People*, vol. 1 (Chicago: Lewis, 1912), 8.
37. Schrantz, *Background of Belle Starr*, 8.
38. R. I. Holcombe, ed., *History of Greene County, Missouri* (Saint Louis, MO: Western Historical, 1883), 179; Michael Wallis, *The Best Land under Heaven: The Donner Party in the Age of Manifest Destiny* (New York: Liveright, 2017), 73. In 1838, Boggs issued an "Extermination Order" and called for all Mormon followers to be purged from Missouri. This led to his attempted assassination against him in Independence, Missouri, in 1842, after he left office. In 1846, Boggs and his second wife, a granddaughter of Daniel Boone, left Missouri for California. For much of the journey, their wagon caravan included members of the ill-fated Donner party. Boggs died in California in 1880.
39. Schrantz, *Background of Belle Starr*, 5.
40. Schrantz, *Background of Belle Starr*, 8.

41. John Suval, "Squatters, Statesmen, and the Rupture of American Democracy, 1830–1860" (PhD diss., University of Wisconsin–Madison, 2021).
42. Livingston, *History of Jasper County Missouri*, 11.
43. Schrantz, *Background of Belle Starr*, 11.
44. Schrantz, *Background of Belle Starr*, 12.
45. Schrantz, *Background of Belle Starr*.
46. "Brief History of Jasper County, Missouri," Ancestry.com. At this meeting of the county road commissioners, it was also decided that each male White person in the county was required to work on the public roads at least two days each year or pay fifty cents.
47. Malcolm G. McGregor, *The Biographical Record of Jasper County, Missouri* (Chicago: Lewis, 1901), 13.
48. Schrantz, *Background of Belle Starr*, 14. In describing this incident, Schrantz added, "Thus the man [John Pennington], who, it appears, later was to become Myra Belle Shirley's maternal grandfather, dedicated the town which Belle Starr was to claim as her birthplace."
49. Shirley Family Association, "31. Peter Shirley (cont.), 1(iii). Christian Shirley."
50. Schrantz, *Background of Belle Starr*, 20, 21.
51. Schrantz, *Background of Belle Starr*, 21, 22.
52. Wallis, *Best Land under Heaven*, xv, 27.
53. Schrantz, *Background of Belle Starr*, 23.

Chapter 2: Young Myra in Carthage

1. Joel Thomas Livingston, *A History of Jasper County, Missouri, and Its People*, vol. 1 (Chicago: Lewis, 1912), 34.
2. Betty M. Shirley, ed., *Belle Starr and Her Roots* (Cupertino, CA: Shirley Family Association, 1989), 1, 4.
3. "Behind the Name Myra."
4. Shirley, *Belle Starr and Her Roots*, 4; Phillip W. Steele, *Starr Tracks: Belle and Pearl Starr* (Gretna, LA: Pelican, 1998), 23. Steele was a proponent of the name Myra Maebelle; Glenn Shirley, *Belle Starr and Her Times: The Literature, the Facts, and the Legends* (Norman: University of Oklahoma Press, 1982), 32. Glenn Shirley gave her name as Myra Maybelle.
5. US National Archives and Records Administration, Milestone Documents, "Treaty of Guadalupe Hidalgo (1848)."
6. US National Archives and Records Administration, "Treaty of Guadalupe Hidalgo."
7. Ward L. Schrantz, *The Background of Belle Starr*, unpublished manuscript, n.d., 30. From the Phillip W. Steele Collection, courtesy of Charlotte Steele and Roy Young.
8. Shirley Family Association, "31. Peter Shirley (cont.), 1(iii). Christian Shirley."
9. Shirley Family Association, "31. Peter Shirley (cont.), 1(iii). Christian Shirley."
10. Livingston, *A History of Jasper County, Missouri*, 155.
11. F. A. North, *The History of Jasper County* (Des Moines, IA: Mills, 1883), 392.
12. Shirley, *Belle Starr and Her Roots*, 3.
13. North, *The History of Jasper County*, 1030–31. Williamson Dunn Alexander was born in Kentucky in 1815 and later moved to Indiana, where he met and married Elizabeth Shirley.
14. Schrantz, *Background of Belle Starr*, 30.
15. Shirley Family Association, "31. Peter Shirley (cont.), 1(iii). Christian Shirley."
16. U.S. Department of the Interior, Bureau of Land Management, Official Land Records Site, MW-1002-108, John Shirley and Harry W. Younger Land Patent (1850).
17. Schrantz, *Background of Belle Starr*, 30–32.
18. Schrantz, *Background of Belle Starr*, 32.
19. Schrantz, *Background of Belle Starr*, 32–33.

20. Schrantz, *Background of Belle Starr*, 33.
21. Betty Shirley, ed., "The Shirley News" 3, no. 5 (Summer 1889): 4.
22. Livingston, *A History of Jasper County Missouri*, 35.
23. R. F. Stringfellow, chairman, The Platte County Self-Defense Association, *Negro Slavery, No Evil; or The North and the South* (Saint Louis, MO: M. Niedner, 1854), 13.
24. Schrantz, *Background of Belle Starr*, 36.
25. Schrantz, *Background of Belle Starr*, 36, 40.
26. Schrantz, *Background of Belle Starr*.
27. Schrantz, *Background of Belle Starr*, 38.
28. Schrantz, *Background of Belle Starr*, 36, 38.
29. Schrantz, *Background of Belle Starr*, 38, 39.
30. Schrantz, *Background of Belle Starr*, 40.
31. Schrantz, *Background of Belle Starr*, 40, 41.
32. Schrantz, *Background of Belle Starr*, 41.
33. Schrantz, *Background of Belle Starr*, 42, 43.
34. Glenn Shirley, *Belle Starr and Her Times: The Literature, the Facts, and the Legends* (Norman: University of Oklahoma Press, 1982), 36.
35. Shirley, *Belle Starr and Her Times*.
36. Helen Katherine Hunter, *Echoes of School Bells: History of Jasper County Missouri Rural Schools* (Carthage, MO: Drop Cap, 2013), 11.
37. Hunter, *Echoes of School Bells*.
38. Schrantz, *Background of Belle Starr*, 47, 49.
39. Schrantz, *Background of Belle Starr*, 49. Charlotte Amanda Shirley wed Jesse Thompson on January 13, 1857, in a civil ceremony presided over by justice of the peace Joseph Thompson. Apparently, Charlotte lost contact with the other members of the Shirley family. It is believed that she and her husband resided in Indian Territory before moving to Matamoros, Mexico.
40. Schrantz, *Background of Belle Starr*, 52.
41. Jerry J. Gaddy, *Dust to Dust: Obituaries of the Gunfighters* (Fort Collins, CO: Old Army Press, 1977), 68. The reference to Myra Shirley's shooting ability first appeared in the February 15, 1889, edition of the *Fort Smith (AR) Weekly Elevator*.
42. Schrantz, *Background of Belle Starr*, 46.
43. Schrantz, *Background of Belle Starr*, 44. Shirley was appointed a county road commissioner on July 24, 1855.
44. Schrantz, *Background of Belle Starr*, 46–47.
45. Shirley, *Belle Starr and Her Times*, 36.
46. Schrantz, *Background of Belle Starr*, 47.
47. Livingston, *A History of Jasper County*, 26.
48. North, *The History of Jasper County, Missouri*, 284.
49. J. Kevin Graffagnino, "Vermont Attitudes Toward Slavery: The Need for a Closer Look," *Vermont History: The Journal of the Vermont Historical Society* 45, no. 1 (winter 1977), 31–34. Many people used the expression "peculiar institution" to defend slavery.
50. Graffagnino, "Vermont Attitudes Toward Slavery," 31–32. On January 18, 1849, Slade delivered the first abolitionist speech ever made in the US Congress. He called for an immediate end of slavery in America.
51. Debra Michals, ed., "Catherine Beecher," National Women's History Museum, 2015. Despite her forward-thinking views concerning women's education, opposition to the Indian Removal Bill, and antislavery stance, Beecher initially opposed women's suffrage. She believed women could best impact society as teachers and mothers and avoid the corruption of politics.
52. Anika Rede and Maryum Ali, "*Uncle Tom's Cabin*: Generating a Rising Tide of Responsibility to End the Institution of Slavery," Weebly.

53. "Politics Make Strange Bedfellows," Sacred Cow WordPress. The quote is attributed to Charles Dudley Warner, an essayist and editor.
54. *First Annual Report of the General Agent of the Board of the National Education Board* (Cincinnati, OH: Ben Franklin Printing House, 1848), 7. The thirty-member board reviewed applications, chose teachers, prepared them for their work, and assigned them to schools. All the teachers were expected to be of "unexceptionable moral and religious character."
55. North, *The History of Jasper County, Missouri.*
56. Ward Schrantz Articles Collection, *Carthage* (Missouri) *Evening Press* files, Powers Museum, Carthage, Missouri. The newspaper articles in this collection are from a local history column that Schrantz began in 1942 and continued until his death in 1958.
57. Schrantz Articles Collection, *Carthage Evening Press* files.
58. Livingston, *A History of Jasper County.*
59. Schrantz Articles Collection, *Carthage Evening Press* files, 53. Schrantz found this advertisement in the sole existing copy of the *Southwest News*, March 29, 1861.
60. Schrantz Articles Collection, *Carthage Evening Press* files.
61. Burton Rascoe, *Belle Starr: The Bandit Queen* (New York: Random House, 1941), 68.
62. Leonard I. Sweet, "The Female Seminary Movement and Women's Mission in Antebellum America," *Journal of the American Society of Church History* 54, no. 1 (Cambridge: Cambridge University Press, 1985), 41.
63. Judith E. Harper, *Women during the Civil War: An Encyclopedia* (New York: Routledge, 2004).
64. Schrantz Articles Collection, *Carthage Evening Press* files, 54, 56.

Chapter 3: "The War That Never Goes Away"

1. The phrase is contained in a lyric of "The Battle Hymn of the Republic," written in 1861 by abolitionist Julia Ward Howe after having visited a Union army camp. The song was published in 1862 and quickly became a rallying cry and the most popular song of the war in the North.
2. Archibald Forbes, *Memories and Studies of War and Peace* (London: Cassell, 1895), 241, quoting Union General Phil Sheridan.
3. David Walsh, "Historian James M. McPherson and the Cause of Intellectual Integrity," World Socialist Web Site, May 18, 1999.
4. Walsh, "Historian James M. McPherson."
5. Donald L. Gilmore, *Civil War on the Missouri-Kansas Border* (Gretna, LA: Pelican, 2008), 43. Senator Stephen A. Douglas of Illinois proposed the Kansas-Nebraska Act. The bill overturned the 1820 Missouri Compromise's use of latitude as the boundary between free and slave territory.
6. Floyd C. Shoemaker, "Missouri's Proslavery Fight for Kansas, 1854–1855," *Missouri Historical Review* 48, no. 3 (Columbia: State Historical Society of Missouri, 1954), 222.
7. Shoemaker, "Missouri's Proslavery Fight."
8. Harold C. Evans, *The WPA Guide to 1930s Kansas* (New York: Viking, 1939), 234.
9. Gilmore, *Civil War on the Missouri-Kansas Border*, 10. In the 1850s, Horace Greeley, founder and editor of the *New York Tribune*, became the chief propagandist for the antislavery movement and has often been credited with coining the term "Bleeding Kansas," from a poem by Charles S. Weyman, published in the September 13, 1856, edition of the *Tribune*. However, there is also a record of the term having been used two months earlier at a political convention in Philadelphia.
10. Gilmore, *Civil War on the Missouri-Kansas Border.*
11. "Beecher Bibles," Kansas Historical Society.
12. Joel Thomas Livingston, *A History of Jasper County, Missouri, and Its People*, vol. 1 (Chicago: Lewis, 1912), 39. Sarcoxie was known to be the first town in Missouri to fly the "Stars and

Bars" flag of the Confederacy. A popular but unsubstantiated story claimed that during the war, the Kansas schoolteacher who had been run out of town returned to Sarcoxie as a Union soldier and took his revenge by burning down the schoolhouse.
13. James M. McPherson, "A War That Never Goes Away," *American Heritage* 14, no. 2, 1990. McPherson wrote, "The poignancy of a brothers' war is the other face of the tragedy of a civil war. In hundreds of individual cases the war did pit brother against brother, cousin against cousin, even father against son. This was especially true in the border states."
14. Ward L. Schrantz, *The Background of Belle Starr*, unpublished manuscript, n.d., 50. From the Phillip W. Steele Collection, courtesy of Charlotte Steele and Roy Young.
15. Schrantz, *Background of Belle Starr*, 44.
16. Schrantz, *Background of Belle Starr*.
17. Schrantz, *Background of Belle Starr*, 48; Michael Wallis, *The Wild West 365* (New York: Abrams, 2011), 70. In later years, Frémont lost his fortune because of poor business decisions and was supported by the writings of his wife, Jessie Benton Frémont. He died in New York in 1890, the same year that the American West he had helped to open was declared closed.
18. F. A. North, *The History of Jasper County* (Des Moines, IA: Mills, 1883), 1034. Benton ran for governor of Missouri in 1856 and lost. He died in 1858.
19. "The 1860 Election in Missouri," Missouri Division.
20. Schrantz, *Background of Belle Starr*, 59.
21. Preston Shirley in the 1860 United States Federal Census, 1860; Census Place: Burleson [County], Texas; Roll: M653_1289; Schrantz, 61–62.
22. Schrantz, *Background of Belle Starr*.
23. The 1860 Census record for Preston Shirley lists his wife, three sons, and C. Dixon, a hired hand. Shirley's personal estate value was $2,500.
24. Schrantz, *Background of Belle Starr*, 60.
25. Missouri, General Assembly, House of Representatives, *Journal of the House of the State of Missouri at the First Session of the Twenty-First General Assembly* (Jefferson City, Missouri: W. G. Cheeney, Public Printer, 1861), 48.
26. "Life in the Ozarks," Historical Marker Database.
27. Elle E. Harvell, "The Struggle for Missouri," *Essential Civil War Curriculum*.
28. "The Civil War in Missouri," Mo Civil War.
29. Schrantz, *Background of Belle Starr*, 65. In the run-up to the 1860 election, Dawson endorsed all the presidential candidates except Lincoln.
30. Schrantz, *Background of Belle Starr*.
31. "Confederate Flags—Historical US Civil War Flags," World Atlas.
32. "Confederate Flags—Historical US Civil War Flags." Harry McCarthy wrote "The Bonnie Blue Flag" in 1861. It became the second most popular song in the South after "Dixie."
33. Livingston, *A History of Jasper County, Missouri*, 48.
34. Schrantz, *Background of Belle Starr*, 64.
35. Schrantz, *Background of Belle Starr*, 64–65.
36. Schrantz, *Background of Belle Starr*.
37. Schrantz, *Background of Belle Starr*, 64.
38. Schrantz, *Background of Belle Starr*.
39. Livingston, *A History of Jasper County, Missouri*, 49.

Chapter 4: All Torn Asunder

1. Diane Fischler, "The War Comet of 1861 or the Great Comet of 1861," *Courier* 4, no. 6, June 2016, 8–9. Samuel C. Upham, a Union printer and promoter and a counterfeiter of Confederate currency, designed a drawing of the comet portraying President Lincoln as the comet's head. Winfield Scott, commanding general of the US Army in 1861, was also depicted at the

head of the Great Comet, with the comet's tail composed of bayonets. The Scott illustration appeared in the October, 31, 1861, issue of *Vanity Fair*.
2. John Beauchamp Jones, *A Rebel War Clerk's Diary at the Confederate State Capital*, vol. 1 (Philadelphia: J. B. Lippincott, 1866), 56.
3. Kenneth E. Burchett, *The Battle of Carthage, Missouri* (Jefferson, NC: McFarland, 2013), 33–35.
4. David C. Hinze and Karen Farnham, *The Battle of Carthage: Border War in Southwest Missouri, July 5, 1861* (Gretna, LA: Pelican), 97. Reportedly, the many southern sympathizers of Sarcoxie had been flying the rebel flag well before the bombardment of Fort Sumter in April 1861.
5. Ward L. Schrantz, *The Background of Belle Starr*, unpublished manuscript, n.d., 77–78. From the Phillip W. Steele Collection, courtesy of Charlotte Steele and Roy Young.
6. Anthony Hodges, "Confederate Quandary: The Fourth of July," *Chattanooga* (Tennessee) *Times Press*, June 30, 2013. According to Hodges, although the boycotting of the July Fourth celebrations was not uncommon, "many Southerners agreed that the Confederacy had a strong claim to the holiday based on what they saw as similarities between 1776 and 1861."
7. Steve Cottrell, *The Battle of Carthage and Carthage in the Civil War* (Carthage, MO: The City of Carthage, 1990), 7–9. The name of James Spring, site of the Union camp, was later changed to Carter Spring. It is in the current Battle of Carthage State Park.
8. Cottrell, *Battle of Carthage*, 3.
9. Cottrell, *Battle of Carthage*, 10.
10. Joel Thomas Livingston, *A History of Jasper County, Missouri, and Its People*, vol. 1 (Chicago: Lewis, 1912), 51.
11. Phillip Rutherford, "The Carthaginian Wars," *Civil War Times Illustrated*, February 1987, 43.
12. Rutherford, "Carthaginian Wars."
13. Rutherford, "Carthaginian Wars."
14. Rutherford, "Carthaginian Wars."
15. Cottrell, *Battle of Carthage*, 8.
16. Schrantz, *Background of Belle Starr*, 89–91.
17. Cottrell, *Battle of Carthage*, 25.
18. Cottrell, *Battle of Carthage*, 12–13.
19. Archy Thomas, "Civil War Battle of Carthage Memoir," n.d., R167, Western Historical Manuscript Collection. State Historical Society of Missouri, Rolla Research Center.
20. Schrantz, *Background of Belle Starr*, 97.
21. Schrantz, *Background of Belle Starr*, 99.
22. Schrantz, *Background of Belle Starr*.
23. Schrantz, *Background of Belle Starr*.
24. Schrantz, *Background of Belle Starr*, 101–2.
25. Schrantz, *Background of Belle Starr*, 102.
26. Schrantz, *Background of Belle Starr*, 103.
27. Cottrell, *Battle of Carthage*, 20.
28. Thomas, "Civil War Battle of Carthage Memoir."
29. Schrantz, *Background of Belle Starr*, 105, 106, 109.
30. Schrantz, *Background of Belle Starr*, 106.
31. Schrantz, *Background of Belle Starr*, 107.
32. Schrantz, *Background of Belle Starr*, 108–9.
33. Cottrell, *Battle of Carthage*, 25.
34. Cottrell, *Battle of Carthage*, 26.
35. Schrantz, *Background of Belle Starr*, 122–23.
36. Schrantz, *Background of Belle Starr*.
37. F. A. North, *The History of Jasper County* (Des Moines, IA: Mills, 1883), 1044.
38. North, *History of Jasper County*. James Hunter was discharged from the Union army at Nash-

ville, Tennessee, on July 21, 1865. On January 13, 1867, he married Catharine H. Issenhower. That same year, Hunter, his wife, and his mother, Mary Shirley Hunter, returned to Jasper County, Missouri. Hunter and his wife raised six children. His mother resided with them until her death on October 3, 1878.
39. Schrantz, *Background of Belle Starr*, 123.
40. Malcolm G. McGregor, *The Biographical Record of Jasper County, Missouri* (Chicago: Lewis, 1901), 19.
41. Schrantz, *Background of Belle Starr*, 127.
42. Sara Coster, "A Balm in Gilead." This spiritual hymn, based on biblical references, gained popularity in the years leading up to the Civil War. The phrase "a balm in Gilead" appears in Edgar Allan Poe's famous poem "The Raven," published in 1845.
43. Coster, "A Balm in Gilead."

Chapter 5: Myra on the Scout

1. Anne Goodwyn Jones, "Belles and Ladies," *The New Encyclopedia of Southern Culture*, vol. 13: Gender. Edited by Nancy Bercaw and Ted Ownby; Charles Reagan, general editor (Chapel Hill: University of North Carolina Press, 2009), 42–49.
2. A native of Vermont, Orestes Brownson was an activist preacher and noted Catholic convert and writer. He died in Detroit in 1876.
3. Orestes Brownson, "The Woman Question," Part I, *Catholic World*, vol. 9, no. 50 (Paramus, NJ: Paulist Fathers, May 1869), 151.
4. Philip S. Foner, ed., *Frederick Douglass on Women's Rights* (Westport, CT: Greenwood Press, 1976), 78.
5. *Liberty* (Missouri) *Weekly Tribune*, August 30, 1861, 4; Ian Spurgeon, "Battle of Wilson's Creek," *Civil War on the Western Border: The Missouri-Kansas Conflict, 1854–1865*, Kansas City Public Library.
6. *Liberty Weekly Tribune*, August 30, 1861; "Lint Societies," Encyclopedia Dubuque. On August 30, 1862, William A. Hammond, surgeon general of the United States, announced the creation of a national program for women and children to assist in the war effort by "furnishing us the means to dress the wounds of those who fall in defence [sic] of their rights and their homes." As a result, "Lint Societies" were formed in many cities and towns.
7. Michael Fellman, *Inside War: The Guerrilla Conflict in Missouri during the American Civil War* (New York: Oxford University Press, 1990), 23.
8. Michael Wallis, *The Wild West 365* (New York: Abrams, 2011), 158.
9. Wallis, *Wild West 365*.
10. "Charles Rainsford Jennison," The Civil War Muse. In summer 1861, Charles R. Jennison formed a company of Kansas state militia that he called the Mound City Sharps Rifle Guards. During their frequent raids into Missouri, Jennison and his troops did not distinguish between secessionists and loyal Unionists. Jennison took command of the Red Legs along with George H. Hoyt, a Massachusetts lawyer who had defended John Brown at his trial after the Harper's Ferry raid. The Red Legs were never considered part of the Union Army.
11. A phrase that often appeared in Civil War accounts that was taken directly from the Bible, Jeremiah 7:11.
12. William E. Connelly, *Quantrill and the Border Wars* (Cedar Rapids, IA: Torch, 1910), 412.
13. Wallis, *Wild West 365*.
14. Albert Castel, "Kansas Jayhawking Raids into Western Missouri in 1861," *Missouri Historical Review* 54, no. 1 (October 1959): 1–11.
15. Ron Soodalter, "A Burning Hell," *Missouri Life* 46, no. 5 (July–August 2019): 55.
16. Donald L. Gilmore, *Civil War at the Missouri-Kansas Border* (Gretna, LA: Pelican, 2006),

134–35; Soodalter, 59. Today, an Osceola cemetery monument reads: "In memory of citizens of Osceola murdered by Kansas jayhawkers and the Union Army."
17. Major S. H. M. Byers, *With Fire and Sword* (New York: Neale, 1911), 14, 22.
18. Wallis, *Wild West 365*, 156.
19. Gilmore, *Civil War at the Missouri-Kansas Border*, 209.
20. Gilmore, *Civil War at the Missouri-Kansas Border*, 213.
21. Wallis, *Wild West 365*, 160.
22. Calvin Duvall Cowles, comp., *The War of the Rebellion: A Compilation of the Official Records of the Union and Confederate Armies*, Series 1, vol. 41 in four parts, Part 2—Correspondence (Washington, DC: Government Printing Office, 1893), 75.
23. Matthew E. Stanley, "Anderson, William 'Bloody Bill,'" Civil War on the Western Border: The Missouri-Kansas Conflict, 1855–1865.
24. Ward L. Schrantz, *The Background of Belle Starr*, unpublished manuscript, n.d., 249–50. From the Phillip W. Steele Collection, courtesy of Charlotte Steele and Roy Young.
25. Schrantz, *Background of Belle Starr*, 171.
26. Schrantz, *Background of Belle Starr*, 249.
27. Article 88, Instructions for the Government of Armies of the United States in the Field, General Orders No. 100, War Department, Adjutant General's Office, Washington, DC, April 24, 1863, in United States War Department, *War of the Rebellion: Official Records of the Union and Confederate Armies*, 128 vols., Series 3, vol. 3 (Washington, DC: Government Printing Office, 1880–1901), 148–64.
28. Schrantz, *Background of Belle Starr*, 173, 175. The terms *spy* and *scout* were often used interchangeably during the war.
29. Schrantz, *Background of Belle Starr*, 158; Joel Thomas Livingston, *A History of Jasper County, Missouri, and its People* (Chicago: Lewis, 1912), 60. In his history of Jasper County, Joel T. Livingston writes about Eliza Vivion, another daring courier for the partisan guerrillas and pro-Confederate soldiers in Jasper County. The granddaughter of Thackery Vivion, considered the first settler in the county, young Eliza came from strong southern sympathizers, and her brother served in the Confederate army. Like Myra, Eliza frequently delivered messages and intelligence to soldiers in the field. According to Livingston, "She was an expert horsewoman, could take a fence on her fiery steed as well as a man."
30. Schrantz, *Background of Belle Starr*, 264.
31. Schrantz, *Background of Belle Starr*.
32. Schrantz, *Background of Belle Starr*.
33. Anne Cope, "Newtonia: Village with a Vivid Civil War History," *Neosho* (Missouri) *Daily News* July 22, 1984, 7.
34. Cope, "Newtonia."
35. Cope, "Newtonia."
36. Wallis, *Wild West 365*, 60.

Chapter 6: Turning Point

1. Ward L. Schrantz, *The Background of Belle Starr*, unpublished manuscript, n.d., 247–50. From the Phillip W. Steele Collection, courtesy of Charlotte Steele and Roy Young.
2. Schrantz, *Background of Belle Starr*.
3. Schrantz, *Background of Belle Starr*, 288.
4. Schrantz, *Background of Belle Starr*, 372.
5. Ward L. Schrantz, *Jasper County, Missouri, in the Civil War* (Carthage, MO: Carthage, 1923), 129.
6. Schrantz, *Jasper County, Missouri*, 130.
7. Schrantz, *Jasper County, Missouri*, 131.

8. Malcolm G. McGregor, *The Biographical Record of Jasper County, Missouri* (Chicago: Lewis, 1901), 139–40.
9. Schrantz, *Background of Belle Starr*, 311–12.
10. Schrantz, *Background of Belle Starr*, 313.
11. Schrantz, *Background of Belle Starr*.
12. Schrantz, *Jasper County, Missouri*, 186.
13. Schrantz, *Jasper County, Missouri*, Appendix B, 26.
14. Schrantz, *Jasper County, Missouri*.
15. Schrantz, *Jasper County, Missouri*, 187–88.
16. Schrantz, *Background of Belle Starr*, 315.
17. Schrantz, *Background of Belle Starr*.
18. Schrantz, *Background of Belle Starr*, 315–16.
19. Schrantz, *Background of Belle Starr*, 316.
20. Schrantz, *Background of Belle Starr*.
21. Schrantz, *Background of Belle Starr*, 317; McGregor, *Biographical Record of Jasper County, Missouri*, 50. In 1870, the Carthage City Cemetery was converted into Central Park. The bodies were to be removed to another location except for some that were left by special request of the families. The remains of soldiers buried during the war were removed to the National Cemetery at Springfield, Missouri. It later became known that many bodies had not been removed. It is likely that Bud Shirley's remains lie in an unmarked grave in the public park.
22. Harry Hansen, *The Civil War: A History* (New York: New American Library, 2002), 347, 400.
23. Schrantz, *Background of Belle Starr*, 321.
24. Schrantz, *Background of Belle Starr*, 322.
25. Schrantz, *Background of Belle Starr*, 323.
26. Schrantz, *Background of Belle Starr*.
27. Schrantz, *Background of Belle Starr*, 324–25.
28. Schrantz, *Background of Belle Starr*, 325.
29. Michael Wallis, *The Wild West 365* (New York: Abrams, 2011), 156.
30. Wallis, *Wild West 365*, 158. Shaken by the war and perhaps feeling some guilt because of his own vicious deeds, Lane shot himself on July 1, 1866, and died ten days later.
31. Richard Cordley, *A History of Lawrence, Kansas, from Earliest Settlement to the Close of the Rebellion* (Lawrence, KS: Lawrence Journal Press, 1895), 195.
32. Carl W. Breihan, *Quantrill and His Civil War Guerrillas* (Denver, CO: Sage, 1959), 135.
33. Breihan, *Quantrill and His Civil War Guerrillas*, 136.
34. Breihan, *Quantrill and His Civil War Guerrillas*, 136–37.
35. Edward E. Leslie, *The Devil Knows How To Ride* (New York: Random House, 1996), 261.
36. Burnt District Monument, Cass County, Missouri, Historical Society.
37. Schrantz, *Background of Belle Starr*, 330.
38. Terry Beckenbaugh, "Shelby's Raid," US Army Command and General Staff College; Derly P. Sellmeyer, *Jo Shelby's Iron Brigade* (Gretna, LA: Pelican, 2007), 302.
39. *Report of Col. Joseph Shelby (CSA) to Major L. A. Maclean, Adjutant-General, Price's Division Headquarters Shelby's Brigade, Camp Price, November 16, 1863*, Roots Web.
40. *Report of Col. Joseph Shelby*.
41. *Report of Col. Joseph Shelby*.
42. Schrantz, *Jasper County, Missouri*, 151.
43. Schrantz, *Jasper County, Missouri*.
44. Schrantz, *Jasper County, Missouri*, 152.
45. Schrantz, *Background of Belle Starr*, 345.
46. Donald L. Gilmore, *Civil War at the Missouri-Kansas Border* (Gretna, LA: Pelican, 2006), 259.
47. Gilmore, *Civil War at the Missouri-Kansas Border*; "Major J. B. Pond Is Dead," *New York Times*, June 22, 1903.

48. Gilmore, *Civil War at the Missouri-Kansas Border*, 260–61.
49. Michael Wallis, *The Real Wild West: The 101 Ranch and the Creation of the American West* (New York: St. Martin's Press, 1999), 102.
50. Schrantz, *Background of Belle Starr*, 346.
51. Gilmore, *Civil War at the Missouri-Kansas Border*, 263.
52. Schrantz, *Background of Belle Starr*, 345.
53. Bowers Mill Collection, "Ozark Civil War."
54. Schrantz, *Background of Belle Starr*, 347.
55. Schrantz, *Background of Belle Starr*.
56. Schrantz, *Background of Belle Starr*.
57. Schrantz, *Background of Belle Starr*, 351.
58. Leon Boyd, "The War in Jasper County, as seen by a Soldier," *Carthage* (Missouri) *Weekly Banner*, 3, no. 42, October 14, 1869, 1.
59. Schrantz, *Background of Belle Starr*, 351–52.
60. Schrantz, *Background of Belle Starr*, 252–54.

Chapter 7: Gone to Texas

1. Michael Wallis, *The Wild West 365* (New York: Abrams, 2011), 34.
2. Wallis, *Wild West 365*.
3. Ward L. Schrantz, *The Background of Belle Starr*, unpublished manuscript, n.d., 356. From the Phillip W. Steele Collection, courtesy of Charlotte Steele and Roy Young.
4. Schrantz, *Background of Belle Starr*.
5. Glenn Shirley, *Belle Starr and Her Times: The Literature, the Facts, and the Legends* (Norman: University of Oklahoma Press, 1982), 66; Kenneth A. Butler, correspondence with Phillip W. Steele, May 23, 1987, Phillip W. Steele Collection, courtesy of Charlotte Steele and Roy Young; "Definition of 'shug,'" Urban Dictionary. Although *Shug* is an old Scottish nickname usually given to people with the first name Hew or Hugh, it became a popular term of endearment in the American South. For many people, *shug* is also the southern pronunciation of the abbreviation of *sugar*.
6. Shirley Families of Dallas Texas, "African-American Lineages," Shirley Association African-American Ancestry Research Center.
7. Shirley Families of Dallas Texas, "African-American Lineages." The Ancestry Research Center was designed to assist Shirley family members in researching their African-American ancestry. The site includes data from sources exclusive to African-Americans and from traditional sources copied from other data pages.
8. Shirley Families of Dallas Texas, "African-American Lineages."
9. DNA Diagnostics Center, Fairfield, Ohio. Although two possible fathers who are related do not share all their DNA (unless they are identical twins), they do share enough that obtaining conclusive results for paternity might be problematic. In addition, a full 50 percent of a son's DNA comes from his father, so if those two men are each the possible father of a child, there is a high possibility of a false-positive result.
10. Shirley Families of Dallas Texas, "African-American Lineages."
11. Ward L. Schrantz, "Shelby Wiggles from Hot Spots in Carthage Fight, October 18, 1863," *Carthage* (Missouri) *Evening Press*, August 3, 1950, 6.
12. Schrantz, "Shelby Wiggles from Hot Spots."
13. Shirley, *Belle Starr and Her Times*, 63–64.
14. Dianna Everett, "Butterfield Overland Mail," *The Encyclopedia of Oklahoma History and Culture*.
15. John W. Bond, "The History of Elkhorn Tavern," *Arkansas Historical Quarterly* 21, no. 1 (Spring 1962): 3–4.

16. William J. Butler, *Fort Smith: Past and Present: A Historical Summary* (Fort Smith, AR: First National Bank of Fort Smith, 1972), 75.
17. "Mudtown: The Story," City of Lowell, Arkansas.
18. "Actions at Fayetteville April 18, 1863," *Encyclopedia of Arkansas*.
19. Butler, *Fort Smith*, 75–76.
20. Edwin C. Bearss, "The Federals Capture Fort Smith, 1863," *Arkansas Historical Quarterly* 28, no. 2 (1969): 156–90.
21. Muriel H. Wright, "Historic Places on the Old Stage Line from Fort Smith to Red River," *Chronicles of Oklahoma* 11, no. 2 (June 1933), 798.
22. Glen Sample Ely, *The Texas Frontier and the Butterfield Overland Mail, 1858–1861* (Norman: University of Oklahoma Press, 2016), 25–26. The Chickasaws were one of the Five Civilized Tribes, a pejorative term that many people, including scholars, ascribed to the Chickasaws, Cherokees, Choctaws, Seminoles, and Creeks. Those tribes had been forcibly removed from their ancestral lands in the southeastern United States and relocated to Indian Territory. Some tribal members emulated White southerners, developed their own plantation system, and acquired enslaved laborers to work the land.
23. Schrantz, *Background of Belle Starr*, 61–62.
24. "Charles Christopher Jackson," *Handbook of Texas Online*.
25. Richard J. Miller, correspondence with Phillip W. Steele, February 20, 1988, Dallas County Tax Assessment Rolls, 1861 and 1862. From the Phillip W. Steele Collection, courtesy of Charlotte Steele and Roy Young.
26. *Times Picayune*, New Orleans, Louisiana, January 6, 1894, 11; "Charles H. Young," *Handbook of Texas Online*.
27. William R. Geise, "Missouri's Confederate Capital in Marshall, Texas," *Southwestern Historical Quarterly* 66, no. 2, (July 1962–April 1963): 193.
28. Geise, "Missouri's Confederate Capital in Marshall, Texas"; Albert Castel, *General Sterling Price and the Civil War in the West* (Baton Rouge: Louisiana State University Press, 1968), 273–79.
29. Assessment of Property Situated in the County of Dallas for 1864, Family History Center, Tulsa (Oklahoma) City-County Library; Rick Miller, correspondence with Phillip W. Steele, February 20, 1988, Phillip W. Steele Collection, courtesy of Charlotte Steele and Roy Young.
30. Shirley Families of Dallas, Texas, "African-American Lineages." When George Shirley died in Dallas, Texas, on June 30, 1951, his death certificate listed Mansfield Shirley as his father.
31. Jasper County, Missouri Deed Record Book "C," p. 151/9-1-1855.

Chapter 8: Armed and Dangerous

1. Suzanne Starling, "Scyene, TX," *Handbook of Texas Online*.
2. Starling, "Scyene, TX."
3. Starling, "Scyene, TX."
4. "Old Scyene Road," Texas Historical Markers, Waymarking.
5. "White Rock Creek," Dallas Pioneer.
6. Ward L. Schrantz, *Jasper County, Missouri, in the Civil War* (Carthage, MO: Carthage Press, 1923), 211–12.
7. Schrantz, *Jasper County, Missouri*, Appendix B, 264.
8. Glenn Shirley, *Belle Starr and Her Times: The Literature, the Facts, and the Legends* (Norman: University of Oklahoma Press, 1982), 65.
9. "Dallas Trinity Trails," Dallas Trinity Trails blog.
10. Aida Lott, "Texas Corn," Texas Escapes.
11. Shirley, *Belle Starr and Her Times*.
12. "When Did the Civil War End?" History on the Net, Salem Media.

13. Jeffrey William Hunt, "Palmito Ranch, Battle of," *Handbook of Texas Online*. Colonel John S. "Rip" Ford acquired his nickname "Rip" during his service in the Mexican War when he wrote the citation "Rest in Peace" at the top of official death notices of slain American soldiers.
14. Robert G. Slawson, "The Story of the Pile of Limbs," National Museum of Civil War Medicine (originally published in *Surgeon's Call* 22, no. 1 [2017]). Use of the slang terms *bones* or *sawbones* to describe surgeons dates to the 1830s.
15. Geoffrey Ward, with Ric Burns and Ken Burns, *The Civil War* (New York: Vintage, 1990), xii.
16. *Manual of Military Surgery Prepared for the Use of the Confederate States Army Illustrated by Order the Surgeon-General* (Richmond, VA: West & Johnson, 1861), 97.
17. Jonathan S. Jones, "Then and Now: How Civil War–Era Doctors responded to their Own Opiate Epidemic," Civil War Monitor.
18. Horace B. Day, *The Opium Habit* (New York: Harper & Brothers, 1868), 6–7.
19. Eric T. Dean Jr., *Shook over Hell: Post-Traumatic Stress, Vietnam, and the Civil War* (Cambridge, MA: Harvard University Press, 1997), 168.
20. R. Gregory Lande, "Felo De Se: Soldier Suicides in America's Civil War," *Military Medicine* 176, no. 5 (2011): 531.
21. Allen Cornwell, "Civil War Vets and Mental Illness: The Tragedy after the War," Our Great American Heritage.
22. Cornwell, "Civil War Vets and Mental Illness."
23. U.S. Congressional Serial 1497, "Retention of Arms by Soldiers," General Orders, No. 101, May 10, 1865, 167–72; Joseph G. Rosa, *Taming of the West: Age of the Gunfighter* (New York: Smithmark, 1993), 106.
24. Dean, *Shook over Hell*, 99, 102.
25. Louis J. Wortham, *A History of Texas from Wilderness to Commonwealth*, vol. 4 (Fort Worth, Texas: Wortham-Molyneaux Company, 1924), 363–66.
26. *Galveston* (Texas) *Daily News*, August 10, 1865, 2.
27. *Dallas* (Texas) *Daily Times Herald*, June 21, 1903, 17.
28. *Dallas Daily Times Herald*, April 6, 1924, 11.
29. *Dallas Daily Times Herald*, June 21, 1903, 17.
30. *Dallas Daily Times Herald*.
31. David W. Blight, *Race and Reunion: The Civil War in American History* (Cambridge, MA: Belknap, 2001), 266.
32. Robert Penn Warren, *The Legacy of the Civil War* (Lincoln: University of Nebraska Press, 1961), 15; Victor Strandberg, "Southern Comfort: Robert Penn Warren and the Art of (the Civil) War," public lecture presented at the Robert Penn Warren Circle annual meeting, Guthrie, Kentucky, 2011.
33. Mark Anthony Frassetto, "The Law and Politics of Firearms Regulations in Reconstruction Texas," *Texas A&M Law Review* 4, no. 1 (2016): 98–99. The Special Committee on Lawlessness and Violence was created on June 6, 1868.
34. Frassetto, "Law and Politics of Firearms Regulations," 99.
35. Shirley Families of Dallas Texas, "African-American Lineages," Shirley Association African-American Ancestry Research Center.
36. Shirley Families of Dallas Texas, "African-American Lineages."
37. Carl W. Breiham, *Quantrill and His Civil War Guerrillas* (Denver, CO: Sage, 1959), 168–74.
38. Michael Wallis, *The Real Wild West: The 101 Ranch and the Creation of the American West* (New York: St. Martin's Press, 1999), 160.
39. Wallis, *Real Wild West*.
40. Wallis, *Real Wild West*, 156.
41. Paul I. Wellman, *A Dynasty of Western Outlaws* (New York: Bonanza Books, 1961), 13.
42. Wallis, *Real Wild West*, 164.

43. T. J. Stiles, *Jesse James: Last Rebel of the Civil War* (New York: Vintage Books, 2003), 119–22.
44. Wallis, *Real Wild West*, 162.

Chapter 9: Jimmy and May

1. Glenn Shirley, *Belle Starr and Her Times: The Literature, the Facts, and the Legends* (Norman: University of Oklahoma Press, 1982), 66.
2. Melinda Rankin, *Texas in 1850* (Boston: Damrell and Moore, 1850), 116. After the outbreak of the Civil War, Rankin left Texas because of her loyalty to the Union. She later taught and opened schools in New Orleans and Mexico. Rankin died in Bloomington, Illinois, in 1888.
3. Debbie Mauldin Cottrell, "Women and Education," *Handbook of Texas Online*.
4. Shirley, *Belle Starr and Her Times*.
5. Shirley, *Belle Starr and Her Times*.
6. Shirley, *Belle Starr and Her Times*.
7. Shirley, *Belle Starr and Her Times*.
8. Shirley, *Belle Starr and Her Times*.
9. Gwen Pettit, *Between the Creeks*, Lindy Fisher, comp., July 2006, University of North Texas Libraries.
10. "Oscar Wilde's West," Literary Traveler. Oscar Wilde stated his views in a letter dated April 19, 1882, nine months after the death of Billy the Kid in New Mexico Territory and sixteen days after Jesse James had been shot and killed in Missouri.
11. Eric Hobsbawm, *Bandits* (New York: Delacorte, 1969), 7.
12. Richard W. Slatta, "Eric J. Hobsbawm's Social Bandits: A Critique and Revision," *A Contracorriente: Magazine of Social History and Literature in Latin America* 1, no. 2 (2004).
13. T. J. Stiles, *Jesse James: Last Rebel of the Civil War* (New York: Vintage, 2003), 165–66.
14. Cole Younger, *The Story of Cole Younger, by Himself* (Chicago: Henneberry, 1903), 121–22.
15. Mark A. McGruder, *History of Pettis County, Missouri* (Topeka, KS: Historical Publishing, 1919), 105.
16. J. B. Johnson, ed., *History of Vernon County, Missouri*, vol. 2 (Chicago: C. F. Cooper, 1911), 604.
17. Johnson, *History of Vernon County, Missouri*.
18. Johnson, *History of Vernon County, Missouri*.
19. Fatima Jane Reed Jones Records (1863–1961), annotated by Verna M. White, Wallis Collection.
20. "Susan Demanda Brock," Paden/Peden Family History and Genealogy.
21. Shelba K. Davis, letter to Phillip W. Steele, December 6, 1992, 2. From the Phillip W. Steele Collection, courtesy of Charlotte Steele and Roy Young.
22. Ward L. Schrantz, *The Background of Belle Starr*, unpublished manuscript, n.d., 356. From the Phillip W. Steele Collection, courtesy of Charlotte Steele and Roy Young.
23. Davis, letter to Phillip W. Steele, December 6, 1992.
24. Clifford D. Gates, *Pioneer History of Wise County from Red Men to Railroads—Twenty Years of Intrepid History* (Decatur, TX: Wise County Old Settlers Association, 1907), 81.
25. Davis, letter to Phillip W. Steele, December 6, 1992.
26. Gates, *Pioneer History of Wise County*, 115–16.
27. Gates, *Pioneer History of Wise County*, 117–19.
28. Davis, letter to Phillip W. Steele, December 6, 1992.
29. Davis, letter to Phillip W. Steele, December 6, 1992.
30. *Clinton* (Missouri) *Eye*, February 23, 1889, 2.
31. Gates, *Pioneer History of Wise County*, 121.
32. Gates, *Pioneer History of Wise County*, 122.
33. Richard A. Ensmiger, contributor, "Quantrill's Guerrillas: Members in the Civil War," Kan-

sas Heritage Group; Richard S. Brownlee, *Gray Ghosts of the Confederacy* (Baton Rouge: University of Louisiana Press, 1958), 259; Paul R. Peterson, *Quantrill in Texas: The Forgotten Campaign* (Nashville, TN: Cumberland House, 2007), 79.
34. Davis, letter to Phillip W. Steele, December 6, 1992.
35. Davis, letter to Phillip W. Steele, December 6, 1992.
36. Davis, letter to Phillip W. Steele, December 6, 1992; "Teague Cemetery, Wise County, Texas," Wise County, Texas.
37. Fatima Jane Reed Jones Records.
38. B. Jane England, "Wise County," *Handbook of Texas Online*.
39. Davis, letter to Phillip W. Steele, December 6, 1992.
40. J. Lee Stambaugh and Lillian J. Stambaugh, *A History of Collin County, Texas* (Austin: Texas State Historical Association, 1958), 69.
41. *Clinton Eye*, February 23, 1889, 2.
42. Pettit, *Between the Creeks*.
43. Richard K. Fox, publisher, *Bella Starr, the Bandit Queen, or the Female Jesse James*, New York: 1889. Facsimile reproduction, R. H. Porter, publisher, Austin, TX: Steck, 1960.
44. Gwen Pettit, "Some Early Weddings Were 'Leaps in the Dark,'" October 5, 1991, entry in *Between the Creeks*, compilation of newspaper columns on local history published 1986–1992 in the *Allen* (Texas) *Leader* and *Allen* (Texas) *American*, compiled and edited by Lindy Fisher, July 2006, 394–95, University of North Texas Libraries; *Texas, Select County Marriage Records, 1837–2015*, vol. 3, Provo, Utah, 2014, 49, Ancestry. Pettit, 395, says James Reed's mother and family lived at what was later Country Club Road (FM 1378) and FM 2170.
45. Pettit, "Some Early Weddings," 395; *Texas, Select County Marriage Records, 1837–2015*, vol. 3.
46. Pettit, "Some Early Weddings," 395.
47. F. M. [Marion] Reed, quoted in an interview in the *Clinton* (Missouri) *Eye*, February 23, 1889, 2.
48. *Texas, Select County Marriage Records, 1837–2015*.
49. Shirley, *Belle Starr and Her Times*, 72.
50. Fatima Jane Reed Jones Records; "Re: Frank James Writes Letter to *The Appeal* . . . Memphis, TN 1882," Genealogy.com.
51. Shirley, *Belle Starr and Her Times*, 72–73, 268, endnote 29. Shirley does not cite sources for this information, but he adds this as endnote 29: "In the late 1920s, Richard H. Reed compiled a narrative manuscript concerning his early life and that of his family, and in it he recalls the marriage of 'brother Jim to Myra Mabelle [sic] Shirley, in Collin County.' He tells of his 'almost constant' association with Myra in his earliest boyhood and of being present at the birth of their daughter in Missouri. The manuscript is in possession of his son at Ashland, Oregon. Richard H. Reed's recollection agrees with Cole Younger's autobiographical statement that he saw Belle in 1868 at the home of Reed's mother in Bates County about three months before the birth of her first child." Richard Henry (Dick) Reed was a younger brother of James C. Reed. The additional source of information cited here on Myra and James Reed's early years of marriage is the F. M. [Marion] Reed interview in the *Clinton* (Missouri) *Eye*. F. M. Reed does not include as much detail about dates and events as Glenn Shirley does.
52. Shirley, *Belle Starr and Her Times*; "James C. Reed," Paden/Peden Family History and Genealogy.
53. Henry Dale, *Adventures and Exploits of the Younger Brothers, Missouri's Daring Outlaws, and Companions of the James Boys*, no. 15, Secret Service Series. New York: Street & Smith, 1890; mentioned in Shirley, Chapter 1: "From Richard K. Fox to Twentieth Century–Fox," 6, 9. The inaccurate book by Henry Dale about the Youngers repeated an erroneous claim about the supposed "marriage" between Cole Younger and Myra Shirley.
54. "A Stillwater Sensation; Cole Younger Says He Never Was Belle Starr's Husband," *Saint Paul* (Minnesota) *Globe*, February 7, 1889, 2.

55. Cole Younger, *The Story of Cole Younger, by Himself*, 95. Although historians consider Cole Younger's autobiography, published after he had served twenty-five years in prison in Minnesota, to be filled with lies in an attempt to portray himself in the best possible light, some matters of chronology and other statements are perhaps accurate.
56. Younger, *Story of Cole Younger*; "A Stillwater Sensation," *Saint Paul* (Minnesota) *Globe*, February 7, 1889.
57. Shirley, *Belle Starr and Her Times*, 77–78.

Chapter 10: On the Scout

1. Betty M. Shirley, ed., *The Shirley News* 1, no. 16 (July 1982): 6. Some sources erroneously claim that Edwin Benton Shirley was killed in 1866 or 1867.
2. Dallas County, Texas, District Court, May 3, 1866, Edward [Edwin] Sherley [Shirley] Cause Number 585, vol. D, 105; Dallas County, Texas, District Court, October 24, 1866, Edward Sherley, Cause Number 587, vol. D, 146; Mansfield Shirley, unknown cause number, vol. D, 147, Richard Miller to Phillip W. Steele, February 21, 1988. From the Phillip W. Steele Collection, courtesy of Charlotte Steele and Roy Young.
3. Randolph B. Campbell, "The District Judges of Texas in 1866–1867: An Episode in Failure of Presidential Reconstruction," *The Southwestern Historical Quarterly* 93, no. 3 (1990): 357–77.
4. Marshall Trimble, "Horse Theft," *True West Magazine*.
5. Robert Turpin, "Horse Stealing—A Hanging Offense," Ezine Articles.
6. *Dallas* (Texas) *News*, January 7, 1894, 3.
7. "Jim Wheat's Dallas County, Texas, Archives," Old Pleasant Mound Cemetery, Free Pages. Edwin Benton Shirley's grave is unmarked. Many other graves in the historic cemetery are also unmarked.
8. Dianna Everett, "Horse Racing," *The Encyclopedia of Oklahoma History and Culture*. The majority of Native American peoples in Indian Territory raced horses as training for life and as a sport. During the territorial era, private matches or race meets frequently took place throughout the territory.
9. Ramon F. Adams, *A Dictionary of the Range, Cow Camp, and Trail* (Norman: University of Oklahoma Press, 1944), 107, 127. According to Adams, many outlaws rode trails "that'd make a mountain goat nervous." Other terms synonymous with "on the scout" include "on the dodge," "among the willows," and "in the brush."
10. Marshall Trimble, "Origin of Owlhoot," *True West Magazine*. According to Trimble, a story from Indian Territory in about 1870 claimed the name *owlhoot* came from Indians who lived in the area and used "owl hoots to signal danger or someone's approach."
11. Gwen Pettit, *Between the Creeks*, Lindy Fisher, comp., July 2006, University of North Texas Libraries.
12. Michele D. Poynter, "The Clay County Savings Association," *James Farm Journal* 30, no. 2 (Spring 2019): 3–4.
13. William A. Settle Jr., *Jesse James Was His Name* (Lincoln: University of Nebraska Press, 1977), 33.
14. W. H. Woodson, *History of Clay County, Missouri* (Topeka, KS: Historical Publishing Company, 1920) 139.
15. T. J. Stiles, *Jesse James: Last Rebel of the Civil War* (New York: Vintage, 2003), 172–73; Elizabeth Prather Ellsberry, comp., *Clay County, Missouri, Cemetery Records*, vol. 1, 1962, John R. Keller Graveyard.
16. Stiles, *Jesse James*, 173–74.
17. Stiles, *Jesse James*, 182.
18. Stiles, *Jesse James*, 186.
19. Jay Clarke, "Missouri Bank Cashes In on Jesse James," *Chicago Tribune*, May 2, 2004.

20. *The Nashville* (Tennessee) *Banner*, March 22, 1868, 1.
21. Marley Brant, *The Outlaw Youngers: A Confederate Brotherhood* (Lanham, MD: Madison Books, 1992), 84–85.
22. Cole Younger, *The Story of Cole Younger, by Himself* (Chicago: Henneberry, 1903), 44.
23. Brant, *Outlaw Youngers*, 87.
24. Francis J. Johnston, "The James Bros. in California," *Odyssey* 8, no. 4 (1986), 50–52. Noted California historian Francis Johnston wrote, "The presence of Jesse and Frank James in California during the years 1868 and 1869 has been documented. Their activities for 1868 and possibly part of 1869 are also fairly well established"; "The Life and Times of Jesse James," The Real Wild West. "In late 1868 Frank and Jesse went to visit their Uncle Drury Woodson James who lived in California so Jesse could spend time in the warm springs of Paso Robles that were reputed to have curative powers"; Jesse James Family Reunion, December 20, 2014, Eric James.
25. Burton Rascoe, *Belle Starr: "The Bandit Queen"* (Lincoln: University of Nebraska Press, 2004), 166.
26. Glenn Shirley, *Belle Starr and Her Times* (Norman: University of Oklahoma Press, 1982), 84–85.
27. Shirley, *Belle Starr and Her Times*, 78.
28. Dee Cordry, "Outlaws and Lawmen of the Cherokee Nation," *Oklahombres: The Journal of Lawman and Outlaw History of Oklahoma* 5, no. 1 (Fall 1993): 1–3, typed transcription.
29. Cordry, "Outlaws and Lawmen of the Cherokee Nation."
30. Cordry, "Outlaws and Lawmen of the Cherokee Nation," 2.
31. R. P. Vann, "Reminiscences of Mr. R. P. Vann, East of Webbers Falls, Oklahoma, September 28, 1932, As Told to Grant Foreman," *Chronicles of Oklahoma* 11, no. 2 (June 1933): 844.
32. Shirley, *Belle Starr and Her Times*, 78.
33. Cherokee Nation, Daniel H. Ross, and J. A. Scales, *Constitution and Laws of the Cherokee Nation*. composed by W. P. Boudinot [St. Louis, R. & T. A. Ennis, printers, 1875].
34. Angie Debo, "John Rollin Ridge," *Southwest Review* 17, no. 1 (Dallas, TX: Southern Methodist University, 1932), 62; Matthew Wynn Sivils, "Ridge, John Rollins," *The Encyclopedia of Oklahoma History and Culture*.
35. President James K. Polk, "April 13, 1846: Message Regarding Cherokee Indians," Miller Center of Public Affairs, Presidential Archives, University of Virginia, Charlottesville. President Polk concluded his message by pejoratively stating, "The Cherokees have been regarded as among the most enlightened of the Indians tribes, but experience has proved that they have not yet advanced to such a state of civilization as to dispense with the guardian care and control of the Government of the United States."
36. Cordry, "Outlaws and Lawmen of the Cherokee Nation," 3.
37. Harry F. O'Beirne and E. S. O'Beirne, *The Indian Territory* (Saint Louis, MO: C. B. Woodward, 1892), 92. Many Cherokees referred to the treaty as "the Tom Starr Treaty."
38. Cordry, "Outlaws and Lawmen of the Cherokee Nation"; Cherokee National Council, comp., *Compiled Laws of the Cherokee Nation*, Chapter 7, Article 1, Section 1 (Tahlequah, Indian Territory: National Advocate Printer, 1881), 193.
39. Shirley, *Belle Starr and Her Times*, 84.
40. Denele Pitts Campbell, "A Little Murder with Your Lemonade?," Denelecampbell. A native of Washington County, Denele Campbell is a journalist and author who focuses on northwestern Arkansas history
41. Ben F. Greer, *Greer Family Reminiscences* (Fayetteville, AR: Washington County Historical Society, 1956), 28.
42. Julia Etter Yadon, Sue Ross Cross, and Randall Ross Viguet, *Reflections of Fort Smith* (Fort Smith, AR: Fort Smith Historical Press, 1976), 101; Department of Justice, National Institute of Law Enforcement and Criminal Justice, *The Development of the Law of Gambling: 1776–1976* (Washington, DC: US Government Printing Office, 1977), 307. Arkansas legalized pari-mutuel betting in 1935.

43. Kenneth W. Hobbs Jr., "Jim Reed, Southwestern Outlaw and Husband of Belle Starr: A Study of the Watt Grayson and San Antonio Stage Robberies" (master's thesis, Texas Christian University, Fort Worth, 1975), 20.
44. Pettit, *Between the Creeks*; Michael Wallis, *The Wild West 365* (New York: Abrams, 2011), 532.
45. Pettit, *Between the Creeks*.
46. "Early Crimes of Washington County, Arkansas," Arkansas Genealogy. This material is sourced from *History of Benton, Washington, Carroll, Madison, Crawford, Franklin, and Sebastian Counties, Arkansas* (Chicago: Goodspeed, 1889).
47. Denele Pitts Campbell, "The Shannon-Fisher Feud," Denelecampbell.
48. *Clinton (Missouri) Eye*, February 23, 1889, 2.
49. *Clinton Eye*, February 23, 1889, 2.
50. "Early Crimes of Washington County, Arkansas," Arkansas Genealogy.
51. Pettit, *Between the Creeks*.

Chapter 11: Southern California: An "Island" in the Sun

1. Glenn Shirley, *Belle Starr and Her Times: The Literature, the Facts, and the Legends* (Norman: University of Oklahoma Press, 1982), 89.
2. Shirley, *Belle Starr and Her Times*, 90. Glenn Shirley pointed out that many questions about the shooting deaths of Noah Fitzwater and Newton Stout remained unanswered. Shirley wrote: "Jim Reed obviously did not kill the two Shannon brothers. Neither is he included among the Fisher gang members for whom [F. M.] Shannon offered a reward. However, it appears that Shannon soon learned that he [Jim Reed] was one of the assassins of Fitzwater and Stout (the 'two Shannon boys' referred to by Francis M[arion] Reed), and this[,] coupled with the federal writ for introducing whiskey into Indian Territory, caused Jim to seek less hazardous climes."
3. Cole Younger, *The Story of Cole Younger, by Himself* (Chicago: Henneberry, 1903), 69.
4. Nancy B. Samuelson to Michael Wallis, personal communications, August 15, 18, 30, 31, September 3, 4, 17, 19, 20, 2019. Samuelson mentions several sources for Confederate activities in the West.
5. Samuelson to Wallis, August 30, 2019.
6. Younger, *Story of Cole Younger*.
7. Roy B. Young, "The Allen H. Parmer Story: Quantrill Guerrilla, Outlaw, Cattleman, Solid Citizen," *Wild West History Association Journal* 11, no. 3 (September 20, 2018): 16, prepared for the 11th Annual Wild West History Association Roundup, July 19, 2018, Springfield, Missouri. Robert Sallee James, father of Jesse and Frank, left his family in Missouri in April 1850 to visit his brother Drury Woodson James, who had already moved to California. Robert James planned to prospect for gold and preach to the gold miners. Shortly after arriving in California in August 1850, he contracted cholera and died. He was buried in an unmarked grave. Probate records show that he had owned six enslaved laborers and had been a commercial hemp farmer.
8. "The Pioneer Past Is Alive," *Los Angeles Times*, June 19, 1997, 38. Although this *Los Angeles Times* article says Jesse and Frank James traveled by boat from New York to San Francisco (implying that they were together), an earlier source gives a more detailed explanation: Both brothers had received wounds that needed to be healed. J. A. Dacus, *Life and Adventures of Frank and Jesse James, the Noted Western Outlaws*, Chapter 13, "On the Pacific Slope" (Saint Louis, MO: W. S. Bryan, 1880), 93; Dan Krieger, "Infamous Brothers Once Stayed in the Area," *Tribune* (San Luis Obispo, CA), Francis J. Johnston, "The James Bros. in California," *Odyssey* 8, no. 4 (October-November-December 1986): 51–54.

9. "The Pioneer Past Is Alive," *Los Angeles Times*.
10. Mary Louise James Burns, "History of Drury Woodson James," dictated to her granddaughter Mary Jean Malley Beamis, 1949; in Eric F. James, "Drury Woodson James by his Daughter Mary Louise James Burns," *Stray Leaves: A James Family in America 1650–2000*.
11. Phil Dirkx, "Paso Robles' Founders: A Vigilante, a Capitalist, and Jesse James' Uncle," *Telegram-Tribune* (San Luis Obispo, CA), October 1, 1987; republished by David Middlecamp.
12. James C. Reed to F. M. Reed, February 5, 1870. Photocopy of original letter, Phillip W. Steele Collection, courtesy of Charlotte Steele and Roy Young. For identification of James C. Reed's brother Jasper Columbus Reed, Fatima Jane Reed Jones Records (1863–1961), annotated by Verna M. White, Wallis Collection. James Reed also had an uncle named Jasper Reed.
13. The Federal Writers' Project of the Works Progress Administration for the State of California, *The WPA Guide to California* (New York: Hastings House, 1939). Republished with a new foreword by Gwendolyn Wright (New York: Pantheon, 1984), 618; "Rancho Cucamonga, California, United States," Encyclopedia Britannica.
14. James C. Reed to [F. M.] Marion Reed, March 25, 1870. Photocopy of original letter, Phillip W. Steele Collection, courtesy of Charlotte Steele and Roy Young. The "Uncle" mentioned in Jim Reed's California letters evidently was his father's much younger brother Henry Reed.
15. James Reed to Marion Reed, March 25, 1870.
16. James Reed to Marion Reed, March 25, 1870.
17. James Reed to Marion Reed, March 25, 1870.
18. US Census Bureau, "Population of the United States in 1870: California," 23, original ledger page reproduced in facsimile in FamilySearch.
19. Betty M. Shirley, ed., *Belle Starr and her Roots* (Cupertino, CA: Shirley Association, 1989), 3. Betty M. Shirley gives Myra and Jim Reed's son's name as Edwin Benton Reed. However, "Various authors have called him James Edward Reed, Jr., James Edwin, Edward Benton and Edwin Benton Reed"; Laurence J. Yadon, "The Mystery of Edwin Reed, Life among the Starrs," *Oklahombres: The Journal of Lawman and Outlaw History of Oklahoma* 12, no. 3 (Spring 2011): 3. Based on court records and contemporary newspaper articles, Edwin Reed mostly used the name Ed Reed, and no instance has been found in which he was referred to as James or James E. Reed.
20. Although western author Richard Patterson (in *Historical Atlas of the Outlaw West*, Boulder, Colorado: Johnson Books, 1985, 21) states (citing Glenn Shirley, *Belle Starr and her Times*) that James Reed "fled the city [Los Angeles] in March 1871, and Belle followed shortly after," the letter from Myra Maibelle and James Reed to Marion Reed seems to indicate that they were still in southern California considerably later than March 1871. In the letter, James Reed mentions money he was due to pay on "the first of January," and Myra refers to the payment as being due "next month." She also mentions that the baby "is teething." The Reeds' son, Eddie, was born on February 22, 1871, and would not normally have been teething by March 1871. Myra also refers to her daughter Rosie knowing the alphabet and learning to read. Rosa would have turned three years old in September 1871. She could have been reading in late 1871 but is not as likely to have done so in early 1871, although that is not impossible either.
21. May [Myra Maibelle Reed] and [James C. Reed] to Marion [Reed], [December 1871?]. Photocopy of original letter, Phillip W. Steele Collection, courtesy of Charlotte Steele and Roy Young.
22. Myra Reed must have meant this reference to Los Nietos being an "Island" in some figurative sense, perhaps alluding to its Spanish background. By the time the Los Nietos land grant was divided, "the grants begun under Spanish rule had produced a scattering of rancho 'islands' on the plain. Small adobe houses, workshops, and servants' quarters clustered next to plowed fields and vineyards. In between were lonely miles of range land, marsh, and seashore"; "Ran-

chos and the Californios," City of Lakewood, California. In the sixteenth century, some Spanish explorers believed California to be a huge island, as shown on early maps. This misconception existed until the late 1680s when Father Eusabio Kino (1645–1711)—a Jesuit missionary, geographer, and cartographer—proved Baja California was a peninsula, not an island. He also established twenty-four Catholic missions throughout California.

23. Reed and Reed to Reed, [December 1871]. Phillip W. Steele transcribed this letter in his book *Starr Tracks: Pearl and Belle Starr* (Gretna, LA: Pelican, 1998, 41), but he misconstrued several words in this passage.
24. Reed and Reed to Reed, [December 1871].
25. Reed and Reed to Reed, [December 1871]. For identification of James C. Reed's younger sisters Susan Demanda (Manda) Reed and Sarah Francis (Sallie or Alice) Reed, see Fatima Jane Reed Jones Records (1863–1961).
26. Reed and Reed to Reed, [December 1871]. Again, in *Starr Tracks* (42), Phillip W. Steele misconstrued some words in his transcription of this part of the letter. For identification of Fatima (Tima) Jane Reed, see Fatima Jane Reed Jones Records (1863–1961); Shelba King Davis, telephone interview by Hazel Rowena Mills, March 22, 2019.
27. Reed and Reed to Reed, [December 1871].
28. Reed and Reed to Reed, [December 1871].
29. Paul R. Spitzzeri, "What a Difference a Decade Makes: Ethnic and Racial Demographic Change in Los Angeles County During the 1860s," *The Branding Iron: The Westerners Los Angeles Corral*, no. 249, fall 2007, 5.
30. Spitzzeri, "What a Difference a Decade Makes."
31. "Los Angeles Revisited—Town of Ramirez, Near Whittier, California," Los Angeles Revisited; John Steven McGroarty, ed., *History of Los Angeles County*, vol. 1 (Chicago: American Historical Society, 1923), 84.
32. J. Albert Wilson, *History of Los Angeles County, California* (Oakland, CA: Thompson and West, 1880, 74.
33. Mike Cox, "Stagecoaching in Texas," *Texas Almanac 2008–2009*.
34. Spitzzeri, "What a Difference a Decade Makes," Tables 1–2, p. 7–8; US Census Bureau, "Population of the United States in 1860: California"; *The WPA Guide to California*, 398.
35. Paul R. Spitzzeri, "All over the Map: Greater Los Angeles in 1872," the Homestead Blog, August 22, 2016, 2.
36. Spitzzeri, "All over the Map."
37. Henry Dwight Barrows, *An Illustrated History of Los Angeles County* (Chicago: Lewis, 1889), 101–2.
38. Barrows, *Illustrated History of Los Angeles County*, 199.
39. Wilson, *History of Los Angeles County, California*, 84.
40. McGroarty, *History of Los Angeles County*, 359, 198–99; US Census Bureau, "Population of the United States in 1870: California."
41. Kenneth W. Hobbs Jr., "Jim Reed, Southwestern Outlaw and Husband of Belle Starr: A Study of the Watt Grayson and San Antonio Stage Robberies" (master's thesis, Texas Christian University, Fort Worth, 1975), 25.
42. Hobbs, "Jim Reed, Southwestern Outlaw," quoting the *Dallas* (Texas) *Daily Commercial*, August 10, 1874.
43. "The Legend of Belle Starr—Queen of the Oklahoma Outlaws," Ron and Sue's Family History Site, Whitsett and Wall.
44. Younger, *Story of Cole Younger*, 95. Younger might have overstated his influence on John Shirley. There is no evidence that Shirley would have had to be persuaded to help his daughter and son-in-law when they returned from California.
45. James C. Reed to F. M. Reed, January 19, 1872. Photocopy of original letter, Phillip W. Steele Collection, courtesy of Charlotte Steele and Roy Young.
46. James Reed to F. M. Reed, January 19, 1872.

Chapter 12: Living the Outlaw Life in Texas

1. Shirley Families of Dallas Texas, "African-American Lineages," Shirley Association African-American Ancestry Research Center. James K. Shirley was listed as age one in the 1870 census and age eleven in the 1880 census. There are no other records for him, and according to the Shirley family records, "He likely died young."
2. Dallas County, Texas, District Court, December 8, 1869, Mansfield Shirley Cause Number 604, vol. E, 381; US Department of Commerce, Bureau of Census, Ninth Census of the United States, 1870: Federal Population Schedules, Dallas County, Texas, National Archives Microcopy No. 593, Roll 1581. Mansfield is listed in the John Shirley household at age seventeen. Also listed are John, 72; Eliza, 52; and John A. [Shug] Shirley, 12.
3. Dallas County, Texas, Mansfield Shirley Cause Number 604.
4. Shirley Family Association, "31. Peter Shirley (cont.), 1(iii). Christian Shirley."
5. Shirley Family Association, "31. Peter Shirley (cont.), 1(iii). Christian Shirley."
6. Shirley Family Association, "31. Peter Shirley (cont.), 1(iii). Christian Shirley." According to Shirley family records, Oliver D. Shirley was unmarried and living with his parents at age twenty-four in the 1880 census for Cooke County, Texas. He was listed in Case Township in Cleveland County, Oklahoma Territory, in 1900; living in Oklahoma City, Oklahoma, by 1910; died 1922, and was buried in Clear Springs Mashak Cemetery, Midwest City, Oklahoma County, Oklahoma.
7. Shirley Family Association, "31. Peter Shirley (cont.), 1(iii). Christian Shirley."
8. Rick Miller, *Tin Star Tales: Law and Disorder in Dallas County, Texas, 1846–1900* (Bloomington, IN: Archway, 2017), 41.
9. Marley Brant, *The Outlaw Youngers: A Confederate Brotherhood* (Lanham, MD: Madison Books, 1992), 87, 89.
10. Brant, *Outlaw Youngers*, 93.
11. Brant, *Outlaw Youngers*, 96.
12. Miller, *Tin Star Tales*, 42.
13. T. J. Stiles, *Jesse James: Last Rebel of the Civil War* (New York: Vintage, 2003), 203–4.
14. Records of Governor Joseph Washington McClurg, Western Historical Manuscript Collection–Columbia, University of Missouri, C1746 Joseph Washington McClurg (1818–1900), telegram, 1869. To [Charles Dougherty], Independence, Missouri, from Jefferson City, Missouri Dec. 24, 1869. Telegram to the sheriff of Jackson County giving instructions for organizing a militia to aid in the capture or killing of Frank and Jesse James.
15. Paul Kooistra, *Criminals as Heroes: Structure, Power & Identity* (Bowling Green, OH: Bowling Green State University Popular Press, 1989), 48.
16. Kooistra, *Criminals as Heroes*.
17. Michael Wallis, *The Wild West 365* (New York: Abrams, 2011), 26. In 1800, it was estimated that as many as sixty million "Monarchs of the Plains" grazed in the West. Ninety years later, that number had been reduced to fewer than six hundred.
18. Wallis, *Wild West 365*, 28.
19. John William Rogers, *The Lusty Texans of Dallas* (New York: E. P. Dutton, 1951), 103; Wallis, *Wild West 365*, 580.
20. *The Texas Almanac for 1872*, and *Emigrant's Guide to Texas*, University of North Texas Libraries.
21. Rogers, *Lusty Texans of Dallas*, 111; Daniel Hardy and Terri Myers, preparers, National Register of Historic Places Multiple Property Documentation Form, 1995, "The Development of East and South Dallas, 1872–1945," 3.
22. Paul Zebe, comp., "Descendants of John Canote and his wife Rosanna (nee Hunse)," Home Pages. The Canote family of the United States was founded by John Canote and his wife Rosanna Hunse. With the exception of the Canote family in California, all Canotes living in the United States today are known to be descendants of this couple. John and

Rosanna had four children who lived to adulthood: Jacob, John Jr., Elizabeth, and Rosannah. In 1796, Rosannah wed Christian Shirley, and they were the parents of John Shirley, Myra's father. The Canotes' other daughter, Elizabeth, married George Sheeks, and their daughter Elizabeth Jane Sheeks Canote wed Daniel Bass. They were the parents of Sam Bass; Shirley Family Association Genealogical Research; "Famous Relations of Berry Towles Canote," Free Pages. This site lists Sam Bass and Myra Belle Shirley as second cousins through the Canote line of descent. Rosanna Canote Shelly (1700s), Genealogy; Lyman Chalkley, *Chronicles of the Scotch-Irish Settlement in Virginia: Extracted from the Original Court Records of Augusta County, 1745–1800*, vol. 1 (Augusta County, VA: Commonwealth Printing, 1912), 412.

23. "Sam Bass," Home of Frontier History, Outlaw Series. The Sam Bass profile is part of the site's "Outlaw Series." It also includes Bass on a top-ten list of "The most dangerous men to have operated on Texas soil."
24. "Sam Bass."
25. Rogers, *Lusty Texans of Dallas*, 148–49.
26. Robert Moorman Denhardt, *Foundation Dams of the American Quarter Horse* (Norman: University of Oklahoma Press, 1995), 144.
27. Lynn Sheffield Simmons, "Speaking of Texas," *Texas Highways Magazine* (February 1995): 3.
28. "How to Pronounce Bosque," Encyclopedia of Santa Fe. Spanish speakers pronounce Bosque as BO-skay, and most English speakers say BAH–skay. Locals mostly pronounce it "boskie."
29. Wallis, *Wild West 365*, 214. The Chisholm Trail was so common that the name often was used indiscriminately for all cattle trails out of Texas.
30. William C. Pool, *A History of Bosque County* (San Marcos, TX: San Marcos Record Press, 1954), 53.
31. Pool, *History of Bosque County*, 51.
32. Sharon E. Whitney, comp. and ed., *The Memories of Will Conine: 1860s to 1890s* (Waco, TX: Texian Press, 1999), 42.
33. Whitney, *Memories of Will Conine*.
34. Whitney, *Memories of Will Conine*.
35. Whitney, *Memories of Will Conine*, viii–v, 121–47. Sharon E. Whitney, Will Conine's great-grandniece, compiled and edited *The Memories of Will Conine*. Conine's detailed account of events in Bosque County in the late 1860s and especially the 1870s provides incredible access to the lives of the Reed family during that time. Conine wrote in pencil on nine tablets that have been preserved by his descendants. Whitney painstakingly researched, documented, and edited the material, which had no punctuation, sentence structure, or paragraphing. To provide further clarity and confirmation, selections of Whitney's documentation were included in the book.
36. Whitney, *Memories of Will Conine*, 42–43.
37. Whitney, *Memories of Will Conine*, 37.
38. Whitney, *Memories of Will Conine*, 37, 96.
39. Whitney, *Memories of Will Conine*, 37.
40. Whitney, *Memories of Will Conine*, 43.
41. Whitney, *Memories of Will Conine*, 88.
42. Kenneth W. Hobbs Jr., "Jim Reed, Southwestern Outlaw and Husband of Belle Starr: A Study of the Watt Grayson and San Antonio Stage Robberies" (master's thesis, Texas Christian University, Fort Worth, 1975), 25.
43. Whitney, *Memories of Will Conine*, 43.
44. T. J. McKechern [Thomas J. McKeehan] enlisted in Pettis County, Missouri, and served as private with Colonel Thomas R. Freeman's Fourth Regiment, Third Missouri Cavalry, until the unit's surrender in 1865; Soldier Details, the Civil War, National Park Service. Records transcribed from the National Archives' original documents and compiled by National Park Service staff at Battle of Pilot Knob State Historic Site.

45. *Vernon County, Missouri, Marriage Book A* (Nevada, MO: Tri-County Genealogical Society, 2006), 110.
46. Glenn Shirley, *Belle Starr and Her Times: The Literature, the Facts, and the Legends* (Norman: University of Oklahoma Press, 1982), 106.
47. "Towns of Bosque County," the US Gen Web.
48. Whitney, *Memories of Will Conine*, 41–43.
49. Whitney, *Memories of Will Conine*, 49.
50. Whitney, *Memories of Will Conine*.
51. Whitney, *Memories of Will Conine*, 50.
52. Whitney, *Memories of Will Conine*.
53. Whitney, *Memories of Will Conine*.
54. Whitney, *Memories of Will Conine*.
55. John Ross, Department of History, Lon Morris College, Jacksonville, Texas, review published on H-Law, May 2007.
56. Whitney, *Memories of Will Conine*, 46.
57. Whitney, *Memories of Will Conine*.
58. Whitney, *Memories of Will Conine*, 44.
59. Whitney, *Memories of Will Conine*.
60. Whitney, *Memories of Will Conine*, 45.
61. Whitney, *Memories of Will Conine*.
62. Whitney, *Memories of Will Conine*.
63. Whitney, *Memories of Will Conine*, 45–46.
64. Whitney, *Memories of Will Conine*, 46.
65. Hobbs, "Jim Reed, Southwestern Outlaw," quoting the *Dallas* (Texas) *Daily Commercial*, August 10, 1874.
66. Hobbs, "Jim Reed, Southwestern Outlaw"; An Inventory of Governor Edmund Jackson Davis Records at the Texas State Archives, 1869–1875, Box 2014/110-28, Folder 325, Correspondence September 1–11, 1873, documents from Bosque County Sheriff John A. Biffle regarding a coroner's inquest, asking for a reward to be offered for the Wheeler murderers, and stating that the Reed brothers are refugees from justice, Texas State Library and Archives, Austin. The reward offered was $250 for each of the two Reed brothers.
67. Chuck Rabas, "The Mysterious Jack Keene," *James Farm Journal*, 30, no. 2 (Spring 2019): 7–8. During his outlaw career, Jesse James often wrote letters proclaiming his innocence for the many crimes he and the James-Younger gang had committed. The 1875 letter from James was eventually published in the May 18, 1882, edition of the *Kansas City* (Missouri) *Journal*, shortly after Charlie and Bob Ford had killed James.
68. Shirley, *Belle Starr and Her Times*, 97.
69. Shirley, *Belle Starr and Her Times*.
70. "Descendants of John Starr Jr.," Genealogy.com.
71. Emmet Starr, *History of the Cherokee Indians and Their Legends and Folk Lore* (Oklahoma City, Oklahoma: The Warden Company, 1921), 160–61; Jon D. May, "Starr, Emmet," *The Encyclopedia of Oklahoma History and Culture*.
72. "John Ritchie (1817–1887)," Descendants of John Starr Jr., Territorial Kansas Online.
73. "Descendants of John Starr Jr." Other pro-Union Cherokees who served in Company C with Squirrel Starr included Mankiller Catcher, Eli Tadpole, Bark Prince, and Littlebear Bigmush.
74. "Starr Genealogy," Red Eagle JW; "Descendants of A-ma-do-ya Moytoy [Nancy Starr]," Genealogy.com. Sallie Baldridge was married three times and spent her entire life in Oklahoma, where she died in 1920.
75. "Thomas Starr Genealogy," We Relate.
76. George Morrison Bell Sr., *History of "Old and New Cherokee Indian Families"* (Bartlesville, OK: Watie Bell, 1972), 480. George Morrison Bell Sr. (1901–1981) was Tom Starr's fourth cousin.

77. Steele Kennedy, "What Time Has Done to Old Younger's Bend," *Tulsa* (Oklahoma) *Daily World*, December 3, 1933; Tulsa (Oklahoma) City-County Library, Tulsa and Oklahoma History Collections, Vertical File, Outlaws—Starr, Belle. The full text of restricted items in not available online. To view these items, visit the Research Center at Tulsa Central Library.
78. Phillip W. Steele, *Starr Tracks: Belle and Pearl Starr* (Gretna, LA; Pelican Publishing Company, 1998), 51–52.
79. Shirley, Belle Starr and Her Times, 84; John Milton Oskison, *Tales of Old Indian Territory and Essays on the Indian Condition* (Lincoln: University of Nebraska Press, 2012), 546.
80. "Descendants of John Starr Jr."
81. Indian Pioneer History Project for Oklahoma, Louise Rider interview with fieldworker Nannie Lee Burns, Interview 13727, April 16, 1938, Goodoowag.

Chapter 13: Sheer Greed

1. *The Times*, Philadelphia, Pennsylvania, December 31, 1893, 10. The article also describes Tom Starr's imposing physical appearance. "He was over six feet in height, with deep chest and splendid breadth of shoulders. His hair was whitening with age, but he stepped with almost the elasticity of youth."
2. *The Times*, Philadelphia, December 31, 1893.
3. Phil Norfleet, "Biographical Sketch of the Family of Thomas Starr (1813–1890)," quoting a September 15, 1937, WPA Indian-Pioneer Project interview with John Henry West (born in 1866) at Vian, Oklahoma.
4. Harry F. O'Beirne and E. S. O'Beirne, *Indian Territory: Its Chiefs, Legislators and Leading Men* (Saint Louis, Missouri: C. B. Woodward Company, 1892).
5. O'Beirne and O'Beirne, *Indian Territory*, 92–96.
6. Kenneth W. Hobbs Jr., "Jim Reed, Southwestern Outlaw and Husband of Belle Starr: A Study of the Watt Grayson and San Antonio Stage Robberies" (master's thesis, Texas Christian University, Fort Worth, 1975), 31. Grayson preferred to be called Watt, a diminutive of his given name, Walter.
7. Hobbs, "Jim Reed, Southwestern Outlaw," 31–32.
8. Carolyn Thomas Foreman, "The Ballentines (Balentines), Father and Son, in 'The Indian Territory,'" *Chronicles of Oklahoma* 12, no. 4 (December 1934): 425–26; Hobbs, "Jim Reed, Southwestern Outlaw," 32.
9. Jon D. May, "North Fork Town," *The Encyclopedia of Oklahoma History and Culture*; Theodore Isham and Blue Clark, "Creek (Mvskoke)," *The Encyclopedia of Oklahoma History and Culture*. The Creek Indians are more properly called the Muscogee, alternatively spelled Mvskoke.
10. Carolyn Thomas Foreman, "North Fork Town," *The Chronicles of Oklahoma* 29, no. 1 (Spring 1951): 79, 87, 92.
11. Foreman, "North Fork Town," 107; David A. Chang, "An Equal Interest in Soil: Creek Small-Scale Farming and the Work of Nationhood, 1866–1889," *American Indian Quarterly* 33, no. 1 (Winter 2009): 106.
12. Claudio Saunt, *Black, White, and Indian: Race and the Unmaking of an American Family* (New York: Oxford University Press, 2005), 15–16.
13. Saunt, *Black, White, and Indian*.
14. Don C. East, *A Historical Analysis of the Creek Indian Hillabee Towns* (Bloomington, IN: Universe, 2008), 87–88.
15. East, *Historical Analysis of the Creek Indian Hillabee Towns*.
16. East, *Historical Analysis of the Creek Indian Hillabee Towns*, 88, 89, 91.
17. East, *Historical Analysis of the Creek Indian Hillabee Towns*, 99.
18. East, *Historical Analysis of the Creek Indian Hillabee Towns*.
19. East, *Historical Analysis of the Creek Indian Hillabee Towns*, 93.

20. John R. Swanton, *Social Organization and Social Issues of the Indians of the Creek Federation* (Washington, DC: US Bureau of American Ethnology, 1928), 31.
21. Saunt, *Black, White, and Indian*, 4.
22. Saunt, *Black, White, and Indian*, 70.
23. *New York Daily Herald*, April 8, 1854, 5. The execution took place three weeks before the *Herald* ran the story, which had first appeared in the *Chickasaw Intelligencer*, published in the Choctaw Nation of Indian Territory.
24. Saunt, *Black, White, and Indian*, 69. According to the author, enslaved workers were a common sight in the Creek Nation. One of every ten Creek families held slaves.
25. Barbara Krauthamer, "Slavery," *The Encyclopedia of Oklahoma History and Culture*. Krauthamer wrote, "Through the rest of the century, blacks in the nation struggled to secure their citizenship and land rights. When the five nations were dissolved under the Curtis Act (1898), both blacks and Indians were compelled to accept land allotments and become residents of the state of Oklahoma."
26. US Congress, 44th Congress, Congressional Record: Proceedings and Debates, vol. 4, part 1 (Washington, DC: United States Printing Office, 1876), 334. Papers relating to the claims of Watt Grayson for compensation for depredations of whites upon the Indian, to the Committee on Indian Affairs; "Benjamin & Eugenia Dev Les Goodere Lang," Dallas Gateway.
27. US Congress, 44th Congress, Congressional Record: Proceedings and Debates, vol. 4, part 1, 1876.
28. US Congress, 44th Congress, Congressional Record: Proceedings and Debates, vol. 4, part 1, 1876.
29. Hobbs, "Jim Reed, Southwestern Outlaw," 34.
30. Hobbs, "Jim Reed, Southwestern Outlaw."
31. Hobbs, "Jim Reed, Southwestern Outlaw."
32. Hobbs, "Jim Reed, Southwestern Outlaw."
33. Hobbs, "Jim Reed, Southwestern Outlaw," 34–35.
34. Hobbs, "Jim Reed, Southwestern Outlaw," 35.
35. Hobbs, "Jim Reed, Southwestern Outlaw."
36. Hobbs, "Jim Reed, Southwestern Outlaw."
37. Hobbs, "Jim Reed, Southwestern Outlaw," 36.
38. US Congress, 44th Congress, Congressional Record: Proceedings and Debates, vol. 4, Part 1, 1876.
39. Document 28804, Creek Court—Supreme file, Indian Archives Division, Oklahoma Historical Society, Oklahoma City, Oklahoma.
40. Saunt, *Black, White, and Indian*, 133; *Indian Journal* (Muskogee, Indian Territory), 1876–1877.
41. US District Court records, Western District of Arkansas, criminal cases, U.S. vs. William D. Wilder, Cause No. 114, Federal Archives and Records Center, Fort Worth, Texas.
42. *U.S. vs. William D. Wilder*.
43. Hobbs, "Jim Reed, Southwestern Outlaw," 38.
44. Glenn Shirley, *Belle Starr and Her Times: The Literature, the Facts, and the Legends* (Norman: University of Oklahoma Press, 1982), 103; Laurence J. Yadon and Dan Anderson, *200 Texas Outlaws and Lawmen, 1835–1935* (Gretna, LA: Pelican, 2008), 208.
45. Hobbs, "Jim Reed, Southwestern Outlaw," 88–89.
46. Hobbs, "Jim Reed, Southwestern Outlaw," 89.

Chapter 14: Jim Reed's Last Hurrah

1. *Dallas* (Texas) *Daily Commercial*, August 10, 1874.
2. Shirley Families of Dallas Texas, "African-American Lineages," Shirley Association African-American Ancestry Research Center.

3. Shirley Families of Dallas Texas, "African-American Lineages."
4. Shirley Families of Dallas Texas, "African-American Lineages." In the 1880 census of Dallas County, Texas, Annie Shirley was conclusively identified, as were her children, living on Canton Street in Dallas.
5. Bosque County, Texas, Deed Actuaries, December 18, 1873, provided by Texas historian Rick Miller. Bosque County Deed Records, vol. N, 5. James H. [sic] Reed and M. M. Reed, his wife, of Dallas County, Texas sold this property to William D. Wilder for $750, December 18, 1873. Bosque County Deed Records, vol. N, 75. Wilder sold the property to Joel A. Lipscomb, Trustee L. C. Upshaw, March 3, 1874, filed March 13, 1874.
6. Bosque County, Texas, Deed Actuaries, December 18, 1873.
7. Bosque County, Texas, Deed Actuaries, December 18, 1873.
8. Rick Miller, "Outlaw Jim Reed," *Wild West History Association Journal* 7, no. 4 (August 2013): 32. Rosanna McCommas Cox (1835–1854), wife of Jessie Cox, was the sister of James Burke McCommas, father of the younger Rosanna McCommas, who was born in Texas in 1855.
9. "History of the Restoration Movement," Restoration Movement.
10. *Memorial and Biographical History of Dallas County, Texas* (Chicago: Lewis, 1892), 960–61.
11. Miller, "Outlaw Jim Reed."
12. *Dallas* (Texas) *Daily Herald*, February 10, 1874, 2.
13. *Dallas Daily Herald*, February 10, 1874.
14. *Dallas Daily Herald*, February 10, 1874.
15. *Dallas Daily Herald*, February 10, 1874; Rick Miller, *Tin Star Tales: Law and Disorder in Dallas County, Texas, 1846–1900* (Bloomington, IN: Archway, 2017), 68.
16. Miller, "Outlaw Jim Reed," 31, 37; Bosque County District Court, vol. D, 26, Minutes, February 12, 1874.
17. Kenneth W. Hobbs Jr., "Jim Reed, Southwestern Outlaw and Husband of Belle Starr: A Study of the Watt Grayson and San Antonio Stage Robberies" (master's thesis, Texas Christian University, Fort Worth, 1975), 42.
18. Hobbs, "Jim Reed, Southwestern Outlaw," 43.
19. *Austin* (Texas) *American-Statesman*, April 17, 1874, 3.
20. Michael Wallis, *The Real Wild West: The 101 Ranch and the Creation of the American West* (New York: St. Martin's Press, 1999), 120; "Legends of the West," Legends of America.
21. Wallis, *Real Wild West*, 121.
22. Wallis, *Real Wild West*, 122.
23. *Dallas* (Texas) *Daily Commercial*, August 10, 1874, 1.
24. Miller, "Outlaw Jim Reed," 32.
25. *Austin* (Texas) *American-Statesman*, April 17, 1874, 3.
26. Harry Sinclair Drago, *Outlaws on Horseback* (Lincoln: University of Nebraska Press, 1964), 101.
27. Hobbs, "Jim Reed, Southwestern Outlaw," 44.
28. *Austin* (Texas) *Democratic Statesman*, April 9, 1874, 1; "Stagecoaching in Texas," Texas Almanac.
29. Miller, "Outlaw Jim Reed."
30. *Austin Daily Democrat Statesman*, April 17, 1874.
31. *Austin Daily Democrat Statesman*, April 17, 1874.
32. *Austin Daily Democrat Statesman*, April 17, 1874.
33. *Waco* (Texas) *Daily Examiner*, April 16, 1874.
34. Miller, "Outlaw Jim Reed"; "Stuart & Mair Mercantile and Exchange Merchants," Austin (Texas) City Directory, Austin Genealogical Society, 1872, 78.
35. *Austin Daily Democrat Statesman*, April 17, 1874; Ramon F. Adams, *The Cowboy Dictionary* (New York: Perigee, 1993), 85. *Cuidado* was a warning shout, meaning "Look out!" or "Take care!"
36. *New York Times*, April 9, 1874, 1.

37. Miller, "Outlaw Jim Reed," 32–33; John W. Payne Jr., "Coke, Richard," *Handbook of Texas Online*.
38. Hobbs, "Jim Reed, Southwestern Outlaw."
39. *Journal of the Executive Proceedings of the Senate of the United States of America* 17 (Washington, DC: US Government Printing Office, 1901), 594.
40. "US Deputy Marshal Henry Frank Griffin," Mark Thacker.
41. Western Americana Collectibles, early historic Texas Colt single action, Online Collectibles Auctions, Deadwood, South Dakota, April 28, 2018, Icollector.
42. Austin (Texas) *American-Statesman*, April 17, 1874.
43. *Austin American-Statesman*, April 17, 1874.
44. *Austin American-Statesman*, April 17, 1874.
45. Hobbs, "Jim Reed, Southwestern Outlaw," 54–55.
46. Drago, *Outlaws on Horseback*, 100–101.
47. Drago, *Outlaws on Horseback*.
48. Glenn Shirley, *Belle Starr and Her Times: The Literature, the Facts, and the Legends* (Norman: University of Oklahoma Press, 1982), 111–12.
49. Glenn Shirley, *Belle Starr and Her Times*.
50. *Galveston* (Texas) *Daily News*, April 17, 1874, 1.
51. *Dallas* (Texas) *Weekly Herald*, April 25, 1874, 1; Philip Lindsley, *A History of Greater Dallas and Vicinity*, vol. 1 (Chicago: Lewis, 1909, 9; "Texas on 66," Texas History Notebook.
52. *Dallas Weekly Herald*, April 25, 1874.
53. *Dallas Weekly Herald*, April 25, 1874.
54. Miller, *Tin Star Tales*, 72.
55. *Dallas* (Texas) *Daily Commercial*, April 27, 1874, 1.
56. *Dallas* (Texas) *Daily Herald*, April 30, 1874, 1.
57. *Dallas Daily Herald*, April 30, 1874.
58. Miller, *Tin Star Tales*.
59. *Dallas Daily Herald*, April 30, 1874.
60. *Dallas Daily Herald*, April 30, 1874.
61. *Dallas Daily Herald*, April 30, 1874.
62. Bob Alexander, *Whiskey River Ranger: The Old West Life of Baz Outlaw* (Denton: University of North Texas Press, 2016), 37.
63. Gwen Pettit, *Between the Creeks*, Lindy Fisher, comp., July 2006, University of North Texas Libraries.
64. Pettit, *Between the Creeks*.
65. Texas State Library and Archives Commission, Austin, Texas Governor Richard Coke: An inventory of Governor Richard Coke Records at the Texas State Archives, 1873–1877, "A letter from Collin County Sheriff W. W. Merritt regarding John T. Morris," Box Numbers 2014/123–1, Correspondence, September 1874, 13–2 (folder 2 of 2). In this official letter about Morris that Sheriff Merritt sent to Governor Coke, it is stated that Morris's "wife was a cousin of Reed's." Other credible sources, including Texas historian Rick Miller, agree that Eliza Morris and Reed were cousins.
66. Petit, *Between the Creeks*.
67. *Dallas* (Texas) *Daily Herald*, May 30, 1874, 1.
68. *Dallas Daily Herald*, May 30, 1874.
69. *Dallas Daily Herald*, May 30, 1874.
70. *Dallas Daily Herald*, May 30, 1874.
71. *Dallas Daily Herald*, May 27, 1874, 1.
72. *Dallas Daily Herald*, May 27, 1874; *Sherman* (Texas) *Patriot*, May 31, 1874, 1.
73. *United States v. Jim Reed et al.*, Case No. 142, U.S. District Court, Western District of Texas, Austin.
74. Glenn Shirley, *Belle Starr and Her Times*, 116–17.

75. Shirley, *Belle Starr and Her Times*.
76. *Cherokee Advocate*, Tahlequah, Indian Territory, July 18, 1874, 1.
77. Letter from Indian agent John B. Jones, included in *U.S. v. Cal Carter, Bill Fisher, and One Reed*, District Court Records, Western District of Arkansas, Richard J. Miller Collection.
78. Letter from Indian agent John B. Jones.
79. Letter from Indian agent John B. Jones.
80. Shirley, *Belle Starr and Her Times*, 118.
81. Pettit, *Between the Creeks*.
82. Miller, "Outlaw Jim Reed," 33.
83. *San Antonio* (Texas) *Daily Express*, July 22, 1874, 3.
84. Pettit, *Between the Creeks*.
85. *Dallas* (Texas) *Daily Herald*, August 2, 1874, 2.
86. *Dallas Daily Herald*, August 2, 1874.
87. Miller, "Outlaw Jim Reed," 34.
88. *Dallas* (Texas) *Daily Commercial*, August 10, 1874, 1.
89. Miller, "Outlaw Jim Reed."
90. Hobbs, "Jim Reed, Southwestern Outlaw," 5.
91. Miller, "Outlaw Jim Reed."
92. Hobbs, "Jim Reed, Southwestern Outlaw," 64.
93. Shirley, *Belle Starr and Her Times*, 119; Hobbs, "Jim Reed, Southwestern Outlaw."
94. Shirley, *Belle Starr and Her Times*.
95. Hobbs, "Jim Reed, Southwestern Outlaw"; Pettit, *Between the Creeks*.
96. Hobbs, "Jim Reed, Southwestern Outlaw."
97. *Dallas Daily Commercial*, August 10, 1874.
98. *Dallas Daily Commercial*, August 10, 1874.
99. Miller, "Outlaw Jim Reed."
100. Miller, "Outlaw Jim Reed."
101. Miller, "Outlaw Jim Reed."

Chapter 15: Repercussions

1. *Dallas* (Texas) *Daily Commercial*, August 10, 1874, 1.
2. S. W. Harman, *Hell on the Border: He Hanged Eighty-Eight Men* (Lincoln: University of Nebraska Press, 1992), 570. Originally published in 1898 by Phoenix Publishing Company, Fort Smith, the book is largely a biography of noted federal judge Isaac C. Parker.
3. Harman, *Hell on the Border*.
4. Harman, *Hell on the Border*.
5. Homer Croy, *Cole Younger: Last of the Great Outlaws* (Lincoln: University of Nebraska Press, 1999), 51.
6. Ramon Frederick Adams, *Six-Guns and Saddle Leather: A Bibliography on Western Outlaws and Gunmen* (Mineola, NY: Dover Publications, Inc., 1998), 280. According to Adams, much of the Harman book is "not too trustworthy," and the material is "unreliable, especially that about Belle Starr."
7. Kenneth W. Hobbs Jr., "Jim Reed, Southwestern Outlaw and Husband of Belle Starr: A Study of the Watt Grayson and San Antonio Stage Robberies" (master's thesis, Texas Christian University, Fort Worth, 1975), 65. According to Hobbs, Sheriff Gose reportedly "testified that the deceased was Reed, and that he knew him during the war as one of the Quantelle [sic] men"; Larry A. Hamblen, "Gose Family History, John A. Gose, Pvt., Co. C, Company Muster-in Roll, Burnet's Battalion, Texas Sharp Shooters," Lamar County, Texas.
8. Hobbs, "Jim Reed, Southwestern Outlaw."
9. *Galveston* (Texas) *Daily News*, August 9, 1874, 1.

10. *Galveston Daily News*, August 9, 1874.
11. Gwen Pettit, *Between the Creeks*, Lindy Fisher, comp., July 2006, University of North Texas Libraries; "Potter's Field Cemetery—McKinney," Collin County, Texas, History. Potter's Field Cemetery is no longer known by that designation and is now part of Pecan Grove Memorial Park. Potter's Field is sometimes called the Hispanic section because of the large number of Hispanic graves. Indigents can be buried free in that section if they are from McKinney.
12. *Kansas City* (Missouri) *Times*, July 19, 1874, 1.
13. *Kansas City Times*, July 19, 1874.
14. Hobbs, "Jim Reed, Southwestern Outlaw," 69.
15. William A. Settle Jr., *Jesse James Was His Name* (Lincoln: University of Nebraska Press, 1977), 16.
16. Michael Wallis, *The Real Wild West: The 101 Ranch and the Creation of the American West* (New York: St. Martin's Press, 1999), 50.
17. Settle, 41, 46. According to Settle, Edwards's "effusive defense and glorification of the James band" continued until his death in 1889.
18. T. J. Stiles, *Jesse James: Last Rebel of the Civil War* (New York: Vintage, 2003), 263.
19. Hobbs, "Jim Reed, Southwestern Outlaw."
20. Hobbs, "Jim Reed, Southwestern Outlaw"; *Dallas* (Texas) *Daily Commercial*, August 26, 1874, 1.
21. *Denison* (Texas) *Daily News*, August 22, 1874, 3.
22. Glenn Shirley, *Belle Starr and Her Times: The Literature, the Facts, and the Legends* (Norman: University of Oklahoma Press, 1982), 120.
23. C. W. Raines, *Year Book for Texas* (Austin, Texas: Gammel-Statesman, 1902), 229.
24. "Samuel Bell Maxey," Lamar County, Texas.
25. *Galveston* (Texas) *Daily News*, August 15, 1874, 2.
26. *Dallas* (Texas) *Daily Herald*, August 15, 1874, 2.
27. Shirley, *Belle Starr and Her Times*, 121.
28. *Austin* (Texas) *Daily Democratic-Statesman*, August 26, 1874, 2.
29. Hobbs, "Jim Reed, Southwestern Outlaw," 67.
30. Shirley, *Belle Starr and Her Times*, 121.
31. Records of the United States District Courts for the Eastern District of Texas, National Archives Southwest District, Fort Worth. Fires destroyed the records of the Paris, Texas, court in 1916 and the Tyler, Texas, court on November 17, 1878. In addition, few Tyler newspapers survive from that time because of the fire.
32. Texas State Library and Archives Commission, Austin, Texas Governor Richard Coke: An inventory of Governor Richard Coke Records at the Texas State Archives, 1873–1877, "A letter from Collin County Sheriff W. W. Merritt regarding John T. Morris," Box Numbers 2014/123–1, Correspondence, September 1874, 13–2 (folder 2 of 2).
33. Texas State Library and Archives Commission, "A letter from Collin County Sheriff W. W. Merritt regarding John T. Morris."
34. Rick Miller, "Outlaw Jim Reed," *Wild West History Association Journal* 7, no. 4 (August 2013): 35.
35. Shirley, *Belle Starr and Her Times*, 122.
36. Shirley, *Belle Starr and Her Times*.
37. Shirley, *Belle Starr and Her Times*.
38. Federal Archives and Records Center, Fort Worth, Texas, Records of the United States District Court, Western District of Arkansas, Fort Smith, *U.S. vs. W. D. Wilder*.
39. *U.S. vs. W. D. Wilder*.
40. *U.S. vs. W. D. Wilder*.
41. *U.S. vs. W. D. Wilder*.
42. *U.S. vs. W. D. Wilder*.

43. *U.S. vs. W. D. Wilder.*
44. Shirley, *Belle Starr and Her Times*, 124.
45. Sharon E. Whitney, comp. and ed., *The Memories of Will Conine: 1860s to 1890s* (Waco, TX: Texian, 1999), 53.
46. Whitney, *Memories of Will Conine.*
47. Whitney, *Memories of Will Conine*, 54.
48. Whitney, *Memories of Will Conine.*
49. Whitney, *Memories of Will Conine.*
50. Whitney, *Memories of Will Conine*, 53.
51. Whitney, *Memories of Will Conine*, 55.
52. Miller, "Outlaw Jim Reed," 36.
53. United States House of Representatives records, Watt Grayson claim file, exhibit H, quoted by Hobbs, "Jim Reed, Southwestern Outlaw," 76.
54. United States House of Representatives records, Watt Grayson claim file.
55. *Fort Smith* (Arkansas) *Weekly New Era*, October 14, 1874, 1.
56. *Fort Smith Weekly New Era*, October 14, 1874.
57. *Galveston* (Texas) *Daily News*, October 11, 1874, 2.
58. Hobbs, "Jim Reed, Southwestern Outlaw," 78.
59. Hobbs, "Jim Reed, Southwestern Outlaw," 79.
60. National Park Service Staff, Fort Smith Historic Site, comps., "Law Enforcement for Fort Smith 1851–1896," *Fort Smith Historical Society Journal* 3, no. 1 (April, 1979): 3. In spring 1873, graft and corruption in the court for the Western District of Arkansas sparked a congressional investigation. Judge Story resigned under fire. Pending the appointment of a new judge, Henry Caldwell presided over the Fort Smith court.
61. National Park Service Staff, "Law Enforcement for Fort Smith 1851–1896." Although Caldwell had been criticized for handing down lenient verdicts, he also sent seven men to the gallows during his tenure in the Western District.
62. Shirley, *Belle Starr and Her Times*, 124.
63. *Fort Smith* (Arkansas) *Weekly New Era*, December 16, 1874, 1.
64. Shirley, *Belle Starr and Her Times.*
65. Riley Kovalcheck, "The Modern Plantation: The Continuities of Convict-Leasing and the Analysis of Arkansas Prison Systems," *College Language Association Journal* 7 (2019): 96–130; Tina Easley, transcriber, "Prisons, Schools, Asylums," *Centennial History of Arkansas—1922*, Genealogy Trails. Used during the Civil War as a federal prison, the old Arkansas State Penitentiary was on the site of the present state capitol, built between 1899 and 1915.
66. Miller, "Outlaw Jim Reed"; United States District Court Records, Western District of Texas, Austin, criminal minutes, ledger no. 122, 576, Federal Archives and Records Center, Fort Worth, Texas.

Chapter 16: Out of the Shadows

1. Katherine McDaniel, for the City of Greeley Museums, "Angels in Black: Victorian Women in Mourning" Exhibit, 2018.
2. Virginia Scharff, "Women of the West," *History Now: The Historian's Perspective*, no. 9, September 2006.
3. Scharff, "Women of the West."
4. Mrs. John A. Logan, assisted by Professor William Mathews, Catherine Owen, and Will Carleton, *The Home Manual: Everybody's Guide in Social, Domestic, and Business Life* (Chicago: H. J. Smith, 1889), 284.
5. Logan, *Home Manual.*
6. Logan, *Home Manual*, 304–9.

7. Thomas J. Schlereth, *Victorian America: Transformations in Everyday Life, 1876–1915* (New York: HarperCollins, 1982), 33.
8. Rebecca L. Ash, "Women in the American West: Blurred Reality."
9. Ash, "Women in the American West: Blurred Reality."
10. Sandra L. Myres, *Westering Women and the Frontier Experience 1800–1915* (Albuquerque: University of New Mexico Press, 1982), 438.
11. Myres, *Westering Women and the Frontier Experience*.
12. Emerson Hough, *The Passing of the Frontier* (New Haven, CN: Yale University Press, 1921), 93–94.
13. *Muskogee* (Oklahoma) *Daily Phoenix*, October 4, 1919, 6.
14. Sharon E. Whitney, comp. and ed., *The Memories of Will Conine: 1860s to 1890s* (Waco, TX: Texian, 1999), 91–92. The surcingle that Will Conine referred to is a strap that fastens around the horse's girth to bind a blanket to the horse's back. Myra Reed apparently not only rode sidesaddle and astride but at times rode astride with only a blanket and surcingle rather than a saddle.
15. Whitney, *Memories of Will Conine*. Will Conine had no use for sidesaddles. "I think sidesaddles were invented by some over nice fool for it was sure hard on the women to ride them a long distance and dangerous too. For they could not ride near as well sideways and it was awful tiresome too"; Patricia Riley Dunlap, *Riding Astride: The Frontier in Women's History* (Denver, CO: Arden, 1995), 59.
16. Glenn Shirley, *Belle Starr and Her Times: The Literature, the Facts, and the Legends* (Norman: University of Oklahoma Press, 1982), 131.
17. Shirley, *Belle Starr and Her Times*; Ann DeFrange, "Historian Lets 'Just the Facts' Enhance Stories," *Oklahoman*, January 21, 1990.
18. Cecilia Rasmussen, "Truth Dims the Legend of Outlaw Queen Belle Starr," *Los Angeles Times*, February 17, 2002.
19. *Dallas* (Texas) *Morning News*, February 8, 1889, 8.
20. "Books: Petticoat Terror," *Time Magazine*, June 2, 1941.
21. Burton Rascoe, *Belle Starr: "The Bandit Queen"* (New York: Random House, 1941), 177–78.
22. Rascoe, *Belle Starr: "The Bandit Queen*," 178.
23. Shirley, *Belle Starr and Her Times*, 23; Rascoe, *Belle Starr: "The Bandit Queen*," 118.
24. Willard H. Smith, Review of *Belle Starr: "The Bandit Queen*," by Burton Rascoe (New York: Random House, 1941), *Journal of American History* 28, no. 2 (September 1941): 311; Judith Rascoe, "A Cautionary Tale for Reviewers," *New York Times*, May 14, 1989, 38.
25. Paula Reed and Grover Ted Tate, *Sam Bass and Joel Collins: The Tenderfoot Bandits, Their Lives and Hard Times* (Tucson, Arizona: Westernlore, 1988), 40.
26. "Isaac McComas (variant spelling) father of Michael, or Mitchell McComas," Geni; "James Burke McCommas, son of Amon McCommas and father of Rosanna McCommas," Geneanet.
27. "Michael or Mitchell McComas (variant spelling), son of Isaac and Sarah Ann McComas, nephew of Elder Amon McComas," Geni.
28. Michael J. McCommas Records, 1850 US Census—Sugar Loaf Township, Crawford County, Arkansas; 1860 U.S. Census—Sugar Loaf Township, Sebastian County, Arkansas; and 1870 U.S. Census—Dallas County, Texas, Richard J. Miller Collection.
29. "Arkansas Genealogy and Boundary Changes."
30. "Arkansas Genealogy and Boundary Changes." United Confederate Veterans was considered the premier Confederate veterans' organization. It was formed on June 10, 1889, and was dissolved on May 30, 1951.
31. "Arkansas Genealogy and Boundary Changes"; "Old Soldier Dead: Confederate Laid Body of Former Comrade under the Sod Today," *Ardmore* (Oklahoma) *Daily Ardmoreite*, May 18, 1913, n.p.
32. "Dallas County, Texas: Pioneers of Dallas," Genealogy Trails. Three brothers of Isaac McCommas—Amon, Stephen, and John—had moved from Missouri to Texas in 1844.

33. "Michael J. 'Mike' McComas, Birth of son William McComas (1869–1869)," Texas, Ancestry.com.
34. U.S. Census—Dallas County, Texas, William McCommas, born 1869," Richard J. Miller Collection.
35. "Isaac Mason McCommas," My Heritage.
36. Richard J. Miller Collection, documentation from various county and census records. Isaac Mason McCommas was married three times: to Jennie Love Hall in Parker County, Texas, on February 5, 1890; to Martha Jane Stofle in Cooke County, Texas, on April 30, 1901; and to Della Lou Norman in Cooke County, Texas, on November 22, 1919. He is listed in the 1910 United States census as a carpenter at Hewitt, Carter County, Oklahoma.
37. *Big Spring* (Texas) *Daily Herald*, June 25, 1940, 6. McCommas had moved to Big Spring, Texas, from Elk City, Oklahoma, in 1929. The obituary spelled his name McComas.
38. Frederick S. Barde, "The Story of Belle Starr," *Sturm's Oklahoma Magazine* 11, no. 1, 1910, 21. First published in September 1905 in Tulsa, Indian Territory, the monthly publication moved to Oklahoma City in 1906. By 1911, the magazine had folded because of financial reasons.
39. William Yancey Shackleford, *Belle Starr, The Bandit Queen: The Career of the Most Colorful Outlaw the Indian Territory Ever Knew* (Girard, KS: Haldeman-Julius, 1946), 26. William Yancey Shackleford was a pseudonym for Vance Randolph.
40. Rick Miller, *Bounty Hunter* (College Station, TX: Creative, 1988), 42.
41. *Dallas* (Texas) *Daily Herald*, February 10, 1874, 2.
42. *Dallas Daily Herald*, February 10, 1874.
43. *Dallas* (Texas) *Daily Herald*, April 15, 1875, 4.
44. *Dallas Daily Herald*, April 15, 1875.
45. *Dallas Daily Herald*, April 15, 1875.
46. *Dallas Daily Herald*, April 15, 1875.

Chapter 17: The Glare of the Limelight

1. Rick Miller, *Tin Star Tales: Law and Disorder in Dallas County, Texas, 1846–1900* (Bloomington, IN: Archway, 2017), 79–80.
2. Miller, *Tin Star Tales*, 80.
3. Roger N. Conger, "Waco, Texas," *Handbook of Texas Online*; Carl Hoover, "Roaring Red Light District Part of Waco's Early History," Waco History Project, November 14, 2005. Waco earned the nickname "Six-Shooter Junction." The city legally recognized, licensed, and regulated prostitution in the Reservation district until 1917.
4. Elizabeth Hayes Turner, Stephanie Cole, and Rebecca Sharpless, *Texas Women: Their Histories, Their Lives* (Athens: University of Georgia Press, 2015), 139.
5. Turner, Cole, and Sharpless, *Texas Women*.
6. Judith Ann Benner, "Ross, Lawrence Sullivan (Sul)," *Handbook of Texas Online*, 2020.
7. Benner, "Ross, Lawrence Sullivan."
8. Michael Wallis, *The Wild West 365* (New York: Abrams, 2011), 238.
9. Wallis, *Wild West 365*.
10. Joaquin Rivaya Martinez, "Review of *Myth, Memory, and Massacre: The Pease River Capture of Cynthia Ann Parker*" by Paul H. Carlton and Tom Crum (2012), *Great Plains Quarterly* 2743.
11. Sharon E. Whitney, comp. and ed., *The Memories of Will Conine: 1860s to 1890s* (Waco, TX: Texian Press, 1999), 134.
12. Whitney, *Memories of Will Conine*, 133–34.
13. Whitney, *Memories of Will Conine*, 134.
14. *Waco* (Texas) *Reporter*, April 28, 1875, 1. The story was picked up by several newspapers, including the *Dallas* (Texas) *Daily Herald* and *San Antonio* (Texas) *Daily Express*.

15. *Waco Reporter*, April 28, 1875. There were no further reports concerning Myra Reed allegedly having had any involvement in a double murder. Unfortunately, Myra Reed's "letters on her person of a startling character" have never been found.
16. Rick Miller, "Outlaw Jim Reed," *Wild West History Association Journal* 7, no. 4 (August 2013): 36. According to Miller, "There is no further mention of this arrest."
17. Miller, "Outlaw Jim Reed."
18. Minutes, Fourteenth District Court, Dallas County, Texas, vol. 1, 54, *State of Texas v. Myra Reed*, cause no. 2873; Rick Miller, *Bounty Hunter* (College Station, TX: Creative, 1988), 44.
19. *Dallas* (Texas) *Morning News*, August 21, 1929, 6.
20. Rick Miller, personal communication to Michael Wallis, July 6, 2020.
21. Mona D. Sizer, *Texas Bandits: Real to Reel* (Dallas, TX: Taylor, 2004), 98.
22. James C. Reed to F. M. Reed, February 5, 1870, photocopy of original letter, Phillip W. Steele Collection, courtesy of Charlotte Steele and Roy Young; US Census Bureau, Population of the United States in 1870: California, 23, original ledger page reproduced in facsimile in FamilySearch; James C. Reed to F. M. Reed, January 19, 1872, photocopy of original letter, Phillip W. Steele Collection, courtesy of Charlotte Steele and Roy Young.
23. Miller, *Tin Star Tales*, 80.
24. Miller, *Bounty Hunter*, 44.
25. Randolph B. Campbell, "A Moderate Response: The District Judges of Dallas County during Reconstruction, 1865–1876," *Legacies: A History Journal for Dallas and North Central Texas* 5, no. 2 (Fall 1993): 10. Judge Barksdale served until spring 1876, when the new Texas constitution went into effect and revised the district court system..
26. Miller, *Bounty Hunter*.
27. *Dallas* (Texas) *Daily Herald*, May 4, 1875, 4.
28. "Silas Hare," Genealogy Trails. Judge Hare's son, Luther Rector Hare, served as an officer in the Seventh United States Cavalry under the command of General George Armstrong Custer. Hare survived the disastrous Battle of the Little Big Horn, June 25–26, 1876.
29. *Austin* (Texas) *Weekly Democratic Statesman*, May 13, 1875, 4.
30. Tom Peeler, "Nostalgia Crooked Cowpokes," *D Magazine*, December 1983.
31. *Dallas* (Texas) *Daily Herald*, July 3, 1875, 4.
32. Cecil Harper Jr., "Cabell, William Lewis," *Handbook of Texas Online*. W. L. Cabell served as Dallas mayor for three two-year terms: 1874–1876, 1877–1879, and 1883–1885. From 1885 to 1889, he was United States marshal for the Northern District of Texas. He died in Dallas on February 22, 1911. A grandson, Earle Cabell, was elected mayor of Dallas in 1961 and was serving on November 22, 1963, when President John F. Kennedy was assassinated in Dallas.
33. Miller, *Tin Star Tales*, 80.
34. *Dallas* (Texas) *Daily Herald*, July 23, 1875, 2.
35. Campbell, "Moderate Response," 4–12.
36. *Fort Worth* (Texas) *Morning Register*, December 1, 1901, 2; *Dallas* (Texas) *Daily Times Herald*, December 8, 1893, 2.
37. Miller, *Tin Star Tales*.
38. *Dallas* (Texas) *Daily Herald*, November 10, 1875, 4.
39. *Dallas Daily Herald*, November 10, 1875.
40. David Crowther, "Words Shakespeare Invented," *The History of England*, July 29, 2017. William Shakespeare invented more than seventeen hundred common words by changing nouns into verbs, changing verbs into adjectives, connecting words never used together before, adding prefixes and suffixes, and devising words wholly original. The word *unsex* was used for the first time in Lady Macbeth's famous soliloquy when she calls on the supernatural to "Unsex me here" and make her crueler to fulfill her plan to murder Duncan.
41. Vicente Edward Clemons, "The New Woman in Fiction and History: From Literature to Working Woman" (M.A. thesis, Pittsburg State University, May 2016), Electronic Theses and Dissertation Collection, 76.

42. Miller, *Tin Star Tales*, 90.
43. *Dallas* (Texas) *Daily Herald*, November 19, 1875, 4.
44. *Dallas Daily Herald*, November 19, 1875.
45. Kenneth W. Hobbs Jr., "Jim Reed, Southwestern Outlaw and Husband of Belle Starr: A Study of the Watt Grayson and San Antonio Stage Robberies" (master's thesis, Texas Christian University, Fort Worth, 1975), 89. Note from Michael Wallis: This citation refers to Myra Reed's deposition, mentioned in Chapter 13 of this book, regarding her knowledge of the Grayson robbery.
46. Hobbs, "Jim Reed, Southwestern Outlaw," 88–89.
47. Hobbs, "Jim Reed, Southwestern Outlaw," 89.
48. Hobbs, "Jim Reed, Southwestern Outlaw."
49. Hobbs, "Jim Reed, Southwestern Outlaw," 90.
50. Hobbs, "Jim Reed, Southwestern Outlaw," 94.
51. Minutes, Fourteenth District Court, Dallas County, Texas, vol. 1, 29, December 22, 1875, Cause No. 2873—*State of Texas v. Myra Reed*—case continued by defendant.
52. *Dallas* (Texas) *Daily Times Herald*, February 7, 1889, 1; Glenn Shirley, *Belle Starr and Her Times: The Literature, the Facts, and the Legends* (Norman: University of Oklahoma Press, 1982), 133. Another yarn told about Myra claimed that she got out of jail by eloping with an enamored jailer who returned "to the bosom of his family a month later, his infatuation, for some cause, having cooled."
53. Miller, "Outlaw Jim Reed," 37.
54. Miller, *Bounty Hunter*, 45.
55. Miller, *Bounty Hunter*.
56. Miller, *Bounty Hunter*.
57. Shirley, *Belle Starr and her Times*, 131.
58. Shirley Families of Dallas Texas, "African-American Lineages," Shirley Association African-American Ancestry Research Center. Some records, such as Laura Shirley's death certificate, list Mansfield Shirley as her father, but law officers had killed him in 1870, six years prior to her birth. Laura lived in Dallas until her death in 1952 at age seventy-five.
59. Miller, *Bounty Hunter*, 45–46.

Chapter 18: The Legend Takes Root

1. S. W. Harman, *Hell on the Border: He Hanged Eighty-Eight Men* (Lincoln: University of Nebraska Press, 1992), 570–72. Harman copied the original letter on October 4, 1898, at Fort Smith, Arkansas. Although Harman's work was often found to be inaccurate and some of his sources were questionable, even his critics, including Glenn Shirley, agreed that the letter, postmarked August 10, 1876, was written by Myra Reed; Glenn Shirley, *Belle Starr and Her Times: The Literature, the Facts, and the Legends* (Norman: University of Oklahoma Press, 1982), 130–31; Rick Miller, "Outlaw Jim Reed," *Wild West History Association Journal* 7, no. 4 (August 2013): 37.
2. Shirley, *Belle Starr and Her Times*, 130.
3. Shirley, *Belle Starr and Her Times*.
4. Harman, 572; Edwin P. Hicks, *Belle Starr and Her Pearl* (Little Rock, Arkansas: Pioneer Press, 1963), 37–38. Hicks wrote that Rosie Reed "had suffered a brain hemorrhage" but offered no proof to back his claim.
5. Shirley, *Belle Starr and Her Times*.
6. Bob Alexander, *Whiskey River Ranger: The Old West Life of Baz Outlaw* (Denton: University of North Texas Press, 2016), 37.
7. Alexander, *Whiskey River Ranger*.
8. Mike Cox, *Texas Ranger History* (Charleston, SC: History Press, 2015), 217.

9. Alexander, *Whiskey River Ranger*, 39.
10. Cox, *Texas Ranger History*.
11. Cox, *Texas Ranger History*.
12. Christina Stopka, Dan Agler, and Fred Wilkins, comps., "Texas Rangers Killed or Died While on Duty" (Waco, Texas: Armstrong Texas Ranger Research Center, 2019), 10.
13. Rick Miller, *Bounty Hunter* (College Station, TX: Creative, 1988), 46.
14. Rick Miller, *Tin Star Tales: Law and Disorder in Dallas County, Texas, 1846–1900* (Bloomington, IN: Archway Publishing, 2017), 80.
15. *Daily Arkansas Gazette*, February 24, 1921, 13.
16. *Daily Arkansas Gazette*, February 24, 1921; Cindy Beckman, "Early Hotels: Looking Back" (Conway: Faulkner County Historical Society, 2016).
17. *Daily Arkansas Gazette*, February 24, 1921. Various sources later claimed that Myra and Rosie Reed lived in Faulkner County, Arkansas, for two to six months.
18. Joel Livingston, *A History of Jasper County, Missouri and Its People* (Chicago: Lewis, 1912), 126.
19. Livingston, *A History of Jasper County, Missouri*, 137.
20. Livingston, *A History of Jasper County, Missouri*, 174.
21. Livingston, *A History of Jasper County, Missouri*.
22. Livingston, *A History of Jasper County, Missouri*, 187. Bruce Younger came to Joplin and worked in the mines under an assumed name.
23. Belle Starr files, Jasper County (Missouri) Archives & Records Center.
24. Richard W. Etulain and Glenda Riley, eds., *With Badges & Bullets: Lawmen and Outlaws in the Old West* (Golden, CO: Fulcrum, 1999), 148.
25. "Colonel Charles Lee Younger (1779–1854)—Genealogy," Geni.
26. "Colonel Charles Lee Younger," quoting the will of Colonel Charles Lee Younger, Jackson County, Missouri, February 26, 1852.
27. "Colonel Charles Lee Younger."
28. "Colonel Charles Lee Younger." In the will, Younger wrote that the children of Parmelia Wilson "are sometimes called by the name of 'Younger' instead of 'Wilson' (and whom I acknowledge as my children by the said Parmelia Wilson their mother)."
29. "Colonel Charles Lee Younger," quoting the codicil to the will of Colonel Charles Lee Younger, Jackson County, Missouri, November 11, 1854. When Charles Lee Younger died in Missouri in 1854, he willed that all his enslaved children and their mothers be freed and given part of his property.
30. "Bruce Younger (1853–1889)," Ancestry.
31. "Paola, Kansas: A 150-year History in Detail," Chapter 3: "The War Is Over, the Indians Are Gone, and Growth Begins!," Think Miami County History.
32. *Memphis* (Tennessee) *Appeal*, August 8, 1876, 1, datelined Saint Louis, Missouri, August 6, 1876.
33. *Chicago Tribune*, August 8, 1876, 5, "Special dispatch to *The Tribune*" from Saint Louis, Missouri, August 7, 1876, citing a "Sedalia [Missouri] special."
34. *Chicago Tribune*, August 8, 1876.
35. *Chicago Tribune*, August 8, 1876. The catalogue of officers and students of the University of Notre Dame for 1867–1868 shows Bruce Younger of Warsaw, Missouri, *Twenty-fourth Annual Catalogue of the Officers and Students of the University of Notre Dame, Indiana, for the Academic Year 1867–68, Annual Commencement, Wednesday, June 24, 1868*, Notre Dame, IN: Ave Maria Steam Power Press Print, 1868, title page, 40. Financial information at Notre Dame for Bruce Younger of Warsaw, Missouri, is recorded in Notre Dame: Index to Financial Ledgers 1841–1869, vol. 5, 361, October 30, 1867, November 14, 1867, January 23, [1868]. Early Notre Dame Student, Class, and Financial Record books, Mercantile Department Day Book, ULDG Day Book, 1864–1911, vol. 2, 150, shows that W. A. McClain was the guardian of Bruce Younger and that "Mr. Johnson

will send" $150; Joseph Smith, archivist, Notre Dame University, personal communication to Rick Miller, September 16, 2020; Joseph Smith, archivist, Notre Dame University, personal communication to Hazel Rowena Mills, September 30, 2020. William Alexander McClain (1816–1878) of Warsaw, Missouri, was a member of the Missouri legislature and law partner of Waldo P. Johnson, executor of Charles Lee Younger's estate; *Poplar Bluff* (Missouri) *Citizen*, November 22, 1878, 2; *Jefferson City* (Missouri) *People's Tribune*, November 27, 1878, 1; Rick Miller, personal communication to Hazel Rowena Mills, September 17, 2020.

36. *Chicago* (Illinois) *Tribune*, August 8, 1876.
37. *State Journal*, Jefferson City, Missouri, August 11, 1876, citing in part the *Sedalia* (Missouri) *Bazoo*, August 6, 1876; *Junction City* (Kansas) *Weekly Union*, August 12, 1876, 2; *Daily Commonwealth*, Topeka, Kansas, August 13, 1876, 1, datelined Saint Louis, Missouri, August 12, 1876; *Weekly Kansas State Journal*, Topeka, Kansas, August 17, 1876; *State Journal*, Jefferson City, Missouri, August 18, 1876, 3.
38. *State Journal*, Jefferson City, Missouri, August 11, 1876.
39. *Empire City* (Kansas) *Echo*, June 20, 1876, 4.
40. *Fort Scott* (Kansas) *Daily Monitor*, June 21, 1878, 4.
41. Nancy B. Samuelson, personal communication to Hazel Rowena Mills, September 23, 2019.
42. Vance Randolph Collection, Library of Congress.
43. William Yancey Shackleford [Vance Randolph], *Belle Starr, the Bandit Queen: The Career of the Most Colorful Outlaw the Indian Territory Ever Knew* (Girard, KS: Haldeman-Julius, Little Blue Book No. 1846, 1946), 28–29. Facsimile reprint, Kessinger, n.d.
44. Shackleford, *Belle Starr, the Bandit Queen*, 29.
45. Shackleford, *Belle Starr, the Bandit Queen*, 29–30.
46. Shackleford, *Belle Starr, the Bandit Queen*, 30.
47. Shackleford, *Belle Starr, the Bandit Queen*.
48. Shackleford, *Belle Starr, the Bandit Queen*, 30–31.
49. Shackleford, *Belle Starr, the Bandit Queen*, 31.
50. *Galena* (Kansas) *Weekly Republican*, June 5, 1886, 5, quoting in part the *Carthage* (Missouri) *Press*.
51. Criminal court minute books, Dallas County (Texas) District Court, cause number 2899, vol. H-2, 492, August 4, 1876; cause number 2519, vol. J, 177, March 16, 1877, arrested with Tom Jones; cause number 2978, vol. J, 179; cause number 2982, vol. O, 86, April 20, 1882, charged with Dave McCommas; Richard J. Miller, attorney at law, to Phillip W. Steele, February 21, 1988, photocopy of original letter, Phillip W. Steele Collection, courtesy of Charlotte Steele and Roy Young; Case number 2978, Shirley, and case number 2982, McCommas and Shirley, "District Court: The Criminal Docket as Set to Date," *Dallas* (Texas) *Weekly Herald*, January 6, 1877, 3.
52. *Galveston* (Texas) *Daily News*, September 19, 1878, 1.
53. *Galveston Daily News*, September 19, 1878. There were no further reports about Lizzie Hall or her child. No record has been found that John Alva "Shug" Shirley ever married; Shirley Association. Letters in the New Albany Public Library (Floyd County, Indiana) written by John Alva Shirley Jr. (born 1881) say his father's name was John Alva Shirley Sr., his grandfather was John Shirley, and his great-grandfather was Christian Shirley of Floyd County.
54. *Pleasanton* (Kansas) *Observer-Enterprise*, July 19, 1879, 2.
55. *Burlington* (Kansas) *Democrat*, April 2, 1880, 3.
56. *Parsons* (Kansas) *Daily Eclipse*, April 7, 1880, 1.
57. *Neodesha* (Kansas) *Free Press*, April 9, 1880, 3.
58. *Junction City* (Kansas) *Weekly Union*, May 8, 1880, 5.
59. *Junction City* (Kansas) *Weekly Union*, May 13, 1880, 3.
60. Office of Probate Judge S. L. Coulter, "true copy" of marriage license for Bruce Younger and Maibelle Reed, May 15, 1880, state of Kansas, county of Labette; digital scan of original printed

form filled out by hand, Labette County District Court, Oswego, Kansas, Lori Davis to Hazel Rowena Mills, January 30, 2019. The marriage was recorded in record volume B, page 361; photocopy of typed transcript of marriages, Dreat Younger to Phillip W. Steele, April 23, 1989, Phillip W. Steele Collection, courtesy of Charlotte Steele and Roy Young. A later transcription of the marriage license contains less information; photocopy of printed form filled out by typewriter, n.d.; Florence Wiley, Colorado Springs, Colorado, to Phillip W. Steele, postmarked August 24, 1987; Phillip W. Steele Collection, courtesy of Charlotte Steele and Roy Young.

61. Dreat Younger, Joplin, Missouri, to Phillip W. Steele, April 23, 1989; Phillip W. Steele Collection, courtesy of Charlotte Steele and Roy Young.
62. *Labette County Democrat*, Oswego, Kansas, June 4, 1880, 8.
63. *Labette County Democrat*, Oswego, Kansas, June 4, 1880, 1.
64. *Parsons* (Kansas) *Weekly Sun*, June 10, 1880, 8.
65. *Western Herald*, Girard, Kansas, June 24, 1880, 3.
66. Janeal Schmidt, "Selfish Intentions: Kansas Women and Divorce in Nineteenth Century America" (master's thesis, Kansas State University, 2009), introduction, xi.
67. Schmidt, "Selfish Intentions," Chapter 2, "Changes in Kansas Divorce Law," 24, 37.
68. General Statues of the State of Kansas 1868, Chapter 80, Article 28, Section 639; cited in Schmidt, 30.
69. *Mail and Breeze*, Topeka, Kansas, July 21, 1899; cited in Schmidt, "Selfish Intentions," Chapter 3, "Concerns about Liberal Divorce Law," 47.
70. Lori Davis, Labette County District Court, Oswego, Kansas, telephone interview by Hazel Rowena Mills, January 30, 2019; Lori Davis, Labette County District Court, Oswego, Kansas, personal communication to Hazel Rowena Mills, January 31, 2019.
71. Office of Vital Statistics, Kansas Department of Health, December 6, 2019.
72. Lauren Leeman, librarian, State Historical Society of Missouri, Center for Missouri Studies, telephone interview by Hazel Rowena Mills, December 9, 2019.
73. Lori Davis, Labette County District Court, Oswego, Kansas, personal communication to Hazel Rowena Mills, January 31, 2019; records of Cherokee County, Kansas, December 30, 2019; Deanna Maynard, chief deputy recorder, Jasper County, Missouri, personal communication to Hazel Rowena Mills, December 30, 2019; Pat Terry, recorder, Saint Clair County, Missouri, personal communication to Hazel Rowena Mills, December 30, 2019; Shelly Baldwin, recorder, Vernon County, Missouri, personal communication to Hazel Rowena Mills, December 30, 2019; Danyelle Baker, recorder, Bates County, Missouri, personal communication to Hazel Rowena Mills, December 31, 2019; Melanie Forquer, Jasper County Circuit Court, Carthage, Missouri, personal communication to Hazel Rowena Mills, January 9, 2019; Nora Goff, recorder, Newton County District Court, Neosho, Missouri, personal communication to Hazel Rowena Mills, January 9, 2019.
74. Mallory Covington, Oklahoma Historical Society, personal communication to Hazel Rowena Mills, September 12, 2019.

Chapter 19: The Birth of Belle Starr

1. Marriage report of Samuel Starr and Mrs. Bell Reed, June 5, 1880, Oklahoma Historical Society Indian Archives Volume 1-B, Court Records of Canadian District December 14, 1869–March 1, 1891, Proceedings of District Court of Canadian District, Cherokee Nation, 297, Microfilm Roll 22, for Canadian District; digital scan of handwritten record, Mallory Covington, Oklahoma Historical Society, to Hazel Rowena Mills, February 14, 2019.
2. Marriage report of Samuel Starr and Mrs. Bell Reed, June 5, 1880. In 1883, Abraham Woodall joined the Cherokee Nation Senate, representing Canadian District.
3. Ronald W. Lackmann, *Women of the Western Frontier in Fact, Fiction, and Film* (Jefferson, NC: McFarland, 1997), 10.

4. Michael Wallis, *The Wild West 365* (New York: Abrams, 2011), 86.
5. Katherine Ellinghaus, *Taking Assimilation to Heart: Marriages of White Women and Indigenous Men in the United States and Australia, 1887–1937* (Lincoln: University of Nebraska Press, 2006), 73.
6. Russell Thornton, *The Cherokees: A Population History* (Lincoln: University of Nebraska Press, 1990), 173.
7. Emmet Starr, *History of the Cherokee Indians and Their Legends and Folk Lore* (Oklahoma City, OK: The Warden Company, 1921), 655.
8. Melville Weston Fuller and Supreme Court of the United States, *U.S. Reports: Cherokee Intermarriage Cases*, 203 U.S. 76.1906, periodical, Library of Congress.
9. James W. Parins, "The Shifting Map of Cherokee Land Use Practices in Indian Territory," *Elohi—Indigenous People and the Environment* 1 (2012): 13–19.
10. Parins, "The Shifting Map of Cherokee Land Use Practices in Indian Territory."
11. Oliver Ray Titchenal, *The Titchenal Cherokee Connection*, edited and converted to web format by Titchenal family members.
12. Will Chavez, "Though No Longer Bustling, Porum Has Rich History," *Cherokee Phoenix*, Tahlequah, Oklahoma, August 10, 2018.
13. Glenn Shirley, *Belle Starr and Her Times: The Literature, the Facts, and the Legends* (Norman: University of Oklahoma Press, 1982), 142, 246.
14. Shirley, *Belle Starr and Her Times*, 142; Indian-Pioneer History Project for Oklahoma, interview with F. W. Keith of Muskogee, Oklahoma, July 31, 1937, interviewer: Florence L. Phillips.
15. Shirley, *Belle Starr and Her Times*, 143.
16. Shirley, *Belle Starr and Her Times*; David Dary, *Stories of Old-Time Oklahoma* (Norman: University of Oklahoma Press, 2015), 120. Dary: "If Big Head's treasure existed, the Starrs apparently never found it. Countless other people have since searched for the legendary $10,000 in gold coins. If anyone found the treasure, they did not brag about it in public."
17. Harry Sinclair Drago, *Outlaws on Horseback* (New York: Dodd, Mead, 1964), 107.
18. Onieta Fisher, "Life in a Log House."
19. Linda D. Wilson, "Barde, Frederick Samuel," *The Encyclopedia of Oklahoma History and Culture*.
20. Kenneth A. Butler, comp., "Some Articles and Items about Belle Starr," Oklahoma City, n.p., October 1987. Oklahoma historian Butler compiled seventy-six pages pertaining to published articles and other material related to Belle Starr. He also included commentary concerning the validity and accuracy of the collection. In describing the importance of Frederick Barde's 1910 article, Butler wrote, "This is the earliest, serious effort that I have found, where the author tried to write his impression of the facts of Belle's life in the Cherokee Nation. Earlier writers seemed to be far more interested in writing a sensational story that would sell big, while I believe that Barde was more interested in providing a record, as near the truth as he could learn."
21. Frederick S. Barde, "The Story of Belle Starr," *Sturm's Oklahoma Magazine* 11, no. 1 (September 1910): 22.
22. Shirley, *Belle Starr and Her Times*, 143.
23. Barde, "Story of Belle Starr," 23.
24. Barde, "Story of Belle Starr," 22–23; Frederick S. Barde Collection, Oklahoma Historical Society. Barde's article in *Sturm's Oklahoma Magazine* was illustrated with photographs of the Starr cabin, the shade trees, and the well enclosed by a fence.
25. Shirley, *Belle Starr and Her Times*, 144, 147.
26. Barde, "Story of Belle Starr," 22.
27. Shirley, *Belle Starr and Her Times*, 144.
28. Victoria Stefani, "True Statements: Women's Narratives of the American Frontier Experience" (PhD diss., University of Arizona, 2000), 114.
29. Stefani, "True Statements."

30. Titchenal, *Titchenal Cherokee Connection*.
31. Linda D. Wilson, "Schools, Subscription," *The Encyclopedia of Oklahoma History and Culture*.
32. University of Oklahoma Libraries Western History Collections, Indian-Pioneer History, George Weaver Interview 6647, Porum, Oklahoma, July 14, 1937, James S. Buchanan, fieldworker.
33. Shirley, *Belle Starr and Her Times*, 147.
34. John F. Weaver, "Belle Starr: A Few Leaves from the Life of a Notorious Woman," *Fort Smith (Arkansas) Elevator*, February 15, 1889, 3.
35. Stefani, "True Statements," 122.
36. Stefani, "True Statements," 123–24.
37. Stefani, "True Statements." Dr. Stefani wrote: "The voice [in the sketch] is distinct from the rest of the article in content and tone, and it is stylistically consistent with Belle's letter to Pearl: direct, grammatically fluid, and correct, employing similar vocabulary and patterns and variations in sentence structure and length. It also resembles the letter in its awareness of the conflict between the values the writer professes and the way others view her."
38. Stefani, "True Statements," 123.
39. Stefani, "True Statements," 127.
40. Shirley, *Belle Starr and Her Times*, 148.
41. Charles D. Anderson, comp. and ed., *Outlaws of the Old West* (Los Angeles, CA: Mankind, 1973).
42. Wallis, *Wild West 365*, 374.
43. Wallis, *Wild West 365*, 382.
44. Wallis, *Wild West 365*.
45. Wallis, *Wild West 365*, 506.
46. Wallis, *Wild West 365*.
47. Shirley, *Belle Starr and Her Times*.
48. Wallis, *Wild West 365*, 316.
49. Wallis, *Wild West 365*.
50. Wallis, *Wild West 365*, 310.

Chapter 20: **Hell on the Border**

1. Eric Leonard, "Myths and Legends Surrounding Judge Parker," Fort Smith National Historic Site, National Park Service.
2. Roger H. Tuller, "Parker, Isaac Charles," *The Encyclopedia of Oklahoma History and Culture*.
3. Edwin C. Bearss, *Law Enforcement at Fort Smith, 1871–1896*, United States National Park Service Library, Denver, Colorado, January 1964, 25–28.
4. Bearss, *Law Enforcement at Fort Smith*, 32.
5. Bearss, *Law Enforcement at Fort Smith*, 44.
6. Bearss, *Law Enforcement at Fort Smith*, 413.
7. Daniel Richard Maher, "Vice in the Veil of Justice: Embedding Race and Gender in Frontier Tourism" (PhD diss., University of Arkansas–Fayetteville, 2013), *Graduate Theses and Dissertations*, 71; Carolyn Pollan and Amelia Martin, eds., "Law Enforcement for Fort Smith 1851–1896," *Fort Smith Historical Society Journal* 3, no. 1 (April 1979): 4.
8. Michael Wallis, *The Wild West 365* (New York: Abrams, 2011), 310, 312.
9. Stephanie Stegman, "The Good, the Bad, and the Legend of the Fort Smith Federal Courthouse," Washington, DC: Ultimate History Project. The author is a professor of history at Texas Wesleyan University, Fort Worth, and special media projects volunteer at the National Archives at Fort Worth.
10. Glenn Shirley, *Law West of Fort Smith: A History of Frontier Justice in the Indian Territory, 1834–1896* (Lincoln: University of Nebraska Press, 1968), 41.

11. Juliet Galonska, "Payment of Deputy Marshals," Fort Smith National Historic Site, National Park Service.
12. Wallis, Wild West 365, 312.
13. Samuel Arthur Galpin, "Report upon the Condition and Management of Certain Indian Agencies in the Indian Territory," United States Office of Indian Affairs (Washington, DC: United States Government Printing Office, 1877), 34.
14. Wallis, Wild West 365, 610, 614.
15. Richard White, "Outlaw Gangs of the Middle Border: American Social Bandits," The Western Historical Quarterly 12, no. 4 (October 1981): 403.
16. Wallis, Wild West 365, 612, 614.
17. Wallis, Wild West 365, 616.
18. Jeffrey Burton, Indian Territory and the United States, 1866–1906: Courts, Government, and the Movement for Oklahoma Statehood (Norman: University of Oklahoma Press, 1995). 65.
19. Shirley, Law West of Fort Smith, 59.
20. Bearss, Law Enforcement at Fort Smith, 43–44.
21. Bearss, Law Enforcement at Fort Smith, 48–49.
22. Bearss, Law Enforcement at Fort Smith, 48.
23. Bearss, Law Enforcement at Fort Smith, 49.
24. Bearss, Law Enforcement at Fort Smith, 47; Stegman, "The Good, the Bad, and the Legend."
25. "The Murder of William Riley Seaboalt, Jr. (1851–1874)," Pioneers of Ellis County, Texas. Much of the text was prepared by William D. Gorman, great-grandnephew of William Riley Seaboalt Jr.
26. "The Murder of William Riley Seaboalt."
27. Bearss, Law Enforcement at Fort Smith, 51.
28. Roger Harold Tuller, "Let No Guilty Man Escape": A Judicial Biography of Isaac C. Parker (Norman: University of Oklahoma Press, 2001), 55. According to the author, when Parker pronounced his sentence on Evans, the judge's "eyes were brimming with tears."
29. Kathy Weiser, "Hanging Judge Parker of Indian Territory," Legends of America.
30. "1875: Six in Fort Smith under Hanging Judge Parker," ExecutedToday.
31. "1875: Six in Fort Smith."
32. New York Times, September 4, 1875, 1.
33. Kenneth W. Hobbs Jr., "Jim Reed, Southwestern Outlaw and Husband of Belle Starr: A Study of the Watt Grayson and San Antonio Stage Robberies" (master's thesis, Texas Christian University, Fort Worth, 1975), 86–87.
34. Wallis, Wild West 365, 314.
35. Marie Bartlett, "Prince of Hangmen?" True West Magazine, May 2015. Some critics of hangman George Maledon contend that he propagated his own myth after his retirement when he toured country towns and cities with his treasured ropes and lectured about the lives and deaths of various outlaws he had hanged.
36. Wallis, Wild West 365.
37. Wallis, Wild West 365.
38. Bearss, Law Enforcement at Fort Smith, 65.
39. "1875: Six in Fort Smith."
40. Maranda Radcliff, "Isaac Charles Parker (1838–1895)," The Encyclopedia of Arkansas.
41. National Park Service Staff, Fort Smith Historic Site, comps., "Law Enforcement for Fort Smith 1851–1896," Fort Smith Historical Society Journal 3, no. 1 (1979): 3.
42. National Park Service Staff, "Law Enforcement for Fort Smith," 68.
43. National Park Service Staff, "Law Enforcement for Fort Smith."
44. Lawrence H. Larsen, American Historical Review 107, no. 2 (April 2002): 550; Adam Crepelle, "Shooting Down Oliphant Self-Defense as an Answer to Crime in Indian Country," Lewis & Clark Review 22, no. 4 (2018): 1800.
45. James C. Thomas, "The Judge," Tulsa Law Review 2, no. 2 (1965): 96.

46. Tom Correa, "Old West: Wyatt Earp—Was Wyatt a Horse Thief?," Net Posse.
47. Bearss, *Law Enforcement at Fort Smith*, 173–74.
48. Jim Hoy, "Cattle Industry," *The Encyclopedia of Oklahoma History and Culture*.
49. Bearss, *Law Enforcement at Fort Smith*, 173.
50. Glenn Shirley, *Belle Starr and Her Times: The Literature, the Facts, and the Legends* (Norman: University of Oklahoma Press, 1982), 156.
51. "Shields Family," Lone Star Genealogy. Nancy Harlan Starr (1779–1841) and Sarah Sally Harlan (1790–1837) were the daughters of Ellis Harlan, a White man, and Kati, the granddaughter of Nanyehi (Nancy Ward), who was known as Ghigau (Beloved Woman) and was a powerful political leader and diplomat of the Cherokee Nation.
52. Bearss, *Law Enforcement at Fort Smith*, 174.
53. Bearss, *Law Enforcement at Fort Smith*, 174–75.
54. "Cassius McDonald Barnes (1845–1925)," Geni.
55. US District Court for the Western Division of Arkansas, Fort Smith Division, National Archives and Records Administration, jacket number 170, 1.
56. Shirley, *Belle Starr and Her Times*, 152.
57. Shirley, *Belle Starr and Her Times*.
58. Shirley, *Belle Starr and Her Times*.
59. Bearss, *Law Enforcement at Fort Smith*.
60. Bearss, *Law Enforcement at Fort Smith*.
61. John Hallam, *Biographical and Pictorial History of Arkansas*, vol. 7 (Albany, NY: Weed, Parsons, 1887), 513–14.
62. Hallam, *Biographical and Pictorial History of Arkansas*, 514.
63. Amelia Martin, ed., "William Murphy Cravens," *Fort Smith Historical Society Journal* 27, no. 1 (April 2003): 9.
64. Martin, "William Murphy Cravens"; Joel Thomas Livingston, *A History of Jasper County, Missouri, and Its People*, vol. 1 (Chicago: Lewis, 1912), 21.
65. Livingston, *History of Jasper County, Missouri*, 23. Judge Jeremiah Cravens had been instrumental in the creation of School District No. 2, the first in Jasper County, and was one of the district's first directors; Martin, "William Murphy Cravens."
66. Ward L. Schrantz, *The Background of Belle Starr*, unpublished manuscript, n.d., 49. From the Phillip W. Steele Collection, courtesy of Charlotte Steele and Roy Young.
67. Schrantz, *Background of Belle Starr*.
68. Schrantz, *Background of Belle Starr*, 52.
69. Martin, "William Murphy Cravens."
70. Martin, "William Murphy Cravens."
71. Martin, "William Murphy Cravens," 9–10.
72. Martin, "William Murphy Cravens," 10.
73. Shirley, *Belle Starr and Her Times*, 153.
74. Criminal Case Procedure in Judge Parker's Court, National Park Service. As clerk of Judge Parker's court, Wheeler issued 18,877 writs for the arrest of persons charged with nearly every crime known.
75. Shirley, *Belle Starr and Her Times*, 153–58.
76. Shirley, *Belle Starr and Her Times*, 160.
77. Shirley, *Belle Starr and Her Times*.
78. Shirley, *Belle Starr and Her Times*.
79. Shirley, *Belle Starr and Her Times*, 160–61.
80. US District Court for the Western Division of Arkansas, jacket number 170.
81. *Fort Smith* (Arkansas) *New Era*, February 22, 1883, 1.
82. Fort Smith *New Era*, February 22, 1883.
83. Bearss, *Law Enforcement at Fort Smith*.
84. Bearss, *Law Enforcement at Fort Smith*, 176.

85. Shirley, *Belle Starr and Her Times*, 161.
86. Bearss, *Law Enforcement at Fort Smith*, 175–76.
87. *Fort Smith New Era*, February 22, 1883.
88. *Fort Smith New Era*.
89. Bearss, *Law Enforcement at Fort Smith*, 176.
90. Shirley, *Belle Starr and Her Times*, 163.
91. US District Court for the Western Division of Arkansas, Fort Smith Division, National Archives and Records Administration, WAR16, Common Law Record Books, 1855–1959, 170, 268–69.
92. Shirley, *Belle Starr and Her Times*, 165.
93. S. W. Harman, *Hell on the Border: He Hanged Eighty-Eight Men* (Lincoln: University of Nebraska Press, 1992), 582–84. Harman's book was originally published in 1898 by Phoenix Publishing Company in Fort Smith. As he also stated regarding other copies of Belle Starr's writings that he published, Harman noted that this letter was copied from the original. It is likely that Harman acquired the letter from Belle's daughter or another family member. Although Harman's book contains many inaccuracies and he, like so many other authors of his time, failed to properly cite sources, historian Glenn Shirley and other Belle Starr biographers considered the letter to be genuine.
94. Harman, *Hell on the Border*, 582–84.
95. Harman, *Hell on the Border*.
96. Victoria Stefani, "True Statements: Women's Narratives of the American Frontier Experience" (PhD diss., University of Arizona, 2000), 119–21.
97. "OrangeManor."
98. Jerry Akins, "Hangin' Times in Fort Smith," *Fort Smith Historical Society Journal* 27, no. 1 (April 2003): 15. Born in Germany, Dell emigrated to the United States in 1846 and settled in Fort Smith in 1859. In 1863, he launched the *New Era*, a weekly newspaper, and published it until his death in 1884.
99. Stefani, "True Statements."
100. *Fort Smith* (Arkansas) *Elevator*, March 23, 1883, 3.
101. *Vinita* (Indian Territory) *Indian Chieftain*, March 30, 1883, citing the *Independent*, Cox Collection. Twenty-one prisoners are listed by name in this article, including two women—Belle Starr and a Mrs. Pearson.
102. Shirley, *Belle Starr and Her Times*, 167.
103. Dianna Everett, "Cassius McDonald Barnes," *The Encyclopedia of Oklahoma History and Culture*.
104. "A Batch for the Pen," *St. Louis* (Missouri) *Post-Dispatch*, March 20, 1883, 6. Twenty-two prisoners are mentioned in this article, but only one woman—Belle Starr. It is not known why the tally does not agree with the number of prisoners listed in the *Vinita Indian Chieftain* article or what happened to Mrs. Pearson.
105. "The Detroit House of Correction: To the Editor of the Detroit Free Press," *Detroit* (Michigan) *Free Press*, March 20, 1883, 6.
106. Susan Marie Garneau, *Imprisoning Chicago: Incarceration, the Chicago City Council, Prisoners, and Reform, 1832–1915* (PhD diss., Loyola University Chicago, 2012), 97–98, footnote 38, citing Inspectors of the Detroit House of Correction, *First Annual Report of the Inspectors of the Detroit House of Correction*, Detroit, Michigan: Advertiser and Tribune Printing House, 1864, 4–5.
107. Frank Richard Prassel, *The Great American Outlaw: A Legacy of Fact and Fiction*, Chapter 11, "The Moll" (Norman: University of Oklahoma Press, 1993), 224–25.
108. Lawrence M. Friedman, *Crime and Punishment in American History*, Chapter 10, "Women and Criminal Justice to the End of the Nineteenth Century" (New York: BasicBooks, 1993), 233.
109. Paul W. Keve, "Building a Better Prison: The First Three Decades of the Detroit House of

Correction," *Michigan Historical Review* 25, no. 2 (Fall 1999): 17. In Keve's article, Belle Starr is the only inmate at Detroit House of Correction mentioned by name.
110. Silas Farmer, *History of Detroit and Wayne County and Early Michigan: A Chronological Cyclopedia of the Past and Present*, 3rd ed. (Detroit, MI: Silas Farmer & Co., published for Russell & Co., New York, 1890), cited in Detroit Historical Society, "Did You Know a Prison and a Cemetery Used To Stand on the Site of Eastern Market?"
111. Harman, *Hell on the Border*, 584.
112. Harman, *Hell on the Border*.
113. Keve, "Building a Better Prison," 18. Keve's footnote 45 contains some inaccuracies about the details of Belle Starr's death.
114. Belle Starr, Detroit House of Correction—Register of Prisoners, 1883, Burton Historical Collection, Detroit [Michigan] Public Library, typed transcription of original ledger record, 2019; Mark Bowden, coordinator of special collections, personal communication to Hazel Rowena Mills, January 18, 2019.
115. Samuel Starr, Detroit House of Correction—Register of Prisoners, 1883, Burton Historical Collection, Detroit [Michigan] Public Library, typed transcription of original ledger record, 2019; Mark Bowden, coordinator of special collections, personal communication to Hazel Rowena Mills, January 18, 2019.
116. Samuel Starr, Detroit House of Correction, Register of Prisoners, 1883.
117. "Moon Phase for Monday January 28, 1884, Nine Planets.
118. "Moon Phase."
119. David Wolfe, "Cherokee Moons," Telliquah.
120. Wolfe, "Cherokee Moons."

Chapter 21: Myth Versus Reality

1. Glenn Shirley, *Belle Starr and Her Times: The Literature, the Facts, and the Legends* (Norman: University of Oklahoma Press, 1982), 169.
2. Michael Wallis, *The Wild West 365* (New York: Abrams, 2011), 66. The term *Manifest Destiny* was first used by journalist John O'Sullivan in *New York Democracy* magazine in 1845.
3. Wallis, *Wild West 365*.
4. "The End of American Exceptionalism: Frontier Anxiety from the Old West to the New Deal," University Press of Kansas.
5. David M. Wrobel, "The Closing Gates of Democracy: Frontier Anxiety Before the Official End of the Frontier," *American Studies* 32, no. 1 (Spring 1991): 61.
6. David W. Teague, *The Southwest in American Literature and Art: The Rise of a Desert Aesthetic* (Tucson: University of Arizona Press, 1997), 60.
7. Wrobel, "The Closing Gates of Democracy," 62.
8. Wrobel, "Closing Gates of Democracy," 61.
9. Wrobel, "Closing Gates of Democracy."
10. "Fort Smith Streetcar History," Fort Smith Trolley Museum; "History Is Electric!" Exhibit, Tulsa Historical Society.
11. Shirley, *Belle Starr and Her Times*.
12. Shirley, *Belle Starr and Her Times*.
13. "The Legend of Belle Starr—Queen of the Oklahoma Outlaws," Ron and Sue Wall's Family History Site, Whitsett and Wall, modified November 23, 2017, 4.
14. Richard W. Etulain and Glenda Riley, eds., *With Badges & Bullets: Lawmen & Outlaws in the Old West* (Golden, CO: Fulcrum, 1999), 151.
15. Flossie [Florence Pearl Epple Hutton], "The Story of Flossie, Belle Starr's Granddaughter," Part II, *Dallas* (Texas) *Morning News*, Feature Section, May 7, 1933, 1. To conceal her iden-

tity, Pearl's daughter identified herself in this article only as Flossie, a nickname, instead of her birth name, adopted name, or married name.
16. Flossie, "Story of Flossie, Belle Starr's Granddaughter."
17. Edwin P. Hicks, *Belle Starr and Her Pearl* (Little Rock, AR: Pioneer, 1963), 114.
18. *Muskogee* (Indian Territory) *Phoenix*, August 13, 1891, 1.
19. Shirley, *Belle Starr and Her Times*, 173.
20. Shirley, *Belle Starr and Her Times*.
21. Burton Rascoe, *Belle Starr: "The Bandit Queen"* (Lincoln: University of Nebraska Press, 2004), 69.
22. Victoria Stefani, "True Statements: Women's Narratives of the American Frontier Experience" (PhD diss., University of Arizona, 2000), 156.
23. Shirley, *Belle Starr and Her Times*, 175.
24. *Muskogee* (Indian Territory) *Indian Journal*, May 28, 1885, 1.
25. *Muskogee Indian Journal*, May 28, 1885.
26. Rick Miller, *Bounty Hunter* (College Station, TX: Creative, 1988), 154.
27. "Outlaw John Middleton," Genealogy.com.
28. Miller, *Bounty Hunter*, 155.
29. Shirley, *Belle Starr and Her Times*, 177.
30. Miller, *Bounty Hunter*.
31. Miller, *Bounty Hunter*; Docket Book, District Court, Lamar County, Texas, Fall Term 1884, vol. 4, 244, 261 (*State of Texas v. John Middleton*, cause nos. 3397, 3398, and 3432).
32. Miller, *Bounty Hunter*, 156.
33. Miller, *Bounty Hunter*.
34. Miller, *Bounty Hunter*, 154. According to Lamar County, Texas, election records, Black prevailed with 2,927 votes to Crook's 1,859.
35. Miller, *Bounty Hunter*.
36. Miller, *Bounty Hunter*, 158–59.
37. Robert K. DeArment, *Man-Hunters of the Old West* (Norman: University of Oklahoma Press, 2017), 135–36.
38. John Wesley Hardin Collection, Southwestern Writers Collection, Texas State University, San Marcos; Miller, *Bounty Hunter*, 82–83.
39. Bob Alexander and Donaly E. Brice, *Texas Rangers: Lives, Legends, and Legacy* (Denton: University of North Texas Press, 2017), 311–12.
40. Kent Biffle, *A Month of Sundays* (Denton: University of North Texas Press, 1993), 114. On the evening of February 9, 1878, Duncan's favorite whore, Hattie Washburn, shot him with his own gun; *Dallas* (Texas) *Daily Times Herald*, March 24, 1880, 4.
41. DeArment, *Man-Hunters of the Old West*, 136.
42. *Fort Worth* (Texas) *Daily Gazette*, November 23, 1888, 5.
43. *Waco* (Texas) *Evening News*, November 29, 1888, 1.
44. DeArment, *Man-Hunters of the Old West*, 137.
45. Shirley, *Belle Starr and Her Times*, 178.
46. Shirley, *Belle Starr and Her Times*; "Killing of J. A. 'Polk' Burris, Lamar County, Texas, Genealogy Trails.
47. Shirley, *Belle Starr and Her Times*, 179–80.
48. Shirley, *Belle Starr and Her Times*. Glenn Shirley concluded that the purported Starr-Middleton robberies were pure "folklore."
49. DeArment, *Man-Hunters of the Old West*.
50. Case Records, United States District Court, Western District of Arkansas (*United States v. Sam Starr and Belle Starr*, 1882).
51. "Shields Family," Lone Star Genealogy; Indian-Pioneer History Project for Oklahoma, interview with Ellis West of Muskogee, Oklahoma, Interview 5177, no date given. Interviewer: Florence L. Phillips, OK Gen Web.

52. Richard Young and Judy Dockery Young, eds., *Outlaw Tales: Legends, Myths, and Folklore from America's Middle Border* (Little Rock, Arkansas: August House Publishers, Inc., 1992), 44.
53. Young and Young, *Outlaw Tales*.
54. "Richard Robert Middleton," Find a Grave, memorial 4077723.
55. Indian-Pioneer History Project for Oklahoma, interview with James Middleton of Briartown, Oklahoma, Interview 5657, May 10, 1937. Interviewer: James S. Buchanan; Shirley, 180. As Glenn Shirley later wrote about Jim Middleton, "With a brother like John, he was careful to keep legitimate and keep his mouth shut."
56. Shirley, *Belle Starr and Her Times*, 182.
57. Miller, *Bounty Hunter*, 170.
58. Shirley, *Belle Starr and Her Times*, 175.
59. Edwin P. Hicks, *Belle Starr and Her Pearl* (Little Rock, AR: Pioneer, 1963), 50. According to Hicks, Belle Starr had many friends in Arkansas and Indian Territory. Some of Jim Reed's relatives lived near Paris, Arkansas, and Belle had other friends or relatives at Conway and near Dardanelle, at Chickalah, and at Burnett Springs, a spa resort community southeast of Paris.
60. Shirley, *Belle Starr and Her Times*, 182.
61. Shirley, *Belle Starr and Her Times*.
62. Shirley, *Belle Starr and Her Times*.
63. S. W. Harman, *Hell on the Border: He Hanged Eighty-Eight Men* (Lincoln: University of Nebraska Press, 1992), 587.
64. Miller, *Bounty Hunter*, 171.
65. Shirley, *Belle Starr and Her Times*, 183.
66. Shirley, *Belle Starr and Her Times*; Harman, *Hell on the Border*. Harman erroneously inferred that the saddle Belle gave to Pearl was a sidesaddle "of peculiar make and was known to every one in that country as the 'Belle Starr' saddle." However, Middleton would not have ridden a sidesaddle but a standard western saddle.
67. *United States v. Belle Starr*, Case No. 1180, US District Court, Western District of Arkansas, Fort Smith. *Nooning* is a word meaning to rest or have a meal at midday.
68. Shirley, *Belle Starr and Her Times*.
69. Shirley, *Belle Starr and Her Times*, 185.
70. Eric Standridge, "Poteau River Flood: A Tale of Wister, Oklahoma," June 18, 2019, Discover.
71. *Fort Smith* (Arkansas) *Elevator*, May 15, 1885, 3.
72. *Fort Smith Elevator*, May 15, 1885.
73. *Fort Smith Elevator*, May 15, 1885.
74. *Fort Smith Elevator*, May 15, 1885. O. D. Weldon also was a correspondent for the *New York Herald*, *Chicago Times*, and *Fort Worth Gazette*, and he occasionally wrote for several other newspapers.
75. *Arkansas Gazette*, May 15, 1885, 1.
76. *Fort Smith* (Arkansas) *Elevator*, May 22, 1885, 3.
77. *Fort Smith Elevator*, May 22, 1885.
78. *Fort Smith Elevator*, May 22, 1885.
79. *Fort Smith Elevator*, May 22, 1885.
80. *Fort Smith Elevator*, May 22, 1885.
81. Cleveland Ferguson III, "Yellow Journalism," *Media*.
82. James L. Baughman, "The Fall and Rise of Partisan Journalism."
83. *Fort Smith Elevator*, May 22, 1885.
84. Harman, *Hell on the Border*, 582–90.
85. Miller, *Bounty Hunter*, 171.
86. *Fort Smith Elevator*, May 22, 1885.
87. *Arkansas Gazette*, May 23, 1885, 1. The newspaper incorrectly placed Wealaka in the Cherokee Nation; Jason Baird Jackson, "Yuchis in Alabama," *Encyclopedia of Alabama*.

88. *Arkansas Gazette*, May 23, 1885.
89. Indian-Pioneer History Project for Oklahoma, interview with J. R. Lewis of Tulsa, Oklahoma, Interview 7653, September 24, 1937. Interviewer: Effie S. Jackson. Beyond his work as a lawyer, S. R. Lewis was considered an authority on Cherokee history. He claimed that he saw Belle only once, in 1887, when he was a boy, and "was impressed with her striking appearance."
90. Muskogee (Indian Territory) *Indian Journal*, May 28, 1885, 5.
91. *Muskogee Indian Journal*, May 28, 1885.
92. Shirley, *Belle Starr and Her Times*, 183.
93. *Muskogee Indian Journal*, May 28, 1885.
94. Miller, *Bounty Hunter*, 174.
95. Miller, *Bounty Hunter*.
96. Case Records, United States District Court, Western District of Arkansas (*United States v. Frank Cook*, cause no. 764, 1885).
97. Miller, *Bounty Hunter*; Luther B. Hill, A *History of the State of Oklahoma*, vol. 1 (Chicago: Lewis, 1908), 15; Case Records, United States District Court, Western District of Arkansas (*United States v. Frank Cook*, cause no. 1497, 1886). After serving most of his sentence at Detroit, Cook was released but was arrested on a charge of horse theft dating to May 1885. He was found guilty on August 21, 1886, and received another one-year sentence, at Southern Illinois Penitentiary at Menard.
98. Fort Smith (Indian Territory) *Elevator*, June 19, 1885, 2.
99. *Muskogee Indian Journal*, May 28, 1885; Richard J. "Rick" Miller, correspondence with author, August 7, 2020. Miller documented Duncan's colorful life in *Bounty Hunter*, published in 1988.

Chapter 22: The Legend Grows

1. Glenn Shirley, *Belle Starr and Her Times: The Literature, the Facts, and the Legends* (Norman: University of Oklahoma Press, 1982), 186.
2. Shirley, *Belle Starr and Her Times*.
3. Shirley, *Belle Starr and Her Times*.
4. *United States v. Sam Starr, Felix Griffin and Richard Hays*, Case No. 59, November 9, 1885, US Commissioner's Court, Western District of Arkansas, Fort Smith.
5. *Fort Smith* (Arkansas) *Elevator*, January 1, 1886, 2; National Penitentiary, Historic American Buildings Survey (Library of Congress Cherokee). Prior to construction of the tribal prison in 1874, the Cherokee Nation punished criminals in one of three ways: fines, flogging, or hanging. Persons in custody for trial were kept in private homes, and residents were paid a fee for room and board.
6. Shirley, *Belle Starr and Her Times*, 187.
7. *Fort Smith* (Arkansas) *Elevator*, January 1, 1886, 2.
8. *Fort Smith Elevator*, January 1, 1886.
9. Fayette Barnett and Belle Starr, Larceny 1885, National Archives at Fort Worth, Defendant Jacket Files for US District Court Western Division of Arkansas, Fort Smith Division 1866–1900, NAID 203713, jacket number 14.
10. Fayette Barnett and Belle Starr, Larceny 1885, National Archives at Fort Worth, NAID 203713.
11. Art T. Burton, "Lawman Legend Bass Reeves: The Invincible Man Hunter," History Net.
12. Burton, "Lawman Legend Bass Reeves."
13. Arkansas Digital Archives, *U.S. v. Bass Reeves*, Item 13_04_017, United States Western District Court of Arkansas records, Arkansas State Archives, Little Rock.

14. Burton, "Lawman Legend Bass Reeves."
15. Burton, "Lawman Legend Bass Reeves."
16. Burton, "Lawman Legend Bass Reeves."
17. Burton, "Lawman Legend Bass Reeves."
18. *Fort Worth* (Texas) *Gazette*, February 17, 1886, 3.
19. Shirley, *Belle Starr and Her Times*, 188; *United States v. Belle Starr*, Case No. 1180, US Western District Court, Western District of Arkansas, Fort Smith.
20. *Fayetteville* (Arkansas) *Weekly Democrat*, February 18, 1886, 4.
21. *Fayetteville Weekly Democrat*, February 18, 1886.
22. *Fayetteville Weekly Democrat*, February 18, 1886.
23. Shirley, *Belle Starr and Her Times*, 190.
24. Shirley, *Belle Starr and Her Times*; *United States v. Samuel Starr* et al., Case No. 1213, US Western District, Western District of Arkansas, Fort Smith.
25. *Fort Smith* (Arkansas) *Elevator*, March 12, 1886, 13.
26. *Fort Smith Elevator*, March 12, 1886.
27. *Fort Smith Elevator*, March 12, 1886.
28. *Muskogee* (Indian Territory) *Indian Journal*, March 11, 1886, 3.
29. Frederick S. Barde, "The Story of Belle Starr," *Sturm's Oklahoma Magazine* 11, no. 1 (September 1910): 20.
30. Shirley, *Belle Starr and Her Times*, 192.
31. Weston Arthur Goodspeed, ed., *The Province and the States*, vol. 7 (Madison, WI: Western Historical Association, 1904), 302–3.
32. Dorothy M. Roberson, ed., "The Duel Across the Mississippi," *Tennessee Genealogical Magazine* 45, no. 1 (Spring 1998): 29–33.
33. University of Arkansas Libraries, Special Collections Department/ MS Un33r 430, US District Court, Arkansas, Western District Records/Records Pertaining to Criminal Cases/Complaints. Defendant(s): Starr, Belle and two others [unknown]; Charge Larceny; Complaint: S. Fay; US Commissioner: James Brizzolara: March 10, 1886.
34. Shirley, *Belle Starr and Her Times*.
35. "A Deputy Marshal Assassinated," *New York Times*, April 16, 1886, 3.
36. "Oklahoma Law Enforcement Memorial."
37. Shirley, *Belle Starr and Her Times*.
38. Shirley, *Belle Starr and Her Times*.
39. Shirley, *Belle Starr and Her Times*.
40. Shirley, *Belle Starr and Her Times*, 194.
41. "A Wild Western Amazon," *National Police Gazette*, May 22, 1886, 16, Library of Congress Prints and Photographs Division, Washington, DC, digital ID cph3b11522//hdf.loc.gov/loc.pnp/cph.3b11522.
42. "A Wild Western Amazon," *National Police Gazette*, May 22, 1886.
43. Brett McKay and Kate McKay, "America's First Popular Men's Magazine: The *National Police Gazette*," Art of Manliness, April 30, 2013, updated November 26, 2017.
44. McKay and McKay, "America's First Popular Men's Magazine."
45. McKay and McKay, "America's First Popular Men's Magazine."
46. Belle Starr, Fort Smith, Arkansas, 1886, original photograph by Roeder Brothers of Fort Smith, Fort Smith National Historic Park, National Park Service.
47. *Muskogee* (Indian Territory) *Indian Journal*, June 3, 1886, 1.
48. *Muskogee Indian Journal*, June 3, 1886.
49. Mrs. Leister E. Presley and the Goodspeed Brothers, *History of Benton, Washington, Carroll, Madison, Crawford, Franklin & Sebastian Counties, Arkansas* (Chicago: Goodspeed, 1889), 1175.
50. "Bluford Duck (1859–1895)," WikiTree.
51. "Bluford Duck (1859–1895)."

52. "Bluford Duck (1859–1895)."
53. "Bluford Duck (1859–1895)."
54. *United States v. Blue Duck and William Christie*, Case No. 1089, United States District Court, Western District of Arkansas, Fort Smith.
55. Shirley, *Belle Starr and Her Times*, 195.
56. Blue Duck and Belle Starr cabinet card, May 23, 1886, Roeder Brothers, Fort Smith, courtesy Frederick S. Barde Collection (4631), Oklahoma Historical Society.
57. *The Public Papers of Grover Cleveland, Twenty-Second President of the United States* (Washington, D.C.: United States Government Printing Office, 1889), 521; Edwin C. Bearss, *Law Enforcement at Fort Smith, 1871–1896*, United States National Park Service Library, Denver, Colorado, January 1964, 232–33.
58. Jerry Akins, *Hangin' Times in Fort Smith: A History of Executions in Judge Parker's Court* (Fayetteville: University of Arkansas Press, 2012), 122. Blue Duck died on May 7, 1895, and was buried in Dick Duck Cemetery near Catoosa, Cherokee Nation, Indian Territory. Some sources question the May 7 date of death.
59. Harry Sinclair Drago, *Outlaws on Horseback* (Lincoln: University of Nebraska Press, 1998), 149. Reprinted from the original 1964 edition by Dodd, Mead, New York.
60. Drago, *Outlaws on Horseback*, xxv.
61. A Map of Kansas Literature, Washburn University, Topeka, Kansas.
62. Paul I. Wellman, *A Dynasty of Western Outlaws* (New York: Bonanza, 1961), 146.
63. Alicja Zelazko, ed., "Did Catherine the Great Have Unusual Sexual Proclivities?," Britannica Beyond.
64. Bearss, *Law Enforcement at Fort Smith*, 212. Historian Edwin Bearss incorrectly wrote that Belle Starr was "Blue Duck's current paramour" at the time of his murder trial; Bill Black, "Belle Starr: A Black Widow?," National Park Service; *Cherokee Advocate*, Tahlequah, Indian Territory, February 6, 1895, 1. A mixed-blood Cherokee, Jim French was a known killer, horse thief, train robber, and whiskey peddler who died in a gunfight on February 5, 1895, at age twenty-two. In 1886, French would have been fourteen years old.
65. *Fort Smith* (Arkansas) *Weekly Elevator*, May 28, 1886, 3.
66. Shirley, *Belle Starr and Her Times*, 198.
67. Amelia Martin, ed., "Fort Smith Press," *The Fort Smith Historical Society Journal* 13, no. 2 (September 1889): 14–25. The article contains biographical information on J. Frank Weaver, O. D. Weldon, and A. A Powe; Shirley, 201. Glenn Shirley writes that the correspondent "may have been" Powe, who in 1898 became editor of the *Fort Smith* (Arkansas) *Evening Call*.
68. *Fort Smith* (Arkansas) *Weekly Elevator*, February 15, 1889, 3.
69. *Dallas* (Texas) *Morning News*, June 7, 1886, 4.
70. *Dallas Morning News*, June 7, 1886.
71. *Dallas Morning News*, June 7, 1886.
72. *Dallas Morning News*, June 7, 1886.
73. Shirley, *Belle Starr and Her Times*, 198.
74. *Dallas Morning News*, June 7, 1886.
75. Shirley, *Belle Starr and Her Times*, 201.
76. Shirley, *Belle Starr and Her Times*.
77. Shirley, *Belle Starr and Her Times*, 202.
78. Shirley, *Belle Starr and Her Times*.
79. *Muskogee* (Indian Territory) *Indian Journal*, June 24, 1886, 3.
80. *Vinita* (Indian Territory) *Indian Chieftain*, July 8, 1886, 1.
81. *Arkansas Democrat*, July 8, 1886, 8.
82. *Arkansas Democrat*, July 8, 1886.
83. Shirley, *Belle Starr and Her Times*, 204.
84. *Arkansas Gazette*, September 20, 1886, 1.

85. *Arkansas Gazette*, September 20, 1886.
86. *Arkansas Gazette*, September 20, 1886.
87. *Arkansas Gazette*, September 20, 1886.
88. Shirley, *Belle Starr and Her Times*, 207.
89. Grant Foreman, "Reminiscences of Mr. R. P. Vann, East of Webbers Falls, Oklahoma, September 28, 1932," *Chronicles of Oklahoma* 11, no. 2 (June 1933): 842.
90. *United States v. Belle Starr*, Case No. 1180.
91. *United States v. Belle Starr*, Case No. 1180.
92. Shirley, *Belle Starr and Her Times*, 206.
93. Shirley, *Belle Starr and Her Times*, 207.
94. Shirley, *Belle Starr and Her Times*, 208.
95. Shirley, *Belle Starr and Her Times*.
96. Shirley, *Belle Starr and Her Times*.
97. *United States v. Samuel Starr* et al., Case No. 1213.
98. *United States v. Samuel Starr* et al., Case No. 1213.
99. *United States v. Samuel Starr* et al., Case No. 1213.
100. *Daily Arkansas Gazette*, October 12, 1885, 2.
101. Paula Bosse, "When the Circus Came to Town—1886," *Dallas* (Texas) *Herald*; Harold Calvin Tedford, "A Study of Theatrical Entertainments in Northwest Arkansas from Their Beginning through 1889" (PhD diss., Louisiana State University Historical Dissertations and Theses No. 1094, 1965), 150–53, 190, DOI 10.31390/gradschool_disstheses.1094.
102. "Sideshow Banner vs. Reality," Show History.
103. *Arkansas Democrat*, October 16, 1886, 2; "Isaac W. Sprague—The Original Living Skeleton," The Human Marvels. The "living skeleton" became a popular sideshow attraction. It was not uncommon, in a feat of inspired promotion, for a sideshow "skeleton man" to marry the local "fat lady" in an extravagant ceremony.
104. Bosse, "When the Circus Came to Town—1886."
105. Joseph G. Rosa and Robin May, *Buffalo Bill and His Wild West* (Lawrence: University Press of Kansas, 1989), 73.
106. Rosa and May, *Buffalo Bill and His Wild West*, 67–68.
107. Bosse, "When the Circus Came to Town—1886."
108. Shirley, *Belle Starr and Her Times*, 209.
109. Shirley, *Belle Starr and Her Times*.
110. *Daily Arkansas Gazette*, October 12, 1886, 2.
111. Marvin VanGilder, "Belle and Hometown Band Entertained Each Other," *Carthage* (Missouri) *Press*, August 7, 2002, 4. VanGilder, often referred to as "the keeper of Carthage history," summarized the news coverage of the 1886 Fort Smith fair in this feature story.
112. VanGilder, "Belle and Hometown Band Entertained Each Other."
113. VanGilder, "Belle and Hometown Band Entertained Each Other."
114. VanGilder, "Belle and Hometown Band Entertained Each Other."
115. *Daily Arkansas Gazette*, October 16, 1886, 2.
116. VanGilder, "Belle and Hometown Band Entertained Each Other," *Carthage Press*, August 7, 2002.
117. VanGilder, "Belle and Hometown Band Entertained Each Other"; S. W. Harman, *Hell on the Border* (Lincoln: University of Nebraska Press, 1992), 593–94.
118. Shirley, *Belle Starr and Her Times*, 210.
119. *United States v. Samuel Starr* et al., Case No. 1213.
120. *Fort Smith* (Arkansas) *Elevator*, November 19, 1886, 2.
121. Robert Barr Smith, *Outlaw Tales of Oklahoma* (Lanham, MD: Rowman & Littlefield Publishing Group, 2013), 103.
122. Smith, *Outlaw Tales of Oklahoma*.

123. *United States v. Thomas Starr,* Case No. 1670 R.L.D. [retail liquor distribution], U.S. District Court, Western District of Arkansas, Fort Smith.
124. Fort Smith Sentence Books, Thomas Starr, Indictment Charge 1670 R.L.D. [retail liquor distribution], Date Incarceration 11/23/1886, Menard, Illinois.
125. Shirley, *Belle Starr and Her Times,* 213.
126. Shirley, *Belle Starr and Her Times.*
127. Shirley, *Belle Starr and Her Times,* 214.
128. *Muskogee* (Indian Territory) *Indian Journal,* December 22, 1886, 1; *Fort Smith* (Arkansas) *Weekly Elevator,* December 24, 1886, 1.
129. Ted Byron Hall, *Oklahoma, Indian Territory* (Fort Worth, Texas: American Reference Publications, 1971), 24.
130. Shirley, *Belle Starr and Her Times*; *Fort Smith* (Arkansas) *Weekly Elevator,* December 24, 1886.

Chapter 23: The Curtain Falls

1. Cherokee Intermarriage Cases, United States Supreme Court, November 15, 1906.
2. Glenn Shirley, *Belle Starr and Her Times: The Literature, the Facts, and the Legends* (Norman: University of Oklahoma Press, 1982), 218.
3. *Muskogee* (Indian Territory) *Journal,* January 30, 1890, 8.
4. Shirley, *Belle Starr and Her Times.*
5. *Rolla* (Missouri) *Herald,* February 14, 1889, 2.
6. Shirley, *Belle Starr and Her Times.*
7. Richard W. Etulain and Glenda Riley, eds., *With Badges & Bullets: Lawmen & Outlaws in the Old West* (Golden, CO: Fulcrum Publishing, 1999), 154.
8. Etulain and Riley, *With Badges & Bullets.*
9. Shirley, *Belle Starr and Her Times,* 220.
10. Oliver Ray Titchenal, *The Titchenal Cherokee Connection,* edited by Titchenal family members, Titchenal. James and Rebecca McClure are listed in the Eastern Cherokee records in 1840, 1851, and 1869. Both are listed in Indian Territory in 1880. Rebecca died in 1882. Only James is listed in the 1890 record with a second wife, Martha. James died in 1897 and was buried in McClure Cemetery.
11. Titchenal, *Titchenal Cherokee Connection.*
12. Phillip W. Steele, *Starr Tracks: Belle and Pearl Starr* (Gretna, LA: Pelican, 1889), 62.
13. Shirley, *Belle Starr and Her Times.* Note: Instead of Belle sending Pearl to friends in Arkansas, Phillip Steele wrote that Pearl "went to her grandmother Reed's home near Rich Hill, Missouri."
14. Shirley, *Belle Starr and Her Times.*
15. Shirley, *Belle Starr and Her Times,* 221.
16. Shirley, *Belle Starr and Her Times,* 222.
17. Kelly Lanko, "Un-Romanticizing the American West: White Frontier Women's Daily Lives, 1860–1900," Scholar Works. In post–Civil War America, stronger antiabortion laws were passed and vigorously enforced. Many people used illegal underground abortion services. Other remedies were also available, including strong purgatives and various douches to bring on an abortion.
18. Steele, *Starr Tracks,* 61–62.
19. Shirley, *Belle Starr and Her Times.*
20. Francis Marion Reed, [S4351] 1850 Federal Census, Bates County, Missouri, Microfilm Image, NARA Series M432, Roll 392.
21. Reed, [S4351] 1850 Federal Census.
22. "Siloam Springs, Arkansas—Historic Sites and Points of Interest," Explore Southern History.

23. "Healing Waters," Shiloh Museum of Ozark History, Springdale, Arkansas.
24. "Siloam Springs, Arkansas," Siloam Springs, Arkansas.
25. "Main Street Siloam Springs," Main Street Siloam Springs, Arkansas. The Crown Hotel, formerly the Lakeside Hotel, remains in operation and was listed on the National Register of Historic Places in 1979.
26. "Healing Waters," Shiloh Museum of Ozark History, Springdale, Arkansas.
27. Steele, *Starr Tracks*, 63.
28. H. A. Hazen, "The Most Destructive Tornadoes Since 1872," *Science* 16, no. 390 (July 25, 1890): 45.
29. Steele, *Starr Tracks*.
30. Flossie [Florence Pearl Epple Hutton], *Dallas* (Texas) *Morning News*, May 7, 1933, Feature Section, 1–2.
31. Shirley, *Belle Starr and Her Times*, 223.
32. *United States v. Bill July alias Jim Starr*, Case No. 103, August 30, 1887, US Commissioner's Court, Western District of Arkansas, Fort Smith.
33. *Bill July alias Jim Starr.*
34. *Bill July alias Jim Starr.*
35. *Bill July alias Jim Starr.*
36. Kenny L. Brown, "Robert Latham Owen," *Encyclopedia of Oklahoma History and Culture*.
37. *Muskogee* (Indian Territory) *Indian Journal*, July 28, 1887, 4.
38. Brown, "Robert Latham Owen."
39. *Bill July alias Jim Starr,* Case No. 103.
40. Shirley, *Belle Starr and Her Times*, 15.
41. Frederick S. Barde, "The Story of Belle Starr," *Sturm's Oklahoma Magazine* 11, no. 1 (1910): 19–20.
42. Barde, "The Story of Belle Starr."
43. Shirley, *Belle Starr and Her Times*, 224.
44. *United States v. Ed Reed (larceny)*, Case No. 3015, July 21, 1888, United States Commissioner's Court, Western District of Arkansas, Fort Smith. James Lewis was known as "Gentleman Jim."
45. *Reed*, Case No. 3015, July 21, 1888.
46. *Reed*, Case No. 3015, July 21, 1888.
47. Larry Yadon, "The Mystery of Edwin Reed, Life among the Starrs," *Oklahombres: The Journal of Lawman and Outlaw History of Oklahoma* 12, no. 3 (Spring 2011): 12.
48. Shirley, *Belle Starr and Her Times*, 225–26.
49. Shirley, *Belle Starr and Her Times*.
50. *Fort Smith* (Arkansas) *Elevator*, August 10, 1888, 1.
51. Yadon, "Mystery of Edwin Reed."
52. *Fort Smith Elevator*, August 10, 1888.
53. Shirley, *Belle Starr and Her Times*, 227.
54. Shirley, *Belle Starr and Her Times*.
55. Mary Jane Warde, "Indian International Fair," *The Encyclopedia of Oklahoma History and Culture*.
56. *Vinita* (Indian Territory) *Indian Chieftain*, October 4, 1888, 2.
57. *Vinita Indian Chieftain*, October 4, 1888.
58. Shirley, *Belle Starr and Her Times*.
59. *United States v. Ed Reed*, Case No. —, October 13 and 25, 1888, US Commissioner's Court, Western District of Arkansas, Fort Smith; *Reed*, Case No. 3015.
60. *Ed Reed*, October 13 and 25, 1888.
61. *Ed Reed*, October 13 and 25, 1888.
62. Shirley, *Belle Starr and Her Times*, 226–27.

63. Shirley, *Belle Starr and Her Times*, 228.
64. Flossie, *Dallas Morning News*, May 7, 1933.
65. Steele, *Starr Tracks*, 92.
66. Steele, *Starr Tracks*.
67. Donald L. Boyd, "Land of the Buckeye."
68. "Wichita Children's Home," End Slavery Now.
69. S. W. Harman, *Hell on the Border: He Hanged Eighty-Eight Men* (Fort Smith, AR: Phoenix. 1898), 605–6.
70. Shirley, *Belle Starr and Her Times*, 229.
71. *Dallas* (Texas) *Morning News*, December 13, 1888, 5.
72. *Arkansas Democrat*, December 13, 1888, 6.
73. *Arkansas Democrat*, December 13, 1888.
74. From the collection of Will Naillion, Challis, Idaho. Attached to the boots are the original repair card and work order, "Keller Dry Goods & Boot Repair of Canadian I. T., January 29, 1889 for Half Soles & Heel Job."
75. Shirley, *Belle Starr and Her Times*, 233.
76. Barde, "The Story of Belle Starr," 22–23.
77. Shirley, *Belle Starr and Her Times*, 234.
78. Shirley, *Belle Starr and Her Times*.

Chapter 24: Who Killed Belle Starr?

1. "Milo 'Frog' Ard Hoyt," My Cherokee Family.
2. *United States v. Edgar A. Watson*, Case No. —, February 22–23, 1889. US Commissioner's Court, Western District of Arkansas, Fort Smith; Criminal Defendant File for Edgar A. Watson, Defendant Jacket Files for U.S. District Court, Western Division of Arkansas, Fort Smith, ARC ID 201532 Murder jacket number: 197. National Archives, Fort Worth, Texas.
3. *Watson*, February 22–23, 1889.
4. *Watson*, February 22–23, 1889.
5. *Watson*, February 22–23, 1889.
6. *Fort Smith* (Arkansas) *Weekly Elevator*, February 4, 1889, 1.
7. *Fort Smith Weekly Elevator*, February 4, 1889.
8. Correspondence from Jack Wallace, Redlands, California, to Phillip Steele, June 5, 1988. Phillip W. Steele Collection, courtesy of Charlotte Steele and Roy Young.
9. Jack Wallace to Phillip Steele, June 5, 1988.
10. *Watson*, February 22–23, 1889.
11. *Tahlequah* (Indian Territory) *Telephone*, March 1, 1889, 1.
12. Jenna Hunnef, "The Cereal Politics of Belle Starr's Outlaw Reputation," *Food and Feast in Modern Outlaw Tales*, edited by Alexander L. Kaufman and Penny Vlagopoulos (New York: Routledge, 2019), 90–91. Some accounts of Belle Starr's burial contend that mourners dropped small pieces of cornbread into the casket.
13. *Tahlequah Telephone*, March 1, 1889.
14. Glenn Shirley, *Belle Starr and Her Times: The Literature, the Facts, and the Legends* (Norman: University of Oklahoma Press, 1982), 241.
15. Shirley, *Belle Starr and Her Times*.
16. Shirley, *Belle Starr and Her Times*.
17. Shirley, *Belle Starr and Her Times*, 231–32.
18. "Edgar J. Watson (1855–1910)," WikiTree.
19. Savannah Oglesby, "The Story of Edgar J. Watson: The Infamous Businessman & Serial Killer," *Coastal Sun Breeze News*, Marco Island, Florida, December 17, 2020.
20. "Ann Mary Watson," Geni.

21. "Jane S. (Dyall) Watson," WikiTree.
22. Oglesby, "Story of Edgar J. Watson."
23. Shirley, *Belle Starr and Her Times*, 241.
24. *Watson*, February 22–23, 1889.
25. *Watson, Fort Worth Gazette*, February 9, 1889.
26. *Van Buren* (Arkansas) *Press*, February 16, 1889, 1.
27. Shirley, *Belle Starr and Her Times*, 232.
28. Shirley, *Belle Starr and Her Times*.
29. Shirley, *Belle Starr and Her Times*.
30. *Fort Worth* (Texas) *Gazette*, February 9, 1889, 4.
31. *Fort Worth Gazette*, February 9, 1889.
32. *Fort Worth Gazette*, February 9, 1889.
33. *Watson, Fort Worth Gazette*, February 9, 1889.
34. *Watson*, February 22–23, 1889.
35. *Watson*, February 22–23, 1889.
36. Norita Shepherd Moss, "Edgar A. Watson," Lee County Florida Family Records, Genealogy Trails.
37. Moss, "Edgar A. Watson."
38. *Watson*, February 22–23, 1889.
39. *Watson*, February 22–23, 1889.
40. *Watson*, February 22–23, 1889.
41. *Watson*, February 22–23, 1889.
42. *Watson*, February 22–23, 1889.
43. *Watson*, February 22–23, 1889.
44. *Fort Smith* (Arkansas) Weekly *Elevator*, March 1, 1889, 3.
45. *Watson*, February 22–23, 1889.
46. Thomas Neil Knowles, "The Everglades' Bandit Killer," *Florida Keys Sea Heritage Journal* 17, no. 4, (Summer 2007): 4, 6.
47. Oglesby, "Story of Edgar J. Watson."
48. Oglesby, "Story of Edgar J. Watson."
49. Oglesby, "Story of Edgar J. Watson."
50. Oglesby, "Story of Edgar J. Watson."
51. "Edna Catherine (Bethea) Burkett (1888–1975)," WikiTree. Edna Catherine Bethea married Edgar Watson on June 20, 1905. The year after his death in 1910, she wed Mortimer Burkett. She died February 20, 1975, in Polk County, Florida.
52. Knowles, "Everglades' Bandit Killer."
53. "The Lessons of Edgar Watson," Free Library.
54. Oglesby, "Story of Edgar J. Watson."
55. David Farris, "The Death of Belle Starr," *Edmond* (Oklahoma) *Life & Leisure*, December 25, 2014.
56. Leroy Towns, ed., *Midway*, Sunday magazine of the *Topeka* (Kansas) *Capitol-Journal*, August 2, 1970, 3–4.
57. Towns, *Midway*.
58. Shirley, *Belle Starr and Her Times*, 252.
59. Shirley, *Belle Starr and Her Times*, 249–50.
60. Shirley, *Belle Starr and Her Times*, 250.
61. Nancy B. Samuelson, "The Murder of Belle Starr and the Murder of Deputy U.S. Marshal William Erwin," *Quarterly of the National Association for Outlaw and Lawmen History, Inc.* 23, no. 1 (January–March 1999): 1.
62. Shirley, *Belle Starr and Her Times*, 246; "Death of a Once Noted Indian Outlaw," *Van Buren* (Arkansas) *Press*, October 25, 1889, 3.
63. Richard Young and Judy Dockery Young, "Belle and the Stuff of Legends," *Outlaw Tales*:

Legends, Myths, and Folklore from America's Middle Border (Little Rock, AR: August House, 1992), 44.
64. Indian-Pioneer History Project for Oklahoma, interview with James Middleton of Briartown, Oklahoma, Interview 5657, May 10, 1937. Interviewer: James S. Buchanan.
65. Jenna Hunnef, "Dangerously Free: Outlaws and Nation-Making in Literature of the Indian Territory" (PhD diss., University of Toronto, 2016), 70.
66. Ron Hansen, "Larger Than Life, Deader Than Dead," *New York Times Book Review*, June 24, 1990, Section 7, 7, review of Peter Matthiessen, *Killing Mister Watson* (New York: Random House, 1990).

Epilogue: **Print the Legend**

1. David Richard Maher, "Vice in the Veil of Justice: Embedding Race and Gender in Frontier Tourism" (PhD diss., University of Arkansas–Fayetteville, 2013), *Graduate Theses and Dissertations*, 168.
2. *New York Times,* February 6, 1889, 1.
3. *New York Times,* February 6, 1889.
4. *New York Sun,* February 6, 1889, 1.
5. "A Wild Western Amazon," *National Police Gazette,* May 12, 1886, 16.
6. "A Coward Got the Drop on Her," *National Police Gazette,* February 23, 1889,
7. "A Coward Got the Drop on Her," *National Police Gazette.*
8. Glenn Shirley, *Belle Starr and Her Times: The Literature, the Facts, and the Legends* (Norman: University of Oklahoma Press, 1982), 4.
9. Maher, "Vice in the Veil of Justice," 168.
10. Burton Rascoe, *Belle Starr: "The Bandit Queen"* (New York: Random House, 1941), 13–14.
11. Shirley *Belle Starr and Her Times,* 5.
12. *Dallas* (Texas) *Morning News,* June 7, 1886, 4.
13. Shirley, *Belle Starr and Her Times,* 198.
14. *Dallas* (Texas) *Morning News,* February 19, 1889, 3.
15. *Dallas Morning News,* February 19, 1889.
16. *Saint Joseph* (Missouri) *Weekly Herald,* February 21, 1889, 5.
17. *Daily Arkansas Gazette,* February 20, 1889, 4.
18. Shirley, *Belle Starr and Her Times,* 6.
19. Shirley, *Belle Starr and Her Times.*
20. Richard Fox, publisher, *Bella Starr or The Bandit Queen, or the Female Jesse James: A Full and Authentic History of the Dashing Female Highwayman* (New York: National Police Gazette, 1889). Note: Author access to rare first-edition copy from the Robert G. McCubbin Collection.
21. Fox, *Bella Starr,* 1.
22. Fox, *Bella Starr,* 7.
23. Fox, *Bella Starr.*
24. H. F. O'Beirne, *Leaders and Leading Men of Indian Territory,* vol. 1, *Choctaws and Chickasaws: With a Brief History of Each Tribe: Its Laws, Customs, Superstitions and Religious Beliefs* (Chicago: American Publishers' Association, 1892), 193.
25. *New York Times,* January 30, 2000, 4; "The Man Who Shot Liberty Valance," Britannica.
26. Cherokee National Records, Verbal Will of Belle Starr, Court Records of Canadian District: October 24, 1876–December 27, 1897, vol. 2, 15.
27. Shirley, *Belle Starr and Her Times,* 221.
28. Cherokee National Records, Verbal Will of Belle Starr.
29. *Dallas* (Texas) *Morning News,* August 22, 1889, 1.

30. Sarah C. Thomas, "Rogers County," *The Encyclopedia of Oklahoma History and Culture*. The county was officially founded prior to statehood in 1907 and was originally named Cooweescoowee (after the Cherokee district that had covered the new county and other areas). Residents protested the name, and the county was renamed Rogers after Clement (Clem) Vann Rogers, a mixed-heritage Cherokee rancher and the father of Will Rogers.
31. *Dallas Morning News*, August 22, 1889.
32. Dan Anderson and Larry Yadon, *100 Oklahoma Outlaws, Gangsters, and Lawmen, 1839–1939* (Gretna, LA: Pelican, 2007), 94–95.
33. Anderson and Yadon, *100 Oklahoma Outlaws, Gangsters, and Lawmen*, 287.
34. Devon A. Mihesuah, *Ned Christie: The Creation of an Outlaw and Cherokee Hero* (Norman: University of Oklahoma Press, 2018), 3–4.
35. *Daily Arkansas Gazette*, January 28, 1890, 1.
36. *Edmond* (Oklahoma Territory) *Sun*, January 30, 1890, 8.
37. *Indian Journal* (Muskogee, Indian Territory), January 30, 1890, 8.
38. *Fort Smith* (Arkansas) *Elevator*, January 24, 1890, 3.
39. *St. Louis* (Missouri) *Post-Dispatch*, February 28, 1890, 2.
40. *St. Louis Post-Dispatch*, February 28, 1890.
41. *Western Herald*, Girard, Kansas, June 24, 1880, 3; *Junction City* (Kansas) *Weekly Union*, May 8, 1880, 5; *Wichita* (Kansas) *Daily Evening Resident*, August 26, 1886, 4; "The Younger Boys," *Daily Commonwealth*, Topeka, Kansas, August 2, 1880, 3.
42. "The Younger Boys," *Daily Commonwealth*, Topeka, Kansas, August 2, 1880.
43. *Topeka* (Kansas) *State Journal*, March 27, 1883, 4; *Wichita* (Kansas) *Daily Times*, March 29, 1883, 1; *Topeka* (Kansas) *State Journal*, April 5, 1883, 6; *El Dorado* (Kansas) *Daily Republic*, June 17, 1887, 4.
44. "Bruce Younger, 1853–1889, Burial at Evergreen Cemetery, Colorado Springs, El Paso County, Colorado," People Legacy. Note: Despite this online source, Evergreen Cemetery has no record of the burial of Bruce Younger.
45. "Timeline—Notre Dame 175," Notre Dame University. Notre Dame opened its doors to women undergraduates for the first time in 1972. That autumn, 365 women were enrolled.
46. *Twenty-Fourth Annual Catalog of the University of Notre Dame, Indiana, for the Academic Year 1867–68, Annual Commencement, Wednesday, June 24, 1868* (Notre Dame University: Ave Maria Steam Power Press Print, 1868), 40. The catalog lists Bruce Younger, Warsaw, Missouri, as a student. Joseph Smith, archivist, Notre Dame University, personal communication to Rick Miller, September 16, 2020, and to Hazel Rowena Mills, September 30, 2020. Financial information at Notre Dame for Bruce Younger of Warsaw, Missouri, is recorded in the Notre Dame: Index to Financial Ledgers 1841–1869, vol. 5, 361, October 30, 1867, November 14, 1867, January 23, [1868]. "Waldo Porter Johnson," Bioguide.
47. *Chicago Daily Tribune*, August 8, 1876, 5.
48. *Twenty-Fourth Annual Catalog of the University of Notre Dame, Indiana, for the Academic Year 1867–68*, 15–18.
49. *Chicago Daily Tribune*, March 6, 1893, 5.
50. *Chicago Daily Tribune*, March 6, 1893.
51. Peter C. Kjaeraard, "The Fossil Trade: Paying a Price for Human Origins," *University of Chicago Press Journals*; "Petrifaction and Stone Giant Hoaxes," Hoaxes.
52. *Arizona Republic*, Phoenix, Arizona Territory, March 11, 1893, 1.
53. "World's Fair 'Mummies,'" World's Fair Chicago 1893.
54. *Colorado Springs* (Colorado) *Gazette*, April 23, 1893, 3. Colorado City, in what is now El Paso County, Colorado, was founded on August 13, 1859, during the Pikes Peak gold rush and was the first settlement in the Pikes Peak region. Colorado City was known for its opium dens, bordellos, and saloons, which were prohibited in adjacent Colorado Springs, which developed later. Colorado City was annexed into Colorado Springs in 1917.

55. *Oakdale* (California) *Leader*, December 14, 1894, 2.
56. Evergreen Cemetery has no record of the burial of Bruce Younger; Kelly Stevenson, director, Evergreen Cemetery, Colorado Springs, Colorado, telephone interview by Hazel Rowena Mills, December 5, 2019. No death certificate was found for Bruce Younger; Vital Records Section, Colorado Department of Public Health and environment, personal communication to Hazel Rowena Mills, December 30, 2019.
57. "Belle Starr's Mother Dead," *Dallas* (Texas) *Daily Times Herald*, January 5, 1894, 8, col. 2–3. This article, published the day after Eliza Pennington Shirley died, consists mostly of an interview with "Aunt" Annie Shirley. In the article, many dates and other statements about the Shirleys' lives are inaccurate. Elizabeth "Eliza" Pennington, Paden/Peden Family History and Genealogy.
58. In 1882, Eliza Shirley sold property in Scyene, Texas: "Eliza Shirley, et. al., to J. A. Pruitt. Lots 5 and 6, in block 2, of the town of Scyene, for [$]175.00," in "Real Estate Transfers," *Dallas* (Texas) *Daily Herald*, February 22, 1882, 7; Rick Miller, personal communication to Hazel Rowena Mills, August 7, 2020.
59. "Belle Starr's Mother Dead," *Dallas Daily Times Herald*.
60. From Ladies Aid Society minutes, Methodist Episcopal Church South [later called First United Methodist Church], Dallas, Texas, January 2 and January 8, 1894, n.p., courtesy of Kelvin L. Meyers, chairman of the history and archives committee, First United Methodist Church, Dallas, Texas, June 10, 2019, and August 11, 2020; personal communications from Kathy Huber, Tulsa (Oklahoma) City-County Library System, manager of Genealogy Center, to Hazel Rowena Mills, June 10, 2019, and August 11, 2020.
61. Ladies Aid Society minutes, Methodist Episcopal Church South.
62. *Dallas* (Texas) *Morning News*, January 5, 1894, 10; *Dallas* (Texas) *Daily Times Herald*, January 5, 1894; Ladies Aid Society minutes, Methodist Episcopal Church South; *Fort Worth* (Texas) *Gazette*, January 6, 1894, 2; Rick Miller, personal communication to Hazel Rowena Mills, August 7, 2020.
63. Ladies Aid Society minutes, Methodist Episcopal Church South.
64. Rick Miller, personal communication to Hazel Rowena Mills, August 8, 2020; "Elizabeth Pennington Hatfield Shirley," Find a Grave, Greenwood Cemetery, Block 4, Lot 35, Space 6, memorial ID 16480340.
65. "*Dallas* (Texas) *Morning News*, June 27, 1889, 5; *St. Louis* (Missouri) *Post-Dispatch*, June 27, 1889, 8; *Daily Arkansas Gazette*, June 27, 1889, 1; *St. Joseph* (Missouri) *Herald*, June 28, 1889, 8; *Ford County Republican* (Kansas), July 3, 1889, 1; *Osceola* (Arkansas) *Times*, July 6, 1889, 2; *St. Louis* (Missouri) *Post-Dispatch*, July 11, 1889, 9.
66. *Daily Arkansas Gazette*, June 27, 1889.
67. *St. Joseph Herald*, June 28, 1889.
68. *St. Louis* (Missouri) *Post-Dispatch*, July 11, 1889, 9; *Fort Worth* (Texas) *Daily Gazette*, July 12, 1889, 1, Cox Collection; *Daily Arkansas Gazette*, July 12, 1889, 1; *Evening Dispatch*, Arkansas City, Kansas, July 12, 1889, 1; *Fayetteville* (Arkansas) *Weekly Democrat*, July 19, 1889.
69. *Fort Worth* (Texas) *Daily Gazette*, July 12, 1889; *Daily Arkansas Gazette*, July 12, 1889; *Evening Dispatch*, Arkansas City, Kansas, July 12, 1889; *Fayetteville* (Arkansas) *Weekly Democrat*, July 19, 1889.
70. *Daily Arkansas Gazette*, August 1, 1889, 1; *Daily Arkansas Gazette*, August 7, 1889, 2; *St. Louis* (Missouri) *Post-Dispatch*, August 7, 1889, 4; *Osceola* (Arkansas) *Times*, August 10, 1889, 2.
71. Reed returned "home two years ago," according to an article headlined "Ed Reed Captured and Taken to Fort Smith Ark.," *Cherokee Advocate*, Tahlequah, Indian Territory, June 12, 1895, vol. 19, no. 35, 2; "Special to the Republic," datelined "Fort Smith Ark., June 7"; Rick Miller, personal communication to Hazel Rowena Mills, June 24, 2020.
72. Dee Cordry, "Outlaws and Lawmen of the Cherokee Nation," *Oklahombres: The Journal of Lawman and Outlaw History of Oklahoma* 5, no. 1 (Fall 1993), typed transcription; Rick Miller, personal communication to Hazel Rowena Mills, December 10, 2020. Cordry's article

lists several sources at the end but does not use citations, so the origin of his statement about Ed Reed having served as guard for the Katy Railroad is unclear.
73. "On a Bender," *Muskogee* (Indian Territory) *Phoenix*, January 23, 1895, 3, Rick Miller, personal communication to Hazel Rowena Mills, June 24, 2020; *Vinita* (Indian Territory) *Indian Chieftain*, January 24, 1895, vol. 13, 4, Rick Miller, personal communication to Hazel Rowena Mills, June 24, 2020; *Muskogee* (Indian Territory) *Phoenix*, January 26, 1895, 5, Rick Miller, personal communication to Hazel Rowena Mills, June 24, 2020; *Muskogee* (Indian Territory) *Phoenix*, May 18, 1895, 3; Rick Miller, personal communication to Hazel Rowena Mills, June 24, 2020; "Ed Reed in Town," *Record-Democrat*, Wagoner, Indian Territory, ___, 1.
74. *Kellogg's Wichita* (Kansas) *Record*, June 8, 1895, 1; *Cherokee Advocate*, Tahlequah, Indian Territory, June 12, 1895; *Blue Rapids* (Kansas) *Times*, June 13, 1895, 2; *Marlow* (Indian Territory) *Magnet*, June 13, 1895, 4, datelined "Fort Smith, Ark., June 7"; Rick Miller, personal communication to Hazel Rowena Mills, June 24, 2020; *Vinita* (Indian Territory) *Indian Chieftain*, June 13, 1895, 3.
75. *Cherokee Advocate*, Tahlequah, Indian Territory, June 12, 1895.
76. *Vinita Indian Chieftain*, June 13, 1895; Criminal Defendant Case File for Daniel Hare, 1895, NRFF-21-3W51-19716, perjury, jacket number 369, National Archives, Southwest Region; Rick Miller, personal communication to Hazel Rowena Mills, June 26, 2020; *Marlow* (Indian Territory) *Magnet*, June 13, 1895.
77. *Vinita* (Indian Territory) *Indian Chieftain*, July 18, 1895, 3.
78. Rick Miller, personal communication to Hazel Rowena Mills, July 24, 2020.
79. Cordry, "Outlaws and Lawmen of the Cherokee Nation."
80. *Alliance Courier*, Ardmore, Indian Territory, August 2, 1895, 1; Rick Miller, personal communication to Hazel Rowena Mills, June 24, 2020; *McAlester* (Indian Territory) *Capital*, October 31, 1895, 2; Mallory Covington, Oklahoma Historical Society, personal communication to Hazel Rowena Mills, June 8, 2020; *Fayetteville* (Arkansas) *Weekly Democrat*, October 31, 1895, 1; *Helena* (Arkansas) *Weekly World*, October 30, 1895, 3; *Cherokee Advocate*, Tahlequah, Indian Territory, October 30, 1895, 2; *Vinita* (Indian Territory) *Indian Chieftain*, October 31, 1895; *Vinita* (Indian Territory) *Leader*, October 31, 1895, vol. 1, no. 33, 1, attributed to the *Sentinel*.
81. *Vinita* (Indian Territory) *Indian Chieftain*, December 17, 1896, 2.
82. *Blanchard* (Oklahoma) *News*, December 17, 1959, 1; Rick Miller, personal communication to Hazel Rowena Mills, July 31, 2020.
83. *Vinita* (Indian Territory) *Indian Chieftain*, December 17, 1896.
84. *Vinita* (Indian Territory) *Indian Chieftain*, March 19, 1896, 2.
85. *Evening Messenger*, Marshall, Texas, December 16, 1896, 2.
86. *Claremore* (Indian Territory) *Progress*, December 19, 1896, 3; Rick Miller, personal communication to Hazel Rowena Mills, June 24, 2020.
87. *Vinita* (Indian Territory) *Indian Chieftain*, March 19, 1896, 2.
88. Charles A. Gibbs III, telephone interview by Hazel Rowena Mills, December 3, 2018; Charles A. Gibbs III, personal communication to Hazel Rowena Mills, February 4, 2019. The firearm is a double-barreled twelve-gauge shotgun made in 1892 by Eclipse Gun Company; Charles A. Gibbs III, personal communication to Hazel Rowena Mills, September 8, 2020.
89. *Evening Messenger*, Marshall, Texas, December 16, 1896, 2.
90. *Daily Ardmoreite*, Ardmore, Indian Territory, December 17, 1896, datelined "Claremont [Claremore], I. T., Dec. 15," 4.
91. *Vinita Indian Chieftain*, December 17, 1896, 2, 3.
92. *Claremore Progress*, December 19, 1896.
93. The US Army Corps of Engineers moved Cochran Cemetery to its present location in Rogers County, Oklahoma, when Lake Oologah was built.
94. Two photographs of the "J. E. Reed" tombstone in Cochran Cemetery, Rogers County, Okla-

homa, courtesy of Pat Waddill, Vinita, Oklahoma, are published in Phillip W. Steele, "Eddie Reed—Belle Starr's Son," *Quarterly of the National Association for Outlaw and Lawman History* 21, no. 1 (July–September 1997): 8, Phillip W. Steele Collection, courtesy of Charlotte Steele and Roy Young. When the photographs were taken, the shaft of the gravestone had been broken off its base.

95. *Blanchard News*, December 17, 1959.
96. *Blanchard News*, December 17, 1959; "Jennie Cochran McDaniel (1875–1959)," Find a Grave, memorial ID 33048843, burial at Blanchard Cemetery, McClain County, Oklahoma, photograph of tombstone added by Charlene Birchfield, n.d.
97. "Belle Starr's Alleged Murderer," Special Dispatch to the Globe-Democrat, *Cherokee Advocate*, Tahlequah, Indian Territory, March 6, 1889, 1, datelined "Fort Smith, Ark., February 20"; personal communication from Rick Miller, August 5, 2020.
98. *Daily Arkansas Gazette*, April 19, 1889, 3; *The Index*, Hermitage, Missouri, April 25, 1889, 1, datelined "Arkansas City, Kan., April 16."
99. *Daily Arkansas Gazette*, May 2, 1889, 6.
100. *Dallas* (Texas) *Morning News*, March 21, 1891, 3, datelined "Gainesville, Tex. March 20," photocopy of original article; personal communication from Rick Miller, August 20, 2020.
101. *Fayetteville* (Arkansas) *Weekly Democrat*, March 27, 1891, 4, datelined "Gainesville, Tex., March 19"; *Allen County Herald*, Iola, Kansas, March 27, 1891, 2, datelined "Gainesville, Tex., March 24."
102. *Kiowa* (Kansas) *News-Review and Kiowa Record*, April 1, 1891, 1; *Oklahoma State Capital*, Guthrie, Oklahoma Territory, May 9, 1891, 8.
103. *Fort Worth* (Texas) *Gazette*, April 2, 1891, datelined "Special to the Gazette; Quanah, Tex., March 25," Cox Collection.
104. *Daily Arkansas Gazette*, April 2, 1891, 2, datelined "Special to The Arkansas Gazette; Fort Smith, April 1."
105. *Arkansas Democrat*, May 4, 1891, 6; photocopy of original article and typed transcription, personal communication from Rick Miller, August 5, 2020.
106. *Muskogee* (Indian Territory) *Phoenix*, August 6, 1891, 1; photocopy of original article, personal communication from Rick Miller, July 7, 2020.
107. *Muskogee* (Indian Territory) *Phoenix*, August 13, 1891, 1; photocopy of original article, personal communication from Rick Miller, July 7, 2020.
108. Juliet Galonaska, "Pearl Starr," "Fort Smith Minutes" series, National Park Service, Fort Smith National Historic Site, US National Park Service, 2.
109. *Fort Smith* (Arkansas) *Times*, April 30, 1901, 4; *Cherokee Advocate*, Tahlequah, Indian Territory, April 15, 1893, 2, photocopy of original article, personal communication from Rick Miller, August 5, 2020; *Fort Smith* (Arkansas) *Times*, May 16, 1901, 1. This article also mentions imminent action in a case against Pearl Starr and Lena Strickland. "Pearl Starr's Escapade: She and Friends Engage in a Row on Train Near Sallisaw," *Fort Smith* (Arkansas) *Times*, July 24, 1901, 1; *Fort Smith* (Arkansas) *Times*, March 23, 1902, 12, photocopy of original article, personal communication from Rick Miller. These are only a sampling of the articles about Pearl's arrests. Benjamin Boulden, *Living under a Red Light: Fort Smith's Bordello Row, 1898 to 1948*, sponsored by a grant from the Arkansas Historic Preservation Program, January 1994, 5, 16.
110. *Fort Smith* (Arkansas) *Times*, March 27, 1906, 6; *Fort Smith* (Arkansas) *Times*, June 12, 1907, 1.
111. *Daily Arkansas Gazette* (Little Rock), May 6, 1911, 2, photocopy of original article, personal communication from Rick Miller; Ross Pendergraft, Donrey Media Group, Fort Smith, Arkansas, to Phillip W. Steele, October 9, 1987, enclosing a handwritten letter from Charles M. Hiner, Fort Smith, Arkansas, to Ross Pendergraft. Hiner says his grandfather's law firm of Hiner and Hiner represented Pearl Starr "in all her affairs [sic] criminal and real estate" and describes some of them in detail; Phillip W. Steele Collection, courtesy of Charlotte Steele and Roy Young.

112. Phillip W. Steele, *Starr Tracks: Belle and Pearl Starr* (Gretna, LA: Pelican, 1998), 82.
113. State of Arkansas, County of Washington, Certificate of Marriage, Mr. Arthur Erbach and Miss Rosie P. Reed, license issued October 9, 1897, ceremony performed October 10, 1897, by N. M. Ragland, recorded October 13, 1897, handwritten ledger, 416, Washington County Marriage Records 1845–1941, photocopy of original ledger page, Ancestry, personal communication from Rick Miller; *Daily Oklahoman* (Oklahoma City, Oklahoma Territory), October 24, 1897, 5, quoting the *Fort Smith* (Arkansas) *Times-Democrat*, photocopy of original article, personal communication from Rick Miller. The *Daily Oklahoman* article refers to the "contracting parties" to the marriage as Arthur Urback [sic] and "Mrs. Sterling Price Harris . . . best known here and all over the Indian Territory as Pearl Starr." *Guthrie* (Oklahoma Territory) *State Capital*, March 25, 1898, 2.
114. E. Arthur Erbach, birth certificate, Sebastian County, Arkansas, August 24, 1898, personal communication from Rick Miller, July 19, 2022.
115. *Fort Smith* (Arkansas) *Times*, September 14, 1898, 8.
116. Steele, *Starr Tracks*, 82–83; Fort Smith City Cemetery (Oak Cemetery) records, handwritten ledger, Arthur E. Erbach (husband), page number missing, entry 145; Arthur E. Erbach (infant), page 168, entry 670. Pearl Starr also paid for the burial in the same cemetery of a two-month-old Smith infant who died on November 19, 1899, and was buried the next day, possibly the child of one of her bordello employees. Burial records are from photocopies of original ledger pages with handwritten annotations by Brookie Craig; Phillip W. Steele Collection, courtesy of Charlotte Steele and Roy Young.
117. Oddly, the marriage license for Dell Andrews and Rosa Pearl Erbach states that both of them were from Paris, Lamar County, Texas; personal communication from Rick Miller, July 21, 2022.
118. *Fort Smith* (Arkansas) *Times*, April 12, 1905, 8, photocopy of original article, personal communication from Rick Miller.
119. Steele, *Starr Tracks*, 84.
120. Request submitted in 1964 for delayed birth certificate, Jennette Steele Andrews, born November 8, 1902, Fort Smith, Sebastian County, Arkansas, personal communication from Rick Miller, July 21, 2022.
121. Steele, *Starr Tracks*, 84–85.
122. Cindy Hayostek to Phillip W. Steele, January 12, 1994, Phillip W. Steele Collection, courtesy of Charlotte Steele and Roy Young.
123. *State of Arizona against "Rosa Reed, alias Pearl Starr," defendant*, April 5, 1918 (also listed in the same document as "Pearl Starr, alias Rosa Reed," and as "Pearl Starr"); Police Court of the City of Bisbee, County of Cochise, State of Arizona: *State of Arizona, plaintiff, vs. Rose Reed, defendant*, proceedings, April 5–17, 1918; Police Court of the City of Bisbee, County of Cochise, State of Arizona: *State of Arizona, plaintiff, vs. Rose Reed, defendant*, appeal bond, April 17, 1918. Rosa Reed (who signed her name on the court documents in that form) was convicted on April 16, 1918, of the misdemeanor of conducting a "disorderly and ill-governed house" in Bisbee and was to be jailed for sixty-eight days or pay a fine of sixty-eight dollars. She appealed the conviction. Superior Court of the County of Cochise, State of Arizona: *State of Arizona, plaintiff, vs. Rose Reed, defendant*, subpoena for Eddie Anderson, Wallace Christwell, and Billy Anderson to appear in court on October 1, 1918. All legal sources are printouts from microfilm of original typed documents, Phillip W. Steele Collection, courtesy of Charlotte Steele and Roy Young. Articles in the *Bisbee* (Arizona) *Review* of April 7, 9, 17, and 18, 1918, comment on the Reed case and mention in the April 7 article a Billie Anderson identified as Rosa Reed's "daughter," in the April 9 article a "Belle Anderson" as the codefendant, and in the April 17 article a "Billie Anderson, her alleged daughter"; typed transcriptions from the *Bisbee Review* are by Cindy Hayostek, Phillip W. Steele Collection, courtesy of Charlotte Steele and Roy Young; typed transcriptions, personal communication from Rick Miller, July 21, 2022. These are the only known mentions of an alleged daugh-

ter named Billie or Belle Anderson (she also might have been the "Billy Anderson" who was subpoenaed as a witness in the above-mentioned court case). Both Ruth Kaigler and Jennette Steele Andrews lived with their mother in Arizona at times. Jennette "chose to enter the business her mother, Pearl, had been so successful in" and was "[a]ssociated with a sporting house known as the Lucky Strike"; Steele, *Starr Tracks*, 99. It is interesting to speculate whether Billy, Billie, or Belle Anderson might have been an alias for Jennette Steele Andrews, but she was only fifteen years old at the time of these incidents in 1918. The *Bisbee Review* of April 18, 1918, specifies that Rosa Reed's "disorderly house" was in Upper Brewery Gulch.

124. *Bisbee* (Arizona) *District Directory*, 1924, 121; Phillip W. Steele Collection, courtesy of Charlotte Steele and Roy Young.
125. *Bisbee District Directory*, 1924, 87–94.
126. Hayostek to Steele.
127. "Mrs. Rosa Reed Dies," undated and unidentified newspaper clipping, photocopy from microfilm, Phillip W. Steele Collection, courtesy of Charlotte Steele and Roy Young.
128. Bureau of Vital Statistics, Arizona State Board of Health, Standard Death Certificate, Rosa Reed, died July 6, 1925, filed July 7, 1925, photocopy from Kathy Huber, manager of Genealogy Center, Tulsa (Oklahoma) City-County Library System.
129. "Mrs. Rosa Reed Dies"; Record of Funeral, Rosa Reed, July 6, 1925, Porter and Ames Mortuary, Douglas, Arizona, photocopy of handwritten ledger page, Phillip W. Steele Collection, courtesy of Charlotte Steele and Roy Young. Annette Saavedra, office manager, Brown-Page Mortuary, Douglas, Arizona, to Brookie Craig, March 27, 1984, photocopy of typed letter, Phillip W. Steele Collection, courtesy of Charlotte Steele and Roy Young.
130. Record of Funeral, Rosa Reed, Porter and Ames Mortuary.
131. Bureau of Vital Statistics, Arizona State Board of Health, Standard Death Certificate, Rosa Reed, gives the date of burial as July 9, 1925, although the funeral was held on July 8; "Rose Lee 'Pearl Starr' Reed (1866–1925)," Find a Grave, memorial ID 7771302.
132. Biographical note, scope and content note, Vance Randolph Collection, Library of Congress.
133. William Yancey Shackleford [Vance Randolph], *Belle Starr, the Bandit Queen: The Career of the Most Colorful Outlaw the Indian Territory Ever Knew* (Girard, Kansas: Haldeman-Julius, Little Blue Book No. 1846, 1946), 28–29.
134. Obituary of Florence Pearl Epple Hutton, *Topeka* (Kansas) *State Journal*, August 9, 1943, 8. The *Journal* stated that Hutton had lived in Topeka for about twenty-five years when she died. For information on Hutton, see Donald L. Boyd, "Land of the Buckeye."
135. Steele, *Starr Tracks*, 97–98.
136. Steele, *Starr Tracks*, 99.
137. Steele, *Starr Tracks*, 98–100.
138. *Dallas* (Texas) *Morning News*, March 20, 1890, 3; *Edmond* (Oklahoma Territory) *Sun*, May 1, 1890, 1. Some news reports erroneously suggested that the "very fine pistol" had once belonged to Cole Younger.
139. Shirley, *Belle Starr and Her Times*, 253–54.
140. Roger Bell, "Women Led the Way in Pioneering Success," *Three Rivers Historian: A Journal of Three Rivers Museum* 17, no. 2 (Spring 2015): 5.
141. Bell, "Women Led the Way in Pioneering Success." Based on what appears to be "J. Daly" carved at the bottom of the monument slab, historian Roger Bell suggests that the stonecutter's name might have been Daly and that he "would be a good candidate as the stonecutter of Belle's grave marker."
142. Shirley, *Belle Starr and Her Times*, 259, 262.
143. Shirley, *Belle Starr and Her Times*, 262.
144. Richard E. Meyer, ed., "Markers XI," *Journal of the Association for Gravestone Studies* (Worcester, Massachusetts: Association for Gravestone Studies, 1994), 197. According to the author,

"Epitaphs—at least the more elaborate, poetic examples—tend most frequently to be found in the sample books available to many marble carvers during this period."
145. *Indian Chieftain*, Vinita, Indian Territory, June 20, 1895, 2.
146. *Indian Chieftain*, Vinita, Indian Territory, June 20, 1895.
147. Frederick S. Barde, "The Story of Belle Starr," *Sturm's Oklahoma Magazine* 11, no. 1 (September 1910): 19–26.
148. Barde, "Story of Belle Starr."
149. *Tulsa* (Oklahoma) *World*, December 3, 1933, 3.
150. Joe Synar and Richard Venator, *Muskogee* (Oklahoma) *Daily Phoenix*, January 5, 1936, 3.
151. Synar and Venator, *Muskogee Daily Phoenix*.
152. Bell, "Women Led the Way in Pioneering Success," 11–12.
153. Bell, "Women Led the Way in Pioneering Success," 12.
154. Bell, "Women Led the Way in Pioneering Success."
155. Bell, "Women Led the Way in Pioneering Success."
156. *Tulsa* (Oklahoma) *World*, April 12, 1959, 22.
157. "Legacy of an Outlaw," *Oklahoma Magazine*, April 25, 2019.
158. Bell, "Women Led the Way in Pioneering Success," 15.
159. Bell, "Women Led the Way in Pioneering Success," 15–16.
160. *Tulsa* (Oklahoma) *World*, June 8, 1986, 8.
161. *Tulsa World*, June 8, 1986.
162. Bell, "Women Led the Way in Pioneering Success," 16.
163. Bell, "Women Led the Way in Pioneering Success," 18.
164. "Legacy of an Outlaw," *Oklahoma Magazine*.
165. "Legacy of an Outlaw," *Oklahoma Magazine*.
166. "Legacy of an Outlaw," *Oklahoma Magazine*.
167. Oklahoma Historical Society marker, Dr. Ron and Donna Hood, erected 2013.

Bibliography

Private Collections

Cox Collection
Richard J. Miller Collection
Wallis Collection

Archives

Assessment of Property Situated in the County of Dallas for 1864, Family History Center, Tulsa City-County Library.
Barde, Frederick S., Collection, Photographs, Research Division, Oklahoma Historical Society.
Creek Court—Supreme file, Doc. 28804, Records of the Creek Nation, American Indian Archives Division, Oklahoma Historical Society.
"Defendants: Starr, Belle, and Two Others Unknown," Box 1, Folder 3, Items 47 and 48, March 10, 1886, Complaints, Records Pertaining to Criminal Cases, Western District Records, no. MS Un33r 430, US District Court, Arkansas, Special Collections Department, University of Arkansas Libraries.
Hardin, John Wesley, Collection, Southwestern Writers Collection, Texas State University, San Marcos.
"History Is Electric!" (exhibit), Tulsa Historical Society.
An Inventory of Governor Edmund Jackson Davis Records at the Texas State Archives, 1869–1875, Texas State Library and Archives, Austin.
An Inventory of Governor Richard Coke Records at the Texas State Archives, 1873–1877. Texas State Library and Archives, Austin.
McClurg, Joseph Washington, governor. Records, no. C1746. Western Historical Manuscript Collection, State Historical Society of Missouri.
McDaniel, Katherine, "Angels in Black: Victorian Women in Mourning" (exhibit), 2018, City of Greeley Museums.
Pettit, Gwen, *Between the Creeks*. Newspaper columns on local history published 1986–92, compiled and edited by Lindy Fisher, July 2006, Portal to Texas History, University of North Texas Libraries.
Polk, James K., president. "April 13, 1846: Message Regarding Cherokee Indians." Miller Center of Public Affairs, Presidential Archives, University of Virginia, Charlottesville.
Randolph, Vance, Collection, Library of Congress.

Schrantz, Ward, Articles Collection, *Carthage (MO) Evening Press* files, Powers Museum, Carthage, MO.
Starr, Belle. Files. Jasper County (MO) Archives and Records Center.
Starr, Belle. Vertical File, Outlaws, Tulsa and Oklahoma History, Tulsa City-County Library.
Starr, Belle, and Samuel Starr. Register of Prisoners, 1883, Detroit House of Correction. Typed transcripts of original ledger records, Burton Historical Collection, Detroit Public Library.
Starr, Samuel, and Mrs. Bell Reed. Marriage report, June 5, 1880, Microfilm Roll 22, Proceedings of the District Court of the Canadian District, Court Records of the Canadian District December 14, 1869–March 1, 1891, Volume 1-B, Cherokee Nation 297, American Indian Archives, Oklahoma Historical Society.
Steele, Phillip W., Collection, Wild West History Association.
Texas Almanac for 1872 and *Emigrant's Guide to Texas*, Portal to Texas History, University of North Texas Libraries.
Thomas, Archy. "Civil War Battle of Carthage Memoir," no. R167, Rolla Research Center, Western Historical Manuscript Collection, State Historical Society of Missouri.

Books

Adams, Ramon F. *The Cowboy Dictionary*. New York: Perigee, 1993.
Adams, Ramon F. *A Dictionary of the Range, Cow Camp, and Trail*. Norman: University of Oklahoma Press, 1944.
Adams, Ramon F. *Six-Guns and Saddle Leather: A Bibliography on Western Outlaws and Gunmen*. Mineola, NY: Dover, 1998.
Akins, Jerry. *Hangin' Times in Fort Smith: A History of Executions in Judge Parker's Court*. Fayetteville: University of Arkansas Press, 2012.
Alexander, Bob. *Whiskey River Ranger: The Old West Life of Baz Outlaw*. Denton: University of North Texas Press, 2016.
Alexander, Bob, and Donaly E. Brice. *Texas Rangers: Lives, Legends, and Legacy*. Denton: University of North Texas Press, 2017.
Anderson, Charles D., comp. and ed. *Outlaws of the Old West*. Los Angeles: Mankind, 1973.
Anderson, Dan, and Larry Yadon. *100 Oklahoma Outlaws, Gangsters, and Lawmen, 1839–1939*. Gretna, LA: Pelican, 2007.
Armitage, Susan. "Through Women's Eyes: A New View of the West." In *The Women's West*. Edited by Susan Armitage and Elizabeth Jameson. Norman: University of Oklahoma Press, 1987.
Barrows, Henry Dwight. *An Illustrated History of Los Angeles County*. Chicago: Lewis, 1889.
Bell, George Morrison, Sr. *History of "Old and New Cherokee Indian Families."* Bartlesville, OK: Watie Bell, 1972.
Biffle, Kent. *A Month of Sundays*. Denton: University of North Texas Press, 1993.
Blight, David W. *Race and Reunion: The Civil War in American History*. Cambridge, MA: Belknap Press, 2001.
Boulden, Benjamin. *Living under a Red Light: Fort Smith's Bordello Row, 1898 to 1948*. Sponsored by a grant from the Arkansas Historical Preservation Program.
Bradbury, John. *Travels in the Interior of America, in the Years 1809, 1810, and 1811*. London: Sherwood, Neely, & Jones, 1817.
Brant, Marley. *The Outlaw Youngers: A Confederate Brotherhood*. Lanham, MD: Madison Books, 1992.
Breihan, Carl W. *Quantrill and his Civil War Guerrillas*. Denver, CO: Sage, 1959.
Brownlee, Richard S. *Gray Ghosts of the Confederacy*. Baton Rouge: University of Louisiana Press, 1958.
Burton, Jeffrey. *Indian Territory and the United States, 1866–1906: Courts, Government, and the Movement for Oklahoma Statehood*. Norman: University of Oklahoma Press, 1995.

Burchett, Kenneth E. *The Battle of Carthage, Missouri*. Jefferson, NC: McFarland, 2013.

Butler, William J. *Fort Smith: Past and Present: A Historical Summary*. Fort Smith, AR: First National Bank of Fort Smith, 1972.

Byers, Major S. H. M. *With Fire and Sword*. New York: Neale, 1911.

Castel, Albert. *General Sterling Price and the Civil War in the West*. Baton Rouge: Louisiana State University Press, 1968.

Chalkley, Lyman. *Chronicles of the Scotch-Irish Settlement in Virginia: Extracted from the Original Court Records of Augusta County, 1745–1800*. Augusta County, VA: Commonwealth Printing, 1912.

Chisolm, J. Julian. *A Manual of Military Surgery, for the Use of Surgeons in the Confederate Army*. Richmond, VA: West & Johnson, 1861.

Connelly, William E. *Quantrill and the Border Wars*. Cedar Rapids, IA: Torch, 1910.

Cordley, Richard. *A History of Lawrence, Kansas, from Earliest Settlement to the Close of the Rebellion*. Lawrence, KS: Lawrence Journal Press, 1895.

Cottrell, Steve. *The Battle of Carthage and Carthage in the Civil War*. Carthage, MO: City of Carthage, 1990.

Cox, Mike. *Texas Ranger History*. Charleston, SC: History Press, 2015.

Cross, Mark H. "How to Pronounce Bosque." In *Encyclopedia of Santa Fe and Northern New Mexico*. Caminito, 2012.

Croy, Homer. *Cole Younger: Last of the Great Outlaws*. Lincoln: University of Nebraska Press, 1999.

Dacus, J. A. *Life and Adventures of Frank and Jesse James, the Noted Western Outlaws*. St. Louis: W. S. Bryan, 1880.

Dale, Henry. *Adventures and Exploits of the Younger Brothers, Missouri's Daring Outlaws, and Companions of the James Boys*. New York: Street & Smith, 1890.

Dary, David. *Stories of Old-Time Oklahoma*. Norman: University of Oklahoma Press, 2015.

Day, Horace B. *The Opium Habit*. New York: Harper & Brothers, 1868.

Dean, Eric T., Jr. *Shook over Hell: Post-Traumatic Stress, Vietnam, and the Civil War*. Cambridge, MA: Harvard University Press, 1997.

DeArment, Robert K. *Man-Hunters of the Old West*. Norman: University of Oklahoma Press, 2017.

Denhardt, Robert Moorman. *Foundation Dams of the American Quarter Horse*. Norman: University of Oklahoma Press, 1995.

Drago, Harry Sinclair. *Outlaws on Horseback*. New York: Dodd Mead, 1964.

Drago, Harry Sinclair. *Outlaws on Horseback*. 1964; reprint, Lincoln: University of Nebraska Press, 1998.

Dunlap, Patricia Riley. *Riding Astride: The Frontier in Women's History*. Denver: Arden, 1995.

East, Don C. *A Historical Analysis of the Creek Indian Hillabee Towns*. Bloomington, IN: Universe, 2008.

Ellinghaus, Katherine. *Taking Assimilation to Heart: Marriages of White Women and Indigenous Men in the United States and Australia, 1887–1937*. Lincoln: University of Nebraska Press, 2006.

Ellsberry, Elizabeth Prather, comp. *Clay County, Missouri, Cemetery Records*. John R. Keller Graveyard, 1962.

Ely, Glen Sample. *The Texas Frontier and the Butterfield Overland Mail, 1858–1861*. Norman: University of Oklahoma Press, 2016.

Etulain, Richard W., and Glenda Riley, eds. *With Badges and Bullets: Lawmen and Outlaws in the Old West*. Golden, CO: Fulcrum, 1999.

Farmer, Silas. *History of Detroit and Wayne County and Early Michigan: A Chronological Cyclopedia of the Past and Present*, 3rd ed. (Detroit, MI: Silas Farmer for Russell & Co., New York, 1890), cited in Detroit Historical Society, "Did You Know a Prison and a Cemetery Used To Stand on the Site of Eastern Market?"

Fellman, Michael. *Inside War: The Guerrilla Conflict in Missouri During the American Civil War*. New York: Oxford University Press, 1990.

First Annual Report of the General Agent of the Board of the National Education Board. Cincinnati, OH: Ben Franklin Printing House, 1848.

Foner, Philip S., ed. *Frederick Douglass on Women's Rights*. Westport, CT: Greenwood Press, 1976.
Forbes, Archibald. *Memories and Studies of War and Peace*. London: Cassell, 1895.
Fox, Richard K. *Bella Starr, The Bandit Queen, or the Female Jesse James: A Full and Authentic History of the Dashing Female Highwayman*. 1889; reprint, Austin, TX: Steck, 1960.
Friedman, Lawrence M. *Crime and Punishment in American History*. New York: Basic Books, 1993.
Gaddy, Jerry J. *Dust to Dust: Obituaries of the Gunfighters*. Fort Collins, CO: Old Army Press, 1977.
Gates, Clifford D. *Pioneer History of Wise County from Red Men to Railroads—Twenty Years of Intrepid History*. Decatur, TX: Wise County Old Settlers Association, 1907.
Gilmore, Donald L. *Civil War at the Missouri-Kansas Border*. Gretna, LA: Pelican, 2006.
Goodspeed, Weston Arthur, ed. *The Province and the States*. Madison, WI: Western Historical Association, 1904.
Goodspeed's History of Newton, Lawrence, Barry and McDonald Counties, Missouri. Chicago: Goodspeed, 1888.
Greer, Ben F. *Greer Family Reminiscences*. Fayetteville, AR: Washington County Historical Society, 1956.
Hall, Ted Byron. *Oklahoma, Indian Territory*. Fort Worth, TX: American Reference Publications, 1971.
Hallam, John. *Biographical and Pictorial History of Arkansas*. Albany, NY: Weed, Parsons, 1887.
Hansen, Harry. *The Civil War: A History*. New York: New American Library, 2002.
Harman, S. W. *Hell on the Border: He Hanged Eighty-Eight Men*. 1898; reprint, Lincoln: University of Nebraska Press, 1992.
Harper, Judith E. *Women During the Civil War: An Encyclopedia*. New York: Routledge, 2004.
Hicks, Edwin P. *Belle Starr and Her Pearl*. Little Rock, AR: Pioneer Press, 1963.
Hill, Luther B. *A History of the State of Oklahoma*. Chicago: Lewis, 1908.
Hinze, David C., and Karen Farnham. *The Battle of Carthage: Border War in Southwest Missouri, July 5,1861*. Gretna, LA: Pelican, 2004.
Hobsbawm, Eric. *Bandits*. New York: Delacorte, 1969.
Holcombe, R. I., ed. *History of Greene County, Missouri*. St. Louis: Western Historical, 1883.
Hough, Emerson. *The Passing of the Frontier*. New Haven, CT: Yale University Press, 1921.
Hunnef, Jenna. "The Cereal Politics of Belle Starr's Outlaw Reputation." In *Food and Feast in Modern Outlaw Tales*. Edited by Alexander L. Kaufman and Penny Vlagopoulos. New York: Routledge, 2019.
Hunter, Helen Katherine. *Echoes of School Bells: History of Jasper County Missouri Rural Schools*. Carthage, MO: Drop Cap, 2013.
Johnson, J. B., ed. *History of Vernon County, Missouri*. Chicago: C. F. Cooper, 1911.
Jones, Anne Goodwyn. "Belles and Ladies." *The New Encyclopedia of Southern Culture*, vol. 13: *Gender*. Edited by Nancy Bercaw and Ted Ownby. Chapel Hill: University of North Carolina Press, 2009.
Jones, John Beauchamp. *A Rebel War Clerk's Diary at the Confederate State Capital*. Philadelphia: J. B. Lippincott, 1866.
Kiebar, John E., ed. *The Kentucky Encyclopedia*. Lexington: University Press of Kentucky, 1992.
Kooistra, Paul. *Criminals as Heroes: Structure, Power and Identity*. Bowling Green, OH: Bowling Green State University Popular Press, 1989.
Lackmann, Ronald W. *Women of the Western Frontier in Fact, Fiction, and Film*. Jefferson, NC: McFarland, 1997.
Leslie, Edward E. *The Devil Knows How to Ride*. New York: Random House, 1996.
Lindsley, Philip. *A History of Greater Dallas and Vicinity*. Chicago: Lewis, 1909.
Livingston, Joel Thomas. *A History of Jasper County, Missouri, and Its People*. Chicago: Lewis, 1912.
Logan, Mrs. John A., et al. *The Home Manual: Everybody's Guide in Social, Domestic, and Business Life*. Chicago: H.J. Smith, 1889.
Madison, James H., and Lee Ann Sandweiss. *Hoosiers and the American Story*. Indianapolis: Indiana Historical Society Press, 2014.

McGregor, Malcolm G. *The Biographical Record of Jasper County, Missouri.* Chicago: Lewis, 1901.
McGroarty, John Steven, ed. *History of Los Angeles County.* Chicago: American Historical Society, 1923.
McGruder, Mark A. *History of Pettis County, Missouri.* Topeka, KS: Historical Publishing, 1919.
Memorial and Biographical History of Dallas County, Texas. Chicago: Lewis, 1892.
Mihesuah, Devon A. *Ned Christie: The Creation of an Outlaw and Cherokee Hero.* Norman: University of Oklahoma Press, 2018.
Miller, Rick. *Bounty Hunter.* College Station, TX: Creative, 1988.
Miller, Rick. *Tin Star Tales: Law and Disorder in Dallas County, Texas, 1846–1900.* Bloomington, IN: Archway, 2017.
Myres, Sandra L. *Westering Women and the Frontier Experience 1800–1915.* Albuquerque: University of New Mexico Press, 1982.
North, F. A., *The History of Jasper County, Missouri.* Des Moines: Mills, 1883.
O'Beirne, Harry F. *Leaders and Leading Men of Indian Territory*, vol. 1, *Choctaws and Chickasaws: With a Brief History of Each Tribe: Its Laws, Customs, Superstitions and Religious Beliefs.* Chicago: American Publishers Association, 1892.
O'Beirne, Harry F., and E. S. O'Beirne, *Indian Territory: Its Chiefs, Legislators and Leading Men.* St. Louis: C. B. Woodward, 1892.
Oskison, John Milton. *Tales of Old Indian Territory and Essays on the Indian Condition.* Lincoln: University of Nebraska Press, 2012.
Patterson, Richard. *Historical Atlas of the Outlaw West.* Boulder, CO: Johnson Books, 1985.
Peterson, Paul R. *Quantrill in Texas: The Forgotten Campaign.* Nashville, TN: Cumberland House, 2007.
Pool, William C. *A History of Bosque County.* San Marcos, TX: San Marcos Record Press, 1954.
Prassel, Frank Richard. *The Great American Outlaw: A Legacy of Fact and Fiction.* Norman: University of Oklahoma Press, 1993.
Presley, Mrs. Leister E., and the Goodspeed Brothers. *History of Benton, Washington, Carroll, Madison, Crawford, Franklin and Sebastian Counties, Arkansas.* Chicago: Goodspeed, 1889.
Raines, C. W. *Year Book for Texas.* Austin, TX: Gammel-Statesman, 1902.
Rankin, Melinda. *Texas in 1850.* Boston: Damrell & Moore, 1850.
Rascoe, Burton. *Belle Starr, "The Bandit Queen."* 1941; reprint, Lincoln: University of Nebraska Press, 2004.
Reed, Paula, and Grover Ted Tate. *Sam Bass and Joel Collins: The Tenderfoot Bandits, Their Lives and Hard Times.* Tucson: Westernlore, 1988.
Rogers, John William. *The Lusty Texans of Dallas.* New York: E. P. Dutton, 1951.
Rosa, Joseph G. *Taming of the West: Age of the Gunfighter.* New York: Smithmark, 1993.
Rosa, Joseph G., and Robin May. *Buffalo Bill and His Wild West.* Lawrence: University Press of Kansas, 1989.
Saunt, Claudio. *Black, White, and Indian: Race and the Unmaking of an American Family.* New York: Oxford University Press, 2005.
Schlereth, Thomas J. *Victorian America: Transformations in Everyday Life, 1876–1915.* New York: HarperCollins, 1982.
Schrantz, Ward L. *Jasper County, Missouri, in the Civil War.* Carthage, MO: Carthage Press, 1923.
Sellmeyer, Derly P. *Jo Shelby's Iron Brigade.* Gretna, LA: Pelican, 2007.
Settle, William A. Jr. *Jesse James Was His Name.* Lincoln: University of Nebraska Press, 1977.
Shackleford, William Yancey [Vance Randolph]. *Belle Starr, the Bandit Queen: The Career of the Most Colorful Outlaw the Indian Territory Ever Knew.* Girard, KS: Haldeman-Julius, 1946. Facsimile reprint, Kessinger, n.d.
Shirley, Betty M., ed. *Belle Starr and Her Roots.* Cupertino, CA: Shirley Family Association, 1989.
Shirley, Glenn. *Belle Starr and Her Times: The Literature, the Facts, and the Legends.* Norman: University of Oklahoma Press, 1982.
Shirley, Glenn. *Law West of Fort Smith: A History of Frontier Justice in the Indian Territory, 1834–1896.* Lincoln: University of Nebraska Press, 1968.

Sizer, Mona D. *Texas Bandits: Real to Reel*. Dallas: Taylor, 2004.
Smith, Robert Barr. *Outlaw Tales of Oklahoma*. Lanham, MD: Rowman & Littlefield, 2013.
Stambaugh, J. Lee, and Lillian J. Stambaugh. *A History of Collin County, Texas*. Austin: Texas State Historical Association, 1958.
Starr, Emmet. *History of the Cherokee Indians and Their Legends and Folk Lore*. Oklahoma City, OK: Warden Co., 1921.
Steele, Phillip W. *Starr Tracks: Belle and Pearl Starr*. Gretna, LA: Pelican, 1998.
Stiles, T. J. *Jesse James: Last Rebel of the Civil War*. New York: Vintage, 2003.
Stringfellow, R. F. *Negro Slavery, No Evil; or The North and the South*. St. Louis: M. Niedner, 1854.
Teague, David W. *The Southwest in American Literature and Art: The Rise of a Desert Aesthetic*. Tucson: University of Arizona Press, 1997.
Thornton, Russell. *The Cherokees: A Population History*. Lincoln: University of Nebraska Press, 1990.
Tuller, Roger Harold. *"Let No Guilty Man Escape": A Judicial Biography of Isaac C. Parker*. Norman: University of Oklahoma Press, 2001.
Turner, Elizabeth Hayes, Stephanie Cole, and Rebecca Sharpless. *Texas Women: Their Histories, Their Lives*. Athens: University of Georgia Press, 2015.
Twenty-Fourth Annual Catalog of the University of Notre Dame, Indiana, for the Academic Year 1867–68, Annual Commencement, Wednesday, June 24, 1868. Notre Dame University: Ave Maria Steam Power Press Print, 1868.
Vernon County, Missouri, Marriage Book A. Nevada, MO: Tri-County Genealogical Society, 2006.
Wallis, Michael. *The Best Land under Heaven: The Donner Party in the Age of Manifest Destiny*. New York: Liveright, 2017.
Wallis, Michael. *The Real Wild West: The 101 Ranch and the Creation of the American West*. New York: St. Martin's Press, 1999.
Wallis, Michael. *The Wild West 365*. New York: Abrams, 2011.
Ward, Geoffrey, with Ric Burns and Ken Burns. *The Civil War*. New York: Vintage, 1990.
Warren, Robert Penn. *The Legacy of the Civil War*. Lincoln: University of Nebraska Press, 1961.
Wellman, Paul I. *A Dynasty of Western Outlaws*. New York: Bonanza, 1961.
Whitney, Sharon E., ed. *The Memories of Will Conine: 1860s to 1890s*. Waco: Texian Press, 1999.
Wilson, J. Albert. *History of Los Angeles County, California*. Oakland, CA: Thompson & West, 1880.
Woodson, W. H. *History of Clay County, Missouri*. Topeka, KS: Historical Publishing Co., 1920.
Wortham, Louis J. *A History of Texas from Wilderness to Commonwealth*. Fort Worth, TX: Wortham-Molyneaux Co., 1924.
Wrobel, David M. *The End of American Exceptionalism: Frontier Anxiety from the Old West to the New Deal*. Lawrence: University Press of Kansas, 1993.
Yadon, Julia Etter, Sue Ross Cross, and Randall Ross Viguet. *Reflections of Fort Smith*. Fort Smith, AR: Fort Smith Historical Press, 1976.
Yadon, Laurence J., and Dan Anderson. *200 Texas Outlaws and Lawmen, 1835–1935*. Gretna, LA: Pelican, 2008.
Young, Richard, and Judy Dockery Young, eds. *Outlaw Tales: Legends, Myths, and Folklore from America's Middle Border*. Little Rock, AR: August House, 1992.
Younger, Cole. *The Story of Cole Younger, by Himself*. Chicago: Henneberry, 1903.

Periodicals

"A Batch for the Pen." *St. Louis Post-Dispatch*, March 20, 1883.
"A Coward Got the Drop on Her." *National Police Gazette*, February 23, 1889.
"A Deputy Marshal Assassinated." *New York Times*, April 16, 1886.

Bibliography

Akins, Jerry. "Hangin' Times in Fort Smith." *Fort Smith (AR) Historical Society Journal* 27, no. 1 (April 2003).
Allen County Herald (Iola, KS), March 27, 1891,
Alliance Courier (Ardmore, Indian Territory), August 2, 1895.
Arizona Republic (Phoenix, Arizona Territory), March 11, 1893.
Arkansas Democrat (Little Rock), July 8, 1886; October 16, 1886; December 13, 1888; May 4, 1891.
Arkansas Gazette (Little Rock), May 15, 1885; May 23, 1885; October 12, 1885; September 20, 1886; October 16, 1886; February 20, 1889; April 19, 1889; May 2, 1889; June 27, 1889; July 12, 1889; August 1, 1889; August 7, 1889; January 28, 1890; April 2, 1891; May 6, 1911; February 24, 1921.
"A Stillwater Sensation; Cole Younger Says He Never Was Belle Starr's Husband." *St. Paul (MN) Globe*, February 7, 1889.
Austin American-Statesman, April 17, 1874.
Austin Daily Democratic-Statesman, April 17, 1874; August 26, 1874.
Austin Democratic Statesman, April 9, 1874.
Austin Weekly Democratic Statesman, May 13, 1875.
"A Wild Western Amazon." *National Police Gazette*, May 22, 1886, digital ID cph3b11522//hdf.loc.gov/loc.pnp/cph.3b11522, Library of Congress Prints and Photographs Division, Washington, DC.
Barde, Frederick S. "The Story of Belle Starr." *Sturm's Oklahoma Magazine* 11, no. 1 (September 1910).
Bartlett, Marie. "Prince of Hangmen?" *True West Magazine* (May 2015).
Bearss, Edwin C. "The Federals Capture Fort Smith, 1863." *Arkansas Historical Quarterly* 28, no. 2 (1969).
Bell, Roger. "Women Led the Way in Pioneering Success." *Three Rivers Historian: A Journal of Three Rivers Museum* 17, no. 2 (Spring 2015).
"Belle Starr's Alleged Murderer." *Cherokee Advocate* (Tahlequah, Indian Territory), March 6, 1889.
"Belle Starr's Mother Dead." *Dallas Daily Times Herald*, January 5, 1894.
Big Spring (TX) Daily Herald, June 25, 1940.
Bisbee (AZ) Review, April 18, 1918.
Bisbee (AZ) Review, April 7, 9, 17, 18, 1918, typed transcriptions by Cindy Havostek. Phillip W. Steele Collection.
Blanchard (OK) News, December 17, 1959.
Blue Rapids (KS) Times, June 13, 1895.
Bond, John W. "The History of Elkhorn Tavern." *Arkansas Historical Quarterly* 21, no. 1 (Spring 1962).
"Books: Petticoat Terror." *Time*, June 2, 1941.
Boyd, Leon. "The War in Jasper County, As Seen by a Soldier." *Carthage (MO) Weekly Banner*, no. 42, October 14, 1869.
Brownson, Orestes. "The Woman Question," pt. I. *Catholic World* 9, no. 50 (May 1869).
Burlington (KS) Democrat, April 2, 1880.
Campbell, Randolph B. "A Moderate Response: The District Judges of Dallas County During Reconstruction, 1865–1876." *Legacies: A History Journal for Dallas and North Central Texas* 5, no. 2 (Fall 1993).
Campbell, Randolph B. "The District Judges of Texas in 1866–1867: An Episode in Failure of Presidential Reconstruction." *Southwestern Historical Quarterly* 93, no. 3 (1990).
Castel, Albert. "Kansas Jayhawking Raids into Western Missouri in 1861." *Missouri Historical Review* 54, no. 1 (October 1959).
Chang, David A. "An Equal Interest in Soil: Creek Small-Scale Farming and the Work of Nationhood, 1866–1889." *American Indian Quarterly* 33, no. 1 (Winter 2009).
Chavez, Will. "Though No Longer Bustling, Porum Has Rich History." *Cherokee Phoenix* (Tahlequah, OK), August 10, 2018.

Cherokee Advocate (Tahlequah, Indian Territory), July 18, 1874; April 15, 1893; February 6, 1895; June 12, 1895; October 30, 1895.
Chicago Daily Tribune, March 6, 1893.
Chicago Tribune, August 8, 1876.
Claremore (Indian Territory) *Progress*, December 19, 1896.
Clarke, Jay. "Missouri Bank Cashes In on Jesse James." *Chicago Tribune*, May 2, 2004.
Clinton (MO) Eye, February 23, 1889.
Colorado Springs Gazette, April 23, 1893.
Cope, Anne. "Newtonia: Village with a Vivid Civil War History." *Neosho (MO) Daily News*, July 22, 1984.
Cordry, Dee. "Outlaws and Lawmen of the Cherokee Nation," *Oklahombres: The Journal of Lawman and Outlaw History of Oklahoma* 5, no. 1 (Fall 1993), typed transcription.
Crepelle, Adam. "Shooting Down Oliphant Self-Defense as an Answer to Crime in Indian Country." *Lewis and Clark Review* 22, no. 4 (2018).
Daily Ardmoreite (Ardmore, Indian Territory), December 17, 1896.
Daily Commonwealth (Topeka, KS), August 13, 1876.
Daily Oklahoman (Oklahoma City), October 24, 1897.
Dallas Daily Commercial, April 27, 1874; August 10, 1874; August 26, 1874.
Dallas Daily Herald, February 10, 1874; April 30, 1874; May 27, 1874; August 2, 1874; August 15, 1874; April 15, 1875; May 4, 1875; July 3, 1875; July 23, 1875; November 10, 1875; November 19, 1875.
Dallas Daily Times Herald, March 24, 1880; February 7, 1889; December 8, 1893; January 5, 1894; June 21, 1903; April 6, 1924.
Dallas Daily Herald, May 30, 1874.
Dallas Morning News, June 7, 1886; December 13, 1888; February 8, 1889; February 19, 1889; June 27, 1889; August 22, 1889; March 20, 1890; March 21, 1891; January 5, 1894; August 21, 1929.
Dallas News, January 7, 1894.
Dallas Weekly Herald, April 25, 1874.
"Death of a Once Noted Indian Outlaw." *Van Buren (AK) Press*, October 25, 1889.
Debo, Angie. "John Rollin Ridge." *Southwest Review* 17, no. 1 (1932).
DeFrange, Ann. "Historian Lets 'Just the Facts' Enhance Stories." *Oklahoman*, January 21, 1990.
Denison (TX) Daily News, August 22, 1874.
"The Detroit House of Correction: To the Editor of the Detroit Free Press." *Detroit Free Press*, March 20, 1883.
Dirkx, Phil. "Paso Robles' Founders: A Vigilante, a Capitalist, and Jesse James' Uncle." *Telegram-Tribune* (San Luis Obispo, CA), October 1, 1987.
"District Court: The Criminal Docket as Set to Date," case no. 2978, Shirley, and case no. 2982, McCommas and Shirley. *Dallas Weekly Herald*, January 6, 1877.
Edmond Sun (Oklahoma Territory), January 30, 1890; May 1, 1890.
"Ed Reed Captured and Taken to Fort Smith Ark." *Cherokee Advocate* (Tahlequah, Indian Territory) 19, no. 35, June 12, 1895.
"Ed Reed in Town." *Record-Democrat* (Wagoner, Indian Territory), 1895.
El Dorado (KS) Daily Republic, June 17, 1887.
Empire City (KS) Echo, June 20, 1876.
Evening Dispatch (Arkansas City, KS), July 12, 1889.
Evening Messenger (Marshall, TX), December 16, 1896.
Farris, David. "The Death of Belle Starr." *Edmond (OK) Life and Leisure*, December 25, 2014.
Fayetteville (AR) Weekly Democrat, February 18, 1886; July 19, 1889; March 27, 1891; October 31, 1895.
Fischler, Diane. "The War Comet of 1861 or the Great Comet of 1861." *Courier* 4, no. 6 (June 2016).
Fisher, Onieta. "Life in a Log House." *Annals of Iowa* 37, no. 8 (1965).
Flossie [Florence Pearl Epple Hutton]. "The Story of Flossie, Belle Starr's Granddaughter," pt. 2. *Dallas Morning News*, Feature Section, May 7, 1933.

Ford County Republican (Dodge City, KS), July 3, 1889.
Foreman, Carolyn Thomas. "North Fork Town." *Chronicles of Oklahoma* 29, no. 1 (Spring 1951).
Foreman, Carolyn Thomas. "The Ballentines (Balentines), Father and Son, in 'The Indian Territory.'" *Chronicles of Oklahoma* 12, no. 4 (1934).
Fort Scott (KS) Daily Monitor, June 21, 1878.
Fort Smith (AR) Elevator, March 23, 1883; May 15, 1885; May 22, 1885; June 19, 1885; January 1, 1886; March 12, 1886; November 19, 1886; August 10, 1888; January 24, 1890.
Fort Smith (AR) New Era, February 22, 1883.
Fort Smith (AR) Times, September 14, 1898; April 30, 1901; May 16, 1901; March 23, 1902; April 12, 1905; March 27, 1906; June 12, 1907.
Fort Smith (AR) Weekly Elevator, May 28, 1886; December 24, 1886; February 4, 1889; February 15, 1889; March 1, 1889.
Fort Smith (AR) Weekly New Era, October 14, 1874; December 16, 1874.
Fort Worth Daily Gazette, November 23, 1888; July 12, 1889, Cox Collection.
Fort Worth Gazette, February 17, 1886; February 9, 1889; April 2, 1891, Cox Collection; January 6, 1894.
Fort Worth Morning Register, December 1, 1901.
Frassetto, Mark Anthony. "The Law and Politics of Firearms Regulations in Reconstruction Texas." *Texas A&M Law Review* 4, no. 1 (2016).
Galena (KS) Weekly Republican, June 5, 1886.
Galveston Daily News, August 10, 1865; April 17, 1874; August 9, 1874; August 15, 1874; October 11, 1874; September 19, 1878.
Geise, William R. "Missouri's Confederate Capital in Marshall, Texas." *Southwestern Historical Quarterly* 66, no. 2 (July 1962–April 1963).
Graffagnino, J. Kevin. "Vermont Attitudes Toward Slavery: The Need for a Closer Look." *Vermont History: Journal of the Vermont Historical Society* 45, no. 1 (Winter 1977).
Guthrie State Capital (Oklahoma Territory), March 25, 1898.
Hansen, Ron. "Larger Than Life, Deader Than Dead." *New York Times Book Review*, June 24, 1990, review of Peter Matthiessen, *Killing Mister Watson*.
Hartog, Hendrik A. "Marital Exits and Marital Expectations in Nineteenth Century America." *Georgetown Law Review* 80 (January 1991).
Hazen, H. A. "The Most Destructive Tornadoes Since 1872." *Science* 16, no. 390 (July 25, 1890).
Helena (AK) Weekly World, October 30, 1895.
Hodges, Anthony. "Confederate Quandary: The Fourth of July." *Chattanooga Times Press*, June 30, 2013.
Indian Chieftain (Vinita, Indian Territory), June 20, 1895.
Indian Journal (Muskogee, Indian Territory), January 30, 1890.
Jefferson City (MO) People's Tribune, November 27, 1878.
Johnston, Francis J. "The James Bros. in California," *Odyssey* 8, no. 4 (October–December 1986).
Junction City (KS) Weekly Union, August 12, 1876; May 8, 1880; May 13, 1880.
Kansas City Times, July 19, 1874.
Kellogg's Wichita Record, June 8, 1895.
Kennedy, Steele. "What Time Has Done to Old Younger's Bend." *Tulsa Daily World*, December 3, 1933.
Keve, Paul W. "Building a Better Prison: The First Three Decades of the Detroit House of Correction." *Michigan Historical Review* 25, no. 2 (Fall 1999).
Kiowa (KS) News-Review and Kiowa Record, April 1, 1891.
Kjaeraard, Peter C. "The Fossil Trade: Paying a Price for Human Origins," *ISIS* 103, no. 2 (June 2012).
Knowles, Thomas Neil. "The Everglades' Bandit Killer." *Florida Keys Sea Heritage Journal* 17, no. 4 (Summer 2007).
Kovalcheck, Riley. "The Modern Plantation: The Continuities of Convict-Leasing and the Analysis of Arkansas Prison Systems." *College Language Association Journal* 7 (2019).

Krieger, Dan. "Infamous Brothers Once Stayed in the Area," *Tribune* (San Luis Obispo, CA), June 4, 2011.
Labette County Democrat (Oswego, KS), June 4, 1880.
Larsen, Lawrence H. "Let No Guilty Man Escape." *American Historical Review* 107, no. 2 (April 2002).
Lande, R. Gregory. "Felo De Se: Soldier Suicides in America's Civil War." *Military Medicine* 176, no. 5 (2011).
Lanko, Kelly. "Un-Romanticizing the American West: White Frontier Women's Daily Lives, 1860–1900," *Undergraduate Research Journal* 6 (2003).
"Legacy of an Outlaw," *Oklahoma Magazine*, April 25, 2019.
Liberty (MO) Weekly Tribune, August 30, 1861.
Mail and Breeze (Topeka, KS), July 21,1899.
"Major J. B. Pond Is Dead." *New York Times*, June 22, 1903.
Marlow Magnet (Indian Territory), June 13, 1895.
Martin, Amelia, ed. "Fort Smith Press." *Fort Smith Historical Society Journal* 13, no. 2 (September 1989).
Martin, Amelia, ed. "William Murphy Cravens." *Fort Smith Historical Society Journal* 27, no. 1 (April 2003).
Martinez, Joaquin Rivaya. Review of *Myth, Memory, and Massacre: The Pease River Capture of Cynthia Ann Parker*" by Paul H. Carlson and Tom Crum. *Great Plains Quarterly* 32, no. 1 (Winter 2012).
McAlester Capital (Indian Territory), October 31, 1895.
McPherson, James M. "A War That Never Goes Away." *American Heritage* 14, no. 2, 1990.
Memphis Appeal, August 8, 1876,
Meyer, Richard E. *Markers: The Annual Journal of the Association for Gravestone Studies* 11 (1994).
Miller, Rick. "Outlaw Jim Reed." *Wild West History Association Journal* 7, no. 4 (August 2013).
"Mrs. Rosa Reed Dies." Undated and unidentified newspaper clipping, photocopy from microfilm. Phillip W. Steele Collection.
Muskogee Indian Journal (Indian Territory), May 28, 1885; March 11, 1886; June 3, 1886; June 24, 1886; December 22, 1886; July 28, 1887.
Muskogee Journal (Indian Territory), January 30, 1890.
Muskogee Phoenix (Indian Territory), August 6, 1891; August 13, 1891; January 26, 1895; May 18, 1895.
Muskogee (OK) Daily Phoenix, October 4, 1919.
Nashville Banner, March 22, 1868.
Neodesha (KS) Free Press, April 9, 1880.
New York Daily Herald, April 8, 1854.
New York Sun, February 6, 1889.
New York Times, April 9, 1874; September 4, 1875; January 30, 2000.
Oakdale (CA) Leader, December 14, 1894.
Obituary of Florence Pearl Epple Hutton, *Topeka State Journal*, August 9, 1943.
Oglesby, Savannah. "The Story of Edgar J. Watson: The Infamous Businessman & Serial Killer." *Coastal Sun Breeze News* (Marco Island, FL), December 17, 2020.
Oklahoma State Capital (Guthrie, Oklahoma Territory), May 9, 1891.
"Old Soldier Dead: Confederate Laid Body of Former Comrade Under the Sod Today." *Ardmore (OK) Daily Ardmoreite*, May 18, 1913.
"On a Bender." *Muskogee Phoenix* (Indian Territory), January 23, 1895.
Osceola (AR) Times, July 6, 1889; August 10, 1889.
Parins, James W. "The Shifting Map of Cherokee Land Use Practices in Indian Territory." *Elohi—Indigenous People and the Environment* 1 (2012).
Parsons (KS) Daily Eclipse, April 7, 1880.
Parsons (KS) Weekly Sun, June 10, 1880.

"Pearl Starr's Escapade: She and Friends Engage in a Row on Train Near Sallisaw." *Fort Smith (AR) Times*, July 24, 1901.

Peeler, Tom. "Nostalgia Crooked Cowpokes." *D Magazine* (December 1983).

Peters, Laura. "Historian: Valley Slavery Story 'Not Pretty.'" *Staunton (VA) News Leader*, November 15, 2015.

"The Pioneer Past Is Alive." *Los Angeles Times*, June 19, 1997.

Pleasanton (KS) Observer-Enterprise, July 19, 1879.

Poplar Bluff (MO) Citizen, November 22, 1878.

Poynter, Michele D. "The Clay County Savings Association." *James Farm Journal* 30, no. 2 (Spring 2019).

Rabas, Chuck. "The Mysterious Jack Keene." *James Farm Journal* 30, no. 2 (Spring 2019).

Rascoe, Judith. "A Cautionary Tale for Reviewers." *New York Times*, May 14, 1989.

Rasmussen, Cecilia. "Truth Dims the Legend of Outlaw Queen Belle Starr." *Los Angeles Times*, February 17, 2002.

"Real Estate Transfers." *Dallas Daily Herald*, February 22, 1882.

Roberson, Dorothy M., ed. "The Duel Across the Mississippi." *Tennessee Genealogical Magazine* 45, no. 1 (Spring 1998).

Rolla (MO) Herald, February 14, 1889.

Rutherford, Phillip. "The Carthaginian Wars." *Civil War Times Illustrated* (February 1987).

Samuelson, Nancy B. "The Murder of Belle Starr and the Murder of Deputy U.S. Marshal William Erwin." *Quarterly of the National Association for Outlaw and Lawmen History* 23, no. 1 (January–March 1999).

San Antonio Daily Express, July 22, 1874.

Scharff, Virginia. "Women of the West." *History Now: The Historian's Perspective*, no. 9 (September 2006).

Schrantz, Ward L. "Shelby Wiggles from Hot Spots in Carthage Fight, October 18, 1863." *Carthage (MO) Evening Press*, August 3, 1950.

Sherman (TX) Patriot, May 31, 1874.

Shirley News 1, no. 16 (July 1982).

Shirley News 3, no. 5 (Summer 1989).

Shoemaker, Floyd C. "Missouri's Proslavery Fight for Kansas, 1854–1855." *Missouri Historical Review* 48, no. 3 (1954).

Simmons, Lynn Sheffield. "Speaking of Texas." *Texas Highways Magazine* (February 1995).

Slatta, Richard W. "Eric J. Hobsbawm's Social Bandits: A Critique and Revision." *A Contracorriente: Magazine of Social History and Literature in Latin America* 1, no. 2 (2004).

Smith, Willard H. Review of *Belle Starr, "The Bandit Queen,"* by Burton Rascoe. *Journal of American History* 28, no. 2 (September 1941).

Soodalter, Ron. "A Burning Hell." *Missouri Life* 46, no. 5 (July–August 2019).

Spitzzeri, Paul R. "What a Difference a Decade Makes: Ethnic and Racial Demographic Change in Los Angeles County During the 1860s." *Branding Iron: The Los Angeles Corral of the Westerners*, no. 249 (Fall 2007).

St. Joseph (MO) Herald, June 28, 1889.

St. Joseph (MO) Weekly Herald, February 21, 1889.

St. Louis Post-Dispatch, June 27, 1889; July 11, 1889; August 7, 1889; February 28, 1890.

State Journal (Jefferson City, MO), August 11, 1876; August 18, 1876.

Steele, Phillip W. "Eddie Reed—Belle Starr's Son." *Quarterly of the National Association for Outlaw and Lawman History* 21, no. 1 (July–September 1997).

Sweet, Leonard I. "The Female Seminary Movement and Women's Mission in Antebellum America." *Journal of the American Society of Church History* 54, no. 1 (1985).

Synar, Joe, and Richard Venator. *Muskogee (OK) Daily Phoenix*, January 5, 1936.

Tahlequah Telephone (Indian Territory), March 1, 1889.

Times (Philadelphia), December 31, 1893.

Thomas, James C. "The Judge." *Tulsa Law Review* 2, no. 2 (1965).
Times Picayune (New Orleans), January 6, 1894.
Topeka State Journal, March 27, 1883; April 5, 1883.
Towns, Leroy, ed. *Midway*, Sunday magazine of the *Topeka Capitol-Journal*, August 2, 1970.
Trimble, Marshall. "What Is the Origin of 'Owl Hoot?,'" *True West Magazine*. Oct 1, 2012.
Trimble, Marshall. "When Did They Stop Hanging Men for Horse Theft?," *True West Magazine*. July 1, 2004.
Tulsa World, April 12, 1959; June 8, 1986.
US National Park Service Staff, Fort Smith Historic Site, comps. "Law Enforcement for Fort Smith 1851–1896." *Fort Smith Historical Society Journal* 3, no. 1 (April 1979).
Van Buren (AR) Press, February 16, 1889.
VanGilder, Marvin. "Belle and Hometown Band Entertained Each Other." *Carthage (MO) Press*, August 7, 2002.
Vann, R. P. "Reminiscences of Mr. R. P. Vann, East of Webbers Falls, Oklahoma, September 28, 1932, As Told to Grant Foreman." *Chronicles of Oklahoma* 11, no. 2 (June 1933).
Vinita Indian Chieftain (Indian Territory), March 30, 1883, Cox Collection; July 8, 1886; October 4, 1888; January 24, 1895, vol. 13; June 13, 1895; July 18, 1895; March 19, 1896; December 17, 1896.
Vinita Leader (Indian Territory), October 31, 1895.
Waco Daily Examiner, April 16, 1874.
Waco Evening News, November 29, 1888.
Waco Reporter, April 28, 1875.
Weaver, John F. "Belle Starr: A Few Leaves from the Life of a Notorious Woman." *Fort Smith (AR) Elevator*, February 15, 1889.
Weekly Kansas State Journal (Topeka), August 17, 1876.
Western Herald (Girard, KS), June 24, 1880.
White, Richard. "Outlaw Gangs of the Middle Border: American Social Bandits." *Western Historical Quarterly* 12, no. 4 (October 1981).
Wichita Daily Evening Resident, August 26, 1886.
Wichita Daily Times, March 29, 1883.
Wright, Muriel H. "Historic Places on the Old Stage Line from Fort Smith to Red River." *Chronicles of Oklahoma* 11, no. 2 (June 1933).
Wrobel, David M. "The Closing Gates of Democracy: Frontier Anxiety Before the Official End of the Frontier." *American Studies* 32, no. 1 (Spring 1991).
Yadon, Larry. "The Mystery of Edwin Reed, Life Among the Starrs." *Oklahombres* 12, no. 3 (Spring 2011).
"The Younger Boys." *Daily Commonwealth* (Topeka, KS), August 2, 1880.
Young, Roy B. "The Allen H. Parmer Story: Quantrill Guerrilla, Outlaw, Cattleman, Solid Citizen." *Wild West History Association Journal* 11, no. 3 (September 20, 2018).

Theses and Dissertations

Clemons, Vicente Edward. "The New Woman in Fiction and History: From Literature to Working Woman." M.A. thesis, Pittsburg State University, May 2016.
Garneau, Susan Marie. "Imprisoning Chicago: Incarceration, the Chicago City Council, Prisoners, and Reform, 1832–1915," PhD diss., Loyola University Chicago, 2012.
Hobbs, Kenneth W. Jr. "Jim Reed, Southwestern Outlaw and Husband of Belle Starr: A Study of the Watt Grayson and San Antonio Stage Robberies." Master's thesis, Texas Christian University, Fort Worth, 1975.
Hunnef, Jenna. "Dangerously Free: Outlaws and Nation-Making in Literature of the Indian Territory," PhD diss., University of Toronto, 2016.

Maher, David Richard. "Vice in the Veil of Justice: Embedding Race and Gender in Frontier Tourism." PhD diss., University of Arkansas–Fayetteville, 2013.
Schmidt, Janeal. "Selfish Intentions: Kansas Women and Divorce in Nineteenth Century America." Master's thesis, Kansas State University, 2009.
Stefani, Victoria. "True Statements: Women's Narratives of the American Frontier Experience." PhD diss., University of Arizona, 2000.
Suval, John. "Squatters, Statesmen, and the Rupture of American Democracy, 1830–1860." PhD diss., University of Wisconsin–Madison, 2021.
Tedford, Harold Calvin. "A Study of Theatrical Entertainments in Northwest Arkansas from Their Beginning through 1889." PhD diss., Louisiana State University, 1965.

Online Sources

"Actions at Fayetteville April 18, 1863," EncyclopediaofArkansas.net.
"A Map of Kansas Literature," Washburn University, Topeka, KS.
"Ann Mary Watson," Geni.
"Anna Elizabeth (Kelker) Shelley (1736–1800)," WikiTree.
"Arkansas Genealogy and Boundary Changes."
Armstrong, Martin A. "Panic 1837," ArmstrongEconomics.com.
Ash, Rebecca L. "Women in the American West: Blurred Reality," AngelFire.com
Baughman, James L. "The Fall and Rise of Partisan Journalism," Ethics.Journalism.Wisc.edu.
Beckenbaugh, Terry. "Shelby's Raid," CivilWarontheWesternBorder.org.
Beckman, Cindy. "Early Hotels: Looking Back," November 21, 2016. FaulknerHistory.org.
"Beecher Bibles," Kansas Historical Society, KSHS.org.
"Behind the Name, Myra."
"Benjamin & Eugenia Dev Les Goodere Lang," Dallas Gateway.
Benner, Judith Ann. "Ross, Lawrence Sullivan (Sul)," Handbook of Texas, Texas State Historical Association.
Black, Bill. "Belle Starr: A Black Widow?" Fort Smith National Historic Site, NPS.gov.
"Bluford Duck (1859–1895)," WikiTree.
Bosse, Paula. "When the Circus Came to Town—1886," FlashbackDallas.com.
Bowers Mill Collection, OzarksCivilWar.org.
"Brief History of Jasper County, Missouri," Ancestry.com.
Brown, Kenny L. "Robert Latham Owen," Encyclopedia of Oklahoma History and Culture, OKHistory.org.
"Bruce Younger (1853–1889)," Ancestry.com.
"Bruce Younger, 1853–1889," Burial at Evergreen Cemetery, Colorado Springs, CO, FindaGrave.com Note: Despite this online source, Evergreen Cemetery has no record of the burial of Bruce Younger.
Burns, Mary Louise James. "History of Drury Woodson James," dictated to her granddaughter Mary Jean Malley Beamis, 1949, in Eric F. James, "Drury Woodson James by his Daughter Mary Louise James Burns," *Stray Leaves: A James Family in America 1650–2000.*
"Burnt District Monument," Cass County Historical Society, CCHSMO.org.
Burton, Art T. "Lawman Legend Bass Reeves: The Invincible Man Hunter," HistoryNet.com.
Campbell, Denele Pitts. "The Shannon-Fisher Feud," DeneleCampbell.com.
Campbell, Denele Pitts. "A Little Murder with Your Lemonade?," DeneleCampbell.com.
"Cassius McDonald Barnes (1845–1925)," Geni.
"Charles Christopher Jackson," Handbook of Texas, Texas State Historical Association.
"Charles H. Young," Handbook of Texas, Texas State Historical Association.

"Charles Rainsford Jennison," The Civil War Muse.
"The Civil War in Missouri," Mo Civil War.
"Colonel Charles Lee Younger (1779–1854)—Genealogy," Geni.
"Confederate Flags—Historical US Civil War Flags," WorldAtlas.com.
Conger, Roger N. "Waco, Texas," Handbook of Texas, Texas State Historical Association.
Cornwell, Allen. "Civil War Vets and Mental Illness: The Tragedy after the War," OurGreatAmericanHeritage.com.
Correa, Tom. "Old West: Wyatt Earp—Was Wyatt a Horse Thief?" July 28, 2011, NetPosse.com.
Coster, Sara. "A Balm in Gilead."
Cottrell, Debbie Mauldin. "Women and Education," Handbook of Texas, Texas State Historical Association.
Cox, Mike. "Butterfield Overland Mail: Stagecoaching in Texas," Texas Almanac.
"Criminal Case Procedure in Judge Parker's Court," National Park Service.
Crowther, David. "Words Shakespeare Invented," July 29, 2017, TheHistoryofEngland.co.uk.
Crumrin, Timothy. "Women and the Law in Early 19th-Century Indiana," Conner Prairie.
"Dallas County, Texas: Pioneers of Dallas," Genealogy Trails.
"Dallas Trinity Trails," DallasTrinityTrails.blogspot.com.
"Descendants of A-ma-do-ya Moytoy [Nancy Starr]," Genealogy.com.
"Descendants of John Starr Jr.," Genealogy.com.
"Did You Know a Prison and a Cemetery Used To Stand on the Site of Eastern Market?," Detroit Historical Society
"The Divorce Mill of the Midwest," September 5, 2011, IndianaPublicMedia.org.
DNA Diagnostics Center, Fairfield, OH, DNACenter.com.
"Donald L. Boyd (1897–1965)," LandoftheBuckeye.net.
"Early Historic Texas Colt Single Action," Online Collectibles Auction, Deadwood, SD, April 28, 2018, Western Americana Collectibles, iCollector.com.
Easley, Tina, transcriber. "Prisons, Schools, Asylums," *Centennial History of Arkansas—1922*, Genealogy Trails.
"Edgar J. Watson (1855–1910)," WikiTree.
"Edna Catherine (Bethea) Burkett (1888–1975)," WikiTree.
"1875: Six in Fort Smith under Hanging Judge Parker," ExecutedToday.com.
"The 1860 Election in Missouri," Missouri Division.
"Elizabeth 'Eliza' Pennington," Paden/Peden Family History and Genealogy.
"Elizabeth Pennington Hatfield Shirley," Memorial ID 16480340, Greenwood Cemetery, Find a Grave.
England, B. Jane. "Wise County," Handbook of Texas, Texas State Historical Association.
Ensmiger, Richard A. "Quantrill's Guerrillas: Members in the Civil War," KansasHeritage.org.
Everett, Dianna. "Butterfield Overland Mail," Encyclopedia of Oklahoma History and Culture, OKHistory.org.
Everett, Dianna. "Cassius McDonald Barnes," Encyclopedia of Oklahoma History and Culture, OKHistory.org.
Everett, Dianna. "Horse Racing," Encyclopedia of Oklahoma History and Culture, OKHistory.org.
"Famous Relations of Berry Towles Canote," FreePages.RootsWeb.com.
Ferguson, Cleveland III. "Yellow Journalism," *Media*.
"Floyd County, Indiana, Marriages, 1802–1892," FHL no. 1411883, Genealogy Trails.
"Fort Smith Streetcar History," Fort Smith Trolley Museum, FSTM.org.
Gorman, William D. "The Murder of William Riley Seaboalt, Jr. (1851–1874)," Pioneers of Ellis County, Sites.Rootweb.org.
Hamblen, Larry A. "Gose Family History," LamarCountyTX.org.
Harper, Cecil, Jr. "Cabell, William Lewis," Handbook of Texas, Texas State Historical Association.
Harvell, Elle E. "The Struggle for Missouri," EssentialCivilWarCurriculum.com.
"Healing Waters," Shiloh Museum of Ozark History, ShilohMuseum.org.

"History of the Restoration Movement," TheRestorationMovement.com.
Hoover, Carl. "Roaring Red Light District Part of Waco's Early History," November 14, 2005, WacoHistoryProject.org.
Hoy, Jim. "Cattle Industry," Encyclopedia of Oklahoma History and Culture, OKHistory.org.
Hunt, Jeffrey William. "Palmito Ranch, Battle of," Handbook of Texas, Texas State Historical Association.
"Isaac Mason McCommas," MyHeritage.com.
"Isaac McComas (variant spelling), father of Michael, or Mitchell McComas," Geni.
"Isaac W. Sprague—The Original Living Skeleton," Human Marvels.
Isham, Theodore, and Blue Clark, "Creek (Mvskoke)," Encyclopedia of Oklahoma History and Culture, OKHistory.org.
Jackson, Jason Baird. "Yuchis in Alabama," EncyclopediaofAlabama.org.
James, Frances. "White Rock Creek," DallasPioneer.org.
"James Burke McCommas, son of Amon McCommas and father of Rosanna McCommas," En.Geneanet.org.
"James C. Reed," Paden/Peden Family History and Genealogy.
"Jane S. (Dyall) Watson," WikiTree.
"Jennie Cochran McDaniel (1875–1959)," memorial ID 33048843, Blanchard Cemetery, McClain County, OK, Find a Grave.
"Jesse James Family Reunion," December 20, 2014, Eric James.
"Jim Wheat's Dallas County, Texas, Archives," Old Pleasant Mound Cemetery, Free Pages.
"John Ritchie (1817–1887)," Descendants of John Starr Jr., Territorial Kansas Online.
Jones, Jonathan S. "Then and Now: How Civil War–Era Doctors Responded to their Own Opiate Epidemic," November 3, 2017, *The Front Line* (blog), *Civil War Monitor*.
"Killing of J. A. 'Polk' Burris, Lamar County, Texas," Genealogy Trails.
Krauthamer, Barbara. "Slavery," Encyclopedia of Oklahoma History and Culture, OKHistory.org.
"Legends of the West," LegendsofAmerica.com.
"The Lessons of Edgar Watson," TheFreeLibrary.com.
"The Life and Times of Jesse James," Real Wild West.
"Life in the Ozarks," Historical Marker Database, HMDB.org.
"Lint Societies," EncyclopediaDubuque.org.
"Town of Ramirez, Near Whittier, California," September 7, 2012, *Los Angeles Revisited* (blog).
Lott, Aida. "Texas Corn," TexasEscapes.com.
Mackenzie, John. "A Brief History of the Mason-Dixon Line," APEC/CANR, University of Delaware.
"Main Street Siloam Springs," MainStreetSiloam.org.
May, Jon D. "North Fork Town," Encyclopedia of Oklahoma History and Culture, OKHistory.org.
May, Jon D. "Starr, Emmet," Encyclopedia of Oklahoma History and Culture, OKHistory.org.
McKay, Brett, and Kate McKay. "America's First Popular Men's Magazine: The *National Police Gazette*," November 26, 2017, ArtofManliness.com.
"Michael J. 'Mike' McComas, Birth of Son William McComas (1869–1869)," Ancestry.com.
"Michael or Mitchell McComas (variant spelling), son of Isaac and Sarah Ann McComas, nephew of Elder Amon McComas," Geni.
Michals, Debra, ed. "Catharine Beecher," 2015, WomensHistory.org.
"Interview of Milo 'Frog' Ard Hoyt and Others on Belle Starr's Death," April 19, 2018, MyCherokeeFamily.wordpress.com.
Moss, Norita Shepherd. "Edgar A. Watson," Lee County Florida Family Records, Genealogy Trails.
"Moon Phase for Monday January 28, 1884," NinePlanets.org.
"Mudtown: The Story," Lowell.Arkansas.gov.
Norfleet, Phil. "Biographical Sketch of the Family of Thomas Starr (1813–1890)," Geni.
"Oklahoma Law Enforcement Memorial," Oklemem.com.
"Old Scyene Road," Texas Historical Markers, Waymarking.com.

"OrangeManor."
"Outlaw John Middleton," Genealogy.com.
"Paola, Kansas: A 150-Year History in Detail," Think Miami County History.
Partridge, Dennis. "Early Crimes of Washington County, Arkansas," June 6, 2014, ArkansasGenealogy.com.
Payne, John W., Jr. "Coke, Richard," Handbook of Texas, Texas State Historical Association.
"Petrifaction and Stone Giant Hoaxes," Hoaxes.org.
Pfeiffer, Lee. "The Man Who Shot Liberty Valance," *Britannica*.
"Politics Make Strange Bedfellows," Sacred Cow.
"Potter's Field Cemetery—McKinney," CollinCountyHistory.com.
Radcliff, Maranda. "Isaac Charles Parker (1838–1895)," EncyclopediaofArkansas.net.
"Rancho Cucamonga, California," *Britannica*.
"Ranchos and the Californios," Lakewood.City.org.
"Re: Frank James writes letter to *The Appeal* . . . Memphis, TN 1882," Genealogy.com.
Rede, Anika, and Maryum Ali. "Uncle Tom's Cabin: Generating a Rising Tide of Responsibility to End the Institution of Slavery," Weebly.com.
"Report of Col. Joseph Shelby (CSA) to Major L. A. Maclean, Assistant Adjutant-General, Price's Division Headquarters Shelby's Brigade, Camp Price, November 16, 1863," FreePages.RootsWeb.com.
"Richard Robert Middleton," Starr Cemetery, Briartown, OK, Memorial ID 5077723, Find a Grave.
"Rosanna Canote Shelly (1700s)," Genealogy.com.
"Rose Lee 'Pearl Starr' Reed (1866–1925)," Calvary Cemetery, Douglas, AZ, Memorial ID 7774203, Find a Grave. Note: Rosa Lee Reed was born in 1868, not 1866.
Ross, John, Department of History, Lon Morris College, Jacksonville, TX. Review published on H-Law, May 2007.
"Sam Bass," Outlaw Series, FrontierTimes.com.
"Samuel Bell Maxey," LamarCountyTX.com.
"Shields Family," LoneStar Genealogy.
"Shirley Families of Dallas Texas: African-American Lineages," October 2022, African-American Ancestry Research Center, Shirley Association.
"Shug," UrbanDictionary.com.
"Sideshow Banner vs. Reality," ShowHistory.com.
"Silas Hare," GenealogyTrails.com.
"Siloam Springs, Arkansas—Historic Sites and Points of Interest," ExploreSouthernHistory.com.
"Siloam Springs, Arkansas," SiloamSprings.com.
Sivilis, Matthew Wynn. "Ridge, John Rollins," Encyclopedia of Oklahoma History and Culture, OKHistory.org.
Slawson, Robert G. "The Story of the Pile of Limbs," December 6, 2018, CivilWarMed.org
Spitzzeri, Paul R. "All Over the Map: Greater Los Angeles in 1872," August 22, 2016, *The Homestead Blog*. HomesteadMuseum.org.
Spurgeon, Ian. "Battle of Wilson's Creek," Border War Encyclopedia, Civil War on the Western Border.
"Stagecoaching in Texas," Handbook of Texas, Texas State Historical Association.
Standridge, Eric, and Sierra Standridge. "Poteau River Flood: A Tale of Wister, Oklahoma," June 18, 2019, Discover.HubPages.com.
Stanley, Matthew E. "Anderson, William 'Bloody Bill,'" Border War Encyclopedia, Civil War on the Western Border.
Starling, Suzanne. "Scyene, TX," Handbook of Texas, Texas State Historical Association.
"Starr Genealogy," Red Eagle JW.
Stegman, Stephanie. "The Good, the Bad, and the Legend of the Fort Smith Federal Courthouse," Washington, DC: Ultimate History Project.

"Stuart & Mair Mercantile and Exchange Merchants," 1872 Austin City Directory, AustinGenealogicalSociety.org.
"Susan Demanda Brock," Paden/Peden Family History and Genealogy.
Teague Cemetery, Wise County, Texas.
"Texas History Notebook," Texas on 66.
Texas, US, Select County Marriage Records, 1837–2015, vol. 3, Provo, Utah, 2014, Ancestry.com.
Thacker, Mark. "US Deputy Marshal Henry Frank Griffin," MarkAThacker.com.
Thomas, Sarah C. "Rogers County," Encyclopedia of Oklahoma History and Culture, OKHistory.org.
"Thomas Starr Genealogy," WeRelate.org.
"Timeline—Notre Dame 175," 175.nd.edu.
Titchenal, Oliver Ray. "The Titchenal Cherokee Connection," Titchenal.com.
"Towns of Bosque County," BosqueCoTXGenweb.org.
Tuller, Roger H. "Parker, Isaac Charles," Encyclopedia of Oklahoma History and Culture, OKHistory.org.
Turpin, Robert. "Horse Stealing—A Hanging Offense," Ezine Articles.
"Johnson, Waldo Porter," Biographical Directory of the United States Congress.
Wall, Ronald N. "The Legend of Belle Starr—Queen of the Oklahoma Outlaws," November 23, 2017, WhitsettandWall.com.
Walsh, David. "Historian James M. McPherson and the Cause of Intellectual Integrity," May 18, 1999, WSWS.org.
Warde, Mary Jane. "Indian International Fair," Encyclopedia of Oklahoma History and Culture, OKHistory.org.
Weiser, Kathy. "Isaac Parker—Hanging Judge of Indian Territory," LegendsofAmerica.com.
Wellington, Jan. "Oscar Wilde's West," August 19, 2007, LiteraryTraveler.com.
"When Did the Civil War End?" HistoryontheNet.com.
"Wichita Children's Home," EndSlaveryNow.org.
Wilson, Linda D. "Barde, Frederick Samuel," Encyclopedia of Oklahoma History and Culture, OKHistory.org.
Wilson, Linda D. "Schools, Subscription," Encyclopedia of Oklahoma History and Culture, OKHistory.org.
Wolfe, David. "Cherokee Moons," Telliquah.com.
"World's Fair 'Mummies' at the Field Museum," WorldsFairChicago1893.com.
Zebe, Paul, comp. "Descendants of John Canote and His Wife Rosanna (nee Hunse)," February 8, 2001, HomePages.RootsWeb.com
Zelazko, Alicja, ed. "Did Catherine the Great Have Unusual Sexual Proclivities?," Britannica Beyond.

Government Documents and Publications (Tribal, City, County, Territorial, State, and Federal)

Barnett, Fayette, and Belle Starr, Larceny 1885, Identifier no. 203713, Jacket no. 14, Defendant Jacket Files for the US District Court Western Division of Arkansas, Fort Smith Division 1866–1900, National Archives at Fort Worth.
Bisbee (AZ) District Directory, 1924.
Cherokee Intermarriage Cases, 203 U.S. 76 (1906).
Cherokee Nation, W. P. Boudinot, Daniel H. Ross, and J. A. Scales, comps. *Constitution and Laws of the Cherokee Nation*. St. Louis, 1875.
Cherokee National Council. *Compiled Laws of the Cherokee Nation*. Tahlequah, Indian Territory, 1881.

Cherokee National Penitentiary, Historic American Buildings Survey. Prints and Photographs Division, Library of Congress.

Common Law Record Books, 1855–1959, WAR16, US District Court for the Western Division of Arkansas, Fort Smith Division, National Archives at Kansas City.

Congressional Record, 44th Cong., vol. 4, pt. 1, 1876.

Cowles, Calvin Duvall, ed. *The War of the Rebellion: A Compilation of the Official Records of the Union and Confederate Armies*. Washington, DC: Government Printing Office, 1893.

Criminal Court Minute Books, Cause no. 2899, vol. H-2, 492, August 4, 1876; Cause no. 2519, vol. J, 177, March 16, 1877, arrested with Tom Jones; Cause no. 2978, vol. J, 179; Cause no. 2982, vol. O, 86, April 20, 1882, charged with Dave McCommas, Dallas County District Court.

Criminal Minutes, Ledger no. 122, 576, US District Court Records, Western District of Texas, National Archives at Fort Worth.

Deed Actuaries, December 18, 1873, Bosque County Deed Records, vol. N, Bosque County, TX.

Deed Record Book C, Jasper County, MO.

Erbach, Arthur. Birth certificate, Sebastian County, AR, August 24, 1898.

Erbach, Arthur, and Rosie P. Reed. Certificate of marriage, license issued October 9, 1897, ceremony performed October 10, 1897, Washington County Marriage Records 1845–1941, County of Washington, State of Arkansas, via Ancestry.com.

Erbach, Arthur E. (husband), entry 145, and Arthur E. Erbach (infant), entry 670. Handwritten ledger, records, City Cemetery (Oak Cemetery), Fort Smith.

Evans, Harold C., and Federal Writers' Project. *The WPA Guide to 1930s Kansas*. New York: Viking, 1939.

Federal Population Schedules, Dallas County, TX, US Census Bureau, 1870, Microcopy No. 593, Roll 1581, National Archives.

Federal Writers' Project. *The WPA Guide to California*. 1939; reprint, New York: Pantheon, 1984.

Galonaska, Juliet. "Pearl Starr." "Fort Smith Minutes" series. Fort Smith National Historic Site, US National Park Service.

Galonsksa, Juliet. "Payment of Deputy Marshals." Fort Smith National Historic Site, US National Park Service.

Galpin, Samuel Arthur. *Report upon the Condition and Management of Certain Indian Agencies in the Indian Territory*. US Office of Indian Affairs. Washington, DC: Government Printing Office, 1877.

Grayson, Watt. Claim file, Exhibit H, Records of the US House of Representatives, National Archives.

Hardy, Daniel, and Terri Myers. "The Development of East and South Dallas, 1872–1945." Multiple Property Documentation Form, 1995, National Register of Historic Places.

Hare, Daniel, Criminal Defendant Case File, 1895, NRFF-21-3W51-19716, perjury, jacket no. 369, National Archives at Fort Worth.

Instructions for the Government of Armies of the United States in the Field, Article 88, General Orders No. 100, April 24, 1863, in US War Department, *War of the Rebellion: Official Records of the Union and Confederate Armies*, 128 vols., series 3, vol. 3. Washington, DC: Government Printing Office, 1880–1901.

Jacket no. 170, US District Court for the Western Division of Arkansas, Fort Smith Division, National Archives and Records Administration, Washington, DC.

Journal of the Executive Proceedings of the Senate of the United States of America. Washington, DC: Government Printing Office, 1901.

Journal of the House of the State of Missouri at the First Session of the Twenty-First General Assembly. Jefferson City, MO, 1861.

December 6, 2019, Office of Vital Statistics, Kansas Department of Health,

Leonard, Eric. "Myths and Legends Surrounding Judge Parker," Fort Smith National Historic Site, US National Park Service.

Marriage Records of Greene County, Indiana, Book C, p. 32, certified copy by Frankie Justus Jr., Clerk of Greene County Circuit Court.

McKechern, T. J. [Thomas J. McKeehan], Soldier Details, the Civil War, US National Park Service. Records transcribed from National Archives.

Minutes, vol. D, February 12, 1874, Bosque County (TX) District Court.

National Institute of Law Enforcement and Criminal Justice, *The Development of the Law of Gambling: 1776–1976*. Washington, DC: Government Printing Office, 1977.

Office of Vital Statistics, Kansas Department of Health, December 6, 2019.

Public Papers of Grover Cleveland, Twenty-Second President of the United States. Washington, DC: Government Printing Office, 1889.

Records of Cherokee County, KS, December 30, 2019.

Records of the US District Court for the Eastern District of Texas, National Archives at Fort Worth.

Reed, Francis Marion [S4351]. 1850 Federal Census, Bates County, MO, Microfilm Image, Series M432, Roll 392, National Archives and Records Administration, Washington, DC.

Reed, Rosa. Standard death certificate, died July 6, 1925, filed July 7, 1925, Bureau of Vital Statistics, Arizona State Board of Health.

Section 639, "Causes for Granting Divorce," in Article 28, "Divorce and Alimony," in Chapter 80, "Procedure, Civil," in *General Statutes of the State of Kansas* (Lawrence, 1868).

Sherley [Shirley], Edward [Edwin]. Cause no. 585, May 3, 1866, vol. D, Dallas County District Court.

Sherley [Shirley], Edward [Edwin]. Cause no. 587, October 24, 1866, vol. D, Dallas County District Court.

Shirley, John, and Nancy Fowler, entry for April 6, 1818, Marriage Record, Book A, p. 21, Marriages, 1808–1897, Clark County, IN.

Shirley, John, and Harry W. Younger. Land patent (1850), Official Land Records Site, MW-1002-108, US Bureau of Land Management.

Shirley, Mansfield. Cause no. unknown, October 24, 1866, vol. D. Dallas County District Court.

Shirley, Mansfield. Cause no. 604, December 8, 1869, vol. E, Dallas County District Court.

Shirley, Preston, in Burleson [County], TX, Roll: M653_1289. 1860 Federal Census.

Starr, Belle. Verbal will, Court Records of Canadian District, October 24, 1876–December 27, 1897, vol. 2, Cherokee National Records, Oklahoma Historical Society.

Starr, Thomas. Indictment Charge 1670 R.L.D. [retail liquor distribution]. Date of incarceration November 23, 1886, Menard, IL, Fort Smith Sentence Books.

State of Arizona vs. Rosa Reed, alias Pearl Starr, April 5, 1918, Police Court of Bisbee, AZ.

State of Arizona vs. Rose Reed, appeal bond, April 17, 1918, Police Court of Bisbee, AZ.

State of Arizona vs. Rose Reed, proceedings, April 5–17, 1918, Police Court of Bisbee, AZ.

State of Arizona vs. Rose Reed, subpoena for Eddie Anderson, Wallace Christwell, and Billy Anderson to appear in court on October 1, 1918, Superior Court of the County of Cochise, State of Arizona.

State of Texas v. John Middleton, Cause nos. 3397, 3398, and 3432, Docket Book, Fall Term 1884, 4:244, District Court, Lamar County, TX.

State of Texas v. Myra Reed, Cause no. 2873, Minutes, vol. 1, p. 54, Fourteenth District Court, Dallas County, TX.

State of Texas v. Myra Reed, Cause no.. 2873, Minutes, vol. 1, p. 29, case continued by defendant, December 22, 1875, Fourteenth District Court, Dallas County, TX.

Stopka, Christina, Dan Agler, and Fred Wilkins, eds. "Texas Rangers Killed or Died While on Duty." Waco: Armstrong Texas Ranger Research Center, 2019.

Swanton, John R. *Social Organization and Social Issues of the Indians of the Creek Federation.* Washington, DC: Bureau of American Ethnology, 1928.

Treaty of Guadalupe Hidalgo (1848), National Archives and Records Administration, Washington, DC.

United States. v. Bass Reeves, Item 13_04_017, Records of the US Western District Court of Arkansas, Arkansas State Archives, Little Rock.
United States v. Belle Starr, Case no. 1180, Records of the US District Court, Western District of Arkansas, Fort Smith.
United States v. Bill July alias Jim Starr, Case no. 103, August 30, 1887, Records of the US Commissioner's Court, Western District of Arkansas, Fort Smith.
United States v. Blue Duck and William Christie, Case no. 1089, Records of the US District Court, Western District of Arkansas, Fort Smith.
United States v. Cal Carter, Bill Fisher, and One Reed, letter of John B. Jones, Indian agent, Records of the US District Court, Western District of Arkansas, Fort Smith.
United States v. Ed Reed (larceny), Case no. 3015, July 21, 1888, Records of the US Commissioner's Court, Western District of Arkansas, Fort Smith.
United States v. Ed Reed, Case no. ___, October 13 and 25, 1888, Records of the US Commissioner's Court, Western District of Arkansas, Fort Smith.
United States v. Edgar A. Watson, Case no. ___, February 22–23, 1889. Records of the US Commissioner's Court, Western District of Arkansas, Fort Smith.
United States v. Frank Cook, Cause no. 1497, 1886, Records of the US District Court, Western District of Arkansas, Fort Smith.
United States v. Frank Cook, Cause no. 764, 1885, Records of the US District Court, Western District of Arkansas, Fort Smith.
United States v. Jim Reed et al., Case no. 142, Records of the US District Court, Western District of Texas, Austin.
United States v. Sam Starr and Belle Starr, 1882, Records of the US District Court, Western District of Arkansas, Fort Smith.
United States v. Sam Starr, Felix Griffin and Richard Hays, Case no. 59, November 9, 1885, Records of the US Commissioner's Court, Western District of Arkansas, Fort Smith.
United States v. Samuel Starr et al., Case no. 1213, Records of the US District Court, Western District of Arkansas, Fort Smith.
United States v. Thomas Starr, Case no. 1670 R.L.D. [retail liquor distribution], Records of the US District Court, Western District of Arkansas, Fort Smith.
United States v. William D. Wilder, Cause no. 114, Criminal Cases, Records of the US District Court, Western District of Arkansas, Fort Smith.
US Census Bureau. "Population of the United States in 1860: California."
US Census Bureau. "Population of the United States in 1870: California."
US Census Bureau. "Population of the United States in 1870: California," original ledger page reproduced in facsimile in FamilySearch.com.
US Congressional Serial 1497, "Retention of Arms by Soldiers," General Orders, No. 101, May 10, 1865.
Watson, Edgar A. Criminal Defendant File, ARC ID 201532 Murder Jacket no: 197. Defendant Jacket Files for US District Court, Western Division of Arkansas, Fort Smith.
Younger, Bruce, and Maibelle Reed. "True copy" of marriage license, May 15, 1880, Office of Probate Judge S. L. Coulter, vol. B, Labette County District Court, Oswego, KS.

Interviews

Burns, Nannie Lee (field worker). Interview by Louise Rider. Interview no. 13727, April 26, 1938, Indian-Pioneer Papers, Western History Collections, University of Oklahoma, Norman.
Davis, Shelba King. Telephone interview by Hazel Rowena Mills, March 22, 2019.
Gibbs, Charles A. III. Telephone interview by Hazel Rowena Mills, December 3, 2018.
Keith, F. W. Interview by Florence L. Phillips, July 31, 1937. Interview no. 7371, Indian-Pioneer Papers, Western History Collections, University of Oklahoma, Norman.

Leeman, Lauren (librarian, State Historical Society of Missouri, Center for Missouri Studies). Telephone interview by Hazel Rowena Mills, December 9, 2019.
Lewis, S. R. Interview by Effie S. Jackson, September 24, 1937. Interview no. 7653, Indian-Pioneer Papers, Western History Collections, University of Oklahoma, Norman.
Middleton, James. Interview by James S. Buchanan, May 10, 1937. Interview no. 5657, Indian-Pioneer Papers, Western History Collections, University of Oklahoma, Norman.
Stevenson, Kelly (director, Evergreen Cemetery, Colorado Springs). Telephone interview by Hazel Rowena Mills, December 5, 2019.
Weaver, George. Interview by James S. Buchanan. July 14, 1937. Interview no. 6647, Indian-Pioneer Papers, Western History Collections, University of Oklahoma, Norman.
West, Ellis. Interview by Florence L. Phillips, n.d. Interview no. 5177, Indian-Pioneer Papers, Western History Collections, University of Oklahoma, Norman.

Oral Presentations

Strandberg, Victor. "Southern Comfort: Robert Penn Warren and the Art of (the Civil) War." Public lecture presented to the Robert Penn Warren Circle annual meeting, Guthrie, KY, 2011.
Suval, John. "Squatters, Statesmen, and the Rupture of American Democracy, 1830–1860." Presentation to the Kinder Institute Colloquium, October 26, 2018.

Unpublished Works

Andrews, Jennette Steele. Born November 8, 1902, Fort Smith, Sebastian County, AR. Request for delayed birth certificate, 1964.
Bearss, Edwin C. *Law Enforcement at Fort Smith, 1871–1896*. National Park Service Library, Denver, Colorado, January 1964.
Brown, David, and Mike Gregory. "Agriculture in the Upper Shenandoah: An Outline from the 18th Century to the Present." Unpublished paper, Washington and Lee University, 2015.
Butler, Kenneth A., comp. "Some Articles and Items about Belle Starr." Oklahoma City, OK, October 1987.
Jones, Fatima Jane Reed. Records (1863–1961), annotated by Verna M. White. Wallis Collection.
Ladies Aid Society, minutes, Methodist Episcopal Church South [later called First United Methodist Church], Dallas, January 2 and 8, 1894.
Mercantile Department Day Book, ULDG Day Book, 1864–1911, vol. 2, Early Notre Dame Student, Class, and Financial Record Books.
Miller, Richard J. February 20, 1988, Dallas County Tax Assessment Rolls, 1861 and 1862.
Notre Dame: Index to Financial Ledgers 1841–1869, vol. 5, 361, October 30, 1867, November 14, 1867, January 23, [1868].
Reed, Rosa. Record of funeral, July 6, 1925, Porter and Ames Mortuary, Douglas, AZ. Photocopy of handwritten ledger page.
Schrantz, Ward L. "The Background of Belle Starr." Unpublished manuscript, n.d., Phillip W. Steele Collection.

Illustration Credits

Page iv (and 260): Courtesy Robert G. McCubbin Collection, Wild West History Association.
Page xi (map): Steve Rice, publisher, Map Ink, Norman.
Page 12: Jasper County, Missouri, insert map. "My Genealogy Hound," Courtesy of Hearthstone Legacy Publications.
Page 52: Courtesy Robert G. McCubbin Collection, Wild West History Association.
Page 65: Courtesy Robert G. McCubbin Collection, Wild West History Association.
Page 89: Courtesy Robert G. McCubbin Collection, Wild West History Association.
Page 90: Courtesy Robert G. McCubbin Collection, Wild West History Association.
Page 94: Courtesy Robert G. McCubbin Collection, Wild West History Association.
Page 100: Texas, Select County Marriage Records, 1837–2015, vol. 3.
Page 105: Courtesy Phillip W. Steele Collection, Wild West History Association.
Page 116: Detail from the Homestead Blog, "All over the Map: Greater Los Angeles in 1872," from the Homestead Museum's collection.
Page 127: Bosque County, Texas, map 1911, from Rand McNally.
Page 139: Courtesy Phillip W. Steele Collection, Wild West History Association.
Page 160: Courtesy Phillip W. Steele Collection, Wild West History Association.
Page 206: LaBette County District Court, Oswego, Kansas, Marriage Records, Vol. B, 36.
Page 209: Oklahoma Historical Society Indian Affairs Archives, Vol. 1-B, Court Records of Canadian District, Cherokee Nation.
Page 211: Courtesy of the Oklahoma Historical Society, Frederick S. Barde Collection, No. 1464.6.
Page 216: Courtesy Robert G. McCubbin Collection, Wild West History Association.
Page 219: Courtesy Robert G. McCubbin Collection, Wild West History Association.
Page 223: Courtesy Robert G. McCubbin Collection, Wild West History Association.
Page 259: *National Police Gazette*, May 22, 1886, 16, Library of Congress Prints and Photographs Division, Washington, D.C., LC-USZ62-63912.
Page 260 (and iv): Courtesy Robert G. McCubbin Collection, Wild West History Association.
Page 263: Courtesy Robert G. McCubbin Collection, Wild West History Association.
Page 290: Courtesy Will Naillion Collection.
Page 291: Courtesy Will Naillion Collection.
Page 302: Courtesy Phillip W. Steele Collection, Wild West History Association.
Page 322: University of North Texas Libraries, the Portal to Texas History, hops://texashistory.uni.edu, crediting Denton (Texas) Public Library.
Page 325: Courtesy Robert G. McCubbin Collection, Wild West History Association.
Page 331: Courtesy of the Oklahoma Historical Society, Frederick S. Barde Collection, No. 1464.1.
Page 335: Courtesy Kassey Weaver Photography.

Index

abolitionism, 18, 23, 25, 30–35, 47, 50, 65, 80, 136, 344n50, 345n1
abortion, 206, 235, 280, 390n17
Acton, Charles, 294–95, 311–12
Adams, Ramon F., 356n9, 368n6
adultery, 7–8, 260
Adventures and Exploits of the Younger Brothers (Dale), 355n53
Adventures of Huckleberry Finn (Twain), 239
Alabama, 140, 141
"Alexander, C. P.," *see* James, Frank
Alexander Mitchell and Company, private bank, Lexington, Missouri, 106
Alexander, Nancy (Nannie) Clorinda Fisher, 188
Alexander, Williamson Dunn, 16, 343n13
American Party (Know Nothing Party), 34
American Revolution, 5
American West, 39, 92–93, 176–77, 346n17
  buffalo/bison, 3, 82, 125–26
  community dances, 258, 267, 287, 293
  fringed buckskin costumes, 3, 178
  frontier burial customs, 295
  Wild West shows, 271–73
  women in the, 176–77, 235, 259
  see also horses; lawlessness; "Wild West, the"; women of the American West
amputations, 84
Anderson, Billie, 400n123
Anderson, Jim, 106
Anderson, Lucy Josephine, 179
Anderson, William H., 170–73
Anderson, William T. ("Bloody Bill"), 54, 88–90, 106, 124–25
Andrew J. Moore store, Blaine, Choctaw Nation, 253

Andrews, Dell, 327, 382n116
Andrews, Jennette Steele, 327, 330, 400n123
Annual Fair of Western Arkansas and the Indian Territory, 271–72
Appomattox, Confederate surrender at, 83
Arizona, 113, 120, 166, 327–28, 399n123
  Bisbee, 328, 399n123
  Douglas, 328–29
Arkansas, 78–79, 98
  during the Civil War, 63, 67
  Conway, 197, 385n59
  Evansville, 110–11, 113
  Fayetteville, 78–79, 227, 326–27
  Fisher gang, 111–12, 113, 131, 149, 358n2
  legalized pari-mutuel betting, 357n42
  Siloam Springs, 289–81, 391n25
  Van Buren, 78, 326
  Western District of Arkansas, 171–74, 218, 229, 255, 370n60
  see also Fort Smith, Arkansas
Arkansas Democrat, 267–68, 325
Arkansas Gazette, 248, 269, 309, 324–25
Arkansas State Penitentiary, 174, 242, 370n65
Arnold, Frank J., 271
Associated Press, 335
Austin American-Statesman, 151
Austin Democratic Statesman, 151–52
Austin, Texas, 80, 151–58, 166, 170, 215

Babb, William, 11
Baldridge, Eli, 136
Baldridge, Sallie, 136, 363n74
Balentine, William H., 140
Ball, Larry, 224
"Balm in Gilead, A" (hymn), 48, 348n42

Barde, Frederick Samuel, 211–12, 283–84, 332–33, 378n20, 378n24
Barkley, James E., 156, 189–92, 194
Barksdale, Hickerson, 189, 373n25
Barnes, Cassius M., 226, 233
Barnes, Robert and Jerusha, 292
Barnett, Fayette, 247, 251, 254–56, 270
Barnhill, Charles Fletcher, 258
Bass, Sam, 126–27, 362n22, 362n23
"Battle Hymn of the Republic" (song), 29, 345n1
Bearss, Edwin C., 223, 226, 227, 230, 388n64
Beecher, Catharine, 25–26, 344n51
Beecher, Henry Ward, 32
"Beecher's Bibles," 32
Bell, John, 34
Bell, Roger, 400n141
Bella Starr, the Bandit Queen, or the Female Jesse James (Fox), 99, 310–11, 329
Belle Starr and Her Pearl (Hicks), 240, 374n4, 385n59
Belle Starr and Her Roots (Betty M. Shirley), 341n6, 359n19
Belle Starr, the Bandit Queen: The Career of the Most Colorful Outlaw the Indian Territory Ever Knew (Shackleford [Vance]), 201–2, 329
Belle Starr (Myra Maibelle Shirley Reed Younger Starr), the lady, xi, xiii–xv, 307–36
　alleged crimes on trial in Fort Smith, Arkansas, 218–29, 236–52, 254–74, 282–87, 290–91, 294, 297
　alleged role in the Farrill robbery, 256, 258, 266–67
　arson trial, 188, 193
　birth and early life, 14–21
　birth of a legend, 208–17
　Bosque County, Texas, *127*, 128–35, 142, 147, 149, 171, 173, 187, 362n28, 363n66, 366n5
　in California with Jim Reed, 113–22
　death of, 277–92, 307, 332, 392, 401
　equestrian skills, 23, 51, 177, 273, 286, 324, 371n14
　falsely associated with the Grayson robbery, 139–46, 147, 149, 153, 156, 158, 170–73, 192–93, 222, 284
　family origins of, 3–13
　first known use of the name Belle, 208
　incarceration in the Detroit House of Correction, 14, 231–36, 238, 251, 383n109
　in Fort Smith, on trial for the Farrill robbery, 256–66
　growing up in Carthage, Missouri, 14–21
　her boots waiting to be picked up, 290–91, 392n74
　her horse Venus, 240, 247, 258–61, 264–65, 268–70, 275, 331
　her last meal of cornbread, 292, 295, 392n12
　horse-theft charge with Sam Starr, 225–37
　Indian International Fair of 1875, 176–77, 286–87
　marriage to Bruce Wilson Younger, 101, 198–207, 208–9, 314–18
　marriage to Jim July, 277–83, 286–91, 294–97, 301, 303–4, 308, 311–14, 324
　marriage to Jim Reed, 95–102, 105–7, 113–22
　marriage to Sam Starr, 208–17, 225–36, 238, 241, 245, 253–76, 278–82, 292, 333
　"mystery years" of, 177–78
　myth versus reality, 238–52
　Newtonia ride, 56–57
　on the scout during the Civil War, 49–57
　piano story, 240–41
　reenacting a stagecoach robbery for the public, 271–73
　relationship with Mike McCommas, 153, 159, 179–82, 185–93
　riding with surcingle and blanket, 177, 371n14
　supposed harboring of wanted criminal John Middleton, 240–52, 254, 270, 385n55, 385n66
　time in Bosque County, Texas, *127*, 128–35, 142, 147, 149, 171, 173, 187, 362n28, 363n66, 366n5
　unsolved murder of, xiii, 293–306
　wanted for the theft of Sam Campbell's gray mare, 225–26, 229
　wanted for theft during the Younger's Bend 1882 spring roundup, 225–37
　widow several times over, 175–82, 277
　in Will Conine's memories, 129–34, 171–73, 177, 362n35, 371n14
Belle Starr (Myra Maibelle Shirley Reed Younger Starr), the legend, xiii–xv, 194–203, 208–17, 253–76, 307–36
　alleged bandit queen of many appetites, 264, 308
　allegedly dressing "like a man," 145, 181, 215, 222, 256, 267, 324–25

Index ✣ 429

compared with Lady Macbeth, 191, 373n40
"female desperado," 308, 333
"hellcat of Dallas," 177
legacy of a legend, 307–36
myth versus reality, 238–52
myths of an affair and child with Cole Younger, 101, 136, 198, 215, 307–8, 324, 330
Newtonia ride, 56–57
tall tales about, 136, 177, 193, 211, 217, 225, 312
"wild Amazon," 191, 259, 293
woodcuts of, 260, 308
Benge, J. M., 99
Benton, Thomas Hart, 34, 346n18
Bethea, Edna Catherine, 302, 393n51
Bidwell, horse thief, 156–57
Biffle, John A., 363n66
Big Head's treasure, 211, 378n16
Billy the Kid, 307, 354n10
Bingham, George Caleb, 66
Bisbee, Arizona, 328, 399n123
Black, James H., 242–43
Black people and communities
  denial of equal citizenship to Creeks with African ancestry, 141
  as freedmen, 87, 142
  genealogical research by the Shirley Family Association, 76–77, 341n6
  Juneteenth, 87
  lawlessness and violence against African Americans, 128
  see also race and racism; slavery
Blaine, Choctaw Nation, 253, 256, 268
"Bleeding Kansas," 30–32, 51, 345n9
Blight, David W., 87
Blossom Prairie, Texas, 242
Blunt, James G., 69
Board of Popular Education, 25
Boggs, Lilburn, 10, 342n38
"Bonnie Blue Flag, The" (song), 37, 346n32
boomtowns, see mining
Boone, Daniel, 6, 227, 342n38
boots, as crime-scene evidence, 221, 251, 304
boots, Belle Starr's, 290–91, 392n74
Border Guards of Medoc, 38–39, 46
Border Rangers of Carthage, 37–38, 45
Border Ruffians, 31
Bosque County, Texas, 127, 128–35, 142, 147, 149, 171, 173, 187, 362n28, 363n66, 366n5

Boswell, William, 149–53, 158, 170, 174
bounty hunters, 153, 243
Boyd, Leon, 71
Bracken, L. E., 149
Bradbury, John, 4
Brant, Marley, 107, 124
Breckinridge, John C., 34
Briartown, Cherokee Nation, 210–14, 230, 239–40, 244–45, 258, 269–70, 274–76, 279, 287, 304, 332, 385
Briartown-Eufaula Trail, 211
Brizzolara, James, 257–58, 284, 287, 299–301
Brock family of Kentucky and Missouri, 95–98, 195, 203–4
Brock, Fatima Jane, 98
Brock, Susan Demanda, 95–96, 98, 195, 203–4, 238, 280–81, 284–85
Brock, William Commodore Perry, 96–97
Brooks, Cassius, 234
Broome, George W., 21, 47
"Brothers' War," 32
Brown, Amelia, 192
Brown, John, 136, 348n10
Brown, Samuel W., 250–51, 253, 368
Brownson, Orestes A., 50, 348n44
Broyles, Gil, 335
Bruce, James H., 136
Buchanan, James, 33–35
"Buffalo Bill," see Cody, William F.
buffalo/bison, 3, 82, 125–26
Building a Better Prison (Keve), 383n109
Bull Run (or Manassas), Battle of, 42
Burch, Milton J., 63–64, 68–70
Burkett, Mortimer, 393n51
Burleson County, Texas, 35, 80
Burlington Democrat (Kansas), 204
"Burns," see Dickens, Marion
Burns, Alex, 271
Burnt District, Missouri, 66–67
Burris, James A. ("Polk"), 244
Burris, W. S., 86
Bush, Charles, 112, 149
bushwhackers, 51–55, 58, 60–64, 68, 71, 88, 105
Butler, Joe, 133
Butler, Kenneth A., 378n20
Butterfield Overland Mail Company stagecoach route, 77–79, 115, 120
Byers, Samuel, 53

Cabell, Earle, 373n32
Cabell, William Lewis, 189, 373n32

Cache, Choctaw Nation, 256–57
Caldwell, Henry Clay, 173–74, 218, 370n60
California
    El Paso Robles, 114, 357n24
    gold rush of 1849, 15–16, 22, 120, 140, 332, 358n7, 396n54
    Jim and Myra Reed in, 113–22
    Los Angeles, 119–21, 358n8, 359n20
    Los Nietos Township, 117–20, 359n22
    San Francisco, 77, 114, 128, 358n8
    Spanish land grants in, 115, 119, 359n22
    wineries, 115
    Younger family in, 113–14
Callahan's Tavern, Arkansas, 78
Campbell, Denele Pitts, 110, 357n40
Campbell, Sam, gray mare owned by, 225–26, 229
Canote family of Virginia, 4–5, 126, 361n22
Carney, Thomas, 66
carpetbaggers, 221
Carr, Albert, 251–52
Carroll, John, 255, 284
Carter, Calvin H. (Cal), 112, 131, 149–51, 153, 157–59, 170, 174
Carthage City Cemetery, 350n21
Carthage Female Academy, 24–27, 38, 76, 91, 213
Carthage Light Guard Band, 272
Carthage, Missouri, 11–12, 14–28
    Border Rangers of, 37–38, 45
    during the Civil War, 33–39, 40–50, 54–57, 58–64, 65–72, 76–79, 83
    Shirley House hotel, 23–24, 28, 29, 42–47, 54–55, 57, 61, 64, 75, 83, 197
Carthage News, 273
Carver, William Frank ("Doc"), 271–72
cash crops, 5, 358n7
Cates brothers from Whitefield, Choctaw Nation, 295–96, 300, 332
Catherine the Great of Russia, 264
Catholicism, 50, 89, 348n45, 360n22
Centralia, Missouri, 88, 90
Chase, C. M., 51–52
Chelson, Mary Arella, *see* Shirley, Mary Arella Chelson
Cherokee Advocate, 158
Cherokee Nation
    Briartown, 210–14, 230, 239–40, 244–45, 258, 269–70, 274–76, 279, 287, 304, 332, 385
    burial practices, 295
    circuit court, 253

Claremore, 312, 321–23
    the Cold Moon, 237
    communal land ownership in the, 136, 210, 225
    Fort Gibson, 108, 144, 158, 282
    Going Snake District, 135, 158
    lighthorsemen of the, 244
    Old Settlers of the, 109–10
    Ross Party, 108–9
    Tahlequah, 138, 158, 253
    Treaty of New Echota, 108
    Vinita, 226
    see also Younger's Bend, Cherokee Nation
Chicago, 234, 317
Chicago Tribune, 199–200, 316
Chickasaw Intelligencer, 365n23
Chickasaw Nation, 79–80, 217, 312, 314, 321, 324, 352n12
Chinese community in Los Angeles, 120
Chisholm Trail, 128, 185, 362n29
Choctaw Nation, 79, 110, 140, 213, 217, 352n12
    Atoka, 309
    Blaine, 253, 256, 268
    Cache, 256–57
    Cates brothers from Whitefield, 295–96, 300, 332
    Jackson Rowe family of, 289–92, 294, 297–99
    McAlester, 225, 240, 320, 326
    store on King Creek, 291
    Tamaha, 325, 326
Christie, Ned, 313
Christie, William, 261–62
citizen scouts, 51, *see also* Jayhawkers; Red Legs
Civil War, 25, 29–39
    attack on Fort Sumter, 37, 347n4
    in Belle Starr country, 40–48, 50–56
    Bull Run (or Manassas), Battle of, 42
    deserters, 63, 301
    Elkhorn Tavern (or Pea Ridge), Battle of, 77–78
    end of the war and Reconstruction, 58–72, 84–85, 87, 93, 103, 190
    "Extermination Order No. 11," 66–67
    female spies during the, 55, 349n29
    Fort Sumter, South Carolina, 37, 347n4
    Fourth of July after the, 41, 347n6
    Gettysburg, 63
    John Shirley's family on the eve of, 33–39
    July 1863 turning point, 63

Missouri during the, 36, 40–42, 47, 66, 77
Myra Shirley's Newtonia ride, 56–57
neutrality in the, 55–56
origins in "Bleeding Kansas," 30–32, 51, 345n9
Osceola massacre of 1861, 52–53, 64–66, 349n15
Palmito Ranch, Battle of, 83–84
Pease River, Battle of, 186
raid on Harper's Ferry, 348n10
the Republican Party, 34–35, 218, 221
Sherman's "March to the Sea," 47
surrender at Appomattox, 83
tragedy of, 346n13
Vicksburg, 63
violence and criminality after the, 92–95
War Comet of 1861, 40, 346n1
Wilson's Creek, Battle of, 50, 90, 228
see also guerrilla warfare
Clabaugh, Samuel Newton, 187
Claremore, Cherokee Nation, 312, 321–23
Claremore Progress, 323
Clark, Edgar, 322
Clark, John, 323
Clay County Savings Association, Liberty, Missouri, 105–6
Clayton, William H. H., 229–30, 273–74
Clement, Archie, 106
Cleveland, Grover, 262–63
Cochran, Alec, death of, 321–23
Cochran, Frank, 261
Cochran, Jennie, 321–23
Cody, William F. ("Buffalo Bill"), 178, 272
Coke, Richard, 153, 169, 180–82, 367n66
Colbert, Benjamin Franklin, 79–80
Colburn, Joe, 326
Cold Moon of the Cherokees, 237
Coleman, John, 112
Colley and Bart, 19–21
Collins, Ann Mary, 297
Collins, Robert Marvin, 97
Colorado City, Colorado, 317–18, 396n54
Colorado Springs, Colorado, 317, 395n44, 396n54, 396n55
Colt revolvers, 59, 240, 248, 264, 323
Comanches, 96, 128, 186
Comet of 1861, 40, 346n1
community dances, 258, 267, 287, 293
Confederate States of America, 29
"Dixie" (song), 346n32
flag of the, 41, 345n12
"Little Dixie," Missouri, 18, 31

Lost Cause, 86, 179
secession, 33–37, 50, 167, 348n10
United Confederate Veterans, 179, 371n30
unreconstructed, 86, 131
view of "states' rights," 86
see also Civil War
Congress, *see* United States Congress
Conine, Will, 129–34, 171–73, 177, 362n35, 371n14
consumption, 262–63, 315
Conway, Arkansas, 197, 385n59
Cook, Frank, 246–47, 250–52, 386n97
Coon Creek, Texas, 129–31, 147–48, 171–72
Cordley, Richard, 65
Cordry, Dee, 397n72
corn, 11, 80, 83, 118, 120
cornbread, 292, 295, 392n12
"Cornerstone Speech" (A. H. Stephens), 29–30
corruption, 93, 133, 370n60
cotton, 80, 83, 185
Coulter, S. L., 204–5, 206, 377n60
"Country of the Six Bulls," 3–4, 9–10, 14, 31, 40
Cox family of Coon Creek, 129, 148, 366n9
Cox, Samuel P., 125
Crane, Andrew, 225–26, 229–30
Cravens & Marcum (law firm), 227–30, 258, 261–62, 274
Cravens, Jeremiah, 381n65
Cravens, Jesse L., 38
Cravens, William, 22, 227–30, 258
Cravey, Dick, 131–33
Creek Nation, 352n12
 Creek communities in Alabama, 140, 141
 Eufaula, 140, 170, 211, 241, 247, 251, 287, 294, 334
 Grayson robbery, 139–46, 147, 149, 153, 156, 158, 170–73, 192–93, 222, 284
 hiding out in the, 268, 284
 murder of William Riley Seaboalt Jr., 221
 Muskogee, 176–77, 251–52, 257, 275–76, 281–82, 286
 Okmulgee, 282
 robbery of the treasury of the, 244
 slave owning among the Creeks, 141–42, 365n25
 theft of Jim Lewis's horse, 284–85, 287, 391n44
 Wealaka robbery, 250–51, 253, 368
 Yuchi (Euchee) tribe, 250
Crook, George Mack, 242–44

Crown Hotel (formerly Lakeside Hotel), Siloam Springs, Arkansas, 280, 391n25
Croy, Homer, 165
Crump, George, 321
Crumrin, Timothy, 7
curatives/"taking the waters," 246, 280–81, 357n24, 385n59
Custer, George Armstrong, 373n28

Daily Arkansas Gazette, 309–10, 324–25
Dale, Henry, 355n53
Dale, John B., 19
Dallas County, Texas, 80–82, 86, 103–4, 147–48, 151, 168, 179–81, 187–90, 194, 197, 366n5
  as a growing city, 86, 123–27
  Kennedy assassination, 373n32
  Kirkpatrick House, hotel on Austin Avenue, 185–87
  Texas & Pacific Railroad to, 126
Dallas Daily Commercial, 121, 131, 149, 155, 164
Dallas Daily Herald, 159–60, 185
Dallas Daily Times Herald, 86
Dallas Morning News, 177, 264–66, 289, 309, 312, 329
Dallas News, 104
Dallas Weekly Herald, 157
Dalton brothers (Bob and Grat), 220
Daviess County Savings Association in Gallatin, Missouri, 124–25
Davis, Edmund J., 135
Davis, Jude Dean, 135
Dawson, Christopher Columbus, 37, 346n29
Day, Horace B., 84
DeArment, Robert K., 243
Delaware tribe, 9–10
Dell, Valentine, 233
Denison Daily News, 159
Denton County, Texas, 122–23, 126–28, *322*
Department of the Missouri, 66
deserters, 63, 301
desperadoes, 131, 162, 181, 233, 243, 308, 333
Detroit Free Press, 234
Detroit House of Correction, 14, 231–36, 238, 251, 383n109
Devena, Nana, 303
Dickens, Marion, 139–46, 149–54, 170–72
Dickerson, J. J., 314
Dictionary of the Range, Cow Camp, and Trail, A (R. F. Adams), 356n9

district court system, 154, 169, 173–74, 190, 217, 228–29, 321, 369n31, 373n25
divorce, 6–7, 136, 188, 206–7, 240, 327
"Dixie" (song), 346n32
DNA genealogy in the Shirley family, 76, 351n9
Doc Carver's Famous Original Wild West Show, 271–72
Doerr, Henry A., 159, *160*
Douglas, Arizona, 328–29
Douglas, Stephen A., 34, 345n5
Douglass, Frederick, 50
Drago, Harry Sinclair, 151, 263–64
Duck, Bluford ("Blue"), 261–64, 388n58
Duncan, John Riley ("Jack"), 243–45, 249–52
Duvall, Benjamin T., 228–29
Dynasty of Western Outlaws, A (Wellman), 90, 263–64

education
  Carthage Female Academy, 24–27, 38, 76, 91, 213
  personal politics of teachers, 32, 345n54, 346n12
  private schools, 22, 26–27
  public schools, 22, 25–26, 91
  reform, 22–23, 25, 345n9
  subscription school, 213–14
  for women, 24–27, 91, 213–14
  women as teachers, 25–26, 321, 344n51
Edwards, John Cummins, 22
Edwards, John Newman, 167, 369n17
Egan, William F. ("Dad"), 126–27
Eighth Missouri State Militia Cavalry, 63–64, 68
El Paso Robles, California, 114, 357n24
electrified streetcars in Fort Smith, Arkansas, 239
Eleventh Missouri Cavalry, 66
Elkhorn Tavern (or Pea Ridge), Battle of, 77–78
Empire City Echo, 200
Encyclopedia Britannica, 264
Enfield rifles, 158
England, Ray, 294, 300
Enrolled Missouri Militia, 67
enslaved workers, *see* slavery
Epple, David, 328
Epple, Florence ("Flossie") Pearl, 328–29, 384n15
Erbach, Arthur E., 327–28, 399n116
Erbach, Arthur E. Jr., infant, 328, 399n116

Eufaula, Creek Nation, 140, 170, 211, 241, 247, 251, 287, 294, 334
Evans, Daniel, 221–22, 380n28
Evans, Sam, 201–2
Evansville, Arkansas, 110–11, 113
"Everglades' Bandit Killer, The" (Knowles), 302
Ewing, Thomas, Jr., 66, 77
executions, 20–21, 53, 55, 221–24, 262, 270, 365n23
"Extermination Order No. 11," 66–67
"Eyewitness, An" (Archy Thomas memoir), 43

Farmer, Harry, 190
farming
    California wine, 115
    corn, 11, 80, 83, 118, 120
    cotton, 80, 83, 185
    hemp, 5, 358n7
    sharecropping, 296–98
    tobacco, 5, 18, 316
    wheat, 5, 130–31
    see also slavery
Farrill, Wilse W., robbery of, 256, 258, 266–67
Fayetteville, Arkansas, 78–79, 227, 326–27
ferry crossings, 78, 79–80, 106, 226, 267, 293
Field, Mary E., 26
Fifteenth Texas Cavalry, 97
Fifth Iowa Volunteers, 53
Figueroa, Jose, 120
Fillmore, Millard, 34
firepower
    Colt revolvers, 59, 240, 248, 264, 323
    Enfield rifles, 158
    gunslingers and crack shots, 23, 111, 243, 264
    Sharps rifles, 31–32, 58–59, 348n10
    Winchester rifle, 296, 313, 324
First Indian Brigade, 109
Fisher, Eliza Jane, 156
Fisher gang in Arkansas, 111–12, 113, 131, 149, 358n2
Fisk, John, 19–21
Fite, Nancy ("Nannie"), 176–77
Fitzwater, Noah, 112, 113, 358n2
Five Civilized Tribes, 352n12, *see also* Indian Territory; Native Americans
Florida, serial killer from, 296–302
Floyd County, Indiana, 6–7, 376n53
folk-hero outlaw archetype, 93–95
Ford, Bob and Charley, 216, 363n67

Ford, John Salmon ("Rip"), 83–84, 353n13
Ford, John, 311
Foreman, Bullet, 267
Foreman, Carolyn Thomas, 140
Fort Blair (Fort Baxter), Kansas, 69
Fort Gibson, Cherokee Nation, 108, 144, 158, 282
Fort Scott Daily Monitor, 200
Fort Scott, Kansas, 37, 47, 58, 69, 71
Fort Smith, Arkansas
    the arm of "the law," 110–11, 149, 171, 173–74, 217, 218–29
    Belle Starr's various crimes before the court in, 218–29, 236–52, 254–74, 282–87, 290–91, 294, 297
    during the Civil War, 69, 78–79
    electrified streetcars in, 239
    Parker, Isaac C., 217, 218–25, 229–31, 236, 241, 252, 255, 261–62, 268, 270, 272–74, 288, 300, 380n28
    Pearl's pregnancy in, 279–80
    Phoenix Publishing Company, 382n93
    Roeder Brothers Photography, 260–62
Fort Smith Elevator, 214, 233, 248–49, 252, 264, 313
Fort Smith Evening Call, 388n67
Fort Smith New Era, 173–74, 229, 229
Fort Smith Times, 255
Fort Sumter, South Carolina, 37, 347n4
"forting up," 96
Fourteenth Kansas Cavalry, 69
Fourth of July, 41, 347n6
Fox, Richard Kyle, 99, 310–11, 329
freedmen, 87, 142
Freeman, Thomas R., 362n44
Free-Staters, 31–32
Frémont, Jessie Benton, 346n17
Frémont, John C., 34, 346n17
French, James Kell, 264, 388n64
"French leave" (evading creditors), 75
fringed buckskin costumes, 3, 178
"frontier anxiety," 238
Frontier Guards, 97
frontier life, *see* American West; farming; lawlessness

Galena, Kansas, 198, 201–2
Galena Weekly Republican, 202
Galonska, Juliet, 219
Galveston Daily News, 85, 173
Galveston, Texas, 87, 142
Garten, Nannie, 328

434 ✤ Index

Gates, Clifford D., 97
General Order No. 11, 66–67
Georgia, 21, 30, 107, 140, 279
German community of Saint Louis, Missouri, 41–42
German Revolution of 1848, 42
Gettysburg, Battle of, 63
Ghigau (Beloved Woman of the Cherokees), *see* Nanyehi
Gibbs brothers' saloon, Claremore, Indian Territory, 322
Gillespie, James T., 196
Gilmore, Donald, 53
Going Snake District of the Cherokee Nation, 135, 158
going "tramping," 85
gold rush of 1849, 15–16, 22, 120, 140, 332, 358n7, 396n54
Gone to Texas ("G.T.T."), 75
Gose, John A., 165, 368n7
Granger, Gordon, 87
Grant, Ulysses S., 83, 87, 218
"gray gold," 15
Grayson, Watt, robbery of, 139–46, 147, 149, 153, 156, 158, 170–73, 192–93, 222, 284
Great Comet of 1861, 40, 346n1
Greeley, Horace, 345n9
Grierson [Grayson], Walter B. (Watt), 140–41
Griffin, Felix, 253–54, 256, 257–58, 267–68
Griffin, Luna, 253
guerrilla warfare, 31, 51–56, 58, 60–71, 77, 83, 88–89, 95, 98, 104
  Border Guards of Medoc, 38–39, 46
  Border Rangers of Carthage, 37–38, 45
  bushwhackers, 51–55, 58, 60–64, 68, 71, 88, 105
  daring courier Eliza Vivion, 349n29
  Iron Brigade, 67–69, 166–67
  "Kansas Brigade," 51–52
  origins of the James-Younger gang, 105–7
  "owlhoots," 105, 111, 356n10
  Red Legs, 51–53, 96, 348n10
  see also lawlessness; outlaws
Gunn, Bill, 243
gunslingers and crack shots, 23, 111, 243, 264

Hall, Lizzie, 203, 376n53
Hamilton, Ada, 335–36
Hamilton, Claude, 333–36
Hammond, William A., 348n6

Haney, Ben B., 97
hangings, 19–20, 49, 105, 143, 221–24
Hannell, Dempsey, 210
Hansen, Ron, 305
Hardin, John Wesley, 243
Hare, Dan, 320–21
Hare, Luther Rector, 373n28
Hare, Silas, 189
Harlan, Sarah Sally, 381n51
Harlan, Nancy, 135, 226, 381n51
Harman, S. W., xiii, 164–65, 231–33, 235, 289, 368, 374n1, 382n93
Harnage, William, robbery of, 158–59
Harper's Ferry, raid on, 348n10
Harris, Newt and Rebecca, 242, 244
Harrison, Mabel, 240
Harrison, William (Will), 240
Hartog, Hendrik, 7
Harvell, Elle E., 36
Harvey, S. M., 162–63, 165
Hays, Richard, 118, 181, 253
health and medicine
  abortion, 206, 235, 280, 390n17
  amputations, 84
  "bones" or "sawbones" to describe surgeons, 353n14
  consumption, 262–63, 315
  smallpox, 120
  "taking the waters," 246, 280–81, 357n24, 385n59
Hell on the Border (Harman), xiii, 164–65, 231–33, 235, 289, 368, 374n1, 382n93
Heresberg, William, 157
Hickey, James, 43
Hicks, Edwin P., 240, 374n4, 385n59
Hicks, William, 247
Higgins, Gertrude, 101–2
highway robbery, 52, 107, 152
Hillabee, Alabama, 141
Hiner and Hiner law firm, 399n111
Historical Atlas of the Outlaw West (Patterson), 359n20
Hobbs, Kenneth W. Jr., 143, 154, 166, 169
Hobsbawm, Eric, 93–94
Hodges, Anthony, 347n6
Holland, George, 171–73
Holman, Lewis, 243–44
Home Manual: Everybody's Guide in Social, Domestic, and Business Life, The, 176
Hood, Norris C., 71
Hood, Ron and Donna, 335, 336, 338
Hornback, George, 11

horse theft, 14, 16, 103–4, 149, 225
    Andrew Crane's bay horse, 225–26, 229–30
    James Lewis's horse, 284–85, 287, 391n44
    McCarty's sorrel mare, 247–48, 251, 254–56, 270, 287
    McCormick's black mare, 282
    Sam Campbell's gray mare, 225–26, 229
horses
    Brown Dick, racehorse, 134
    demand for, 16
    Jenny, Sam Bass's "Denton Mare," 127
    racing, 127, 133–34, 176–77, 199–200, 356n8
    Rondo, Jim Reed's horse, 161–62, 165, 175, 195, 222
    the Shirley family's fine Kentucky horses, 8, 23
    thoroughbreds, 47
    Venus, Belle Starr's favorite horse, 240, 247, 258–61, 264–65, 268–70, 275, 331
    women riding sidesaddle, 23, 102, 177–78, 240, 260, 260–61, 371n14, 371n15, 385n66
    see also horse theft
Horton Hotel, Conway, Arkansas, 197
hot springs, 246, 280–81, 357n24, 385n59
hotels
    Carthage Hotel (Shirley House), 23–24, 28, 29, 42–47, 54–55, 57, 61, 64, 75, 83, 197
    Elk House, popular hotel in McAlester, Choctaw Nation, 240
    Evans Hotel, North Galena, Kansas, 201–2
    Horton Hotel, Conway, Arkansas, 197
    Kirkpatrick House, hotel in Dallas, Texas, 185–87
    Lakeside Hotel, Siloam Springs, Arkansas, 280–71, 391n25
    Savoy Hotel, Douglas, Arizona, 328–29
Hough, Emerson, 176
"Howard, G. W.," *see* James, Jesse
Howe, Julia Ward, 345n1
Hoyt, George H. ("Frog"), 293–94, 296, 298, 303, 348n10
Hughes, Benjamin Tyner, 257–58, 260, 261, 270–71
Hughes, John T., 50
Hughes, Simon P., 271
Hunse, Rosanna, 4, 361n22
Hunter, Cornelius and Thomas, 47
Hunter, James, 38–39, 46–47

Hunter, Mary Shirley, 38, 46, 348n38
Hunter, Richard, 17, 33
Hurley, D. P., 27
Hutchins, James Robert ("Bob"), 312–14
Hutton, Florence ("Flossie") Pearl Epple, 328–29, 384n15
Hutton, Flossie Mae, daughter of Robert Hutton, 330
Hutton, Robert, 328, 330

Illinois, 51–52, 262, 274, 386n97
imperialist and racist views, 238
Indian International Fair of 1875, Muskogee, 176–77
Indian police, 244, 253, 257, 267, 269–70, 281, 286
Indian Removal Bill, 108, 279, 344n51, 352n12
Indian Territory (Oklahoma)
    Chickasaw Nation, 79–80, 217, 312, 314, 321, 324, 352n12
    "Five Civilized Tribes," 352n12
    Indian lighthorsemen, 217, 244
    Indian police, 244, 253, 257, 267, 269–70, 281, 286
    Oklahoma land rush, first (Unassigned Lands), 124, 324
    Oklahoma statehood, 10, 79, 283, 365n25
    Seminole Nation, 244, 342n82
    tribal courts/tribal law, 210, 217, 270
    see also Cherokee Nation; Choctaw Nation; Creek Nation
Indiana, 4, 6–8, 16–17, 23, 46–47
    Floyd County, 6–7, 376n53
    Shirley family in, 3–8
    University of Notre Dame, 200, 315–16, 375n35, 395n46
"Iron Brigade," 67–69, 166–67
Irwin, William H., 257–58
Issenhower, Catharine H., 348n38

Jackson, C. L., 299–301
Jackson, Claiborne Fox, 36, 39, 41, 45
James, Drury Woodson, 114, 357n24, 358n7
James-Younger gang, 92, 94–95, 105–8, 114–15, 124–25, 135, 166–67, 200, 357n24
    Civil War origins of the, 105–7
    Daviess County Savings Association, Gallatin, Missouri, 124–25
    disastrous Northfield, Minnesota, raid, 200–201, 314

James-Younger gang (*continued*)
  Ford brothers, Bob and Charley, 216, 363n67
  glorification of the, 369n17
  guerrilla warfare and origins of the, 105–7
  Jesse James's visits to Younger's Bend, 215–17
  Jim Reed's alleged connections to the, 97–98, 107–8, 121
  links between the families, 92–95, 101, 105–8
  true identity of "James White," 107–8
  wanted for a robbery in Russellville, Kentucky, 107–8, 114
  wanted for a train robbery at Blue Cut, Missouri, 215–16
  wanted for robbery of Clay County Savings Association, Liberty, Missouri, 105–6
Jayhawkers, 51–54, 65, 67, 96, 349n15
Jefferson City, Missouri, 26, 200
Jefferson, Texas, 82
Jennings, Edmund, 3–4
Jennison, Charles R. ("Doc"), 51, 67, 348n10
John Kettle Settlement, 210
Johnson, James, 247
Johnson, Waldo P., 200, 376n35
Johnston, Francis, 357n24
Jones, Anne Goodwyn, 49
Jones, John Beauchamp, 40, 158
Joplin, Missouri, 15, 198–201, 375n22
Journal of American History, 178
July, Jim, 277–83, 286–91, 294–97, 301, 303–4, 308, 311–14, 324
Junction City Weekly Union, 204
Juneteenth, 87

Kaigler, Charles, 326
Kaigler, Ruth D., 326, 329, 330, 400n123
Kansas
  Baxter Springs, 69–71, 79
  "Bleeding Kansas," 30–32, 51, 345n9
  divorce in, 206–7
  Fort Scott, 37, 47, 58, 69, 71
  Galena, 198, 201–2
  Lawrence, 65–66, 69
  state militia of, 348
  statehood of, 10, 30–31, 35
  Wichita, 284, 288–89, 328
Kansas and Texas Railway ("the Katy"), 140, 241
"Kansas Brigade," 51–52
Kansas City Journal, 363n67

Kansas City Star, 167
Kansas City Times, 166–68
Kansas-Nebraska Act, 30, 345n5
Kansas Pacific Railway train robbery, Muncie, Missouri, 135
Kelker (Kolliker), Anna Elizabeth, 4
Keller, Levie, 290, 392n74
Kendrick, W. B., 77
Kennedy, Henry, 113
Kennedy, John F., 373n32
Kentucky, 4–6, 8–10, 34, 37, 86
  Brock family of Kentucky and Missouri, 95–98, 195, 203–4
  Russellville robbery, 107–8, 114
Kerry, Hobbs, 199
Keve, Paul W., 383n109
King, A. J., 111–12, 113, 131, 149, 358n2
Kino, Eusabio, 360n22
Kiowa Indians, 96, 128
Kirkpatrick, Naomi, 185–87
Kirkpatrick, Sophronia Lee Younger, 317
Kneeland, Samuel D., 27
Know Nothing Party (American Party), 34
Knowles, Thomas Neil, 302
Kraft, Morris, 311–12
Krauthamer, Barbara, 365n25

Labette County Democrat, 205
Ladies Aid Society, 319
Lady Macbeth, 191, 373n40
Lake Eufaula, Oklahoma, 334
Lakeside Hotel (later Crown Hotel), Siloam Springs, Arkansas, 280–71, 391n25
Lane, James Henry, 51–53, 65, 350n30
law enforcement, 218–24
  Arkansas State Penitentiary, 174, 242, 370n65
  being "on the scout," 105–6, 356n9
  boots as crime-scene evidence, 221, 251, 304
  bounty hunters, 153, 243
  community dances as alibis and crime scenes, 258, 267, 287, 293
  corruption, 93, 133, 370n60
  Detroit House of Correction, 14, 231–36, 238, 251, 383n109
  district court system, 154, 169, 173–74, 190, 217, 228–29, 321, 369n31, 373n25
  executions, 20–21, 53, 55, 221–24, 262, 270, 365n23
  first Black federal lawman west of the Mississippi, 126–27, 362n22, 362n23

"gone rogue," Dalton brothers of Missouri, 220
hangings, 19–20, 49, 105, 143, 221–24
Indian lighthorsemen, 217, 244
offers of immunity, 243–44
Southern Illinois Penitentiary, 262, 274, 386n97
tarring and feathering, 32
tribal courts/tribal law, 210, 217, 270
U.S. marshals and their deputies, 110, 144, 149, 153–59, 170–74, 192, 218–21, 226–27, 233–34, 252, 255–58, 322, 373n32
Western District of Arkansas, 171–74, 218, 229, 255, 370n60
Western District of Texas, 153
see also Fort Smith, Arkansas
lawlessness
adultery, 7–8, 260
Florida serial killer, 296–302
highway robbery, 52, 107, 152
homicide rates, 85, 87
how wars breed crime and criminals, 89
lynchings, 18–20, 65, 87–88, 128, 149, 174
opium, 84, 396n54
prostitution, 235, 243, 325–27, 372n3, 396n54, 399n116
scalpings, 54, 88, 90
"squatter sovereignty," 11, 219
taking "French leave" (evading creditors), 75
vigilante committees, 18–20, 87, 128, 133, 149, 180, 217
violence against African Americans, 128
violence and criminality after the Civil War, 92–95
see also James-Younger gang; liquor
Lawrence, Kansas, 65–66, 69
lead mining, 15–16, 198
Lear, Ed, 319–20
Lee, Robert E., 63, 83, 87
Leech, William, 255
Lewis, James, horse stolen from, 284–85, 287, 391n44
Lewis, S. R., 250
Liberty, Missouri, 105
Liberty Tribune, 125
Lightfoot, Henry W., 168
Lincoln, Abraham, 34–38, 40, 46, 83, 87, 346n29, 346n1
"Lint Societies," 348n6
liquor

feuds over the whiskey-running trade, 111
in New Mexico Territory, 270
poisoning from bad liquor, 322
quart house distillery stores, 131, 134
selling illicit liquor, 274
selling "spirituous liquors" to Indians in Indian Territory, 12, 219, 251, 274, 322, 358n2
Little Big Horn, Battle of the, 373n28
"Little Dixie," Missouri, 18, 31
"living skeletons," 271, 389n104
Livingston, Hugh L., 7
Livingston, Joel T., 349n29
Lomax, Susan Frances, 128
Long, Ben, 142, 145, 170
Los Angeles, California, 119–21, 358n8, 359n20
Los Angeles Times, 358n8
Los Nietos, California, 117–20, 359n22
Lost Cause, 86, 179
Louisiana, 82, 354n2
Louisiana Purchase, 10
Love, Robert, 106
lunatic asylums, 85
lynchings, 18–20, 65, 87–88, 128, 149, 174

Macbeth (Shakespeare), 191, 373n40
MacDonald, Emmett, 38
mail/postal service, *see* U. S. Postal Service
Maledon, George, 222–24, 380n35
Man Who Shot Liberty Valance, The (film), 311
"Manifest Destiny," 13, 383n2
Mansfield, Thomas, 17
Maples, Dan, 313
Marcum, Thomas, 227–30, 258, 261–62, 274
Marks, Lemuel Walker, 226–27
Marshall, Pete, 246–47, 279
Marshall, Texas, 80–81
Martin, John Hunter, 188
Martin, Sam, 157
Mason-Dixon Line, 4, 30, 36, 341n5
Maurice, Charles E., 168
Maxey, Samuel Bell, 168
May, Robin, 272
McAlester, Choctaw Nation, 225, 240, 320, 326
McAntz, Andy, 294
McCarthy, Harry, 346n32
McCarty, Albert G., 247–48, 251, 254–56, 270, 287

McClure, Mamie (Florence ["Flossie"] Pearl Epple Hutton), 279–81, 284–86, 288–89, 328
McClure, Robert, 278–81, 288–89, 390n10
McClurg, Joseph W., 125
McCommas family, 148, 179–80, 203, 366n9
McCommas, Mike, 179–82, 185–93
McCommas, Rosanna (Rosa), 148, 151, 153–56, 159–60, 168, 170, 179, 366n9
McCormick, J. H., 282
McCoy, Arthur, 166, 167
McCoy, Eleanor (Nellie), 136
McDaniel, Alexander Lewis, 323
McDaniel, Katherine, 175
McGilberry, Lila, 256–57, 267
McKeehan, Thomas John Jr., 131, 362n44
McLaughlin, "Mamma Mc," 231
McPherson, James M., 346n346
Meador, Timothy, 21
Medoc, Missouri, 15, 37–39
Meek, Will, 287
Mellette, William Moore, 299, 300
Memories of Will Conine, The, 129–34, 171–73, 177, 362n35, 371n14
men in "new marriages," 6–7
Meridian, Texas, 129, 132, 134
Merritt, William W., 157, 161, 165, 169, 367n66
Mershon, J. H., 313
Methodists, 13, 120, 318–19
Mexican rule over California, 120
Mexican-American War, 13, 15, 42, 189, 353n13
Mexico border, 171
Meyers, Alton B., 308–11
Middleton, James F., 245, 252, 304, 385n55
Middleton, John, 240–52, 254, 270, 385n55, 385n66
Miller, Rick [Richard D.], 161, 173–74, 188, 191, 197, 245, 321
Milsap, J. H., 244–45, 249–52
Minehart, John Henry, 173
mining
  Bisbee, Arizona, copper boomtown, 328, 399n123
  boomtown culture, 198
  gold rush of 1849, 15–16, 22, 120, 140, 332, 358n7, 396n54
  lead mining, 15–16, 198
  zinc mining, 198
Missouri Compromise of 1820, 3–4, 19, 30, 51, 341n5, 345n5

Missouri State Cavalry, 66–67, 70, 362n44
Missouri State Guard, 43, 50, 90
Missouri
  Burnt District, 66–67
  "Country of the Six Bulls," 3–4, 9–10, 14, 31, 40
  Jefferson City, 26, 200
  Joplin, 15, 198–201, 375n22
  Kansas Pacific train robbery, Muncie, 135
  Liberty, 105
  "Little Dixie," 18, 31
  Medoc, 15, 37–39
  Neosho, 67–68, 77, 122, 228
  Newtonia, 56–57
  Otterville train robbery, 199–200
  "Outlaw State," 88
  Pleasant Gap, 203–4
  Prairie Point, 96, 98
  public-domain state, 10–11
  Saint Louis, 36, 40–42, 47, 66, 77
  Sarcoxie, 9, 32, 37, 40, 60–62, 68, 345n12, 347n4
  Shirley's Ford, 10, 16
  slave state, 3–4, 19, 30, 51, 341n5, 345n5
  see also Carthage, Missouri
Mitchell, Sarah Ann, 179
mixed-race individuals, 140–41, 209–10, 263, 388n64, 395n30
Mormons, 342n38
Morris, John T., 156–79, 195–97, 222, 367n66
Mound City Sharps Rifle Guards, 348n10
Mouse, Katy (Caty), 135
Muncie, Missouri, train robbery, 135
murder
  of Ambrose Wheeler, 133–35, 142, 149, 363n66
  of Belle Starr, xiii, 293–306
  of Benjamin Vore, 108–9
  of Dick Cravey, 131–33
  of John Fisk, 19–21
  of Newton C. Stout, 112, 113, 358n2
  of Noah Fitzwater, 112, 113, 358n2
  of Samuel Wyrick, 261–62
  of Thomas P. Nigh, 196–97
  of William H. Irwin, 257–58
  of William Leech, 255
  of William Riley Seaboalt Jr., 221
Murphy, M. J., 234
Musgrave, Sarah Scott, 60–62
Muskogee, Creek Nation, 176–77, 251–52, 257, 275–76, 281–82, 286

Muskogee Daily Phoenix, 325–26, 333
Muskogee Indian Journal, 251, 257

Nanyehi (Nancy Ward), 381
National Cemetery, Springfield, Missouri, 350n21
National Police Gazette, 258–60, 308
National Register of Historic Places, 391n25
Native Americans
    Battle of the Little Big Horn, 373n28
    "Five Civilized Tribes," 352n12
    horse racing among, 356n8
    Indian Removal Bill, 108, 279, 344n51, 352n12
    see also Indian Territory (Oklahoma); specific Native American tribes and nations
needlework, as women's work, 27, 91
Neodesha Free Press, 204
Neosho, Missouri, 67–68, 77, 122, 228
"new marriages," 6–7
New Mexico Territory, 270, 312, 315, 354n10
New Orleans, Louisiana, 354n2
New York Sun, 308
New York Times, 42, 152, 222–24, 305, 307–8
New York Tribune, 345n9
Nicholson, Joseph, 234
Nieto, Manuel, 119–20
Nigh, Thomas P., 196–97
Nocona, Peta, 186
Norris, Milt, 60–61
North, F. A., 16
Northfield, Minnesota, raid, 200–201, 314
Notre Dame, University of, 200, 315–16, 375n35, 395n46
Nye, Edgar Wilson, 239

O'Beirne brothers (Harry F. and E. S.), 110, 138–39, 309, 311
Oglesby, Savannah, 301–2
Oklahoma land rush, first (Unassigned Lands), 124, 324
Oklahoma, statehood of, 10, 79, 283, 365n25, *see also* Indian Territory
Okmulgee, Creek Nation, 282
Old Settlers in the Cherokee Nation, 109–10
"on the scout," 105–6, 356n9
opium, 84, 396n54
"Origin of Owlhoot" (Trimble), 356
Osage tribe, 10, 95, 227
Osage War, 10
Osceola massacre, 52–53, 64–66, 349n15
O'Sullivan, John, 13, 383n2

Otterville train robbery, 199–200
outlaws, 16, 86–90, 92–95
    folk-hero outlaw archetype, 93–95
    "on the scout," 105–6, 356n9
    "social bandits," 93–94
    see also James-Younger gang; lawlessness
Owen, Robert Latham, 282–83, 286
"owlhoots," 105, 111, 356n10

Palmer, Frank, 257–58, 267–68
Palmito Ranch, Battle of, 83–84
Panic of 1837, 8, 13
paramilitary factions, 51–52, *see also* guerrilla warfare
Paris, Texas, 159, 165–66, 168, 242–43, 313–14, 369n31
Parker, Cynthia Ann, 186
Parker, Isaac C., 217, 218–25, 229–31, 236, 241, 252, 255, 261–62, 268, 270, 272–74, 288, 300, 380n28
Parsons Daily Eclipse, 204
Parsons Weekly Sun, 205
Passing of the West, The (Hough), 176
patriarchy's shadow on women's stories, 264
Patterson, Richard, 359n20
Peak, Junius ("June"), 155
Pease River, Battle of, 186
Pennington, John, 9–12, 343n48, *see also* Shirley, Elizabeth Pennington
Perryman, July, 277
Perryman, Mose, 284–87
"petrified corpse" in New Mexico Territory cave, 316–17
Pettit, Gwen, 99
Petty, James, 58–60
Phoenix Publishing Company, Fort Smith, Arkansas, 382n93
photography
    Belle and Sam Starr's home, 212, 378n14
    Belle Starr, 260–64
    Belle Starr misidentified in, 159–60
    Henry A. Doerr of San Antonio, 159, *160*
    in investigating crimes, 155
    Pearl, 327–28
    proof of death, 88–89
    Roeder Brothers Photography, Fort Smith, 260–62
    Sam Starr misidentified in, *260*
    W. H. Catterlin Studio, Claremore, Cherokee Nation, *322*
Pickett, George Bible, 97
Pikes Peak gold rush, 396n54

Platte County Self-Defense Association, 18
Pleasant Gap, Missouri, 203–4
Pleasanton Observer-Enterprise, 203
Polk, James K., 13, 15, 109, 357n35
Pond, James Burton, 69
"popular sovereignty," 30
Porter, Jim, 132–33, 181
Porter, W. H., 332
Prairie Point, Missouri, 96, 98
prostitution, 235, 243, 325–27, 372n3, 396n54, 399n116
Purcell, Chickasaw Nation, 198
Purcell, Sarah Sullivan, 198
Purnell, Thomas, 153–56, 161, 170

Quantrill, William Clarke, 53–56, 64–70, 88–89, 90, 94–95, 97–98, 106
quart house distillery stores, 131, 134

race and racism
    Chinese riot in Los Angeles, 120
    imperialist and racist views in westward expansion, 238
    lynchings, 18–20, 65, 87–88, 128, 149, 174
    mixed-race individuals, 140–41, 209–10, 263, 388n64, 395n30
    southern exceptionalism and White supremacy, 86
    see also slavery; Native Americans
railroad
    Blue Cut train robbery, Missouri, 215–16
    Kansas and Texas Railway ("the Katy"), 140, 241
    Kansas Pacific Railway train robbery, Muncie, Missouri, 135
    Otterville train robbery, Missouri, 199–200
    region's first railroad, 120
    Texas & Pacific Railroad, 126
    transcontinental railroad, 78
Rancho Cucamonga, California, 115
Rancho Los Nietos, California, 117–20, 359n22
Rancho Santa Gertrudes, California, 120
Randolph, Vance (William Yancey Shackleford, pseudonym), 180, 201–2, 329
Rankin, Melinda, 91, 354n2
Rascoe, Burton, 177–78, 241
rawhide necklace of dried earlobes, 109
Reconstruction, 58–72, 84–85, 87, 93, 103, 190
Red Legs, 51–53, 96, 348n10

Reed, Eliza W., infant daughter of Jim and Myra Reed, 117
Reed family
    after Belle Starr's death, 319–30
    Brock family of Missouri and the, 95–98, 195, 203–4
    Canote family of Virginia and the, 4–5, 126, 361n22
    in Denton County, Texas, 122–23, 126–28, *322*
    in Missouri, 95–96
Reed, Fatima Jane, 119
Reed, Franklin Marion, 97, 99–100, 111–12, 114–22, 232, 280–81
Reed, James Commodore (Jim), 97–100, 104, 112–16, 122, 139–43, 159–60, 163, 230
    alleged confession of, 166–67
    alleged connections to the James-Younger gang, 97–98, 107–8, 121
    attempted murder by Mose Perryman, 284–87
    in California, 113–22
    relationship with Rosanna (Rosa) McCommas, 148, 151, 153–56, 159–60, 168, 170, 179, 366n9
    on the scout, 105–12
    in Texas, 122–23, 128–38, 159–60, 166, 168, 170, 181, 215, *322*
    Tom Starr and, 108–11, 113, 125, 135
    wanted for the Grayson robbery, 139–46, 147, 149, 153, 156, 158, 170–73, 192–93, 222, 284
    wanted for the murder of Ambrose Wheeler, 133–35, 142, 149, 363n66
    wanted for the robbery of William Harnage, 158–59
    wanted for the theft of Jim Lewis's horse, 284–85, 287, 391n44
Reed, James Edwin (Ed, Eddie; Belle Starr's son), 16, 22, 117, 103, 123, 164, 194–97, 204, 213, 232, 238, 241, 246–47, 289–90, 294, 296–97, 319–23, 330–31, 356n1, 359n20
    marriage to Jennie Cochran, 321–23
Reed, Jennie Cochran, wife of Ed Reed, 321–23.
Reed, Richard H., 355n51
Reed, Rosa (Rosie) Lee (Pearl Reed, Pearl Younger, Pearl Starr; Belle Starr's daughter), 100–101, 104, 129, 202, 250, 265–81
    as the alleged illicit child of Cole Younger, 324, 330

Belle Starr's letter from prison, 231–33
charge of illegal cohabitation with Joe Colburn, 326
death of her mother, 284–92, 293–97, 303, 308, 330–32, 344
her daughter Jennette Steele Andrews, 327, 330, 400n123
her daughter Mamie McClure (Florence ["Flossie"] Pearl Epple Hutton), 279–81, 284–86, 288–89, 328–29, 384n15
her daughter Ruth D. Kaigler, 326, 329, 330, 400n123
her son Arthur E. Erbach Jr., infant, 328, 399n116
later life as a prostitute and bordello operator, 323–30
marriage to Dell Andrews, 327, 382n116
marriage to Arthur E. Erbach, 327–28, 399n116
marriage to Will Harrison, 240
relationship with Charles Kaigler, 326
relationship with Robert McClure, 278–81, 288–89, 390n10
visiting Chickalah, Arkansas, 246–47
visiting Eliza Shirley in Eufaula, Indian Territory, 241
at Younger's Bend, 213, 253–55, 258, 266, 268, 274
Reed, Samuel Benton, 98
Reed, Sarah, 118–19, 131
Reed, Scott, 111–12
Reed, Solomon Lafayette, 95–98, 122, 131, 133–35, 142, 149, 363n66
Reed, Susan Demanda, 95–96, 98, 195, 203–4, 238, 280–81, 284–85
Reed, William Scott, 97, 111–12
Reese, Catherine, 136, 310
Reese, Charles Tasker, 136, 137
Reese, Eleanor (Nellie) McCoy, 136
Reeves, Bass, 254–55
Remington, Frederic, 238–39
Republic of Texas, 148
Republican Party, 34–35, 218, 221
Revolutionary War, 6
Reynolds, Thomas C., 80–81
Rider, Louise Norwood, 137
Ridge, John Rollin, 109
Riley, Glenda, 198, 240
Ritchey, H. M., 56
Ritchie, John, 136
Ritter, Moses, 8
robberies, *see* horse thievery; lawlessness

Robertson, Mark, 13
Robinson, A. J., 303
Robinson, Riley, 201
Roeder Brothers Photography, Fort Smith, 260–62
Rogers, Clement (Clem) Vann, 395n30
Rogers, John William, 125–27
Rogers, Will, 395n30
Rogers, William H., 144
Rondo, Jim Reed's horse, 161–62, 165, 175, 195, 222
Rosa, Joseph G., 272
Ross, John, 133
Ross, Lawrence Sullivan, 186–87, 193
Ross Party, 108–9
Rowe family of the Choctaw Nation, 289–92, 294, 297–99
Russell, Henry, 159–61, 168–69
Russellville, Kentucky, 107–8, 114

S. T. Scott Company stagecoach robbery, 151–53, 157–58, 170
Sac and Fox tribe, 95
Saint Louis, Missouri, 36, 40–42, 47, 66, 77
San Antonio, Texas, 127, 148–51, 159–60, 166, 168, 170, 181, 215
San Francisco, California, 77, 114, 128, 358n8
Sandels, Monti Hines, 273, 288
Santa Catalina Island, California, 121
Sarcoxie, Missouri, 9, 32, 37, 40, 60–62, 68, 345n12, 347n4
Saunt, Claudio, 141
scalpings, 54, 88, 90
Scharff, Virginia, 175
Schofield, John M., 66
Schooling, Gilbert, 61
Schrantz, Ward Loren, 9, 17, 19, 21, 26, 28, 33, 38, 41–47, 54–56, 58–64, 68, 70–71, 343n48
Scott, John J., 19–20
Scott, Margaret Ann "Peggy," 96
Scott, Winfield, 346n1
Scyene, Texas, 81, 82–86, 91–92, 95, 99–101, 124–26, 135, 147–51, 155–56, 177, 180–81, 185–90, 193, 195–96, 318
Seaboalt, William Riley Jr., 221
Second Indian Home Guard, 136
Second Indiana Volunteer Cavalry, 47
Seminole Nation, 244, 342n82
Seventh Missouri Provisional Enrolled Militia, 60–61, 136, 363n73

Seventh United States Cavalry, 373n28
Sewall, W. J., 272
Shackleford, William Yancey (pseudonym of Vance Randolph), 180, 201–2, 329
Shakespeare, William, 191, 373n40
sharecropping, 296–98
Sharps rifles, 31–32, 58–59, 348n10
Shawnee Indians, 10
Sheets, David L., 126
Sheets, John W., 125
Shelby, Joseph O. ("Jo"), 67–70, 77, 166–67
Sheridan, Phil, 29
Sherman, Texas, 127, 157, 166, 244
Sherman, William T., 47
Shields, John P., 204–5
Shirley, Annie, 14, 45, 62, 76–77, 81, 87–88, 123, 147, 193, 318, 366n4, 396n57
Shirley, Betty M., 341n6, 359n19
Shirley, Charlotte Amanda, 8, 13, 22, 318, 344n39
Shirley, Christian T., 4–6, 15, 362
Shirley, Clarissa, 6, 7, 342n22
Shirley, Cravens (John Alva, or "Shug"), 22, 44, 76, 92, 123, 194, 202, 203, 227, 351n5, 376n53
Shirley, Elizabeth (Eliza) Pennington (Belle Starr's mother), 4, 8–13, 14–17, 24, 27, 43–45, 62, 72, 75–76, 123, 147, 189
  her family origins, 9–12, 343n48
  after John Shirley's death, 193, 195, 238, 241, 289, 308, 318–19
  possible view of Annie Shirley, 87–88, 147, 396n57
Shirley family
  DNA genealogy in the, 76, 351n9
  gone to Texas after the war, 75–81, 82–85
  tracing the African American genealogy of the, 76–77, 341n6
  Younger family's links to, 16, 101, 121, 124
Shirley, George Washington, 81, 87
Shirley, Glenn, 92, 108, 110, 177, 213–17, 220, 239–41, 266, 287, 298, 309n4, 358n2, 374n1, 382n93, 385n55, 388n67
Shirley, James K., 123, 361n1
Shirley, John (Belle Starr's father)
  adultery, 7–8
  as county road commissioner, 13, 23, 343n46, 344n43
  on the eve of the Civil War, 33–39
  family origins in Indiana, 3–8
  fine horses of, 6, 8, 11, 16

  his Carthage Hotel (Shirley House), 23–24, 28, 29, 42–47, 54–55, 57, 61, 64, 75, 83, 197
  marriage to Nancy Fowler, 6
  migration to Missouri, 3–21
  settling in Carthage, 21–24
Shirley, John Allison M. ("Bud"), 12–13, 17, 22–23, 38, 42, 45, 49–51, 55–63, 71, 76, 175, 266, 272, 350n21
Shirley, Laura, 374n58
Shirley, Mansfield, 17, 22, 44, 76, 92, 103, 123, 352n90, 361n2, 374n58
Shirley, Mary Arella Chelson, 13, 80
Shirley, Michael, 5–6
Shirley, Myra Maibelle, see Belle Starr, the lady; Belle Starr, the legend
Shirley, Peter (Johann Peter Shalle), 4–5, 341n10
Shirley, Preston, 6, 8, 10, 13, 15–17, 33–35, 46, 79–80, 92, 123–24, 346n23
Shirley, Robert E. Lee, 147
Shirley, Sterling Price, 147
Shirley's Ford, Missouri, 10, 16
Shoemaker, Floyd C., 22, 31
Shreveport, Louisiana, 82
sidesaddle, 23, 102, 178, 240, 260, 260–61, 371n14, 371n15, 385n66
sideshows, 271, 389n104
Sigel, Franz, 41–45
Siloam Springs, Arkansas, 289–81, 391n25
Simpson, Elizabeth, 199
Simpson, John F., 221
Sinnugee, Creek girl, 141
Sixkiller, Sam, 267
Sixth Kansas Regiment Volunteer Cavalry, 37–38
Sixth Missouri State Militia Cavalry, 70
Slade, William, 25, 344n50
slavery
  abolitionism, 18, 23, 25, 30–35, 47, 50, 65, 80, 136, 344n50, 345n1
  "Bleeding Kansas," 30–32, 51, 345n9
  importance of enslaved workers, 5–8, 10–11
  "popular sovereignty," 30
  slave ownership and intermarriage, 141
  slave owning among the Creeks, 141–42, 365n25
  Uncle Tom's Cabin (Stowe), 25, 32
  Underground Railroad, 30, 136
smallpox, 120
Smith, Frank, 267

Smith, Jeff, 132–34
Smith, Willard H., 178
"social bandits," 93–94
South
   Mason-Dixon Line, 4, 30, 36, 341n5
   southern exceptionalism and White supremacy, 86
   violence and criminality after the Civil War, 92–95
   without slavery, 86–90
   see also Civil War; slavery
"southern belle, the," 49–50
Southern Democrats, 34
Southern Illinois Penitentiary, 262, 274, 386n97
Southwest News, 37–38
Spaniard, Jack, 258, 264, 267–68
Spanish empire, California land grants, 115, 119, 359n22
"squatter sovereignty," 11, 219
"squaw men," 209
St. Joseph Weekly Herald, 309
St. Louis Globe-Democrat, 248, 261
St. Louis Post-Dispatch, 233–34
stagecoach travel, 77–79, 114
   Belle Starr reenacting a stagecoach robbery for the public, 271–73
   Butterfield Overland Mail Company stagecoach route, 77–79, 115, 120
   see also trailblazing/travel; U.S. Postal Service
Starr, Gene, 336
Starr, James, 108
Starr, James Jr., 228
Starr, Nancy Harlan, 135, 226, 381n51
Starr, Sam, 208–17, 225–36, 238, 241, 245, 253–76, 278–82, 292, 333
   death of, 274–76
   life with Belle Starr in Younger's Bend after prison, 238–41
   theft during the Younger's Bend 1882 spring roundup, 225–37
   wanted for burglaries in Blaine, Choctaw Nation, 253–54
   wanted for the robbery of Brown's mercantile, Wealaka, Indian Territory, 250–51, 253, 368
   wanted for the theft of Sam Campbell's gray mare, 225–26, 229
   see also Younger's Bend, Cherokee Nation
Starr, Squirrel, 135–36, 363n73

Starr, Tom, 108–11, 135–40, 153, 159, 228, 274, 364n1
   jailed for whiskey running, 274
   Jim Reed and, 108–11, 113, 125, 135
   marriage to Catherine Reese, 136, 310
   murder of Benjamin Vore, 108–9
   rumor that he had killed Belle Starr, 304
   see also July, Jim; Younger's Bend, Cherokee Nation
"Stars and Bars," Confederate flag, 41, 345n12
State Journal (Jefferson City, Missouri), 200
"states' rights," 86
Statham, Benjamin, 294, 297
Stefani, Victoria Lee, 215, 233, 241, 379n37
Stegman, Stephanie, 219n9
Stephens, Alexander H., 29–30
Stiles, T. J., 167
Story of Cole Younger, The (C. Younger), 107, 355n51, 356n55, 360n44
Story, William, 173–74, 218
Stotts, Green C., 60
Stout, Newton C., 112, 113, 358n2
Stowe, Harriet Beecher, 25
Strickland, Lena, 398n109
Sturm's Oklahoma Magazine, 212, 333, 372n38, 378n24
surcingle, 177, 371n14
Surratt, Lucy and Henry, 275, 292
Synar, Joe, 333

Tahlequah, Cherokee Nation, 138, 158, 253
Talbot, A. J., 39
Tallay, Henry, 247–49
Tapía, Tubercio, 115
tarring and feathering, 32
Taylor, Fox, 282
Tennessee, 3–4, 96, 107, 136
Terry, Ansel D., 300
Texas
   Austin, 80, 151–58, 166, 170, 215
   Blossom Prairie, 242
   Bosque County, *127*, 128–35, 142, 147, 149, 171, 173, 187, 362n28, 363n66, 366n5
   Burleson County, 35, 80
   Confederates from, 83–85
   Coon Creek, 129–31, 147–48, 171–72
   Galveston, 87, 142
   homicide rate in, 87
   Jefferson, 82
   Marshall, 80–81

Texas (*continued*)
   Meridian, 129, 132, 134
   Paris, 159, 165–66, 168, 242–43, 313–14, 369n31
   as a republic, 148
   San Antonio, 127, 148–51, 159–60, 166, 168, 170, 181, 215
   Scyene, 81, 82–86, 91–92, 95, 99–101, 124–26, 135, 147–51, 155–56, 177, 180–81, 185–90, 193, 195–96, 318
   Sherman, 127, 157, 166, 244
   Waco, 185–86, 190, 372n3
   Western District of Texas, 153
   Wise County, 96–98
   see also Dallas County, Texas
Texas & Pacific Railroad, 126
Texas Almanac, 126
Texas Constitutional Convention of 1868, 87
Texas Rangers, 127, 186, 193, 196, 243, 282
Texas Road, 70, 79
Third Missouri Cavalry, 362n44
Third Wisconsin Cavalry, 69
Thomas, Archy, 43, 44
Thomas, Heck, 313
Thompson, Charlotte Amanda, *see* Shirley, Charlotte Amanda
Thompson, Jesse B., 22, 344n39
Thompson, T. F., 20
Thornton, Henry P., 7
thoroughbreds, 47
Titchenal family, 378n11, 390n10
tobacco, 5, 18, 316
Toney, Nancy, 198
trailblazing/travel, 6
   Briartown-Eufaula Trail, 211
   Chisholm Trail, 128, 185, 362n29
   ferry crossings, 78, 79–80, 106, 226, 267, 293
   "forting up," 96
   going "tramping," 85
   stagecoach travel, 77–79, 114
   Texas Road, 70, 79
   Wilderness Trail through the Cumberland Gap, 6
   see also railroads
Trainor, Bud (Bub), 313–14
transcontinental railroad, 78
treasure hunting, 211, 333, 337, 378n16
Treaty of Guadalupe Hidalgo, 15
Treaty of New Echota, 108
tribal courts/tribal law, 210, 217, 270
Trimble, Marshall, 356

True Republic Sentinel, Sycamore, Illinois, 51–52
Tufts, John Quincy, 281–82
Turpin, Robert, 104
Twain, Mark, 239
Tyler, Texas, 168–69, 369n31
Tyson, G. G., 284–86

Uncle Tom's Cabin (Stowe), 25, 32
Underground Railroad, 30, 136
United Confederate Veterans, 179, 371n30
United States
   American Revolution, 5
   election of 1856, 33–34
   election of 1860, 34–35, 346n29
   Mexican-American War, 13, 15, 42, 189, 353n13
   Office of Indian Affairs, 220
   Revolutionary War, 6
   see also American West
United States Congress, 15, 109
   Indian Removal Bill, 108, 279, 344n51, 352n12
   Kansas-Nebraska Act, 30, 345n5
   Know Nothing Party (American Party), 34
   Republican Party, 34–35, 218, 221
   Southern Democrats, 34
   stagecoach service authorized by, 77
University of Notre Dame, 200, 315–16, 375n35, 395n46
unreconstructed Confederates, 86, 131
Upham, Samuel C., 346n1
U.S. Army
   cavalry units of the, 37–38, 47, 66–71, 362n44, 373n28
   Corps of Engineers, 334, 398n93
   Department of the Missouri, 66
   Seventh Missouri Provisional Enrolled Militia, 60–61, 136, 363n73
U.S. marshals and their deputies, 110, 144, 149, 153–59, 170–74, 192, 218–21, 226–27, 233–34, 252, 255–58, 322, 373n32
U.S. Postal Service, 77–79
   Butterfield Overland Mail Company stagecoach route, 77–79, 115, 120
   intercepting, 289
   newspaper lists of unclaimed mail, 206, 314
   post offices, 82, 120, 126, 206, 253, 256, 303
   S. T. Scott Company stagecoach robbery, 151–53, 157–58, 170

Van Buren, Arkansas, 78, 326
Vance, Randolph (William Yancey Shackleford, pseudonym), 180, 201, 329
VanGilder, Marvin, 389n112
Vanity Fair (magazine), 347n1
Vann, H. J., 208, 311–12
Vann, R. P., 109, 269
Vann, William, 257, 267–69, 395n30
Venable, George, 44
Venator, Richard, 333
Venus, Belle Starr's favorite horse, 240, 247, 258–61, 264–65, 268–70, 275, 331
"Verbal Will of Belle Starr," 311
Vermont, 25, 26, 344n49, 344n50
Vicksburg, Battle of, 63
Vicksburg, Mississippi, 63
Victorian ideals, 15, 175–76, 191
vigilante committees, 18–20, 87, 128, 133, 149, 180, 217
Vignolo, Delores, 330
Vinita Indian Chieftain, 233, 286, 321, 382n101, 382n104
violence, *see* lawlessness
Virginia, 4–6, 33, 36, 83
Vivion, Eliza, 349n29
Vore, Benjamin, 108–9

W. H. Catterlin Studio, Claremore, Cherokee Nation, 322
W. W. Cole's New Colossal Show, a circus, 271
Waco Daily Examiner, 152
Waco Reporter, 187, 373n15
Waco, Texas, 185–86, 190, 372n3
Waite, Stand, 109
Walker, Alice, 27
Walker, George B., 59–60
Wall, Ron and Sue, 240
Walt, Veleska Myra, 330
War Comet of 1861, 40, 346n1
War of 1812, 15
Ward, Geoffrey C., 84
Ward, Nancy (Nanyehi), 381
Warren, Robert Penn, 87
Watson, Edgar Artemus, 292, 296–305, 312, 324, 393n51
Wealaka, Creek Nation trading center, 250–51, 253, 386n87
Weaver, Elizabeth ("Lizzy"), 279
Weaver, John F., 214, 264–65
Weldon, O. D., 248–50, 261, 385n74
Wellman, Paul I., 90, 263–64

West, Frank, 30, 226, 245, 269–70, 275–76, 292
West, John C., 230–31, 244–45, 249–52, 253–54, 257, 275, 281–82
West, John Henry, 138
"westering women," 176
Western District of Arkansas, 171–74, 218, 229, 255, 370n60
Western District of Texas, 153
westward expansion, 13–15, 238
  exploration of the West, 34
  Louisiana Purchase, 10
  the Wild West, 89, 92–93, 238–39, 307
  see also railroads; trailblazing/travel
Weyman, Charles S., 345n9
Whaley, Thomas, 97
wheat, 5, 130–31
Wheeler, Ambrose, 133–35, 142, 149, 363n66
Wheeler, Stephen, 226, 228–29, 270, 297, 381n74
White, Alf, 293–95
"White, James," 107–8
White people and communities
  intermarriage with Native Americans, 209
  "settlers and squatter sovereignty," 4, 11, 219
  southern exceptionalism and White supremacy, 86
  see also slavery; *specific locations and communities*
Whitney, Sharon E., 362n35
Wichita Children's Home, 288–89, 328
Wichita, Kansas, 284, 288–89, 328
"Wild West, the" 89, 92–93, 238–39, 271–73, 307
  imperialist and racist views, 238
  and the mostly male subscribers of pulp magazines, 258
  Victorian ideals in the, 15, 175–76, 191
  Wild West shows, 271–73
Wilde, Oscar, 93, 354n10
Wilder, William D., 139–45, 148–49, 153, 155–56, 170–74, 181, 192, 366n5
Wilderness Trail through the Cumberland Gap, 6
Wilkins, S. M., 99–100
Wilson, Parmelia Dorcas, 198–99, 375n28
Wilson's Creek, Battle of, 50, 90, 228
Winchester rifles, 296, 313, 324
wineries in California, 115
Wise County, Texas, 96–98

women in the American West, 15, 176–77, 191, 233, 235, 259
   Carthage Female Academy, 24–27, 38, 76, 91, 213
   divorce among, 6–7, 136, 188, 206–7, 240, 327
   domesticity, 176, 307
   dressing "like a man," 145, 215, 222, 256, 267
   the importance of riding sidesaddle, 23, 102, 177–78, 240, 260, 260–61, 371n14, 371n15, 385n66
   intermarriage with Native Americans, 209
   needlework, as women's work, 27, 91
   in "new marriages," 6–7
   patriarchy's shadow on the stories of, 264
   as perpetual juveniles, 7
   prostitution, 235, 243, 325–27, 372n3, 396n54, 399n116
   riding "astride," 177, 371n14
   rights of, 25, 50, 344n51
   the "southern belle," 27, 49–50
   as spies during the Civil War, 55, 349n29
   as teachers sent to educate the West, 25–26, 321, 344n51
   Victorian ideals, 15, 175–76, 191
   "westering women," 176
   White women captives of Native Americans, 186
   see also Belle Starr, the lady; Belle Starr, the legend
Woodall, Abe, 208
Wooten, Thomas Callaway, 61
World's Columbian Exposition of 1893, Chicago, 317
Wright, Muriel H., 79
Wymore, George, 106
Wyrick, Samuel, 261–62

Yankees, 88
   carpetbaggers, 221
   running "Yankee lovers" out of town, 46
   Yankee do-gooders., 26
   "Yankee Dutch," 43–45
Yates, Jim, 243–44
Young, Mamie Reed, 281, 284–86, 288–89, 328
Younger, Bruce Wilson, 101, 198–207, 208–9, 314–18, 375n35, 395n46
Younger, Bursheba, 124
Younger, Charles Lee, 198–99, 375n28, 375n29
Younger, Cole, 90, 94–95, 97–98, 101
   in California, 113–14
   his autobiography, 107, 355n51, 356n55, 360n44
   Jim Reed and, 97–98, 121
   myths of Belle Starr's affair and child with, 101, 136, 198, 215, 307–8, 324, 330
   in Texas, 107, 124
Younger, Coleman, 16, 113
Younger family
   in California, 113–14
   James family's links to, 92–95, 101, 105–8
   Shirley family's links to, 16, 101, 121, 124
   in Texas, 107, 124
   see also James-Younger gang
Younger, Henry (Harry) Washington, 16, 198
Younger's Bend, Cherokee Nation, 136–37, 138–42, 197
   Belle and Sam Starr settle in, 210–17
   after Belle Starr's death, 311–12, 330–36
   Belle Starr's relationship with Jim July in, 277–78, 288–93
   horse theft during the 1882 spring roundup, 225–37
   the hunt for wanted killer John Middleton, 240–52, 254, 270, 385n55, 385n66
   hunting for Big Head's treasure, 211, 378n16
   Jesse James's visits to, 215–17
   life for Belle and Sam Starr after prison, 238–41
Yuchi (Euchee) tribe, 250

Zelazko, Alicja, 264
zinc mining, 198